HAMMER OR ANVIL?

Modern Germany 1648–Present

HAMMER OR ANVIL?

Modern Germany 1648–Present

HOLGER H. HERWIG
University of Calgary

D. C. Heath and Company
Lexington, Massachusetts *Toronto*

Address editorial correspondence to:

D. C. Heath and Company
125 Spring Street
Lexington, MA 02173

Acquisitions Editor: James Miller
Developmental Editor: Lauren Johnson
Production Editor: Renée M. Mary
Designer: Alwyn R. Velásquez
Photo Researcher: Billie Ingram
Art Editor: Diane Grossman
Production Coordinator: Charles Dutton

Photo Credits:

Bildarchive Preußischer Kulturbesitz: pp. 15, 21, 30, 91, 118, 141, 151, 157, 165, 176, 197, 207, 244, 255, 281, 294, 298, 301, 303, 307, 408, 417, 436; *Archiv für Kunst und Geschichte:* pp. 44, 48, 52, 67, 74, 95, 102, 106, 169, 219, 220, 238, 259, 278, 335, 346, 369, 379, 382, 387, 412, 421; *Historical Pictures / Stock Montage:* p. 150; *Magnum Photos:* p. 304; *Austrian National Library:* p. 320; *Sovfoto / Eastfoto:* pp. 262, 341, 350; *Volkswagen America:* p. 388; *Bettmann Newsphotos:* p. 397; *The Bettmann Archive:* p. 433; *Sygma / A. Tannenbaum:* p. 448; *Sipa Press / Cham:* p. 450.

Published simultaneously in Canada.

Printed in the United States of America.

International Standard Book Number: 0-669-21877-4.

Library of Congress Catalog Number: 92-83833.

10 9 8 7 6 5 4 3

For Brooke and Lars

About the cover

Born in 1867 in the German-speaking part of what was then part of Southern Denmark, Emil Nolde grew up in an environment that is clearly evident in the cover painting "Friesland Farm under Red Colors." The landscape is one known for its harsh winters, mild summers, and frequent fogs envelop the spacious farms. The uncluttered and vast expanses of land serve as a broad stage for the dramatic climate. The weather and the land are of constant concern to the farmers who depend on both for their livelihood, and who develop almost a religious relationship with them. Nolde was never happy when away from this environment.

Unlike his contemporaries, Nolde was not an intellectual painter, and was proud of his peasant roots. He liked solitude, preferring to speak and interact with his canvases rather than to socialize with other artists. He strongly resented the label "expressionist" that contemporaries applied to him, and he defended his work by saying that he was more subordinate to colors than to his personal need for expression. "I delighted in colors," he said, "and it seemed to me that they loved my hands."

An early member of the Danish Nazi Party, Nolde felt a fervent sense of alliance with what he saw as the emerging German ideal. Idealistically, he had an urgent need to portray the people whom he saw as part of the new, vigorous, and joyous German culture emerging under National Socialism. He felt that art "had to become German" and represent Germany. "My art is German, strong, austere, and sincere," he said. Nevertheless, his work was received with disfavor by the leaders of the Third Reich. When his work was exhibited in a show along with other "degenerate" works of his contemporaries, Nolde was devastated. The art that Hitler and Goebbels supported was sentimental, idealistic, and superficial, and the power of works by Nolde and other German artists was severely criticized.

During the Hitler years, Nolde, like his contemporaries, had to continue his work in secret. The works he produced, which he called "unpainted pictures," were not available to the public until well after the war. By then his acceptance was again assured, but the experiences of his clash with the leaders of the country he loved are clear in his statement, "Clever people master life; the wise illuminate it and create fresh difficulties."

PREFACE

Twice in this century, Gemany made what historian Fritz Fischer called a "bid for world power"; twice, at tremendous cost, a powerful global coalition defeated it. Yet for an entire generation born, as I was, either during or shortly after World War II, the proverbial "German question" — whether Germany would be a stable and reliable factor in European affairs — did not exist. Germany's division by 1949 into the German Democratic Republic (GDR) and the Federal Republic of Germany (FRG) seemed an appropriate nemesis for the German declarations of war of 1914 and 1939. As long as Moscow controlled its satellite state at East Berlin and the United States its client state at Bonn, and as long as the GDR remained securely anchored in the Warsaw Pact and the FRG in the North Atlantic Treaty Organization (NATO), European security seemed ensured. As British general Hastings "Pug" Ismay, the first head of NATO, succinctly put it, the alliance had been founded for the express purpose "to keep the Americans in [Europe], the Russians out, and the Germans down."

This comfortable, if potentially dangerous, bipolar world came crashing down with the German revolution of 1989-1990. Entrenched alliances dissolved and unspoken assumptions evaporated overnight. The Soviet empire disintegrated. France lost its cherished role as mediator between Moscow and Washington. U.S., British, and Soviet troops no longer were welcome (or needed) on German soil. The Warsaw Pact collapsed; NATO struggled to define its new role. The dollar and the pound sterling plummeted against the rising deutsche mark. Remembrances, often not so fond, of Frederick the Great, Otto von Bismarck, and William II resurfaced as West Germans rushed to pay homage to the Prussian legacy at Potsdam, largely denied them by the existence of the East German state. Uneasy memories of Hitler stirred as racial riots erupted in former GDR towns and cities.

The unified Federal Republic will be preoccupied with reconstructing eastern Germany until the next century. Will it be content thereafter to submerge its national interests into those of the European Community? Or will it seek to go a separate way? Whatever the case, the "German question" is with us once more.

In the wake of the revolution of 1989-1990, the time is propitious for another look at German history. Germany will be a major world player after the reconstruction of eastern Germany is complete, and we can ill afford to ignore Germany's past. We need to understand how the nation was forged by Prussia on the anvil of war between 1864 and 1871; why it gambled on war in 1914; why it turned to fascism in 1933; and how it ravaged Europe after 1939. We need to grasp how the past has shaped and will continue to shape Germany's future, and how the "Auschwitz complex," to name but the most obvious national liability, affects both our views of Germany and Bonn's freedom to maneuver on the political stage.

Why title this book *Hammer or Anvil?* rather than something blander and more generic, like *History of Modern Germany*? Germany's most celebrated writer, Johann Wolfgang von Goethe (1749–1832), in Act 2 of *Der Gross-Coptha* gave literary expression to this "hammer or anvil" theme in German history:

> *You must either conquer and rule or lose and serve,*
> *suffer or triumph, and be the anvil or the hammer.*

In December 1899 State Secretary of the Foreign Office Bernhard von Bülow, shortly before becoming chancellor, borrowed heavily from Goethe to continue the metaphor: "In the coming century, the German nation will be either the hammer or the anvil." And today, historian Michael Stürmer, a part-time speech writer for Chancellor Helmut Kohl, argues that Germany's geographical location at the center of Europe, between France and Russia, forced the question of hammer or anvil on the German states. Obviously, using *Germany* in the title as I have is misleading, for the German Empire did not come into being until 1871; and from 1949 to 1990 there existed two German states. I use the term principally for simplicity.

Further, why begin the book at 1648? Clearly, one could argue that any history of the German states would be incomplete without a full discussion of the medieval period, of the Salian, Staufen, and Hohenstaufen dynasties. But students can also jump into German history in 1648 — at the conclusion of the Thirty Years' War — and pick up the threads of nation-state building, the Austro-Prussian rivalry, the growth of cities and commerce and industry, and the formation of the modern Prusso-German bureaucratic and military state.

I wrote this book first and foremost for students. Having taught German history for twenty years in the United States and Canada, I have tried to address students' concerns about what a history textbook should be. The work is based on more than two decades of research in numerous Austrian, East German, and West German national, regional, and city archives. Above all, this book derives from countless hours of musings over the subject of my life's work; I hope that it will convey to readers my ongoing excitement about the teaching and research of Germany's history. For me, that story has lost none of its allure, mystery, and wonder.

Writing a text of this scope was a daunting task. German history from Frederick II and Maria Theresa to Erich Honecker and Helmut Kohl is a complex story, full of subtleties and exceptions to every generalization. A field rich in historical treatments, it almost defies single-author analysis. The manuscript reviewers that D. C. Heath engaged for each chapter constantly reminded me of the difficulty of the undertaking. Fortunately, I was able to lean on many superb studies. Although the *Suggested Readings* at the end of each chapter contain only English-language works available to undergraduates, I relied heavily on recent German scholarship as well as on my archival work. I owe intellectual debts to too many people to mention here.

Every author who surveys three centuries of history faces critical decisions about what to include and what to exclude. I have selected topics on the basis of their importance to the major themes developed in the work. For example, one chapter focuses entirely on World War I, and two are devoted to the history of the Third Reich. These decisions reflect my belief that students are most interested in these explosive eras of Germany's past. Indeed, what makes German history so distinct is not its literary heritage or regional quaintness but rather its aggressive, militaristic actions against Europe and the rest of the world. Nor have I pursued a strictly chronological treatment. Instead, I have highlighted developments that seemed critical to me. One writer's omission is often another's hobbyhorse, and I hope that my readers understand the necessity of this selection process.

Naturally, the book reflects my own areas of specialization: political, social, and diplomatic-military history. Yet I have offered students a broader sampling of the history of art, architecture, literature, and women, as well as the history of everyday life. Perhaps most important, I designed the book as a resource work around which instructors can build their own discourses on German history. Put differently, the book is intended to supplement in-class instruction, to serve as a guide for further enrichment and elaboration.

I undertook this project partly because of my children, Brooke (born 1978) and Lars (born 1982). I want them to have some idea of my side of their heritage. Their paternal great-grandfather fought and died in World War I. Their grandfather marched to Stalingrad and ended World War II as a prisoner of war picking oranges in Oxnard, California. Their father was born in 1941 in Hamburg just as the aerial *Blitz* of that proud and beautiful Hanseatic city was about to climax in Operation Gomorrah. May their lives be more sanguine.

I thank history editor James Miller of D. C. Heath for his persistent persuasion that I undertake this project; development editor Lauren Johnson for her good work and support as I wrote and revised the chapters; my wife, Lorraine, for her constant sagacious critique of the manuscript; and the Social Sciences and Humanities Research Council of Canada for the generous grant that has allowed me for the past three years to conduct archival research in Austria and Germany. Last, I extend many thanks to the following reviewers for their helpful suggestions throughout the project: Kenneth Barkin, *University of California, Riverside*; David F. Crew, *University of Texas at Austin*; Hannah S. Decker, *University of Houston*; Stephen G. Fritz, *East Tennessee State University*; Michael E. Geyer, *University of Chicago*; Theodore Hamerow, *University of Wisconsin, Madison*; Peter Hayes, *Northwestern University*; David W. Hendon, *Baylor University*; Jonathon B. Knudsen, *Wellesley College*; Mary Jo Maynes, *University of Minnesota*; Allan Mitchell, *University of California, San Diego*; Gordon R. Mork, *Purdue University*; Donald L. Niewyk, *Southern Methodist*

University; Johannes M. Postma, *Mankato State University*; Diethelm Prowe, *Carleton College*; Marion Rappe, *San Francisco State University*; Benjamin C. Sax, *University of Kansas*; Douglas A. Unfug, *Emory University*; and Franklin C. West, *Portland State University*.

H. H. H.

CONTENTS

M A P S

CHAPTER

1

GERMANY IN THE EIGHTEENTH CENTURY: SOCIETY AND STATE

THE GERMAN EMPIRE

Germany? But where does it lie? I do not know how to find that land. Where learning begins, politics end.

GERMAN NATIONAL CHARACTER

You Germans hope in vain to develop yourselves into a nation; instead — and you can do it — develop yourselves more freely into human beings.

Goethe and Schiller, *Xenien* (1795–1796)

For modern-day readers, eighteenth-century Germany appears as a hodgepodge of confusing and often conflicting institutions, traditions, standards, and states. The terms *Zersplitterung* (disunity) and *Kleinstaaterei* (particularism) are most often used by German historians to refer to the fact that more than three hundred states of varying size and importance, each sovereign and independent, each with its own army and regulations, constituted the loose union called the Holy Roman Empire of the German Nation (*Heiliges römisches Reich deutscher Nation*, or *Regnum teutonicum*), often called simply the Empire or the Reich. Within this conglomerate realm, there existed not simply "Germans" but a diverse array of other nationals, such as Danes and Dutch, Flemish and Walloons (Belgians), Czechs and Swiss, as well as religious groups such as French Huguenots and Swiss Mennonites, many of whom had come to the German lands to escape religious and ethnic persecution at home.

Eighteenth-century Germany was especially burdened with the consequences of its recent history. The Thirty Years' War (1618–1648), and its accompanying outbreaks of dysentery, typhus, and bubonic plague, had ravaged the land and almost halved its population: estimates of losses range from 33 percent in the cities to 40 percent in the countryside. Apart from the breakdown in the social order engendered by more than a generation of warfare, the Thirty Years' War also created a rigid socioeconomic system. Feudal barriers arose anew in 1648 where such obligations had long ceased to exist as rulers sought to prevent further erosion of population and skills. Free peasants were tied to the land to varying degrees in the German states, burdened with the onus for proving "free" legal status. Obligatory servitude brought about virtual enslavement of the peasantry; in Bohemia, for example, manual service (the *robot*) owed the lord increased from 8 to 122 days per year.

More generally, the Thirty Years' War, a titanic struggle between Protestant Reformation and Catholic Counter Reformation, as well as between estates and monarchy, deprived the Empire of religious unity because the Peace of Westphalia in 1648, as already earlier the Peace of Augsburg[1] in 1555, enabled each ruler to choose the religion for his holdings. Violent internal struggle in northern German lands meant that trade in that region fell almost by default to the Dutch, the English, and the Swedes. Even the mouths of Germany's principal rivers remained in foreign hands: the Swedes controlled the Oder and Weser, the Danes the Elbe, and the Dutch the Rhine. Internal tariffs crippled commerce as they dissected rivers and subdivided some three hundred states.

Whereas England and France had steadily progressed toward national unity since the twelfth century, Germany remained marked by disunity and particularism. There existed no emperor powerful enough to establish a system of common law; no central representative body like the British Parliament; no common literature as in pre-Elizabethan England; no national industry like British textiles; no effective system of taxation to draw the Empire together into an economic unit. And where German developments did parallel those in England and France — in the growth of a professional bureaucracy and royal standing army, the introduction of a monetary system, and the spread of secular education — they favored local princes rather than the emperor. A Scottish traveler in Germany, David Hume, noted in 1748 that the country was "full of industrious honest people, and were it united, it would be the greatest power that ever was in the world." Unification would come only in 1871; centralization would take an additional half-century.

The Holy Roman Empire

From 1512 to 1806, the Holy Roman Empire comprised ten imperial districts, encompassing 314 sovereign territorial states, as well as the lands of more than 1,400 independent imperial knights. According to the imperial articles of

[1] The major outcome of the peace was that territorial princes gained the right to determine (and change) the religion of their lands, thereby breaking the medieval unity of Christendom.

1521, there also existed 85 imperial cities; in reality, their number had shrunk to 51 cities "free" of imperial control by the middle of the eighteenth century. These ranged in size from Hamburg with a population of 130,000 to Buchau with fewer than 1,000 people. The Empire stretched from the Duchy of Holstein on the North Sea to the Bishopric of Trent on Lake Garda then part of Austrian Tyrol; from the Bishopric of Lüttich in the west to the Grand Duchy of Austria and the Kingdom of Bohemia in the east. Its vast territories amounted to 672,000 square kilometers; its population in 1762 was estimated at 24 million by Johann Peter Süssmilch, Germany's first demographer.

Polycentrism characterized the Empire; there existed no cultural, political, or economic center comparable to London or Paris. As late as 1784, the enlightened journalist Johann Pezzl still wrote of "the misery of polycentrism":

> There sits many a princeling upon a throne who would not be competent to rule over twelve chickens: but he wants to shine, wants to remain in step with the grand princes; must have his own cooks, horses, dogs; his own viziers and troops, even if the entire army consists of four grenadiers, six musketeers, and two cavalrymen — and in order to bring all this into being, he fleeces his small herd of serfs mercilessly.

The Empire's highly patchworked structure is hardly surprising. Since 1663, the Imperial Legislature (Reichstag) had convened at Regensburg; the Imperial Chancellor resided at Mainz; the Imperial High Court of Justice met at Wetzlar; and election as well as coronation of the emperor, or Kaiser, took place at Frankfurt. It is little wonder that a contemporary scholar, Samuel von Pufendorf, called the Holy Roman Empire an irregular monstrosity. After the Peace of Westphalia in 1648, the Reich was so powerless that its very existence had to be secured by two great states, France and Sweden; in 1779, Russia was added to the list of "guarantors." In every sense, then, the *regnum teutonicum* was both the heart of the "German question" — that is, the debate over the future territorial form of the German lands — and a European problem.

The Golden Bull (1356) of Holy Roman Emperor Charles IV — in many ways, the critical document determining the nature of the Reich — had stipulated that the Empire was an elective institution. The election of the Kaiser was to be undertaken by four secular and three religious rulers: the electors of the Palatinate (after 1777, Bavaria), Saxony, Brandenburg, and Bohemia, as well as the archbishops of Cologne, Mainz, and Trier. An eighth vote was granted Braunschweig-Lüneburg, which after 1709 voted for Hanover, when the latter's rulers ascended the English throne. The Golden Bull has accurately been described as "legal anarchy" because it perpetuated political division through formal law.

With the exception of Emperor Charles VII, a Bavarian who ruled only between 1742 and 1745, the crown of Charlemagne belonged from 1440 to 1806 to the House of Habsburg, a dynasty established as dukes and archdukes of Austria after 1282. In fact, few other aspirants vied for the role. In his Political

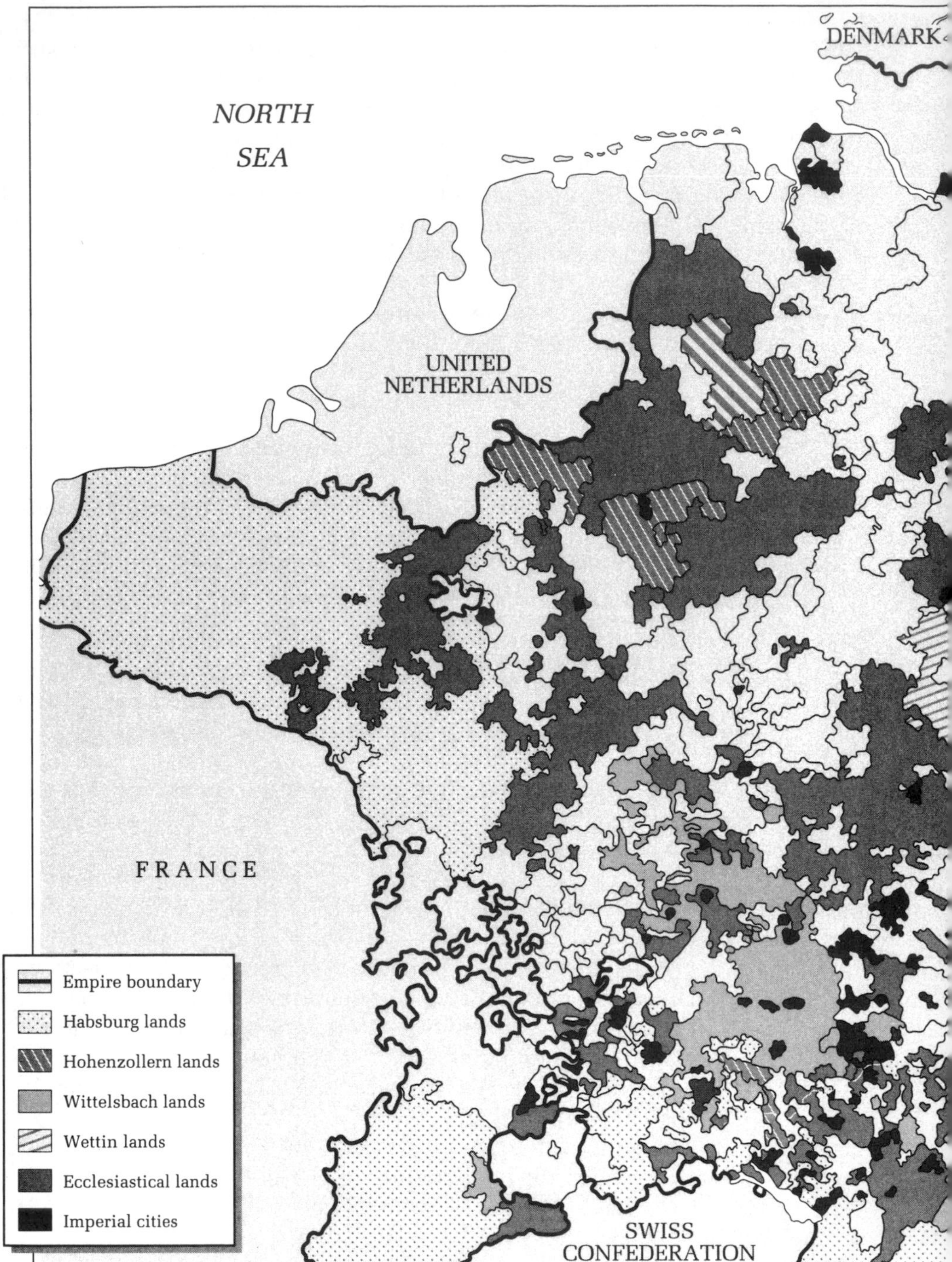
DENMARK
NORTH
SEA
UNITED
NETHERLANDS
FRANCE
SWISS
CONFEDERATION
Empire boundary
Habsburg lands
Hohenzollern lands
Wittelsbach lands
Wettin lands
Ecclesiastical lands
Imperial cities

PIRE, 1648

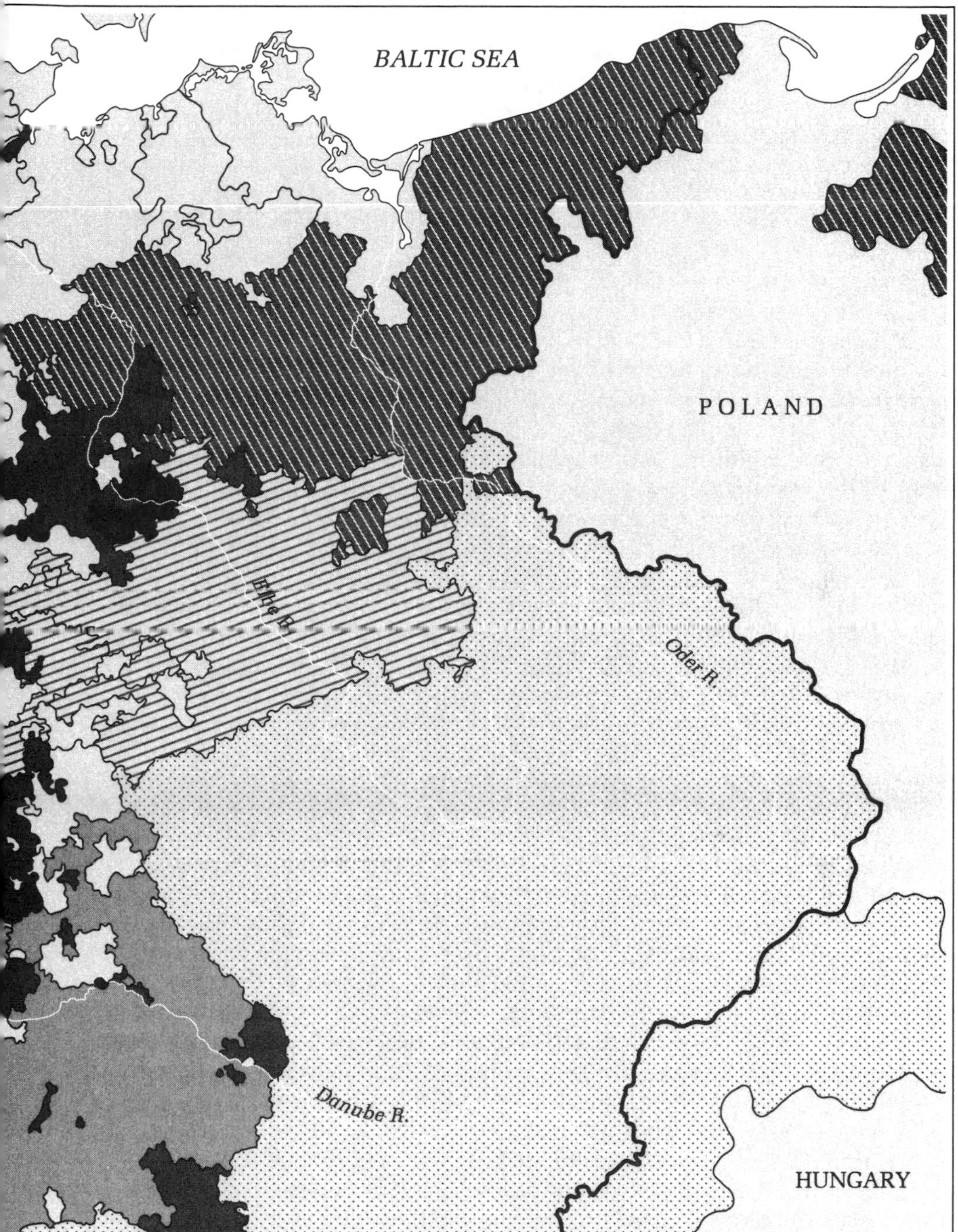

Testament, Frederick II of Prussia (1740–1786) admonished his successor not to seek "empty titles" but rather to acquire "a rich province." Frederick's contemporary, the lawyer Johann Jacob Moser, said of the Kaiser that he "had not a foot of land or a single subject; no country was governed in his name, nor was a source of revenue to him." The title was an expensive luxury that few could afford; the Habsburgs paid for it mainly out of their Austrian and Bohemian revenues.

The states of the Empire were supposed to provide income for the crown. Yet as late as 1750, only 58,000 gulden, the income of a small state, or half the amount requested of the Reichstag by the Emperor, was raised. By the end of the Seven Years' War in 1763, just two rulers, the archbishop of Trier and the elector of Hanover, still paid their assessments. The Empire's army existed largely on paper, a polyglot collection of aged warriors whose various uniforms reflected the quilting of the German map. The truth was that the electors worked on behalf of the Reich only to the extent that this suited their own purposes. As a result, the imperial army generally consisted of superannuated soldiers of questionable quality, a sort of police watch at best.

True sovereignty, then, rested with the regional rulers rather than with the Emperor. The nineteenth-century British historian James Bryce caustically suggested that the Reich was neither holy, nor Roman, nor an empire. It survived only as long as it served its primary purpose: to leave undisturbed the territorial integrity and sovereignty of its roughly three hundred princes.

Serfs and Subjects

Of the slightly more than 20 million people inhabiting the Holy Roman Empire in the eighteenth century, 6.1 million lived in the Habsburg lands in 1754. By 1805 that figure would climb to 9.3 million. Much of the new growth stemmed from settlers attracted mainly from south and southwest Germany to Hungary and the Carpathian regions. Military conquest and the two partitions of Poland in which Austria participated (1772 and 1795) would bring the Habsburgs the populations of Galicia and the Bukovina. During the reign of Maria Theresa (1740–1780), 47,000 colonists reportedly were added to the Habsburg possessions. Under Emperor Joseph II (1780–1790), another 38,000 settlers were attracted, in part by the Decree of Tolerance of 1781, which appealed mainly to Protestants.

Brandenburg-Prussia, the second major power in the Empire, used the combination of tolerance and conquest with notable success to increase its population. The Potsdam Decree of Tolerance in November 1685 had drawn 20,000 industrious Huguenots (French Protestants denied religious freedom by Louis XIV that year through revocation of the Edict of Nantes) to the lands of Frederick William, the Great Elector. After the conquest of Silesia in 1740, Prussia's population stood at 3.5 million. A staggering 284,000 colonists were

THE HABSBURG LANDS, EIGHTEENTH CENTURY

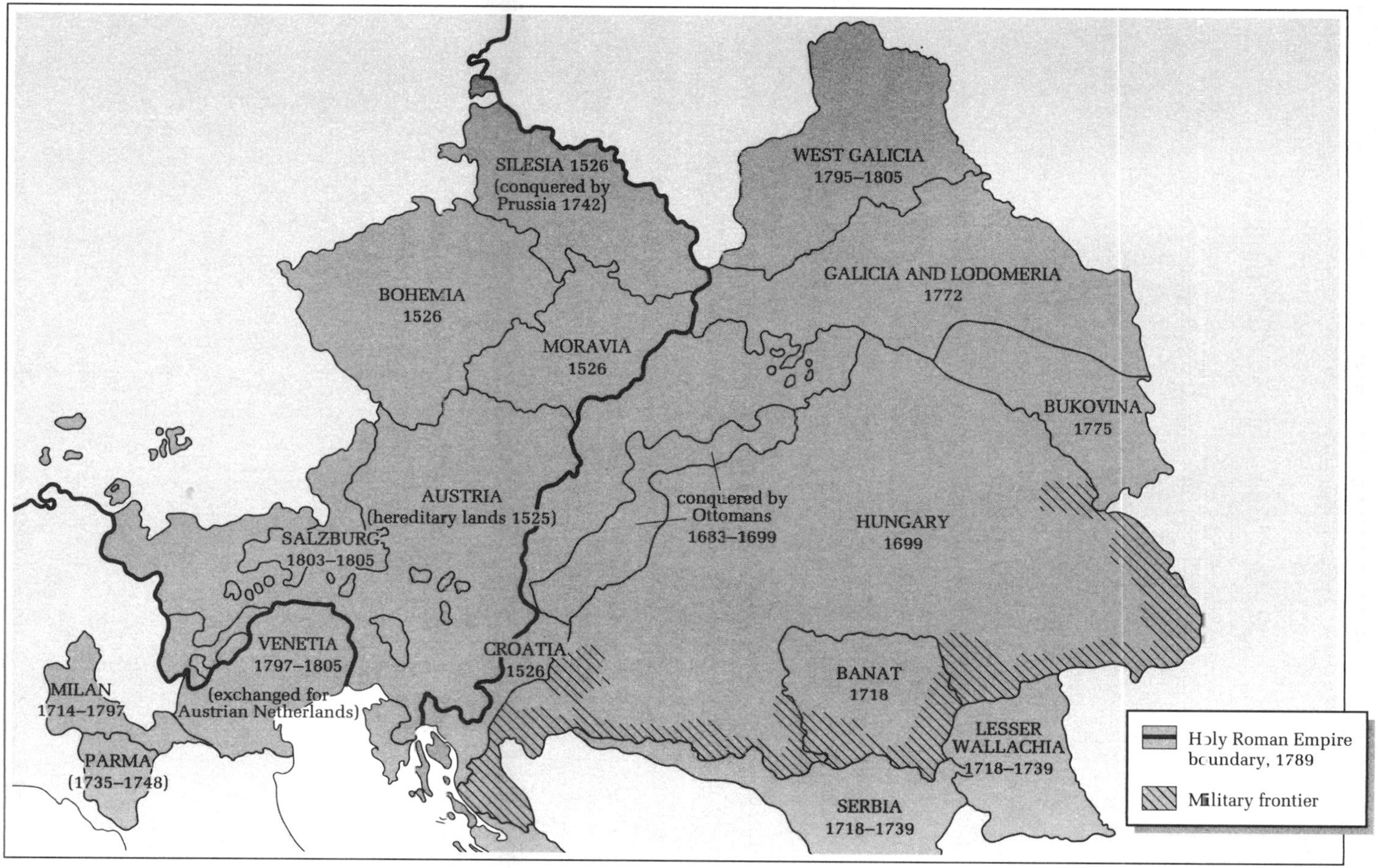

BRANDENBURG-PRUSSIA, EIGHTEENTH CENTURY

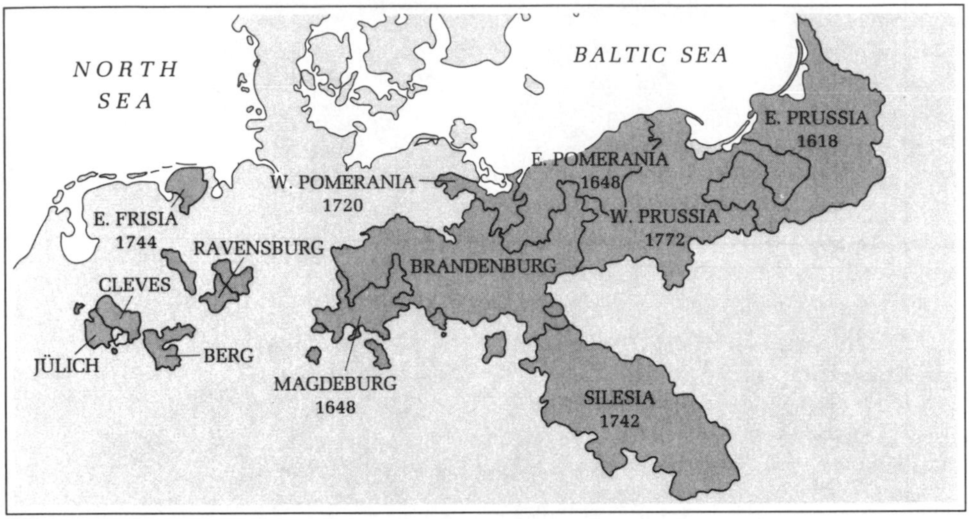

brought to Prussia during the reign of Frederick II alone. The first Polish partition added still more, with the result that the Prussian population by 1789 had risen to 5.7 million.

Conversely, many Germans left their homeland, mainly to escape poverty and lack of opportunity. Most well known were the emigrations from Westphalia to the Netherlands and from Swabia to the lower Danube and Black Sea regions. Over the course of the eighteenth century, it is estimated that 200,000 people left Germany. Nearly half of these opted for the thirteen British colonies in North America. Of special interest are the 29,000 young German men sold by their princes as soldiers to Britain to wage war against the rebellious colonies in North America between 1775 and 1783. Only 17,000 returned from the United States. Landgrave Frederick III of Hesse-Kassel was most active in the mercenary trade, selling 17,000 young men to Britain for just over 6 million pounds sterling.

Germany was home to a wide variety of religious denominations. In 1792 about 16 million Catholics and 10 million Lutheran Protestants resided in the Holy Roman Empire. In addition, 2 million Calvinists (Reformed) inhabited mainly the Rhineland, Hesse, Westphalia, and Brandenburg, where Elector Johann Sigismund had converted to Calvinism in 1613. Of the 200,000 Jews in the Reich, about 80,000 lived in the Habsburg lands. Some cities excluded "Israelites" altogether; others permitted them, but only if they lived in ghettos.

German cities paled in comparison with London and Paris. By 1800 the former boasted a population of 1 million, the latter just over half a million. The largest German city in 1800 was Vienna, with 232,000 people. Berlin followed with 172,000, and Hamburg came third with 130,000. Königsberg and Dresden each had 60,000 residents, Cologne 50,000, and Frankfurt 48,000. Bremen, Leipzig, and Munich each possessed only about 40,000 people.

Four of every five subjects lived on the land, eking out a primitive and meager existence. As late as 1800, less than half the land in Prussia was cultivated; 25 percent lay fallow at any given time, and 40 percent was considered infertile. In the villages there was no running water, no sanitation, and no medical care, apart from the occasional bloodletting performed by surgeons, who doubled as barbers.

Disease ran rampant. The last great wave of pestilence passed through Brandenburg early in the eighteenth century, claiming about one third of the population. Smallpox replaced the plague thereafter as the most lethal epidemic: in 1777, smallpox claimed 16,000 Prussian lives (of 118,000 deaths that year). Nearly one in every ten deaths in Berlin in the 1780s was of a child infected with smallpox. In Württemberg, the figure was one death in every thirteen among children. Pneumonia, spotted fever, and vertigo followed smallpox on the list of epidemics. These cold, impersonal statistics take on life when put in human terms by Ulrich Bräker, a chronicler of the 1780s, who recalled his father's death:

> At first he only pricked his thumb with a thorn; it came up. He bound fresh cow-dung onto it; then the whole hand swelled up. He felt a terrible heat in it, went to the pump and washed the dung off under the tap. But that had dreadful consequences. He soon had to lie down, and took a dropsy. He got himself tapped off; the fluid ran down into the cellar. After he'd lain about 5 months he died.

Nutrition was primitive at best; two out of every three peasants, it is estimated, received insufficient nutrition. In central Germany, a typical day's ration for a peasant consisted of a watery bread soup and some milk for breakfast, boiled potatoes soaked with curdled milk for lunch, and watery bread-soup for dinner. Beer was far more than a beverage. Regarded in some parts of Germany as "liquid bread," annual intake in the eighteenth century stood at 300 liters per head, twice the current level of consumption in Germany today.

Introduction of the potato revolutionized central European diets by the end of the eighteenth century, but this process took time. As late as the 1770s, Berliners still viewed the potato as fodder; peasants refused to eat it, believing that it gave rise to scrofula, rickets, consumption, and gout. When Frederick II introduced the potato at Kolberg in 1744 in the wake of a severe famine, local farmers refused to plant it: "The things have no smell and no taste, and not even dogs will eat them." It did not help that they had tried to eat the potatoes raw. Frederick II tried again the following year, this time successfully, by having a guard of royal grenadiers supervise the planting. By 1800 this one crop had become a dietary staple and within a generation had almost erased absolute famine. No longer were peasants dependent on the uncertainties of cereal grain production.

Typical for preindustrial Europe, average life expectancy ranged from as low as twenty-nine years in France to as high as thirty-three years in Sweden. Child mortality was alarming in mid-eighteenth-century Sweden. Of every one hundred children born, only seventy-eight survived their first year and sixty-six their fifth; a mere fifty-seven reached the age of twenty. Women gave birth on average every two and a half years; most adult females under the age of forty were either pregnant or nursing. Infants faced chancy survival. In numerous German regions, as many as one of every three newborns died. Seven of ten did not survive their fourteenth year. As a result, despite multiple childbirths, it was unusual for a family to raise more than two children to maturity. Finally, given the economic plight of the general populace, only half the women and one-third of the men in Europe reportedly married by age thirty. The average age at marriage for men was thirty-three, for women about twenty-two.

Women were not deemed legal persons, and their lot, especially in the countryside, was abysmal. The Prussian Civil Code of 1794 stated clearly that "the man is the head of the conjugal community and his decision is final in matters affecting that community." The wife required the husband's consent to pursue a career; her dowry and any claim to an inheritance automatically passed to him upon marriage; children were subject "primarily" to his authority; and only illegitimate children bore the wife's name. The code unequivocably stated the purpose of marriage as "the procreation and raising of children."

The Prussian state under Frederick II based matrimony on the contract theory of marriage and natural law. Grounds for separation were similarly codified: "impermanent bitterness against each other" or "insurmountable antipathy," with the result that the partnership "procreated no children." The king could grant divorce for the wife's adultery, willful desertion, attempted murder, insanity, infertility, and "persistent and obdurate denial of conjugal duties." Above all, though, the state needed recruits. To allow for a steady supply, Prussia enacted the most liberal divorce laws in Europe. Even the enlightened philosopher Immanuel Kant, a lifelong bachelor, described marriage as consisting of no more and no less than "a contract concluded between two people of the opposite sex which regulated the use of sexual characteristics." Passionate love existed mainly in novels, such as Johann Wolfgang Goethe's *The Sorrows of Werther* (1774) and August Wilhelm von Schlegel's *Lucinde* (1799).

Around 1800, Heinrich von Kleist stated bluntly that the aim of every female was "to become a mother, and to provide the world with virtuous people." Nor were the German romantics less calculating. The novelist Novalis (Friedrich Baron von Hardenberg) depicted marriage and the family as the heart and soul of a state and hence proclaimed that the woman's role was that of "house mother." In 1765 Goethe's compatriot, Christoph Martin Wieland, described the ideal wife as being "without moods, even-tempered, calm, agreeable, easy to amuse, used to an almost monastic way of life. . . . She fits in effortlessly . . . with my taste, my mood, and my way of life." What was required of women in the educated middle class was "a couple of polonaises, the odd jig on the piano, a couple of songs . . . reading and writing for the purpose of housekeeping." Finally, he noted, "I do not require a grain of intellect from my wife. I have plenty of that in my books." For those of means, marriage was an act of social and material enhancement, to be planned with all the precision of a military operation. For the nobility, it was an instrument of statecraft.

One bright spot in this otherwise depressing picture was the special salons that allowed noble and nonnoble women alike to air the literary, cultural, and philosophical issues of the day. By and large patterned after Parisian salons, these German centers became havens for enlightened intercourse among men and women. In Vienna, Fanny Arnstein and Karoline Pichler hosted Clemens Prince von Metternich, Friedrich von Gentz, and Felix Mendelssohn. At Jena, Caroline Schlegel opened her home to Novalis, Goethe, Friedrich Schiller, and Johann Gottfried von Herder. By 1800 Berlin boasted fourteen salons catering to about a hundred regulars. Henriette Mendelssohn, Rahel Varnhagen, and Henriette Herz provided the private settings where they could discuss the philosophy of the Enlightenment with Heinrich Heine, Friedrich Nicolai, Moses Mendelssohn, Jean Paul, Friedrich Schlegel, and Alexander, as well as Wilhelm von Humboldt. Interestingly, many of these Jewish women, under the influence of the romantics, converted to Christianity, particularly to Catholicism. Moreover, Henriette Herz arguably became the first German feminist by translating Mary Godwin Wollstonecraft's *A Vindication of the Rights of Women* (1792) into German.

An almost perverse dichotomy separates the Berlin salons of the late eighteenth century, whose focal point was usually a highly educated and cultured woman, and what has been called the dominant "male-bonding" element in German history. The latter was manifested by the "tobacco parliament" of Frederick William I and the intellectual circle at Sans Souci under Frederick II, the officer *Kasinos,* and the university fraternities. This dominant male culture, as we shall see, would reappear in virtually all subsequent phases of German history.

The Estates and the Social Order

The accident of birth proved decisive in the strict hierarchical society of eighteenth-century Germany. It determined one's religion and culture, education and occupation, family and social status, even clothing and nutrition. Mobility was not only greatly restricted but also highly individualistic: people achieved horizontal mobility by migration, either overseas or from the countryside into the city, and vertical mobility by a fortunate marriage, advanced education, meritorious service, or purchase of high office. When Kant suggested in 1793 that every person ought to rise to the level that talent, work, and luck permitted, he meant this only within the legal parameters allowed by the state. He even defined the concept of equality strictly in terms of the subject's legal relationship with the established executive authority, or *Obrigkeit*, as the Germans would term it well into the twentieth century.

Whereas France had only three tiers of society, or estates — clergy, nobility, and everyone else — the German lands, with their numerically much smaller middle class, recognized four distinct estates, or *Stände*: clergy, nobility, burghers, and peasantry. Although each group exhibited numerous gradations, for the sake of simplicity, these four categories suffice to afford a meaningful insight into the social structure of the *ancien régime* (the "old order" before the coming of the French Revolution).[1]

In 1800 the clergy (*Klerus*) was numerically the smallest estate, comprising but 1 percent of the population in Prussia. Elsewhere, it ranged from 0.4 percent in Saxony to 2.6 percent in the principality of East Frisia. In the Catholic lands, the picture was muddied by the number of high-ranking clerics who were also secular rulers: the electors of the archbishoprics of Cologne, Mainz, and Trier, as well as a host of princely bishops, abbots, and abbesses. By one estimate, as late as the end of the eighteenth century, no fewer than 1,200 to 1,400 ecclesiastical benefices (ecclesiastical offices yielding revenues from an endowment) dotted the Holy Roman Empire to provide for the sons and daughters of the nobility.

In the top echelons of the Catholic clergy, an air of superiority and caste discrimination dominated. Admission into the ranks of the church-princes usually required a minimum of four noble ancestors. Masked balls given by the archbishop-prince of Mainz, for example, were open only to those who could certify sixteen quarterings of blue blood.

In Catholic Bavaria, about 7 percent of the clergy came from the nobility and 30 percent from the civil service. The lower clergy was recruited predominantly from the ranks of middle-class and artisan families. The Bavarian church also wielded significant economic power; it owned about one-third of all land. A great number of its countless monasteries, in fact, were major agrarian producers. None paid taxes. As early as 1704, the Wittelsbach dynasty had sought to curb donations of land to the church in order not to lose these revenues, but after 1764 the state forbade all such transactions. Because the Catholic clergy could not marry, or acquire, or inherit property, it never approximated the social and educational homogeneity of its Protestant brethren.

[1] The term *ancien régime* defines the period of royalist absolutism before 1789. The French Revolution generally is considered a watershed because it created a centralized state in which local and social privileges yielded to the powers of an omnipresent and omnipotent secular state.

In fact the Protestant clergy was distinguished by bourgeois origins, educational elitism, and self-perpetuation. With the exception of a few renowned collegiate churches, which required pedigrees listing no fewer than thirty-two noble ancestors for honorary canons in cathedral chapters, the Protestant church offered none of the rich sinecures that the Roman church reserved for the nobility. Moreover, since the Reformation, a close tie had linked pastor and state, with the former customarily reading aloud the latter's decrees to subjects during Sunday services. Over time, pastors tended to form a closed shop: by the end of the eighteenth century, more than 44 percent of pastors in Württemberg were sons of pastors, and more than 80 percent were middle class. In Prussia, church offices, from simple abbot to superintendent of the High-Consistory, tended to be staffed by members of sharply defined social and economic circles.

The advent of Pietism in Prussian Protestant circles — that is, of a return to a simpler Christianity based on the Scriptures — and its institutionalization at the University of Halle under Christian Thomasius and August Hermann Francke, greatly attracted Prussian rulers. King Frederick William I (1714–1740), especially, saw merit in harnessing this fundamentalism to state service; he recruited pastors and educators from Halle and sent administrators there for further training. The king thus reinforced the old Lutheran tradition of a church subservient to the state. The Prussian ruling house of the Hohenzollerns for the first time forged a closer union between the dynasty and the world of academic learning.

Protestant north Germany was dominated for much of the eighteenth century by deism. Harking back to the sixteenth-century writings of advocates of state rights over special group interests such as Herbert of Cherbury and Jean Bodin, the noted Hamburg deist and theologian Hermann Samuel Reimarus argued that although God was indeed the creator of the universe, he no longer had any influence over it. "Natural" or objective religion came into vogue. In his *Critique of Pure Reason* published in 1781, Kant explained that the deist believes in a God, the theist in a living God. For the apostles of reason, there was no longer room for a dominant, controlling God because human beings were now quite able to direct their own affairs.

The Holy Roman Empire's second estate, the nobility (*Adel*), almost defies categorization due to its diversity. It broke down into the higher nobility — the rulers, princes, counts, and dukes who congregated at royal courts — and the lower nobility — hereditary and recently patented nobles, sword as well as robe, both urban and rural. But whatever their level, the nobility was international rather than German; its language of choice was French, and its music Italian. Goethe lamented that nobles were reduced to cursing in French for lack of a national oath.

The nobility constituted about 1 percent of the Reich's 24 million people around 1800. In raw figures, this amounted to 250,000 persons among 50,000 noble families. This 1 percent broke down into two regional groups. In the southwest, the *Adel* stood directly under the legal patrimony of the Kaiser and hence had the right to cast votes — one each for every prince and count, four collectively for the rest — at the Reichstag. In the north, the nobility was a freeholding squirearchy (called Junkers in Prussia) that derived its status directly from the land. On another level, the nobility was divided by its relationship to the princely court. In Austria the emperors preferred to draw the nobility to court and thereby to tie it to the Habsburg cause. In Prussia the Hohenzollerns sought to bind the nobility to the crown by forcing it to serve in the royal administration and army.

The court nobility rigidly followed a routine that sought to emulate Louis XIV and his court at Versailles. Court ritual, in fact, became an end in itself. The sun revolved around the ruler in his palace. Nature was shaped according to his will in formal gardens and parks. His every move gave occasion to rumor and speculation. His every act, from rising to retiring, became a spectacle worthy for the privileged to behold.

In Saxony under King Augustus the Strong, there existed in 1716 no fewer than ninety ranks of court nobility. The official state calendar contained fifty-three pages listing court offices: the court chamberlain, high officials ranging from falconer to stablemaster, common chamberlains, pages, a French choir and music staff, a Polish orchestra, a ballet, a theater company, lackeys, and cooks. One of the king's generals could entertain 190 guests with a four-course repast without having to borrow silver or porcelain.

At Vienna the court calendar obeyed the rigid etiquette of the Spanish Counter Reformation. Year in and year out, the Habsburg Kaiser observed the same ritual of banquets, saints' days, and fast days. Each day was specified whether he would reside at Schönbrunn, Laxenburg, or the Hofburg. Every movement of every audience was carefully orchestrated according to prescribed ceremony. Courtly life was anything but spontaneous.

Court ritual demanded overwhelming quantities of food. At Trier, when the archbishop entertained, the tables were so laden with game and meat that they bent to the floor. Offering guests fewer than six main courses was considered a gross insult. In Vienna, twenty-four courses customarily characterized formal banquets. An English traveler, Lady Mary Wortley Montagu, counted no fewer than fifty meat dishes served with eighteen wines at one state dinner. Pastries were so elaborate as to require the services of an architect and sculptor. Drink, especially at ecclesiastical courts where romantic gallantry was forbidden, was out of hand; guests recorded that they rarely managed to escape sober. Visitors to Würzburg concurred that one could not avoid being drunk twice a day, so numerous were the toasts of and to the archbishop.

Every German prince constructed his own Versailles. At Mannheim, Karlsruhe, Nymphenburg, and Ludwigsburg, their palaces drained enormous sums from their surrounding lands. The duke of Pfalz-Zweibrücken, to mention but one case, built a modest "pastoral" residence that quickly developed into stables for a thousand horses, kennels for a thousand dogs, a riding school, an

Outdoor sport for the aristocracy: Boar hunting (1750).

orangerie, zoological gardens, a theater, and barracks for fourteen hundred men, at a cost of 14 million gulden — nearly twenty times the annual revenue from his lands. The landgrave of Hesse-Kassel financed his palace at Wilhelmshöhe and an outstanding art collection by selling his male subjects to Britain for use against the Americans after 1776. Finally, each palace relied heavily on a large circle of gold and silver smiths and makers of luxury items, such as lace, hats, snuff, cards, ribbons, and porcelain.

Frederick II of Prussia later heaped ridicule on contemporary princes, noting that the smaller the land was, the greater was the opulence of its court's architecture, opera, and painting:

> Most small princes, particularly the German ones, ruin themselves with reckless extravagance, misled by the illusion of their imagined greatness. . . . The youngest son of the youngest son of an endowed dynasty imagines that he is of the same stamp as Louis XIV. He builds his Versailles, keeps his mistresses, and has an "army" — one perhaps strong enough to fight an imaginary battle on the stage at Verona — at his beck and call.

All of a noble's titles and privileges stemmed from the land. These advantages included freedom from taxation, special legal status, the right to exercise patrimonial justice, special church patronage, the right to levy land-usage fees, exclusive hunting and fishing rights, and the sole right to own land. And they had the privilege of choosing for themselves beheading by sword rather than hanging by rope in capital cases.

The country nobility, especially in northeast Germany, often differed little in appearance and work from their peasants. Prussian Junkers, it was said, "sweep and milk and make butter." They usually lived in unpretentious timber-and-brick houses euphemistically called "castles." Very few read newspapers or discussed cultural and literary affairs. Their lives centered on dogs and horses, local fairs, and shooting parties. Their meals typically consisted of weak onion soup, beef and pork courses, and goose or hare, served with a watery beer that was washed down by brandy or grain spirits (*Schnaps*). For health, the Junker was either bled regularly or induced to vomit. He attended church on Sunday and once a week acted as local magistrate. He maintained few domestic servants, consumed what he produced, made his own tools, brewed his own beer, and distilled his own liquor. His major preoccupation was to preserve his honor, and hence he took ample opportunity to duel; in time of war, the duel was usually to the death, otherwise until blood was first drawn.

Dress set the high nobility apart from the other social orders. Only the privileged few could wear silk stockings, powder their hair, don plumed hats, and carry a sword. Moreover, the nobility alone put their servants into special livery, displayed family coats of arms, used special seals, and insisted on being addressed by a plethora of titles. No one else could afford the brocades, silks, lace embroidered with jewels, towering coiffures, and hooped skirts. In the eighteenth century, to be natural meant to be dull and plebeian.

Strict laws governed public outings. In the theater nobles sat apart from commoners. At church they had their own pews and burial vaults. Universities segregated noble from bourgeois students in lecture halls. At court the grand nobles surrounded their seats with a number of empty chairs equal to their perceived social status. Many were certain that even heaven reserved special places for them.

Nobles sought above all to live a life of elegance and splendor. It was beneath their dignity to engage in commerce or business. Scholarship was anathema to them; their education focused on riding, fencing, and dancing, as well as a modicum of legal Latin. Widely denouncing universities as "scholastic monasteries," nobles received rudimentary training in carving at the dinner table, playing card games, paying compliments, dressing according to the occasion, and behaving properly at court balls. The highlight of any noble's upbringing was the Grand Tour, preferably to England, France, Holland, and Italy. Frederick III of Gotha, for example, undertook the tour accompanied by fourteen servants, including his personal chef and chaplain, at a cost of 6,500 thaler, or one month's income of his father's realm, over eighteen months.

The nobility was not, however, a permanent, unchanging elite. The male line in most noble clans typically lasted about three hundred years. Natural attrition played a large role in clan longevity. In Brandenburg only one in four medieval noble families still existed in 1800. In Silesia just three hundred of an original two thousand medieval noble families survived to 1800. Whereas the three Silesian wars fought between 1740 and 1763 deprived numerous noble clans of male heirs, downright poverty by 1840 destroyed at least eighteen historic families in Brandenburg. The ravages of syphilis, for which there was no cure, also took their toll on countless noble families throughout central Europe.

Dynasts were acutely aware of the threats to the upper class and constantly sought to replenish the nobility by ennobling middle-class officials of long standing and meritorious service. Since 1741 the Hohenzollerns held the right to ennoblement without the emperor's consent. Joseph II of Austria routinely enhanced not only the ranks of his *Adel* but also his coffers through the sale of noble titles: 20,000 gulden for an earldom and 6,000 for a baronetcy, amounts beyond the reach of all but the wealthiest in society.

The high clergy of the Catholic church remained exclusively noble to 1803. Another special group consisted of the patriarchy of the imperial cities. Although technically members of the middle class, the "noble" families of Nuremberg, Münster, and Frankfurt had simply selected "patricians" from within their own ranks since the end of the seventeenth century, who were accorded social status commensurate with that of the lower nobility. Nuremberg was a special case. Since the sixteenth century, its patricians had bought land estates, and since 1667 they had used nobiliary participles (*auf, von, zu*) in front of their middle-class names. Since 1697 the twenty leading families were free to use the title *Edel* ("noble" or "wellborn").

The German middle class (*Bürgertum*, or burghers) formed the third estate. Hardly a privileged order, this group was predominantly urban, by 1800 comprising about one in every four citizens, or just under 6 million people. Conversely, middle-class residents enjoying full legal status as free citizens (*Bürgerrecht*) made up roughly 10 to 12 percent of the population of most major cities. These urban citizens, or *Bürger*, could not vote at the Reichstag. Rather, they cast their ballots indirectly through their local city deputation.

As with the nobility, the urban middle class was marked by heterogeneity. The Prussian Civil Code of 1794 vaguely defined *Bürger* as all those who "belong neither to the nobility nor to the peasantry." At the top stood an upper echelon of about 3 to 6 percent of the urban population: wealthy merchants and tradesmen, manufacturers, high-ranking civil servants, lawyers, doctors, clerics, and professors, as well as a few nobles who maintained city residences.

By far the vast majority of the bourgeoisie belonged to the middle layer — about 40 percent of most urban populations — consisting of artisans, craftsmen, small merchants, low-ranking civil servants, and service personnel. Of special importance were the closed-shop guilds, whose masters since the fourteenth century had the right to sit on city councils. In fact, the guilds dominated town governments and held exclusive rights to market their products in towns. In addition, the masters restricted admission to the guilds, supervised training standards, and set wages and prices. The number of citizens enjoying full legal status, or *Bürgerrecht*, varied from city to city. In eighteenth-century Augsburg, for example, it ranged as high as 6,000 out of 30,000 inhabitants.

The lower rungs of the bourgeoisie made up anywhere between 40 and 60 percent of the urban and 20 to 25 percent of the general population. This *petite bourgeoisie* ranged from domestic servants, seamstresses, and washerwomen to unskilled and day laborers. In addition, the lower bourgeoisie included widows, tailors, weavers, dyers, fullers, shoemakers, and impoverished artisans, none of whom paid taxes because they had little real income.

The *petite bourgeoisie* faced harsh lives. In Berlin artisans toiled in the summer from 6:00 A.M. until 7:00 P.M.; in the winter, they began at 7:00 A.M. and labored until 8:00 P.M. Around 1800 a brick mason required about three-fourths of his income for food, and more than half of that went for bread alone. Preindustrial pauperization was rampant: on average, one in every four city dwellers resorted to begging. Only a few centers such as Halle and Leipzig had permanent asylums, orphanages, and poorhouses designed to alleviate the plight of the downtrodden. For the most part, the destitute were left to their own devices.

Because the German middle class was primarily urban, it is useful to take a close look at several representative German cities. In 1784 Berlin boasted 145,000 inhabitants divided into six societal orders: members of the military; the educated, privileged upper-middle class; the German middle class; a French Huguenot colony; a Bohemian colony; and Jews. The Huguenots numbered just over 5,000 and the Jews over 3,000. More than 7,000 beggars roamed the city. One in every five citizens was listed as a legally and economically independent head of a household. Almost one in five belonged to the group of domestic servants. Most urban dwellers still owned small plots of land. Whereas police in Frankfurt repeatedly warned residents not to let their pigs run loose on city streets, townspeople in Berlin still maintained pigsties in their front yards as late as 1800. In neither city were the streets swept.

The Hanseatic city of Hamburg represented yet another distinct category, recognizing neither nobility nor patriarchy. Nobles could not purchase property within city limits, become legal *Bürger*, or find employment in the city administration. At best, they could enlist in its militia. Theoretically all citizens enjoyed legal equality. In reality, however, full legal status as free *Bürger* was bestowed upon only about 9,000 residents out of a total population in 1800 of 130,000. These few were thus entitled to vote in municipal elections. Of the 9,000, roughly 3,000 to 4,000 constituted a resident elite that selected the city's 650 office-holders. As part of the so-called golden triangle of Amsterdam-London-Hamburg, the city's middle class was practically divided into an upper and lower middle class according to wealth. A single family, Amsinck, provided fully two-thirds of all members of the senate in the mid-eighteenth century.

Vienna, the largest city in the Empire, was dominated by the nobility. Since the middle of the sixteenth century, Vienna had served as the administrative center of the Holy Roman Empire and the Habsburg possessions. Since 1619 it also functioned as the administrative seat for Austria, Bohemia, and Hungary. Thus, more than any other German city, its character as a royal residence was determined by its role as an imperial and royal administrative hub. Its population climbed from 175,000 in mid-century to 232,000 by 1800.

Sixty percent of Vienna's residents in 1730 belonged to privileged social orders: 20 percent were court personnel, 18 percent members of the nobility, 12 percent civil servants, and 10 percent the city guard. Forty percent of the city's inhabitants were deemed middle class — persons such as doctors, fixed-income earners, artisans, merchants, and innkeepers.

The Habsburgs were adept at ensuring social mobility for urban burghers. Both Empress Maria Theresa and her son, Emperor Joseph II, generously rewarded the prosperous and meritorious middle class. Of those ennobled between 1740 and 1780, 7 percent belonged to the industrious middle class. In the decade of his rule after 1780, Joseph II raised that figure to 18 percent. The contrast to Prussia is illuminating. While four out of every ten persons ennobled by Maria Theresa were civil servants, in Prussia between 1790 and 1806 more officers than civil servants received titles of nobility.

Poverty plagued Vienna too. Most of the indigent were women and children, financially cast adrift by the death of a husband and father. In 1790, for example, two of every three persons stricken in this manner reportedly were reduced to begging. According to another estimate from that year, two of every three lower-class Viennese whose corpses arrived at the morgue had possessed but the rags on their bodies.

The German princes exercised patriarchal guardianship — law and order in today's parlance — over both the physical and moral well-being of their subjects. Public order was maintained in German cities by local police, who additionally were responsible for maintenance of the water supply, sanitation, garbage removal, supervision of midwives and pharmacists, prohibition of begging, and regulation of prices, wages, hours, and conditions of work. Because most German princes also controlled the moral education of their subjects, police were empowered to enforce such ordinances as those forbidding servant girls in Brunswick from wearing gold or silver ornaments in public, using silk as dress material, and wearing shoes made of anything but plain black leather. In Posen (today Poznań, in Poland), police saw to it that middle-class women refrained from wearing capes and from letting their hair hang down their backs. Landgrave Karl Friedrich of Baden considered it his "fatherly duty" to teach his subjects "even against their will how to order their domestic affairs" or, as he put it on another occasion, "to make them, whether they like it or not, into free, prosperous and law-abiding subjects."

Most middle-class homes were modest. In Silesia, one of the richest provinces in the Empire, two-thirds of all houses still had thatched straw roofs at the time of the Seven Years' War. Only one-third of the residents could afford sturdier fireproof tile roofs. The homes were mainly simple wooden structures, often half-timbered with mud and straw walls. The few who could afford carpets usually purchased them from Belgium and France. Tapestries came from Paris and Lyon. Furniture styles, dictated by the main princely residential centers of Berlin, Dresden, Munich, and Vienna, were produced in manufacturing plants established at Aachen, Brunswick, Lüttich, Mainz, and Würzburg. The popular Louis XVI style dominated until around 1800. Six years later, the new *empire* style of Napoleon I began to achieve prominence at courts, and the English furniture manuals put out by Thomas Chippendale, Robert and James Adams, George Hepplewhite, and Thomas Sheraton dictated bourgeois tastes. The new rage for *Bürger* was the spittoon, which made its way from France to Germany late in the eighteenth century.

The last estate in the Reich was that of the peasantry (*Bauern*). Serfdom (*Leibeigenschaft*) pervaded this estate, proving harshest in Holstein and the Wendish lands of eastern Germany, moderate in Westphalia, and least severe in Hesse and Swabia. Around 1800, three Germans in every four, or roughly 18 million people, lived on the land. Of these, an estimated 40 percent were propertyless, and 35 percent were freeholders (mainly in south and west Germany). Recent estimates of land dwellers in western German lands suggest that half were peasants and smallholders, intermingled with smaller groups of artisans, as well as landless and homeless laborers. The Swiss chronicler Ulrich Bräker left a vivid account of rural life in the 1780s:

> The worst for me by far was leaving my warm little bed so early in the morning, and tramping poorly clad and barefoot out into the cold fields. . . . Then I'd freeze . . . and feel pains in my feet, even though they were hard as shoeleather. Most of the time I also had injuries or bruises somewhere or other on me; and when one wound was healed then I went and got myself another, either by landing on a sharp stone and losing a nail or a piece of flesh from a toe, or else giving my hand a gash with one of my tools.

For centuries, the manorial system (*Grundherrschaft*) defined legal and social landownership. The village with its people and surrounding farmlands constituted a manor, the estate of a lord. A mutual or reciprocal relationship existed between lord and serf. The lord owed his vassals protection and the administration of justice; the vassals worked the lord's fields and owed him part of their own production. Serfs were thus bound to the soil under this system. Lesser landowners within the manor could freely buy, sell, lease, bequeath, or inherit land, in return for certain rents and fees payable annually in recognition of the manor lord's eminent property rights. Recent studies of villages in the western German lands have revealed that peasant fees and contributions on average amounted to between one-fifth and one-third of all produce and that seven of every ten farmers there struggled at the bare subsistence level.

The idealized "beast of burden" (1750).

In the eastern German lands, self-managed Junker estates (*Gutsherrschaft*) dominated. The dominant feature was the extension of noble control over the peasants. In its strictest form, *Gutsherrschaft* dictated the peasants' movement, marriage, and even servitude of their children. The unfortunates under this system also owed the lords special manual labor — in the Habsburg lands ranging from one hundred to two hundred days per year — as well as a head tax, death tax, marriage tax, and part of their production. The Prussian Civil Code of 1794 clearly defined the legal obligations incurred under *Gutsherrschaft*. Even in a progressive state such as Bavaria, where serfdom was relatively mild, farmers owned but 4 percent of all land, compared to 56 percent for the clergy, 34 percent for the nobility, and 13 percent for the crown.

The peasants were truly the beasts of burden. Most were illiterate; they left few records describing the misery of life on the land. The Enlightenment writers habitually depicted peasants as brutish and dumb, coarse and dishonest, drunken and quarrelsome. *Der dumme Bauer* ("the dumb farmer") became a byword for "stupidity." Veneration of rustic clothing and life-styles would not become fashionable in central Europe until the nineteenth century. Austrian folklore had it that the peasantry, like grass, needed to be mowed down frequently in order for it to regenerate.

Few peasants possessed furniture, utensils, or tools of any kind. Most lived in one-room cottages that served as living and sleeping quarters, kitchen, storage shed, and barn for humans and animals alike. In summer, the peasants slept en masse in haylofts; in winter, in crowded barns kept warm only by the body heat of animals. Incest was extremely high, and its customary results were usually not even recorded. Most peasants consumed at least two-thirds of all they produced and made their own clothing and the few rudimentary tools they needed. In the case of rare surplus crops, they bartered them for such items as spices and metal tools.

Perhaps a contemporary, Goethe's great-uncle, Johann Michael Baron von Loen, best described the German peasantry of 1771:

> Today, the peasant is the most miserable of all creatures: the farmers are slaves and their farmhands are almost indiscernible from the animals they tend. One sees villages where the children run about half naked, and hail travelers for alms. Their parents scarcely have a rag with which to cover their nakedness. A few haggard cows must till their fields and give them milk. Their barns are empty, and their cottages threaten to collapse in a heap at any moment. They [the peasants] look pathetic and miserable; one would pity them, if their wild and brutish appearance did not seem to justify their hard lot.

Apart from death or emigration, the only hope for a peasant was to be the subject of an enlightened ruler. The peasants on the Hohenzollern crown lands were legally emancipated by Frederick William I of Prussia as early as 1718. The king even gave his subjects their homes and tools "from Christian intention." In 1777 his son, Frederick II, decreed that about fifty thousand royal peasants would have their possessions guaranteed by the state — not only for themselves but also for their children. Naturally, the king demanded payments in return, as the revenue from crown lands amounted to no less than one-fourth of all Prussian income. Yet the Prussian case remained isolated. Most peasants did not shed their servitude until the first decade of the nineteenth century, and in Austria not until 1848–1849.

Land usage patterns had not changed much since the days of Rome. The Slavic wooden plow enjoyed widespread use. Germans considered deep-plowing, as practiced in Britain, harmful and unnatural. The three-field system was standard: one field, plowed in autumn, would be sown with wheat or rye; another field, plowed early in the new year, would be sown with spring grain such as barley, oats, beans, or peas; and because fertility soon gave out, the third field had to be left in fallow to recuperate. Crop rotation — first flax, then turnips, then oats undersown with clover — as developed in Flanders by the mid-seventeenth century (and thereafter adopted in Britain as the Norfolk system) was unknown in the German lands. In Bohemia, soil manuring was held to be a crime. The open-field system, which paid no attention to pasture lands, afforded little fodder, and in the spring, animals often were so weak that farmers had to drag them to pastures on sleds. When Dutch fodder crops arrived in

Austria, they were such a success that the man responsible was raised into the nobility as "knight of the clover." By 1800 the Norfolk system came to Germany, whereby the field habitually used for spring plantings of barley and oats was now allowed to recover, either by supporting other crops, such as fodder, or by lying fallow. A truly scientific understanding of farming would not come until around the time of the French Revolution.

Commerce and Communications

Lack of uniform commercial and communications systems severely hampered trade in eighteenth-century Germany. Circulating coinages, especially, proved baffling. Thaler and groschen dominated in north Germany, and the gulden and kreuzer reigned south of the Main River. Although both Lübeck and Prussia used a kurantfuss, the former's was valued at 34 gulden and the latter's at 21 gulden. And whereas the Austrian konventionsfuss was set at 20 gulden, the Bavarian koventionsfuss was slightly higher, at 24 gulden. A plethora of gold coins such as the carolin (Bavaria), souvrain d'or (Austria), or ducat, max d'or, louis d'or, and pistole circulated the land, varying in value from 4.5 to 13.5 gulden.

Banks of issue were almost unknown in a society that conducted the majority of its commercial transactions in barter or precious metals. The first such institution was founded in Berlin in 1765 by Frederick II as the Royal Transfer and Loan Bank. Two years later in Munich, the Electoral Land Bank of Bavaria followed. Perhaps the need for financial paper transfers grew from the fact that most states spent the major portion of their revenues at home directly on the military. Under Frederick II of Prussia, that amount was estimated at 80 percent. In Vienna it came to half of all revenues, and in Bavaria it was lowest at one-third of the monies collected.

Monetary values are virtually impossible to translate into current terms.[1] It might help to note that English travelers in Germany recorded that an unskilled laborer could earn six or seven pence a day, at a time when bread cost one pence, and beef, lamb, or pork four pence per pound. Whereas a good cook or servant man could earn thirty shilling per year, a pound of coffee went for one shilling. An experienced tutor might receive a salary of between three and eight pounds sterling per annum, but a fine lady's dress averaged ten pounds. Such monetary values obviously are valid only in relationship to each other. Further, salaries and wages fluctuated wildly from one state to another, defying meaningful comparisons.

Inconsistent weights and measures, like coinage, also hampered trade. The south German pound was 22 percent heavier than the English pound, but the

[1] Roughly, 1 gulden was equal to 2 shillings, or 2 reichsmark.

north German pound was only 3 to 5 percent heavier. The ell, the unit of linear measurement, was generally set at two feet, but although the Prussian foot roughly equaled the English foot, in Vienna it was longer and in Hamburg shorter than the English unit. Some German states even used various ells for different materials. The German "common mile" was 4.6 English statute miles, thus making the German square mile the equivalent of 21.25 English square miles. Still more baffling, the German mile (*Meile*), when converted to the metric system after the French Revolution, ranged from seven to nine kilometers.

The state of German roads represented a third impediment to commerce and communications. Carriage gauges varied, and ruts in roads were wider in the east than in the west, with the result that drivers often found it easier to travel over open fields than on roads. The latter, especially in Prussia, were sandy in summer and muddy in winter. There existed few stone bridges; most were made of differing qualities of wood and thus were susceptible to fire and flood. Travelers had to ford small streams and to rely on unstable floating bridges on the larger rivers. Public boats were neither sturdy nor seaworthy. When David Hume traveled down the Danube by private boat in 1748, he was surprised to see that the craft was "pulled to pieces in Vienna. The wood is sold and the watermen return to Regensburg on foot. We lie on shore every night."

Pack horses remained the most reliable method of moving light goods. Primitive rafts transported heavier cargoes, but rapids and shallows restricted the use of rivers and the construction of many canals until the nineteenth century. By 1744 the postal system was a monopoly in the hands of the prince of Thurn und Taxis of Regensburg, who received imperial fiat to undertake this exasperatingly slow service. At best the post could cover fifty miles per day. The journey from Frankfurt am Main to Berlin took nine days. Roadside inns were dirty, and the food and drink served there were of poor quality.

Internal tariffs created yet another impediment. The fifty-mile stretch of the Rhine from Koblenz to Mainz bristled with a toll station every mile. No fewer than sixteen additional tariff barriers inhibited trade between Koblenz and Holland. On the Elbe River, fourteen toll stations stood between Magdeburg and Hamburg, and on the Main River no fewer than thirty-three barriers marked the route between Mainz and Bamberg.

The states of the Empire traded mainly with France but also with Britain and the Netherlands. By the end of the eighteenth century, German exports consisted of 60 percent of textiles and only 10 percent of cereal grains. Hamburg became the major German seaport of the eighteenth century, and most of its commerce lay in foreign hands. Of the 2,000 ships that called at Hamburg every year, only 160 belonged to local merchants. Hamburg virtually became a British satellite, a clearinghouse where British merchants transferred their wares to the rest of the Continent. As a result, Hamburg possessed the first coffeehouses, published the first political journals like the *Spectator*, boasted the first Masonic lodge, and became a breeding ground for British political and economic theories.

Leipzig served as the primary inland commercial center, where trade routes from east and west met. Poles and Jews, Russians and Greeks, Dutchmen and Englishmen mingled there at the thrice-annual trade fairs. It was not unusual for seven thousand merchants to congregate at these fairs or for English traders to report turnovers of 1 million pounds sterling. Moreover, Leipzig became a publishing center for Germany. Since Pope Pius IV had created the Index of Prohibited Books in 1570, and since the Imperial Book Commission at Frankfurt applied this censorship rigorously, Protestant Leipzig, which eschewed official censorship, developed a lucrative book printing trade that lasted well into the early twentieth century.

German domestic manufacturing was miniscule by British standards, employing but 7 percent of the work force. Textiles led the way, with 3 percent of the labor pool. Much of the German production came from seasonal and part-time cottage industries: linen from Silesia, clocks from the Black Forest, toys from Thuringia, and crystal glass from Bohemia. The largest state industries produced luxury items; Germany boasted no fewer than sixty porcelain manufactories. The most famous arose in Meissen (1710), Vienna (1718–1719), Nymphenburg (1747), Fürstenberg (1753), and Berlin (1760).

Mercantilism, as espoused in France by Louis XIV's controller-general, Jean-Baptiste Colbert, prevailed in the Reich. Protectionistic, monopolistic, and highly dependent on government subsidies, this economic theory stressed the cultivation of new industries, markets, trade routes, and trading companies. To stimulate overseas commerce, merchants looked to colonies as sources of raw materials and as markets for finished products. In the German lands, mercantilism took a special form known as cameralism, a term derived from a word denoting economic and fiscal policies devised in the chambers of the princely court and administration. But given the Reich's polycentrism, cameralism by definition was particularist rather than national.

By the latter part of the eighteenth century, a countervailing influence came to Germany from across the North Sea. Adam Smith's *An Inquiry into the*

SOURCES OF NATIONAL INCOME IN GERMANY, 1800

Source	Income (reichsthaler)
Cultivated farmland	50,656,000
Pastures, meadows	19,652,000
Forest and wood products	6,500,000
Gardens	2,782,000
Manufacturing	1,638,000
Fishing	749,000
Hunting	665,000
Mining	300,000

Nature and Causes of the Wealth of Nations (1776) was warmly received in Germany and appeared in translation between 1794 and 1796. It appealed primarily to the three Hanseatic cities of Bremen, Hamburg, and Lübeck, as well as to the imperial city of Frankfurt. These four commercial centers had effectively practiced free trade and had possessed free market economies well before Smith's classic work on the subject.

Culture: Official and Popular

The eighteenth century has been variously called the Age of Absolutism, the Age of Reason, and the Age of the Enlightenment. It was also an age of German classical literature and classical music, an age of baroque and rococo architecture, and an age of letters in which noted scholars filled eighty or more volumes with their collected works. Writers such as Klopstock and Herder, Goethe and Schiller, composers such as Mozart and Haydn, Beethoven and Händel, are the most legendary. An adequate analysis of these men and their works goes far beyond the limits of this book, but a few comments on their role in eighteenth-century Germany are in order.

The learned and elite culture of central Europe found its zenith in the Enlightenment. Centered mainly in west and central Europe, the *Aufklärung*, the German phase of the Enlightenment, emphasized emancipation of the individual from convention, prejudice, religion, and tradition. The movement's leading figures were of varied regional and social origins and people of great talents from a narrow layer of society: some from the nobility, some from the middle class, and a very few from the lower middle class. Their interests ranged over literature, mathematics, history, political theory, economics, and philosophy. A number were recently baptized former Jews. All shared a common commitment to intellectual freedom as well as a belief that the religious traditions of the Roman Catholic church and the "dark ages" of the medieval past especially thwarted human intellectual fulfillment. Their battle cry was simple: use reason to its full potential. Kant, in an article entitled "What Is Enlightenment?" defined the movement's purpose: "*Dare to know!* Have courage to make use of your own understanding."

Although the Enlightenment was limited to the most literate citizens — and hence to less than 10 percent of the population — it nevertheless wielded significant influence through the high administrative offices held by some of its apostles, such as Gerhard van Swieten, Samuel von Cocceji, and Joseph von Sonnenfels. Collectively, the leading figures of the German Enlightenment conducted a written campaign against dogmatism, intolerance, and superstition in religion and ignorance, inequality, and prejudice in society.

Absolutism (actually a nineteenth-century term), the theory that power should emanate from one ruler, was a close relative of the Enlightenment, especially in central Europe. The historical territorial fragmentation and the peculiar political structure of the Holy Roman Empire, whereby a prince could be both absolute in his own state and yet representative in the Reichstag, prompted German Enlightenment writers to associate their political freedom with strong princely authority. As a result, there was little subject-ruler antagonism in the German *Aufklärung*. Both ruler and philosopher sought to rationalize princely power. Both favored secularization. Both championed the economic and political power of the central state against the church. And both accepted the "social discipline" of an order of estates (*Stände*) as natural.

One of the most brilliant minds of the early eighteenth century, Gottfried Wilhelm von Leibniz, argued that because dissension tended to reduce the power of the individual states within the Empire, rulers and subjects alike needed to present a strong, united front to the outside world to avert political chaos. While there was no shortage of tyrannical hereditary rulers, Leibniz suggested that the evils caused by rebellion far outweighed any princely abuse.

A great trio of German *Aufklärung* theorists — Samuel von Pufendorf, Christian Thomasius, and Christian von Wolff — agreed that princes were responsible for education, economy, and welfare services (including orphanages and poor houses) in their realms. All three concurred that some nebulous form of a contractual basis for princely rule existed and needed to be observed. Yet none showed any enthusiasm for Charles de Secondat Montesquieu's notion of a division of powers or the concept of aristocratically limited monarchy as set out in his *Esprit des lois* (The Spirit of Laws) in 1748. None of the three German thinkers urged constitutional safeguards or conceived of alternatives to unlimited princely powers.

The relationship between enlightened philosophers and rulers remains an open question. One may well ask to what extent Maria Theresa and Joseph II, for instance, used Enlightened tracts only to the degree that such writings served to underpin and strengthen royal absolutism. Or, at another level, while acknowledging that Frederick II at Sans Souci surrounded himself with a cadre of enlightened thinkers and devoured the works of the French *philosophes*,[1] one may well argue that the Prussian ruler pursued domestic policies that were all but indistinguishable from those of his father — a most "unenlightened" ruler in purely intellectual terms. It is well known that Catherine II of Russia purchased the twenty-eight volumes of Denis Diderot's *Encyclopédie* and read and annotated them, yet she kept the collection under lock and key. Perhaps the absolute rulers of central Europe exploited the works of the Enlightenment theorists only to the extent that their thoughts served to support princely power.

[1] The *philosophes* were French progressive thinkers who argued that Europe in the eighteenth century was finally emerging from a long twilight, an age of darkness and barbarism. The term is generally applied to French men of letters, popularizers, and publicists.

Official and elite culture, especially architecture and music, revolved around courts. Whether prince or archbishop, a ruler sought to enhance his status by surrounding himself with palaces and gardens, vivid displays of his power over nature and humanity alike. By welding castles and abbeys into one form, baroque architects strove to symbolize an imperial dignity supported by a universal religious faith.

Dresden had long led the way in German architecture. Under Augustus the Strong, Matthäus Pöppelmann and Georg Bähr had turned the Saxon capital into a baroque city, and its magnificent art collection and Italian opera gave rise to Dresden's reputation as the Florence on the Elbe. Vienna's premier architect, Johann Bernhard Fischer von Erlach, developed a building style known as "imperial baroque." The Habsburg residence at Schönbrunn, built between 1696 and 1730 and remodeled for Maria Theresa in the 1740s, perhaps best exemplifies this style; other examples grace Prague and Salzburg. The lesser German princes similarly sought to express their power through lavish residences at Herrenhausen, Ludwigsburg, Mannheim, Nymphenburg, and elsewhere. Those who could not afford their own "Versailles," such as the rulers at Brunswick, Karlsruhe, Mühlhausen, Stuttgart, and Wolfenbüttel, settled for less extravagant wooden palaces and town houses.

Royal residences were designed to be fit for heroes. Consequently, Olympian motifs of classical gods abounded. Humanity's greatness received careful attention. Royal portraits, especially, gave visible expression to the newfound Olympus. Perhaps most representative is Hyacinthe Rigaud's picture in Dresden of Augustus III. The proudly poised head, the overly erect figure, the leonine state wig, the shining armor, the silk and ermine cloak swelling in the breeze against a stormy sky — all depict a baroque Jupiter with one hand on his swordhilt, the other on his marshal's staff. For a court painter to have suggested less would have amounted to an insult, and probably permanent unemployment as well. It mattered little that Augustus III was a lazy and ineffectual idler.

Ecclesiastical baroque dominated in Bohemia and Silesia, Bavaria and Austria, Swabia and Franconia, as well as in the German states along the Rhine. The prince-bishops created ornate residences at Bonn, Bruchsal, Pommersfelden, and Würzburg — the last completed by Balthasar Neumann in the 1740s and featuring the exquisite fresco paintings of Giovanni Battista Tiepolo. Other noted architects designed the grand Austrian abbeys of Melk, St. Florian, Admont, and Göttweig, the Bavarian Ettal, the Swabian Weingarten, Ottobeuren, and the Silesian Grünau.

Baroque castles of Christ, these abbeys reflected classical styles and constituted but an extension of Renaissance art forms. The baroque church was designed to direct the attention of the faithful toward transcendental truth and joy. The interior, composed as a single entity, sought to lift the believer from this earth up toward heaven. A central cupola flooded the altar with sunlight; to worshipers looking upward, the cupola seemed the very panorama of heaven. Cherubs and saints suspended from walls and columns in ideal space invited mortal believers to exaltation. Never before had Christianity offered such sensual attraction to stir the faithful to greater devotion.

In south and southwest Germany, baroque reached its opulent climax in rococo after the end of the Seven Years' War[1] in 1763. Derived from the France of Louis XIV, rococo displayed a supreme concentration of detail. Every pillar in a church was adorned with angelic figures painted in rich, lush colors and brushed with gold or hung with gold brocade. Biblical scenes depicted the church's ceiling as the very gates to heaven. This most lavish portrayal of Christian exuberance, wealth, and triumph became the trademark especially of François Cuvilliès in Bavaria. His greatest accomplishments included the monasteries of Schäftlarn and Diessen, castle Falkenlust near Brühl, and the Munich residence. The Wies church in southern Bavaria is perhaps the most famous rococo structure in Germany.

North Germany, by contrast, generally escaped the baroque influence. Only under Frederick I of Prussia (1701–1713) was there a brief flirtation with using architecture to glorify the royal dignity that the Hohenzollerns had gained in 1701. Andreas Schlüter built the Armory as well as the royal palaces in Berlin and at Charlottenburg. Thereafter, a stark classicism prevailed through the "rococo classicism" of Georg Wenzeslaus von Knobelsdorff (Sans Souci and the Neues Palais) and the "Prussian" and "Dutch" classicism of Karl Gotthard Langhans (Brandenburg Gate).

Sculpture by and large was uninteresting. German artists roamed Italy with sketchbooks in hand, taking detailed notes of Italian models, most of them inferior copies of Greek and Roman originals. Imitation thus was further imitated. Led by Johann Joachim Winckelmann, German sculptors strove to reproduce a noble and superior spirit in their classical works. The urban middle class found the imitations pleasing and filled gardens, parks, and public squares with such monuments. In Berlin only Gottfried Shadow challenged this blind veneration of classical culture and instead produced realistic representations in both portraits and statues.

German painters did not share this veneration of classical culture. Instead, artists such as Wilhelm von Kobell and Joseph Anton Koch offered realistic portrayals of German landscapes. They combined keen observation and great sensitivity to convey a natural, lively atmosphere through the use of light and shade. Heinrich Tischbein's famous painting *Goethe in the Campagna* (1787) shows the great writer as a citizen of the world against an Arcadian background; his wide white traveling cloak evokes the Roman toga, and the broad-rimmed hat depicts the reflective humanist of the eighteenth century. Bridging the period before and after the French Revolution is the work of Caspar David

[1] The Seven Years' War was fought between Austria and Prussia between 1756 and 1763. It will be discussed in Chapter 2.

Citizen of the world: Heinrich Tischbein's *Goethe in the Campagna* (1787).

Friedrich, whose paintings depicted human beings as transient parts of creation and nature. Friedrich contrasted human beings with nature to show how insignificant and powerless people are in the face of nature's strength. Guided by a deep yet simple piety, Friedrich developed an insatiable longing to understand the universe and to use its august majesty as a source of inspiration.

Elite culture also found expression in eighteenth-century music, another art form of the aristocracy in general and of the church-princes in particular. Vienna, finally liberated from Italian guardianship, dominated as the musical capital of Europe, claiming as its own Joseph Haydn, Wolfgang Amadeus Mozart, and Ludwig van Beethoven. Northern Germany counted Johann Sebastian Bach and Georg Friedrich Händel (who eventually settled in England) as their own.

Johann Sebastian Bach, born in 1685, served after 1723 as cantor at the Thomas Church at Leipzig. A deeply pious man, Bach sought in his *Passions* to reveal the reflections and moods of fundamental Christian ideas. For Lutheran Germany, Bach struggled to make visible the deepest substance of Christian religion. A brief visit with Frederick II — himself a notable flutist and composer — at Potsdam in 1747, which Bach described as the climax of his career, resulted in Bach's famous *Musical Offering*, a composition extemporized upon a theme given the composer by the king. Bach's great secular work, the six *Brandenburg Concertos*, remains a musical tribute to the land of the Hohenzollerns.

Georg Friedrich Händel, like Bach born in 1685, moved to England in 1714 after a brief career in Germany and Italy. There he anglicized his name to Handel. After the English public lost its interest in Italian opera (at which Handel excelled), he turned to the oratorio, depicting the Bible as the record of God's relations with his elected people (*Messiah* and *Judas Macabaeus*). Handel moved the setting for his musical theodicies for heroically minded Christians out of the English churches and into the concert halls, thereby attracting an enthusiastic new public to his music, which appealed especially to a nation still mired in the Stuart insurrection. Händel is the only German buried at Westminster Abbey.

For years, Franz Joseph Haydn served the great Hungarian magnates, the Princes Paul and Nicholas Esterházy, as personal musician. In the process, he developed the classic sonata form and integrated the various instruments of the string quartet into the full orchestra, a single sound-body. At heart a Pietist, Haydn's religious view reflected that of the Enlightenment, the grateful worship of a God who was the creator of a world full of beauty and joy. Haydn's great oratorio, *The Creation*, composed in 1798 and adapted from John Milton's *Paradise Lost*, attested to his deeply pious outlook.

Wolfgang Amadeus Mozart, by contrast, was a tragic figure. Born in Salzburg to a family of Augsburg artisans, Mozart accepted employment as a musician at the court of the prince-archbishop. After Mozart lost the patronage of the ruler, he remained poverty stricken until his death in 1791 at the age of thirty-five. This towering genius of eighteenth-century music was the first to compose some of his operas in German and included all strata of society. Many of his characters received realistic, almost Shakespearean stature. In his unfinished *Requiem Mass*, Mozart acknowledged the existence of life and death as the will of the creator but expressed confidence that human beings could progress toward a higher state of virtue and love. Like Haydn, Mozart was truly a prodigy of the Enlightenment. Vienna, however, rejected him, and the French complained about "too much music" (that is, too many notes) in his works.

The age of German classical music sought to bridge the traditional gap between secular and religious music. International and cosmopolitan in approach and substance, its exuberance and celebration of the human spirit musically paved the way for the French Revolution's ideals of freedom, equality, and brotherhood. Ludwig van Beethoven's stirring chorale in the Ninth Symphony, based on Friedrich Schiller's "Ode to Joy," perhaps best typifies this humanitarian approach.

German literature, in contrast, remained primarily a middle-class product and suffered financial instability. The first German daily newspaper, the *Leipziger Zeitung*, did not appear until 1660. Playwrights usually had to finance the staging of their own plays, often losing their meager resources as a result. No copyright laws existed in Germany before 1871; hence plagiarism was a constant threat.

If France was the model for the German nobility, England became the guiding star for the German bourgeoisie's tastes. The latter's love of things English ranged from the "discovery" of William Shakespeare by Johann Elias Schlegel and Gotthold Ephraim Lessing in the early nineteenth century to English gardens and country manors, and from the English journals of Joseph Addison and Richard Steele to enlightened English writers such as John Locke and (the Scot) David Hume.

Perhaps the greatest problem for German writers was the absence of any national symbols. Late in life, the German poet Friedrich Gottlieb Klopstock had turned to northern mythology as a symbol of a new German school of poetry and had attempted to liberate the German language from French and Latin domination, but his efforts would have to await Richard Wagner's *Nibelungen* for a revival of the Teutonic (musical) drama. And while Goethe saw Frederick II of Prussia as the first "German" heroic figure and Kant spoke of the eighteenth century as "Frederick's century," the Prussian king did not reciprocate these feelings. In fact, Frederick II rejected both the German language ("One speaks German to the dogs") and its practitioners. Frederick's Enlightenment was French; his models came from ancient Greece and Rome. He especially despised what he termed "the awful plays of Shakespeare translated into our language," calling these works "absurd farces, fit only for the savages of Canada." Goethe's *Götz von Berlichingen* (1773), a play of Shakespearean stature set in the German Middle Ages and replete with heroic action, earned from Frederick a ringing rebuke: "A detestable imitation of those wretched English plays." German literature, as a result, was "the almost miraculous creation of a soul without a body."

Frederick's French myopia was most unfortunate, for Germany was approaching its age of classical literature. Lessing's *Minna von Barnhelm* (1767) constituted the first work of a north German national character, depicting the plight of Prussian veterans and families after the Seven Years' War. Lessing's *Miss Sara Sampson* (1755) and *Emilia Galotti* (1772), compassionate treatments of the restricted role of females in eighteenth-century Germany, became bourgeois classics. His *Nathan the Wise* (1779), based on St. Paul's First Letter to the Corinthians, was a heart felt plea for tolerance and humanity.

Friedrich Schiller's historical dramas, such as *Don Carlos* (1787), *Maria Stuart* (1800), *Die Jungfrau von Orleans* (1801), and *Wilhelm Tell* (1804), were European in scope and national in their settings. In bold, clear lines, Schiller, who taught history and philosophy at Jena University, sought to convey to his readers unambiguous moral lessons. His enthusiastic optimism especially appealed to Germans in later, more troubled times. His early protest play (1772–1778) *Die Räuber* (The Robbers) was a runaway success that challenged even Goethe in popularity, if not durability. Above all, Schiller became the champion of freedom. He advocated human solidarity and detailed its longing for progress, perfection, and liberty. The ultimate goal of civilization was a free state of reason, its highest stage that of simple humanity.

In 1776 Friedrich Maximilian von Klinger's drama *Sturm und Drang* inadvertently gave name to the "storm and stress" period of German literature. Writers now rebelled against what they termed the precision, logic, and lack of emotion that for them characterized the Age of Reason and sought instead to emphasize feelings, emotions, fantasy, and nature. One critic has summarized their stance as follows: With Shakespeare and Rousseau against Voltaire!

The ensuing "period of genius" was dominated by Goethe, Germany's greatest lyric poet. Born in 1749 the son of a prosperous innkeeper who had married the daughter of the lord mayor of Frankfurt, Goethe served as minister of finances and mines at the court of Karl August of Weimar and was ennobled in 1782. His literary activity spanned the periods of classicism, "storm and stress," and romanticism. He witnessed the French Revolution, the Napoleonic wars, and even the birth of German liberalism before his death in 1832.

Goethe's *The Sorrows of Young Werther* (1774) became the representative *Sturm und Drang* piece, wherein a sensitive soul is quashed by the conflict with reality and eventually commits suicide. *Werther* sounded the opening shot in the revolt of the young generation against the Enlightenment. Indeed, the polarity between the individual and society emerged as a standard literary theme starting with this work. *Werther* became a cult novel. Napoleon devoured it and when he met and praised its author in 1806 at Erfurt, he declared: "Here is a man!" In Vienna there were annual "Werther fireworks." Elsewhere, an epidemic of "Werther" pants, blue dress-coat, and yellow vest raged. Germany was also swept by a wave of "Werther" suicides.

Perhaps of greater impact on German literature and history was Goethe's *Faust* trilogy (1773, 1806, and 1832). *Faust,* called the "divine comedy" of eighteenth-century humanism, is the story of the magician and charlatan Dr. Faust, who, accompanied by Mephistopheles (the Spirit of Denial), makes a compact with the devil, bartering away his soul for a definite period of superhuman power and knowledge, but finally triumphs over the powers of evil. It became the archetypal German tragedy: the dialectic of good and evil, God and the devil, guilt and redemption, reality and myth, triumph and defeat — a heady mix of history, war, politics, and the state that was to become a *Leitmotiv* down to Thomas Mann's novel *Doktor Faustus* in 1947.

Finally, inspired by Johann Gottfried Herder's *Journal of My Journey of 1769*, romantic writers such as Jean Paul, Friedrich Hölderlin, Heinrich von Kleist, and Novalis (Friedrich von Hardenberg) rediscovered and glorified Germany's medieval past as a period of peace and harmony, a spiritual empire led by a wise church.[1] This religious beauty and truth, they declared, had been

[1] The romantic school championed the freedom of the individual, the undivided sensuousness and intelligible nature of people, and poetic aesthetic sense. It rejected the dominance of general laws and ideals and the existence of a system of general truth.

destroyed by the Reformation and the Age of Reason. Rational scientific thought as expressed in deism had dethroned God and reduced him to a mere bystander. Emboldened by Novalis's *Christendom and Europe,* published in 1799, many romantics converted to Catholicism and embraced cosmopolitanism. Eventually they would succumb to French revolutionary rhetoric.

Almost all of these writers emphasized humanity, not nation, and when they spoke of the German community, they meant a cultural, not a political, community. Many scholars have seen the romantics as the forerunners of the "Good European," persons who placed the greater European community above their narrow national feelings. Goethe rejected "national hatred" even during the wars of liberation against Napoleon. He simply asked "whether people are civilized or barbarous." Herder cried out for the cause of "humanity," while Schiller "embraced millions" with his "universal kiss" in the "Ode to Joy." Kant even devised a plan for a European "league of nations." Goethe and Schiller combined to answer their critics with the dicta in *Xenien*, two of which provide this chapter's epigraphs.

Whether such cosmopolitan and humanitarian traits served merely to help Germans escape from political impotence and territorial particularism at home remains open to debate. Was classicism primarily a means to flee the narrow world of the fractured Reich to an ancient Greece that Germans imagined as free and graced by noble simplicity and serenity? Certainly these writers did not openly challenge the established order but merely sought to appeal to the princes' hearts to reform evil and abuse. All championed the cause of the middle class; none intended to incite it to revolt. Nor did the classical age of literature address contemporary trends. One would search high culture in vain for treatment of what we would call the "Prussian spirit," the world of commerce and industry, of capitalistic enterprise, or of the peasant village and traditional peasant life.

Popular culture in Germany found expression mainly in primary education and religious cultism. In sharp contrast to the Olympian accomplishments of the Enlightenment and the classical age of literature, general education and literacy remained appallingly rare in mid-eighteenth century Germany. On average, only one in every ten subjects could read, a figure that rose slowly to 15 percent in 1770 and 25 percent by 1800. Among the literate, tastes changed over the course of the century. Theological readings declined from 40 to 6 percent, philosophical inquiries doubled to 40 percent, and poetry climbed from 9 to 27 percent of available reading materials. By the end of the eighteenth century, two-thirds of all new books dealt with literature and philosophy.

The root of the low rate of literacy lay in the abysmal elementary educational system. Joseph II in Austria in the 1780s discovered that only one in three school-aged children attended classes. Despite his strenuous efforts to encourage literacy, the attendance figure for Bohemia in 1790 had risen to only 42 percent. A Prussian survey in 1732 found that only 10 percent of all children had even the most rudimentary schooling, and that was restricted mainly to memorizing scripture and the catechism. Part of the problem was that the schools all too often were not conducive to learning. In Württemberg, for example, the predominantly convent schools meted out such harsh discipline that, according to a contemporary estimate, one teacher over half a century of work administered 911,527 blows with a stick, 124,000 with a switch, and 136,715 by hand.

The educated elite read enlightened tracts such as John Locke's *Some Thoughts Concerning Education* (1693) and Jean-Jacques Rousseau's *Emile, ou de l'éducation* (1762), but the lessons contained in these works escaped official attention. Frederick II's General School Regulation of 1763, in fact, constituted the first instance when a state, rather than the church, insisted on formal education for all children from the ages of five to thirteen. Yet even in this "progressive" state, a random inspection of district teachers revealed that most were incompetent. The majority had received no training to teach. They had been appointed without qualifying examinations, and once employed, they possessed neither the books nor the money to educate themselves. Most continued to work at outside jobs such as tailors, toll or tax collectors, organists, and distillers. Attendance in schools remained irregular, and in times of planting and harvesting, as well as in summer, the buildings usually stood empty.

German universities were little better. Professors routinely lectured twenty to twenty-four hours per week, often augmenting their pitiful salaries with second jobs. Students were renowned mainly for alcoholism, indiscipline, and brawling. And while the general population was increasing throughout the eighteenth century, the number of university students actually declined to less than 1 percent of the populace. In 1790 the Holy Roman Empire had thirty-seven universities. Fourteen had been founded or refounded in the period from 1648 to 1789. Prussia in 1804 boasted seven universities with 1,873 students: 868 studied law, 623 theology, 164 medicine, 130 philosophy and mathematics, 82 cameralism, 4 economics, and 2 military science.

Most students were sons of nobles and civil servants. Of Göttingen University's roughly one thousand students at the end of the eighteenth century, 18 percent were noble. At the Erlangen University, 13 percent were noble, and fully half came from the academic middle class. Education was conducted in Latin, and law was the desired subject for young men preparing to enter princely administration. At Ingolstadt University, 61 percent of all law students came from privileged groups like the nobility and the high-ranking civil service. Riding, fencing, and dancing were required subjects, a remnant from the days of the old boarding schools for aspiring knights.

The 1770s and 1780s saw a popular religious cult, the Freemasons, permeate German society, from the educated middle class to the nobility and even the courts. Although dedicated to the general goal of instilling humanitarian ideals through elite education, German Freemasons realistically hoped to reshape society by attracting to their ranks influential ministers and members of ruling houses. Secret Masonic societies, however, espoused the principle of equality of all people, as well as humanitarian and cosmopolitan ideals. Most secret societies dedicated themselves to fighting what they considered to be the clandestine and enduring influence of the church in general and Jesuits in particular. Deistic in religious conviction, the Freemasons relished the irrational. A cult of secrecy permeated their rituals, from initiation to the sixty secret grades to the identity of the Grand Master. This secrecy provoked fantastic rumors extolling the group's invisible power and influence. The first lodge in Vienna had been founded in 1742; an additional thirteen had sprouted by 1795. Prussia boasted no fewer than forty-three lodges during the period 1741 to 1781. Even Frederick II was seduced by the Masonic movement in 1738 while crown prince.

The Illuminati constituted a second secret society. Founded in 1776 by Adam Weishaupt, a lecturer in canon law at Ingolstadt, this group also followed a cult of secrecy and relied on mysticism to gain influence over high-ranking members of the court. Its strength remained concentrated in Bavaria, where it recruited about six hundred to seven hundred members from the ranks of the nobility and the middle class, and especially from the lists of Freemasons. Outside Bavaria, its august recruits included the dukes of Brunswick, Sachsen-Gotha, and Sachsen-Weimar, as well as the landgraves of Hesse-Kassel and Hesse-Homburg. As with the Freemasons, the Illuminati reached well into the titans of the Enlightenment; Goethe, Herder, Klopstock, Nicolai, and Sonnenfels all became members.

The Illuminati sought to inculcate both daily life and politics with a higher morality and a code of ethics. Weishaupt instilled in his followers an unshakable belief in the power of reason to lift the veil of confusion and ignorance that had enveloped Europe since the Middle Ages. A rigid program of learning letters and the useful arts would permit human beings to understand their true nature, rooted in equality and rationality. Thereafter, enlightened subjects could work through benevolent princes toward an amelioration of society. The Illuminati's appeal lay in secrecy and, hence, in their perceived power and influence at court.

A third secret society was that of the Rosicrucians. Their power and influence, unlike that of the Freemasons and Illuminati, were well known. Frederick William II of Prussia (1786–1797) was recruited into the society by two of his ministers, Hans Rudolf von Bischoffswerder and Johann Christoph von Wöllner, the reputed Grand Master of the society. Lesser chapters also existed in Austria and Bavaria. The Rosicrucians saw themselves as sort of a political club with a mission to influence domestic affairs, personnel politics, and general culture. At worst, their emphasis on spiritualistic seances tainted the movement with irrationality bordering upon the occult.

The French Revolution constituted the death knell for the secret societies. The Freemasons and the Illuminati, especially, were suspected allies of the Jacobins — and little wonder. The scale and violence of the changes brought about after 1789, ranging from regicide to the Terror and finally to continental war, seemed to defy conventional explanation. Plot theories of history thrive in times such as these. How could the swiftness and completeness of the French Revolution be explained other than in terms of millenarian expectation, providential design, divine retribution — or secret plots? The very secrecy surrounding the European cult movement from its inception after 1789 proved its greatest threat.

Karl Baron vom Stein in 1791 bluntly informed Frederick William II from Mainz that the Illuminati, under cover of cosmopolitanism, were scheming to "subvert all order." The government of Saxony barred all suspected French sympathizers from its lands and instituted strict controls over "subversive" literature. In the end, ex-Illuminati turned over their former comrades to state authorities. Their ready embrace of Napoleon Bonaparte as the great liberator and progressive hardly endeared them to successive German patriots.

Central Europe in the eighteenth century was an amorphous collection of more than three hundred kingdoms, duchies, archbishoprics, Hanseatic cities, and imperial fiefs loosely gathered in the Holy Roman Empire of the German Nation under the Habsburg dynasty. Most rulers lived well beyond their means and possessed little sense of purpose or mission beyond maintaining their lavish palaces and life-styles. The Empire lacked a political center that could have initiated political, economic, or agrarian reforms. The middle class, its prosperity limited, remained concentrated in the Hanseatic cities such as Bremen, Hamburg, and Lübeck and the free imperial city of Frankfurt. The vast majority of people lived on the land, on the verge of poverty.

Change was championed mainly by the writers of the Englightenment, who argued that reason and logic could end the darkness that had descended on Europe during the medieval period. Hailing primarily from the middle class, these writers challenged established religious, political, and socioeconomic policies and traditions and hoped to inspire princely rulers to undertake extensive reform. Their idea of freedom was both political and intellectual: they yearned to throw off the chains of feudal servitude and religious orthodoxy.

By the middle of the eighteenth century, a new chapter in German history opened: Austro-Prussian dualism, or the struggle between Austria and Prussia for preeminence in Central Europe. Straddling the Danube River, the Habsburg Empire was the premier German power. Largest in territory and population, it dominated the other 360 states on the basis of both history and tradition. The Habsburgs wore the ancient crown of Charlemagne as well as those of St. Stephen (Hungary) and Wenceslas (Bohemia). But with the accession to the Prussian throne of Frederick II in 1740, Austria detected a rival in Brandenburg-Prussia. The Hohenzollern possessions centered on the largely desolate stretches of sand and pine surrounding Berlin, as well as the wild forests and marshes of East Prussia stretching east from Königsberg. At first, Austria had little to fear from this northern rival, but the indomitable determination of

Frederick II to expand his possessions in 1740 threatened Habsburg complacency and supremacy.

Suggested Readings

English-language scholars have woefully neglected the history of Germany before the French Revolution. The most detailed overview of German affairs is still Hajo Holborn, *A History of Modern Germany, 1648–1840* (New York, 1969), reprinted in paperback by Princeton University Press in 1982. James J. Sheehan's splendid *German History, 1770–1866* (Oxford, 1990), remains beyond the pale of most students and scholars, in terms of both cost and length. With regard to Austria, two excellent paperback surveys exist: Robert J. W. Evans, *The Making of the Habsburg Monarchy, 1550–1700* (Oxford, 1979), and Robert A. Kann, *A History of the Habsburg Empire, 1526–1918* (Berkeley and Los Angeles, 1974). The early history of Prussia has been analyzed by Francis L. Carsten, *The Origins of Prussia* (Oxford, 1954).

German constitutional developments have been examined by Francis L. Carsten, *Princes and Parliaments in Germany from the Fifteenth to the Eighteenth Century* (Oxford, 1959). James Bryce, *The Holy Roman Empire* (New York, 1904), remains the classic with regard to the Empire. Students also should consult Geoffrey Barraclough, *The Origins of Modern Germany* (New York, 1963); Part V deals with the final phase of the Empire. Gerhard Benecke, *Society and Politics in Germany, 1500–1750* (London and Toronto, 1974), is a fine companion volume to Carsten, Bryce, and Barraclough. Two regional studies are James A. Vann, *The Making of a State: Württemberg, 1593–1793* (Ithaca and London, 1984), and Charles W. Ingrao, *The Hessian Mercenary State: Ideas, Institutions and Reform Under Frederick III* (Cambridge, 1987).

The close connection between German literature and society has been expertly scrutinized by Walter H. Bruford, *Germany in the Eighteenth Century: The Social Background of the Literary Revival* (Cambridge, 1965), and his *Culture and Society in Classical Weimar, 1775–1806* (Cambridge, 1962). The world of music is surveyed in Claude V. Palisca, *Baroque Music* (Englewood Cliffs, N.J., 1981); the connection between music and the Englightenment has been analyzed by Ira C. Singleton, "The Rationality of Eighteenth Century Musical Classicism" (Ph.D. diss., New York University, 1954). Two general works by Christian Norberg-Schulz introduce eighteenth-century architecture: *Baroque Architecture* (New York, 1972) and *Late Baroque and Rococo Architecture* (New York, 1985). More specific is Henry R. Hitchcock, *Rococo Architecture in Southern Germany* (London, 1968). A brief survey of the German arts is offered by Gottfried Lindemann, *History of German Art: Painting Sculpture Architecture* (New York, 1971).

Relatively little work has been done on women in eighteenth-century Germany, apart from the general overview by Ute Frevert, *Women in German History: From Bourgeois Emancipation to Sexual Liberation* (New York, 1988).

The same comment applies to the German peasantry, with the exception of Richard J. Evans, *The German Peasantry: Conflict and Continuity in Rural Society from the Eighteenth to the Twentieth Centuries* (London and Sydney, 1986). At a more general level, students should consult Louise Tilly and Joan Scott, *Women, Work and Family* (New York, 1978). Everyday rural life is richly portrayed in Ulrich Bräker, *The Life Story and Real Adventures of the Poor Man of Toggenburg* (Edinburgh, 1970).

A fine short survey of the Enlightenment is Norman Hampson, *A Cultural History of the Enlightenment* (New York, 1968). Peter Gay's two-volume *The Enlightenment: An Interpretation* (New York, 1966, 1969), offers a good synthesis, as well as a detailed bibliographical essay. Ernst Cassirer, *The Philosophy of the Enlightenment* (Boston, 1955), may be too abstract for most people, as is definitely the case with Leonard Krieger, *The German Idea of Freedom* (Boston, 1957). On Austria, see Paul P. Bernard, *Jesuits and Jacobins: Enlightenment and Enlightened Despotism in Austria* (Urbana, Ill., 1971); on Prussia, Henri Brunschwig, *Enlightenment and Romanticism in Eighteenth-Century Prussia* (Chicago, 1974). Secret societies have been analyzed by J. M. Roberts, *The Mythology of the Secret Societies* (London, 1972). Charles McClelland, *State, Society and University in Germany, 1700–1914* (Cambridge, 1980), explores higher education in the German states; Lawrence Stone, ed., *Schooling and Society* (Baltimore, 1976), offers several essays on primary education. Finally, Koppel Pinson, *Pietism as a Factor in the Rise of German Nationalism* (New York, 1934), remains the most useful of books on this subject.

C H A P T E R

2

FROM RIVALRY TO SURVIVAL: PRUSSIA AND AUSTRIA, 1740–1815

Boundary, n. *In political geography, an imaginary line between two nations, separating the imaginary rights of one from the imaginary rights of the other.*

Ambrose Bierce, *The Devil's Dictionary*

The period from the death of Frederick William I of Prussia in 1740 to the reordering of Europe at the Congress of Vienna in 1815 saw almost constant wars and geographical gerrymandering. Crowns were lost and gained with regularity. Territories were created, destroyed, or altered at random. Even the venerable Holy Roman Empire ceased to exist, replaced by a new and untried German Confederation. The Austro-Prussian dynastic struggle of 1740–1763 exerted its influence beyond even the Continent, for, as the British prime minister, the Elder William Pitt noted, Canada was won on the fields of Silesia.[1] Johann Wolfgang Goethe in 1824 could well look back upon his long life as a time of great global decisions: the Seven Years' War, the American Revolution, the French Revolution, the Napoleonic furor, and finally the restoration at the Congress of Vienna. The age of reason, enlightenment, and refinement was also marked by brutal aggression and cynical deception. No one understood this better than Frederick II of Prussia.

[1] German historians usually speak of the "Three Silesian Wars": the first took place between 1740 and 1742, the second between 1744 and 1745, and the third between 1756 and 1763. Anglo-Saxon scholars refer to these wars as the First and Second Wars of the Austrian Succession and the Seven Years' War (1756–1763).

Enlightened Despotism: The Prussian Case

In 1740 Frederick II inherited the Prussian state created by his father, Frederick William I. A corpulent man of violent temper and prodigious energy, the "Soldier King" had labored tirelessly from 1713 to 1740 to establish his absolute rule on the twin principles of army and bureaucracy. "Salvation is of God," he once announced, "everything else is my affair." The king insisted on controlling everything, from the market price of eggs and meat to the cost of a new canal or cannon. He traveled throughout the year to inspect regiments, meet with royal officials, and check up on tax collectors — and earned the sobriquet "king of the highways" from George II of England.

Frederick William I had clearly laid out the goals of his reign in 1713 to his friend Leopold, prince of Anhalt-Dessau: "I am the finance minister and field marshal of the King of Prussia; this will be sufficient to uphold the King of Prussia." He might as well have added that he would also be his own minister of economics, internal affairs, and industry.

Frederick William's first task was to streamline and rationalize his administration. Revenues from the domains, post, mint, and customs were united in a General Board of Finance; those from the land tax (contribution) and the consumer tax (accise) in the hands of the War Commissariat. In 1723 the king established the General Directory as "a supreme board" entrusted with matters affecting the military, police, finances, revenues, and commerce. The General Directory's orders were carried out at the local level by royal provincial chambers and intendants, in the process demolishing the last vestiges of local autonomy and feudal authority. Minimum standards of education were introduced for these royal agents, and former soldiers were generally favored as tax collectors, policemen, and teachers. Frederick William I promised to treat his bureaucrats "in a tyrannical manner." "They shall dance to my music or the devil take me," he once boasted. Special agents called Fiscals regularly spied on the royal civil service for the king.

Frederick William's first love was the military. During his reign, the size of the army doubled to eighty thousand troops; although Prussia was tenth in size and twelfth in population in Europe, it possessed the fourth largest military, after France, Russia, and Austria. Discipline not seen since the days of Rome — the club, running the gauntlet, the wheel, the axe, and the noose — kept the unruly recruits in a state of fear. The monarch established a royal treasury as a war reserve. "One will always be obliged to court the favor of a prince," Frederick William lectured his eldest son, "who has a standing army of 100,000 men and 25 million Crowns to support it in action."

Most important, Frederick William in 1733 introduced the canton system designed to end desertions (which ran as high as three thousand per year) and to replace brutal press gangs and mercenary contractors. Under its provisions, the kingdom was divided into districts and these, in turn, into cantons, each of which was to supply one regiment. It was a revolutionary innovation: officers and men alike were now stationed in their home districts. The distinction between private and military life was removed: the Junker was both lord and officer, the peasant both serf and recruit. Even when off duty working the fields during planting and harvest seasons, the peasant recruit wore a red cap denoting his reserve status and unit. Service with foreign armies was forbidden. "The King of Prussia," Frederick William announced, "is as good as the King of France." Cadet schools such as the one at Lichterfelde in Berlin were founded to train young nobles. Orphanages were established at royal expense for sons of fallen soldiers.

Prussia was the only state in Europe to possess a service nobility. "The authority of the Junkers shall be destroyed," Frederick William I had decreed. "I shall establish my sovereignty like a rock of bronze." In return for service, the king elevated the new nobility of the sword to "the first estate in the realm." Frederick II later commented that, under his father, Prussia had become the Sparta of the north. The Frenchman Mirabeau noted that Prussia was the one country where the army, in fact, possessed a state. "To work for the King of Prussia" became a contemporary byword, denoting hard work and little reward.

To pay for this expanded military, Frederick William I turned to cameralism, whereby the state assumed control over the economy. Subjects were "encouraged" to work more diligently; established industries were expanded and new ones founded; domestic production was protected by high tariffs; and colonists were attracted to Prussia by promises of land and exemption from military service. Frederick William's strategy lured nearly seventeen thousand newcomers from Austria, Poland, Russia, Saxony, and Swabia. The king established chairs of cameralism at Halle in 1723 and at Frankfurt/Oder in 1727 to promote his economic policy.

Textiles became the new state industry. The king founded a royal warehouse (*Lagerhaus*) in Berlin through which all wool had to pass. Royal inspectors ensured quality, set prices for raw materials and finished products, and supervised all aspects of production, from dyeing and fulling to spinning and weaving. Guilds were abolished or placed under royal authority. To attract the best workers, Frederick William offered above-scale wages. The export of wool was forbidden, under penalty of death, and quality was enhanced through the importation of merino sheep from Spain. To create a market for the finished product, in 1713 the king ordered all regimental commanders to use only royal blue cloth for their troops. Even the dead were to be wrapped in Prussian blue for burial.

Frederick William I also demanded that justice be meted out more quickly and more justly than before. He required lawyers to study jurisprudence and sent judges to the University of Halle to sharpen their skills. In 1737 he appointed Samuel von Cocceji as minister of justice. Whereas the black toga previously had been forced on lawyers so that honest citizens could recognize (and avoid) them in public, Cocceji transformed them into robes of distinction.

Frederick William I's "Tobacco Parliament" (1730s).

Cocceji was also charged with drawing up a civil and criminal legal code for Prussia. This code would be finished only much later under Frederick II, who even abolished torture designed to elicit confession in all cases save treason and murder. Cases involving witchcraft were severely curtailed when Frederick William I demanded that all stakes upon which accused witches had been burned be removed from public squares. Penalties nevertheless remained both severe and equal, regardless of gender. Branding, pinching with hot tongs, beheading, drawing and quartering, breaking on the wheel, and hanging were practiced. Infanticide was punished by sewing women into leather bags and casting them in rivers to drown.

Public education in Prussia was rudimentary by modern standards but set the standard in eighteenth-century Europe. Frederick William I built more than eleven hundred schools during his reign; by 1732 one child in ten reportedly possessed some kind of education. This achievement is all the more astonishing because teachers, who were often retired soldiers, artisans, or blacksmiths, were untrained and underpaid. Moreover, schools were little more than one-room houses where students studied the Bible, hymns, and the Lutheran catechism. As Frederick William I instructed his teachers, "Christianity, reading, writing, and arithmetic is enough; everything else is tomfoolery." A simple man, Frederick William I pursued simple goals. "The password of this world," he asserted, "is nothing more than effort and work." This became a true Prussian motto.

This was the state that Frederick II inherited in 1740. He did little to change it and instead built upon his father's reforms. To improve the royal administration, for example, he expanded the General Directory in 1740 to include a fifth department for commerce and manufacturing. Six years later, he added a sixth department for army supplies. Brutally honest annual fitness reports were demanded of all civil servants.

On the economic front, Frederick II followed his father's cameralist policies. Foreign goods, especially those from Austria and Saxony, were subjected to prohibitive import duties. The interconnection of the Oder, Havel, and Elbe rivers by canals, begun under Frederick William the Great Elector (1640–1688), and the dredging of Swinemünde at the mouth of the Oder in order to accommodate a thousand ships per year were completed. Frederick II later claimed that in this way he gained an entire province by peaceful measures. Colonists continued to flock to Prussia, attracted by state subsidies for farms, homes, and businesses. Established industries were encouraged and new industries founded: linen in Silesia, porcelain in Berlin, and in 1751 a silk company for the China trade. In 1749 Frederick II became his own minister of trade within the General Directory, and he decreed that precise records (*Acta Borussica*) be kept for all aspects of the state's activities.

In 1746 the king gave Samuel von Cocceji royal license to proceed with his legal reforms. Ennobled and promoted to grand-chancellor, Cocceji was free to remove recalcitrant judges, reform court procedures, and create a uniform system of fines and punishments. Corruption in awarding judgeships gave way to state training and licensing. Higher pay resulted in a decrease in bribery. The system whereby brokers brought cases to trial in return for a percentage of potential awards was abolished. Although Cocceji's great Civil Code would not be completed until 1794, throughout Frederick's reign the law was brought under royal control at the expense of local patrimony. And while the king in all cases remained the highest court of appeal, Frederick promised to respect lower court decisions in civil cases.

Frederick William's military system continued some practices but underwent change too. Annual maneuvers were continued to test commanders and tactics. Cantonal regiments were inspected annually by the king. The cavalry was reformed to fight in mass formation, to charge fast and hard, to use the saber instead of the carbine, and generally to act as shock troops to demoralize enemy infantry. Artillery remained unchanged; infantry was drilled to fire muskets only once and thereafter to advance with fixed bayonets. But the notion of decisive battle began to supplement the traditional art of elaborate maneuver. In place of the standard three-deep linear formations, Frederick II introduced the *ordre oblique*, whereby the army advanced in slanted formation, permitting last-minute concentration on either side to turn an enemy's flank. Frederick himself led from the front, perhaps the last king personally to command troops on Europe's battlefields.

The major difference between the two great Prussian monarchs of the eighteenth century, however, lay in their policies regarding the nobility. Whereas the Soldier King had striven to break the power of the Junkers and to recruit nonnobles for his administration, Frederick II clearly favored the landed aristocrats. He reestablished the office of *Landrat* — as royal officials but elected by fellow Junkers — as a symbol of local self-rule. Under Frederick, the nobility dominated high-level appointments, especially in the army. Between 1700 and 1806, for example, twelve members of the von Kleist family were promoted to general, along with eleven each of the von Schwerin and von der Marwitz clans. By 1900 the von Schwerins had supplied Prussia with 280 officers (and six Ph.D.s).

The cost of service was high. During the Austro-Prussian wars (1740–1763), the von Wedel family lost seventy-two male offspring and the von Kleist family fifty-eight. A number of other ancient Prussian noble clans were deprived of male heirs by the wars. A grateful Frederick II noted: "It is their sons who are defending the land; their race is so good that it deserves to be conserved at all costs." This bond of blood between state and nobility would survive until the last months of the Third Reich. As Paul von Hindenburg, chief of the General Staff in the last years of World War I, once caustically noted with regard to the privileges of his Junker class, theirs was the right to be first to die.

Frederick II preferred social rigidity to social mobility. In 1749 he devised the *Bauernschutz* — literally, "peasants' protection" — whereby serf and noble alike were tied to the soil; neither could buy or sell rural property. Landownership by middle-class aspirants was prohibited. Even the king himself could not acquire additional domains. Because the canton system relied on a guaranteed supply of serf recruits and noble officers, the king was not about to imperil the agrarian-military order by opening the way to capitalist land speculation.

Frederick II's self-appointed role as enlightened ruler perhaps was demonstrated best during the reconstruction period (*rétablissement*) after the last of his wars with Austria ended in 1763. At the age of fifty-one, having spent the previous six years in the field commanding his armies, Frederick personally toured his ravaged lands, distributing seventeen thousand bushels of grain and thirty-five thousand army horses, as well as a last cash reserve of 29 million thaler.[1] He established state monopolies on tobacco and coffee as well as a state lottery to bring in much-needed revenues. He ordered construction to begin on a Neues Palais at Potsdam to provide work for unemployed craftsmen. In 1760 he purchased a bankrupted porcelain factory and transformed it into the Royal Prussian Manufactory, which soon became the largest state industry, with five hundred workers. Over 40 million thaler from royal coffers went to help veterans and invalids make the transition to civilian life. The new State Bank made extensive credits available to Junkers so that they could rebuild their estates. The king even established a Grain Bank to protect his subjects from the vicissitudes of the marketplace: the crown bought up cheap grain in time of good harvests and sold grain below market value in time of bad harvests to stabilize prices.

The old cameralist policies continued. The state drained swamps, dredged rivers, and expanded canals. New fodder crops were planted, pasture lands expanded, and the so-called Norfolk three-crop-rotation system introduced. No fewer than three hundred royal villages were turned into private farms. Frederick II estimated that during his reign, more than fifty-seven thousand families moved to Prussia at state expense.

What historians have termed "Prussian socialism" perhaps can best be understood by the case of Frederick's acquisition of West Prussia in 1772. After touring his new possession, Frederick II called it a "piece of anarchy" and likened it to Canada. Thereupon, he went to work. Each year he established fifty new villages and earmarked 100,000 thaler for new cities. Meanwhile, eleven thousand colonists were attracted to West Prussia by grants of land, homes, and exemption from military service; most came from German states such as Franconia, Mecklenburg, the Palatinate, Swabia, and Salzburg, as well as from Bohemia and Poland. Frederick II established eight hundred schools in West Prussia for their children.

Frederick's philosophy was Hobbesian.[2] "This polished century is still very ferocious," he noted near the end of his reign. "Man is an untamable animal when he gives rein to his passions." Frederick preferred what he called the contemplative life of reading and writing "as a Cartusian monk" at his modest palace, Sans Souci, in Potsdam. There, surrounded by such luminaries

---

[1] These figures should be measured against Prussia's annual revenues, which during Frederick II's reign rose from 7 million thalers in 1740 to 29 million by 1786.

[2] Thomas Hobbes in England had sided with the king against Parliament in the civil wars of the 1640s and generally argued that human beings have no capacity for self-government. In his major book, *Leviathan* (1651), Hobbes concluded that life generally is "solitary, poor, nasty, brutish and short."

The philosophers of Sans Souci: Frederick II and Voltaire (1750–1753).

as Maupertuis and Voltaire, the composer Carl Philipp Emanuel Bach, and other major Enlightenment figures, Frederick became the self-styled "philosopher of Sans Souci." His sister, Wilhelmine, referred to Sans Souci as a monastery, with her brother the resident abbot. Neither wife, nor mistress, nor children appealed to the king. Nor did any God guide man's fortunes:

> I have lived over seventy years in this world and during that time I have seen nothing but the strange freaks of fortune which mingles many painful happenings with a few that are favorable. We toss without ceasing between many anxieties and certain moments of satisfaction. That is the lot of common man.

To the end, Frederick's notion of kingship was one of service to the state. Kingship, he argued, was not derived from God. Indeed, in his *Political Testament* of 1768 he called Christianity "an old metaphysical fairy tale, full of miraculous legends, paradoxes, and nonsense." Kingship, he believed, stemmed from some ancient (and undefined) agreement between ruler and people. Under this contract theory, probably taken from French constitutional theorists and refined in Prussia by Christian Wolff, Samuel von Pufendorf, and Carl Gottlieb Suarez, Frederick described himself as the "first servant of the state." His person meant nothing; his office everything. Princes, Frederick once stated, were but "the slaves of their means. . . . The welfare of the state is their law."

The *Political Testament* concluded that wisdom was derived solely from the philosophical laws and moral ideals of the Enlightenment. Yet although that same philosophy taught Frederick II that the ultimate goal of a policy directed by reason ought to be the advancement of human welfare, experience dictated that power alone provided security. Not even the "philosopher of Sans Souci," the erstwhile author of the *Anti-Machiavelli*, managed to reconcile that contradiction.[1]

Royal Absolutism: The Austrian Case

In Austria, Maria Theresa and her son, Joseph II, sought to reform the Austrian state to make it a worthy competitor in the Age of Reason, but peculiarities of the Habsburg state militated against centralization and reform: Hungarian historical rights had to be respected, and the Catholic church enjoyed a privileged status as landholder, censor, and educator. As a result, most Austrian reforms were limited to the so-called German historic lands — Austria and Bohemia. The overall design of the reforms paralleled those in Prussia: to establish the ascendancy of the centralized royal government over the still-feudal estates institutions. More specifically, Maria Theresa and Joseph II sought to curtail the powers of the noble estates, to limit the narrow self-interests of the guilds, and to curb the arbitrary patrimonial jurisdiction of the lords.

Given the alarming regularity of Austrian defeats at the hands of Frederick II between 1740 and 1763 (discussed in the next section), it is not surprising

[1] In 1739, Crown Prince Frederick had refuted the rational principles espoused in Machiavelli's *Prince*, arguing instead that morality, religion, and law restrained "the horrible beast *raison d'état*" (reason of state).

that the Habsburgs looked to Berlin for a model. Queen Maria Theresa even selected the scion of a Silesian family, Friedrich Wilhelm Count von Haugwitz, governor of Austrian Silesia, to undertake administrative reform. Haugwitz first centralized the financial, military, and political agenda of the crown lands — the so-called *gubernia* after 1762 — under the Court Chancery in Vienna, which he now headed. As early as 1746, Maria Theresa had emulated Frederick's fifth department of the General Directory by establishing the Universal Directory of Commerce. Three years later, she created the *Directorium in publicis et cameralibus*, almost an exact copy of the Prussian General Directory. In 1760 a Council of State was established to serve both as brain trust for Maria Theresa and as watchdog over her subjects.

An expanded professional bureaucracy obviously was needed to staff these offices. Thus, a new type of school, the Theresianum, arose to train especially the sons of the nobility. A Silesian, Johann Andreas Felbiger, and Anton Count Pergen proved instrumental in reforming the Habsburg elementary and general intermediate schools. Under Gerhard van Swieten, the Jesuit influence in the medical school of the University of Vienna was reduced in 1749, and other departments thereafter followed suit.

With an eye not only to the Prussian model (Samuel von Cocceji) but also on neighboring Bavaria, which, under Elector Max III Joseph, had promulgated criminal, civil, and land tenure codes between 1751 and 1753, Maria Theresa set out after 1753 to devise a unified legal code for her diverse lands. The *Constitutio criminalis theresiana* was completed in 1766 and the *Codex iuris civilis* two years later. Both were revised by Joseph II in 1787 and received final form in 1811. As in Prussia, penalties remained harsh. Life sentences of hard labor, such as pulling ships or treading mills, were common for all segments of society.

Constantly on the verge of bankruptcy, the Habsburg state also turned to a form of Prussian cameralism. Under the guidance of Joseph von Sonnenfels, professor of cameralism at Vienna University from 1763 until 1791, new industries sprouted up: textiles in Bohemia and in Upper and Lower Austria, glass in Bohemia, porcelain in Vienna, iron mining in Styria, lead mining in Carinthia, mercury mining in Carniola, and silk in Lombardy. The Oriental Academy opened in Vienna in 1754, designed to boost the China trade. The Commercial Academy followed in 1770 to strengthen the new cameralism. Technical colleges sprang up to advance understanding of the applied sciences. Above all, Maria Theresa sought to introduce the principle that church as well as nobility should pay taxes beyond the occasional "free gift." Haugwitz, in fact, levied a tax of 1 percent on the nobility and 2 percent on the peasantry to pay for a standing army of 108,000 soldiers. But even this paltry assessment, spread over ten years, was bitterly opposed in most states. Hungary continued to reject the principle of royal taxation until the nineteenth century.

Opposition to Haugwitz's taxation scheme was easy to organize because land was concentrated in relatively few hands. In Bohemia, for example, some fifty princely families held title to 80 percent of the land. The church owned three-eighths of all the land in Austria as well as more than two thousand monasteries. All six thousand monks, as well as their property, were tax exempt.

The abysmal performance of the Austrian armies in Maria Theresa's wars with Frederick II between 1740 and 1763 necessitated military improvements. Prince Joseph Wenzel von Liechtenstein reformed the Austrian artillery into one of the finest in Europe. Leopold Count von Daun in 1752 established a military academy at Wiener-Neustadt and two years later an engineering academy to train future officers. Hard on the heels of the end of the Seven Years' War, Austria adopted the Prussian canton system under the so-called soul conscription of 1763 whereby the peasantry, in addition to bearing the burden of the *robot* (manual labor for up to 120 days of the year), provided the recruits for the Austrian army. Permanent military camps, annual maneuvers, standardized uniforms and equipment, and a new manual of drills and tactics (copied from the Prussian) circulated to the troops all served to sharpen the army's skills. Yet despite this feverish activity, the nobility of the Habsburg lands, perhaps the richest and most ostentatious in Europe, never became a military service nobility on the model of the Prussian Junkers. The very diversity and separate historical traditions within the lands of the Habsburg Empire militated against uniformity. Regardless of their ethnic and religious differences, aristocrats were united in opposing the centralization efforts of the crown in Vienna.

Maria Theresa's reforms were but the prelude to the far more ambitious efforts of her son, whom she rightly accused of "flirting with the spirit" of the Enlightenment. Co-regent since 1765, Joseph II issued no fewer than six thousand reform edicts during the period of his sole rule from 1780 to 1790. In this one decade, he tried to recast the entire Austrian domestic firmament. He thought in utilitarian terms and sought to centralize royal power. Two of the main pillars of that state, the Roman Catholic church and the Magyar nobility in Hungary, he especially targeted for reform. The general populace even coined the term *vulgar Josephinism* to depict a policy that they perceived to be liberal and anticlerical.

Joseph no longer willingly accepted the church as an institution separate from and equal to the state. He strove for nothing less than to establish an Austrian national church in which Vienna rather than Rome dominated. To this end, he insisted upon his right to appoint bishops, to place church educators under state control, and to transfer jurisdiction in marriage questions to the state. He abolished all contemplative orders as well as more than seven hundred monasteries — about one in three of which were in the Habsburg lands. Not even burial rites or Sunday observances escaped his reformist attention.

Europe's First Family: Maria Theresa, Francis I, and the future Joseph II (fifth from right) at Schönbrunn Castle.

In October 1781, Joseph II issued his famous Edict of Tolerance, which granted all non-Catholics virtual freedom to practice their religion. Free to choose, more than 70,000 people openly stated their preference for Protestantism in the first year alone. Four months later, he granted Jews the rights of full citizens and freedom of trade and occupation and relieved them of all distinctive dress codes. The decree affected the 70,000 Jews of Bohemia especially, as well as the 200,000 Jews in Galicia acquired in 1772. Unlike his mother, Joseph II did not regard his Jewish subjects as "the worst pest for the state," although his hopes that Jews would now assimilate fully into the Austrian state and society remained unfulfilled.

Joseph II similarly assaulted Hungary's special status. He refused to be crowned at Pozsony (Pressburg, today Bratislava) and to swear to uphold the ancient Hungarian constitution. He moved the Crown of St. Stephen, given to the Magyar's first king by the pope in the year 1001, to Vienna and the Magyar capital to Budapest.[1] Hungary was divided into ten districts, and a royal governor for each was appointed from Vienna. Most galling of all for the Magyars, who still conducted their politics in Latin and would continue to do so until 1848, Joseph decreed in 1784 that German was to be the official language of his lands.

Joseph II also proceeded to cement centralism. He outlawed local assemblies in Hungary, Lombardy, and the Austrian Netherlands and consolidated the thirteen major administrative departments at Vienna into a United Court Chancellery. A pervasive police spy network, reminiscent of the Fiscals in Prussia, went on the alert to ascertain whether the royal decrees were being enforced.

Agrarian reform in Austria proved a thorny issue given both the diversity and the power of local nobles. Peasants fell into two basic groups: tenants or dominicalists, who had some sort of a contractual relationship with their lord, and the rusticalists, a much larger group of hereditary unfree peasants on lords' estates. In legal terms, the former came under the heading of *Unterthänigkeit*, or lord-subject relationship, and the latter under that of *Leibeigenschaft*, or lord-serf relationship. In 1775 Maria Theresa had issued the Robot Patent, limiting personal service owed the lord by the peasant to three days per week, and she abolished serfdom on crown lands.

In November 1781, Joseph II went one step further, abolishing all hereditary serfdom in Bohemia and Galicia. This measure, which he extended to Hungary in 1786, effectively freed the peasants, who could now leave the land, marry at will, and choose occupations. In return for this legal relief, however, the peasants were required to pay about 30 percent of their income in rents and tributes: two-thirds of it to the lord and one-third to the crown. Because the local lord was at once owner of the land, judge, police chief, recruitment officer, and tax collector, Joseph's reforms did not truly free the peasants.

Opposition to Joseph II developed quickly, aided, ironically, by his own relaxation of censorship. Countless political tracts attacked his reforms. Devout Catholics of all social strata despised his Edict of Tolerance. Magyars resented the removal of their ancient crown to Vienna and the institution of the German language throughout the empire. The Austrian nobility and the middle class opposed toleration of Jews. Virtually all lands objected to the abolition of local parliaments.

Matters came to a head in 1787 when Joseph II joined Catherine II of Russia in a war against the Ottoman Empire. Their assay ended in disaster as Habsburg armies reeled from one defeat to another. The Austrian Netherlands rose in revolt that same year. Hungary rebelled from 1788 to 1790. Plagued by military defeat and tuberculosis, Joseph in January 1790 restored local assemblies

[1] The Magyars (called "Hungarians" in Latin) had settled the middle Danube around 900.

in Hungary, agreed to be crowned at Pozsony, and swore to uphold Hungary's ancient constitution. The most brilliant failure in Habsburg history, he died the following month. Wenzel Anton Count von Kaunitz, the architect of Austrian foreign policy during the second half of the eighteenth century, noted laconically: "It was time."

Austro-Prussian Dualism: "The Rape of Silesia"

On a cold December night in 1740, the newly crowned Prussian king, Frederick II, hosted Europe's envoys to his court at a masked ball in Berlin. The next morning, December 13, he personally led twenty thousand Prussian troops across the border into Austrian Silesia, where he promised his officers "a rendezvous with destiny." With that march, Frederick II initiated what historians have called the Austro-Prussian "dualism" in Germany — a contest for preeminence that did not reach resolution until 1866. What began in 1740 as an overt act of territorial piracy, stemming from Frederick's admitted craving for fame and glory, would develop into more than two decades of mortal combat between the Hohenzollerns and the Habsburgs. When the Silesian wars finally ended in the Peace of Hubertusburg in 1763, Prussia had ascended into the ranks of the great powers. By Frederick's calculations, the expense had been staggering: the dynastic struggle from 1756 to 1763 alone had taken 500,000 Prussian lives (as many men as had been lost during the entire Thirty Years' War) and had cost the state more than 125 million thaler.

Yet Frederick II had not acted alone in 1740, nor had he acted without at least a fig leaf of legality to cover his overt aggression. In April 1713, the crowned heads of Europe had agreed to conclude (and honor) a so-called Pragmatic Sanction with Emperor Charles VI, whereby they recognized the succession of his daughter, Maria Theresa, in the absence of direct male offspring.[1] Frederick's father, Frederick William I, had signed the Pragmatic Sanction in 1728 in return for a vague Austrian promise that Prussia would acquire Berg and Jülich in the Rhineland upon the death of the current ruler, Elector Carl Philip, who had no male issue. When Austria announced in February 1739 that the territories would go not to the Hohenzollern but rather to the Palatinate branch of the Wittelsbach royal family, Frederick William I felt deeply betrayed by Austria. His son was determined to avenge that perceived Austrian treachery.

[1] Confusion surrounded primogeniture, in both 1740 and later in 1837, when Queen Victoria of England had to surrender her claims to the Kingdom of Hanover in Germany. While German constitutional scholars stress that the so-called Salic Law of the medieval Franks was primarily a penal code and did not specifically preclude female succession, in practice Salic Law was consistently applied to prevent female succession in both Germany and France.

SILESIA, 1740

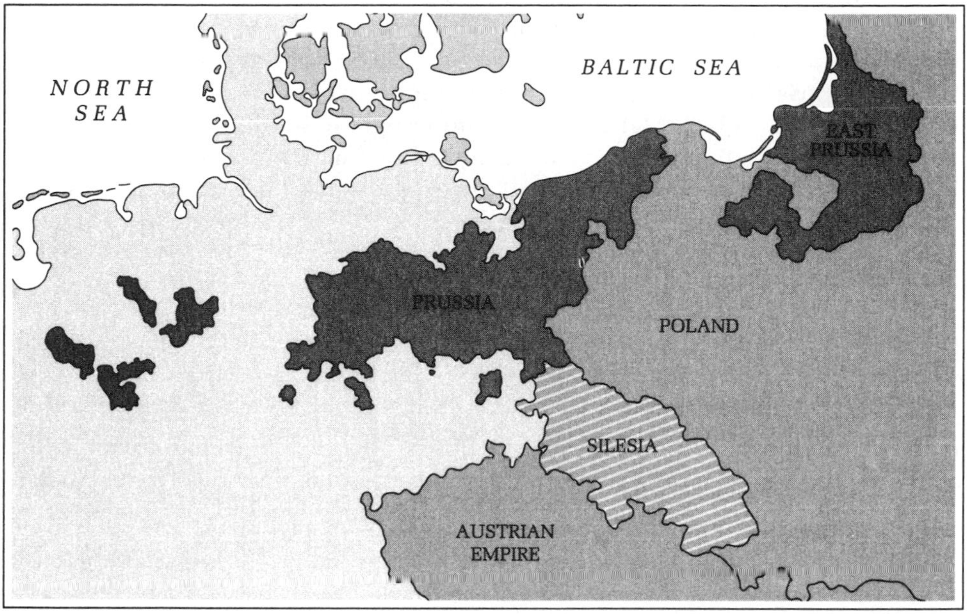

In 1740 Bavaria and France had joined Prussia with self-serving relish in embarking upon the "war of Austrian succession." In due course, the conflict would escalate to global dimensions, as its many names attest: the War of Jenkins' Ear; King George's War; the French and Indian War; the War of Hanoverian Succession; the First, Second, and Third Silesian Wars; the War of Austrian Succession; and finally the Seven Years' War. The struggle raged from central Europe to the Ohio Valley, from Canada to India. When this first truly world war ended in 1763, Prussia had emerged as a major player in Europe and Britain had established its maritime supremacy by ousting France from all lands east of the Mississippi River, Canada, and India and evicting Spain from Florida.

Frederick's theft of Silesia in 1740 resulted from a calculated risk. Acquiring Austria's richest province would increase Prussia's population by half and almost double its annual revenues. Moreover, Frederick realized, Prussia could aspire to become a great power only in opposition to Austria, never in unison with it. Finally, Frederick II thirsted for success.

Given the element of surprise and Prussia's highly disciplined force of eighty-three thousand troops, the outcome was scarcely in doubt. Prussian forces quickly occupied Silesia and in April 1741 defeated an Austrian army at Mollwitz. Frederick added insult to injury by casting his vote for Holy Roman Emperor for Charles Albert of Bavaria, who took the title Kaiser Charles VII in

January 1742, thereby depriving the Habsburgs of the crown of Charlemagne for the only time in the long history of the Empire. A second major defeat of Austrian forces at the hands of Frederick at Chotusitz in May 1742 convinced Maria Theresa of the need for peace. In a preliminary treaty signed at Breslau in June, Austria agreed to surrender Upper and Lower Silesia and the Duchy of Glatz to Prussia. In fact, Maria Theresa had bought breathing space in the final Peace of Berlin, signed in July, to concentrate against Bavaria and France.

The peace lasted barely two years. In August 1744 Frederick II launched the Second Silesian War — also called the Second War of the Austrian Succession — by invading Bohemia. This time the Prussians did not benefit from the element of surprise as they had in 1740. Although Frederick's forces readily occupied Prague, winter, starvation, and desertion thereafter plagued his army. Saxony's decision to join Austria against Prussia and the advance into Bohemia of Maria Theresa's brother-in-law, Prince Charles of Lorraine, at the head of the Austrian Army of the Rhine, forced Frederick to withdraw to Silesia by December 1744. In January 1745 Maria Theresa enjoyed an unexpected windfall when the death of Charles VII ended the state of war between Austria and Bavaria. In September, Maria Theresa's husband, Francis I, was crowned German Emperor, and the imperial dignity of the House of Habsburg was restored.

Confident of success, Austrian forces crossed the mountains into Silesia. At Hohenfriedberg on the morning of June 5, 1745, however, Frederick II routed the armies of Charles of Lorraine. The Prussian king for the first time was hailed as "Frederick the Great." (Ironically, a march composed in honor of the battle would become the favorite of an Austrian, Adolf Hitler.) Frederick pressed the advantage and in September won another victory against the Austrians at Soor; Prince Charles thereupon withdrew his forces behind the Bohemian mountains. On Christmas Day 1745 Frederick occupied Dresden and in the Saxon capital concluded a peace with Austria that again left Silesia in his hands. The "second war of Austrian succession" was over. Frederick II returned to Potsdam to write a history of the two Austro-Prussian conflicts. The *Sturm und Drang* period of his life came to a close; he no longer sought glory in battle. "Happily, I am cured of this passion; the intoxication is over."

But Frederick's travails were not to end. The king remained a prisoner of his action of 1740. His seizure and then defense of Silesia ran like a tragic thread through the next two decades of his life. He would not give up the territory; Maria Theresa would not let it go. Both staked their crowns and reputations upon their victory. In fact, Maria Theresa started work at Schönbrunn on a great victory arch, the Gloriette, that was to commemorate her eventual triumph over Frederick, whom she called a "charlatan" and the "monstrosity" ruling in Berlin.

Apart from the fact that both were strong personalities with indomitable will, the two major players in the struggle over Silesia could hardly have been more antithetical in character. Maria Theresa was a woman of noble character and deep religious faith; Frederick was a cynic and an atheist. She was the mother of sixteen children; he a misogynist. She believed in the rightness of her cause; he in the fickle fortune of fate. Only after two decades of warfare had passed did each develop a grudging respect for the other.

In Count Kaunitz, Maria Theresa found a cold, calculating diplomat who shared her desire to reconquer Silesia and to further the cause of the "august House of Habsburg." Kaunitz understood that the traditional European system of alliances between Austria and Great Britain, on the one hand, and France and Prussia, on the other, was being strained to the breaking point by events in North America. There, the French attempt to link their possessions in Canada with Louisiana by way of a chain of forts in the Allegheny Mountains threatened to cut off possible western expansion for the British settlers who lived along the Atlantic coast. For almost two years, a state of undeclared war existed between Britain and France in the Ohio Valley before London declared war on France in May 1756. Would Prussia support its historic ally, France? And would Austria side with its traditional partner, Britain?

In September 1755 Frederick II learned that Britain, to head off any possible Prussian threat to Hanover, had concluded a subsidy agreement with Russia, whereby the latter was to maintain fifty-five thousand soldiers near the borders of East Prussia. Greatly alarmed and determined to cut British subsidies to Russia, Frederick offered himself as guarantor of Hanover's independence. The Convention of Westminster, concluded between Britain and Prussia in January 1756, stipulated that Berlin and London would act jointly to keep foreign troops out of Hanover. In reality, this meant that Prussia would defend Hanover against potential aggression in return for subsidy payments. Prime Minister Pitt of Great Britain, for his part, refused to send "a drop of blood to the Elbe, to be lost in that ocean of gore."

Frederick II had miscalculated badly. France saw the Convention of Westminster as an act of treachery, and the Franco-Prussian alliance was allowed to lapse. Count Kaunitz seized the opportunity to launch the great "diplomatic revolution." Frederick's invasion of Silesia in 1740, coupled with the Anglo-French colonial struggle, had jeopardized the European balance of power. Frederick's alliance with the British drove Austria and France into one another's arms.

Other powers quickly joined the anti-Prussian camp. Sweden took up the struggle against Prussia in order to regain its former German territories. Most of the lesser German states, arguing that Frederick's theft of Silesia in 1740 had offended the notion of the "imperial peace" within the Holy Roman Empire, sided with Austria after 1756. Brunswick, Gotha, and Hesse-Kassel alone remained neutral. Hanover, through both dynastic ties and the Convention of Westminster, stood with Britain.

Russia was the wild card in this diplomatic game. Since the time of Peter the Great, Russian expansion had moved in two directions: south into Turkey to gain access to the Black Sea and west into northern central Europe to dominate the Baltic region. Thus, Turkey and Prussia posed barriers to Russia's push. Finally, the Convention of Westminster nullified the earlier Anglo-Russian subsidy treaty, greatly angering Empress Elizabeth of Russia. The way was now clear for Russia to join Kaunitz's grand coalition for "the total destruction of Prussia."

Frederick was now fighting for survival. He no longer had illusions of further aggrandizement by military means: either Prussia remained a great power through the acquisition of Silesia, or it would lose and face partition. For Maria Theresa, the issue was more complex. In July 1759 she informed her military commander, Count von Daun, that the root of the struggle lay "not simply in the reconquest of Silesia and Glatz, but also in [restoring] the happiness of the human race and in the preservation of Our sacred religion, for which I offer almost the only support in Germany." Above all, she was driven by the notion of a just war. If there was a God in heaven — and she was certain not only that he existed but that he was Catholic — then the outcome of this war to avenge the wrong of 1740 could never be in doubt.

Outnumbered, outgunned, and outflanked, Frederick II invaded Saxony on August 29, 1756, without even issuing a declaration of war. He explained his action precisely: "Better to preempt than to be preempted." The parallel to the outbreak of World War I in 1914 (discussed in Chapter 6) is obvious and was first pointed out by the great German novelist Thomas Mann in an article entitled "Frederick and the Grand Coalition" (1915). Mann compared Frederick's military strategy with the preemptive character of the Schlieffen plan, the sudden invasion of Belgium, and the all-or-nothing calculus behind the strategic concept.

The everyday experience of battle was vividly captured by Ulrich Bräker's "poor man of Toggenburg" at the battle of Lowositz in Bohemia on October 1, 1756. Frightened at the approach of Austrian cavalry, the Prussian infantry emptied their brandy flasks. "Then all my courage sank into my breeches; my only wish was to creep into the bowels of the earth." The two sides exchanged artillery; then the Prussian cavalry charged:

> And what a clash! what a rattling and glinting, as they laid into them. It scarcely lasted a quarter of an hour, however, before our horsemen returned, beaten back by the Austrian cavalry, harried almost under the muzzles of our cannon. You never saw such a spectacle! — horses with riders hanging from the stirrups, others trailing their guts along the ground.

The main infantry units engaged around mid-afternoon:

> And now the battle recommenced on the plain. But who shall attempt to describe it? — the smoke and fumes that now went up from Lowositz, the crashing and thundering as if heaven and earth were about to melt away, the incessant rattle of many hundreds of drums, the clangour of martial music of

> all kinds, rending and uplifting the heart, the shouts of so many commanders and roars of their adjutants, the moans and groans from so many thousands of wretched, mangled, half-dead victims of this day: it dazed all the sense!

Over the next few years, Frederick experienced both the heights of brilliant victories (Rossbach and Leuthen in 1757) and the depths of dark defeats (Kolin in 1757 and Kunersdorf in 1759). After 1759 he was permanently on the defensive, trying to meet his adversaries' thrusts with as much force and for as long as possible on the various fronts. He escaped annihilation only through his enemies' inability to forge a coordinated plan of attack.

In 1760 Frederick was at the nadir of his reign. On October 9, a combined Austro-Russian force occupied Berlin. Soldiers ransacked the king's castles, and the city was forced to pay an indemnity of 2 million thaler. But Frederick's reputation by now had taken on almost mystical proportions, and at the mere rumor of his impending counterattack, the Austrians and Russians fled the capital. The second blow of the year also came in October, with the death of George II in Britain. George III at once replaced Pitt with his favorite, John Stuart, earl of Bute. Bute, tired of war and horrified by its financial cost, called an end to the United Kingdom's subsidies to Prussia. Frederick survived financial ruin in the short run only by debasing his precious-metal coins, to the tune of 29 million thaler.

By 1761 Frederick was truly desperate. He pressed students into service as officers and hauled young cadets out of school to command troop formations. Fourteen-year-old nobles became instant lieutenants. To maintain morale, the king slept with the troops on straw under the open skies and ate thin field soups with them, all the while contrasting his life with that of his primary opponents, Maria Theresa at Vienna, Tsarina Elizabeth at St. Petersburg, and the marquiese de Pompadour at Paris. As a last resort, Frederick tried to incite the Turks to renew their historic drive on Vienna and the Tatars to strike against Russia. Huddled in his winter quarters, his army on the point of collapse, Frederick vowed to force the issue in the coming spring.

On January 5, 1762, Tsarina Elizabeth of Russia died. She was succeeded by Peter III, a fervent admirer of Frederick the Great. Peter quickly concluded first a separate peace (May 5) and then an alliance (June 19) with Prussia. This so-called miracle of the House of Hohenzollern decided the war. Sweden concluded a separate peace with Frederick on May 22. One by one, the smaller German states began to negotiate with Prussia for an end to the war. Maria Theresa wondered how long she could hold on. Despite having received more than 60 million livres in French subsidies, the Habsburg debt had tripled to 136 million gulden as a result of the war. It was time to strike a deal.

The twenty-three-year struggle over Silesia ended, as it had begun, on a cold December day. In the ruins of Augustus III's baroque hunting lodge at Hubertusburg near Leipzig, Austrian and Prussian plenipotentiaries agreed to conclude the Seven Years' War on the basis of the *status quo ante bellum*. The treaty was formally signed on February 15, 1763. Silesia remained Prussian. Frederick agreed to cast his vote for Joseph II as Holy Roman Emperor. That same month, Great Britain concluded peace with France and Spain to end the global struggle. In awe, the great Prussian philosopher Immanuel Kant spoke of "Frederick's century." Strangely, sixty-five years passed before a statue was erected in honor of his accomplishments.

The Peace of Hubertusburg ushered in three decades of peace in central Europe. Austro-Prussian relations remained charged with suspicion and animosity, but both sides were too exhausted to renew the struggle. Moreover, both Frederick II and Joseph II were alarmed by the territorial ambitions of Empress Catherine II of Russia. In addition to putting her own candidate, Stanisław August Poniatowski, on the Polish throne and supporting him with Russian troops, Catherine sought to wrest the provinces of Moldavia and Wallachia from Turkey. Joseph II objected vehemently. Frederick, allied with Russia since 1763, was treaty bound to support Russia against Austria.

In 1772 Frederick resolved this dilemma by convincing Austria and Russia to join Prussia in "taking Holy Communion in the one Eucharist body that was Poland." Under the terms of this first partition of Poland, Frederick II acquired West Prussia, an area on the lower Vistula River, thereby linking Brandenburg and Pomerania to East Prussia. (Much of this newly acquired territory would form part of the Polish Corridor after 1918.)

Austro-Prussian relations reached the flash point, on the other hand, when Joseph II sent Austrian troops into Bavaria in January 1778 to claim it in the name of his second wife — and to try to offset the loss of Silesia. Frederick the Great countered in July with an invasion of Bohemia. The only serious casualties of the war were the potatoes plundered by the armies. In the end, Bavaria went to Karl Theodor of the Palatinate line of the Wittelsbach dynasty. Austria was assuaged with a strip of land along the right bank of the Inn river, between Salzburg and Passau, which included the city of Braunau (future birthplace of Adolf Hitler). Nor did Joseph's more subtle plan to exchange the Austrian Netherlands for Bavaria find favor with his fellow German princes.

The so-called Potato War alarmed the lesser German states, which realized that their survival depended on German dualism. They could exist, that is, only as long as Berlin and Vienna balanced each other. Frederick II played on these fears by charging that Joseph was seeking "to establish a tyrannical despotism throughout the German lands." The ruse worked: in July 1785 Prussia, Hanover, and Saxony, soon joined by fourteen other states, created the German Princes' League (*Fürstenbund*) to uphold the sanctity of the Reich.

Many contemporaries and some subsequent historians have depicted the league as a first expression of nationalist sentiment and reformist aspirations. Habsburg scholars have countered by arguing that Frederick II sought nothing less than to destroy the Holy Roman Empire and to offer himself as a possible "anti-Kaiser." Both views are inaccurate. Frederick II had not the slightest emotional attachment to the Holy Roman Empire, which he ridiculed as an institution designed merely to "preserve the privileges, possessions, and the freedoms of this republic of princes." To him, the Empire played a necessary role only to the extent that it maintained the balance of power between Austria and Prussia. It needed to survive as long as it fulfilled that single purpose. The Prussian school of history, which saw the Princes' League as the genesis of the later non-Austrian ("little German," or *Kleindeutsch*) unification, also lacks credibility: Frederick II thought not in national but purely in dynastic terms.

Defeat, Reform, Liberation: Germany and the French Revolution

The educated middle class of Germany cast covetous eyes across the Rhine in 1789 as they watched the French Constituent Assembly abolish the nobility, nationalize church property, strike down feudal dues, ban guilds, introduce a land tax, secularize education, and promulgate not only a constitution but also the Declaration of the Rights of Man and Citizen. Numerous Germans, including the scions of such noble clans as von Moltke, von Schlabrendorff, and von Tronck, embraced the egalitarian ideals of the French Revolution and traveled to Paris to see firsthand what Kant called the "dawn of civilization." Others, including Johann Gottfried von Herder, Friedrich Gottlieb Klopstock, and Christoph Martin Wieland, lent their venerable names to the German supporters of "French ideas." The revolution, in turn, included on its august list of "honorary" citizens the names of a handful of notable Germans such as Klopstock and Friedrich Schiller, as well as the German-Swiss Johann Heinrich Pestalozzi, along with George Washington and Thomas Paine.

The German middle class that was initially seduced by "French ideas" consisted mainly of university-educated civil servants — judges, lawyers, professors, teachers, doctors, pastors — a privileged social elite. The Prussian Civil Code of 1794, for example, had been created by and for them: a special category of so-called *Eximierte*, that is, educated middle-class members enjoying preferred legal status and exemption from military service. Their world centered on journals and books, literary and philanthropic societies. They gathered at coffeehouses, Masonic lodges, and private salons (such as the Wednesday Society in Berlin) to discuss the pressing questions of the day. Not surprisingly, they quickly embraced the radical reform movement that was sweeping the French capital. The philosopher Friedrich von Schelling planted a "tree of liberty" at Tübingen University. His professional colleague, Johann Gottlieb Fichte, proclaimed that "the dark ages are over." And Klopstock announced that the French Revolution constituted nothing less than "the noblest deed of the century."

The initial enthusiasm in the German states for the great events then taking place in France was not restricted to the middle class. The mid-nineteenth-century story collector Gottfried Teller passionately detailed the warm reception that the French Revolution received in the home of the Zurich tailor Kaspar Hediger,

> for he was a bitter partisan and sanctioned the Terror after the event. . . . Against the bookcase leaned a well-kept, shining musket. . . . This was *his* hunting-piece, with which he went gunning not for hare and partridge, but for aristocrats and Jesuits, for constitution-breakers and betrayers of the people.

Their initial enthusiasm, however, waned as the revolution in Paris turned ugly. A republic was declared in September 1792. In January 1793, Louis XVI was beheaded, and Marie Antoinette, the "widow Capet," shared her husband's fate in October 1793. Most alarming, the revolution turned on its own. In September 1793 alone, the Jacobin terror claimed a thousand victims. During the following six months, Maximilien Robespierre's Committee of Public Safety dispatched an additional sixteen thousand Frenchmen under the blade of the guillotine at what later became the Place de la Concorde and elsewhere. And before the Committee of Public Safety had finished its grisly work, forty thousand victims, including many of the early German supporters, now denounced as "foreigners," had been executed in the name of the nation.

Shocked by this thirst for blood, the German middle class turned its back on France. Only a few hundred in Hamburg and Mainz remained loyal to "French ideas," and the much-heralded "Republic of Mainz," imposed at the point of French bayonets, lasted only twenty-three days — as long, that is, as French troops occupied the city. The "age of democratic revolutions," as this period has been called, basically remained confined to America and France.

Most of the German states saw only sporadic revolutionary activity sparked by the events in France. After a brief period in which peasants attempted to storm manorial houses to burn feudal records, ultraconservatism regained the upper hand. Many peasants were imprisoned or hanged. In Silesia, they were forced to run the gauntlet in army fashion. In a few isolated instances, East Elbian Junkers led cavalry charges against rebellious serfs. In short, Germany proved unready for its own revolution from below.

The French Revolution, however, cast a long shadow over subsequent German history. In time, it elicited a visceral, negative response to all that 1789 had stood for rather than a positive response to change. Subsequent generations saw the French Revolution as a shock wave that destroyed forever an idyllic and highly romanticized German past of social harmony and political calm. "Foreign" concepts such as revolution, atheism, civil strife, immorality, and political rationalism had invaded and polluted the German polity. The revolution's fierce attacks on religion and property, denounced stridently by the English writer Edmund Burke in his *Reflections on the Revolution in France*, published in 1790 and translated into German in 1792, were singled out as patently "un-German" and "alien." Indeed, numerous scholars have depicted much of subsequent German history as one long, sustained reaction against the "French ideas" of 1789.

Yet, for much of the 1790s, German statesmen such as Count Kaunitz in Austria and Count von Hertzberg in Prussia studiously ignored the potential threat to Germany of French internal developments. Instead, they viewed the revolution only in terms of its effect on the European concert. To secure the stability of the international order, they conducted no fewer than four coalition wars against France between 1792 and 1806. The two leaders abandoned the Austro-Prussian dualism of 1740 in the face of the common danger. Preliminary conventions at Reichenbach in July 1790 and at Pillnitz in August 1791 paved the way for an alliance between the Habsburgs and the Hohenzollerns in February 1792. Symbolically, the last Holy Roman Emperor, Francis II, was crowned on July 14, 1792, the third anniversary of the storming of the Bastille in Paris.

But neither Austria, which fielded 100,000 troops, nor Prussia, which offered 42,000 soldiers, was prepared for war. After the allied commander, the duke of Brunswick, issued a stern manifesto warning the French that the allies would "extract a vengeance that will live in memory forever by delivering the city of Paris to military execution and complete destruction," the famous "cannonade of Valmy" on September 20, 1792, proved indecisive because the duke preferred not to fight in rain and mud. Moreover, Prussia revealed its basic lack of interest in French affairs by turning east. In January 1793, it joined Russia in a second partition of Poland, netting the Hohenzollerns an additional one million Polish subjects in Posen, Thorn, and Danzig (now Poznań, Toruń, and Gdańsk).

The militant government at Paris now harnessed the nation to drive the foreigners from French soil and to secure the republic. The National Convention, which met at Paris after September 1792 to reorder the French state, following the policy of Louis XIV decreed that the Alps and Rhine constituted France's "natural borders." French armies under the comte de Custine invaded Germany and occupied Mainz, Speyer, and Worms. His army's stirring marching song of 1792 would become France's national anthem, "La Marseillaise." In August 1793 Lazare Carnot drafted the famous *levée en masse*, which directed young men and married men and even women, children, and old men, to serve the nation "until the day the enemy is driven from the soil of the French Republic." France was about to plunge Europe into two decades of almost uninterrupted warfare.

Still, Berlin and Vienna leisurely went about their normal business. The allies generated not a single national reform or military recruitment to meet the threats of the Convention. In the spring of 1795, Prussia, totally ignoring the revolutionary danger from France as well as its alliance commitments to Austria, signed a separate peace with France at Basel. Austria turned east, joining Russia in the third Polish partition. It was only due to the grace of Catherine II of Russia that Prussia received another 1 million Poles in October 1795, mainly between East Prussia and Warsaw, in what was called "New East Prussia." This most recent acquisition was sheer madness, a cynical deal cut by dynasts in total ignorance of the national sentiments seething throughout Europe in the last decade of the eighteenth century.

In 1799 the revolution in France entered a new phase when Napoleon Bonaparte seized power. The "world spirit on horseback," as the philosopher Hegel called him, launched into more than sixty great battles in his ever-escalating drive for hegemony in Europe. In just two years, between 1803 and 1805, Napoleon's shrewd combination of brilliant military victories and political blackmail brought the southern German states of Baden, Bavaria, and Württemberg under his control and created the grand duchy of Berg on the right bank of the Lower Rhine under his brother-in-law Joachim Murat. Eventually, France annexed the left bank of the Rhine as well as extensive territory in northwestern Germany and incorporated them as departments of France.

In Germany, the Napoleonic years saw radical change as well as high hopes and deep disappointments. Napoleon proved to be at once destroyer of the Holy Roman Empire and the modernizer of Germany. Few other men could claim to have streamlined and rationalized Germany as much as Napoleon. His introduction in 1804 of the Civil Code (often simply called the *Code Napoléon*) alone guarantees him a place in German legal history. Its 2,281 articles were adopted in their basic contours by Anhalt, Baden, Berg, and Frankfurt, not to mention the French satellite states (the Kingdom of Westphalia and the Confederation of the Rhine). Furthermore, Bonaparte's ruthless policy of secularizing church lands found great resonance in both Protestant Prussia and Catholic Bavaria. These radical innovations, culminating in Napoleon's self-coronation on December 2, 1804, as emperor of the French, provoked fundamental organizational changes for the German states.

Anticipating Napoleon's imperial designs, Emperor Francis II had in August 1804 already collected all Habsburg territorial possessions under the new rubric of "Austrian Empire," thereby in effect supplanting the Holy Roman Empire. And when he lost the so-called three emperors' battle of Austerlitz on December 2, 1805, he was forced to agree to the elevation to kingdomhood of Napoleon's allies, Bavaria and Württemberg. On July 12, 1806, Napoleon created the Confederation of the Rhine (*Rheinbund*) — all told, sixteen middle and small states of what was now called the "Third Germany." The French plan was at once transparent: the confederation, in conjunction with the newly created Kingdom of Westphalia under Napoleon's brother Jérôme, was to serve as a counterbalance to Prussia and Austria.

The end of the old order in Germany was at hand. On August 1, 1806, the states of the Confederation of the Rhine seceded from the Holy Roman Empire. Five days later, Francis II laid down the crown of Charlemagne, now a meaningless coronet. Henceforth, he became Francis I, emperor of Austria. A millennium ended as the Holy Roman Empire evaporated. Surprisingly few

Germans mourned the Reich's passing as they rushed headlong to institute reforms and secularize their society.

Secularization of church property harked back to Joseph II, who had disbanded at least seven hundred monasteries in the 1780s. After 1803 the movement was led by territorial princes, interested in their own sovereignty and aggrandizement, who took their cue in foreign policy from the French dictator. Napoleon's German policy had two salient features: at the diplomatic level, he worked to play Austria off against Prussia, and within Germany he sought to create a new confederation of states to act as a counterweight to the dominant position of Austria and Prussia within the Reich. Additionally, he brought to the German states the irreligion and anticlericalism of the French Revolution.

Secularization took two forms: abrogating the worldly powers of clerical princes and confiscating their lands and property. The Principal Decree of the Imperial Deputation in April 1803 reordered the Holy Roman Empire by stripping church princes of their voting powers and thereby virtually abolishing the Catholic church as the official church of the Empire. In the process, the decree greatly diluted Austria's Catholic majority in the Reich. With a stroke of a pen, ancient ecclesiastical states, prince-bishoprics, imperial abbeys, and monasteries were turned over to the princes of what later were called the German middle states.

At the heart of what has been called the "legal revolution" of 1803 lay the "mediatization" of forty-five free cities and two hundred monasteries, as well as the confiscation of the lands of about fourteen hundred imperial knights. This process, which transferred confiscated lands to the surrounding states, affected roughly 3.2 million people and added 21 million gulden in annual revenues to secular coffers. Between one day and the next, nearly one German in ten found themselves citizens of a new secular state. Erstwhile subjects of princely clans such as Hohenlohe, Fürstenberg, and Leiningen became residents of Baden, Bavaria, Hesse, and Württemberg. Dialects, districts, creeds, and historical traditions were intermingled. Catholics were absorbed into Protestant states, and vice versa. All Catholic universities save Freiburg, Munich, and Würzburg were closed by imperial fiat. Rationalization ran rampant as the erstwhile three-hundred-plus states of the Holy Roman Empire were combined into thirty-five.

Who benefited from secularization? On a general level, the social chasm that had separated the high clergy (noble) and the low clergy (nonnoble) gradually disappeared in favor of a more egalitarian and responsive popular church (*Volkskirche*). Affluent local townspeople — and not foreigners and Jews, as was sometimes claimed — were best positioned to purchase most of the former church lands. In the Rhine-Mosel Department, for example, they bought as much as 16 percent of all arable land.

The greatest winners were the secular states, both Catholic and Protestant, whose rulers had spearheaded the movement. Bavaria, although forced to surrender the Palatinate to the Confederation of the Rhine, managed not only to consolidate its scattered territorial holdings but also to increase them by adding "mediatized" lands from Franconia, Swabia, and Lower Bavaria, as well as the secularized archbishoprics of Augsburg, Bamberg, Freising, Passau, and Würzburg. As a result of this reordering, the Wittelsbach dynasty acquired 880,000 new subjects, and Bavaria became the third largest German state, after Austria and Prussia. After 1803, nearly 65 percent of all Bavarian peasants reportedly became legal tenants of the state. Baden and Württemberg made smaller gains. Prussia, which had forfeited 127,000 subjects and all its lands west of the Rhine to the Kingdom of Westphalia, acquired through secularization nearly 560,000 new subjects and land areas five times the size of those lost.

Losers far outweighed winners in the drive to secularize. Apart from the Roman church, the principal loser, thousands of Catholics had to accept Protestant rulers overnight. The landed nobility was stripped of its claims to more than seven hundred high ecclesiastical sinecures. States affected by secularization and its accompanying upheavals lost countless art collections and libraries to theft and willful destruction. Day laborers, vintners, and smallholders in west and southwest Germany were pauperized when they were unable to purchase the lands they had worked for the church. Those previously employed by the monasteries suffered the same fate. The effects of this secularization became permanent features of Germany's socioeconomic makeup.

In Prussia's case, the gains proved transitory. Having cleverly, if not wholly ethically, steered a middle course between Austria and France and having gained Hanover, Prussia declared war on France on October 9, 1806, when it appeared that London and Paris were about to renegotiate Hanover's future. It was a disastrous decision. Napoleon routed the old Frederican armies at Jena and Auerstädt on October 14. His forces entered Berlin on October 27. While Minister Karl Baron vom Stein managed to remove the treasury to East Prussia, the capital's military governor, General Friedrich Wilhelm von der Schulenburg, allowed all weapons and ammunition to fall into French hands. He admonished Berliners: "Calm is the first duty of the citizen." Accordingly, the Prussian bureaucracy swore allegiance to Napoleon. Civic courage was in short supply at Berlin in 1806.

Napoleon dictated peace to Frederick William III (1797–1840) at Tilsit on July 9, 1807, in terms that were draconian by any standards. Prussia lost half its lands and 5 million subjects. Its western possessions largely went to the Kingdom of Westphalia, and its ill-gotten gains from the second and third Polish partitions helped create the Grand Duchy of Warsaw, a French satellite state placed under the newly elevated Frederick Augustus I, king of Saxony. Danzig was transformed, not for the last time, into a "free" city. Prussia also had to surrender all fortifications, reduce its army to forty-two thousand men, join Napoleon's continental blockade against Britain, and pay the occupation costs for fifteen thousand French soldiers. An initial indemnity of 120 million thaler soon ballooned four- and fivefold as the French ravaged the land to help

The "World Spirit on Horseback": Napoleon greets Queen Luise of Prussia at Tilsit as Alexander I of Russia and Frederick William III of Prussia look on (July 1807).

pay for Napoleon's megalomania. The Hohenzollern fortunes had reached a nadir.

Defeat often drives reform, however, and so it did to varying degrees in the German states after the Napoleonic onslaught. The two French "model states," the Kingdom of Westphalia and the Confederation of the Rhine, were thoroughly reorganized according to French ideas. The *Code Napoléon,* for example, was immediately adopted in the Kingdom of Westphalia, in most states of the Confederation of the Rhine, and throughout north Germany. In Baden, Sigismund Baron von Reitzenstein modified the code, bringing it into line with local custom. Over time, however, French reforms were doomed to failure. In Westphalia, Jérôme, like his famous brother, lost his revolutionary zeal and sought legitimacy by marrying into royalty — in his case, the House of

Württemberg. The king's lavish life-style as well as his brother's plundering soon reduced Westphalian revenues by half. Peasants rose up in protest. Despite French occupation, the socioeconomic fabric of the Kingdom of Westphalia and the Confederation of the Rhine remained basically unaltered.

We can identify three other major groups of German reform states. Austria and Saxony represented one extreme, where little reform took place. Saxony's role as Napoleon's ally protected it against French demands; moreover, Saxony's monarch served a useful function as titular head of the Grand Duchy of Warsaw. Austria escaped huge territorial losses and indemnities partly by assuaging Napoleon and partly by joining coalitions against him whenever possible. Nor did Austria hurt its chances of survival by providing the French emperor with a Habsburg bride. Above all, the pace of Joseph II's frenetic reform movement in the 1780s had soured most Viennese bureaucrats on the idea of change. While Minister Johann Philipp Count von Stadion sought at least to centralize the imperial administration, Francis I flatly stated that he viewed the empire as nothing more than a Habsburg "family entailment."

The second group of reform states consisted of those that sought to combine the tradition of change from the Enlightenment with that of the French Revolution. In the process, these states became the "modern" entities of today. Bavaria perhaps best represents this group. Under the guiding hand of Maximilian Joseph Count von Montgelas, a Savoyard and former Illuminato who had once served in the French army, Bavaria reformed its basic structures. Following the Prussian lead, Montgelas forged a policy of bureaucratic centralism based on a newly created professional civil service. After 1799 a special ministry composed of five departments handled Bavarian affairs. Four years later, Montgelas abolished serfdom and introduced freedom of the press. In October 1806 he granted freedom of religion to the three major Christian denominations (Catholicism, Protestantism, and Calvinism). Seven years later, the Edict of Tolerance permitted Jews to establish their own religious communities. The Bavarian constitution of May 1808 guaranteed personal freedom as well as private property. And to this day, the name of Montgelas is still ardently connected with the ruthless secularization of Catholic monasteries throughout Bavaria.

Prussia exemplified the third type of reform state. Thoroughly disgraced by the forces of the French Revolution, Prussia had no choice but to change its system from the ground up. Frederick William III chose mainly non-Prussian statesmen such as Baron vom Stein, Baron von Hardenberg, and Generals Gerhard von Scharnhorst and Neithardt von Gneisenau, to undertake the effort, while relying on a reactionary court clique to temper the reform zeal. Stein, who stemmed from a family of imperial knights at Nassau, became the driving force of reform. Educated at Göttingen University, he had been influenced not only by Montesquieu's doctrine of the separation of powers and the establishment of a balanced and harmonious society but also by Edmund Burke's refutation of natural law and popular sovereignty. Stein was, above all, a product of the Enlightenment. Both its optimistic moralism and rationalism appealed to him, and he described the ideal state as featuring citizens' devotion to the betterment of human beings. The thoroughness of the Prussian defeats in 1806 gave him the chance to dismantle the Frederican state and to reshape it according to his own ideas.

In October 1807 the Reform Edict, drafted by Stein with the assistance of several Königsberg professors who sought to enact Adam Smith's free market policies, established the free use and sale of land, thereby abolishing the old *Bauernschutz* and ushering in an era of agrarian mobility. Having already released fifty thousand royal peasants from serfdom in 1799, the Hohenzollerns now decreed that as of 1810 "there shall exist only free people." But no provisions were made for peasants to obtain land other than by paying astronomical compensation to noble landlords that, according to one estimate, amounted to 12 billion mark spread over fifty years. In reality, 10 percent of all free farmers lost what little land they possessed to wealthy speculators. Those dispossessed were pauperized when the Reform Edict abolished all responsibility for the Junker to feed, clothe, and care for the newly liberated peasants, most of whom were transformed overnight into migratory day laborers. The East Elbian squirearchy also managed to enhance its holdings by purchasing former communal lands, now put on the market by the state. A rudimentary agrarian capitalism thus ended a millennium of patrimonial land tenure.

In November 1808 Stein's Municipal Ordinance abolished the traditional separation between city and countryside, as well as the old consumer (or accise) tax. Cities were accorded self-government: full citizens (those with annual incomes of 150 to 200 thaler, or slightly fewer than one in ten) elected representatives, who in turn selected the town council. Later, the town council opted to elect mayors to run urban affairs. Cities now acquired control over budgets, education, and police. As Stein put it, his ideal was "to teach the nation to conduct its own business."

In October 1810 Prussia established freedom of trade and occupation, abolishing the guild structure. All citizens were now at liberty to practice or open any trade. Former guild restrictions on production and entry were outlawed. As with the abolition of serfdom, the Freedom of Trade and Occupation Acts impoverished countless carpenters and joiners who could neither afford to open their own shops nor hire additional helpers. And whereas guild restrictions had already disappeared in the Kingdom of Westphalia in 1808, they nevertheless remained in effect in Saxony until 1861, Baden and Württemberg until 1862, and Bavaria until 1868. Stein's attempt to introduce a land tax to replace the old contribution, however, was effectively thwarted by the Junkers.

Jews were emancipated in Prussia in March 1812, two decades after Joseph II had raised them to nearly full legal status in Austria. Once more, it was hoped that legal reform would "assimilate" them into the mainstream Protestant Prussian culture.

Given the magnitude of the Prussian military defeat, it is not surprising that the most thorough reforms took place in the army. After 1806 Napoleon limited the size of the Prussian Army to forty-two thousand men, and emancipation of the serfs effectively undermined the canton system. In order to evade the French limitations, Hermann von Boyen, the war minister, introduced a scheme whereby a small percentage of each regiment's older soldiers were sent on home leave, making room for additional raw recruits. The latter were widely referred to as *Krümper* due to their sloppy (*krumm*) appearance, but they nevertheless permitted the military to expand its forces by an extra twenty thousand men. In 1813 the system was replaced by universal male conscription.

Other military reforms followed. Corporal punishment was abolished. The old officer corps was purged of several hundred officers, with their replacements now to come from all social strata and selected according to merit. In 1810 General Neithardt von Gneisenau, a Saxon from a middle-class family, along with General Gerhard von Scharnhorst, a Hanoverian from peasant stock, created a special War Academy at Berlin under Carl von Clausewitz in order to teach officers the scientific nature of modern warfare. Scharnhorst, especially, an unassuming scholar of great profundity of mind, sought "to bring army and nation into a close union." Like Stein, Scharnhorst believed that without liberating the serfs and abolishing the political separation of social classes, the German states could never achieve domestic freedom — and domestic freedom alone could generate both military power and human dignity.

War Minister von Boyen also wished to create a "nation in arms," but the concept proved too revolutionary for Frederick William III. Instead, the reformers resorted to a three-tiered administrative structure: a royal standing army, a citizen army composed of all able-bodied men (*Landwehr*), and a home defense force composed of those not fit for regular service (*Landsturm*). Once the immediate danger of Napoleon had been removed by 1815, however, the reformers quickly lost influence. Clausewitz was shunted aside in 1815 as a "Jacobin," Gneisenau had to resign his command one year later, and Boyen was forced to yield as war minister in 1819. Prime Minister von Hardenberg desired only what he termed "revolution in the good sense of the term," that is, moderate reform.

In education, Wilhelm von Humboldt, head of the Prussian Ministry of Education in 1809–1810, looked to ancient Greece for his neohumanistic ideals and struggled to develop a curriculum that would incorporate art, literature, and philosophy into a liberal arts education. Brother of the famous explorer and naturalist Alexander von Humboldt and scion of a Brandenburg Junker family, Wilhelm had studied at Göttingen University and then at Jena with Goethe and Schiller. In 1810 he united the institutions of the Berlin Academy of Sciences, as well as some of the capital's other medical facilities, into the University of Berlin. His efforts were eagerly emulated at Heidelberg, Breslau, and Bonn. Although the University of Berlin fully developed only after the peace of 1815, Humboldt's notion of the seminar method and of the free exchange of research data quickly dominated German universities well beyond 1945. Johann Gottlieb Fichte, the first rector of the University of Berlin, described academic freedom in October 1811 as the "heavenly air" and the guiding spirit of the university. On the other hand, by placing the university under state supervision, Humboldt allowed royal bureaucrats great influence over the selection and promotion of faculty.

Humboldt, relying on ideas developed by the Swiss Christian-humanitarian reformer J. H. Pestalozzi, proved instrumental also in changing the general educational scheme in Prussia. He introduced a tripartite system featuring a universal "people's school" (*Volksschule*), a "higher" school (*Gymnasium*) designed for university-bound students, and universities. Educators emphasized individual achievement in the traditional liberal arts subjects. In 1810 Humboldt made state examinations for high school teachers mandatory and introduced the *Abitur* as a graduation certificate granting the right to enter a university.

The boldness of the Prussian reforms is especially surprising in the light of the fact that they stemmed solely from the royal bureaucracy. The middle class developed no initiative of its own in areas other than literature, poetry, and learning. For the most part, Prussian *Bürger* found the state-initiated changes alarming and felt helpless to shape them. The Prussian middle class had not asked for — much less fought for — such sweeping reforms. The movement was truly a "revolution from above." It was also a deliberate rearguard action designed to preserve as much of the old Prussian social order as was possible by adopting only the most necessary radical reforms.

While Prussia underwent rigorous reform, Napoleon decided to challenge the one major European land power that defied his control. In June 1812, a gigantic army of 700,000 men, including 30,000 Austrians and 20,000 Prussians, invaded Russia. Napoleon entered Moscow on September 14, only to abandon it five weeks later in the face of an unusually early winter. His *grande armée* lost 380,000 men during the Russian campaign. The Confederation of the Rhine collapsed without a shot being fired. On December 30, 1812, Prussian General Ludwig Yorck von Wartenburg seized the moment to conclude a neutrality pact with Russia at Tauroggen, at the border of East Prussia, thereby taking Prussia out of Napoleon's war. Throughout Germany, the wars of liberation (to rid the land from French occupation) were about to unfold.

The Prussian mood in 1813 was a mixture of monarchism and antiforeign feeling, vaguely nationalistic and quasi-religious. The apathy of 1806 was replaced by a new patriotism, motivated by both a hatred of the foreign oppressor and a desire to restore normal economic life. People east of the Elbe were animated by Prussian loyalties, and many still regarded the Hohenzollern dynasty as the supreme authority, ordained by God. Moreover, traditional forms of religion proved much stronger than the elitist literature of the age would indicate. The new motto, "With God for King and Fatherland," and the freshly minted Iron Cross, patterned after the Maltese Cross, reflected this unusual symbiosis.

In 1807 the philosopher Fichte had delivered his immortal "Addresses to the German Nation" at the Berlin University, demanding the creation of a national will to resist the foreign occupier. Only the "devouring flame of higher patriotism," Fichte intoned, could liberate the German states. The philosopher tried to inculcate Germans with a new sense of sacrifice, service, and duty that transcended particularism and dynastic loyalties. While his brand of nationalism should not be confused with the narrow and chauvinistic varieties of the next two centuries, it nevertheless helped to develop the concept of the nation as a living community with an urge (and a right) to grow and expand.

Thus patriotism, partly national and partly particularist, abounded, as did a willingness to sacrifice. Junker families sold heirlooms to raise troops. Nearly 30,000 young men volunteered at once for the army, and by 1813 more than 280,000 troops had been mobilized. The militia was activated in March 1813. On March 17 Frederick William III issued a ringing proclamation "To My People!" in which he called upon all "Germans and Prussians" to throw off the foreign yoke. Ludwig van Beethoven, who had originally dedicated his Third Symphony to Napoleon, now turned against the emperor and offered the *Eroica* to Frederick William III for his part in the wars of liberation. The composer dedicated his Third, Fifth, and Ninth symphonies to the cause of "humanity," a clear tribute also to the lingering cosmopolitan spirit of the age.

On October 16, 1813, the greatest military battle of the Napoleonic wars took place at Leipzig. After a series of indecisive engagements in Silesia and Bohemia, Napoleon and his Saxon ally were forced to make a stand along the Elbe against the combined forces of Austria, Prussia, and Russia, augmented by a small Swedish contingent under Napoleon's erstwhile marshal, crown prince Bernadotte of Sweden. Half a million men clashed in the so-called Battle of Nations. Allied losses reached an astounding 54,000; the French lost 37,000 soldiers in battle, and 35,000 were captured. The Kingdom of Westphalia collapsed overnight. The king of Saxony became an allied hostage. Paris fell on March 30, 1814. The conflict stimulated a great outpouring of German national enthusiasm, and radicals called for the dismemberment of France. British diplomats spoke of a "militant republican spirit" in the Prussian Army. More moderate statesmen, however, struggled to regain control of the wars of liberation to channel them back into the traditional cabinet wars conducted by diplomats for dynasts.

Napoleon, banished to the island of Elba in the Mediterranean Sea, escaped and landed in France on March 1, 1815. On June 18, 1815, his army of 125,000 men was decisively defeated at Waterloo by the duke of Wellington and Gebhard Leberecht Prince Blücher. The Corsican surrendered again on June 22. This time, the British removed him to the rock of Ste. Helena in the Atlantic Ocean. Europe's nightmare of war and revolution was finally over.

A World Restored? The Congress of Vienna, 1815

Two emperors, six kings, more than a hundred princes, and over two hundred diplomats gathered at Vienna to sort out the damages done by twenty-three years of almost uninterrupted warfare. Most of the borders of central Europe had been redrawn, ancient dynasties toppled, new monarchies created, and much of Europe laid waste. Three million men had died in battle. The task of restoring Europe rested primarily with four men: Alexander I, tsar of Russia, Lord Castlereagh of Great Britain, Chancellor Klemens Lothar Prince von Metternich of Austria, and Prime Minister Karl August von Hardenberg of Prussia. In the wings stood Charles-Maurice Talleyrand, head of a provisional government in France and future foreign minister of the restored Bourbon regime.

The Congress of Vienna was not actually a congress. It met only once, to sign the final accords. The real work was conducted behind the scenes by the representatives of Austria, Britain, Prussia, and Russia in salons and drawing rooms, as well as by the thirteen committees entrusted with reordering Europe. Intrigue and bribery ran rampant. The Austrian secret police kept Prince von Metternich abreast of most developments. For the vast majority of delegates, the congress consisted of a glittering array of balls, banquets, feasts, hunts, and parades, costing the Habsburgs an estimated 20 million gulden. Not since 1648 had there been such an august gathering (the next would come at Paris in 1919).

The Congress of Vienna was deeply divided from the start. To be sure, the participants generally agreed to uphold the principle of dynastic legitimacy and to restore the balance of power among the great powers. Even Metternich and his ideological mentor and chief councilor, Friedrich von Gentz, realized that the clock could not be turned back to 1789. Both accepted not only the dissolution of the Holy Roman Empire but secularization and "mediatization." Beyond these views, however, the major powers shared little else. While Metternich struggled to combat revolution in all its devious guises, Viscount Castlereagh of Britain fought to preserve the balance on the Continent. Alexander I of Russia and Frederick William III of Prussia pursued much more specific goals, centering on the so-called Saxon question. The Russians wanted to annex the Grand Duchy of Warsaw, and the Prussians coveted the Kingdom of Saxony. Neither Metternich nor Castlereagh was willing to condone such drastic territorial revisions in eastern Europe. In January 1815 Austria and Great Britain concluded a secret alliance designed to head off the vast aggrandizement schemes of the two eastern monarchs. In the process, Metternich and Castlereagh opened the door for the French delegate, Prince Talleyrand, to exploit allied dissension and obtain moderate peace terms for France — the borders of 1792.

Resolving this chaos required a compromise, and the congress worked diligently to find solutions designed to satisfy all of the principal powers to

Reshaping Europe: An irreverent view of the Congress of Vienna (1814).

some degree. Prussia was assuaged with two-fifths of Saxony, Posen and Thorn, Swedish Pomerania, its erstwhile Rhenish lands, and most of the Kingdom of Westphalia. Russia took solace in reconstituting a good deal of the Napoleonic Grand Duchy of Warsaw in a new Kingdom of Poland, ruled by the tsar. Bavaria received Prussia's former holding of Ansbach-Bayreuth, as well as Nuremberg and Augsburg. Austria shifted its center of gravity from central to southeastern Europe by obtaining Tyrol, Salzburg, Trieste, Istria, Dalmatia, and Lombardy, as well as Venice. The United Kingdom regained an enlarged Hanover, the North Sea island of Helgoland, Ceylon, Malta, and other overseas bases. Metternich's caustic comment that "Italy" was but a geographical expression accurately reflected his determination not to pander to the popular clamor for the creation of "nation-states" in Europe. The call of Fichte and others for a united German empire fell upon deaf ears.

The question of the future organizational form for the German states remained. Preliminary agreements led by May 1820 to the Vienna Final Act, establishing a loose German Confederation (*Deutsche Bund*) with its seat at Frankfurt. The confederation's primary task was "to preserve Germany's external and internal security and the independence and integrity of the several German states" — in other words, the status quo of 1815. It comprised thirty-five sovereign states and four "free" cities. Three foreign monarchs also

GERMANY, 1815

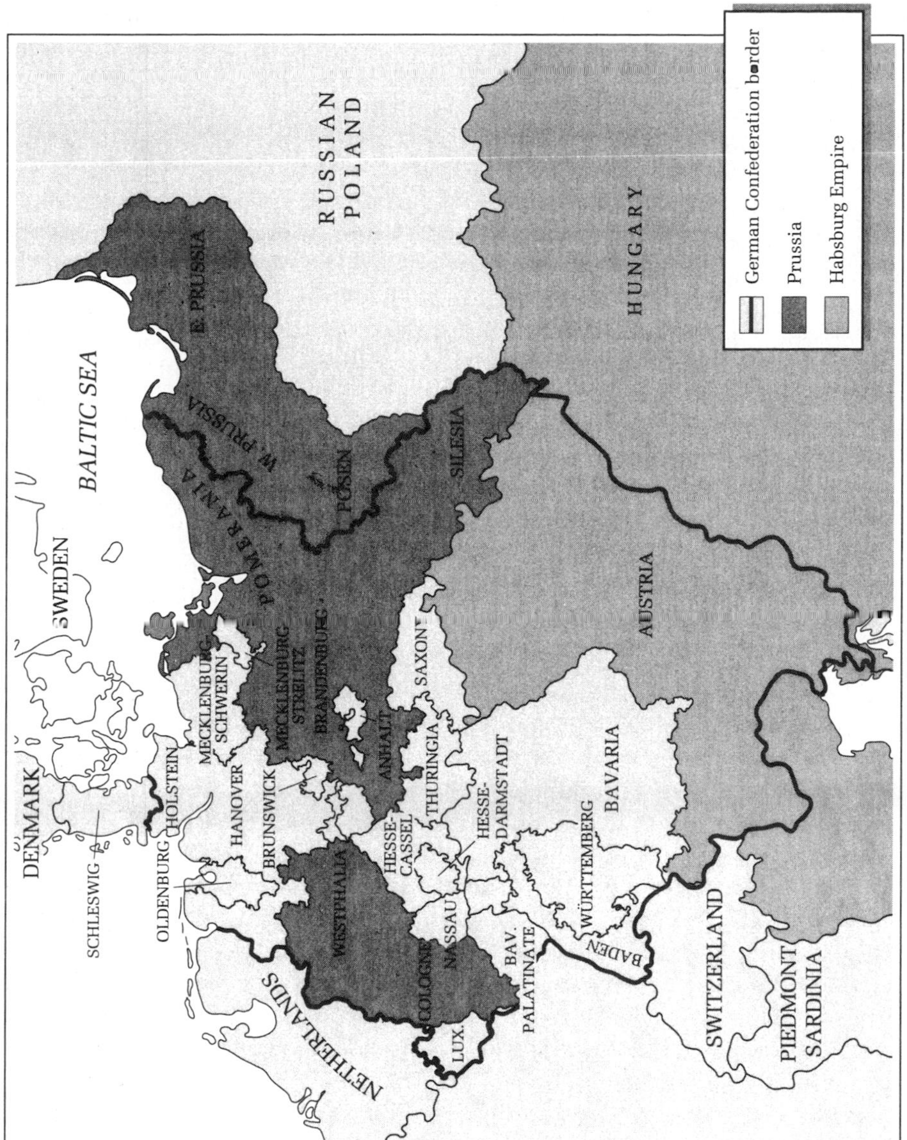

became members: Britain voted for Hanover, Denmark for Holstein, and the Netherlands for Luxembourg. All signatories to the final accords swore to promulgate constitutions in their various lands. Only the rulers of Baden, Bavaria, and Württemberg kept that promise.

The settlements at Vienna were largely the work of Metternich. Descendant of an old Rhenish noble family and erstwhile ambassador to the court of Napoleon, Metternich had become Austrian foreign minister in 1809. He brought to this post both cold skepticism and a strong belief in the old European state system. He believed in balance: among the European states as well as between the forces of progress and continuity. Blessed with great social gifts and charm, Metternich at the Congress of Vienna also displayed a certain calculated disingenuousness and love of intrigue. He understood that nationalism was potentially fatal to the multinational Austrian Empire that straddled the European map, from lands inhabited by German and Italians to those peopled by Poles and Rumanians. And fearing its potent strength, Metternich struggled to build barriers against its further development.

Many scholars have viewed the settlements reached at Vienna as ill guided. Dynasts redrew borders without reference to popular wishes. Some states were rewarded, others punished. Austria gained Italian and Slavic subjects; Prussia once more annexed Poles; Great Britain kept Hanover; Denmark maintained stewardship over Holstein and Schleswig; and Bavaria expanded into Franconia and Swabia. In all cases, the men of Vienna, led by Metternich, sought to suppress the virulent power of national sentiment aroused after 1792. Yet it is not unfair to ask whether the men of Vienna truly believed that they could suppress nationalism (and liberalism) with a wave of a pen. They would find the answer to that question during the next half-century.

In all fairness, it should be pointed out that Metternich was not the archvillain that especially later Prussian historians made him out. He did agree, after all, to allow the German states to promulgate their own constitutions. Can he be blamed for the failure of most to renege on that promise? Above all, Metternich rightly discerned the disruptive and potentially deadly allure of nationalism with regard to the multinational empire that he represented at Vienna. The dynastic wars of the eighteenth century were one thing, the national wars of Napoleon quite another. Austria, which encompassed at least thirteen ethnic groups, could ill afford to be seduced by yearnings for nationhood. For understandable reasons, Metternich chose not to let the genie of nationalism out of the bottle.

In the autumn of his life, Goethe expressed the feelings of many in central Europe when he mused in an exchange with the historian Heinrich Luden: "Yes, the German people offer promise for and possess a future. The destiny of the Germans, in the words of Napoleon, has not yet been fulfilled. . . . But has the [German] *Volk* been awakened? Does it know what it wants and what it is capable of doing?" Half a century would pass before Goethe's interrogation of 1813 was answered.

Suggested Readings

For general background, John Gagliardo, *Reich and Nation: The Holy Roman Empire as Idea and Reality, 1763–1806* (Bloomington, Ind., 1980), traces the Empire's history during its final half-century. Carlile A. Macartney, *The Habsburg and Hohenzollern Dynasties in the Seventeenth and Eighteenth Centuries* (New York, 1970), offers a collection of documents on the dynastic politics of the age. Leonard Krieger, *An Essay on the Theory of Enlightened Despotism* (Chicago and London, 1975), introduces the reigns of Frederick II and Joseph II, among others.

The intellectual history of the age of enlightened despotism can be gleaned from Ernst Cassirer, *The Philosophy of the Enlightenment* (Boston, 1951), and Peter Gay, *The Enlightenment: An Interpretation*, 2 vols. (New York, 1966–1969). The Austrian scene is surveyed by Robert A. Kann, *A Study of Austrian Intellectual History: From Late Baroque to Romanticism* (New York, 1960). The romantic movement in Germany has been assessed by Hans S. Reiss, *The Political Thought of the German Romantics, 1793–1815* (Oxford, 1955). And the development of a rudimentary political process was first pointed out by Reinhold Aris, *History of Political Thought in Germany from 1789 to 1815* (London, 1936).

Austrian affairs are sketched by Robert A. Kann, *A History of the Habsburg Empire, 1526–1918* (Berkeley and Los Angeles, 1974), and Victor S. Mamatey, *Rise of the Habsburg Empire, 1526–1815* (Huntington, N.Y., 1978). Austrian military affairs during the Silesian Wars are detailed by Christopher Duffy, *The Army of Maria Theresa* (New York, 1977), and Paul R. Bernard, *Joseph II* (New York, 1968), has analyzed the reform fervor of Maria Theresa's son. Legal reforms in eighteenth-century Austria have been dealt with by Henry Strakosch, *State Absolutism and the Rule of Law: The Struggle for the Codification of Civil Law in Austria, 1753–1811* (Sydney, 1967). Agrarian policies are examined in Edith M. Link, *The Emancipation of the Austrian Peasant, 1740–1798* (New York, 1949).

Prussian affairs are surveyed by Hansjoachim W. Koch, *A History of Prussia* (New York, 1978), and, in greater sophistication, by Sidney B. Fay and Klaus Epstein, *The Rise of Brandenburg-Prussia to 1786* (Malabar, Fla., 1981). The classic treatment of the Prussian royal bureaucracy was written by Hans Rosenberg, *Bureaucracy, Aristocracy, and Autocracy: The Prussian Experience, 1660–1815* (Cambridge, Mass., 1958). Hubert Johnson, *Frederick the Great and His Officials* (New Haven and London, 1975), is also worth consulting. David B. Horn, *Frederick the Great and the Rise of Prussia* (London, 1964), is a relatively recent interpretation of the reign of Frederick II. The latter's military has been scrutinized by Christopher Duffy in *The Army of Frederick the Great* (London, 1974) and *The Military Life of Frederick the Great* (New York, 1986).

The impact of the French Revolution on the German states was first laid out by George P. Gooch, *Germany and the French Revolution* (London, 1920).

Two more recent assessments for the Rhine area are by T. C. W. Blanning: *The French Revolution in Germany: Occupation and Resistance in the Rhineland, 1792–1802* (Oxford, 1983), and *Reform and Revolution in Mainz, 1743–1803* (London and New York, 1974). The Prussian reform period in the wake of the twin defeats of 1806 has been studied by Walter M. Simon, *The Failure of the Prussian Reform Movement, 1807–1819* (Ithaca, N.Y., 1955), and Marion W. Gray, *Prussia in Transition: Society and Politics Under the Stein Reform Ministry of 1808* (Philadelphia, 1986). There still is no comprehensive treatment of Prussian military reforms: Peter Paret, *Yorck and the Era of Prussian Reform, 1807–1815* (Princeton, 1966), concentrates on tactics; Gordon A. Craig, *The Politics of the Prussian Army, 1640–1945* (Oxford, 1955), devotes but parts of two chapters to the reformers. The subsequent wars of liberation are explained in Friedrich Meinecke, *The Age of German Liberation, 1789–1815* (Berkeley and Los Angeles, 1977).

The standard treatment of the Congress of Vienna has long remained Harold Nicolson, *The Congress of Vienna: A Study in Allied Unity, 1812–1822* (London, 1946). Henry A. Kissinger's somewhat more recent *A World Restored: Metternich, Castlereagh and the Problems of Peace, 1812–22* (Boston, 1957) has become sort of a cult book for American policymakers. Metternich's role at the Congress has been exhaustively examined by Enno E. Kraehe, *Metternich's German Policy*, vol. 2, *The Congress of Vienna, 1814–1815* (Princeton, 1983).

Once again, glimpses into the everyday life of common people are provided by Ulrich Bräker, *The Life Story and Real Adventures of the Poor Man of Toggenburg* (Edinburgh, 1970). The lives of the common people in the early nineteenth century are described by Gottfried Keller in *Stories* (New York, 1982).

C H A P T E R

3

FROM LIBERALISM TO NATIONALISM, 1815–1862

Time hurtles forward. It would be vain to attempt to arrest its stormy course. All that the friends and protectors of order can do is to mitigate its destructiveness. . . . Our aim is very simple to define: nothing more and nothing less than the preservation of the world as we know it. . . . To this end, [we] must bend all individual efforts and all public endeavors by those who share similar interests and outlooks.

Clemens Prince von Metternich, 1820

The period between the Congress of Vienna in 1815 and the decline of the mental health of Frederick William IV, king of Prussia, by 1861 was pregnant with choice. The old order could not possibly be restored fully after the tumultuous events of the French Revolution and the Napoleonic era. Conversely, neither the Terror nor the Empire remained in favor. In fact, the legitimate rulers of the petty German states returned to their thrones in 1815, in many cases with the enthusiastic support of their subjects. But a current of high expectations — of a constitution, a liberalization of the press and assembly, economic progress and tariff easing, and national unity — also ran through everyone's minds. In short, the question of the future form of "Germany" lay wide open.

While the Prussian school of history after 1871 claimed that Prussia's triumph over Austria was inevitable, any thinking person in 1815 would probably have looked to Vienna rather than to Berlin for leadership. The Habsburgs were the older and more established dynasty, and their territorial holdings extended much farther than those of the Hohenzollerns. Vienna rather than Berlin had hosted Europe's first modern diplomatic congress, and Austrian rather than Prussian statesmen continued to set the tone in inner-German affairs. Austria's permanent chairmanship of the German Confederation (*Deutsche Bund*) from 1815 to 1866 confirmed the primacy of the Danubian monarchy in central Europe. The only question was whether Metternich's Austria was prepared and able to lead. Few looked to Berlin for guidance. Even fewer believed that the smaller states (the "Third Germany") offered a viable alternative to Vienna or Berlin.

The period after 1815 is often depicted as the birth of ideologies. Liberalism first appeared on the German scene in the 1770s as a revolt of the intellectuals against the sale of soldiers to Great Britain. Thereafter, it received impetus from the victory of the American revolutionaries over George III of Great Britain. For most Germans, however, liberalism was a British import. The notions of civil liberty and parliamentary government, as embodied in such constitutional landmarks as the Magna Carta and the U.S. Bill of Rights, had been introduced mainly through Göttingen University in Hanover. For Germans, classical nineteenth-century liberalism, while broad and vague, translated politically into freedom of the press, separation of church and state, freedom of trade, establishment of a militia, habeas corpus,[1] and a written constitution. German liberals, then, looked to Britain as their model; only a few radical democrats glanced across the Rhine at France.

German conservatism found its champion in Britain's Edmund Burke, whose *Reflections on the Revolution in France* appeared in 1790. Conservatives abhorred the French Revolution with its bloody excesses and its eventual benefactor, Napoleon Bonaparte. They denied the very principle of revolution, opposed romanticism,[2] and sought to end secret societies. They railed against the individualism of the "liberals," who taught free competition and an end to state intervention in the economic sector. Without the discipline imposed by church, monarchy, and nobility, the conservatives argued, human beings would descend into corruption, decay, and disorder. The natural order was historical and traditional; democracy translated into social anarchy.

Fioally, the French armies that had marched through the German states brought with them a third "ism," nationalism. As a young man, Fichte had defined German nationalism in cosmopolitan terms — as expressing the highest ideals of humanity. But in later life he developed the concept of a nation as a living community with a desire and a right to grow and expand. A subsequent generation would define a stronger, untrammeled nationalism. Beginning with the notion of cultural nationalism, which held that each people has its own culture, history, and language, these thinkers quickly moved on to political nationalism, which held that each people should create for itself a

---

1 Habeas corpus ("you should have the body") denotes various common law writs issued to bring a person before a court or judge, thus guarding against illegal imprisonment.

2 While conservatism and romanticism were linked early in the nineteenth century, most German conservatives over time rejected romanticism's universalist message that no nation enjoyed special status or offered special benefits.

sovereign nation in order to preserve this national culture. Ernst Moritz Arndt, especially, the son of serfs from the Swedish-held island of Rügen, and Friedrich Ludwig Jahn, founder of patriotic gymnastics clubs,[1] nurtured an antiforeign attitude and an ancient Germanic folk spirit (*Volksgeist*). Their speeches and writings sowed the seeds of a virulent form of nationalism that would emerge full-blown only after unification in 1871.

The Political Dialectic: Liberal Challenge and Conservative Reaction

In 1815 "Germany" consisted of thirty-five princely states and four free cities (Frankfurt and the Hanseatic cities of Bremen, Hamburg, Lübeck) loosely incorporated into a German Confederation and inhabited by 30 million people. Three-quarters lived on the land as yeoman farmers (30 percent), small holders (30 percent), landless laborers (30 percent), and nonguild craftsmen (10 percent). The quarter of the population that resided in the twenty-five hundred towns, of which only 70 had more than ten thousand inhabitants, consisted of merchants, guild masters, and day laborers.

Austria, with nearly 10 million inhabitants, was the most populous state in central Europe. Metternich, a Rhinelander by birth who had married into the prestigious Austrian house of Kaunitz, was the Continent's most prominent statesman. To run the affairs of state, he relied on an efficient spy network that censored the mails, monitored all communications, stole diplomatic codes with regularity, and exercised surveillance over all resorts and spas (hence, Metternich's decision in 1819 to hold a German ministerial conference at Karlsbad). The poet Franz Grillparzer noted that censorship was so pervasive that he could read Goethe's works only in 1809 during the French occupation of Vienna and that even Beethoven's musical compositions were scrutinized.

Austria's semifeudal system prevailed despite a patchwork of nationalities. Its 9.4 million German subjects mingled with 14.8 million Slavs, 5.3 million Magyars, and 4.5 million Italians, among others. Any concession to nationalism would threaten the Habsburgs' dynastic rule, as well as the very existence of the Austrian Empire. Thus, Emperor Francis I wished to turn the clock back to the days of Maria Theresa, viewing the monarchy as an entailment that he ruled as feudal lord. It is little wonder, then, that Metternich set out after 1815 to deny the very principle — much less, the existence — of nationalism.

[1] Brooding on Prussia's humiliation at the hands of Napoleon while a teacher in Berlin in 1809, Jahn conceived the idea of restoring the old Germanic prowess and liberty by developing the physical and moral powers of his countrymen through gymnastics. He opened his first gymnastics club in Berlin three years later to achieve emancipation from French rule.

GERMAN POPULATION, 1818 (IN THOUSANDS)

Major States		Lesser States	
Austria	9,500	Lippe	70
Prussia	7,900	Waldeck	52
Bavaria	3,560	Bremen	49
Württemberg	1,400	Anhalt-Köthen	32
Hanover	1,300	Schaumburg-Lippe	24
Saxony	1,200	Hesse-Homburg	20
Baden	1,000	Liechtenstein	6

By contrast, Prussia was now a secondary power but one with promise. Frederick William III was a weak ruler, dominated by an aristocratic clique at court. As his wife, Queen Luise, aptly noted: "We fell asleep on the laurels of Frederick the Great." In 1815 Prussia emerged from defeat and liberation with its population doubled but also with 1.5 million Polish subjects. Under Baron von Hardenberg, a rudimentary ministerial system was established in 1817. The new *Staatsrat*, described as a "parliament of bureaucrats" to advise the king, consisted of the royal princes, leading civil servants, and commanding generals, as well as an additional thirty-four prominent men appointed by the monarch. Prussian policy rested on a triad of bourgeois self-government in the cities, aristocratic rule in the countryside, and bureaucratic centralism at Berlin. The army, the pillar of the Prussian state, was torn between the concepts of a traditional royal standing army officered by the leading Junker families and that of a militia headed by a middle-class meritocracy of education and property. Carl von Clausewitz, denounced by fellow aristocrats as a "Jacobin" in 1815 for championing the latter, in semiretirement between 1816 and 1830 penned his classic *On War*.[1] A precise definition of the nature of the Prussian Army would come only after 1862 under Otto von Bismarck.

Finally, there was the Third Germany. Apart from the four free cities, this term covered the thirty-three German states other than Austria and Prussia. They fell into three political groups: Bremen, Frankfurt, Hamburg, and Lübeck already possessed modern, liberal constitutions by 1815; Hanover, Mecklenburg, and Saxony reneged on their promise at Vienna to promulgate constitutions; and Weimar (1816), Baden (1818), Bavaria (1818), Württemberg (1819), and Hesse-Darmstadt (1820) honored their pledges of constitutional reform. Generally, these states introduced bicameral systems, with a hereditary (aristocratic) upper house and a lower house chosen through indirect, male elections by about 5 percent of the population on the basis of property owner-

[1] *On War* is a brilliant exposition of the relationship between politics and the military in the state, wherein its author argued that war is but the continuation of politics by other means. In addition, Clausewitz stressed the uncertainty of war and warned both politicians and military professionals against predicting either its course or its outcome.

ship. The complicated nature of suffrage in early nineteenth-century Germany was perhaps best exemplified by the Bavarian election of 1818–1819, which returned an assembly comprising large landowners, university professors, clerics, city aldermen, and mayors, as well as small landholders ranging from wine merchants to millers. Finally, German cities began to realize their full potential as independent, self-governing economic units as Baron vom Stein's urban reform of 1808 (see the previous chapter), was extended from Prussia to Bavaria (1818), Württemberg (1819–1822), and Hesse (1829) — typically against the determined opposition of local guilds.

Briefly after 1815, diplomats from the Third Germany sought to rally what they called the "purely German states," that is, those without major non-German ethnic groups, around the twin banners of federalism and liberalism in an effort to offer a viable alternative to Berlin and Vienna. But their attempts quickly collapsed after Metternich's turn against liberalism. The Austrian chancellor had no desire to permit the more liberal states of the Third Germany to set the pace and tenor of the national and constitutional debate, and he used Austria's preeminence within the German Confederation at Frankfurt to dictate policy to the other German states.

A special group of "mediatized" princes within the Third Germany also deserves mention. About eighty princely and ducal families had been deposed as sovereign rulers when Napoleon dissolved the Holy Roman Empire in 1806. Under Article 14 of the Act of Confederation of 1818,[1] however, they retained their special diplomatic standing, legal privileges, social rights, titles, and even civil servants. Thus, they constituted a veritable state within a state. One example was the princely house of Fürstenberg at Donaueschingen, which retained twenty-one hundred square kilometers of land from the Black Forest to Lake Constance as well as eighty-five thousand subjects. A relic from the feudal past, these houses did all within their power to ward off integration into a nation state.

As successor to both the Hohenstaufen Empire[2] and the Holy Roman Empire, the German Confederation offered little more than the formal trappings of national unity. Under permanent Austrian leadership, it eventually stipulated that 1 percent of the "German" population, that is, about 301,000 men, should be formed into ten army corps — of which there were to be three each Austrian and Prussian — for the national defense. Command of this army in case of war would be decided by majority vote in the confederation. It is probably just as well that this force was never tested in battle.

[1] The Act of Confederation was completed in rough draft and incorporated into the Vienna Treaty on June 8, 1815. It created the German Confederation. The act was refined and formally adopted by the *Deutsche Bund* in 1818.

[2] The medieval empire of the Hohenstaufen dynasty reached its zenith under Emperors Frederick I, Henry VI, and Frederick II between 1152 and 1250. It therefore fell within the extended period of the Holy Roman Empire (962–1806).

For all its prestige, the German Confederation radiated little sense of permanence. At Frankfurt it continued to rent the town palace of the Thurn und Taxis family of Regensburg. Until 1848 it devised neither crest nor banner of its own. Even with the military apparatus, its staff consisted of a paltry twenty-seven bureaucrats. And while it published its protocols in emulation of the English *Hansard*, it was revealing that the cook of the Thuringian envoy at Frankfurt sold secret protocols to her butcher as wrapping paper. But for Metternich, the German Confederation was *his* creation, through which he hoped to impose his will on the other German states: "To attack it would be akin to killing my own child."

The German Confederation achieved many successes. It served as an important arena for the development of international cooperative institutions such as unencumbered river navigation, the postal union, and railroad coordination. Most important, the confederation helped to maintain relative peace for nearly half a century. Its architects at Vienna, after all, had erected it primarily as a means "to preserve Germany's external and internal security."

Metternich received much support in his conservative stance from Alexander I of Russia. Together, they had concocted the Holy Alliance in 1815 — the "international fire brigade," as the German historian Heinrich von Treitschke would ridicule it nearly half a century later — with the stated purpose "to defend justice, peace and religion" and to "provide succor and support in any place" against liberal and democratic activities. Alexander sought to preserve the God-given order on the basis of a true Christian alliance; Metternich was too cynical to accept such an idealistic interpretation. Yet both men espoused the doctrine of solidarity. Metternich excised the adjectives *of peoples* and *of citizens* from the preamble of the Holy Alliance in favor of the term *of monarchs*. More concretely, Alexander decreed a two-power standard to ensure his influence over central Europe: the Russian Army at all times was to be the size of the Austrian and Prussian armed forces combined. With great fanfare and enthusiasm, the two leaders sought to keep the established order in power by crushing liberal uprisings in Naples and Piedmont (1821), Greece (1821–1822), Spain (1822), and Poland (1830–1831).

But their vision was not to materialize. Disappointment over broken promises of liberal reform and nation building erupted at the Wartburg[1] on October 18, 1817, the fourth anniversary of the Battle of Nations at Leipzig and the tercentenary of Martin Luther's Reformation. Radical students, organized into fraternities (*Burschenschaften*) first at Jena and Giessen and later at other universities, launched a liberal offensive by founding their own papers and journals, circulating reform petitions, and mobilizing the educated elite, especially in the south German parliaments. Their platform centered on freedom of

[1] After Martin Luther had refused to retract his writings at the Diet of Worms in 1521, he took refuge at the Wartburg Castle near Eisenach in Thuringia under the protection of the Saxon elector. At the Wartburg, Luther translated the Greek New Testament into German.

the press, assembly, and trade; respect for human rights through an end to torture, corporal punishment, political arrest, and the death sentence; abolition of royal standing armies and their replacement with militias; and separation of church and state, including emancipation of Jews who were willing to assimilate into the mainstream German culture. At the Wartburg, students burned lists of reactionaries — Metternich and Alexander I not surprisingly headed them — and carried the black-red-gold banner of a nationalistic fraternity founded at Jena in 1815. In their romantic way, the *Burschenschaften* hoped to "recapture" a dream that had gone astray "in the larger world," and to establish a "German national state based on freedom and unity."

On March 23, 1819, Karl Sand, a theology student at Mannheim, assassinated the playwright and Russian councillor August von Kotzebue as a suspected "spy." Metternich, on a visit to Rome, was outraged. In July he had nationalist leaders such as Jahn at Berlin and Arndt at Bonn arrested. Joseph Görres, who had in 1819 published an inflammatory pamphlet, *Germany and Revolution*, barely escaped to France.

The full weight of Metternich's wrath came down on his enemies during a special ministerial council held at Karlsbad between August 6 and 31, 1819. Three decrees stand out. The University Decree banned the *Burschenschaften*, instituted a system of "supervising" university lecturers, and provided for the dismissal of those found wanting in conservative vigor. The Press Decree reestablished eighteenth-century prepublication censorship: all papers, journals, and books up to 320 pages long required formal permission to be published. Both decrees remained in effect until 1848. The Search Decree established a special Central Office of Investigation at Mainz to look into "the revolutionary intrigues uncovered in several German states." In addition, the colors black-red-gold were forbidden in public, and parliaments were to be closed as being "un-German," apparently the first use of this spurious term.

The Karlsbad Decrees set the political tone within the German Confederation for the next two decades. In Vienna, Metternich, aided by the arch-conservative Friedrich Gentz, stamped out all demands for reform. In Berlin, Hardenberg's death in 1822 ushered in an era of conservative reaction, without the constitution that had been promised in 1815. Gentz, no friend of Protestant Prussia, was satisfied with the political wind that blew in Berlin: "This state lacks nothing other than to be Catholic in order to be the strongest pillar of the world order next to us." Even in the Third Germany reaction triumphed. Bavaria, Württemberg, Baden, and Hesse-Darmstadt all came under royal as well as bureaucratic repression and a general curtailment of debate and freedom.

The novel process of political participation, albeit by only a professional elite, had raised fears and sparked resistance, especially at Vienna. In addition, the radical nature of the reform movement accorded Metternich the unique chance to quash the more moderate reform movements in Prussia and the Third Germany. He deployed what has been termed the "principle of political-social immobilization" to maintain the status quo in central Europe. But Metternich was again to be disappointed by events.

The July Revolution[1] of 1830 in France, the successful Belgian independence movement that year, and the Polish uprising of 1830–1831 agitated central Europe. In response, Brunswick, Hanover, Electoral Hesse, and Saxony sought to forestall any further radicalization of politics by promulgating liberal constitutions. From Paris the so-called Young Germany literary movement of Heinrich Heine and Ludwig Börne issued clarion calls for radical reforms in Germany: civil emancipation, civil rights for Jews, freedom of the press, equality of men and women, sovereignty of the people, and establishment of a unitary republic on the French model. Börne's "Letters from Paris" demanded that Germans rise up and wrest their freedom from the autocratic princes.

Spurred on by the radical liberals Philipp Jakob Siebenpfeiffer and Johann Georg August Wirth, between twenty thousand and thirty thousand people gathered at the castle ruins of Hambach in the Rhenish Palatinate on May 27, 1832, waving the national colors of black-red-gold. This mixed gathering comprised middle-class intellectuals, civil servants, students, workers, Polish refugees, and — for the first time ever in Germany — women. The more radical students demanded full democracy, the deposition of the princes, and a European union of republics. Nationalists among them called for the return of Alsace-Lorraine to German sovereignty. Critical scholars have called the "Hambach festival" nothing more than "agitated somnambulism," but its importance as the first mass political meeting in German history cannot be disputed.

Metternich's reaction was predictable. After an immediate wave of hundreds of political arrests, on June 28, 1832, the confederation passed the "Six Articles": they banned public demonstrations and the wearing of the national colors, reduced the powers of regional parliaments, strengthened censorship of the press, and established a new Central Office of Investigation, this time at Frankfurt, with instructions to head off popular festivals. From Paris Heine reacted with his *Grand Book*, of which entire pages were blackened out by an imaginary censor, leaving only the words "The German censors . . . *Dummköpfe*" ("blockheads").

The next round of protest struck close to home. In 1833 a group of Heidelberg students stormed the main Frankfurt police station, killing six gendarmes. Prussian troops eventually restored order and handed down draconian sentences to nearly two hundred students. In June 1834 Metternich drafted at least sixty articles to tighten restrictions on speech, assembly, and publication. From his deathbed, an alarmed Emperor Francis I admonished his feeble-minded successor, Ferdinand I, in 1835: "Do not disturb a single piece of the foundation of our political system. Govern and change nothing!" This was a true Habsburg motto.

[1] On July 26, 1830, Charles X had issued four ordinances that dissolved the newly elected chamber, imposed censorship on the press, reduced the suffrage of the middle class of banking and industry, and demanded new elections based on the new suffrage. Three days of rioting in Paris removed Charles X from office in favor of the "citizen-king" Louis Philippe.

Perhaps most dramatic of all was the crisis of the so-called Göttingen Seven in 1837. Hanover had been part of the United Kingdom since 1714, but when the British king, William IV, died in 1837 and his niece Victoria ascended the throne, the popular interpretation of German Salic Law demanded male succession in Hanover. William's brother, Ernst August, until then the duke of Cumberland, readily obliged. On November 1, 1837, Ernst August celebrated his coronation in Hanover by dissolving its parliament and abolishing the constitution of 1833. Seven prominent professors at the University of Göttingen who protested this political coup d'état were dismissed from their posts. Further, the historians Friedrich Christoph Dahlmann and Georg Gottfried Gervinus, as well as the philologist Jakob Grimm, were expelled from Hanover. The German Confederation did nothing to restore the constitution. "Göttingen Societies" sprang up in Great Britain, Switzerland, and the United States but to no avail. Ernst August brushed the entire episode off with the comment: "Professors, actors, and whores one can always get."

The political arena was not the only place where liberalism was making a determined showing. What might be called economic and religious liberalism also challenged the established order. The former threatened Austria's political and diplomatic dominance in central Europe. The latter called into question the orthodoxy of both the Roman Catholic and Protestant Christian churches. Combined, they would prove highly effective in transforming the nature of German society.

The loosening of Napoleon's grip on the Continent's economy had brought a flood of English machine-made products into central Europe. Prussia reacted first to this threat by abolishing all internal tariffs and duties in 1818 and generally encouraging free trade within the German Confederation. Hesse-Darmstadt in 1828 and Bavaria in 1829 followed suit. But several Prussian economic advisers set about crafting an economic strategy designed to bring about nothing short of "an independent German union policy," apart from or against the Austrian-dominated Confederation at Frankfurt. Finance Minister Friedrich Christian von Motz in particular propagated the notion of "a free Germany under the protection and umbrella of Prussia."

In 1832 Motz received support from an unlikely source, Friedrich List, a German economist serving as U.S. consul in Germany.[1] List not only designed a plan for a national railroad system and spoke out fervently for a German free trade zone but became the first apostle of the concept of a German-dominated central Europe. As early as 1819, he had demanded "the erection of a general tariff" for the German Confederation in order to restore "national trade and industry," and he continued to champion high import duties designed to shield German industries from other, more advanced industrial countries. Not surprisingly, List's strident protectionism evoked an equally sharp reaction from free traders. Led by John Prince Smith, the free traders demanded the

[1] At the time the U.S. government sometimes appointed foreigners to serve as its consuls abroad.

reduction of existing tariffs and argued against further trade barriers designed to protect fledgling and vital industries. Only the free market economy, unfettered by governmental controls, they argued, could unleash the latent power of German trade and industry. The Prussian government tended to side with the protectionists, but it studiously avoided making a clear decision in this first fiscal controversy.

To be sure, Austria remained wedded to eighteenth-century protective tariffs and blithely ignored its commercial ties to the German states. Thus, when Johann Joseph Prechtl, the head of the Polytechnical Institute at Vienna, developed an export strategy for the Habsburg state in 1819, his eye was on Russia, the Near East, and the Mediterranean; the German states did not even receive mention in his document. One year later, Adam Müller, Austrian diplomat and economist, rejected the introduction of the British factory system by stressing that Germany had traditionally been the home of cottage industry. The "uniformity of factory-produced goods," he argued, was antithetical to the creative spirit of the Germans.

Prussia, rather than Austria, became the economic leader among the German states. Its two earlier acquisitions, Silesia and the Rhineland, were blessed with natural resources; it controlled many of Germany's most important rivers (Elbe, Oder, and Rhine); and it recognized the obvious advantages to be gained from economic consolidation. On January 1, 1834, the Prussian-led customs union (*Zollverein*) took effect. It included not only the major north German states but also the lesser ones of Saxony and Thuringia. Baden, Nassau, and Frankfurt joined in short order, but Austria remained an economic outsider. Twenty-five million Germans now had gathered into one trading block, which soon established formal ties with Great Britain, the Netherlands, and Turkey.

In religion, the first half of the nineteenth century saw a weakening of the ideals of the Enlightenment, a return of orthodoxy, and, finally, a Pietist revival. Once more worshippers turned to the Scriptures rather than the official churches for spiritual guidance. Above all, the churches remembered their duty toward the poor. On the Protestant side, Pastor Theodor Fliedner established a special deaconess (nurses') institution at Kaiserswerth, near Düsseldorf on the Rhine, that tended to the needs of the downtrodden. In the process, these women set female emancipation within the Christian community in motion. In 1830, on the two hundredth anniversary of Gustavus Adolphus's landing in Germany during the Thirty Years' War,[1] a special Gustav-Adolf Association was established that also strove to alleviate the plight of the less fortunate. Meanwhile the tense theological disputes, which had split and

[1] To stem the tide of the Catholic Counter Reformation, Gustavus Adolphus, king of Sweden, landed in Germany in 1630 with an army of forty thousand troops. He died in defense of the Protestant cause at Lützen in 1632.

ZOLLVEREIN, 1834

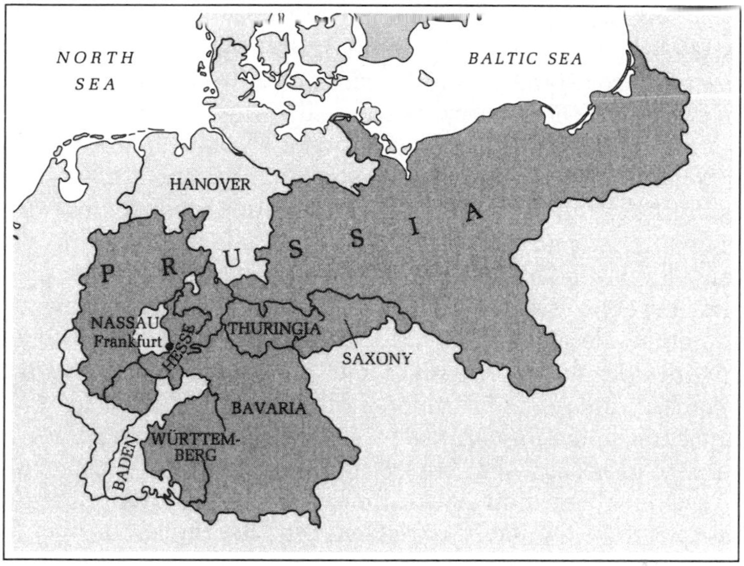

resplit the church in the sixteenth century, receded. In October 1817 Frederick William III united the Lutheran and Reformed (Calvinist) wings of Protestantism into the Evangelical church. In the 1840s the neo-Pietist Friends of Light movement called for a return to a simpler Christianity based on scripture and a turn away from what it deemed to be the stifling orthodoxy of the church's synod.

Renewal of inner faith and care for the indigent also figured prominently in the Catholic reform movements at Munich (Johann Michael Sailer) and Vienna (Clemens Maria Hofbauer). These changes reached a peak in 1844 when the Holy Shroud of Jesus Christ became the object of a pilgrimage of almost 1 million persons to Trier. A secessionist movement of seventy thousand "German Catholics" under Johannes Ronge quickly developed among those Catholic liberals who desired no reminder of what one termed "a modern indulgence racket."[1] Their program demanded the establishment of a German national church with German liturgy and rejection of confession, fasting, pilgrimages, indulgences, and celibacy of the clergy.

[1] One of the practices of the Catholic church that Martin Luther had denounced in 1517 was the sale of indulgences, whereby the church offered remission of temporal punishment of sins in this life and in purgatory for a monetary sum. The practice, based on the doctrine of "treasure of the church," had led to widespread abuse.

Biedermeier Germany: Transition and Transformation

The term *Biedermeier*, coined in 1855, refers sarcastically to the modest bourgeois life-style of the pre–1848 era. Today it describes in nostalgic fashion the *gut bürgerlich*, or comfortable middle class, culture of the age. Karl Wildhagen's *German-English Dictionary* offers the adjectives "plain, homely, old-fashioned" for the German term. In fact, *Biedermeier* was a culture dominated by middle-class values of cleanliness, decency, morality, and strong family bonds. Houses and furniture of the period showed simple, clean lines with a modicum of ornamentation and utilization of cheaper construction affordable to the middle class. Flower boxes, parks, and Sunday family outings became hallmarks of the new style. The painter Carl Spitzweg represented the *Biedermeier* outlook in pictures describing the quiet happiness of flowers in seclusion and the odd, quaint, and downright scurrilous characters he discovered in backyards, old houses, and remote corners of the land.

In a larger sense, the *Biedermeier* era conjures up an image of a moderate, middle-of-the-road society that sought to avoid conflict in favor of compromise, one that remained innocent of the ways in which early capitalism and industrialism were beginning to transform the "nation." Sobriety of manners, moderation in action, balance in judgment: these were the outward values of this patriarchal and hierarchical society of rather temperate and serious Germans.

At the apex of that society reigned academia. First and foremost stood the name Georg Wilhelm Friedrich Hegel. This God-seeking seminarian of Tübingen University absorbed the writings of Immanuel Kant, Johann Gottlieb Fichte, and Friedrich Wilhelm von Schelling. At Berlin he became the dominant intellectual force of the first half of the nineteenth century. Hegel sought nothing less than to explain all human activity. In his system, a rather nebulous "world spirit" guided human civilization through a dialectical progression: a struggle of self-assertion (thesis) and self-opposition (antithesis) that always achieved resolution through synthesis. Hegel's new scientific "historicism" insisted that history was in a constant state of flux. Change, and its accompanying manifestations such as famine and flood, war and pestilence rather than peace and harmony, was the norm. Newly created synthesis immediately aroused new conflicts and new struggles and eventually asserted itself in yet another synthesis. And so on. The ultimate goal that Hegel sought to achieve, in the words of a recent historian, was demanding: the reconciliation of all contradictions, leading to boundless freedom through absolute justice, complete knowledge, the incarnation of reason on earth, and the presence of God. In his system of historical evolution, any given point in history by definition constituted humanity's highest plateau of cultural achievement. He thus laid the foundations of modern German intellectual conservatism.

The agent of historical change for Hegel was the state. Its interests alone decided what was right. Only through the state's existence was humanity's existence justified. What fateful words Hegel would pass on to his successors!

The "World Spirit" at the lectern: G. F. W. Hegel at the University of Berlin (1828).

"Man owes all that he is to the state, and in this is his essence. Man derives his value and spiritual reality from the state." Hegel admonished his fellow citizens: "The state does not exist for the burgher; instead, the state is the goal, and the burgher is the means." In his own time he saw the apex of human development in the Prussian *Rechtsstaat* — that is, a state built on the rule of law — of Frederick William III.

In seeking a greater transcendental truth, the great philosopher had much in common with historian Leopold von Ranke, a colleague at Berlin. Like Hegel, Ranke believed in the progressive revelation of God in history. God, he suggested, expressed the very essence of humanity when he created the peoples of the world. Ranke argued that each historical epoch is related directly to God (that is, each has its own logic and should be judged on its own terms). For both Berlin professors, human beings could seek to interpret the past — "as it actually was," in Ranke's famous and often misunderstood words — only in order to gain a glimpse into their present status. The future was left to God.

It was all the more ironic that a following generation of so-called Young Hegelians would discover in the devout monarchist Hegel the algebra of revolution. Among these *Junghegelianer*, best-known, Karl Marx, would become their guiding light. Initially a student of philosophy at Bonn, Berlin, and Jena, and briefly editor of the *Rheinische Zeitung* in 1842, Marx soon abandoned pure philosophical contemplation with the famous comment: "In the past philosophers have only interpreted the world in different ways; the real task is to change it." While in exile in Brussels, Marx met Friedrich Engels, son of a prosperous businessman from Barmen, and there, his theoretical powers and Engels' knowledge of early industrialism in Britain fused.

In February 1848 that union produced a spectacular polemic, *The Communist Manifesto*. Published in London, the book sold only five hundred copies and brought its authors negligible royalties: two pounds, thirty shilling, and nine pence. By 1975 it had reportedly surpassed the Bible in total sales. It began with a daunting if satirical prognosis: "A specter is haunting Europe — the specter of Communism." It ended with an apocalyptic prophecy: "Let the ruling classes tremble at a Communist revolution. The proletarians have nothing to lose but their chains. They have a world to win. Workingmen of all countries, unite!"

Marx initiated a radical philosophical departure from Hegel. The latter had remained a pure philosopher; Marx sought to become a practical social scientist. While retaining the master's dialectical framework, Marx substituted for Hegel's "world spirit" as the driving force of history the means of production and the resulting social stratification and tensions instead — that is, class struggle. And whereas Hegel had been content to understand the past, Marx predicted the future: a classless proletarian society wherein, in the words of V. I. Lenin, each person was given liberally according to his or her needs, and each contributed freely according to individual abilities. From the British economist David Ricardo, Marx and Engels borrowed the theory of prices and wages to explain to the workers that their world held a dilemma: the true value of their labor was at all times siphoned off by the capitalists in the form of surplus value. The ameliorative forces of parliamentary action, public as well as private morality, and established religion ("the opiate of the people") failed to fit into Marx's monocausal, deterministic scheme of world affairs, and he brushed them aside. History would prove him wrong.

As a final irony, Marx would spend most of his life in exile from Germany in Paris, Brussels, and London. His point of reference remained *The Condition of the Working Classes in England*, which Engels had written in 1845. Marx directly witnessed nothing of the technological and demographic transformation of Germany after the revolts of 1848. He despised the peasantry ("the idiocy of rural life"). He never became the leader of a German "socialist" movement. Carl Schurz, an incisive contemporary and future revolutionary of 1848 as well as eventual U.S. statesman, perhaps summed Marx up best:

> What Marx said was in fact full of substance, logical and clear. Yet I have never seen a man behave with such offensive, unbearable arrogance. He brushed aside any opinion that differed substantially from his own. Anybody who contradicted him, he treated with barely concealed contempt.

Marx and Engels gave the newly emerging industrial workers a historical view of themselves as "proletarians," that is, as a class of wage earners engaged in industrial production whose chief source of income is derived from the sale of their labor. No longer were they merely members of the large and indistinct group of the poor and dispossessed. In addition, the two authors offered workers a utopian vision of victorious struggle, first against the landed nobility and eventually against the capitalist middle class. The Soviet version of their rigid system would be transplanted to German soil by the Red Army in 1945, almost exactly a century after the publication of the *Manifesto.*

Indeed, it was a shame that Marx would spend so much of his life in the library of the British Museum rather than in his native Germany as the German states underwent nothing short of first a demographic and then a technological and industrial revolution. The population of German-speaking central Europe increased by 15 million in half a century, producing a steady exodus from the countryside to the new industrial urban centers. Tens of thousands sought to escape rural poverty by emigrating overseas: the tiny state of Baden, for example, spent 300,000 marks subsidizing emigration between 1840 and 1849 in an effort to elude the Malthusian nightmare of overpopulation.

A good part of the population explosion resulted from advances in the agrarian sector. Emancipation of the serfs had led to the creation of an impoverished class of day laborers, but it had also brought about the abolition of communal lands, which, thanks to the Rhenish village mayor Friedrich Wilhelm Raiffeisen's agrarian credit institutions, were quickly bought up by prosperous farmers. Arable land usage in Prussia, for example, doubled between 1815 and 1864. The three-crop rotation system, the development of a manure industry, and the importation of Swiss and Dutch cows brought further gains. Grain yields in Prussia rose 50 to 60 percent for the same period, milk production doubled, and new Emmental and Limburg cheeses were introduced. The expansion of potato and sugar beet planting helped alleviate hunger. The simple practice of bringing hogs indoors and feeding them potato products doubled per capita meat consumption to thirty kilograms per year by 1870.

The excess population that could not be absorbed by the agrarian sector — and chose not to emigrate — now sought its livelihood in the newly forming industrial centers. Pauperization resulted. By 1844 one-third of all German communities reportedly struggled with poverty. Four years later, Cologne registered more than one-quarter of its ninety-five thousand inhabitants on welfare lists. Another source suggests that by mid-century 20 to 30 percent of the 45 million Germans lived below the poverty line, which fluctuated between 6.50 and 10.50 mark income per week. This led to widescale exploitation of child and female labor as families struggled to survive. Even in progressive Prussia, urban living conditions were wretched: in seven new Berlin tenements completed before the revolution of 1848, twenty-five hundred people were huddled into four hundred rooms.

The cause of this pauperization is unclear. In his classic account of working-class conditions in Britain, Friedrich Engels laid the blame squarely at the feet of early capitalism, but more recent analyses suggest that a combination of the holdover of eighteenth-century rural poverty, the population explosion after 1815, and the relatively slow increase in industrial production (and wages) was at fault. Whatever the cause, Germany passed through a transitional phase of early capitalism entailing only moderate growth (1815–1850) before an actual take-off period (1850–1873).

Clearly industry and technology were on the march in *Biedermeier* Germany. This was the era of the founding generation of German industrialists such as Borsig, Henschel, Hoesch, Krupp, Stinnes, and Stumm. Whereas in some regions such as Bohemia and Silesia the great feudal landowning barons such as the Donnersmarck, Hohenlohe-Ingelfingen, Ballestrem, Pless, and Schaffgotsch financed the industrial age, in western Germany nearly 60 percent of the future entrepreneurs hailed from working- and lower middle-class backgrounds. A case in point is Ludolf Camphausen, the son of a Rhinelander trader, who transformed a modest oil and corn business into a commercial empire of banks in Cologne, steam navigation on the Rhine, and railroads. In 1848 Camphausen headed Prussia's first liberal ministry. Nearly three of every four major German industrialists in the nineteenth century were Protestant, lending credence to the sociologist Max Weber's thesis concerning the special work ethics of the achievement-oriented and plan-and-save-ahead Lutherans.

Banks fueled German industrial development. Before 1846 only four institutions had the right of note issue, including Frederick II's State Bank as well as the Prussian *Seehandlung*, or Overseas Trading Company. The latter, established in 1772 to promote foreign trade and private industry, quickly developed into a domestic credit bank and specialized in placing Prussian state loans on the financial market. The *Seehandlung* also worked to promote Prussian trade — for example, by sending the sailboat *Mentor* on two voyages around the globe in search of new markets for Prussian manufactures. Yet by the fourth decade of the nineteenth century, these financial institutions were unable to meet industry's demand for capital. New institutions based on the *Crédit mobilier* in France emerged: the Schaffhausen'scher Bankverein in 1848, the Diskontogesellschaft in 1851, the Darmstädter Bank in 1853, and the Berliner Handelsgesellschaft in 1856.

These banks, which first appeared in the Rhenish lands, were large joint-stock institutions created to mobilize capital. They were a combination of commercial and investment bank, as well as investment trust backed by a central bank. The banks participated directly in establishing industrial firms, and their officers sat regularly on the boards of directors of these corporations. By providing large lines of credit, the new financial institutions encouraged the expansion of industry beginning in the 1840s.

One can glean some insight into this new industrial age by looking at transportation. The first continental railroad, albeit horse-drawn, opened in

Geographical barriers fall: Inauguration of the Leipzig–Dresden Railroad (1837).

1832, connecting Linz with Budweis (now České Budějovice, in Czechoslovakia). Three years later, steam-driven engines powered a short line linking Nuremberg with Fürth. By 1840 major lines stretched between Leipzig and Dresden, Munich and Augsburg, Mannheim and Heidelberg. Ten years later, the German states boasted six thousand kilometers of railroad track, more than in France. In Austria, rails soon linked Vienna with Brünn (now Brno), Prague, Cracow, and even Trieste. Rail travel lowered transportation costs by as much as 80 percent, opened up new markets for regional products, and extended mobility to much of the populace.

The new railroads brought the postal monopoly of the Thurn und Taxis family to an end. Now, steam-driven trains and ships carried the mail, affixed with state postage stamps. By 1848 Prussia, which in the 1830s had established the first long-distance optical telegraph system between Berlin and Koblenz, had linked its capital to Frankfurt by means of an electrical telegraph developed by Werner Siemens and Johann Georg Halske. In the early 1850s, Britain was connected to central Europe by the first underwater telegraph cable. News agencies such as Havas (1835), Wolff (1849), and Reuter (1851) further reduced the old geographical barriers of communication.

The German labor force doubled between 1832 and 1848 to 1 million. Although most workers remained concentrated in artisan and family-operated small businesses, a modern industrial work force nevertheless arose in the mining and railroad sectors. Each employed roughly 100,000 people by 1848. Not surprisingly, the new machine age threatened cottage crafts and guilds, and violence directed against steam-driven machines erupted at Eupen in 1821, Aachen and Leipzig in 1830, and Mühlheim in the Ruhr in 1838. Perhaps the bloodiest assault on mechanization took place in Silesia in June 1844, where linen weavers for three days attacked factories; twelve people died in the fracas.

Little or no organized protection existed against labor exploitation. The modern German trade unions developed only sporadically before 1848; most perished during the political reaction of the 1850s. Both the early Christian trade unions established by the Catholic church and the Hirsch-Duncker unions founded by the liberals attracted only a small share of the industrial work force. While the latter viewed trade unions as vehicles to bring about concrete material gains such as better wages, job opportunities, and job security, artisans by and large expected state assistance in their plight and restoration of the old corporate order. Socialist trade unions were not formed until after unification in 1871.

Hand in glove with the technological advance came an educational revolution. More people than ever before could read. In time, education became not only the surest means of upward mobility for the untitled classes but a requirement for many state positions. In Prussia the *Abitur* was required by all universities after 1834 in place of entrance examinations. Prussia's population increased roughly by half between the Congress of Vienna and the revolutions of 1848, but the number of students rose by 73 percent and that of teachers by nearly 70 percent. In Austria, by contrast, many institutions of higher learning after 1815 remained firmly in church hands. Hence, whereas Vienna maintained but two lending libraries on the eve of the revolutions, Prussia boasted 656; even Electoral Hesse had no fewer than 19.

Reform also extended to nonuniversity education. In the 1830s special *Realschulen* were established at the secondary level for those who chose to ignore the pure liberal arts curriculum of the *Gymnasium* in favor of more practical subjects related to the new technologies of early industrialism. Polytechnic institutes, created first at Prague (1806) and Vienna (1815), were emulated by the mid–1830s at Karlsruhe, Berlin, Darmstadt, Dresden, Hanover, Kassel, and Münster.

The new literacy found expression not only in the expansion of the so-called penny press (daily newspapers) but with Friedrich Koenig's invention of rapid typesetting. At Leipzig and Gotha, the famous Brockhaus publishing company produced 300,000 sets of the encyclopedia that bore its name before German unification, to be emulated quickly between 1840 and 1852 by *Meyers Konversationslexikon.* The Catholic publisher Herder immediately followed suit with its own *Konversationslexikon* (1853–1857). Karl Baedecker and

Joseph Meyer published travel guides for the newly mobile German populace. The thirst to read and the hunger for knowledge extended even to the rural strata in Prussia, and hence to the bulk of its military. Less than 4 percent of the recruits who fought against Austria at Königgrätz in 1866 were illiterate. Although a close relationship already existed between factory and barracks, industrialism and militarism in Prussia before even 1848, Germany did not fully experience a massive industrial revolution until after the unification of 1871.

The combination of population explosion and early capitalism had a special impact on women and children. In the countryside, child mortality remained at nearly 50 percent during the critical first year of life owing to nutritional problems, inadequate hygiene, and medical incompetence. Among those who survived, only 60 percent attended school past age twelve. In Prussia work for children between the ages of nine and sixteen was "limited" to no more than ten hours per day.

For girls, life in the country was simple: apprenticeship as maids gave way to work as farmhands and finally to marriage. For most of the fifty years after 1815, half a million females annually worked as maids and servants in Prussia's countryside. Those who migrated to the cities usually found employment as domestic servants. By 1871 one in every four households in Bremen and Hamburg and one in every five in Berlin employed maids. These women faced rampant exploitation. Communal servants' regulations established no fixed (much less, minimum) wages, accorded no right to time off, and established no fixed work schedule. Sexual exploitation of these women escapes statistical analysis.

In social life, females were excluded from athletics, museums, professional organizations, and even singing clubs. Their earliest pleas for admission to such professions of caring as medicine, pharmacy, teaching, and welfare went unanswered. In 1822, for example, 620 women were employed in Prussian primary and secondary education, compared with 21,886 men. When women did find work, it was generally in the lowest-paid textile, clothing, food, paper, services, and tobacco industries, where they worked twelve hours per day, Monday through Saturday. The Bielefeld linen industry, for instance, was staffed 55 percent by women, whose annual pay ranged at only 500 to 600 mark. Yet even this work was often begrudged by males fearful of losing their higher-paying jobs. Opposition to female labor ran strongest among cigarmakers, tailors, and cotton printers. At the urging of labor leader Ferdinand Lassalle, unions for tobacco workers and tailors banned female labor. As late as 1892, women made up only 2 percent of the membership of the Free Trade Unions.

Females also suffered blatant moral discrimination. In 1808 a councillor of the Royal Prussian Supreme Court stated that men, "endowed with unbridled passions," could indulge in extramarital affairs with legal impunity. Thirty years later, the Prussian minister of justice decreed that because a woman's "value" lay primarily in her "moral and sexual purity," her employment entailed sacrifices of marriage, home, and children.

Perhaps most tragic in human terms was the role of domestic servants. A typical maid in a German city could expect to earn 150 mark per year, less than one-third the income of her sister in the Bielefeld linen industry. For these workers, there was but one precarious escape from poverty: prostitution. By 1870 Berlin faced a new phenomenon, mass public prostitution on its streets by about sixteen thousand women. State-administered medical examinations and identity papers further humiliated and stigmatized these so-called control girls, who had little chance at a normal life thereafter.

More affluent middle-class women found an outlet for their energies in community welfare. In 1832 Amalie Sieveking's Women's Association for the Care of the Poor and the Sick, soon augmented by the Elizabeth Associations in the Catholic Rhineland, offered relief for the less fortunate through soup kitchens, nurseries, rudimentary education, cookery schools, Sunday schools, and health care. In Rhineland-Westphalia, the Protestant Association of Deaconesses undertook similar work in hospitals, poorhouses, infirmaries, and orphanages.

Mention should be made of the German Jewish sector. Numerically, the picture was rosy. Those of the "Israelite belief" increased in German-speaking Austria between 1820 and 1850 from 85,000 to 130,000 and in Prussia as well as in the Third Germany from 270,000 to 400,000. Germany's Jews worked as dry goods and livestock traders, as well as moneylenders. In the cities they gained increasing visibility as grocers and textile merchants (tailors and furriers). But the great hope of assimilation, as envisaged by reformers after 1806, remained a mirage. Jews continued to suffer exclusion from positions in the civil service as well as the officer corps, and they were denied participation in the electoral process. As the poet Heinrich Heine (himself a converted Jew) bitingly put it, the Christian baptismal certificate remained "the entrance ticket to European culture."

The Turn to Nationalism: 1840

The year 1840 was a watershed in the development of German nationalism. As usual, external developments, in this case French, prodded internal German events. Whereas the Napoleonic invasions had led to the first gush of patriotic fervor in the German states, in 1840 a French diplomatic offensive designed to secure control of Algeria, Egypt, and Syria ironically precipitated a second eruption of the *furor Teutonicus*. In the wake of a British ultimatum to use force to repel French incursions in Egypt, French foreign minister Adolphe Thiers threatened not only to revise the "accords of 1815" but also to extend France's "natural" borders to the Rhine and the Alps.

This piece of French chauvinism was met in kind by Germany, evoking a virulent Francophobia that would poison relations between the two nations for the next century. A flood of patriotic songs and poems expressed the resurgent German nationalism. Nikolaus Becker penned his famous *Rheinlied*: "They shall not have it, the free German Rhine." By one estimate, as many as two hundred variations on the theme followed in short order. Max Schneckenburger composed perhaps the most fervently nationalistic poem of the era, *Die Wacht am Rhein* ("The Watch on the Rhine"), which would gain immortality a generation later when put to music by Karl Wilhelm. In 1841 Hoffmann von Fallersleben wrote the text of what eventually became the nation's official anthem: the *Deutschlandlied*, with music taken from Haydn. Its first stanza (not sung publicly by Germans since 1945) enunciates the expanse of German language and culture; for subsequent generations it defined the nation's still-unrealized physical parameters: from the Maas (River Meuse) to the Memel (River Niemen), and from the Etsch (River Adige in Tyrol) to the Belt (Baltic sea channel north of Schleswig). In the 1840s *Deutschland über Alles* was but the musical expression of an ebullient and optimistic nationalism. It would be transformed into a clarion call for world domination only by later generations.

At the same time, the Germans "rediscovered" their language and literature. National conferences of professors of German language and literature (*Germanistentage*) convened first in 1846 at Frankfurt and one year later at Lübeck. There, representatives of the educated middle class demanded "unity and freedom" within a national state. In the process, the group abandoned the universalist philosophy of cosmopolitanism as well as Francophilia and subordinated liberalism to nationalism. Helmuth von Moltke — able essayist, translator of Edward Gibbon's monumental *Decline and Fall of the Roman Empire*, and future military leader of the Prusso-German wars of unification — spoke openly in the 1840s of a justified German war against France. In doing so, he fell back on Ernst Moritz Arndt's strident reminder of 1813–1814 that the Rhine was "Germany's river, not Germany's border."

The new wave of nationalism permitted a reversal of the earlier arrests of patriots. Frederick William IV (1840–1861), king of Prussia, anxious to close the wounds left by the antinational policies of the past, liberalized censorship and granted amnesty to the "demagogues" of German nationalism. Ernst Moritz Arndt was restored to his professorship at Bonn. Ludwig Jahn, founder of the student fraternities and head of the nationalistic gymnastic societies, returned to teaching (at Berlin). In 1847 he proclaimed the founding of a national gymnastic club (*Turnerbund)* as a first step toward the formation of a national militia. Frederick William IV invited the Göttingen University liberals and philologists Jakob and Wilhelm Grimm to join the prestigious Prussian Academy of Science, and he offered their fellow protester of 1837, Professor Friedrich Christoph Dahlmann, a chair at Bonn University. Near Regensburg, high above the Danube River, Ludwig I, king of Bavaria, sought to give concrete expression to the new nationalism by constructing a massive Greek-inspired temple, the "Walhalla," dedicated to "Germanic" heroes, who in fact turned out to be mainly Bavarian.

This outpouring of nationalism worked to the detriment of the Habsburg monarchy. Ruling a polyglot empire of thirteen major ethnic groups and possessing extensive holdings in both Germany and Italy, Emperor Ferdinand I

(1835–1848) could ill afford to give free rein to national aspirations. The situation, as usual, was extremely critical in Hungary. As early as 1825, Stephan Count Széchenyi broached the issue of liberal reforms in Hungary, and seven years later, with the help of the national revival leader Ferenc Deák, he tendered a comprehensive program of economic, political, and social reforms for the Magyar state. Within another decade, these modest beginnings would turn into the radical liberalism of Louis Kossuth, who argued that the political control of Vienna was the main stumbling block to reform in Hungary.

Meanwhile, the founding of the Bohemian National Museum at Prague in 1818 led to revival of the ancient Czech language and literature. Most closely associated with the name of the historian František Palacký, who proudly described himself no longer as a German but rather as "a Bohemian of the Slavic tribe," the Czech literary revival would transform itself by 1848 from a cultural into a political movement for independence. Similar nationalistic stirring in Austria's Italian holdings (Lombardy, Venetia) and Polish possessions (Galicia) served notice that nationalism and the Habsburg Empire were incompatible.

The Hinge of Fate: 1848

It was against this background of nationalistic activity that news of insurrections abroad reached the German states. First came tidings of the Swiss revolt in 1847 over the admission of Jesuits to the educational system; then, of the Paris revolution[1] of February 24, 1848. Conflicting expectations rose in the German states, ranging from political reform to social justice to relief from misery and servitude. While a shared hostility to the established order united both moderate liberals and radical democrats, a deep gulf nevertheless separated the two. The former desired a British-style constitutional monarchy, while the latter demanded a republic as well as separation of church and state. Social protests also came to the fore in 1848: workers against employers, journeymen against masters, students against teachers, and peasants against landowners.

The German revolts varied, colored largely by regional politics. In central and north Germany, they were carried out by a middle-class intellectual elite. In southwest Germany, especially Baden, they had a radical, democratic impetus under the leadership of Gustav von Struve and Friedrich Hecker. In Saxony the movement became serious briefly under Robert Blum and Julius Fröbel but then turned comic-opera with Mikhail Bakunin and Richard Wagner.[2] In

[1] On February 21 the government of Louis Philippe forbade a planned great banquet in Paris for the following day. That night barricades went up, the National Guard refused to move against them, and on February 24 the king abdicated. The deeper causes of the revolution ranged from fraud and corruption in the government to radical demands for universal suffrage and a republic.

[2] Bakunin, who hoped to turn the European revolutions against the Russian state, organized revolutionary forces in Dresden; Wagner, who wanted freedom to write serious music at the Saxon court, drafted revolutionary leaflets. Wagner wisely rejected Bakunin's suggestion that in case the Prussians stormed Dresden, they blow themselves up with gunpowder as a final act of disdain and rejection of this world.

Bavaria the "revolution" revolved around Ludwig I and his colorful mistress, Lola Montez. It was in Berlin and Vienna, however, that the revolts would determine the future of "Germany."

The revolutions throughout central Europe followed similar patterns. Initial demonstrations met with limited armed force, whereupon rulers generally panicked and agreed to the rebels' liberal and nationalistic demands. After a frenetic pace of radical legislation, the liberals ran out of steam and support. Counterrevolutionary forces — the military, bureaucracy, nobility, and crown — thereupon seized the initiative and regained control, with or without the use of force. In the end, reaction triumphed.

The causes of revolutions usually bedevil analysts, and this is true as well of 1848. Liberal and nationalistic reform movements contributed to the momentum. Potato blight and failed harvests between 1845 and 1847 produced mass food riots in Berlin, Stuttgart, Ulm, and Vienna, where women ransacked bakeries and food stores. In Upper Silesia, eighty thousand people suffered hunger-induced spotted fever, and sixteen thousand died of the disease. Revolution often develops also as an outgrowth of rising expectations, and certainly real per capita income rose sharply in 1848 and 1849. But did it precipitate revolution? We know that the revolutions remained primarily urban: after an initial surge of seizing and burning manorial records, the peasantry virtually disappeared as a revolutionary force.

Turmoil first plagued Vienna when, on March 13, street fighting broke out. Fired up by Louis Kossuth's liberal and patriotic speeches before the Hungarian parliament, students, workers, apprentices, and *Kleinbürger* (lower middle class) poured out into the streets that day. Guildsmen occupied factories and destroyed machines to protest early industrialism. Peasants stormed manor and customs houses to destroy feudal records. The national black-red-gold banner soon flew from St. Stephan's Cathedral. Barricades went up. The army was called out, and nearly sixty persons fell as martyrs to the national cause. The royal family hastened to quieter surroundings at Innsbruck in the Tyrol.

In Prussia money once again proved a factor in bringing about change. Frederick William IV wished to build a railroad from Berlin to Königsberg at a cost of 30 million thaler. He convened the "United Diet" in 1847 to secure the requisite loans, only to discover that the price was a constitution clearly defining the power of the purse. The king refused to allow a "piece of paper" to come between him and his subjects, and parliament declined to finance the railroad. Frederick William's attempts to draw attention away from his domestic problems by calling for the creation of a joint Austro-Prussian national state from Kiel to Trieste fell on suspicious ears. It earned from Metternich the caustic comment that the king of Prussia's policies were works of "fiction."

These tensions exploded in Berlin on March 19, 1848. Students, apprentices, workers, and *Kleinbürger* seized the streets and built barricades at the Alexanderplatz. An army confronted the mob. Shots rang out. More than 230 people fell dead. A stunned Frederick William IV at once issued an appeal for law and order "To My Dear Berliners!," donned the national colors for a tour

"My Dear Berliners": Revolutionaries in Berlin (March 1848).

of the capital, reviewed the corpses at the barricades, and proclaimed that "henceforth Prussia will merge into Germany." In time, however, conservative leaders blocked further concessions to the revolutionaries by persuading the king to retire to Potsdam.

Despite the initial military triumphs, euphoria reigned only briefly. In Berlin as well as in Vienna, constituent assemblies convened and set to work drafting liberal constitutions. Freedom of press and religion, of assembly and speech was guaranteed. Reformers demanded equality of the sexes, free education, a progressive income tax, and a people's militia. The more radical reformers, such as the lawyer Gustav von Struve in Baden, called for abolition of all royal armies and bureaucracies, separation of church and state, deposition of hereditary rulers, abolition of monasteries, and creation of a federal union on the model of the United States. In Berlin U.S. president James K. Polk's representatives to "Germany" assisted the reform cause by passing out food and drink and by lighting the embassy building at night. At Constance, Friedrich Hecker, like Struve a lawyer from Mannheim, proclaimed a German republic.

The year 1848 brought the first appearance of organized labor. Stephan Born, a twenty-three-year-old printer, was the best-known labor leader in Berlin. Born had worked to provide rudimentary education to workers and in 1847 had met Marx and Engels in Paris. That same year he had organized a tiny Workers' Congress in the capital. Its program called for free secular education, housing for workers, equality for women, a ten-hour workday, unemployment insurance, and consumer cooperatives. But neither Born's newly founded "Central Committee of Workers" nor Marx's "Union of Communists" played a significant role in the revolutions. Indeed, Born wrote to Marx that he would be laughed out of town if he declared himself a Communist. As late as 1846–1847, industrial workers constituted but 3 percent of the German work force.

These small numbers notwithstanding, the emergence of an organized labor force in 1848 frightened the middle classes. The workers behind the barricades in Berlin presented a sufficient threat to prompt the citizens of Berlin to cast their lot with the king at Potsdam. They preferred the new *Kreuzzeitung*, the major newspaper of Prussian conservatives, to Marx's *Neue Rheinische Zeitung*, which was banned in May 1849. The historian Dahlmann was correct to state that the German middle class of property and education (*Besitz- und Bildungsbürgertum*) "wanted national and liberal reform" but without "revolution, which would endanger property and education."

The year 1848 also witnessed the first organized women's movement in Germany. Although women were still not allowed in clubs and political organizations, they assisted the revolution not only by passing out food but by carrying cobblestones to rooftops and helping mold bullets in the streets. Although few women actually took part in the fighting, many worked through the Democratic Women's Association in Berlin to improve the plight of seamstresses, lacemakers, knitters, and tailors. In 1848 females everywhere formed democratic women's associations, raised funds for victims of the fighting and their dependents, and established female gymnastic clubs to further the national cause. Women grew especially active in the publishing trade. In April 1848, Luise Otto founded the *Frauen-Zeitung* and called for "the participation of women in the life of the nation." Although Otto did not favor full emancipation and did not demand full social and economic equality for men and women, her actions and those of countless others attested to the fact that some women were eager to become active citizens.

Then hard reality set in. The reformers discovered that they had neither the money nor the soldiers to boost their programs. The peasants remained passive. In several cases, a timely opening of the princely or royal wine cellars pacified the soldiers. The middle class in Berlin became alarmed at the presence of nine hundred workers in their midst, and nearly seventy thousand *Bürger* voted with their feet by joining the king at Potsdam. Creature comforts quickly disappeared. By the autumn of 1848, Vienna lacked light and water, coal and food. Liberals discovered to their horror that good intentions alone could not change the course of events. As the euphoria of the spring of 1848 turned into frustration, disappointment, and bitterness, a large segment of the middle class turned back to the traditional values of law and order, property and prosperity, as manifested by the dynastic state. Civil courage yielded all too easily to personal safety in 1848, as it had in 1806.

Reaction returned. In Baden, Württemberg troops defeated Hecker's army of twelve hundred adventurers at Kandern in the Black Forest. The "German Legion" of the exiled poet Georg Herwegh, which had come from Paris to Baden costumed like soldiers of the Thirty Years' War, met the same fate at Dossenbach. In Munich Ludwig I at first argued lamely that his relationship with his mistress, Lola Montez, was purely platonic, which earned him the cruel cut, "That makes his folly all the greater," from the Prussian envoy to Bavaria. Thereafter the king abdicated and Lola disappeared to the California gold fields. Berlin, to the consternation of General Friedrich Baron von Wrangel, who spoiled for a fight, yielded to his troops without a shot being fired. Government soldiers reinstated martial law, revoked all liberal and national reforms, and meted out harsh verdicts, especially to student leaders, ranging from hanging to army service for life.

Suppression of Austria's revolutions was particularly severe, for the Habsburgs exploited nationalism in a most cynical manner. Joseph Count Radetzky, a Bohemian, defeated the rebellious Italian forces at Custozza on July 25. Alfred Count von Windischgrätz, a German, smashed the Czech revolt at Prague. And from Croatia, Joseph Baron von Jellačić combined with Windischgrätz's new Czech units to retake Vienna on October 26 in the bloodiest episode of 1848. The artillery fire was so intense that neither side could make the other out for long periods. The great copper roof of the Augustine Church melted under the heat. The Croats ransacked the city with women warriors at their sides, fencing with the students and then casually slitting their throats. Black-red-gold banners disappeared, as did the revolutionary long hair and beards. About a dozen reform leaders, including Robert Blum, were executed. Thousands of students found themselves pressed into the army for life. Martial law was declared for five years. Almost as an afterthought, the generals forced the abdication of the feeble-minded Ferdinand I, who was succeeded on December 2 by eighteen-year-old Francis Joseph I. What remained of the liberal parliament at Kremsier was dissolved by the new premier, Felix Prince zu Schwarzenberg. The latter was emboldened in his reactionary course in part by Tsar Nicholas I, who encouraged the Austrians to suppress revolutionary activities.

As these regional revolutions raged, elections were held throughout the German-speaking lands of central Europe for a "German Constituent Assembly" to draft a constitution and bring about unification. The delegates were chosen proportionally, either directly or indirectly, at the rate of roughly one for every fifty thousand citizens and comprised a middle-class preserve of bureaucrats and legal scholars, not the gathering of "fifty mad professors," as derisively depicted by the British Conservative leader Benjamin Disraeli. All members were males, although as a sign of their "progressive" outlook on women's rights, the organizers at the Paulskirche reserved two hundred seats in the galleries for women.

The National Assembly convened on May 18, 1848, at the ancient imperial city of Frankfurt to the accompaniment of ringing church bells and cannon fire. Surely, it seemed, the German educated elite would be able to hammer out a constitution and to lay the foundations for unification. The men who met at the Paulskirche (St. Paul's Church) at Frankfurt were to influence the future of Germany profoundly. With these leaders in mind, the British historian A. J. P. Taylor, referring to Germany's failure to embark upon a parliamentary constitutional course, percipiently called 1848 the turning point at which Germany "failed to turn."

The national parliament that gathered was the first and only freely elected assembly of delegates from so many German lands. Its members ranged from Silesian princes to Austrian peasants, Polish nobles to Baden farmers. Neither the ultraconservative right nor the socialist left was represented. Palacký refused to permit the Czech delegates from Bohemia and Moravia to attend. On May 19 the National Assembly chose Heinrich von Gagern of Hesse-Darmstadt as its leader. At his suggestion, by a vote of 436 to 112, the parliament elected Archduke Johann, the liberal-minded youngest brother of the late Emperor Francis I of Austria, as imperial administrator. The Austrian representatives

FRANKFURT PARLIAMENT

Profession	Number	Percentage
Governmental civil servants	157	19.7
Lawyers (other than judges)	130	16.3
Teachers (all levels)	123	15.4
Judges, public prosecutors	119	14.9
Businessmen	75	9.4
Landowners	68	8.5
Clergy	45	5.6
Writers, journalists	36	4.5
Medical practitioners	25	3.1
Army officers	15	1.9
Other	6	0.7
TOTAL	799	100

The Hinge of Fate: The National Assembly convenes at the Paulskirche in Frankfurt (May 1848).

hoped, albeit in vain, to bring Charlemagne's crown to Frankfurt as a tangible symbol of German unity.

The Frankfurt parliament began with great disappointment: the major European powers refused to recognize it. As expected, Nicholas I of Russia firmly opposed the creation of a liberal German national state in the heart of Europe. Britain declined formal recognition of the national parliament. Most embittering, France, the home of revolution, withheld support. Foreign minister Jules Bastide reassured the Prussian envoy at Paris that France would combat "the triumph of democratic and unitary tendencies in Germany." Although some of the lesser European states (Switzerland, Sweden, Belgium, Holland, Naples, Greece, Sardinia) and the United States extended diplomatic recognition to Frankfurt, their gesture held little consequence.

Despite this initial setback, the parliament forged ahead and drafted a constitution. The representatives of classical nineteenth-century liberalism upheld the principles of individual freedoms, the sanctity of private property, and the notion of secular education (while guaranteeing the right of the 23 million Catholics to private schools). They opted for a federal union headed by a monarch endowed with an imperial title but with his power tempered by an elective assembly and responsible ministry. The monarch, to be chosen from among the German princes, would conduct foreign policy, declare war and conclude peace, and command the armed forces. Under a bicameral system, the House of States would consist of delegates equally divided between those appointed by state governments and those elected by state parliaments. The People's House, by contrast, was to be elected by direct, secret, and universal manhood suffrage. This lower house, to be elected every three years, would have authority to promulgate laws, levy taxes, and define the budget. It could override any veto by the monarch. Finally, a national supreme court would be established to settle conflicts between individual states as well as between the central government and the states.

The greatest issue facing the Frankfurt parliament was that of defining the nation. From July 24 to 27 the debate centered on Poland. Although most delegates greatly sympathized with the Poles for the injustices done to them by the three recent partitions, they nevertheless resolved that Posen and West Prussia should remain German. Wilhelm Jordan set the tone for the majority when he pronounced the "superiority of the Germans over most of the Slavic tribes" as a "natural historical fact." Despite Palacký and his Pan-Slav Congress at Prague, the National Assembly agreed overwhelmingly to include most Habsburg possessions, especially Bohemia and Moravia, in the new Germany. Moreover, the delegates voted to incorporate the "German harbor of Trieste," an Italian-speaking city, into the new state. The conservatives defended these actions by stressing the principle of Germanic hegemony in central Europe; the left-liberals justified their views with humanitarian and cultural phrases upholding the duty of "progressive" peoples to uplift and civilize more "backward" peoples.

The decisive moment for these national aspirations came in July and August. The Danish king, Frederick VII, sought to exploit the German chaos by annexing the twin duchies of Schleswig and Holstein. The Paulskirche responded as if to a national cause. Prussia tried to head off an outburst of nationalism by occupying Holstein. British and Russian opposition, however, forced Frederick William IV on August 26 at Malmö to recall his troops. Thereupon, matters proceeded to get out of hand at Frankfurt. On September 17 thousands of angry young men denounced as treason Frankfurt's acceptance by a vote of 238 to 237 of the Malmö agreement. The next day, the parliament had to call in Austrian and Prussian troops to restore order. Barricades once again went up. A mob stormed the Paulskirche. Soldiers deployed artillery against the demonstrators, killing eighty people. The grand nationalist cause died in the streets of Frankfurt.

The final act of the Frankfurt parliament came on March 27, 1849, when, by a vote of 267 to 263, the group decided to offer the imperial crown to the Hohenzollerns and to seek unity without Austria. Once more accompanied by the pealing of church bells and the thunder of cannon fire, the message was transmitted to Berlin over Europe's first modern telegraph. National unity, albeit in a limited version, lay within reach. But Frederick William IV, true to character, declined to accept a "crown from the gutter," that is, from parliamentary hands. He would later speak of the offered dignity as a pig's crown, a fictitious coronet baked of mud and clay, of an iron collar of servitude.

Disappointment and dissension ravaged the land anew. In Prussia Frederick William IV dissolved parliament. In Austria Francis Joseph I invited Nicholas I to help suppress the Hungarian revolt led by Kossuth. By contrast, a third revolution broke out in Baden under Lorenz Brentano and the Polish insurgent Ludwik Mierosławski. It suffered the same fate of its two predecessors. On July 23 fifty-six hundred Baden rebels surrendered to Prussian forces at Rastatt. They were treated as criminals, forced to lay down their arms, and imprisoned or pressed into army service for life. More than eighty thousand citizens of Baden, one in eighteen, now turned their backs on their homeland and emigrated, mainly to the United States. Smaller uprisings in Saxony and the Palatinate were crushed by the Prussian military.

It is difficult to explain why the Frankfurt parliament failed so spectacularly. Apart from the shortage of support from the major European powers, the Frankfurt parliament lacked a central, powerful executive to carry through its reform program, as well as any source of income with which to finance its administration. It possessed no military might with which to ward off the counterrevolutionary thrusts of Austria and Prussia. Even the projected fleet of Prince Adalbert of Prussia failed to materialize as a national symbol of unity. Perhaps the very polycentrism of the German revolutions militated against success because no single outcome would have satisfied all of "Germany."

Nationalism proved the most important cause of failure for the 1848 uprisings. Nationalists of all shades felt deeply perplexed by, and divided over, the issue of whether the future homeland should include Austria (the *Grossdeutsch* solution) or simply rest on Prussia and the Third Germany (the *Kleindeutsch* solution). The debates concerning Poland, South Tyrol, and the Czech lands of Bohemia and Moravia were but the outward manifestations of this uncertainty. Francis Joseph declared words such as *nation*, *freedom*, and *German unity* to be "revolutionary" concepts, and hence alien to his vocabulary. Few realized in the dark days of 1849 that this declaration would eventually convince German nationalists that the road to unification did not pass through Vienna.

Into the Political Doldrums: The 1850s

Reaction ruled after 1849. Frederick William IV turned his back on Berlin, where he customarily spent much of the winter, and spent his remaining years almost exclusively at Potsdam, determined to eradicate what he termed "the democratic filth of the year of shame." His famous comment that only soldiers would get rid of the democrats set the political tone in Prussia.

Throughout the German states, even uttering such terms as *democrat* and *socialist* sufficed to cast suspicion on their users, who soon became enemies of the state. Reactionaries, such as Prime Minister Otto Baron von Manteuffel and General Leopold von Gerlach, also cleverly exploited the very failure of the revolutions as an argument against allowing liberals any degree of influence in government. These strategists proclaimed the brief use of force in March 1848 as the "natural" consequence of change.

For some of those who had fought for change and lost, emigration provided an escape. In the five years after 1849, more than 1 million people left Germany, most of them for the midwestern United States. There they transferred their German liberalism to the cause of emancipation of the slaves in the southern states. Friedrich Hecker ended up on a farm in Illinois, Lorenz Brentano became a congressman, and Carl Schurz fled Rastatt through a sewer and emigrated to Missouri, where he became a senator and one of the founders of the Republican party. Almost to a man, they fought with the Union against slavery and the Confederacy during the Civil War.

Despite the complete victory of the forces of reaction by late 1849, the twin issues of constitutional reform and national unity refused to disappear from the political stage. Both had moved from the streets and parliaments to professional associations such as the Congress of German Economists (1858), the National Union (1859), the German Jurists (1860), and the National Chamber of Commerce (1861). Significantly, most of these professional associations were headquartered in Prussia; Austria, by definition, seemed "reactionary" to most German liberals and nationalists.

In 1849 Francis Joseph I renounced his predecessor's promise of a constitution. Two years later, he formally "withdrew" the constitution of 1849, which had never actually been put in place. In addition, he abolished the office of prime minister, and in place of a cabinet he installed a neoabsolutist Imperial Council (Reichsrat) to augment his personal rule. Prussia put in place a constitution based on the so-called three-class voting system in 1850 that would survive until 1918. Under its provisions, the male electorate by indirect ballot would send three numerically equal delegations to the *Landtag*: one-third of the deputies were elected by those in the highest tax class (4.7 percent of eligible voters), another third by the middle group of taxpayers (12.6 percent of voters), and the last third by the lowest class of taxpayers (82.7 percent of eligible voters). The upper chamber (*Herrenhaus*) remained an exclusive preserve of the nobility.

Austria suffered in comparison with Prussia in the economic sector especially. Not only was the *Zollverein* renewed in 1852–1853 after bitter negotiations, again with the exclusion of Austria, but the Habsburg monarchy lagged far behind its Hohenzollern rival in production and efficiency. By the mid–1860s Austria, with double Prussia's population of 19 million, produced only the same amount of cereal grains and half the tonnage of pig iron. Most noticeably, with nearly equal annual incomes, the Austrian state debt stood at 1,670 million thaler, that of Prussia at a paltry 45 million thaler. When one keeps in mind that the total cash reserves of Prussian banks doubled to 375 million thaler between 1851 and 1857, it is readily apparent which state was better positioned to lead "Germany" into the industrial age.

Furthermore, Francis Joseph I had hardly boosted his popularity among liberals and nationalists when he concluded a concordat with Rome in 1855. Not even his grandiose rebuilding of Vienna after 1859 with the magnificent Ring Strasse featuring stately edifices such as an opera house and parliament — perhaps as a future capital for "Germany"? — advanced his reputation as a progressive leader.

Finally, there remained the national question. In his heart of hearts, Frederick William IV still lusted after the German crown. As early as May 1849 he had initiated negotiations with Austria for some sort of loose federal structure embracing Austria, Prussia, and the Third Germany without specific divisions of imperial and royal dignities. But the Austrian prime minister Schwarzenberg brusquely rejected such talks.

Largely at the urging of his personal and cabinet adviser in German affairs, Joseph Maria von Radowitz, Frederick William IV now altered tactics. In the spring of 1850, he convened an imperial Reichstag at Erfurt and managed to persuade Saxony and Hanover to endorse his dream of German unity by royal fiat. By May, ten other states from the Third Germany joined the plan. Then disaster struck: on November 28, Schwarzenberg threatened military action against the Prussian "union policy." Next he engineered a military alliance against Prussia with Bavaria, Hanover, Saxony, and Württemberg. And last, he invited the German states to reconvene the confederation at Frankfurt.

Prussia refused to accept the invitation to Frankfurt. Moreover, Prussian troops had occupied parts of Schleswig and Holstein in the wake of the two duchies' rebellion against Danish rule. An alarmed Nicholas I demanded that Prussia withdraw all support from the "rebels" and dispatched a naval squadron to the area. The combination of Prussia's union plans and its refusal to withdraw from Schleswig-Holstein convinced the tsar that his brother-in-law, Frederick William IV, had abandoned conservative principles.

Schwarzenberg spied his chance. He invited the Prussian prime minister, Baron von Manteuffel, to Olmütz (now Olomouc) in Moravia, where on November 29 Prussia had to renounce all union plans and to accept Austrian leadership at Frankfurt (the so-called Punctation of Olmütz). A lame Prussian attempt to salvage at least co-leadership with Austria over the confederation failed at a ministers' conference at Dresden in the spring of 1851. Prussia had been publicly humiliated. Schwarzenberg later confessed regret that the issue had been resolved without recourse to arms. Few in Vienna realized in their moment of victory, however, that Minister Karl von Bruck's plan for a Habsburg empire "of seventy millions" in central Europe had also died at Olmütz. As the new Prussian envoy to Frankfurt, Otto von Bismarck, put it, obstruction of any and all reform plans was now official policy. If Austria "hitched a horse in front" of the German cart, Bismarck observed, Prussia would have to "hitch one behind."

Bismarck was one of the few Prussian leaders delighted at the turn of events at Olmütz. He had viewed Frederick William IV's union plan with suspicion; it smelled too much to him of liberalism and romanticism. German unification, Bismarck believed, could come about only if Prussia was willing to contest primacy in Germany with Austria in battle. The year 1850 was not propitious, and Frederick William IV was not prepared for such a bold course. The union plan, in Bismarck's views, had been a cause outside Prussia's interests. Thus, Olmütz had cleared the air. The clock had been turned back to 1740, when Frederick the Great had challenged Austria by invading Silesia.

Austro-Prussian dualism was a fact of life. There was no more talk of Germanic brotherhood, national parliaments, or union plans. Prussia's only legitimate policy, Bismarck stated with reference to Olmütz, should be based on "egoism rather than romanticism." In a famous letter to his political patron in Berlin, Leopold von Gerlach, Bismarck bluntly noted that Austria's policy was one of "strict hegemony" over the German Confederation. Prussia, whose sole area of vital interest was Germany, stood in the way: "There is no room for both . . . thus we cannot get along over the long haul. We steal each other's breath. One must yield or be 'forced to yield' by the other; until then, we must remain adversaries."

For the time being, this was mostly wishful thinking on the part of Bismarck, a radical outsider in 1853. Would Frederick William IV ever consider entrusting the fate of Prussia to a man whose character he had summarized in 1848 with the comment, "red reactionary, smells of blood, to be used only when the bayonet reigns"? Before that question could be answered, the European powers fell out over Russia's repeated attempts to extend its influence over the Ottoman Empire in general and the Balkans in particular. Nicholas I's invasion of Wallachia and Moldavia (which would unite to form Rumania in 1858) also raised the sensitive issue of the protection of Christians in the Ottoman Empire, including those at Jerusalem. While Britain fought Nicholas I to uphold the Ottoman Empire against Russia, France claimed a special right of protection over Ottoman Christians and had long been a major financial backer of the Porte.

The Crimean War (1853–1856) accorded Prussia an unexpected opportunity to put the shame of Olmütz behind. Frederick William IV resisted the repeated efforts of his brother, Prince William, and the conservative lobby at court, to join Britain and France against Russia. Francis Joseph I, on the other hand, was beset by fears that Russia might conquer the Balkans and seize

Constantinople. In December 1854 he sided with the Western powers against Russia, though not as an active belligerent. Austrian mobilization sufficed to compel the Russians to withdraw their forces from Wallachia and Moldavia. Then, after the Western allies invaded the Crimea and ground down the Russian army, the new tsar, Alexander II, sued for peace in early 1856. Once again, Austria's threat to enter the fray against Russia helped tip the balance.

Almost despite itself, Prussia emerged as the chief beneficiary of the Crimean War. Alexander II, well remembering Russian assistance to Austria in 1849–1850 in putting down the Hungarian revolution, never forgave Francis Joseph I for the "treachery" of December 1854. Moreover, the conservative tsar distrusted France, the country of Napoleon and revolutions, which harbored a strong desire to reconstitute Poland. On the other hand, Alexander II appreciated that Prussia alone of the major European powers had remained neutral during the Crimean War. He also understood that Prussia and Russia shared a mutual desire to prevent the restoration of Poland. On a larger scale, the Crimean War destroyed the European concert as well as the Holy Alliance established at Vienna in 1815.

In 1857 Frederick William IV suffered a series of strokes, and his mental health rapidly deteriorated as well. His brother William, prince of Prussia, was appointed regent in 1858. The next year Count Camillo Cavour of Piedmont-Sardinia, aided by the French emperor Napoleon III, declared war on Austria. While Cavour sought to unify Italy by wresting the provinces of Lombardy and Venetia from Francis Joseph I, Napoleon III wished to destroy the main pillar of the Vienna concert of 1815. Prince William, although sympathetic to the plight of his fellow German monarch at Vienna, nevertheless pressed the advantage he gained by the Austrian defeats at Magenta and Solferino and demanded control over all German forces along the Rhine. Fearful for its position in central Europe, Austria concluded peace with Napoleon III at Villafranca and ceded Lombardy to Cavour.

Prussia had ordered mobilization of its army at the height of the Italian War in the summer of 1859, only to discover that it was grossly understaffed, poorly organized, and badly led. In fact, mobilization had turned into chaos. Prince William now turned his full and undivided attention to his army, determined to reform it from top to bottom and thereby to accord Prussia the respect that William felt it deserved in Europe. In December he chose General Albrecht von Roon to undertake this important assignment. Unknown to Prince William, Roon had an ace up his sleeve: his friend and fellow Junker, Otto von Bismarck, who was quite prepared to shoulder the burden of reform. And more.

Suggested Readings

There is no thorough treatment of *Biedermeier* Germany in English. E. J. Hobsbawn, *The Age of Revolution, 1789–1848* (Cleveland and New York, 1962), is a basic introduction to the period. For those seeking intellectual challenge, Max Weber, *Economy and Society: An Outline of Interpretative Sociology*, 3 vols. (Berkeley and Los Angeles, 1978), is recommended.

The development of a uniquely German historicism was first analyzed in survey form by G. P. Gooch, *History and Historians in the Nineteenth Century* (Boston, 1959), and more recently by Georg C. Iggers, *The German Conception of History: The National Tradition of Historical Thought from Herder to the Present* (Middletown, Conn., 1983). Eda Sagarra, *Tradition and Revolution: German Literature and Society, 1830–1890* (New York, 1971), offers a broad sweep of German writers and their society, and Jonathan Sperber, *Popular Catholicism in Nineteenth Century Germany* (Princeton, 1984), is a valuable counterbalance to the Protestant, Prussian school of history. Koppel S. Pinson, *Pietism as a Factor in the Rise of German Nationalism* (New York, 1934), is still valuable. Students of Hegel would do well to consult John E. Toews, *Hegelianism: The Path toward Dialectical Humanism 1805–1841* (Cambridge, 1980); those of Marx, David McLellan, *Karl Marx: His Life and Thought* (London,1973). Charles E. McClelland, *State, Society, and University in Germany, 1700–1914* (Cambridge, 1980), is valuable for the development of the German university system. Finally, Peter Paret, *Clausewitz and the State* (New York, London, and Toronto, 1976), remains central for understanding the theory of civilian-military relations.

Political currents have found adequate treatment. While Klaus Epstein, before his tragic early death, sought to analyze *The Genesis of German Conservatism* (Princeton, 1966), James J. Sheehan, *German Liberalism in the Nineteenth Century* (Chicago, 1978), and Donald G. Rohr, *The Origins of Social Liberalism in Germany* (Chicago and London, 1963), offered evaluations of classic nineteenth-century liberalism in Germany. John L. Snell, *The Democratic Movement in Germany, 1789–1914* (Chapel Hill, 1976), has provided a useful survey of the forces of democratic reform from the French Revolution to World War I.

Little exists on the history of the peasantry apart from Richard J. Evans, *The German Peasantry: Conflict and Continuity in Rural Society from the Eighteenth to the Twentieth Centuries* (London and Sydney, 1986). Mack Walker, *German Home Towns, Community, State, and General Estate, 1648–1871* (Ithaca, N.Y., 1971), is superb for an understanding of German urban life, and his earlier treatment, *Germany and the Emigration, 1816–1885* (Cambridge, Mass., 1964), does much to explain the immense exodus out of Germany for most of the nineteenth century.

Austrian affairs have received their share of attention. David F. Good has analyzed *The Economic Rise of the Habsburg Empire, 1750–1914* (Berkeley and Los Angeles, 1984), while Enno E. Kraehe's monumental sweep of *Metternich's German Policy*, 2 vols. (Princeton, 1963, 1983), is likely to remain the standard. The events of 1848 are best described by R. John Rath, *The Viennese Revolution of 1848* (Austin, Texas, 1957); see also Alan Sked, *The Survival of the Habsburg Empire: Radetzky, the Imperial Army, and the Class War, 1848* (London, 1979). Events in Hungary are masterfully depicted by István Deák, *The Lawful Revolution: Louis Kossuth and the Hungarians, 1848–1849* (New York, 1979).

With regard to Prussia, John R. Gillis, *The Prussian Bureaucracy in Crisis, 1840–1860: Origins of an Administrative Ethos* (Stanford, 1971), has examined the genesis of the royal Prussian bureaucracy. W. O. Henderson, *The Zollverein* (Cambridge, 1939), remains useful. Otto Pflanze, *Bismarck and the Development of Germany: The Period of Unification, 1815–1871* (Princeton, 1963), is still a handy guide.

Several regional studies are worthy of mention: Frank Tipton, *Regional Variations in the Economic Development of Germany during the Nineteenth Century* (Middletown, Conn., 1976); Lloyd E. Lee, *The Politics of Harmony: Civil Service, Liberalism, and Social Reform in Baden, 1800–1850* (Newark, Del., 1980); and W. Robert Lee, *Population Growth, Economic Development, and Social Change in Bavaria, 1750–1850* (New York, 1977). The role of women in *Biedermeier* Germany requires further study. Two essay collections are offered by John C. Fout, ed., *German Women in the Nineteenth Century: A Social History* (New York and London, 1984), and Ruth Ellen Joeres and Mary Jo Maynes, eds., *German Women in the Enlightenment and Nineteenth Centuries: A Social and Literary History* (Bloomington, Ind., 1986). Ute Frevert, *Women in German History: From Bourgeois Emancipation to Sexual Liberation* (New York, 1988), constitutes the best available survey. The "anguish of assimilation" of German Jews after 1815 has been dealt with by Jacob Katz, *Out of the Ghetto: The Social Background of Jewish Emancipation, 1770–1870* (Cambridge, Mass., 1973), and David Sorkin, *The Transformation of German Jewry, 1780–1840* (New York, 1987).

The revolutions of 1848, unsurprisingly, are blessed with a rich literature. Rudolf Stadelmann's *Social and Political History of the German 1848 Revolution* (Munich, 1948), remains unrivaled; Theodore S. Hamerow, *Restoration, Revolution, Reaction: Economics and Politics in Germany, 1815–1871* (Princeton, 1958), basically followed Stadelmann's analysis. P. H. Noyes, *Organization and Revolution: Working-Class Associations in the German Revolutions of 1848–49* (Princeton, 1966), is central for the role of labor during the revolutions. Frank Eyck, *The Frankfort Parliament, 1848–1849* (London, 1968), is essential to any understanding of the Paulskirche.

CHAPTER

4

THE GERMAN REVOLUTION: THE PRIMACY OF PRUSSIA, 1862–1890

Let me impress upon the attention of the House the character of this war between France and Germany. It is no common war. . . . This war represents the German revolution, a greater political event than the French revolution. . . . You have a new world, new influences at work, new and unknown objects and dangers with which to cope. . . . The balance of power has been entirely destroyed.

Benjamin Disraeli, 1871

What Disraeli called the "German revolution" — more accurately, the three wars of unification that Prussia fought against Denmark (1864), Austria (1866), and France (1870–1871) — indeed constituted a "new world" in that it reshaped Europe. From the German perspective, the nefarious policy of French leaders from Louis XIV to Napoleon III to maintain the disunity of central Europe came to an abrupt end. The European balance of power, the cornerstone of British foreign policy for the past two centuries, had been firmly reestablished at the Congress of Vienna in 1815. But the Crimean War had killed it, and Bismarck's wars of unification buried it with full honors. By 1871 a powerful, united Germanic bloc straddled the European plain from the Meuse to the Vistula. For the first time since 1815, Europe was devoid of major alliances. What, if anything, would take the place of the Metternichian order?

To the casual outside observer the "German revolution" spearheaded by Protestant Prussia was thorough and complete. Catholicism was in full retreat; militant Protestantism was on the rise. A unified customs union (*Zollverein*) under Prussian leadership was poised to dominate the heart of Europe economically from Denmark to Italy and from France to Russia. For the first time in modern history the major rivers of northern central Europe — the Elbe,

Oder, Rhine, and Weser — lay under the control of a single Germanic power. In short, no longer was central Europe to be the military drill square of the major powers.

But few observers realized that deep fissures divided the new state. The south German states, historic entities with their own proud independent history, would require time and understanding to adjust to the new Reich. A host of citizens involuntarily incorporated into the new empire — Danes, French, Hanoverians, and Poles — faced a period of adjustment. Industrial development throughout the German states dislocated ancient rural populations and created new centers of production almost overnight. Would the urban work force be assimilated into the new state? And how would the national liberals of 1848 react to a Prussian-dominated Germany?

Nation Building, Prussian Style

The radical transformation of Europe that Disraeli depicted was primarily the work of one man, Otto von Bismarck-Schönhausen. His life spanned the nineteenth century. Born in the year of the Congress of Vienna, he died in 1898, the year before the outbreak of the Boer War in South Africa.[1] To this day the "Iron Chancellor" has remained an enigma to scholars. Character conflicts abound. A brilliant parliamentary speaker, Bismarck nevertheless devoted most of his life to combating parliamentarism. A devout conservative, he destroyed the European balance through creative antirevolution. A pragmatist, he spent his later years plagued by the nightmare that the Reich was on the verge of dissolving. An honorary general who habitually wore uniform in parliament and who spoke of letting the guns do the talking, he nurtured a lifelong distrust of the military. Even the diversity of his career and policies reflected the complexity of character: from the "red reactionary" of 1848 to the "white revolutionary," or crisis manager as prime minister, after 1862.

Still more apparent conflicts confuse scholars: "Brandenburg vassal" and German nationalist, anticolonialist and founder of the Reich's first overseas empire, antisocialist and creator of the world's first social security system, anti-Catholic and yet holder of the Order of Jesus Christ with Diamonds, "honest broker" and devious manipulator of alliances. Bismarck was well aware of the conflicts. "Faust complains of having two souls in his breast. I have a whole squabbling crowd. It goes on as in a republic."

Part of the answer to this paradox lies in Bismarck's birth. His father was a typical East Elbian country squire whose life revolved around his fields and flocks at Schönhausen. The mother was a Mencken, product of a long line of

---

[1] For three years Britain fought the Afrikaners-Dutch (Boers, or farmers) in the Transvaal and the Orange Free State under Paul Kruger. Most European states vociferously championed the Boer cause.

nonnoble bureaucrats and professors who had served Prussia since the days of Frederick II.[1] Her world was that of the English Utilitarians, the French Positivists, and the German liberals — a world of progress, science, and balance. She sent her son to Göttingen University, hearth of English liberalism; he dropped out after several semesters. An unproductive civil service career left him bitter, cynical, and neurotic. Phlebitis, insomnia, jaundice, convulsions, gastric ulcers, shingles, and nervous facial pain were but a few of the outward symptoms of the conflicts that raged within this complex man. He found an anchor — albeit his was planted firmly in the Old Testament — in his devoutly Pietist wife, Johanna von Puttkamer. His role models were the German theologian Martin Luther and the English republican Oliver Cromwell.

A succession of high-level appointments saved Bismarck from obscurity. In 1852 he was appointed ambassador to the German Confederation at Frankfurt, the only ambassador in Prussian history ever given such an important post without formal training or prior service. Frederick William IV obviously was delighted to be rid of the "red reactionary" of 1848, but he also saw in Bismarck the champion of the prerevolutionary order. In 1859 the king's mental health had deteriorated to the point that his brother Prince William was appointed regent (until 1861). Bent on improving Austro-German relations, Prince William removed the abrasive Bismarck to St. Petersburg. After a brief stint as ambassador to Paris, Bismarck became prime minister of Prussia in 1862 — without an influential circle of social friends and without ever having served in any cabinet.

Bismarck's high-level entrée into Prussian politics in 1862 came about ironically as the result of a bitter domestic dispute. William I (1861–1888) loved nothing better than his army and, as we have seen, had been appalled by the chaotic mobilization of 1859 during the Italian War. Above all, William I, along with War Minister Albrecht von Roon, insisted that the army remain an instrument of royal power, officered by the very landed nobility that Frederick William I had recruited for the military. Soldiers served for three years with the line, two in the reserves, and eleven in the militia (*Landwehr*).

Since the days of reform after 1806, the liberals had a different vision. They regarded the *Landwehr*, especially, as the symbol of democratic nationalism and wished to see it officered by their own bourgeois offspring, with regular service limited to two years. Thus, two quite distinct visions of the Prussian military existed by the mid-nineteenth century. In theory the Prussian army adhered to universal male conscription. But while Prussia's population had doubled since 1815, the annual draft of recruits taken in had remained steady at forty thousand. Put differently, some twenty-three thousand eligible young men annually escaped service with the colors. The liberals

[1] The American critic (and rabid Germanophile) H. L. Mencken (1880–1956) was also a descendant of this family, a member of which emigrated to the United States after the 1848 revolution.

The White Revolutionary: Bismarck in Cuirassier uniform (1874).

were not inclined to provide funds to train additional recruits as long as the government refused to reform the military system.

But the issue was not really military. General Helmuth von Moltke, chief of the General Staff, conceded that five weeks sufficed to train a recruit. The army required the remaining time to "educate" the minds and hearts of the draftees along disciplined, monarchical lines. The army was to be the "school of the nation." The liberals wanted the role of teacher in that school. When it was denied them, they refused to pass the annual army budget. Bismarck was appointed prime minister in 1862 in large measure to resolve this impasse.

Bismarck brought to his new office what few others possessed: a clear concept of Prussia's role in future German affairs and an iron will to execute that policy. Anyone who reads his letters and official documents sees not only a masterful style but also a brilliant understanding of European affairs. Bismarck knew what he wanted, and he appreciated the concerns that motivated the other players on the European chessboard. He understood the dialectic of action and reaction. His position papers were precise, disciplined, and cold. A smattering of foreign phrases attested to his linguistic skills in Greek, Latin, French, English, and Russian.

Bismarck saw the state as a historic entity, an organ of power, the executor of the national will. At the time of the Punctation of Olmütz in 1850, he had given a clear expostulation of his views: "The only sound basis of a great state is egoism, not romanticism; it is beneath the dignity of a great state to fight for a cause which lies outside its own interest." This sentiment would later be celebrated as *Realpolitik*. When it came to furthering Prussia's "own interest," he could be flexible in his approach yet brutal in his methods. He never forgot; he never forgave. He loved to spend his nights in bed hating. He kept a file with the names of all who in his opinion had ever wronged him — and he hounded them into, and even beyond, the grave.[1]

The guiding principle of Bismarck's policies is summed up in a comment from his early career: "Prussian I am, and Prussian I want to remain." Thus he had gone out of his way at the German Confederation to bait the Austrians. Harking back to the days of Austro-Prussian dualism under Frederick II, he fervently believed that Prussia should not merge with the other German states. Prussia was not to play second fiddle to Austria but rather to settle the issue of primacy in Germany as in 1740 by a test of arms. That was the gist of his famous declaration before the budget commission of the Prussian parliament in 1862: the "great issues of the day" would be decided not by speeches and majority votes, as attempted at Frankfurt in 1849, but rather by "iron and blood," on the field of battle. And when William I, in reference to Oliver Cromwell's act of regicide in 1649, shrank back in horror — "I see how it will end — on the gallows. You will suffer the fate of Strafford and I of Charles I" — Bismarck coldly admonished his king, "Better that than surrender."

The constitutional crisis engendered by the impasse over passage of the annual army budget demanded immediate attention. Bismarck did not accept the necessity of three-year military service, but he firmly believed that the army needed to be preserved as an instrument of the crown. General Edwin von Manteuffel put it brutally: the military demanded to know whether "the law and no longer the king was its lord." The liberal deputy Hermann Schulze-Delitzsch countered by declaring that the constitutional conflict could not be resolved until "parliament is backed by a people's army standing amid an

[1] When the liberal leader Eduard Lasker died in 1884 while visiting the United States, Bismarck not only refused to convey to the German parliament an official message of condolence from the House of Representatives but used the opportunity to vilify Lasker's role in German politics.

armed people." Therewith, the struggle became one over a parliamentary versus a royal army.

Bismarck resolved the impasse with a piece of constitutional chicanery. Because under the Prussian bicameral system funds could be expended only with the consent of the king as well as both the House of Lords and the House of Deputies and because the latter now refused to fulfill its constitutional obligation, Bismarck argued that a gap existed in the constitution. There remained no other course for the government but to run the affairs of state in lieu of consent. Parliament repeatedly refused to pass a budget, and just as often, it was dissolved. But taxes were collected, and the army was expanded. At the height of the conflict, Bismarck even toyed with the notion of using the "red menace" to frighten the liberals. In the end he desisted, realizing that Ferdinand Lassalle's tiny General German Workers' Association lacked the power to act as shock agents. "What could the poor devil offer me?" Bismarck mused.

In 1864 the Schleswig-Holstein question resurfaced in time to launch Bismarck onto the national stage. Its complexity was legendary. Lord Palmerston in England perhaps put it best when he stated that only three men had ever grasped its ramifications: one was dead, the second had been driven mad by it, and he, the third, had forgotten all about it. The long and the short of it was that the two duchies were in personal union with the Danish royal house, while only Holstein was officially part of the German Confederation. Schleswig, the center of Danish nationalist agitation, possessed a German minority. In March 1863 Frederick VII, king of Denmark, sought to annex Schleswig outright and to promulgate a new constitution for Holstein. His successor, King Christian IX, moved to enact Frederick VII's annexationist program in November. This provoked a wave of national protest throughout the German lands.

Bismarck cared little for Schleswig-Holstein ("It is no concern of ours whether the Germans of Holstein are happy") and even less for Frederick Duke of Augustenburg, the rival German claimant to the duchies. But he worried that the disputed territories might become the object of a German national outburst as they had in 1848–1849, and any renewed demand for national self-determination might sweep away more than the two duchies. He chose to deal with the matter purely as one of international law, denouncing Denmark's annexation of Schleswig as a clear violation of the Treaty of London (1852), which had decreed Danish administration of the duchies. This shrewd move not only prevented the interested powers, particularly Britain and Russia, from interfering in the matter but also attracted Austria as an ally to uphold the international order and to combat national self-determination in Germany.

On January 16, 1864, Berlin and Vienna demanded that Copenhagen rescind the annexation of Schleswig as well as the constitution for Holstein. Denmark refused. Five days later, Austrian and Prussian troops, aided by Saxon and Hanoverian units, occupied Holstein. Early in February they entered Schleswig. On April 18, after a tenacious defense of the fortifications on the Düppel peninsula, Danish forces capitulated and withdrew to Alsen Island off Schleswig. Their defeat on June 28 effectively ended the war. King Christian IX gave up his claims to Schleswig-Holstein in favor of Austria and Prussia. Under the terms of the Bad Gastein Convention (August 1865), Berlin and Vienna agreed to separate administration for the two duchies.

In January 1866, partly to offset indignation in Germany over the curt manner in which the claims of the duke of Augustenburg had been ignored in Vienna, the Austrian administration in Holstein permitted popular agitation on behalf of the duke. Bismarck at once denounced this action as a breach of the Gastein Convention. He countered the Austrian initiative in April by demanding that a German parliament, elected by universal, equal, and secret manhood suffrage, be convened at once. In June Austria blocked this course by bringing the Schleswig-Holstein question before the German Confederation. Prussia reacted by occupying Austrian Holstein.

There is little doubt that Bismarck desired war with Austria. "The clock of German dualism," he informed an associate, "has to be put right by war." The chancellor secured an alliance with Italy and reminded Russia not only of Prussia's benevolent neutrality during the Crimean War of 1853–1856, when Austria had sided with Britain and France against Russia at the last moment, but also of Prussia's recent support of Russia during the Polish uprising of 1863.

Prussian forces invaded Bohemia on June 21. General von Moltke used the superior north German railroad system speedily to mobilize his forces, ranging from east Prussia to the Rhineland, and to concentrate them against the hesitant, defensive-minded Austrian general, Ludwig August von Benedek. By using his telegraph system effectively, Moltke advanced against the Austrians in two formations, thereby concealing his true strength from Benedek. On July 3, 1866, the Prussians handed the Austrians a crushing defeat at Königgrätz (Sadowa) on the Elbe. One-quarter of the Habsburg army was lost, and the rest retreated toward Vienna. Emperor Francis Joseph sued for peace at Nikolsburg on July 26. Bismarck proved magnanimous in victory and took no territory from Austria, for he had achieved his major purpose: Prussia was now the premier German power.

The Austro-Prussian War of 1866 was a brilliant vindication of the Prussian military system but a German tragedy. One-half million soldiers had fought for the two major German states at Königgrätz that July 3, and one in four became a casualty of this civil strife. Austria surrendered its primacy in Germany, thereby ending the period of dualism launched by Frederick II in 1740, and reached a Compromise (*Ausgleich*) with the Magyars of Hungary. Vienna also rerouted its interests down the Danube toward the Balkans and the Black Sea.

The states of the so-called Third Germany that had sided with Austria were the principal losers: the kingdoms of Bavaria, Hanover, and Württemberg; the grand duchies of Baden, Hesse-Kassel, Hesse-Darmstadt; and the

PRUSSIA BEFORE AND AFTER THE AUSTRO-PRUSSIAN WAR

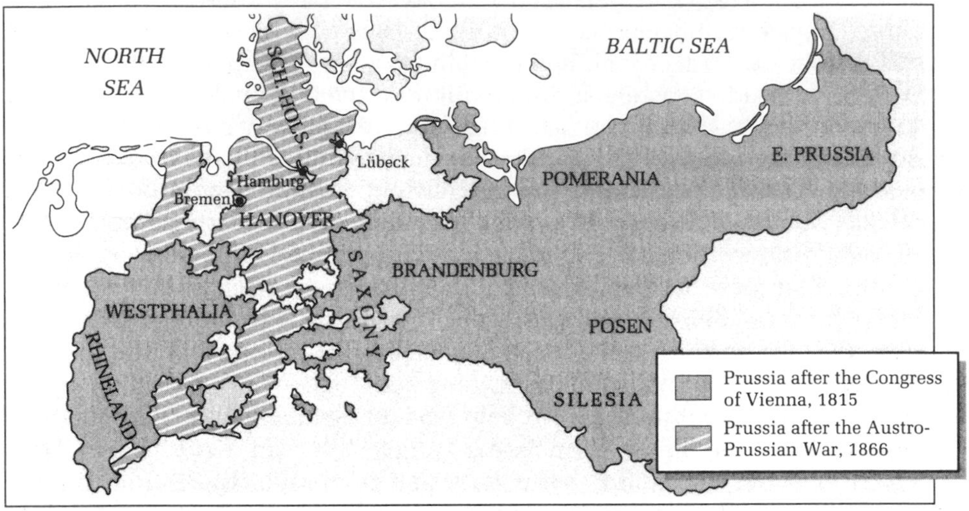

imperial city of Frankfurt, which was forced to pay Prussia an indemnity of 31 million gulden. Other losers included the Catholics (covered in more detail later), the notion of a unitary state (*Einheitsstaat*), the desire of conservatives such as Leopold von Gerlach and Friedrich J. Stahl to restore Metternich's European concert of 1815, and the very principle of legitimacy. Bismarck summarily deposed George V, king of Hanover, and seized his royal revenues.[1] The slogan of the anti-Prussian party in Württemberg — "Pay taxes. Shut up. Become soldiers" — neatly sums up the cost of Königgrätz to the Third Germany.

The most obvious winner was Bismarck, who received a grant of 400,000 thaler[2] with which he purchased an estate at Varzin. His "lesser German" (*Kleindeutsch)* solution to national unity had triumphed. Prussia annexed Schleswig-Holstein, Hanover, Hesse-Kassel, Nassau, and Frankfurt and engineered military alliances with the three south German states of Baden, Bavaria, and Württemberg. The Prussian historian Heinrich von Treitschke crowed: "Our revolution is being completed as it was begun, from above." Yet with the accuracy of historical hindsight, it also is obvious that historic Prussia was among the losers: it swallowed up alien lands that its bureaucrats were unable to digest, it extended its financial, judicial, and military systems to states that did not desire them, and forced its economic domination after 1868 on those same states under the umbrella of the *Zollparlament.*

---

[1] Bismarck used this so-called reptile fund to influence the press and foreign states.

[2] Or 1.2 million marks in the new currency about to be introduced.

The battle of Königgrätz also marked the end of Bismarck's conflict with the Prussian liberals. On September 3, 1866, the Prussian parliament passed an indemnity bill by a vote of 230 to 75. Bismarck conceded that he had ruled illegally since 1862, and parliament forgave him that malfeasance. Most liberals agreed that their political and national aims could more easily be accomplished within a national state. Only a small democratic minority insisted that might did not necessarily make right and vowed to fight on as a "vigilant and loyal opposition." With the benefit of historical hindsight, it is clear that the Prussian landed gentry managed to cling to power in Prussia-Germany for several more decades as a result of the liberals' surrender to Bismarck in 1866, that the military was elevated to a position of great power within the new state, and that socioeconomic tensions of the first magnitude were created by Bismarck's triumph over the forces of liberalism.

Finally, the German Confederation at Frankfurt ceased to exist. In its place Bismarck created the North German Confederation comprising a swollen Prussia and its recently annexed territories together with the few remaining north German states. The chancellor took great care to draft its constitution in order to ensure Prussian domination of the confederation. He opted for a bicameral system. The king of Prussia, William I, not only became the crowned head of the North German Confederation but was accorded exclusive power to decide foreign and military policy. Only the king could appoint (and dismiss) ministers. The Federal Council (*Bundesrat*) consisted of forty-three representatives of the north German states. Each had a single vote, but Prussia had seventeen votes because it exercised the votes of its recently annexed lands. And since any constitutional change required a two-thirds majority, Prussia's seventeen ballots gave it veto power. The Federal Council exercised control over defense and foreign policy, domestic and foreign economic policy, and communications and commercial law. The size of the standing army was set at 1 percent of the population and funded at the rate of 225 thaler per recruit.

The lower house (Reichstag) was elected by the most liberal franchise in Europe: universal, secret, manhood suffrage. Its members enjoyed immunity from legal prosecution, had the right to petition the Federal Council, and annually voted the budget. Reichstag deputies were not paid because Bismarck feared that salaries would create a special class of professional politicians. The chancellor, who presented the government's proposed legislation to parliament, was assisted by a host of state secretaries and served at the pleasure of the Prussian king. In this way the chancellor sought to evade the notion of "cabinet responsibility" as existed in Britain.

Bismarck pursued a policy of economic freedom within the confederation. People were free to move and to form commercial companies as well as coalitions of workers. Internal tariffs were dismantled. A unified patent and copyright law and a unified criminal law code were promulgated. A federal postal and telegraph service was created. Religious freedom was proclaimed and all bureaucratic obstacles to marriage removed. The Prussian tax system, civil laws, and military service were extended to the territories annexed in 1866. Finally, a new flag was devised for the North German Confederation. Bismarck rejected the liberal black-red-gold colors out of hand and instead fused the Prussian black and white with the Hanseatic red and white to create the new national tricolors.

The chancellor accomplished much of this domestic reform with the assistance of the National Liberal party. Initially founded by Rudolf von Bennigsen in Hanover, the National Liberals' strength lay in the states recently annexed by Prussia. The party drew its support mainly from industrialists, merchants, and the educational elite. After Königgrätz it made its peace with Bismarck. A group of dissident liberals — men such as Rudolf Virchow, Theodor Mommsen, and Hermann Schulze-Delitzsch — continued to uphold the liberal position espoused during the constitutional conflict and to view Bismarck with suspicion.

Bismarck posed a conundrum also for the Conservatives. Many of its august leaders, including the chancellor's erstwhile supporters Leopold and Ludwig von Gerlach, were shocked by what they considered the lawlessness of the recent Prussian annexations. As monarchists they were especially outraged by the deposition of the Hanoverian king. Moreover, they berated Bismarck for failing to use the military victory over Austria to destroy parliamentarism. To their horror the chancellor after 1867 moved ever closer to liberalism. Yet as Prussian royalists, they could not go into open opposition. Instead, they grumbled about lost opportunities and the chancellor's lack of Christian-Germanic morality. Their strength lay with the Lutheran feudal gentry (Junkers) of historic Brandenburg, Pomerania, and East Prussia.

A more open-minded and flexible minority faction, comprising predominantly rich Rhenish and Silesian noblemen (mainly Catholic or nonreligious) who had combined agrarian and industrial interests, seceded from the Conservative party to found the Free Conservative Union. Less parochial and dogmatic than the old-line Conservatives, these Free Conservative Unionists were able to attract a good many conservative voters from the non-Prussian lands. They exerted their influence mainly through their great wealth.

Bismarck was quick to realize that he had let the genie of nationalism out of the bottle. One day after the battle of Königgrätz, the French emperor, Napoleon III, after initially promising to remain neutral in this German civil war, had threatened to intervene. His asking price for neutrality had been Belgium and Luxembourg. Bismarck, while denying Napoleon these territories, took note: "We shall need the national swindle later as protection against French demands."

The opportunity to use this "protection" arose over the Spanish throne candidacy. When the Spanish parliament (Cortes) at Madrid in February 1870 picked Prince Leopold, a member of the Catholic branch (Sigmaringen) of the House of Hohenzollern and a Prussian army officer, the French objected. For centuries they had fought what they had conceived to be Habsburg dynastic "encirclement" by Austria and Spain. Were they now about to face Hohenzollern "encirclement" from Prussia and Spain? Moreover, the Hohenzollern-Sigmaringen family had extremely intimate ties to the thrones of Portugal and Rumania. By law, the decision rested with William I as head of the Hohenzollern clan. William was "utterly against the affair" and in May gained an agreement from Prince Leopold not to pursue the Spanish offer of a crown. But France was not content with this diplomatic triumph. The French foreign minister, the duke de Gramont, instructed his ambassador to Prussia, Count Benedetti, to go to Bad Ems, where the Prussian king was taking the cure, and induce William I "if not to order, at least to advise" Leopold or any other Hohenzollern against going to Spain in the future. In case of a negative reply, Gramont informed Benedetti, "It is war." Above all, Gramont demanded that Benedetti extract from William I "assurances that he will not authorize a renewal of the candidacy."

William I naturally declined to make a binding decision for the future on behalf of the Sigmaringen branch of the family. He informed Bismarck by telegram of what had transpired and left it to the chancellor's discretion to inform the French. Bismarck spied his chance. He carefully edited the king's communication by excising all conciliatory phrases from it, leaving only the passages that conveyed William's refusal to have further dealings with Count Benedetti. The so-called Ems Dispatch, when published in the press, uncorked the forces of nationalism in both France and Germany. Howling crowds in Paris surged through the streets screaming: "To Berlin!" "Down with Prussia!"

Where does the responsibility for the war lie? Bismarck's most exhaustive biographer, Otto Pflanze, concludes that there is no decisive answer as to what motivated Bismarck to push the Spanish throne candidacy to the brink of war. Pflanze surmises, however, that Bismarck seized the moment in order to provoke either war with France or a French diplomatic humiliation. In the chancellor's view, national unity could be achieved only at the expense of France. In a candid moment Bismarck spoke of the "unavoidable necessity" of a war with France: Napoleon III needed war to shore up his unstable regime, Bismarck in order to mobilize German national sentiment behind Prussia. On July 19, 1871, France declared war on Prussia.

The Franco-Prussian War of 1870–1871 was perhaps the most bitter struggle since the Napoleonic wars of 1799–1815, and its ramifications lasted for more than three generations. The French invaded Germany with cries of "revenge for Sadowa" and fought to maintain their primacy — real or imagined — on the Continent. The Prussians fought to erase their defeats at the hands of Napoleon at Jena and Auerstädt in 1806 and to complete the process of unification. Whereas the Austro-Prussian War of 1866 had been an old-fashioned cabinet war, pitting one dynasty and royal army against another, the Franco-Prussian War was a people's war, conducted with all the passion and animosity that such struggles can engender.

The war proved costly. The new Krupp breechloading steel guns and the Dreyse needlegun, as well as French repeating rifle (*chassepot*), took a heavy toll of infantry. Cavalry was decimated by massed rifle power. The spectacular

GERMANY, 1871

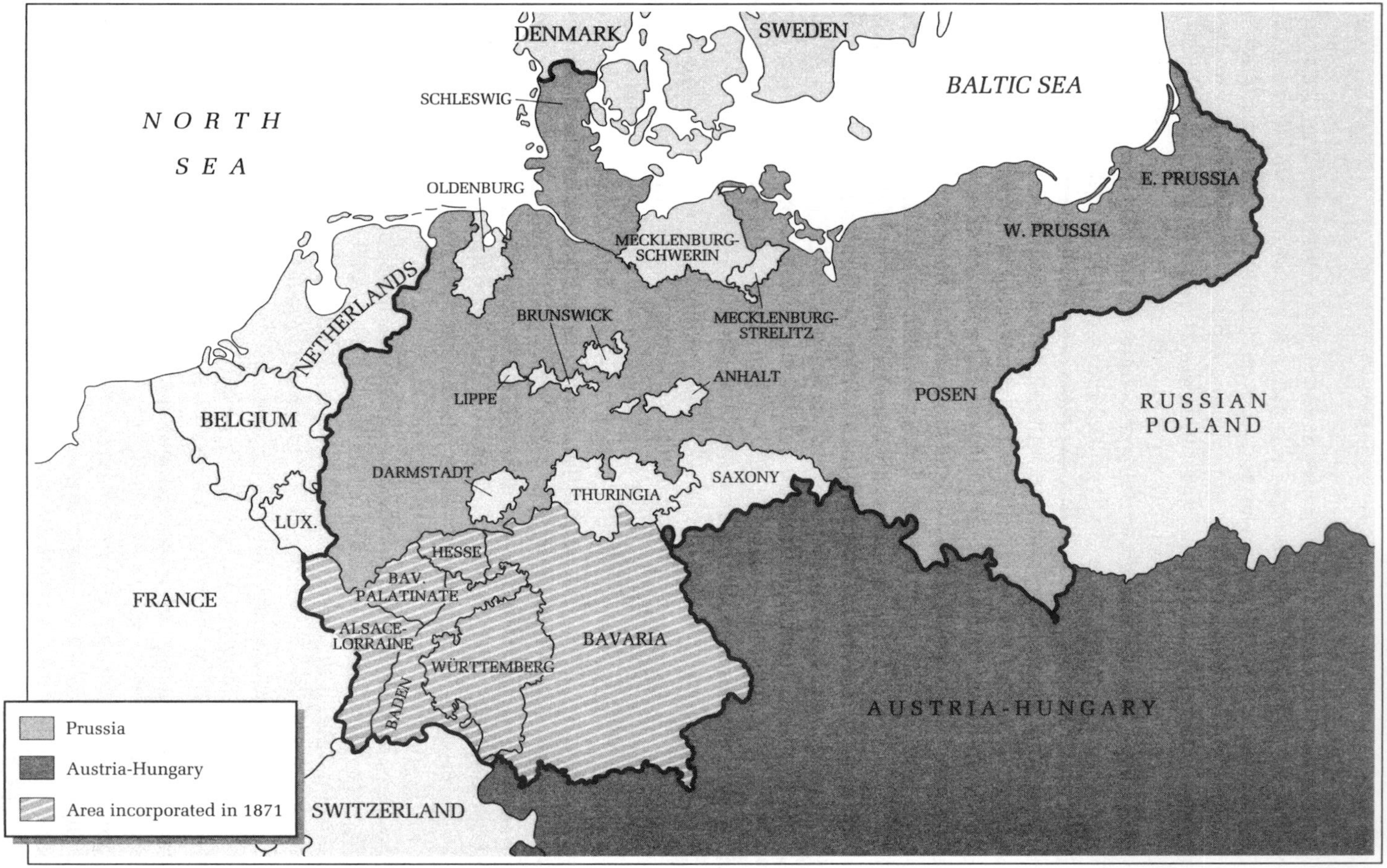

German victory at Sedan on September 2, 1870, was followed not by peace but by guerrilla warfare and a popular uprising organized by Léon Gambetta and Jules Favre of the newly created Government of National Defense in France. Paris was besieged, bombed, and starved. National hatreds flamed on both sides.

Ultimately, a deep clash developed within the German ranks. Bismarck, wary lest the other European powers intervene, pushed the military for a quick end to the war, if need be by bombing Paris into submission. Moltke, reversing Clausewitz, demanded that the military decide national strategy during wartime. German security, in Moltke's mind, could be guaranteed only by total victory over all French forces. When the French capitulated, William I was spared from making a fundamental decision whether statecraft or military considerations deserved primacy during times of national emergency. His failure to make this decision had dire consequences in subsequent German history.

The passions engendered by this war precluded a simple return to the *status quo ante bellum*. Strassburg and Alsace, Metz and Lorraine were minimum demands put forth by both the generals and the public in the name of national security. The hawks in Germany wanted nothing less than to dismember France. An army victory parade through the conquered capital, a gesture that Bismarck forbade at Vienna in 1866, was demanded by the generals to show the new order in Europe. An indemnity, calculated per capita to the reparations imposed on Prussia by Napoleon after 1806, was levied against the new French Republic. And on January 18, 1871, William I was crowned German emperor in the Hall of Mirrors at Versailles Palace, a further insult to French pride. The historian Pflanze has accurately depicted the coronation as the union of three powerful traditions: Hohenzollern authoritarianism, Prussian militarism, and German nationalism.

Germany justified the annexation of Alsace-Lorraine on the ground that both were former territories of the Holy Roman Empire. Moreover, they were strategically important salient heights on the left bank of the Rhine river. But the argument for annexation quickly took on a shrill tone as German nationalists demanded the provinces on the basis that their inhabitants were German by language and race. The historian Treitschke declared that French rule in Alsace-Lorraine had constituted "a crime against the reason of history, a subjugation of free men by half-educated barbarians."

In the long run, annexation proved a heavy burden on Germany's future. France never forgot the loss. The statues of Strassburg and Metz at the Place de la Concorde in Paris remained draped in black until 1918. Cries of revenge for the "gap in the Vosges" never died. The annexation, combined with the French insistence on regaining the provinces, committed Germany to a future policy of isolating France and denying it alliances.

Nor was the annexation Prussian policy: it was an act of German nationalism. The national euphoria clamored for the return of the crown of Charlemagne from Vienna. Even the throne of Henry III (1017–1056) had to be brought to Berlin from Goslar to signify continuity from the "first" to the "second" Reich. Yet the last representative of ancient Prussia, William I, reportedly depicted his imperial coronation at Versailles as the saddest day of his life. "Today we carry the Old Prussia to its grave."

The three south German states succumbed equally to what Bismarck sardonically called the "national swindle" and merged with the North German Confederation to form the German Empire. Bavaria did so only after Bismarck reached deep into the Hanoverian "reptile funds" of 1866 to finance Ludwig II's castle-building mania. Bismarck personally also fared well. He was created a prince and received the Duchy of Lauenburg, just outside Hamburg today, with his residence at Friedrichsruh.

Why had Bismarck, the arch-Prussian, gone down the path of national unity? Part of the answer lies in the fact that for all his indomitable will, Bismarck was basically a determinist. He viewed history, as he once put it, as a mighty river that flowed inexorably toward an unknown end. The great statesman could at best act as helmsman, throwing the rudder left or right, but he could not reverse course. On yet another occasion Bismarck avowed that he could but try to discern God's grand design, take hold of the hem of his gown, and follow his footsteps. Put into the context of Germany in the 1860s, this meant that the great force of nationalism could not be denied; unification would come. The only question was who would carry it out. Bismarck was determined that Prussia should become the agent of unification. Was it not better to control the process than to watch others carry it out? "Let us, so to speak, put Germany in the saddle," he had stated in March 1867; "it will know how to ride." In keeping with this rustic imagery, the Iron Chancellor often proclaimed that in every situation there was always a rider and a horse. There was no question which he preferred to be.

"Honest Broker" or Metternich Reincarnate?

Bismarck, having in Disraeli's words "entirely destroyed" the European balance, worked after 1871 to consolidate the gains of his first nine years in office. He had no desire to overthrow the European pentarchy of powers but only wished to be a major part of it. "When there are five," he proclaimed, "try to be one of three." The recurrent outbreak of territorial squabbles in the Balkan region,[1] especially, convinced him that European affairs needed to be run through some sort of clearing-house, say, at Berlin. Only in this manner, Bismarck reasoned, could the territorial aspirations of Austria-Hungary, Italy, and Russia in the Balkans be held in check.

Bismarck was nagged by doubts concerning the viability of the new Reich. He questioned Prussia's leadership capabilities beyond the military. He was

[1] The lands of southeastern Europe lying between Hungary and Greece were the object of intense interest on the part of Austria-Hungary, Italy, Russia, and the Ottoman Empire.

not certain whether nationalism was a sufficient bond to tie Bavarian to Prussian, Saxon to Rhinelander. In May 1872, at one of his famous political evenings featuring a drink called "black velvet" (half beer, half champagne), shrimp, and maraschino cherries — all devoured simultaneously — Bismarck gave free rein to his fears: "Sleep brings me no rejuvenation, when I sleep at all." Dark visions of impending doom haunted him. "The other day I saw a map of Germany before me, and there appeared one blotch of foul decay after the other. Finally, they all peeled off the map."

Bismarck's greatest fear was a new Kaunitz coalition as in 1756 consisting of Austria and France (and possibly Russia) for "the total destruction of Prussia." French newspapers taunted the chancellor by writing of his "nightmare of coalitions" — possible diplomatic plots that France could engineer against the Reich. Frederick II had answered similar threats in 1740 and again in 1756 with war. What would Bismarck do? He toyed with three possible options: offer compensation to the other European powers for Prussia's recent gains, resort to preemptive strikes to establish German hegemony on the Continent, or preserve the status quo and maintain a permanent defensive.

In March 1875 the French Chamber passed the Army Organization Law raising the number of battalions per infantry regiment from three to four. The General Staff in Berlin panicked. The newspaper *Post* brought out an anonymous lead article, most likely placed by either the chancellor or the military: "Is War in Sight?" It caused a run on the stock markets. War fever ran high. Paris turned to London and St. Petersburg and received assurances that neither Britain nor Russia would allow a second German defeat of France. Bismarck quickly realized the limitations on his freedom of diplomatic maneuver.

In 1875–1876 Bulgaria, Serbia, and Montenegro revolted against Turkish rule in the Balkans. Alexander II of Russia, driven by pan-Slav agitation at home, declared war against Turkey early in 1877. Once again, events in the Balkans threatened the European balance. Bismarck reacted with alacrity. In June 1877 he convened the equivalent of an academic retreat at Bad Kissingen. There, ostensibly to shed their annual winter fat, Bismarck and his son Herbert assessed Germany's potential, liabilities, and options.

The resulting Bad Kissingen Dictate is a model of clarity and simplicity. Bismarck conceded that the "nightmare of coalitions" was a perennial danger. Germany was wedged in between two powerful land powers, France to the west and Russia to the east. Britain was on guard to preserve the balance of power against further erosion. As a result, Bismarck ruled out any new territorial aggrandizement. Germany, he argued with reference to Metternich, was "saturated" and did not need any more Danes, French, or Poles. The Iron Chancellor decided to be satisfied with the Reich's present position of "semi-hegemony" in Europe.

Bismarck's ideal was a Europe in which "all the powers except France need us, and thus will be deterred as far as possible from coalitions against us by their relations to one another." In simple terms, France was to be isolated diplomatically while the other major powers were to be brought into a web of alliances radiating out from Berlin. As long as Germany did not build a fleet, Bismarck reasoned, British vital interests would not be threatened. When it was suggested to him that in case of a new war on the Continent London might land an army in Denmark, Bismarck caustically stated that he would send a police officer and ten men to arrest it. Nor did he fear hostility from the other major continental powers. Russia and Prussia-Germany were united by a common bond, Polish territory. And Austria had accepted the defeat of 1866. It had surrendered its erstwhile leading role in Germany, reached a compromise with the Magyar nobility, and redirected its efforts down the Danube. The time seemed ripe to secure the Reich through alliances.

If Bismarck needed further inducement, he received it in March 1878 when Russia imposed humiliating peace terms on Turkey in the Treaty of San Stefano. Austrian and British protests against Russian incursions into the Balkans raised the specter of a new European war. That Germany was now the diplomatic center of Europe was evidenced by the Congress of Berlin, convened in the capital in June 1878. Arm-in-arm with "the old Jew" Disraeli, Bismarck concocted one of those devious European deals that later would so agitate U.S. president Woodrow Wilson. Austria-Hungary received administrative control of Bosnia and Herzegovina; Russia was forced to surrender most of its military gains save the Bessarabian lands; and the disputed provinces of Moldavia and Wallachia were recognized as united, independent Rumania under a German prince. While Bismarck basked in his role as "honest broker," Gerson Bleichröder, his banker, curtly reminded the chancellor: "There is no such thing as an honest broker!"

Bismarck now proceeded with his alliance plans. In October 1879 he concluded the Dual Alliance with Austria, expanded in 1882 to include Italy and in 1883 Rumania. While grumbling about tying "Prussia's trim little frigate" to Austria's "worm-eaten man-of-war" and curbing Italy's "ravenous appetite" for land, Bismarck nevertheless entered into firm alliances with Vienna and Rome in order to tie both to Berlin, thereby precluding their individual adventures in the Balkans. The capstone of the alliance system was the Reinsurance Treaty with Russia in 1887. Its very name indicates its centrality in Bismarck's diplomacy. Both powers agreed to remain neutral if one of them was at war with a third power — except if Russia or Germany started a war against Austria-Hungary or France. Bismarck thereby thwarted a possible Franco-Russian alliance and assured himself a mediating role between Vienna and St. Petersburg.

Historians later spoke of a *pax Germanica*. To be sure, Germany became the pivotal center of Europe; all "wires" ran through Berlin. Bismarck's goal was to freeze the status quo. Although secret, all treaties were leaked to concerned parties as a further deterrent to war. Codicils appended to each treaty stated that it was null and void if the other contracting power upset the balance in the Balkans. Bismarck was determined that no single power should dominate that area. If Austria-Hungary were displaced there by Russia, Germany would face Russia on three sides, making a future struggle between

Berlin and St. Petersburg inevitable. One ought not create a power vacuum, Bismarck argued, without being willing to fill that void. Germany was not prepared to do so in the Balkans; hence, the chancellor's quip that the area was not worth "the bones of a single Pomeranian grenadier." Austria-Hungary would have to be upheld as a major power but reined in, so to speak, by Germany.

The "nightmare of coalitions" no longer haunted Bismarck. Where could the French desire for revenge for 1870–1871 (*revanchisme*) find fertile soil? Denmark? Holland? Luxembourg? Liechtenstein? As Bismarck lectured William I: "We, situated in the center of Europe, must not be exposed to isolation." Two cardinal axioms drove the chancellor's policy: no conflicts among the major powers in central Europe, and German security without German hegemony. It was collective security, decades before the term was coined.

In the mid–1880s overseas developments briefly diverted Bismarck's attention from central Europe. German merchants such as Adolf Lüderitz of Bremen and Adolf Woermann of Hamburg had acquired property and established commercial stations along the coast of western Africa. Carl Peters, the adventurous son of a Lutheran pastor, concurrently convinced some African chieftains along the southern east African coast to recognize his "protection" of the area. Lüderitz, Woermann, and Peters, fearing possible British enmity, appealed to Bismarck for formal recognition of their holdings. When London refused to take seriously Bismarck's request that it accept Germany's new position in Africa, the chancellor in April 1884 established protectorates over German South-West Africa (today Namibia), Togo, and the Cameroons. In February 1885 he granted a patent of protection for German East Africa (today Tanzania). And three months later he extended German protection to Adolf von Hansemann's possessions in northeastern New Guinea (Kaiser-Wilhelms-Land and the Bismarck-Archipelago).

One reason behind the Iron Chancellor's brief flirtation with colonial ventures lies in his European diplomacy. He knew well that Britain and France were on a collision course in Egypt, the Sudan, and Indochina, and he spied a chance to play Paris off against London. In the words of the English historian A. J. P. Taylor, Bismarck's colonial policy was no more than "the accidental by-product of an abortive Franco-German entente" directed against Britain. Overseas competition was simply the extension of Bismarck's European security policy to the periphery.

Bismarck was also influenced by the national enthusiasm for colonies as an expression of great power status. The founding of the Colonial League in 1882 by Peters and such academic luminaries as Gustav Schmoller, Heinrich von Sybel, and Heinrich von Treitschke, and its endorsement by a large segment of the educated and propertied middle class, no doubt impressed him. But he dropped the colonial game the minute that it no longer served its purpose of separating France from Great Britain. When pressed by Eugen Wolff in 1888 to define a bold colonial policy, Bismarck lectured the German explorer:

"Your map of Africa is very nice, indeed. But my map of Africa lies here in Europe: here is Russia, and here lies France; and we are in the middle. That is my map of Africa." In May 1889 he offered to sell all the Reich's possessions in Africa to Italy.

What distinguished Bismarck's foreign policy from that of his successors was that he was content to accept German semihegemony in Europe and to eschew a Napoleonic policy of hegemony. He understood the dialectic of European diplomacy: every piece on the diplomatic chessboard interacted with every other piece; none moved in isolation from the others. Most important, he appreciated that Germany's security as a land power situated at the geographical heart of Europe depended on avoidance of conflict in central Europe. It was really as simple as that.

Constitutional Engineering, Catholics, and Workers

Bismarck was less successful in domestic politics. It would not be unfair to state that many of the ills that plagued Germany after unification were a direct consequence of his heavy-handed style. The statesman who could juggle the five balls of the European pentarchy in the air with such dexterity never developed the concept of compromise within the peculiar German semiconstitutional system. Bismarck set out from the start to establish his command over internal affairs. Once more his goal was to ensure the dominance of Prussia within the new Reich, to secure the Protestant agrarian order of his aristocratic class, and to retard parliamentary development along British lines.

Bismarck was fully aware of the importance of constitutional law, and he studied the constitutions of the United States and the Frankfurt Parliament of 1849 before setting out to draft a document for Germany. The constitution of the North German Confederation (1867–1871) was extended to the German Empire on April 16, 1871, creating a federal rather than a unitary state. The locus of political power remained the Federal Council (*Bundesrat*), where the representatives of twenty-five states (*Länder*) and free cities sat. Legislation was first introduced and debated in this upper house before being passed on to the lower house for approval. As Paul Laband, the noted constitutional scholar of the day, noted: "The German Empire is not a legal body of 40 million members, but rather of twenty-five members." Prussia maintained its veto in the Federal Council, thereby precluding sudden, unwanted constitutional changes.

The Reichstag, in contrast to the Prussian lower house (where the three-class suffrage remained in effect until 1918), was elected by the most progressive franchise in Europe: universal, secret, equal, direct, manhood suffrage. Its members enjoyed immunity but remained unpaid until 1906. The Reichstag's greatest power was that of the purse. Every four years — after 1874, every seven years — it had the duty to approve or reject the army budget. And because Prussia territorially constituted two-thirds of Germany, the head of the

Krupp empire at Essen was equal only to a single one of his male workers in German elections but more than equal to all his work force combined in Prussian elections.

Given that Prussian elections were open and indirect, it can easily be seen how rural voters, especially, could be persuaded to vote for the local Conservative. Hellmuth von Gerlach left a vivid description of the formally secret and direct Reichstag elections in the Prussian countryside:

> There sat the honorable lord at the end of the table as head of the local election committee. At the lunch hour, the workers would be brought in direct from the fields to the voting place, led by the inspector and overseer. Before entering, everyone received the "proper" ballot outside. None dared exchange it for another under the watchful eyes of the honorable lord and his adjutants.

The Bismarckian constitution, then, was a blend of the Prussian and German systems. The king of Prussia, William I, served as hereditary German emperor. The Prussian prime minister customarily served as German chancellor and, during Bismarck's tenure, often as foreign minister and economics minister of both territories. The Prussian prime minister also presided over the Federal Council, where fourteen votes — Prussia cast seventeen out of fifty-eight, far below its proportional territorial and population ratio within the Empire — sufficed as veto. The national flag continued to be black-white-red.

The king of Prussia/German emperor in his capacity as hereditary president of the Federal Council had an exclusive right to conclude alliances and treaties, to accredit ambassadors, to promulgate laws, to declare war, and to make peace. He exercised a command function (*Kommandogewalt*) as supreme commander of the armed forces and controlled all promotions and appointments. With the advice of the chief of the Prussian General Staff, he bore sole responsibility for the national security. The kings of Bavaria, Saxony, and Württemberg retained their armies in peacetime, but during war these troops would become part of a national force under the command of the Hohenzollern monarch and the Prussian (now Great) General Staff. The navy, on the other hand, was created as a federal German force from the start.

The Prussian prime minister and German chancellor served at the pleasure of the monarch. The executive branch of the government — in Prussia, the prime minister and his ministers of state, and in Germany, the chancellor and his state secretaries — was responsible first and foremost to the crown. The monarch alone could appoint and dismiss his prime minister/chancellor. Federalism had been designed to ease the entrance of the south German states into the Prussian-dominated union, but it had come at a cost. The federal government could not levy direct taxes but rather had to do with indirect surcharges on exports and imports as well as road and canal use fees. Berlin could call on the twenty-five states and cities to contribute to the federal budget in times of need, but these state assessments (*Matrikularbeiträge*) hardly constituted a secure financial basis. The imperial chancellor and his state secretaries were given but skeletal staffs, with the (intended) result that they depended highly on the royal Prussian bureaucracy to execute their policies. Most important, Bismarck's constitutional system contained sufficient checks and balances to protect Prussia against any possible German initiatives in constitutional, financial, or military affairs.

It is perhaps ironic, given this conservative Prussian constitutional dominance, that Bismarck in the 1870s became one of Europe's great economic liberals. Political unity in fact led to economic unity. Bismarck streamlined the Prussian-German system in a decade, thereby ending the crippling administrative, economic, financial, and legal particularism (*Zersplitterung*) that had dominated the states of the former Holy Roman Empire. A uniform civil and criminal legal code had been promulgated for the Reich by 1873 and a High Court of Appeals established at Leipzig by 1879. Bismarck nationalized the German railroads in 1875, established a unified postal system (save for Bavaria and Württemberg), and mandated universal elementary education.

To expedite commerce, both at home and abroad, Bismarck replaced the hodgepodge of medieval weights and measures with the metric system. A national treasury and central bank (Reichsbank) after 1875 transformed thirty-three regional currencies into the mark, regulated the supply of money, set interest rates, and monitored the gold standard. The thirty or more regional banks in time were reduced to the four "Big D" banks — Deutsche, Dresdner, Diskonto, and Darmstädter — as well as a residue of private, mainly Jewish, firms, such as Bleichröder, Rothschild, Seligman, and Warburg. All internal tariff barriers were eliminated. Indigenous industry was protected from foreign competition by modest tariffs. The Prussian administrative system and military draft were extended to the other German states. Prussian bureaucrats quickly came to dominate the highest levels of the civil service, judiciary, and diplomatic corps of the Reich.

Much of this reform work was carried out, as previously under the North German Confederation, with the enthusiastic support of the National Liberal party and its leader, Rudolf von Bennigsen. Heirs to the old National Union (*Nationalverein*) of 1859, which had been established at the height of the Italian War in order to awaken the people's interest in the urgency of national unification, the Liberals championed a state built on law (*Rechtsstaat*), a parliamentary state, a constitutional as well as national state. Their members came mainly from the Rhineland, south Germany, and other states of the Third Germany. They had made their peace with Bismarck in 1867. Liberals who continued to cling to the democratic and republican ideas of 1848 and of the constitutional conflict of 1862–1867 remained in the Progressive party (*Fortschrittspartei*), now under the leadership of Eugen Richter. The Progressives sought a parliamentary state on the English model. They championed progress, both social and economic. The National Liberals and Progressives, then, occupied the German political stage from Left-Center to Right-Center. They shared that pivotal spot with the Catholic Center party and were flanked by the Conservatives on the Right and the Social Democrats on the Left.

The Center party (*Zentrumspartei*), led by Ludwig Windthorst, was unique to German politics. Created first in Prussia as a Catholic faction, in 1870 it formally organized itself as a national political party in the German Empire solely to safeguard Catholic rights in a predominantly Protestant state. These special rights concerned Catholic schools, youth groups, lay organizations, and seminaries. The Center party represented about 40 percent of Germans and was strongest in Bavaria, Baden, Silesia, Westphalia, and the Rhineland. Additionally, it embraced the Poles and the new residents of Alsace-Lorraine. Finally, several splinter groups such as the unreconciled Danes from Schleswig and the Hanoverians (Guelphs) completed the Bismarckian political spectrum.

To the right of the Center party stood the Conservative party, by and large an unhappy group: unhappy over the formation of the North German Confederation, the Indemnity Bill, unification, and Bismarck's liberal economic policies of the 1870s. Although the Conservatives were members of Bismarck's socioeconomic group, they nevertheless continued to view with suspicion what they termed Bismarck's lack of political morality. The Free Conservatives, now led by industrialists such as Wilhelm von Kardorff and Karl Baron von Stumm, proved more supportive of the Iron Chancellor. A party basically of the rich, the Free Conservatives consisted of aristocratic agrarians and great industrialists.

To the left of all the political parties stood the Social Democratic party of Germany (*Sozialdemokratische Partei Deutschlands).* In 1875 the SPD emerged through a fusion of Lassalle's General German Workers' Association of 1863 and August Bebel and Wilhelm Liebknecht's Social Democratic Workers' party of 1869. The latter gave the SPD its openly Marxist theoretical framework, and the former imbued it with a sense of political activism. It rose directly in response to the growth of German industry and the accompanying process of urbanization.

After unification, German industrial development took off. In the first three years after the founding of the German Empire alone, no fewer than 857 corporations with a combined capital of 3.3 billion marks were established. During these founding years of the Reich, more iron smelting and iron working firms were established than in all the previous years of the nineteenth century. Rich coal deposits were exploited in the Ruhr, Westphalia, the Saar, Upper and Lower Silesia, and at Zwickau in Saxony. Alsace brought potash and textiles, Lorraine iron deposits. New industrial empires were founded: Krupp in Essen, Thyssen in Mühlheim, Stumm-Halberg in the Saar, Henckel von Donnersmarck in Silesia. And despite economic depressions in 1873 and 1877, the flood of workers from the countryside to the city continued. An additional 300,000 foreign laborers, most of them from Austria-Hungary and Russia, came to Germany every year seeking work.

The SPD flourished as a result. Whereas in 1871 August Bebel was the party's only Reichstag deputy, three years later there were nine and in 1877 twelve SPD parliamentary delegates. The party's national vote increased from

102,000 in 1871 to 352,000 in 1874. SPD membership stood at 30,000 in 1875; its trade unions had attracted only 45,000 workers, less than 1 percent of the work force. The SPD obviously was not a threat to the social and political stability of the German Empire, yet its shrill Marxist rhetoric suggested to Bismarck as well as to many Germans that the SPD constituted a new "red menace." The party seemed to be a combination of all that was evil and threatening: the French Revolution, the Forty-Eighters, and the Paris Commune of 1871.[1] Pacifist, internationalist, class oriented, Marxist in theory, the SPD disavowed the Reich and the Reich disavowed the SPD.

What the new German Empire required most was a transition period of calm and understanding. A host of conflicting administrative, economic, judicial, and military systems needed to adjust to each other. Historic political and religious opposites such as Bavarians and Prussians were being asked overnight to put aside ancient animosities. Germans of all political persuasions had to become accustomed to parliamentary concepts such as cooperation and compromise. Danes, French, and Poles would have to be assimilated into the new state. The German Empire, for its part, needed to accept the emergence of a highly organized urban working class and to integrate that force into the national polity.

It never had this adjustment period. Bismarck chose instead to assume the political offensive at home, singling out the Center party for attack. As guardian of "Catholic interests in the parliaments," this group was extremely vulnerable. The German Liberals had been outraged as early as 1864 by Pope Pius IX's *Syllabus of Errors*, in which the pontiff had declared it heretical for Catholics to embrace the new secular concepts of "progress, liberalism, and modern civilization." Six years later, at the very moment that Protestant Prussia was fighting Catholic France, a Vatican Council, against the votes of German prelates, promulgated the dogma of papal infallibility. And although the doctrine of infallibility was hotly contested in every European state, Bismarck gave what the Liberal deputy Rudolf Virchow termed a *Kulturkampf* ("struggle of civilizations") a special twist by turning it against the Center party. In short, Bismarck attacked not religion in general or the Catholics in particular but rather the Center party, which emerged from the elections of 1871 as the second largest political party in Germany. The Iron Chancellor launched the struggle by citing Martin Luther: "If I follow the pope, I will lose my eternal salvation."

---

[1] For seventy-two days in the spring of 1871, lower-middle-class and proletarian radicals fought with the government of Thiers in Paris. Twenty thousand died in this bloodiest civil clash in French history. In 1878 Bismarck linked the Commune to the SPD. "From that moment I recognized the Social Democratic elements as an enemy against which state and society are obliged to defend themselves."

REICHSTAG ELECTIONS UNDER BISMARCK

Parties	1871	1874	1877	1878	1881	1884	1887
CONSERVATIVE							
Vote (%)	23.0	14.1	17.6	26.6	23.7	22.1	25.0
Seats	94	55	78	116	78	106	121
LIBERALS							
Vote (%)	46.1	39.3	37.4	32.5	35.9	35.2	35.2
Seats	201	207	176	135	153	118	131
CENTER, GUELPHS, ALSACE-LORRAINE							
Vote (%)	24.7	38.1	34.3	31.6	31.7	30.8	27.5
Seats	83	124	126	133	143	141	130
SOCIAL DEMOCRATS							
Vote (%)	3.2	6.8	9.1	7.6	6.1	9.7	10.1
Seats	2	9	12	9	12	24	11
OTHERS							
Vote (%)	3.0	1.7	1.6	1.7	2.6	2.2	2.2
Seats	2	2	5	4	11	8	4
TOTAL SEATS	382	397	397	397	397	397	397

Bismarck's assault on the Center party, which began in Prussia and was then extended to the rest of Germany, consisted of a host of governmental regulations: state rather than church supervision of schools, prohibition of new Jesuit centers in Germany, and abolition of the Catholic Department of the Prussian Ministry of Culture and Education. Perhaps most ominously, a "pulpit paragraph" was added to the criminal code, making it a crime for clerics to discuss matters of state "in a manner threatening to the public peace."

Bismarck insisted that the Prussian minister of ecclesiastical affairs and education, Adalbert Falk, seize the initiative. The so-called Falk Laws of 1873 struck the articles guaranteeing the independence of the Catholic church from the Prussian Constitution. They made state examinations at state schools mandatory for all candidates for church office and created a state court for church affairs. The laws withdrew all financial support from the Catholic church in Prussia. The following year a new ordinance made state marriage mandatory. Only William I's opposition kept Bismarck from introducing state divorce.

It is difficult to comprehend, much less to explain, the *Kulturkampf.* Why would Bismarck choose to antagonize nearly half the population? Why would he, a recent convert to Pietism, choose to attack the ancient Christian faith? Part of the answer lies in the secular spirit of the nineteenth century, which sought to remove religious influences from public life. Bismarck's temporary liberal allies had a long-standing tradition of anticlericalism. Another part of the answer lies in foreign policy, for Bismarck had always considered France to be the traditional protector of the Roman Catholic church. Thus the Center party, by upholding Catholic rights at all costs, seemed to be placing itself squarely with Prussia's recent enemies (Austria, France) and with its unreconciled domestic opponents.

The close bond between Prussia's Polish subjects and the Church of Rome worried Bismarck, and he did his level best to stamp out Catholic-Polish influences in Prussian schools, to the point of forcefully "resettling" Poles from the Prussian-Polish "border strip." Unreconciled French (Catholic) monarchists and Austrian (Catholic) Habsburgs added fuel to the flames of the *Kulturkampf.* Finally, there was the element of personality. Windthorst, the Center's leader, was a formidable opponent, and Bismarck detested him. "I have my wife to love," the chancellor once stated, "and Windthorst to hate." Bismarck added a particularly nasty aspect to the battle by branding Windthorst an "enemy of the state" (*Reichsfeind*).

The Catholic church reacted with a call to arms. It threatened ecclesiastics and laymen who obeyed the Falk Laws with excommunication. Catholic newspapers and lay organizations were created overnight to buttress the faith. Neither fines, arrests, nor imprisonment demoralized the Catholic clergy, even at a time when in 1878 half its bishops had been deposed and many parishes were without priests. In fact, many conservative, aristocratic Protestant Prussian Junkers rallied to the Catholic cause. They saw in the Falk Laws an assault not only on Catholicism specifically but also on Christianity generally. Bismarck's peers, the one hundred eldest families in Prussia, took out an advertisement in 1876 in the archconservative *Kreuzzeitung* denouncing the "cultural struggle."

The *Kulturkampf* was a disaster for Bismarck in the short run and for Germany in the long run. The Center party increased its seats from fifty-two to ninety in the Prussian elections of 1873, and it did equally well in the federal elections the next year, raising its representation in the Reichstag from sixty-three to ninety-one deputies. The legacy of what Bismarck termed a "contest between the king and the priesthood" was one of internal divisiveness, bitterness, and dissension. The Center party would remember it well in 1933, when Adolf Hitler asked its leaders to grant him emergency powers. As will be shown later, few Catholics in 1933 wished a return to the confrontational politics of the *Kulturkampf.*

There was a cruel twist of cynicism at the end of this sordid affair. In 1878 Leo XIII succeeded Pius IX, and the "struggle of civilizations" ended almost overnight with accord and congeniality. Priests agreed to register with the state. The Falk Laws were relaxed. The Catholic church was allowed to run its seminaries and to staff its sees. Bismarck asked the pontiff to arbitrate a dispute between Germany and Spain over the Caroline Islands; Leo XIII ordered the Center party to vote for the army budget in 1887. Windthorst was mortified: "Shot in the field! Shot in the back!" The truth of the matter is that Leo XIII viewed the new kingdom of Italy as Rome's most immediate danger, and hence he was willing to reach an accommodation with distant Prussia.

At the same time that Bismarck was winding down the *Kulturkampf*, he also jettisoned liberalism. Part of the reason was that classical nineteenth-century liberalism had run its course; its basic tenets (constitution, free speech, free press, free trade, trial by jury) had been implemented. Liberalism suffered a severe setback in England with the defeat of William Gladstone's first and greatest Liberal ministry in 1874. Other liberal administrations fell in Italy in 1876 and Austria in 1879. In the late 1870s Bismarck was already moving to conserve the newly founded Reich through a system of alliances with Rome, St. Petersburg, and Vienna. The time had come to move to the right on domestic issues.

Bismarck's ideal was to rule with a "reliable majority" of moderate Conservatives, Free Conservatives, and National Liberals. By 1878 he felt that the National Liberals had acquired a "dominating position" since they alone were able to form coalitions with the Right, Center, or Left of the political spectrum. Bismarck suspected them of demanding nothing less than sharing power in the national government. He felt that Left liberals such as Eduard Lasker and Ludwig Bamberger, especially, were "systematically undermining all pillars of the monarchical state."

Bismarck decided to end the liberal era. National patriotism was turned against the Liberals as Bismarck worked to regroup parliamentary forces in the interest of conservatism. Ministers, deputies, and courtiers who obstructed his will were to be cowed by a national referendum on the Iron Chancellor's popularity. The electorate did not disappoint him: the National Liberals lost twenty-nine seats and the Progressives nine; the Conservatives and the Free Conservatives gained nineteen seats each.

Landowners, bankers, industrialists, farmers, merchants, and shopkeepers rallied to abandon liberal free trade and to bring back the interventionist state. In fact, for the first time in German history, the economic interests of western industry and eastern and southern agriculture were identical. Agriculture demanded protection against foreign competition on the world grain market, and industry clamored for high tariffs against foreign goods. "Protection of iron and grain" became the rallying cry of Conservatives, Free Conservatives, and Centrists. As an added bonus for Bismarck, higher tariffs translated into greater state revenues.

Economics were never far from Bismarck's mind. The "Great Depression," starting in 1873–1874 and extending to 1896, prompted industrialists to clamor for protection from British manufactured products and Junkers to demand protection against cheap American and Russian grains. Bismarck tentatively sought to establish a "rye-iron alliance," a union of big business and agriculture directed against the common threat of the "red menace." Once more Bismarck's policy was part of a wider global development. Austria, France, Russia, and the United States were all abandoning free trade in favor of some protectionism.

Two assassination attempts against William I in 1878 by anarchists gave Bismarck the opportunity to launch what has been described as the "refounding of the German Empire." Bismarck first dealt with the Liberals. He knew that these free trade supporters would reject his proposed tariffs on iron, wood, grain, and livestock, as well as government levies or monopolies on tobacco, coffee, tea, sugar, and alcoholic beverages. Thus, he turned to yesterday's adversaries, Windthorst and the Center party, to force his protectionist program through parliament. The Liberals splintered into factions. A minority of National Liberals remained loyal to Bismarck, but the majority joined the Progressive party to form the German Liberal party (*Deutsch Freisinnige-Partei*).

Bismarck's assault on liberalism was intimately tied to his concomitant attack on socialism. Labor had begun to organize under the protection of the Industrial Code of 1869, and every new blast furnace and kilometer of railroad track laid brought a new flood of workers from the countryside into the cities. Indeed, 75 percent of the growth of the German population between 1873 and 1895 — estimated at 10 million — took place in cities of over two thousand people. And, once in the industrial cities, German workers were easily attracted to the SPD. Strikes were illegal but began to crop up with regularity, slowly increasing to more than two hundred per year by 1890.

Bismarck disliked the SPD's revolutionary Marxist domestic program as well as its pacifist, internationalist foreign policy. He had been enraged in 1875 by the uncompromising declaration of the SPD leader Wilhelm Liebknecht in the Reichstag: "Not a penny for the present system." His anger rose to fever pitch as he learned of the efforts of prominent German academics ("socialists of the chair") to work for amelioration of working conditions after 1873 through the Association for Social Policy. Were Liberals and Socialists from the same camp?

The Iron Chancellor decided to strangle Social Democracy in the crib. In October 1878 the Reichstag passed the Law Against Social Democratic Activities Dangerous to the Public Welfare by a vote of 221 to 149. The regulations outlawed all organizations serving Social Democratic purposes and provided stiff fines for those that disregarded the law. Public meetings and distribution of printed materials were proscribed, party functionaries subject to arrest in case they violated the new decrees. The so-called Anti-Socialist Laws were enacted for three years and were regularly renewed until 1890. At the height of the parliamentary debate, Bismarck pressed to destroy the National Liberals by painting them with a red brush for their initial reluctance to persecute the SPD.

The Red Revolutionaries: Liebknecht, Hepner, and Bebel of the SPD in the docket (1872).

The other side of the coin was Bismarck's attempt to woo the workers from Social Democracy by enacting a state-sponsored program of social security. In the process the Prussian arch-conservative laid the foundations for the modern European welfare state. Bismarck offered the "soldiers of labor" national health insurance in 1883, with two-thirds of the premiums paid by employers and one-third by employees. Accident insurance, paid for solely by employers, followed the next year. Disability and old-age insurance with costs shared equally by employers, employees, and the state came in 1889. Matters such as maximum hours of work, child and female labor laws, and arbitration would wait until the next century.

The chancellor was motivated by a combination of paternalism and shrewd politics. Pressure for labor reforms from both the SPD and the Association for Social Policy was brought to bear in parliament, but Bismarck's sense of applied Christianity also played a role. And he appreciated the simple reality garnered from observing his own laborers that a healthy worker was a productive worker. Above all, he hoped to take the wind out of the sails of the

SPD by having the state grant the workers relative economic and financial security.

But the crusade against Social Democracy, like the *Kulturkampf,* failed. After an initial drop, the SPD's popular vote in national elections soared to 763,000 in 1887 and 1.43 million by 1890. Its seats in the Reichstag increased from nine in 1878 to thirty-five in 1890. Membership in the SPD's free trade unions rose more than fivefold to 278,000 during this period of proscription. Most important, the SPD survived this period of proscription by turning its back on the state and going underground. Party leaders met in Zurich, Switzerland. Pamphlets and newspapers were illegally printed and distributed. Cells of 5,000 people were organized throughout the country. In Hamburg, for example, this clandestine organization was so effective that the city had to be kept under martial law from 1878 to 1890. Industrial violence increased. There were no fewer than 1,000 strikes involving 400,000 workers alone in the period from January 1889 to April 1890.

The SPD turned to what sociologists have termed "negative integration." If Bismarck refused to integrate the workers into the state, then the SPD would at least integrate them into its party apparatus. Thus, the SPD assumed the role of the state, providing its members with cradle-to-grave services. Party newspapers, libraries, glee clubs, theater and opera performances, sporting associations, kindergarten, schools, savings unions, and the like shielded the workers from both state and society. Overt suppression of labor, as practiced in Russia, was out of the question because Germany was still a state based on law (*Rechtsstaat*). Although about fifteen hundred party members eventually were jailed, there were no mass transportations, deportations, or camps. Nor did Germany possess a Siberia. When the SPD leader August Bebel went to prison, he took along his library and pet canary, and unionized workers of the national railroad lined the platform to salute him.

Bismarck's last years in office, then, were characterized by danger and uncertainty. Unable to engineer a lasting reliable majority, the Iron Chancellor was forced to organize negative coalitions of diverse conservative faction against "enemies of the state" — first the Catholics, then the Left-Liberals, and finally the Socialists. Part of the problem was that Bismarck had lost touch with this age of rapid industrialization and urbanization. His world remained that of rural Prussia, his contacts limited to civil servants and agrarian laborers on his estates. He never toured the western industrial regions of the Empire, visited a coal mine, or saw a Krupp foundry. Although Karl Marx was a contemporary — Marx died in 1883 — Bismarck never bothered to read his works. And when the chancellor visited the Hanseatic port of Hamburg in 1896, he was put off by its hustle and bustle, its crass materialism, its cranes and ships. "It is a new and different world," he sadly noted, "a new age."

"A Mystagogue of Culture"?

The cultural and intellectual stage of Bismarck's new Reich reflected a mixture of elitism and populism, especially with regard to education. Most Germans had eight years of primary education (*Volksschule*), with the result that illiteracy stood at less than 1 percent by the turn of the century. In the 1870s the Prussian curriculum was broadened beyond the basic three Rs to include geography, geometry, history, and the natural sciences. Higher education was still reserved for the elite. Nine of ten students reached university by acquiring the *Abitur* from one of the humanistic high schools, a *Gymnasium*. Eight out of ten came from the ranks of civil servants, lower and higher government officials, teachers, and officers. Many took advantage of the *Einjährig-Freiwillige* option, under which they could bypass army conscription by volunteering for a one-year stint after completing six years of secondary education, whereafter they became eligible for the cherished reserve officer commission.

The state's ideal was not to educate as many of its citizens as possible beyond primary school but rather to concentrate on the select few destined by birth and social station to enter state service after university. It shared the views of a celebrated outsider, Friedrich Nietzsche, who called for the "education of individually selected people" in order to maintain "the natural order of rank in the kingdom of the intellect." Since Wilhelm von Humboldt's university reforms of 1809–1810, the state had maintained an active role in higher education. It had the right to confirm the nomination of university rectors and to appoint university professors. State support for university education increased fourfold to 16 million marks between 1871 and 1907. The state made sure that the educators of the nation's future governing elite were loyal and devoted servants of the Hohenzollern monarchy. Innovators and dissenters were not welcomed.

At the top of the university system stood the eminent chair holders, many of whom refused to retire. They were by and large a conservative lot, lavishing praise on the new Reich and celebrating the Bismarckian fusion of power and state. One of academia's most influential representatives was Treitschke, who trumpeted Bismarck's praise from the lectern, glorified war as an expression of cultural superiority, and in a celebrated article in the *Preussische Jahrbücher* in November 1879 referred to the Jews as "our national misfortune."

A host of followers and imitators echoed the views of this *preceptor Germaniae*. Ernst Haeckel, the Jena zoologist, popularized Charles Darwin's findings in Germany. David Friedrich Strauss, the erstwhile liberal deputy of 1848, like Treitschke embraced arch-conservatism under Bismarck. Strauss rejected Christianity as the "Old Faith" and upheld classic German literature and music, as well as modern science, factories, and laboratories as the "New Faith." Alfred von Tirpitz, future architect of German navalism; Friedrich von Bernhardi, popular writer on war; Carl Peters, African explorer; and Heinrich Class, future head of the Pan-German League, all adopted Treitschke's

Weltanschauung (world view) and became what Nietzsche termed "mystagogues of culture"[1] to the next generation.

The churches played an impressive statistical role in the German Empire. Of its nearly 50 million subjects, 31 million were Evangelical (Lutheran), 17.7 million Catholic, 570,000 Jewish, and about 150,000 members of other Christian sects. These statistics reveal that large numbers of Germans maintained church membership due to habit. They paid their mandatory church taxes and probably left it at that. Popular religious culture remained largely outside the synods. Wilhelm Emmanuel von Ketteler, bishop of Mainz, preached the doctrine of social Catholicism, that is, using church wealth and influence to aid the poor, the downtrodden, the neglected. Court chaplain Adolf Stöcker less generously founded the Christian Socialist party in an attempt to woo the workers from Marxism. Stöcker enthusiastically embraced Bismarck's Anti-Socialist Laws as well as social security system but in the end put out a message that was mainly antisocialist and antisemitic. Stöcker, like Treitschke, viewed the Jews as a "national misfortune."

Antisemitism was on the rise and changing in the 1870s. Traditional, ritualistic, religious antisemitism, a residue of snobbery and suspicion toward a people viewed to be different, mercenary, and inferior, now rigidified into an unshakable hostility toward Jews. The latter were accused not only of having economic might but also the power to corrupt Germans morally, eugenically, and sexually. In 1873 Wilhelm Marr's *The Victory of Judaism over Teutonism*, which went through twelve printings in three years, introduced the term *antisemitism* and laid the foundation for a "Jewish conspiracy" thesis. Marr depicted Jews as being biologically inferior and possessing specific physical characteristics: dark, greasy hair, hooked nose, thick lips, and short, obese body. Rich Jews at best were useful and conservative, poor ones radical and subversive.

The 1870s proved receptive to such mental gymnastics. Modernization had wrought sweeping change in Germany's political institutions. Industrialization and urbanization had frightened many Germans, especially those recently off the land. The *Kulturkampf* had unsettled established religious beliefs. Aristocratic landowners were increasingly impoverished, laborers haunted by unemployment, and artisans threatened by industrial plants. A populace shaken by the economic crash of 1873 wondered why Jews, who made up less than 5 percent of the Reich's population in the 1880s, constituted 26 percent of money managers and 46 percent of wholesalers, retailers, and shippers. A host of antisemitic organizations sought to transform that fear and suspicion into political action designed to curb the power of the Jews. The League of German Students, founded in 1881, was but one such organization.

[1] Nietzsche used the term to refer to persons who practiced or interpreted mystical doctrines.

It remained for the trappings of "scientism" under the guise of social Darwinism[1] to make racism, a popular and xenophobic myth, respectable.

The newfound German nationalism received visible expression in popular architecture. A nationwide flurry of monument construction, designed to preserve in stone the great deeds of the men of 1866 and 1871, especially deserves attention. These monuments were expressions of the popular sentiment, and they represented the view of artists, judges, critics, students, propagandists, and planners — in short, the general populace. Additionally, they served a specific national psychological purpose. Three examples merit attention.

In 1875 Ernst von Brandel completed the *Hermannsdenkmal* in the Teutoburger Forest, where the Germanic chieftain Hermann (Arminius) had defeated Varus' Roman legions in the year A.D. 9. Largely paid for by a national subscription, the monument depicts Hermann with winged helmet and upraised sword both as "savior and founder" of the nation and guarantor of its continued existence, ready to do battle with its enemies.

Ten years later Johannes Schilling unveiled his *Niederwalddenkmal* on the banks of the Rhine across from Bingen. A huge statue of a female Germania, holding the crown of Charlemagne, celebrates German unity. Friezes on the massive pedestal honor the German rivers Rhine and Mosel, as well as the ideals of war and peace. When a national subscription failed to raise more than a quarter of the cost, veterans' associations eventually banded together in a special Kyffhäuserbund to complete the task. Its one million members not only finished the Bingerbrück monument but in 1896 completed another on the Kyffhäuser Mountain in Thuringia. Built in the shape of a fortress centered on a statue of Emperor William I, the stone edifice is topped by a German crown. A large platform in front of the main monument served as "sacred space" for pilgrims. Below the monument, in the depths of the Kyffhäuser Mountain, the medieval emperor Frederick Barbarossa allegedly slept, waiting to restore his Reich.

Nor was the Second Reich's founder forgotten. Wilhelm Kreis designed and built 500 Bismarck stone towers throughout the land. Modeled on the tomb of the Gothic king Theodoric at Ravenna, Kreis' towers symbolized continuity between the First and the Second Reich. By using simple pillars of stone, Kreis sought to imitate the manner in which ancient Saxons had honored the graves of their heroes. But time can upset the best of plans. The mammoth Bismarck statue in Hamburg, patterned after the famous statue of the knight Roland in Bremen, today looks down with stern countenance upon Europe's most renowned sin strip, the Reeperbahn.

---

[1] Social Darwinists applied to human society Charles Darwin's notion of biological evolution in general and of the struggle for survival of the fittest in particular.

These stone monuments were designed to keep in memory both the folklore of the ancient Germanic past, as in the case of the *Niederwalddenkmal*, and the heroic deeds of the nation's most recent founding fathers, as in the case of the Bismarck towers. They served to remind Germans of continuity in their turbulent history and to uplift their level of patriotism in an age of nation-states. Funding was secured through public subscriptions, designed to stress that the entire nation, regardless of class or region, participated in commemorating its heroes, both past and present.

The heroic, militant ambience of these monuments also revealed a degree of uncertainty about the national consciousness. Why this need to immortalize in stone Germanic heroes from Arminius to Bismarck? Why the frenetic building pace? Perhaps Germans in the 1880s and 1890s were trying to compensate for centuries of political disarray. Perhaps they wished to express in stone that there had always been a "German nation," at least in spirit if not in form. Perhaps present-day German historians seek to give literary expression to this Johnny-come-lately mentality of the late Bismarckian period when they entitle their national histories "the delayed nation-state."

Two titans of elitist culture perhaps best represent the power and ambivalence of the new German state created by Bismarck. Both outsiders who did their major work in Switzerland, they would be idolized and emulated by hosts of pseudo-intellectuals. And both cast a long shadow on the subsequent history of Germany. Richard Wagner had manned the barricades at Dresden in 1848 and was exiled from Germany between 1849 and 1861. He wrote his tetralogy of the Teutonic hero Siegfried in Switzerland; his monumental *Ring* opera romanticized the distant Germanic past as portrayed in the *Nibelungenlied*.[1] With the help of Ludwig II of Bavaria, Wagner built a shrine at Bayreuth where future generations of the Wagner clan would receive Oriental potentates, German industrial millionaires, and eventually Adolf Hitler.

Wagner's music was brilliant. If one lays aside the tedious poetic lines and hackneyed plots (which grievously distort the medieval German epics), there remain the feelings, intensity, and expressiveness of the symphonist. His music was dazzling, exotic, and intoxicating. Above all, it was new. The pure passion and dramatic pathos of his orchestral music overpowered listeners accustomed to the religious reverence of Bach, the balanced tenderness of Mozart, and the moral nobility of Beethoven. In the words of the great novelist Thomas Mann, it was "heavy, pessimistic, laden with sluggish yearning," constantly seeking to wrest human beings "out of the darkness and confusion to

[1] The *Nibelungenlied*, in its most popular form, is a collection of ancient Germanic sagas gathered at the court of the Bishop of Passau between 1200 and 1205. Its two salient themes are Siegfried's courtship of Kriemhild and his death, and the end of the Burgundians at the court of King Etzel.

redemption in the beautiful." To be sure, others were not as understanding.[1]

Our interest in Wagner, however, goes beyond his music. His writings condemned Jewish influence in music and endorsed the philosophy of prominent social Darwinists. Wagner's *Bayreuther Blätter* featured Paul de Lagarde's vitriolic dislike of Liberals and Jews, as well as a call for the creation of a "greater Germany" stretching well into Russia. The paper welcomed the pseudo-scientific racial theory of the French Comte Joseph Arthur de Gobineau and paved the way for Wagner's English-born son-in-law, Houston Stewart Chamberlain, to proclaim the superiority of the Nordic race and transform Jesus Christ into a Teuton. As a youth in Vienna, Adolf Hitler had compared his own disappointments and lack of recognition to those of Wagner's early years and yearned for his own "glory of world fame." Nevertheless, it would be overly simplistic to translate either Wagner's music or his antisemitism into the intellectual genesis of Hitler's brand of National Socialism.

The other great outsider of Wilhelmian culture was Friedrich Nietzsche, professor of classical philology at the University of Basel. The son of a Saxon clergyman, Nietzsche prophesied a century of world wars, revolutions, and eternal turmoil. In his apocalyptic vision, everything that was weak would be crushed, everything that was false stamped out. Radical cultural changes and a nihilistic rule of terror dominated his writings. Nietzsche warned in his last major work, *Ecce Homo*: "There will be wars, such as there have never been in this world." Out of the chaos would come a new order built on rule by the ideal artist-warrior genius.

One would have expected Nietzsche to embrace the Germany of Bismarck and Moltke. He refused, and instead condemned his era as "the age of the masses," the Reich as "a new tower of Babel." Contemptuous of racialism in general and of antisemitism in particular, Nietzsche was the avowed enemy of national chauvinism, intellectual snobbery, mass culture, and hypocrisy. He hated what he termed the petty little man who reveled in the smug stuffiness of the new Reich. He declined either to "improve" humanity or to create new "idols." He sought philosophical truth with a passion, in the process willing to challenge all the assumptions on which Western Civilization was based. Nietzsche yearned to "seek out everything alien and questionable, everything which hitherto has been banned by morality." He disdained cultural arrogance — in vogue in Germany after the "national" victory over France in 1871 — and argued that Prussian virtues such as discipline and military might were not synonymous with culture. Instead, he dreamed of a Germany of poets and thinkers, of Goethe rather than of Bismarck.

[1] After attending a performance of Wagner's opera *Lohengrin* in Germany, the great American humorist Mark Twain (Samuel L. Clemens) commented: "The banging and slamming and booming and crashing were something beyond belief."

Ironically, Nietzsche celebrated the very virtues that he lacked: the ruthless vitality of the renaissance prince, the Prussian officer, the "blond beast," the superman. He lacked even a semblance of moderation, generosity, or charity. And as his mind lost its grip on sanity, his polemic became ever more strident, the aphorisms ever more conflicting. Nietzsche condemned religious attitudes, philosophical thought, democracy and socialism, generals and industrialists, and even the romantics. He bequeathed to future generations his phobia of democracy, insistence on the privileges of the elite, strident irrationalism, and fervent belief in the ability to force change through sheer willpower.[1]

The most cruel fate awaited Nietzsche: emulation and popularization by a circle of sycophantic writers and poets and self-proclaimed personification in the 1930s by the greatest criminal in German history. This folly was due in large measure to the deliberate fabrication of a "Nietzsche legend" by his sister, Elisabeth, who edited his writings to suit the image she wished to create. It would be a disservice to Nietzsche to accept her depiction of Adolf Hitler as the "true son" of her brother's philosophical musings.

Neither Wagner nor Nietzsche developed meaningful relations with women. Though romanticized love and death dominated Wagner and his music, in private life he suffered a tragic marriage, and in his advanced years sought mainly companionship. Nietzsche often tendered marriage proposals to women he barely knew — only to be rejected. Thereafter he would denounce women as "God's *second* mistake" and as more barbarous than men in revenge and love. "The Germans are like women," Nietzsche bitterly wrote, "you can scarcely ever fathom their depths — they haven't any." It remains questionable whether either man understood the true role of women in Bismarckian society.

It must be remembered that half the population in the Bismarckian state was not invited to play a major part beyond the traditional homemaker. The electoral laws of 1808 and 1831 denied women the vote, with the exception of special cases in which an extremely rich widow or spinster could be given dispensation from this legal restriction. Nor could women stand for political office. The Prussian Law of Association of 1851, which remained in effect for half a century and was copied in Bavaria and Saxony, barred their participation in political organizations and trade unions. On the other hand, the liberal south German states of Baden and Württemberg, as well as the Hanseatic cities of Bremen and Hamburg, allowed women to join political movements. Bebel's attempt in 1895 to have the Reichstag grant female suffrage was easily rejected.

[1] It should not be overlooked that Nietzsche's adulation of "willpower" in large measure harked back to Arthur Schopenhauer (1788-1860), who had argued that time, space, and causality were "nothing more than functions of the brain."

The Center Party deputy Carl Bachem justified his negative vote by citing St. Paul.[1] Bismarckian Germany was a male-dominated society, and its male guardians were determined that it remain so. The Iron Chancellor undoubtedly expressed the mood of his ruling bureaucratic and political elite when he stated that he had a decided horror of clever women.

Education throughout modern history has been the one reliable vehicle of social advancement. In Imperial Germany this avenue was closed to women. Whereas women had gained the right to become full-time students in the United States in 1853, France in 1861, and Britain in 1878, in Germany women were barred from the *Gymnasium* and hence from universities. Only in 1896 did Prussia allow women to take a special test (*Reifezeugnis*) equivalent to high school graduation and university entrance. But German universities to 1900 remained open only to women from abroad. German women who wished to pursue higher learning were directed to what one historian has called the "insipid pabulum" of special private schools for girls, an elite training ground for matrimony and motherhood. As late as 1901, 1,133 of these special schools still existed, 869 in Prussia alone. And although women staffed many of these private preparatory schools, they comprised only 14,000 of the 90,000 elementary and secondary school teachers in Germany around the turn of the century. Men held the vast majority of administrative positions in education.

By far the largest number of women employed worked the land. Of the 1.9 million female laborers in the Prussian work force in 1861, 500,000 were listed as "maids or servants" and an equal number simply as agricultural workers. Only 90,000 women (less than 10 percent of the nonagricultural labor force) worked in factories. That same year 93,000 of the 164,000 women gainfully employed in Saxony were registered as "domestic servants and farmhands." It was exceptional for a woman to own or run a farm. The 1861 census for Saxony revealed that only 1,900 (4.6 percent) of 41,000 people listed as estate owners, renters, or vintners were women.

Yet agitation for women's rights seethed under the surface. In October 1865 Luise Otto and 150 other women launched the feminist movement by founding the General German Women's association. Its twin demands centered on greater educational opportunities for women in general and admission to the medical profession in particular. The association peaked in size with 11,000 members by the mid–1870s. Thereafter it stagnated and by 1914 could point to only a modest gain of 3,000 members.

The movement for women's rights received a great boost in 1883 when Bebel published *Woman Under Socialism*, which went through fifty reprints.

[1] See St. Paul's First Letter to Timothy 2: 11-12. "Let a woman learn in silence with all submissiveness. I permit no woman to teach or to have authority over men; she is to keep silent."

Women networking: Needlework class in the 1880s.

The leader of the SPD was well aware that women stood at their machines six days a week for up to fourteen hours per day. Most were employed in semiskilled work in spinning and weaving mills, laundries, and clothing stores; the vast majority were single and under twenty-five years of age. Factory work for women by definition constituted a blatant transgression of custom and morality. Women received the minimum wage in most jobs, and ill health and unemployment were common. Only 8.6 percent of the women who worked were in trade and industry; nearly 20 percent were employed as servant girls. And while the socialist free trade unions embraced one worker in every five by 1890, women made up a paltry 1.8 percent of their membership.

Despite Bebel's literary efforts, a basic distrust developed between the association and the SPD. The latter accused the former of elitism, of seeking only ladies' suffrage (*Damenwahlrecht*) as opposed to the vote for all women regardless of socioeconomic status. Additionally, fragmentation plagued the women's movement. By the turn of the century no fewer than 850 organizations with 500,000 members worked in behalf of women's rights.

The Legacy

In April 1890, at age seventy-five, Bismarck left Berlin for retirement at Friedrichsruh with three hundred boxes of state documents and thirteen thousand bottles of wine. The English weekly magazine *Punch* depicted Bismarck as the pilot leaving the ship, with the gloating captain William II watching from the rail. The imagery was on the mark. William II immediately informed the king of Saxony that a new era was at hand. "I am now the officer of the watch on the ship of state. The course remains the same. Full steam ahead!"

A true sense of loss pervaded Germany and Europe. A titan had departed. The German military attaché in St. Petersburg reported a local drop in "self-confidence," a feeling in Russian ruling circles that, without Bismarck, "control of Europe's fate" no longer seemed secure. "Great upheavals and profound changes" were certain to follow the Iron Chancellor's departure. Even the usually hostile French press expressed "concern" for the future without the steadying hand of Bismarck. With "the skilful master" no longer on the scene, the German chargé d'affaires reported, the French feared "European controversies [that] could develop into insoluble conflicts."

"Dropping the Pilot": A British view of Bismarck's dismissal (September 1890).

Bismarck cast a long shadow over his successors. Who could possibly have followed him? Who could have matched his great deeds? All would be judged against him: "What would Bismarck have done?" "How would Bismarck have reacted?" "Bismarck never would have permitted that." It hardly helped that near death in 1898, the legend predicted the end of the German Empire of William II in twenty years. That percipient Prussian observer, Theodor Fontane, in May 1890 caught the mood well: "The world has rarely seen a greater genius, rarely a man of greater courage and character, and rarely a greater humorist. But he did lack one thing: generosity." That lack of generosity would plague the nation well beyond Bismarck's retirement in 1890.

The truth is that Bismarck had to go. The ninety-nine-day rule of Emperor Frederick III in 1888 already had raised in Bismarck fears of a British-style liberal regime in Germany. While it is doubtful that Frederick III could have substantially altered the peculiar Prussian-German system, his brief reign nevertheless brought into question many of the basic assumptions of the Bismarckian state. For the Reich's founder displayed a grim inflexibility on the "social question," pushing to renew the Anti-Socialist Laws in 1890. Unable to control parliament after the electoral victory of the Center, Progressives, and Social Democrats in February 1890, he toyed with the notion of overthrowing the existing constitutional order and replacing the Reichstag with an Economic Council of the well-to-do. He even revived the "gap theory" of 1862: because Prussia had been created by the princes, Bismarck rationalized, it could also be dissolved and reconstituted by them. He was prepared to accept a bloodbath in the process and had alerted the army's commanding generals to stand by. Above all, he failed utterly to appreciate that William II desperately wanted to direct German policy.

Germany was in the throes of another constitutional crisis by 1890. There existed only three alternatives: complete repression of the SPD by abolishing parliament or promulgating a new franchise law based on property; democratization by integrating the SPD into the national community and giving parliament a voice in government; or staying the Bismarckian course of isolating labor and the SPD for as long as possible. The decision fell to the thirty-one-year-old William II.

Suggested Readings

The biographies of Bismarck are legion. Of the older books, A. J. P. Taylor, *Bismarck: The Man and the Statesman* (London, 1960), remains highly readable and entertaining, and Erich Eyck, *Bismarck and the German Empire* (London, 1950), in many ways has not been surpassed in terms of sharp analysis. Alan Palmer, *Bismarck* (London and New York, 1976), Bruce Waller, *Bismarck* (Oxford, 1985), and Edward Crankshaw, *Bismarck* (New York and London, 1981) merely retell a well-known tale. The recent Lothar Gall, *Bismarck: The White Revolutionary*, 2 vols. (London, 1986), stands out. Gall has used the Iron

Chancellor's personal records deposited at Friedrichsruh and has offered what amounts to the first major reinterpretation of Bismarck since World War II. And most recently, Otto Pflanze has completed four decades of work on Bismarck with the masterful three-volume *Bismarck and the Development of Germany* (Princeton, 1990).

A second genre of books takes up the general theme of Bismarck and his age. George O. Kent, *Bismarck and His Times* (Carbondale, Ill., 1978), reflects this trend, as does D. G. Williamson, *Bismarck and Germany, 1862-90* (London, 1986). James J. Sheehan, *German Liberalism in the Nineteenth Century* (Chicago and London, 1978), places Bismarck within the age of liberalism, and Stewart A. Stehlin, *Bismarck and the Guelph Problem 1866–1890: A Study in Particularist Opposition to National Unity* (Amsterdam, 1973), analyzes the chancellor's less savory domestic maneuverings. Bismarck's entry into Prussian politics at the national level is dealt with by Eugene N. Anderson, *The Social and Political Conflict in Prussia 1858–1864* (Lincoln, Neb., 1954). Fritz Stern's brilliant *Gold and Iron: Bismarck, Bleichröder and the Building of the German Empire* (New York and London, 1977), details the complicated relationship between the chancellor and his private banker.

The economic aspects of the Bismarckian era are well handled by J. H. Clapham, *Economic History of France and Germany, 1815–1914* (Cambridge, 1921); William O. Henderson, *The Zollverein* (London, 1968); Ivo N. Lambi, *Free Trade and Protection in Germany, 1868–1879* (Wiesbaden, 1963); and Gustav Stolper, *The German Economy from 1870 to the Present* (London, 1967). Socioeconomic aspects of the Bismarckian era can be gleaned from Theodore S. Hamerow's *Restoration, Revolution, Reaction: Economics and Politics in Germany 1815–1871* (Princeton, 1958), and his two-volume opus, *The Social Foundations of German Unification* (Princeton, 1969, 1972). A highly revisionist treatment is offered by Eckart Kehr, *Economic Interest, Militarism and Foreign Policy: Essays on German History*, tr. Gordon A. Craig (Berkeley, 1977).

Bismarck's misunderstanding of the German labor movement is recounted in Helga Grebing, *History of the German Labour Movement from 1848 to the Present* (Leamington Spa, 1985). Vernon L. Lidtke, on the other hand, traces the effect of Bismarck's Anti-Socialist Laws upon the SPD: *The Outlawed Party: Social Democracy in Germany, 1878–1890* (Princeton, 1966) and *The Alternative Culture: Socialist Labor in Imperial Germany* (Oxford, 1985). And although there remains no acceptable English-language treatment of the *Kulturkampf*, Margaret L. Anderson, *Windthorst: A Political Biography* (Oxford, 1981), at least tackles the problem from the perspective of the Center party's leader during that struggle. John C. Fout, ed., *German Women in the Nineteenth Century* (New York, 1984), offers a collection of essays designed to survey the newly emerging studies of women in German history; a straightforward history is Ute Frevert, *Women in German History: From Bourgeois Emancipation to Sexual Liberation* (New York, 1988).

Books on Bismarck's foreign policy abound. A. J. P. Taylor's *The Struggle for Mastery in Europe, 1848–1919* (Oxford, 1954), has stood the test of time. Two other older treatments have similarly remained in favor: Eber M. Carroll, *Germany and the Great Powers, 1866–1914: A Study in Public Opinion and Foreign Policy* (Hamden, Conn., 1966), and Werner E. Mosse, *The European Powers and the German Question, 1848–1871, with Special Reference to England and Russia* (Cambridge, 1958). Special treatments include William N. Medlicott, *Bismarck, Gladstone, and the Concert of Europe* (London, 1956); George F. Kennan, *The Decline of Bismarck's European Order: Franco-Russian Relations, 1875–1890* (Princeton, 1979); and Bruce Waller, *Bismarck at the Crossroads: The Reorientation of German Foreign Policy after the Congress of Berlin, 1878–1888* (London, 1974). Imanuel Geiss, *German Foreign Policy, 1871–1914* (London, 1975), provides a recent West German perspective. Finally, A. J. P. Taylor's *Germany's First Bid for Colonies, 1884–1885: A Move in Bismarck's European Policy* (London, 1938), remains valid after half a century of research into the subject.

Bismarck's wars and his relations with the Prussian military are stepchildren of German historiography. Gordon Craig's *The Politics of the Prussian Army, 1640–1945* (Oxford, 1955), is badly in need of updating, but no other survey of the subject for this period has emerged in English. Craig's *The Battle of Königgrätz* (London, 1964), and Michael Howard's *The Franco-Prussian War: The German Invasion of France, 1870-71* (New York, 1979) remain valid if dated. On a brighter note, William Carr's recent *The Origins of the Wars of German Unification* (London and New York, 1991), is a welcome addition to the field.

CHAPTER

5

IMPERIAL PROMISE: WILHELMIAN GERMANY, 1890–1914

We must grasp that the unification of Germany was a youthful spree, indulged in by the nation in its old age; it would have been better if it had never taken place since it would have been a costly extravagance, if it was the conclusion rather than the starting point of German power-politics on a global scale.

Max Weber, 1895

Wilhelmian Germany was a paradox. On the surface it exuded power and confidence. Its army seemed invincible, its industry unstoppable, and its emperor unflappable. Real wages rose, running water and electricity enhanced the quality of life even for the poor, and the more affluent enjoyed the comforts of central heating and the telephone. Taxes remained negligible by present-day standards. Freedom of speech and assembly were guaranteed, and the rule of law was sacrosanct. Even the notorious cases where authors were tried for offending the emperor's dignity merely brought the accused greater fame.

Education became the most visible adornment of this state. Especially in the sciences, German academics garnered more than their fair share of Nobel prizes, and the foundation in 1911 of the Kaiser-Wilhelm-Society (today's Max-Planck-Society) to further scientific knowledge was an important part of this trend. Largely due to the support of the Kaiser, German "technical" universities on January 9, 1900, achieved the right to confer doctorates. German universities attracted a global elite, one that gained academic laurels in the Reich and thereafter transported Wilhelm von Humboldt's system of higher education to their native lands. Not without reason was it commonly asserted that every academician had two homelands: his own and Germany.

Within a generation the Reich cast off its continental chains. The new buzzword was *Welt*, or "world." It became fashionable to speak of the world city Berlin, the German world economy, world politics, and world power.

"The German Reich," William II crowed, "has become a *Weltreich*." Companies such as AEG, Friedrich Krupp, Siemens & Halske, Robert Bosch, Carl Zeiss, Bayer, and Hoechst achieved global recognition. American millionaires and British statesmen rushed to the Continent to witness the new phoenix.

But below the surface Wilhelmian Germany was insecure, unsure of its new role, and troubled about its future. Would France forget the defeat of 1871 and accept the loss of Alsace-Lorraine? Would Britain allow the Reich to expand into Africa, Asia, and South America? Would Catholics and Social Democrats become reconciled with the post-Bismarckian state? And would the Reichstag remain content with its modest budgetary powers?

An official display of self-satisfaction and smugness sought to plaster over these cracks in the imperial edifice. Arrogance and superiority permeated especially the military. Pompous martial displays and gaudy national festivals, especially the annual Sedan-Day celebrations on September 2, reassured Germans of their new-found status. Antisemitism seduced those who felt threatened by industrialization. A crass and brash new elite of bourgeois bankers and entrepreneurs sought entry to the court by purchasing noble estates and titles. The traditional Prussian gentry who had staffed army and bureaucracy since the days of Frederick William I began to feel threatened, swamped by the new elite based on wealth.

Theodor Fontane brilliantly captured the change in his novel *Der Stechlin*, published posthumously in 1899. The protagonist, Dubslav von Stechlin, is a retired army major and lord of Castle Stechlin in the Mark Brandenburg. With charm and humor, decency and modesty, he watches the transformation of Old Prussia under William II into a crude, materialistic society. Dubslav's son, Woldemar, is swept away by the tide of materialism, and his electoral district falls to the Social Democrats. Throughout all, Stechlin, in sharp contrast to the ruling elite in Berlin, maintains balance and simplicity of manners.

A Nation at Odds: Crown, Industry, and Workers

William II (1888–1918), German emperor and king of Prussia by grace of God, as he fervently believed, took center stage of this seemingly grand era. "My position and duties," he lectured his Brandenburg vassals in a curious oration on February 24, 1892, wherein he raised Prussia's ally, God, to general's rank, "have been conferred upon me by Heaven." The tragic death of William's father, Emperor Frederick III, in 1888 after only ninety-nine days on the throne had brought the not-yet thirty-year-old William to power well ahead of schedule. To say that he was poorly prepared for the burdens of office is an understatement.

In his soul, the last of the Hohenzollerns reflected the clash of influences, traditions, and dreams that also plagued the nation at large: liberalism and absolutism, love of peace and sabre rattling, imperial romanticism and modern industrialism, oriental ostentation and Prussian frugality. Basically not an evil

"The Most Brilliant Failure in History":
William II (1902).

man, William II began his reign in 1890 as the self-styled "king of the beggars." He cancelled not only the Anti-Socialist Laws of 1878 but also the hated Reinsurance Treaty of 1887 with despotic Russia. Yet within the span of a few years William would struggle to out-Bismarck Bismarck. British Foreign Secretary Sir Edward Grey once likened the Kaiser to a powerful battleship with full steam up, propellers churning, but without a rudder.

William II's fateful illusion was that he took his central constitutional role seriously. He truly believed that all power emanated from him, that all Germany yearned to do his bidding. He cherished his role as supreme war lord and insisted on signing every military appointment and promotion. Ministers and state secretaries existed only to carry out imperial decrees. William II combined in his person the roles of German emperor, king of Prussia, duke of Brandenburg, commander-in-chief of the armed forces, successor to Charlemagne, heir to Frederick the Great, national censor, and global arbitrator. Consistency was not one of his assets. He could in the same instant elevate his grandfather to the status of "William the Great" and demote General von Moltke to that of a "secretarial slave" or "stooge." One of his biographers depicted the period after 1890 as consisting of William's "personal regime."

At heart William was an actor, lazy and incapable of sustained hard work. His life revolved around an endless procession of banquets, parades, reviews, and toasts. He lavished attention on minute uniform changes and loved to receive the ambassador from the Court of St. James's in the uniform of admiral of the fleet. He attended *Swan Lake* dressed as a Russian Cossack general. According to one estimate, the Kaiser spent nearly a third of his life — at times as many as two hundred days of the year — on the imperial yacht *Hohenzollern*, whose accoutrements he had goldplated every three years. Regattas and reviews at Spithead, Cowes, and Kiel fascinated William, who spared no expense to race his yachts against those of Krupp, Vanderbilt, and Lipton.

More seriously, the Kaiser never read the constitution and referred to the Reichstag as "oxen" or "donkeys." Liberal and Social Democratic newspapers were banned from the court and from army barracks alike. Clumsily copying Frederick the Great's habit of appending tart and cynical comments to state papers, William filled the margins of official documents with juvenile notes. He denounced the Americans as "parvenus," the French as "mad Gauls," the Japanese as "great apes." And William II measured his indispensableness and diligence by counting the number of signatures he was required to append to state documents every year.

The Kaiser's public utterances were grist for the mills of the daily press. On November 23, 1891, for example, William reminded recruits being sworn in at Potsdam that they might have to gun down "relatives, brothers, yes, even parents" in defense of their monarch. Four years later he advised Nicholas II, tsar of Russia, that the day might soon come when they would have to hang the Jews, Socialists, and Catholics who dominated their respective societies. At the height of a transport strike at Berlin in 1900, William II openly cabled his troop commander that he expected "at least 500 corpses" to litter the streets by nightfall. A never-ending procession of courtiers and yes-men were on the spot to defend, indeed to encourage, such destructive behavior.

It is easy to be critical, indeed caustic, in assessing the domestic landscape of the Wilhelmian era, but Imperial Germany was probably no worse, and in many cases much better, than other states in dealing especially with labor and civic unrest. The historian David Schoenbaum has shown vividly that the standards for industrial violence were set in the United States with the Haymarket Affair (1886) as well as the Homestead (1892) and Pullman strikes (1894). Additionally, the brutal suppressions of the Paris Commune in 1871 and the workers' demonstration at St. Petersburg in 1905 set the tone for what Schoenbaum calls the "continuation of politics by bloody means." But the German case was especially notorious because of its lack of consistency and direction. In a never-ending, zigzag course of domestic toleration and repression, various imperial governments sought to solve the "social question." A contemporary journalist aptly described the Reich as "the best administered, worst governed country in Europe."

William II truly represented this new German age. Prussia had little business in China, Africa, or South America; *Weltpolitik* was a German policy. William, whose first memories were of the Franco-Prussian War, knew well that his generation was tired of hearing of Bismarck, the great deeds of 1866 and 1871, and the "saturated" Reich. This new generation thirsted for action and deeds of its own. The Bismarckian state had been forged on the anvil of success; the Wilhelmian state required more of the same to sustain it.

The Kaiser's comical theatrics would have been amusing on the part of the ruler of a small state. Coming as they did from the head of the most powerful European country, they could not be taken lightly, for behind William II stood the power and influence of German industry. Coal production rose between 1871 and 1913 from 38 to 179 million tons. Steel production of 13 million tons by 1910 was second only to that of the United States. Other major branches of the economy such as electricity, chemicals, textiles, and machine making experienced fourfold or fivefold expansion between unification and the Great War. German exports flooded global markets to such an extent that the British in 1896 appointed an official blue-ribbon panel to investigate the "Made in Germany" alarm.

The spectacular growth of German banking financed not only this domestic production but also numerous overseas ventures. The thirty-three private banks that before unification had issued their own bank notes had been absorbed by the "Four D" industry giants (Deutsche, Dresdner, Darmstädter, and Diskonto banks) by 1874. Assured of government guarantees for overseas investments, the German banks could afford to tackle even the most risky of speculative investments. Whereas in the United States industry founded its own banks, in Germany the banks financed industry and placed their directors on industrial boards. Thus, the Dresdner Bank funded Krupp, the Deutsche Bank financed railroads in Turkey, and Diskonto built the Greater Venezuelan Railroad. Limited-liability laws served a dual purpose in fueling economic growth: they allowed the small investor and rentier to tap into the financial

KEY INDUSTRIES: RELATIVE PRODUCTION (1913 = 100)

Year	Coal	Lignite[a]	Iron	Steel
1870	13.9	8.7	7.2	6.0
1880	24.7	13.9	14.1	10.9
1890	36.9	21.9	24.1	18.0
1900	57.5	46.4	43.6	33.4
1910	80.4	77.5	76.6	75.8
1913	100	100	100	100

[a] German statistics differentiated between bituminous coal used in industrial plants and locomotives and lignite (or brown) coal used for home heating.

market and simultaneously protected financial and industrial enterprises — some seventeen thousand by 1909 — against disastrous bankruptcies.

German stock companies by 1912 grew to more than five thousand with total holdings of over $3.4 billion. Government fostered the development of cartels or trusts to ensure stability in the financial and industrial sectors. The example of the United States and its Sherman Anti-Trust Act of 1890, which in fact was more symbolic than effective, failed to find favor with either government or industry in the Reich. By 1900 chemical, coal, and steel industries were firmly in the hands of giant cartels that sought to regulate costs, prices, production, and wages. The Central Union of German Industrialists gained special notoriety for both its aggressive lobbying and antiunion activities.

Industry required cheap and plentiful labor. The Reich's population rose 60 percent, to 67 million, between 1871 and 1914, to the great concern especially of France. Germany's birthrate remained a healthy 1 percent per year while the death rate fell from 28 to 16 per thousand between unification and World War I. The continuing flow of people from countryside to urban industrial centers tripled the population of major cities and more than doubled the urban population during the same period. The terms *mobility of population* and *urbanization* aptly describe Imperial Germany. One historian has compared Germany under William II to an anthill constantly on the move, constantly working.

The overall population growth resulted partly from the fact that emigration slowed to almost a trickle. Two million Germans had left their homeland between 1871 and 1890, with the most dramatic exodus (200,000 people) occurring in 1881–1882. Under William II the annual number of emigrants dropped to around 20,000. Medical advances, better nutrition, and earlier marriages also guaranteed that the Reich's population growth would continue unabated.

POPULATION OF MAJOR GERMAN CITIES (in thousands)

City	1800	1850	1880	1900	1910
Berlin	172	419	1,112	1,889	3,730
Hamburg	130	132	290	706	932
Munich	30	110	230	500	595
Leipzig	40	63	149	456	588
Dresden	60	97	221	396	547
Cologne	50	97	145	373	516
Breslau	60	114	273	423	512
Frankfurt	48	65	137	289	415
Düsseldorf	10	27	95	214	358

Along with the rise in population, the number of persons employed in all sectors of the economy jumped from 22.4 to 31 million during William II's reign. The Social Democratic party and its trade unions benefited most directly from these dramatic changes. Membership in the Free Trade Unions leaped from 269,000 in 1895 to 1 million by 1902 and 2.5 million by 1913. Whereas most workers enrolled in the socialist Free Trade Unions, others opted for the Christian (Catholic) Unions as well as the liberal-national Hirsch-Duncker Unions. Collective bargaining was established in 1906, and nearly 14 million employees enjoyed the benefits of the national social security system on the eve of World War I. Annual wages in industry, trade, and transport on average rose from 650 marks in 1890 to 1,083 marks in 1913. The workweek had been reduced to just under sixty hours. Finally, the last nineteen years of peace under William II witnessed fourteen of boom and only four of economic downturn. The Kaiser's pledge upon wresting power from Bismarck to lead the nation "toward glorious times" apparently was being fulfilled.

The growth of the German economy compared with those of the other European powers was both spectacular and alarming. With the exception of the United States, which by the mid–1920s would have equaled the entire European production, Germany's total industrial output by 1913 had surpassed that of all the European powers.

Germany accounted for 13 percent of global trade in 1913. Great Britain still led with 15 percent, and France had fallen to 8 percent. How much longer would the new industrial giant be content with the Iron Chancellor's cautious policy of continental semihegemony? When would the Reich, in Max Weber's words, tire of this "youthful spree" and seek to expand its influence across the oceans and conduct "power-politics on a global scale"?

TOTAL INDUSTRIAL POTENTIAL OF MAJOR POWERS[a]
(Britain in 1900 = 100)

Country	1880	1900	1913	1928
Britain	73.3	[100]	127.2	135
France	25.1	36.8	57.3	82
Russia	24.5	47.5	76.6	72
Austria-Hungary	14	25.6	40.7	—
Germany	27.4	71.2	137.7	158
United States	46.9	127.8	298.1	533

[a] The economic historian Paul Bairoch includes in this complex index coal and steel production, energy consumption, chemical and electrical production, domestic and foreign trade, and goods and services.

The unenviable task of leading Germany beyond Bismarck fell to General Leo von Caprivi, a decent soldier without political experience. After 1890 Caprivi launched the German Empire's second period of liberal reform. Protective legislation for workers was extended to prohibit Sunday work. Employment of children under thirteen years of age in factories was barred, and generally minors were limited to a ten-hour workday. Female factory work was restricted to eleven hours per day. Optional industrial courts of arbitration were created to deal with wage disputes. In Prussia Caprivi restructured commercial as well as inheritance taxes and set in motion, albeit unsuccessfully, efforts to introduce an inheritance tax and even a progressive income tax. In a break with the Bismarckian precedent, after 1892 Chancellor von Caprivi no longer served as Prussian prime minister. In the area of foreign policy he let it be known that he opposed overseas adventures: "The less of Africa, the better." He equated the proposed construction of a battle fleet to national suicide.

Perhaps most important, Caprivi reversed Bismarck's foreign economic policy. Realizing that the Reich was ever more dependent on exports, Caprivi negotiated liberal trade pacts with Austria-Hungary and Italy in 1892, as well as with Belgium, Rumania, and Switzerland the following year. The tariff wars with Russia were suspended. The 1879 levies on wheat and rye, lumber and livestock, were reduced dramatically through the German-Russian trade treaty of 1894. The SPD for the first time voted for a government bill, much to the outrage of the Conservatives. But when the Social Democrats failed to show what William II considered proper gratitude for Caprivi's social legislation, the Kaiser and his court swiftly abandoned the chancellor's liberal course. In its place they demanded a neo-Bismarckian surge of confrontation with the Social Democrats.

William II led the way in vituperation, denouncing the SPD as the "party of revolution" and its leaders as "rabble," not worthy "to carry the name German." Once again, as under Bismarck, domestic opponents were labeled *Reichsfeinde*. In 1894 Botho Count zu Eulenburg, the Prussian prime minister, drafted a "revolutionary bill" giving the government sweeping powers to jail perceived as well as actual political offenders. And while the bill was rejected by the Reichstag, General von Waldersee, destined to succeed Moltke as chief of the general staff, demanded a government order "to gun down the rabble." The Kaiser, obsessed with the "red menace," declared that he "dare not dispatch a single soldier from German soil" for fear of thereby endangering domestic peace. "First gun down the Socialists, then behead them and render them harmless, if need be by a bloodbath," the monarch counseled, "and then war outside our borders. But not the other way around and not too soon."

This patently absurd rhetoric was accompanied by a reversal of Caprivi's liberal trade policies. Bismarck's 1879 levies on iron and grains were reintroduced and raised. Russia replied in kind. Buoyed by a new trade accord with France, St. Petersburg in 1893 slapped special import duties of between 20 and 30 percent on German products. The German Federal Council, in a classic case of tit for tat, countered with a 50 percent levy on all Russian imports, which prompted the Russians to raise their import fees on German goods by the same margin. It was a detrimental step for both sides. Germany was Russia's best trading partner, taking 28 percent of its exports and supplying an equal portion of its imports (France ranged far behind Germany with 5 percent and 8 percent, respectively). As Caprivi had put it, the Reich needed to export: "Either we export goods or we export people."

Germany became ever more dependent on foreign trade. After 1890 foodstuffs and raw materials comprised 75 percent of all imports, and manufactured goods made up nearly 70 percent of all exports. The Reich's total trade in 1890 stood at an impressive 7,500 million marks, but trade deficits of 863 million marks per year were common throughout the 1890s. Although Germany began to recover from the "Great Depression" of 1873 in 1894–1895, the alarming trade deficit nevertheless continued unabated. In an effort to solve this intolerable situation, Berlin resorted to greater protectionism.

In 1890 Johannes von Miquel, the former Liberal lord mayor of Frankfurt, became Prussian finance minister. Miquel had a plan: to revive Bismarck's erstwhile rye-and-iron alliance under the guise of an aggressive union of agrarians and industrialists (*Sammlungspolitik*). Politically, Miquel sought to reestablish the alliance of Conservatives and National Liberals that had existed before the "refounding" of the Reich after 1878. The new constellation was directed against the Social Democrats, Progressives, and Left Liberals. Miquel also mobilized the fledgling antisemites to scare the "left" wing. The nascent German fleet, as will be shown later, became a major beneficiary of "the politics of concentration."

Although the middle class in Germany steadily increased its economic power, it remained without clout in the Reichstag. At the local level it was swept from office by the tide of SPD ballots. Prussian Junkers and agricultural interests continued to dominate the Prussian lower house through the three-class voting system. Throughout Germany, the Liberals managed just barely to cling to their traditional seats of power in small towns and rural villages.

The middle class became ever more conservative under William II and threw its support behind the crown and its twin pillars of bureaucracy and army. The bureaucracy, although officially apolitical, clearly identified itself by the last third of the nineteenth century with the state, conservative and monarchical. Various ordinances from the Ministry of the Interior in the period from 1849 to 1890 demanded that civil servants encourage activities and organizations that endorsed the Hohenzollern monarchy and combat those that did not. Thus by 1890 the very bureaucracy that had championed reform for the past century had become a stolid opponent of democratization and parliamentarization. Bismarck, never an admirer of bureaucrats, had warned of their power as well as autonomy and had suggested sardonically that "every three years several ministers, a few generals, and a dozen councillors be shot; one ought to chase all civil servants from office on their fiftieth birthday."

REICHSTAG ELECTIONS UNDER WILLIAM II

Parties	1890	1893	1898	1903	1907	1912
CONSERVATIVES						
Vote (%)	19.1	19.1	15.5	13.4	13.6	12.3
Seats	93	100	79	75	84	57
LIBERALS						
Vote (%)	32.2	25.4	22.7	22.1	24.2	26.0
Seats	108	90	87	81	96	87
CENTER, GUELPHS, ALSACE-LORRAINE						
Vote (%)	25.0	24.7	25.2	25.5	25.2	22.0
Seats	143	130	135	131	133	123
SOCIAL DEMOCRATS						
Vote (%)	19.8	23.3	27.2	31.7	28.9	34.8
Seats	35	44	56	81	43	110
OTHERS						
Vote (%)	3.9	7.5	9.4	7.3	8.1	4.9
Seats	18	33	40	29	41	20
TOTAL SEATS	397	397	397	397	397	397

The state continued to view the Social Democrats as its primary adversary. Under the euphemism of the "social question," various governments attempted to curb what appeared to be the inevitable rise to power of the SPD via the ballot box. The party's venerable leader, August Bebel, was widely regarded as the "anti-Kaiser" who seemed to have replaced the Christian moral dialectic ("the least shall be the first") with the Marxian materialistic dialectic ("to each according to his need, from each according to his ability"). Allegedly without a fatherland, the Social Democrats risked being excluded from the national community.

The caretaker government of Chlodwig Prince zu Hohenlohe-Schillingsfürst, who succeeded Caprivi in 1894, sought to repeat another of Bismarck's reliable stratagems. While supporting Miquel's right-of-center coalition, Count von Posadowsky-Wehner of the Ministry of the Interior sought to steal the Social Democrats' thunder by expanding the Iron Chancellor's social security system. In short order he improved the sickness and accident insurance programs, made state subsidies for housing available to workers, extended the child labor laws to cottage industries, and made the industrial courts of arbitration mandatory for all communities of more than twenty thousand inhabi-

Sinews of Empire: Casing factory of AEG Berlin (1900).

tants. The domestic zigzag course between the poles of repression and toleration was thus set in motion once more.

Posadowsky-Wehner's seductions notwithstanding, the Social Democratic party grew by leaps and bounds. It emerged from the federal elections of 1912 as the largest political party in Germany with a total raw vote of 4.5 million and 110 seats in the Reichstag. Trade union leaders accounted for one-third of these seats. Indeed, the Free Trade Unions, first founded in the 1860s and united in the 1890s in the General Commission of Free German Trade Unions, were the largest in Europe, with 2.5 million members. Women made up 16 percent of the SPD's rank and file and 10 percent of the Free Trade Unions. (The corresponding figures for Austria were 11 percent in both categories.) By 1912 the SPD had captured the city halls of virtually every German city through the ballot box, and in many they attained 80 percent of the popular vote during local and regional elections.

Part of the SPD's electoral success was due to deplorable housing and workplace conditions. Tenement buildings in the major cities were grimy, drab square cement blocks consisting of confined space and lightless misery — breeding grounds for discontent and revolutionary fervor. Factories were built as cheaply as possible: gray, ugly, unhealthy industrial barracks. Nor were conditions in early industrial labor exemplary. Noise, dirt, heat, cold, and physical as well as psychic brutality dominated the workplace. Chest and lung diseases flourished.

A contemporary account of workers' plight in the Rhenish cotton mills is revealing: "The noise level in the mill was very high. The rattling and screaming machines caused noises almost unbearable for the newcomer." The greatest danger came from moving belts and machine parts; protective casings were considered superfluous, uneconomical, or unbuildable. Nightshift laborers toiled by poor light. "Because of the great danger of fire, the oil lamps — which in any case gave off only a faint light — were set up in the smallest number possible." There were no separate rooms where workers could change, wash, or eat. "The sanitary and hygiene conditions defied description." The most numerous diseases were "consumption, tuberculosis, inflammation of the eyes, nose, throat, and lungs as well as abscesses on legs" due to dust, humidity, and standup work. Adults suffered from chronic backaches because the sewing machines were built to accommodate child labor.

The SPD remained wedded to its Marxist doctrine. The party's leaders espoused the dogma of class warfare and refused to fund national defense. But to those who knew the SPD well — and none knew it better than the Prussian police — the party was anything but united behind its program. Rising economic conditions after 1894 combined with local and regional electoral triumphs to bring into question the party's program. Eduard Bernstein, who had edited the SPD's newspaper from exile during the years of Bismarck's Anti-Socialist Laws, in 1898 challenged the validity of Marx's theory of the inevitable collapse of capitalism and the eternal impoverishment of the proletariat. Bernstein suggested instead that capitalism was alive and well and that the conditions of workers had actually improved. In place of class warfare he urged workers to press for reform within the existing economic and political system. "We dare not hazard the destiny of the movement," Bernstein wrote, "we have built too much and what has been built is too valuable."

This reformist rather than revolutionary stance incensed the party leaders August Bebel and Wilhelm Liebknecht, but it appealed to the Free Trade Unions, whose members would have to man the barricades in case of class warfare. Bernstein's "revisionism" split the SPD; its rhetoric remained revolutionary but its daily regimen became evolutionary. In time a new generation of leaders such as Friedrich Ebert and Philipp Scheidemann proved unwilling to jeopardize the gains of decades of struggle for the mirage of revolutionary activism.

The emerging debate between Marxists and "revisionists" focused on the general strike. Initially embracing the general strike as the workers' best weapon in their struggle with the state, trade union leaders, especially, began to have second thoughts. At the SPD's Mannheim conference in 1906, they firmly rejected the tactic of the general strike as espoused by such party radicals as Rosa Luxemburg and Wilhelm Liebknecht's son, Karl. The following year Gustav Noske, who later boasted that he had never used the word *Marx-*

ism in speeches or articles, suggested that the workers had a duty to defend their homeland. In 1913 the SPD voted not to differentiate "the use to which receipts from taxes were put," that is, whether for military or educational purposes. Above all, the party was patently anti-Russian, seeing in that state the hearth of reaction and suppression of workers. When Bebel proclaimed that "the Socialists shall march to a man" in case of war with Russia, he merely reiterated Friedrich Engels' earlier stance.

The right wing of the party under Eduard Bernstein, Gerhard Hildebrand, and Paul Singer eventually embraced the concept of "social imperialism," arguing that overseas expansion was necessary for the continued steady employment of the proletariat. Was it not better, they asked, for German rather than foreign shipyards to build the merchant ships that carried German trade — and the naval vessels that protected them? Scheidemann, who as vice-president of the Reichstag caused a scandal in 1912 by refusing to pay the customary call on the Kaiser, waxed lyrical about the Berlin-to-Baghdad Railway. Noske welcomed the German colonial empire.

Yet the party was unwilling to come out from under Marx's long shadow and to jettison what many of its younger leaders considered the antiquated revolutionary rhetoric of the *Communist Manifesto.* Its radical image remained. As a result, most German state governments regarded the SPD as a revolutionary organization and sought to curtail its electoral success by restricting the suffrage. Saxony adopted the Prussian three-class voting system in 1896 and Lübeck in 1903–1904. In 1906 Hamburg decided to go Prussia one better by dividing its electorate into four classes on the basis of wealth and property.

The Three K's: *Kinder, Küche, Kirche*

The Kaiser set the tone also for the political debate concerning the German women's movement. His infamous comment in London that the woman's role be restricted to children, kitchen, and church was not an isolated gaffe. In 1910 William II lectured an audience at Königsberg that woman's task lay in "quiet work in the house and in the family." However, a growing number of female activists refused to restrict themselves, as one put it succinctly, to "involuntary producers of cannon fodder."

In March 1894 Auguste Schmidt became president of the newly founded Federation of German Women's Associations (BDF), whose membership quickly rose to seventy thousand by 1901. Through its periodical *Die Frau* and other lobbying efforts, the BDF fought for equal secondary education, access to all institutions of higher learning, legal and economic protection for marriage and motherhood, equal pay for equal work in factories, greater opportunities for professional women, government protection for prostitutes, the right to vote, the right to stand for jury duty, equal property rights, assured child support, and equal parental guardianship laws.

Perhaps as a result of these intensive efforts, the revised Civil Code of 1900, which remained in effect until 1945, for the first time established women as "legal persons." Husbands no longer were the legal guardians of their spouses, nor could they lay claim to the earnings of their partners. In 1908 the Law of Association allowed women to become active in political clubs. And women finally stormed the gates of academia. The first full-time female students were admitted at Freiburg and Heidelberg in 1901; Prussia followed suit in 1908. There were 4,126 full-time female students enrolled in German universities on the eve of World War I. The first German woman to earn a Ph.D., the historian Ricarda Huch, however, had to journey to Switzerland to acquire an advanced degree. Finally, the Civil Code of 1900 brought a reversal in divorce law. Because the introduction of universal male conscription in 1813 had guaranteed the state sufficient recruits for the army, lawmakers in 1900 felt sufficiently confident to remove from the books the 1794 provision for divorce by consent for childless couples.

Women's struggle to gain the right to vote escalated. In 1902 the German Union of Women's Suffrage (DVF) was created by radical feminists led by Anita Augspurg. Twelve years later, at a time when the DVF boasted ten thousand members, the renowned English suffragist Sylvia Pankhurst came to Germany to agitate for the vote. To Pankhurst's dismay, the city fathers of Berlin and Dresden banned her from their territory.

Proletarian women had not been invited to the founding of the German Women's Associations in 1894, and they took no part in the debate over the Civil Code of 1900 to protest what they considered the "bourgeois class character of the women's movement," but their plight did not go unnoticed. Novelists Anna Croissant-Rust, Gabriele Reuter, Helene Böhlau, and Clara Viebig exposed the desperate situation of urban working-class and peasant women. In 1891 Clara Zetkin, an early supporter of the SPD, had founded the paper *Equality* to lecture proletarian women that economic self-sufficiency was the necessary precondition for social and political equality.

Working-class women made several attempts to organize. In 1893 they established thirty-three local associations with more than three thousand members, but the police dissolved most of these for being "political." The associations were reconstituted in 1907, however, in nearly a hundred educational organizations boasting more than ten thousand members. Working women were most active at the local level in the areas of health service, education, welfare for the sick and unemployed, care for infants and orphans, day care, and maintenance of housing and food standards. The Law of Association in 1908 finally permitted women to join the SPD as members with "equal rights."

The vast majority of working women as late as 1907 toiled as either permanent or seasonal agrarian laborers (50 percent) or as domestic servant girls (16 percent). They enjoyed none of the gains of proletarian women (18 percent of the labor force) such as the maximum ten-hour workday, work-free Sundays and nights, and (after 1908) eight-week leave during pregnancy.

Champion of working women:
Clara Zetkin of the SPD (1912).

Women's lot on the land was hard. Many peasant farmers supplemented their income by working in factories, leaving their wives to look after the farm. Pregnancy complicated an already harsh existence. As late as 1912, a local doctor in the Zeitz district of Saxony near Leipzig noted that many a countrywoman did not have sufficient food to "maintain her own strength or that of the child that she carries in her womb." Infant mortality remained high as a result.

> Their diet is poor in fat and protein. This is harmful to pregnant women, to unborn infants and to women in childbed. Debility of the newborn, a short breast-feeding period and a premature use of artificial baby foods, with all their disastrous consequences for the infant, are the result.

The steady influx of seasonal migrant workers from the eastern regions of Prussia and from western Poland depressed agrarian wages and constituted stiff competition for German women.

The middle-class women's movement, like German society at large, experienced a radical shift to the right in the last decade of peace. In November 1904 Ruth Bré created the League for the Protection of Motherhood at Leipzig. Its manifesto left no doubt as to its social Darwinist leanings. The league promised to establish "mother colonies" for unmarried mothers and their children in the countryside with state support for the general "improvement of the nation" by way of "breeding the healthy" and thereby contributing to Germany's "racial health." Academic luminaries such as Max Weber, Werner Sombart, and Sigmund Freud endorsed the league's effort. The German Colonial Women's League, with twelve thousand members by 1911, struggled to preserve the purity of the white race in the German colonies, both present and future.

In 1910 Gertrud Bäumer took charge of the 170,000-member BDF. A disciple of both Adolf Stöcker and Friedrich Naumann, founder of the National Social Association in 1895, Bäumer wanted the feminist movement to be at once national and social. She argued that marriage and motherhood were to take precedence over admission to "male professions." Bäumer, following Bré, refused to support the feminist call for abortion upon demand, save in cases where the embryo was likely to be "inferior."

Another stalwart of the BDF, Maria Lischnewska, did both Bré and Bäumer one better. The nation's will, she declared in Nietzschean language, was synonymous with its birthrate. Lischnewska depicted the French as a "dying, sinking people" and predicted doom for the United States, where white women had recourse to abortion — albeit not legally — while the black population increased at an alarming rate. "The future of the nation," she trumpeted, "lies in the will of the woman to motherhood." Lischnewska demanded forced sterilization of alcoholics, disfranchisement of the illiterate and the mentally defective, compulsory medical examinations for couples intending to marry, and prohibition of racially mixed marriages.

The tone of the debate within the feminist movement had radically shifted. Whereas Auguste Schmidt and Helene Lange had sought to protect marriage for social and moral reasons, Bré and Lischnewska sought to protect matrimony for reasons of "racial hygiene." One wonders whether the irony of their French and Slavic names ever dawned on the German nationalists Bré and Lischnewska.

A male backlash against the various women's activities was not long in coming. In 1912 the League for the Struggle Against the Emancipation of Women was founded. Comprising admirals, generals, and professors, the group's more illustrious leaders included the court painter Anton von Werner, General August Keim of the Navy League, Professor Dietrich Schäfer of the Pan-German League, and Ludwig Schemann of both the Richard Wagner circle at Bayreuth and the Pan-Germans. The broad spectrum of "cultural pessimists" (discussed later in this chapter) joined ranks in this organization. Its foot soldiers consisted largely of the 100,000 members of the German National Commercial Employer's Union, a group that conveniently linked the feminist movement to the alleged Jewish "world conspiracy."

Politics by Pressure Groups

Domestic politics, apart from the unequal treatment of men and women under the Civil Code of 1900, was dominated by the dichotomy between the middle class's economic clout and its political impotence. While some wealthy bourgeois families managed to gain access to the court by purchasing titles of nobility or land and marrying their daughters to impoverished Junkers, the vast majority chafed under their perceived lack of influence on national decision making. This dichotomy was partially alleviated by the transfer of the political process from parliament to external pressure groups. Every conceivable interest group, ranging from the Anti-Semitic League to the Union to Combat Social Democracy, took its cause to the public through mass movements.

The most famous pressure groups were founded by the new national bourgeois right. The various veterans' associations, in 1899 united in the Kyffhäuserbund,[1] lobbied for veterans' rights, stronger national defense, and an aggressive foreign policy. Their ranks swelled from 1.5 million in 1897 to 2.8 million in 1913. By the eve of World War I, the German Navy League, founded in 1898, boasted 1.1 million members, while its sister lobby for ground forces, the German Defense League (1912), could claim 360,000 members by 1914. Women rallied behind Admiral von Tirpitz's fleet building in the German General Women's Association. Closely allied to the Navy League was the German Colonial League. Founded in 1887, its membership rose to 42,000 by 1914. That same year the Pan-German League (founded in 1891), which sought to unite all German speakers under one national umbrella and to spread German culture globally, claimed about 20,000 highly influential and vocal members. Finally, the Agrarian League, founded in 1893, lobbied the government for high tariffs on imported grains. With 328,000 members in 1914, it became the voice of the Prussian Junkers. While the Agrarian League generally preferred to endorse Conservative candidates sympathetic to agrarian interests in federal elections, usually helping to elect seventy to eighty such delegates, it nevertheless was quite willing to run and finance its own candidates when allied Conservatives failed to give proper respect.

These extraparliamentary mass movements pursued their goals — high tariffs on eastern grains, a powerful navy, larger land forces, overseas colonies, the spread of German culture, and others — through public meetings, magazines and newspapers, and lobbying Reichstag deputies. In the process they contributed to the vulgarization of politics and the brutalization of debate. With their combined memberships well in the millions, no government dared ignore them.

---

[1] Both the monument of 1896 and the veterans' movement of 1899 were associated with the Hohenstaufen castle ruin on the Kyffhäuser hill in Thuringia partly because of the legend that the medieval emperor Frederick Barbarossa was asleep under the hill, awaiting the day to lead the German people to victory over their enemies.

Anglo-Saxon historians have viewed this German societal substructure with its chauvinistic mentality and feudal-minded agrarian capitalists as a historical deviance. "Normative" societies such as those in Britain, France, and the United States, they suggest, had managed to shed their feudal past through some sort of bourgeois revolution. In Germany, however, the lack of a liberal revolution, the subservience of the middle class to feudal remnants, and the retarded, somewhat premodern social structure combined to distort national development. This divergence from the West has prompted some historians to detect a special or separate path (*Sonderweg*) in German history, one that ultimately led to the catastrophe of the Third Reich (1933–1945).

Whatever the case, the constitutional glue that held the chaotic domestic sector of the Second Reich together was the crown. William II's role was pivotal. The monarch appointed all Prussian ministers and German state secretaries, decided military policy, dabbled in foreign policy, and had the power to declare war and to make peace. The reins of power in both Prussia and Germany came together in his hands alone. Imperial Germany never possessed a national coordinating body such as the Committee of Imperial Defence in Britain or the National Security Council in the United States. Thus the Kaiser's crucial role as clearinghouse for both domestic and foreign policies in large measure determined the national polity.

Max Weber stated that Imperial Germany had three types of legitimate rule: rational, traditional, and charismatic. By 1900 William II represented the last. His personal rule was a unique combination of prestige and power politics, of a craving for popularity and mesmerization with technology. William II transformed the old legitimate Prussian monarchy into a "cult of charismatic leadership" (*Führertum*) that was to centralize decision making and integrate the realm's diverse regional, religious, and ethnic units into the national polity. But William lacked both the simple modesty of his grandfather and the brilliance of his forefathers such as the Great Elector or Frederick II. The Kaiser's career was to be undermined by three great scandals that clearly defined his limited talents and exposed the nation's political immaturity.

In 1907 Maximilian Harden in his critical journal *Zukunft* implicated Phillip Prince zu Eulenburg, William's close personal adviser and confidant, in a homosexual scandal with the city commandant, Count von Moltke. In a series of four spectacular trials that brought a procession of pimps, thieves, and morons to the witness stand, the German public learned of allegedly "disgusting orgies" in the aristocratic Guards regiment. And while similar episodes involving homosexuality rocked Britain (Oscar Wilde) and Austria (Archduke Ludwig-Viktor), the Eulenburg affair was notorious because it reached into the highest echelons of court and army. In the process, the Kaiser's judgment and "divine right" to rule were brought into question.

More serious, in 1908 William II gave an interview to the London newspaper *Daily Telegraph*, in which the half-English monarch informed the British that while he loved them, this sentiment was not shared by his subjects. The Kaiser further confided that the German fleet was being built not against Britannia but against America and Japan. Finally, William II claimed that during the Boer War he had headed off Franco-Russian plans to forge a continental block against London and that the Prussian General Staff had drafted the plans that finally brought victory over the Boers. These sensational (and unfounded) statements brought forth a storm of protest. The Reichstag denounced William's actions and demanded that he recognize constitutional limits on his power. The Kaiser weathered the storm by slaying fox on the Fürstenberg estates at Donaueschingen, where his chief of the military cabinet, General von Hülsen-Häseler, died of a heart attack trying to amuse his monarch by dancing in a ballerina costume in the summer heat. The so-called *Daily Telegraph* affair hardly enhanced the crown's aura.

Finally, in 1913–1914 an ugly civil-military confrontation occurred at Zabern (Saverne) in Alsace when a Prussian subaltern officer hurled an offensive ethnic slur at a local civilian. The matter turned into a cause célèbre when the Prussian army and government, as well as Crown Prince William, refused to censure the officer. As during the *Daily Telegraph* affair, the Reichstag passed a vote of no confidence (293 to 54) in the government and, by implication, the crown. William II sloughed the matter off as being "purely military" and hence falling solely within his exclusive command authority.

All three cases severely eroded the crown's prestige. All three would have led to the government's resignation under a democratic system. All three revealed that William was not up to the central task of governing. But all three came to naught because under the Bismarckian system, final authority rested with the monarch rather than with parliament. Nevertheless, few in Germany doubted that a constitutional crisis lurked on the horizon.

Nor was Imperial Germany's prestige enhanced by the Kaiser's previously noted uniform fetish. Whereas Frederick William I and Frederick II had worn simple Prussian blue, William II looked more like a peacock. And his veneration of uniforms extended to society in general. The Kaiser's premier ministers appeared in parliament in military uniform, blade at their side, and often delivered major speeches with one hand on the hilt of their sword. German children habitually were clothed (and photographed) in sailor's suits. Professors, squeezed into their reserve lieutenant's uniform, delivered patriotic lectures at national fêtes. Many obituaries for academic "mandarins" listed the deceased's reserve lieutenant's commission before membership in august academies of learning. In Carl Zuckmayer's *Der Hauptmann von Köpenick* ("The Captain from Köpenick"), which satirized this slavish devotion to things martial, the reserve officer attentively listens as the tailor proclaims: "So, you have managed to become a reserve lieutenant, that is the main thing. . . . the doctorate is the visiting card, but the reserve commission is the open door — that's the essential thing these days!" The crown relegated university rectors to forty-seventh place on its social ladder of sixty-two rungs.[1] The German thirst for status and prestige, however, was not limited to the domestic scene.

A Place in the Sun: The New Course of Bülow and Tirpitz

Imperial Germany's foreign policy was, in a word, disastrous. It was not so much that the Reich behaved more aggressively or was more devious in conducting its foreign policy than other European powers, but rather that lack of consistency exasperated friend and foe alike. Germany was much like an unbridled wild stallion until about 1905–1906, forcing every issue, demanding a voice in every decision, and constantly clamoring for recognition by the established world powers. Thereafter, Berlin retreated into a dour defensive and pessimistic posture, viewing war as the only course left open by repeated slights and rebuffs on the part of the established powers.

The truth is that the men who succeeded Bismarck shared Weber's conviction that unification, rather than constituting the end of an era of European nation building, was but "the starting point of German power-politics on a global scale." William II and his minions rejected the notions of a "saturated" Reich, semihegemony on the Continent, and security through alliances — the principles enunciated in Bismarck's Bad Kissingen Dictate. They sought instead to preserve a free hand among the powers, to exploit every crisis for gain. They jettisoned *Realpolitik* for a hybrid mix of *Idealpolitik* based on emotionalism, racialism, and prestige. Pyrrhic victories over neighbors became ends in themselves. Means and goals were never coordinated. No grand design guided the national polity.

The expansion of the German colonial empire under William II in many ways symbolized both the glory and the misery of *Weltpolitik*. Nauru Island, Palau, the Carolines and Marianas, the exchange of Zanzibar for Helgoland Island, the acquisition of a leasehold at Kiaochow and Shantung peninsula: these prestigious gains amounted to a mere net increase of 0.18 percent over Bismarck's colonial empire. At no time did they constitute the lucrative source of raw materials and market for finished goods that imperial historians and Marxists alike claim. In 1914 the colonies accounted for 0.5 percent of the Reich's total trade and 3.8 percent of its overseas investments. Only one of every 1,000 emigrants — a grand total of 5,495 civilians — chose the colonies. Above all, the colonies were a major drain on imperial finances. By 1913 Kiaochow alone had swallowed 200 million marks. The suppression of the Boxer Rebellion[2] in

[1] Reichstag deputies ranked fifty-eighth.

[2] Dangerous antiforeign rebellions broke out in China in the summer of 1900, and the Boxers laid siege to the embassy compound at Beijing. William II dispatched General von Waldersee as part of an international force to restore order. The Kaiser exhorted his troops to give no pardon, take no prisoners, and make a name for themselves as Attila the Hun had once done.

1900 cost the German taxpayers 100 million marks, and that of the Herero tribe in German Southwest Africa between 1904 and 1907 an additional 323 million marks. Matthias Erzberger of the Center party caustically noted that such sums would have sufficed to make the "finest garden even out of the Mark Brandenburg."

It should be noted in all fairness that even a contemporary critic such as Hans Delbrück vociferously endorsed overseas expansion. "The nation which comes away empty-handed," Delbrück warned his fellow countrymen, "will in the next generation cease to be in the ranks of the great nations." Max Weber also embraced the new cult of expansionism: "Power alone will have a decisive influence on the extent to which individual nations will share in the economic control of the world."

William II, through a complex composite of motives, actively pursued *Weltpolitik*. Apart from the simple economic impulse of competing for world markets, raw materials, and investments, the Kaiser sought to overcome Germany's purely continental power position by expanding overseas. Closely allied to this goal, the Reich strove for recognition from the established colonial powers as an equal in world affairs. Imperial Germany struggled to show the flag, to boast its prestige as a major global player. In the oration to his Brandenburg subjects in 1892 mentioned earlier, William II had promised to lead them "towards glorious times." "Great things," the monarch had assured them, were headed their way. In 1898 the Kaiser's foreign minister, Bernhard von Bülow, promised William that he could assume the role of global arbitrator.

The Imperial German Navy became the most obvious manifestation of "world politics." It, more than any other single development or policy, came to represent the shift away from the Continent. The navy manifested the burning desire for a "place in the sun," the craving for recognition, and the willingness to confront recognized powers for a piece of the colonial pie. It became the symbol of German power projection. And the navy, unlike the various royal armies, was a national German entity, a throwback to the heady euphoria of the Paulskirche of 1848–1849. As such it was the darling of the German middle class.

The fleet was virtually synonymous with the name Alfred von Tirpitz (ennobled 1900). A child of the Industrial Revolution born to middle-class parents, the admiral was bedazzled by its technological wonders: armored plates, torpedoes, turbines, diesel engines, explosive shells, optical range finders, and electrical systems. An astute politician, Tirpitz realized that Miquel's attempt to rally the right-of-center parties into a national coalition (*Sammlungspolitik*) could serve the fleet, while the fleet could serve the nation as a "strong palliative against Social Democrats." A symbiotic relationship developed among naval expansion, industry, agriculture, and the state. Industrialists would benefit from shipbuilding contracts and expanded global markets; agrarians would be rewarded for their support of fleet building with high tariffs designed to preserve their social preeminence.

The "Luxury" Fleet: German warships in the Baltic Sea (1907).

But Tirpitz's vision of "navalism" was much more than a dose of social imperialism designed to plaster over the cracks in the Reich's domestic veneer. The admiral had absorbed from Charles Darwin's continental popularizers the notion of struggle for survival and from the American Captain Alfred Thayer Mahan the message that true wealth lay with sea power. Tirpitz, along with William II, had learned the notion of "perfidious Albion" from the historian Heinrich von Treitschke. Britain, so the argument went, was untrustworthy, driven by greed as well as envy of German accomplishments. It alone stood in the way of German overseas expansion.

In 1897 Tirpitz described sea power as "a question of survival" for Germany. He sought to propel the Reich into the ranks of the superpowers by the early 1920s. The future was clear: either Germany broke its continental chains with a powerful fleet, or it would sink back to the status of a "poor farming country." The dominant issue of the coming century, Tirpitz stated, would be the decline and eventual partitioning of the British Empire: "four world powers: Russia, England, America, and Germany." Who would seize the lion's share of the projected spoils? William II expressed the prevailing mood in an address to the Berlin garrison on January 1, 1900, when he stated that just as William I had raised Prussia into the ranks of the great continental powers with his army, he, William II, would "attain that place which [Germany] has not yet reached" in world affairs with a navy.

Two navy bills in 1898 and 1900, augmented by supplementary bills in 1906, 1908, and 1912, were to provide Germany with a fleet of sixty capital ships concentrated "between Helgoland and the Thames."[1] No friend of the hated "parliamentary fleet" of 1848, the admiral promised his Kaiser not only "a great overseas policy" but also a removal of "the disturbing influence of the Reichstag" from naval affairs. A so-called iron budget, stipulating automatic replacement of ships every twenty years, would achieve that goal. Tirpitz financed naval construction through indirect taxes on consumer and luxury items to avoid arousing the antipathy of the Conservatives for what they called the "ghastly fleet." For the same reason, naval outlays were closely indexed to the projected growth of the German economy.

There is no doubt that the fleet was built first and foremost against Britain. During his first month in office, Tirpitz described Britain to William II as "the most dangerous enemy at present." On another occasion the admiral likened his naval plan to "the patient laying of brick upon brick." A "danger zone" of naval construction would have to be traversed safely. The "bear skin," Tirpitz slyly suggested, could not be divided up "before the bear is slain." German diplomacy would have to shield the nascent fleet from a preemptive British strike ("to Copenhagen" it, as Admiral Nelson had done to the Danish fleet in 1801).

In the meantime, the Reich's foreign policy, as Bülow put it, "stood to a certain degree in the service of the fleet." The truth is that Berlin simply could not restrain itself, seeking to push the advantage at each and every international flash point. Germany vied with Britain and the United States for pieces of Samoa in 1889 and 1899 and almost went to war with the United States in 1898 over the Philippines. In 1900 the Reich demanded an active role in the international expedition to China. Two years later, in conjunction with Britain and Italy, Germany challenged the Monroe Doctrine by blockading Venezuela. On each occasion, Berlin managed to alienate a major power without achieving significant gains.

Bülow's ideal was a policy of the free hand. Germany, he declared, could afford to sit back and await major suitors. In reality, however, he pursued two policies: bullying and cajoling the British into an alliance on Germany's terms, while courting the Russians into reconstituting Bismarck's Reinsurance Treaty of 1887. Neither policy succeeded. The British refused to be pressured into making significant colonial concessions to the Germans and more than matched Tirpitz's fleet building. And when William II and Nicholas II in 1905

---

[1] Helgoland is a small island in the North Sea, not far from the mouth of the Elbe River, acquired from the British in 1890 by exchanging it for Zanzibar in East Africa.

at Björkö cheerily signed a Russo-German alliance, their respective governments in Berlin and St. Petersburg rejected the accord as incompatible with the Austro-German Alliance of 1879 and the Franco-Russian Alliance of 1893. Germany, as William II noted, ended up "sitting between two stools."

Yet for a brief moment in 1905–1906, it appeared as though Germany was in the driver's seat. In February 1904 Russia went to war with Britain's ally Japan, leaving France isolated. Crippling Russian defeats both on land and at sea temporarily removed that country as a threat to Germany. William II and Bülow decided to press their advantage. Was the moment not ripe to demand colonial concessions from France and to test the strength of the recently concluded Anglo-French entente of 1904? And was not Joseph Chamberlain, the British minister of colonies, touting a "Teutonic alliance" embracing Britain, Germany, and the United States to regulate the world's affairs? The Germans were so confident of victory that they demanded a European conference to demonstrate their power and to humiliate France.

It was not to be. The conference, held at the Spanish sea resort of Algeciras in January 1906, was a major diplomatic defeat for Germany. Supported only by Vienna, Berlin was forced to acknowledge the strength of the Anglo-French accord. Even Italy, since 1882 a member of the Triple Alliance, deserted Austria-Hungary and Germany in order to court Britain and France in pursuit of its North African plans of conquest. Within a year the Anglo-French entente was extended to include Russia. Cries of encirclement arose in Germany.

The harsh reality is that Berlin possessed no consistent foreign policy. The Foreign Office staggered from crisis to crisis, seeking only to gain from the misfortunes of others. In 1905–1906 it fumbled away perhaps its only chance to restore the primacy of politics by seeking a firm tie in either the east (Russia) or the west (Britain). In London Chamberlain soon spoke of a propitious moment's slipping away. Concurrently, British Admiral Sir John Fisher launched a technological revolution by introducing the all-big-gun, one-calibre *Dreadnought* and *Invincible,* therewith inaugurating a heated naval arms race with Germany. At the Hague in 1899 and again in 1907, Germany made a mockery of disarmament talks.

The mood in Berlin turned dark and pessimistic. William II equated the situation to 1756 and Kaunitz's Austro-French-Russian coalition against Frederick II: "The Coalition is de facto here." The cries of encirclement became ever more shrill. Few were willing to accept that Germany, in reality, had excluded itself from the concert of Europe. Popular pundits began to discern an air of *finis Germaniae* — "the end of Germany."

The Reich's diplomatic isolation in Europe inspired the desperate logic of the Schlieffen plan. In the winter of 1905 and spring of 1906, Alfred von Schlieffen, chief of the General Staff, drafted two contingency plans designed to rescue Germany from its foreign policy predicament by military means. The general sought nothing less than to defeat the Reich's two major enemies, France and Russia, on two separate fronts within a span of forty days. Arguing that France was the more industrialized power with a more extensive railroad system for rapid mobilization, Schlieffen planned to defeat it first before turning against the more slowly mobilizing Russian forces. The German armies were to march through northern France via Belgium and southern Holland, skirt the English Channel, turn in behind Paris from the west, and drive the capital's garrison as well as the main French army against the "anvil" of German forces stationed in Alsace-Lorraine. Military prowess was to rescue failed statecraft.

The Schlieffen plan was a child born of desperation. With Austria-Hungary as the only real ally — no one in Berlin seriously expected Italy to fulfill its treaty obligations in case of war — Germany's options were reduced to one: military action. German planners from Caprivi to Schlieffen, in fact, were convinced that war alone could break what Caprivi had called "a devil's circle of armaments and counter-armaments, coalitions and counter-coalitions, in a climate of mistrust and fear." Schlieffen was convinced that Europe was already aflame by the turn of the century. France still yearned for revenge for 1870–1871, Russia was beset by "racial antipathy between Slavs and Teutons," Britain was obsessed with envy of German trade, and Italy was driven by a naked lust for expansion. Austria-Hungary and Germany alone remained chivalrous and peaceable. The general developed a near-paranoidal worst-case scenario to buttress his notion of the unavoidability of war:

> At the given moment, the gates will be opened, the drawbridges let down, and the [enemy] armies of millions of men will pour into Central Europe across the Vosges, the Meuse, the Königsau, the Niemen, the Bug, and even across the Isonzo and the Tyrolean Alps in a wave of devastation and destruction.

But the Reich did nothing to support Schlieffen's panacea. No new allies were courted; no reassessment of existing alliances was undertaken; no dramatic expansion of the armed forces took place. Even when it dawned on the General Staff in 1912 that the requisite forces for the planned march around Paris existed only on paper, proposals to expand land forces by 300,000 men were scuttled for fear that the army would be forced to recruit the requisite active-duty officers from "undesirable" social circles. The Reichstag spent the last years of peace discussing not national security but such matters as officer elections in regiments, the duel, preferential treatment of nobles in prestigious regiments, the army's boycott of known SPD pubs, and the lack of Jewish active officers in the corps.

After 1905–1906 Germany clung desperately to a failed strategy. Admiral von Tirpitz accepted the British "dreadnought" challenge and began a feverish arms race with "perfidious Albion," one that Germany could not possibly win. German diplomats sought in vain by various means to break the Anglo-French-Russian ring. The much-ballyhooed Berlin-to-Baghdad railroad never reached Baghdad, nor did it remain in German hands. In 1911 Germany tried again to break the entente. Foreign Secretary Alfred von Kiderlen-Wächter dispatched the gunboat *Panther* to the Moroccan port of Agadir in order to "protect" German iron interests in western Morocco against French incursions. Once more Germany was isolated. The British cabinet inaugurated joint staff talks with France and warned Berlin that it would not tolerate such German pressures against France. The German public, which had expected to gain western Morocco, had to be content with a strip of French colonial territory near the Cameroons.

Bismarck had played chess; William II played poker. But even the Kaiser noted that his foreign policy was in serious trouble by 1914. "World politics" had been scaled back to "Balkan politics." As William II put it: "Either the German flag will soon fly over the fortifications on the Bosphorus or I shall share the sad fate of the great exile on St. Helena." The emperor's new chancellor, Theobald von Bethmann Hollweg, was equally pessimistic and forbade his son to plant new trees on his estate of Hohenfinow along the Oder: "In a few years the Russians will be here."[1]

The political vocabulary also changed in Germany. Both William II and Bethmann Hollweg spoke ever more frequently in racial and social Darwinistic terms. In 1912, for example, William II informed the chancellor of his firm belief in an "eventual struggle for survival" that would pit the "Germans in Europe (Austria, Germany)" against "the Latins (Gauls) supported by the Slavs (Russia), with the Anglo-Saxons on the side of the Slavs." Bethmann Hollweg lectured parliament about an "inevitable showdown between Slav and Teuton." Theodor Reismann-Gronne of the Pan-Germans couched the struggle in futuristic language as one between "the blonds" and the "Slavs" and demanded a new vocabulary: "*Volk* instead of kingdom . . . and race instead of humanity." Popular writers as well as government officials reduced the future to a life-and-death struggle between Austria-Hungary and Germany on the one hand, and Britain, France, and Russia on the other. Few bothered to inquire whether the ally at Vienna was prepared for such a showdown.

"Nervous Splendor": Austria-Hungary to 1914

The Habsburg monarchy in the late nineteenth century was the epitome of elegance. Vienna glittered as the social and cultural jewel of Central Europe. People then and later nostalgically spoke of the days when Francis Joseph I administered a dazzling multinational empire in the heart of Europe. It was the time of Strauss waltzes and grand operas, the poems of Hugo von Hofmannsthal and the plays of Arthur Schnitzler, the Burgtheater and the cafés, the imperial and royal army, the countless courtiers and councillors, the endless court balls, and the pioneering psychology of Sigmund Freud. For most

[1] In fact, the Russians did arrive in 1945.

citizens, the rule of law, political freedom, legal security, and a great deal of toleration reigned.

But *fin de siècle* Vienna also exuded what the American novelist Frederic Morton aptly called a "nervous splendor." The dazzling facade belied reality, for the monarchy and the state were living on borrowed time. Bismarck had closed Austria out of his *Kleindeutsch* state. Denied their historic role in the German lands, the Habsburgs redirected their attention down the Danube valley and the Balkan peninsula. Above all, within the monarchy no fewer than eleven major and sundry nationalities sought various forms of self-government. Increasingly, only two institutions, army and crown, held the Austro-Hungarian Empire together.

But beneath this cultured veneer lurked sheer hatred. The lower classes hated the Jews; the middle classes hated the Social Democrats; the nationalities hated each other; and the upper classes hated all but themselves. Demagogues exploited these hatreds. Not even the ethnic Germans were united: pro-Habsburg in Vorarlberg, Tyrol, and Carinthia, they were pro-German in Bohemia as well as in Lower Austria, and divided in allegiance between Berlin and Vienna in the capital itself.

The physical parameters of the Habsburg empire had been decided in the wake of their crushing defeat at the hands of Prussia in 1866. The Magyars, still bitter over Austria's use of Russian forces to break their rebellion under Louis Kossuth, seized the occasion to wring from Vienna the Compromise Agreement of 1867. Thereby the state was officially divided into two halves: "the Kingdoms and Lands Represented in the Reichsrat" at Vienna and the "Lands of the Hungarian Holy Crown" — in short, Austria and Hungary. Each

NATIONALITIES OF THE AUSTRO-HUNGARIAN EMPIRE, 1910

Nationality	Number	Percentage
Germans	12,006,521	23.36
Magyars	10,056,315	19.57
Czechs	6,442,133	12.54
Poles	4,976,804	9.68
Serbs, Croats	4,380,891	8.52
Ruthenes (Ukrainians)	3,997,831	7.78
Rumanians	3,224,147	6.27
Slovaks	1,967,970	3.83
Slovenes	1,255,620	2.44
Italians	768,422	1.50
Others	2,313,569	4.51
TOTAL	51,390,223	100.00

had its own constitution and cabinet, responsible to its own legislature, but ministries of finance, law, and commerce common to both. A customs union and a common bank of issue further united the two halves of the dual monarchy economically. Semiannually, alternating between Budapest and Vienna, sixty delegates from each state, sitting separately and communicating only in writing, met to deal with issues of common interest.

Matters of state were the domain of the emperor-king, the two prime ministers, and a rather nebulous joint council of ministers. An Austrian minister of war administered the so-called Joint Army, the Austrian National Guard (*Landwehr*), and the navy. The official language of command in the armed forces was German. A Hungarian minister of war headed the Hungarian militia, or *honvédség*. Its language of command was Magyar, but one of its components, the Croatian-Slavonian Hrvatsko Domobrantsvo, obeyed only Serbo-Croatian orders. The Compromise Agreement, in the words of a recent historian, "did not satisfy anybody, which assured its survival."

Francis Joseph I, emperor of Austria and king of Hungary, was the cement that held the multinational state together. In youth he had conducted an active foreign policy and fancied himself to possess military abilities. In old age he sought to avoid war and administer his diverse provinces as long as possible. Francis Joseph's personal life was tragic: he lost both Elizabeth of Bavaria, the wife he loved but who did not return his passion, and Rudolf, his son and heir, who chose suicide over succession. Honest, reliable, considerate, and tolerant but also unimaginative, inflexible, and boring, Francis Joseph was the consummate guardian of legitimacy in his realm. The emperor reduced his world to rigid court ceremony dating from the Spanish Counter Reformation. Controversies were drowned in a sea of paper and emotions reduced to mere ceremonial and bureaucratic routine.

There was little hope for the future. The heir apparent, Archduke Francis Ferdinand, although seen by many historians as a potential reformer and possible savior of the multinational empire, in fact was a man of rigid principles and little compromise. A bigoted Catholic, rabid antisemite, and confirmed absolutist, the archduke allowed his anti-Hungarian sentiments to dominate him to such an extent that he actually crossed that ancient land in his railroad car with the curtains drawn.

Was there a viable solution to the Empire's dilemma? Probably not. Francis Joseph I knew well that any concession to the forces of nationalism would unravel his empire. Even the Magyars, who did as little as possible for the Habsburg possessions and who were an ethnic minority even within their own lands, agreed with Francis Joseph. For how could the national revolts of dissatisfied intellectuals and lawyers be resolved? Where they constituted a majority, the ethnic groups had already been granted use of their own language and culture in schools. Additionally, they dominated their regional assemblies and conducted business in their native tongues.

But Francis Joseph realized that the dissatisfied intellectuals wanted more. The Czechs had rediscovered a national culture and now demanded not only their own national militia but also that the ancient kingdom of Bohemia be reconstituted by and for them. The Serbs wished to reestablish a medieval kingdom, a great south Slav nation. The radicals in Belgrade gave clear expression to their anti-Austrian, separatist ambitions. The Poles clouded the picture further by seeking to deploy the Habsburg armies against their primary adversary, Russia.

The Hungarian parliament practiced sheer obstructionism. Its position was simple: not a penny and not a man to the Habsburg defense until Hungary attained its own armed forces and language of command. The Imperial Council (Reichsrat) at Vienna, elected by universal male suffrage after 1906, hardly behaved better. German Liberals, Social Democrats, and Pan-Germans fought with Czech liberals, socialists, and radicals, as well as with a bewildering host of Italian, Rumanian, Ruthenian, and Slovene nationalists, over the military, which was variously denounced as being corrupt, feudal, Germanic, Hungarophile, inefficient, Jesuit-ridden, Judaized, pro-Slav, reactionary, and even spendthrift. Paralyzed by this petty bickering, the Reichsrat was effectively checkmated. Business was conducted instead by a series of dictatorial cabinets that ruled by an emergency article of the Constitution.

Internationally, the Austro-Hungarian Empire faced Russian (and Italian) expansionism in the Balkans, as well as British retreat from the Near East. Berlin alone stood with Vienna. With each crisis that swept across southeastern Europe, like the one following Vienna's annexation of Bosnia and Herzegovina in 1908, the two Germanic powers were driven ever closer into each other's arms. An emotional bond based on racial closeness — the so-called *Nibelungen* loyalty between Hohenzollerns and Habsburgs — replaced the cold logic of Bismarckian diplomacy. More and more, the Dual Alliance of 1879 became a desperate instrument to maintain the German presence in Central Europe. Berlin and Vienna were pushed closer and closer, and proclaimed that they stood "shoulder to shoulder" against a perceived tide of entente resentment and aggression.

The Austro-German alliance was solidified by close ties between William II and Francis Joseph, and especially between William and Archduke Francis Ferdinand, the Habsburg heir apparent. State visits, royal hunts, staff talks, and joint military maneuvers buttressed the Berlin-Vienna connection. But there were also areas of concern. Francis Joseph was dismayed by William's obsession with navalism and *Weltpolitik*, by the Kaiser's frequent attempts to reconstitute the Russian alliance of 1887, and by his failure to appreciate the South Slav (Serbian) problem. In addition, Habsburg diplomats were annoyed that their German counterparts continued to court the Italians and that German economic interests sought to penetrate the Balkans, an area that Austria-Hungary coveted for itself. Yet in the end, however much they may have disliked

AUSTRIA-HUNGARY IN 1914

German policies and attitudes, few statesmen and soldiers in Vienna could deny the economic and military might of the German ally. Germany remained the monarchy's major trading partner, a reliable source of capital, and a military deterrent against Russia.

The second unifying factor in the Empire, the Joint Army, was in a sad state of neglect. Although the population had grown nearly 50 percent between 1870 and 1914, the army's budget had increased a mere 15 percent. In terms of manpower, the result was that while the populace had expanded by

10 million between 1889 and 1912, the annual intake of recruits had remained stagnant at 125,500. The Joint Army thus fell ever further behind its European rivals in force strength. Whereas the Empire in 1906 conscripted 0.29 percent of the population, France took in 0.75 percent, or more than twice as many young men proportionally.

Not even the War Services Act of 1912, instituted mainly by the realization that the monarchy's defenses were woefully inadequate and by Hungarian prime minister István Tisza's willingness to spend on the Habsburg army, brought much timely succor. It raised the annual intake of recruits by forty-two thousand men; provided for emergency measures to mobilize the labor, goods, and services of both parts of the monarchy; and ordered twelve batteries of 30.5-cm heavy howitzers from the Skoda Works in Bohemia. Yet the Habsburg army in 1914 fielded fewer battalions than it had against Italy in 1859. The joke of 1914 — that in Germany the situation was "serious but not hopeless," whereas in Austria-Hungary it was "hopeless but not serious" — certainly was not far off the mark.

The term *nervous splendor* also applies to the Joint Army's leadership. Its dominant personality, Chief of Staff Conrad von Hötzendorf, was convinced that only a successful war could revitalize the Empire. Indefatigable, Conrad turned his attention to improving artillery, education, command and control, and mountain warfare. But the general was beset by both pessimism and social Darwinism. In 1907, for example, he seriously suggested that Austria-Hungary not send a delegate to the Second Hague Conference on Disarmament because it was already in a state of de facto disarmament. Yet Conrad busied himself drafting contingency war plans against Russia, Serbia, Rumania, Italy, and Montenegro, or any combination thereof. From Darwin and Nietzsche, Conrad had accepted notions such as survival of the fittest, the "will to live," and the struggle for life. "The struggle for existence," Conrad was fond of saying, was "the only real and rational basis for policy making." A generation of younger staff officers raised under him accepted these views as dogma.

DEFENSE APPROPRIATIONS OF THE MAJOR POWERS (in $ millions)

	1890	1900	1910	1914
Britain	157	253	340	384
France	142	139	188	197
Germany	121	168	204	442
Italy	79	78	122	141
Russia	145	204	312	441
Austria-Hungary	64	68	87	182

Cultural Pessimism

Germany's cultural life, like its political and industrial life, reflected the stresses and strains of modernization. The old vied with the new, the established with the arriviste. Much of what in the 1920s would be celebrated as "Weimar culture" in fact had its genesis in the last decades of the Second Reich.

Wilhelmian "official" art — art that received private and state funding — featured manly portraits, romanticized battle scenes, idealized rural landscapes, and heroic equestrian statues. But even artists within this group were striking out in new directions. Adolph von Menzel, perhaps best known for his illustrations depicting the epical life of Frederick the Great, was not above showing the seamier side of German life. Menzel's painting *The Rolling Mill* portrayed the dirty, unhealthy atmosphere of a factory and workers' heavy labor. Karl Blechen, a contemporary, shared Menzel's realism in his own painting *Rolling Mill*, wherein he showed the ugly landscape around Eberswalde, an industrial city northeast of Berlin, dominated by smoking chimneys and grimy factories.

Art was in full revolt by 1894 when a group of Munich painters (Blue Rider[1]) refused to abide by the Academy of Art's decision concerning which pieces should go on public display. Instead, they "seceded" from the academy and exhibited their own works. Four years later, the dean of German painters, Max Liebermann, founded the *Sezession* in Berlin to protest the dictating of styles by the Academy of Art and the established salons. Liebermann painted not monarchs and generals but artisans and peasants, workers and women in factories, fields, and homes.

Architecture underwent its own, albeit more modest, "secession." Banks and government buildings continued to be built in the official Wilhelmian style: massive structures adorned with pseudo-classical facades. Villas of wealthy industrialists, like Alfried Krupp's Villa Hügel in Essen, followed suit and were pretentiously decorated like princely palaces. Even middle-class urban residences abounded with gilded exteriors. "Railway station Gothic" was what popular wags termed the official style for schools and barracks, mansions and railway stations. But by the end of the 1890s a new school of architects designed leaner, uncluttered buildings that combined function with grace. Under the guidance of Peter Behrens, the *Jugendstil*, as it was known, stressed clarity of design and utilized steel, stone, and glass to advantage. One of Behrens' students, Walter Gropius, personified the transition from the *Jugendstil* to the *Bauhaus* school of the 1920s.

---

[1] In 1910 Wassily Kandinsky and Franz Marc published a book, *The Blue Rider*, and in 1911 organized an exhibition by that name in Munich.

German youth also was in revolt. In 1901 Karl Fischer, a university student from the Spandau suburb of Berlin, founded the *Wandervögel* ("hiking birds") to protest the hierarchical and materialistic order of German schools, homes, and society. His movement spread rapidly throughout Germany, and his friend Hans Breuer published an edition of folksongs, *Der Zupfgeigenhansl* ("The Guitarist's Companion"), no doubt to ease the rigors of hiking. Adorned with the blue flower of romanticism, the *Wandervögel* visited medieval castles and sang traditional folksongs around campfires in an attempt to transform Bismarck's Reich into a true national community. Much of what transpired has a highly contemporary flavor: organic food over artificial flavoring, fruit over meat, natural over chemical. The Youth Movement even encouraged abstinence from tobacco and alcohol at its founding session on the Hohen Meissner, a hill near Kassel — youth's answer to the gaudy centenary celebrations honoring the Battle of Nations in 1813. Unfortunately, many of the youth groups endorsed anti-semitism because they saw the Jews as the personification of materialism.

The established literary culture of Wilhelmian Germany featured an almost uncritical acceptance of vulgarized versions of Friedrich Nietzsche's thoughts. In fact, a host of neo-Nietzschean pundits tried to exhort youth, especially, toward greater freedoms and influence. Julius Langbehn, for example, sought to remove the "new intellectual life of Germans" from academic mandarins and to transfer it to the Reich's restless youth. His book, *Rembrandt as Educator,* went through thirty-nine printings in 1890–1891. Langbehn's challenge to youth to be "aristocratic" rather than plebeian in their outlook and actions was also taken up by the poet Stefan George.

Through a strangely erotic relationship between master and students established during séances held in darkened Berlin salons, George became the self-styled awakener of a "heroic manly youth," a renegade who looked toward the charismatic rule of the esoteric. George called on his disciples to resist the influence of schools, factories, barracks, and satanically inspired American culture — long before the advent of American jeans, fast food, and rock music. He passed to youth his aversion to Weimar: democracy, liberalism, rationalism, socialism, mass culture, and mass politics. George demanded nothing less than that his young followers create a new form of romanticism by refounding the Reich, entrusting it to a charismatic leader (Führer), uplifting the nobility of force, and deriding women's role in society. George represented an extreme reaction against industrialization and modernization. A splinter group in Munich headed by Alfred Schuler and Ludwig Klages introduced the archsymbol of regeneration, the swastika, to George's circle of admirers. Was this icon a harbinger of the future?

Several German novelists and playwrights of the period undertook serious attempts to draw attention to the dislocation and alienation caused by modernization and industrialization. In 1902 Thomas Mann, utilizing his experiences in growing up in the Hanseatic city of Lübeck on the Baltic Sea, published his Nobel Prize-winning novel *Buddenbrooks*. In point-counterpoint, Mann depicted the humanistic values and family traditions of the established German middle class of property and education during the period 1830 to 1900 against a backdrop of inevitable decline and decay. Industrialization, materialism, urbanization, and alienation ate at the root of the Buddenbrooks' traditional middle-class values.

Thomas Mann's elder brother Heinrich, who was born in the year of the founding of the Reich (1871), was savage in his critique of Wilhelmian Germany. In the novel *Der Untertan*, begun in 1907 and published in English in 1945 as *Little Superman*, Heinrich Mann depicted a crass materialistic state devoid of taste, with artificial social conventions and ostentatious public displays of pomp. Racist fraternities, bigoted students, haughty yet fear-ridden professors, and arrogant officers dominated Heinrich Mann's writing.

Cultural pessimism also extended into the realms of economics and politics. The economist Werner Sombart observed in 1912 that the grandiose national idea exemplified in unification had exhausted itself. The "great ideals" of the founders of the Reich had faded, while nothing had replaced the enthusiasm of 1866 and 1871. "Empty phrases," Sombart stated, "serve to cover up the spiritual void." Ridiculous farces and public rituals abounded. The nineteenth century, Sombart asserted, had closed with "an enormous deficit of idealist enthusiasm." Materialism and class distinctions had replaced idealism. A "dreary opportunism, an uninspired business mentality" dominated German political life. The noble concepts of Stein and Hardenberg, Humboldt and List, the sparkling parliamentary debate of Bennigsen and Lasker, Windthorst and Bebel, were things of the past. The present represented "the nadir of political life" in modern Germany, a sobering and largely fair analysis.

Sombart's bleak conclusion was confirmed when the British secretary for war, Lord Haldane of Cloan, visited Berlin in 1912 in an abortive attempt to arrange an end to the Anglo-German naval arms race. A graduate of Göttingen University and translator of Hegel and Schopenhauer, Haldane visited the graves of Fichte and Hegel, only to find them neglected and run down. When he informed William II of this at dinner, the Kaiser replied with a cold sneer: "Well, there is no room in my empire for characters like Hegel and Fichte."

The flip side of the coin of cultural pessimism was the "cult of inevitability" of war, which extended from Pan-Germans to Social Democrats. An ever-increasing number of Germans regarded force as a vital element in international relations and justified war as a historical necessity. For many, war was the only means to fend off the nation's perceived physical and psychological decay. Fatalistic expectations of war in time became a self-fulfilling prophecy. It had become clear to many observers in Germany well before 1914 that war was as much apocalyptic hope as it was apocalyptic threat. The only question was whether William II was up to it.

German newspapers taunted the Kaiser's lack of aggressive consistency with cries of "valiant chicken" and "William the timid." Heinrich Class, head of the Pan Germans, published an anonymous book, *If I Were Kaiser*, in which he demanded suppression of domestic freedoms and debate, curtailment of Jewish influence in Germany, military preparedness, martial law, racial hygiene, and an elitist dictatorship (*Führerdiktatur)* along supposedly Nietzschean lines.

In short, less than a half-century after unification, Imperial Germany found itself in dire straits. In July 1914 Kurt Riezler, Chancellor von Bethmann Hollweg's political councillor, reflected on a failed foreign policy:

> The earlier errors of a Turkish policy against Russia, a Moroccan against France, fleet against England, irritating everyone, blocking everybody's way and yet not really weakening anyone. Basic cause: lack of planning, craving for petty prestige victories.

Worst of all, Bismarck's successors failed to understand that Germany could not expand in Europe without destroying the established order. Cultural pessimists by and large, they reduced the complex international situation to a simplistic either-or: either victory or defeat, either world power or decline. Even the octogenarian ruler of Austria-Hungary, Francis Joseph I, was prepared to limit his options. "If we must perish, we should do so with honor."

Suggested Readings

There are numerous works dealing with William II in both English and German. Michael Balfour, *The Kaiser and His Times* (New York, 1972), remains acceptable. Isabel V. Hull, *The Entourage of Kaiser Wilhelm II, 1888–1918* (Cambridge, 1982), offers a fascinating look at William II and his court. Lamar Cecil's first volume of the biography, *Wilhelm II: Prince and Emperor, 1859–1900* (Chapel Hill and London, 1989), makes superb reading for the Kaiser's career to the turn of the century. A broad perspective of William II is offered by the selections in John C. G. Röhl and Nicolaus Sombart, eds., *Kaiser Wilhelm II: New Interpretations. The Corfu Papers* (Cambridge, 1982).

The social and political history of the Second Reich has received its fair share of attention recently. James J. Sheehan, ed., *Imperial Germany* (New York and London, 1976), is a useful general introduction. Arthur Rosenberg, *Imperial Germany: The Birth of the German Republic, 1871–1918* (Boston, 1964), provides a critical perspective that remains worth reading. Hans-Ulrich Wehler, *The German Empire, 1871–1918* (Leamington Spa, 1985), presents a critical, if exclusively domestic, analysis of the Second Reich.

The period immediately after Bismarck's dismissal is dealt with by J. C. G. Röhl, *Germany without Bismarck: The Crisis of Government in the Second*

Reich, 1890–1900 (London, 1967); the domestic fabric after the Iron Chancellor can be gleaned from Richard J. Evans, *Society and Politics in Wilhelmine Germany* (London, 1978). Stanley Suval, *Electoral Politics in Wilhelmine Germany* (Chapel Hill, 1985), surveys the complex area of domestic politics and elections. Bourgeois right-wing radicalism has been analyzed by George L. Mosse, *The Nationalization of the Masses: Political Symbolism and Mass Movements in Germany from the Napoleonic Wars Through the Third Reich* (New York, 1975), and Geoff Eley, *Reshaping the German Right: Radical Nationalism and Political Change after Bismarck* (New Haven and London, 1980). The bastardization of Charles Darwin's ideas in Germany has been taken up by Alfred Kelly, *The Descent of Darwin: The Popularization of Darwinism in Germany, 1860–1914* (Chapel Hill, 1981).

The economic aspects of William II's reign are explored in Kenneth D. Barkin, *The Controversy over German Industrialization, 1890–1902* (Chicago, 1970), and in Thorstein Veblen, *Imperial Germany and the Industrial Revolution* (New York, 1915). The Social Democrats have been examined by Peter Gay, *The Dilemma of Democratic Socialism: Eduard Bernstein's Challenge to Marx* (New York, 1952); Carl E. Schorske, *German Social Democracy 1905–1917: The Development of the Great Schism* (Cambridge, Mass., 1955); and Roger Fletcher, *Revisionism and Empire: Socialist Imperialism in Germany, 1897–1914* (London, 1984). Students should also consult the general histories of the German economy and the SPD listed in the preceding chapter.

The erratic foreign policy of the Second Reich has been well scrutinized. Imanuel Geiss, *German Foreign Policy, 1871–1914* (London, 1976), Ludwig Dehio, *Germany and World Politics in the 20th Century* (New York, 1959), and L. L. Farrar, *Arrogance and Anxiety: The Ambivalance of German Power, 1848–1914* (Iowa City, 1981), are three broad surveys of the period. Norman Rich, ed., *Friedrich von Holstein: Politics and Diplomacy in the Era of Bismarck and Wilhelm II*, 2 vols. (Cambridge, 1965), remains the classic treatment of the Foreign Office's "grey eminence." Woodruff D. Smith, *The German Colonial Empire* (Chapel Hill, 1978), analyzes that component of *Weltpolitik*, and Paul Kennedy, *The Rise of the Anglo-German Antagonism, 1860–1914* (London, 1980), and Holger H. Herwig, *Politics of Frustration: The United States in German Naval Planning, 1889–1941* (Boston and Toronto, 1976), detail the effects of "global policies" upon the Anglo-Saxon powers. Fritz Fischer, *War of Illusions: German Policies from 1911 to 1914* (New York, 1975), examines the chaotic last years of peace.

There is no single treatment in English of the German military under William II; we remain reliant upon Gordon A. Craig, *The Politics of the Prussian Army 1640–1945* (Oxford, 1955). Jehuda L. Wallach, *The Dogma of the Battle of Annihilation: The Theories of Clausewitz and Schlieffen and Their Impact on the German Conduct of Two World Wars* (Westport, Conn., 1986), gives great insight into the strategic and operational planning of German land forces under William II. Karl Demeter, *The German Officer Corps in Society and State, 1650–1945* (London, 1965), and Martin Kitchen, *The German Officer Corps, 1890–1914* (Oxford, 1968), provide expert treatment of the army's premier corps. For the navy, that service is rendered by Holger H. Herwig, *The German Naval Officer Corps: A Social and Political History, 1890–1918* (Oxford, 1973). The building of the German fleet was first analyzed in terms of its domestic function by Eckart Kehr, *Battleship Building and Party Politics in Germany, 1894–1901* (Chicago, 1973), and more generally by Jonathan Steinberg, *Yesterday's Deterrent: Tirpitz and the Birth of the German Battle Fleet* (London, 1965). A more recent treatment is by Holger H. Herwig, *"Luxury" Fleet: The Imperial German Navy, 1888–1918* (London and Atlantic Highlands, N.J., 1987). Ivo N. Lambi, *The Navy and German Power Politics 1862–1914* (London, 1984), has given a voluminous account of German strategical and operational planning in the Tirpitz era.

The role of women under William II can be studied in Richard J. Evans, *The Feminist Movement in Germany, 1894–1933* (London, 1976); A. K. Hackett, *The Politics of Femininism in Wilhelmine Germany* (New York, 1979); Ute Frevert, *Women in German History: From Bourgeois Emancipation to Sexual Liberation* (New York, 1988); and Barbara Franzoi, *At the Very Least She Pays the Rent: Women and German Industrialization, 1871–1914* (Westport, Conn., 1985). The various youth movements are covered by Peter D. Stachura, *The German Youth Movement, 1900–1945: An Interpretative and Documentary History* (London, 1981), and Walter Laqueur, *Young Germany: A History of the German Youth Movement* (New York, 1962). The classic treatment of cultural pessimism remains Fritz Stern, *The Politics of Cultural Despair: A Study in the Rise of the German Ideology* (Garden City, N.Y., 1965); see also Roger Chickering, *We Men Who Feel Most German: A Cultural Study of the Pan-German League, 1886–1914* (London, 1984).

Austrian foreign policy has been sketched by Alfred F. Pribram, *Austrian Foreign Policy, 1908–18* (London, 1971), and Peter J. Katzenstein, *Disjointed Partners: Austria and Germany Since 1815* (Berkeley, 1976). The mood in Vienna in the two decades before the Great War has been expertly revealed by Frederic Morton, *A Nervous Splendor: Vienna 1888/1889* (New York, 1979), and *Thunder at Twilight: Vienna 1913–1914* (New York, 1989). A more scholarly approach is offered by Carl E. Schorske, *Fin-de-Siècle Vienna: Politics and Culture* (New York, 1980). The role of the army in the Austro-Hungarian Empire remains with Gunther E. Rothenberg, *The Army of Francis Joseph* (West Lafayette, Ind., 1976); that institution's officer corps has recently been examined by István Deák, *Beyond Nationalism: A Social and Political History of the Habsburg Officer Corps, 1848–1918* (New York and Oxford, 1990).

C H A P T E R

6

FINIS GERMANIAE? WAR AND REVOLUTION, 1914–1918

Eight to ten million soldiers will strangle each other and in the process decimate Europe as no swarm of locusts ever did. The ravages of the Thirty Year's War [will be] telescoped into three or four years and extended to the entire Continent: famine, pestilence, and the general barbarization of both armies and peoples . . . ending in general bankruptcy; the collapse of the old states and traditional statecraft . . . to such an extent that dozens of crowns will roll in the streets and no one will want to pick them up.

Friedrich Engels, 1887

The American diplomat and historian George Kennan called World War I the "great seminal catastrophe of this century." For four long, bloody years the flower of Germany's male youth was slaughtered on the battlefields of France and Russia. The Reich's finances were devastated almost beyond repair, and defeat brought revolution and chaos. Nationalism, social Darwinism, and plain hatred among peoples and nations flourished. Starvation and disease ravaged the population. Dismemberment threatened the Bismarckian state.

How had this disaster come about not even half a century after Bismarck's brilliant campaigns and diplomacy? Few knew — or were willing to assess openly—the causes for war and defeat. Instead, the nation's conservative elite did its level best to shift blame for the debacle to the domestic *Reichsfeinde* (enemies of the state): Jews and Marxists. It even destroyed the diplomatic record for July 1914. A special division within the Foreign Office systematically "ordered" its files so as to obscure the Reich's role in the origins of the war. But largely through the efforts of the Hamburg historian Fritz Fischer and his students, it is possible to piece together the story of Germany's role before and during World War I with accuracy.

1914: "A Leap into the Dark"

A river of ink has been spilled over the origins of World War I. One historian counts more than three thousand works alone on the assassination of the Austro-Hungarian heir apparent, Archduke Francis Ferdinand, at Sarajevo on June 28, 1914. To retell the story of the July crisis blow by blow would be redundant at best. Instead, the following discussion seeks to assess German motivations and, unavoidably, German "war guilt" as later defined in Article 231 of the Treaty of Versailles (1919).

The European tragedy was set in motion at Sarajevo. Serbia resented Austria-Hungary's annexation of Bosnia-Herzegovina in 1908 and longed to create a "Greater Serbia" at the expense of the Habsburgs. In 1914 Colonel Dragutin Dimitrijević-Apis, chief of Serbian Military Intelligence, recruited a band of students to assassinate Francis Ferdinand in order to make public Serbia's discontent with existing conditions. One of the students, Gavrilo Princip, carried out the regicide at Sarajevo on June 28.

Shortly before his death in 1898, Otto von Bismarck had warned that "one day the great European War would come out of some damned foolish thing in the Balkans." Europe's leaders in 1914 were acutely aware of the potential ramifications of that "damned foolish thing" of June 28. Albert Ballin, head of the German Hamburg-America Line, dined with Winston S. Churchill, First Lord of the Admiralty, in London, and the two men sketched out the most likely scenario after Sarajevo. What would Nicholas II, tsar of Russia do, Ballin mused, if Austria chastized Serbia? "If Russia marches against Austria, we must march; and if we march, France must march, and what would England do?" Churchill finally responded, "It would be a mistake to assume that we should stand out of it whatever happened." The dinner conversation between Ballin and Churchill became reality with dramatic suddenness.

The ball was squarely in Vienna's court after Sarajevo. Archduke Francis Ferdinand, never much loved in Vienna, was quickly forgotten and his body dispatched to his country estate in the dead of night. But Foreign Minister Leopold Count Berchtold and General Franz Conrad von Hötzendorf decided not to let the moment slip past for what they termed "a final reckoning with Serbia." Both men joined forces and convinced Emperor Francis Joseph that war against Serbia was the only honorable recourse. The Empire's aim, as Berchtold put it, was to "eliminate Serbia as a political power factor in the Balkans." A victorious war would destroy Serbia and retard the forces of nationalism in general and of pan-Slavism in particular. It might also lead to the annexation of Montenegro, Albania, and the Sanjak of Novi Bazar.[1] Conrad von Hötzendorf had counseled war at any price in 1905, 1907, 1908, 1911, 1912, and 1913.

[1] The Sanjak was a strip of territory annexed by Serbia in 1912; it had previously been under Turkish rule and had separated Serbia from Montenegro.

To be sure, obstacles stood in the way of a quick war with Serbia. The Hungarian prime minister, Count István Tisza, desired no additional Slavs in the Empire. He was brought on board by the war party by two promises: Vienna agreed not to annex any new Slav territories and to present Belgrade with an ultimatum designed to bring the murderers to swift justice, if need be with the assistance of Habsburg authorities. Above all, Conrad von Hötzendorf knew full well that Austro-Hungarian forces were woefully unprepared for a major conflagration. On July 1 and 2 Vienna sent messages to Berlin requesting unconditional backing for any actions it deemed necessary against Serbia.

At that moment the center of attention shifted to Berlin. Under the terms of the Dual Alliance of 1879, Germany was obliged to come to Austria-Hungary's defense only if the latter was attacked by Russia. In June–July 1914 most German diplomatic, military, and political leaders were away from Berlin on vacation. But the Kaiser was at Potsdam. On July 3 William II noted "now or never" on a telegram announcing that the Austrians were prepared to march against Serbia. Two days later the Kaiser assured the Viennese that he would honor their request for full support even if "some serious European complications" — a diplomatic euphemism for war — should result. William II realized, as Ballin and Churchill did, that a war in the Balkans involving one or more of the major powers could not be localized but would quickly demand responses from the other powers. Chancellor von Bethmann Hollweg was hurriedly recalled from his estate at Hohenfinow and endorsed the Kaiser's actions. On July 6, while dining with Gustav Krupp von Bohlen und Halbach, William II pathetically reassured the head of the giant German armaments firm, "This time I will not cave in."

The German military had been convinced for some time that war in Europe was inevitable. The chief of the General Staff, Helmuth von Moltke, was fatalistic about the inevitability of war. In May 1914 he had summarized his position for the head of the Foreign Office, Gottlieb von Jagow:

> Russia will have completed its rearmament program in 2–3 years. The military superiority of our enemies will then be so great that I do not know how we will be able to master them. At present we are still able to match them somewhat. I am of the opinion that we have no alternative but to conduct a preemptive war in order to defeat our adversaries while we are still able to do so.

Only Admiral Alfred von Tirpitz counseled restraint, arguing that the fleet would not be ready before the early 1920s. No one listened.

It is also possible to reconstruct the imperial chancellor's reasoning during the July crisis. Bethmann Hollweg was as pessimistic and fatalistic as Moltke. "The future," he dourly predicted, "belongs to Russia, which grows and grows and rests on us like a nightmare." Might this not be the last chance, Bethmann Hollweg mused, to stabilize Austria-Hungary's position in the Balkans, perhaps without threatening Russia's vital interests in the region? Might not a quick surgical strike against Belgrade preempt the other European powers? And in the highly likely case that Russia intervened on behalf of Serbia, might this not rally the Social Democrats at home to defend their fatherland, keep Britain out of a war designed to avenge a regicide, and impress the neutrals?

Bethmann Hollweg revealed to his closest associates the political rationale behind the so-called calculated risk that he was prepared to accept. If war came "from the east" and Germany entered it in order to preserve the Habsburg monarchy, "then we have the prospect of winning it." But should Russia remain idle, "then we have the prospect of having outmaneuvered the entente in this matter." In short, victory was possible either on the field of battle or at the conference table. Bethmann Hollweg was quite prepared to take what his political councillor, Kurt Riezler, called "a leap into the dark." When the British declined to play the passive role accorded them by the Germans, William II returned his uniforms of admiral of the fleet and field marshal to George V: "This is the thanks for Waterloo."

Fritz Fischer has suggested that war in 1914 was the result of a premeditated German bid for world power (*Griff nach der Weltmacht*), but the evidence does not support such a bold thesis. Rather, the decision for war was taken in an attempt to solidify, and if possible expand, the gains of 1871. Once more, as during the Moroccan crises of 1905 and 1911, German leaders in 1914 sought first and foremost to break the entente ring that seemed to encircle the Reich.

All plans were predicated on Germany's being first to mobilize and on the war's being of short duration. Although railroad mobilization timetables did not cause this war, they certainly contributed to the speed of its unfolding. When the Kaiser at the last moment thought about shrinking back from the precipice of a two-front war against France and Russia and suggested mobilization against only Russia, Moltke firmly declined. A decade of fine-tuning mobilization plans for millions of men could not be jettisoned on the spur of the moment. "Your uncle," William II maliciously lectured Moltke with reference to the victor of Königgrätz (1866) and Sedan (1870), "would have given me a different answer." The Schlieffen plan thus remained the only option. Germany remained committed to a lightning march through the southern Netherlands and Belgium, encirclement of Paris, and defeat of the French armies against the "anvil" of stationary German forces somewhere in Alsace-Lorraine.

But consistency was lacking in Berlin even at this critical stage of the July Crisis. On July 30 Vienna received two conflicting telegrams, one from Chancellor von Bethmann Hollweg requesting Habsburg armies to "halt in Belgrade," the other from General von Moltke charging Vienna to "mobilize also against Russia." At Vienna Foreign Minister Berchtold inquired in exasperation: "Who rules in Berlin? Moltke or Bethmann?" The Schlieffen plan continued to unfold.

Formal declarations of war crisscrossed Europe almost in anticlimactic fashion. On July 28 Austria-Hungary declared war against Serbia. Germany announced that a state of war existed with France on August 1 and with Russia

Off to Paris: The first volunteers leave Berlin (August 1914).

on August 3. Britain declared war against Germany on August 4. Italy refused to honor its alliance obligations to Berlin and Vienna, arguing that its national interest was not involved in the struggle — which, it feared, would be a long one — and that it saw no clear advantage in deploying three army corps along the Rhine (as stipulated in its alliance commitments). Instead, the Italian government opted for neutrality — and thereafter sounded the major powers out to see what territorial offers they were willing to make in return for Italy's support. Rome joined the entente in April 1915 when it became clear that Britain and France could readily offer what neither possessed: Austro-Hungarian lands. General von Moltke bitterly denounced "Italy's felony" and swore vengeance on the Italian "knaves" later.

With clockwork precision, German troops marched west in August 1914. A troop train crossed the Hohenzollern bridge at Cologne every ten minutes. In the east, Habsburg forces assembled against Russia in Galicia (A-Staffel) and in the south against Serbia along the Danube (Minimalgruppe Balkan). Somewhere, in either northeastern France or southern Poland, the decisive battle of encirclement would take place. After this "cleansing thunderstorm," as Churchill termed it, the armies would head home. Business as usual would then resume.

THE GERMAN ATTACK IN THE WEST, AUGUST 1914

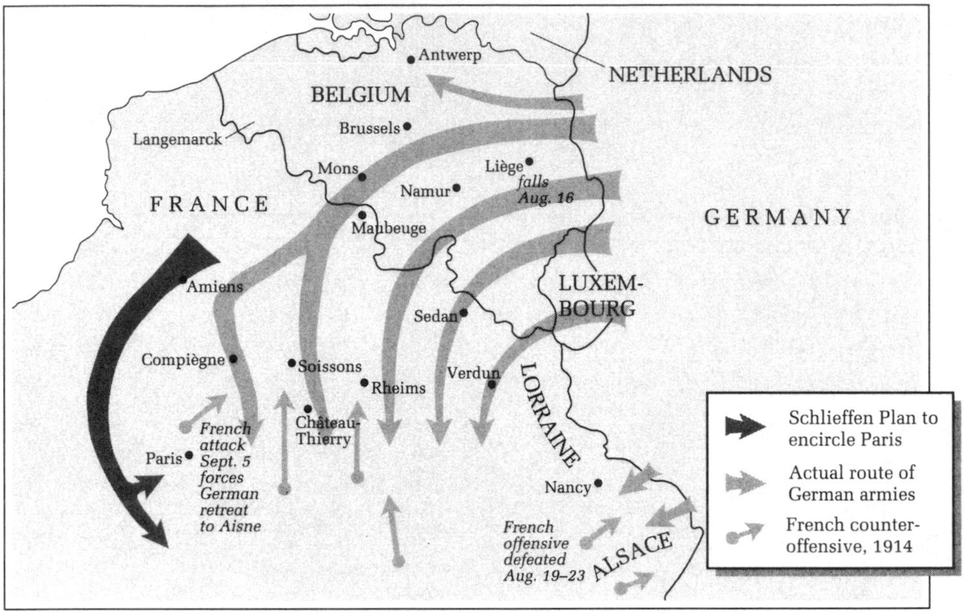

Reality proved otherwise. Although German advance units pressed forward to within eighteen kilometers of Paris's outer fortresses, they could not deliver the decisive blow. The narrow advancing front, enemy destruction of transportation and communications, and the sheer inability of units to march three hundred miles in forty days to the Channel and around Paris while living off the land militated against success. The German army of 1914 was neither materially equipped nor tactically prepared for a war of mobility. Moltke was fired. His successor, General Erich von Falkenhayn, decided to press the advantage instead in Flanders, outflanking the Anglo-French forces there in a last-minute attempt to snatch victory from the jaws of defeat.

One place name would forever symbolize this effort: Langemarck. There, on November 10, regiment after regiment of hastily trained raw recruits, the cream of German youth, advanced over fog-enshrouded fields against seasoned British professionals armed with machine guns. The boys moved up into the line singing the national anthem, "Deutschland über Alles." Eighty thousand of them fell on the field of battle. It is little wonder that the future French premier, Georges Clemenceau, commented: "These people love death."

The eastern front brought mixed results. From August 26 to 31 Generals Paul von Hindenburg and Erich Ludendorff, following a plan devised by General Max Hoffmann, destroyed three-fifths of the Russian Narev Army of 200,000 men. They next moved against the Russian Niemen Army and defeated it between September 9 and 10 at the battle of the Masurian Lakes.

THE GERMAN ATTACK IN THE EAST, 1914

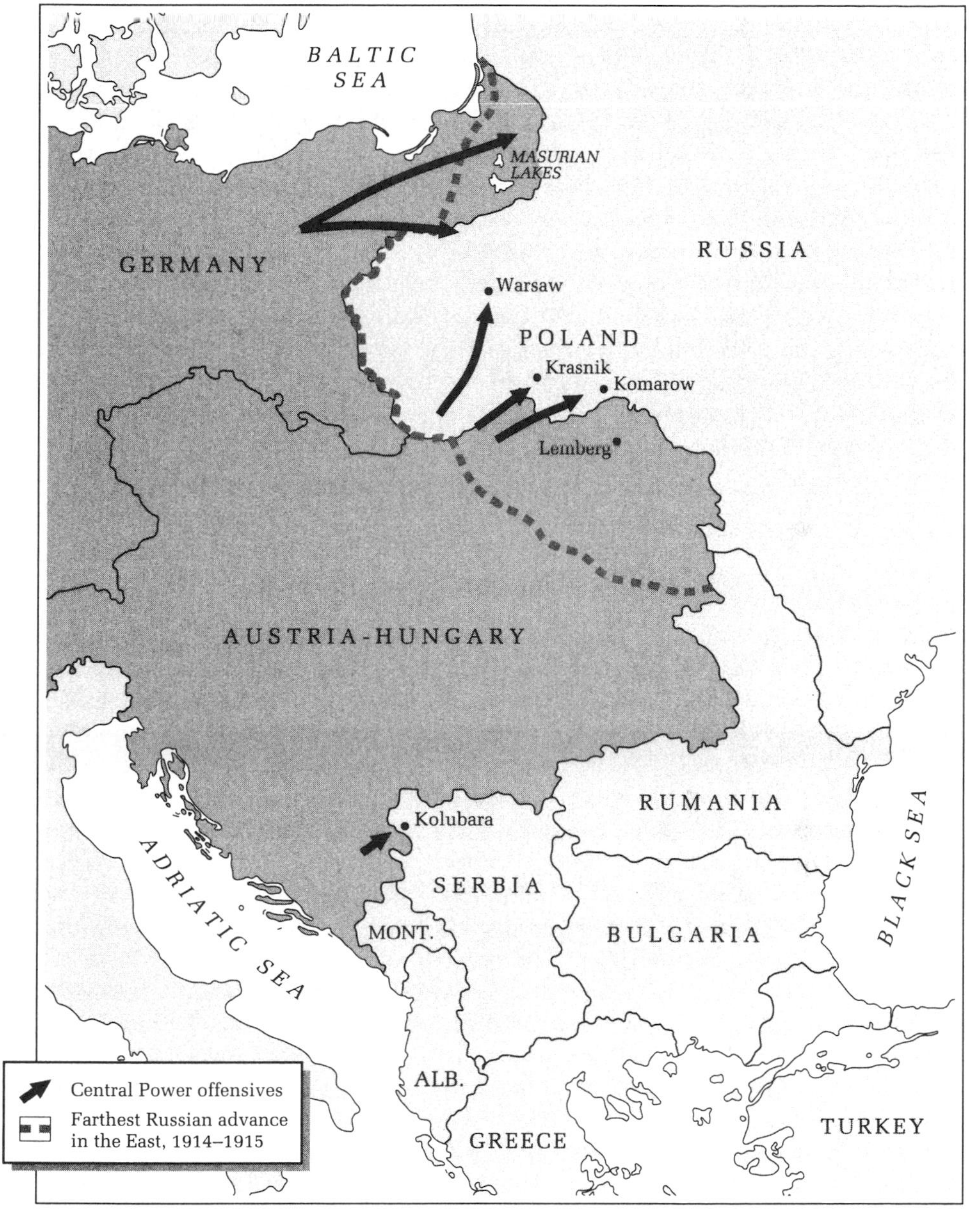

These twin battles established the legends of Hindenburg and Ludendorff, but they could not save the Austro-Hungarian army from disaster. Conrad von Hötzendorf's forces, after initial successes, were broken at Lemberg in Galicia by September 12, losing one-third of their troops (250,000 casualties and

100,000 prisoners of war). The Austro-Hungarian army would never recover. The strategic grand design of the Central Powers, as Austria-Hungary and Germany now were called, had failed. A line of trenches stretching from Switzerland to the English Channel symbolized the stalemate.

Surely now was the time for Germany and Austria-Hungary to reassess. The Schlieffen plan had failed. Conrad's twin blows against Russia and Serbia had been brutally repelled. Manpower and material resources favored the entente powers. Berlin and Vienna could not possibly win a prolonged war. But no council of war took place in either Berlin or Vienna. The two Germanic powers had resolved to fight the war to conclusion without fully weighing its consequences. They made no attempt to coordinate the war effort, created no common command, hammered out no common strategy. They did not even coordinate their political aims. Each was resolved to fight to the bitter end on its own terms and for its own ends. In the process, Berlin and Vienna crossed the threshold from limited cabinet wars as under Bismarck into the *terra incognita* of total war.

Burgfrieden and the "Ideas of 1914"

The German nation united for a brief moment in 1914. Although recent studies suggest that not every hamlet was beset by war fever, Germans by and large rallied to the national colors. Bands played. Men marched off to conquer Paris. Women pinned white flowers (to symbolize cowardice) on those who did not immediately volunteer for war service. The Social Democrats abandoned Marx and voted for bonds and loans to finance the war. One of them, Gustav Noske, claimed that he would have been beaten to death at the Brandenburg Gate had he voted otherwise.

The Kaiser dramatically announced that henceforth partisan politics would end; all Germans were brothers in the face of war. In an antiquated medieval allusion, William II proclaimed domestic "peace in the German castle" (*Burgfrieden*). A new sense of national community was forged. More than a million patriotic poems were penned in August 1914 alone. The nation obviously had tired of Bismarck's enforced prolonged peace. A sense of adventure, a chance to end the stifling atmosphere of the "saturated" Reich, and an opportunity for courageous deeds combined to make war a welcome option in 1914.

Just as German academics in the 1890s had rallied behind Tirpitz's naval program, in 1914 they tackled the issue of war aims with equal relish. As early as October 16, 1914, academia submitted a petition with 3,016 signatures to the government justifying the war as a blatant British attempt to drive a wedge between "Prussian militarism" and "German academia." The professors firmly rejected such an artificial division. The nation, after all, was united.

The theologian Reinhold Seeberg handed the government a document, signed by 352 professors in the summer of 1915, that differed little on the war aims question from similar treatises to be compiled later by the military. In order to secure the Reich "for generations," the Seeberg Address noted, Germany would have to acquire French territories from Belfort to the English Channel. Belgium would have to become a German protectorate and Russia reduced to "an agrarian colonization land" in order to ensure future German population growth. The latter demand was seconded even by a critic of Imperial Germany, Hans Delbrück, who called for the transformation of Russia's western provinces into a "German India."

Above all, the war soon took on tones of international hatred. Certainly France remained the archenemy to many, but the German academic community trained its pens especially on Great Britain. The slogan "perfidious Albion" was revived from Tirpitz's days. "God punish England" became a major war slogan. The noted economist Werner Sombart depicted the conflict as one between "merchants and heroes," with Germans obviously cast as the latter. The classical scholar Ulrich von Wilamowitz-Moellendorff spoke even less kindly of Britain: "There is the real driving evil spirit that has called this war up from Hell, the spirit of jealousy and the spirit of deceit."

At the official level, Chancellor von Bethmann Hollweg gave credence to such musings with his infamous shopping list of German war aims on September 9, 1914. Calling for German security in Europe "for all imaginable time," the chancellor demanded that France be destroyed as a great power, Russia reduced to the dimension it had reached under Peter the Great, Luxembourg annexed outright, Belgium reduced to a "vassal state," and a great "Central African Colonial Empire" created as a German reservoir of raw materials. And while the basic mid-nineteenth-century concept of a grand central Europe under German dominance lay at the heart of Bethmann Hollweg's program, the German military spoke openly of vast annexations in the east designed to "resettle" Poles and Jews from the "Polish border strip," to "resettle" as well the Baltic lands with meritorious German veterans, and to transform the Crimea into a "German Mediterranean." The navy dreamed of bases as far away as the Faeroe and Cape Verde islands in the Atlantic, Tahiti in the Far East, Madagascar in the West Indian Ocean, and one of the major Dutch islands in the East Indies.

Finally, in what has been called "grotesquely anachronistic notions," the German ruling houses jockeyed for their share of the anticipated spoils. Bavaria demanded parts of Alsace-Lorraine, Saxony sought Lithuania, Prussia desired Flanders, Württemberg wanted nothing less than the Polish crown, and Hesse coveted the throne of Finland. The list could easily be expanded.

These grandiose aims were not the reason that Germany went to war in 1914, but once the heavy loss of blood and treasure set in, war aims from Bethmann Hollweg's "September Program" of 1914 to the last desperate demands of autumn 1918 became the means with which to rally the populace behind the war effort. Political and social stability, the argument ran in ruling circles, could be achieved only through vast annexations. Conversely, demands for domestic reform — and especially of the notorious Prussian three-class voting system — could be headed off only by a victorious peace.

It should not be forgotten that the war aims issue increasingly was couched in racial terms. General Ludendorff as early as December 1915 had spoken of acquiring the requisite "breeding stations" for future generations and struggles in the east. General von Hindenburg sought not only to annex the Baltic states for the vital left flank in future wars but also to reserve the "eastern territories" as settlement estates for German soldiers. And when the old Pan-German League and the newly founded Union of the Eastern Marches joined Ludendorff's call for the ruthless "resettlement" of Slavic populations and the "reallocation" of their land to German settlers, the bridge to Adolf Hitler's call of 1933 for the "ruthless Germanization" of eastern lands perhaps was put in place. Indeed, if there exists continuity in any aspect of German history, it surely lies in the field of war aims from Ludendorff to Hitler.

But the war aims question badly divided the nation. On July 19, 1917, by a vote of 212 to 126, the Reichstag passed its famous "peace resolution" calling for an end to the war without annexations and indemnities. The German professorate rallied once more to denounce the parliamentary effort. More than one thousand professors signed a "Declaration Against the Reichstag Majority"; fewer than one hundred rallied to support the parliamentary resolution. The issue became moot in 1918 when Hindenburg and Ludendorff imposed draconian terms in the conquered east. On March 3, 1918, Russia recognized the loss of the Baltic states (Latvia, Lithuania, and Estonia), Poland, and the Ukraine at Brest-Litovsk. On May 7, by the Treaty of Bucharest, Rumania was forced to cede to Germany a trade monopoly on oil as well as control of navigation on the Danube, the national railroads, and grain production. The chasm between these treaties and the Reichstag's "peace resolution" revealed a deep domestic split. Which would be the harbinger of future developments?

Total War

In 1914 Germany had made no preparations for a prolonged struggle. Its utter lack of economic mobilization argues not only against the notion of a long-planned war of expansion but buttresses that of the short-war illusion. Stories abounded before 1914 that Germany had stored a fabled treasure — in reality, the remnants of the French reparations of 1871 — in the Julius Tower of the Spandau citadel for just such an event. The alleged treasure amounted to 205 million marks — enough to run the war for but two days.

An anticipated short war proved to be no immediate fiscal obstacle. On August 4 the Reichstag passed an enabling act covering the direct costs of the war, about 155 billion marks, mainly through long-term war bonds. But when the war was not over by Christmas, as expected, thirteen separate bank note issues had to be approved. A new paper currency, issued at the rate of 3 billion to 4 billion marks per month, replaced gold and silver. By 1919 the national debt stood at 156 billion marks.

The question quite naturally arose, Who would pay for the war? Whereas in Britain higher taxes covered about one-third of the cost of running the war, in Germany taxes were not raised for this purpose. Instead, a vicious financial circle developed. The government paid industry whatever it saw fit to charge for war goods, and industry used the excessive profits from armaments sales to purchase the state's war bonds, fully expecting that still larger returns would accrue later on the monies thus invested. Profits piled on profits, all to be financed by either the defeated powers or the German taxpayers.

Profits for most German joint stock companies doubled between 1914 and 1917. Gains were most noticeable in war production. Although dividends in investments overall remained at around 6 percent, those in the iron and steel sector nearly doubled to 15 percent and in the chemical branch to 12 percent by 1917. Only in 1916 was any modest tax on war profits introduced, producing 4.8 billion marks in 1917 and only 2.5 billion marks in 1918. Overall, barely 16 percent of the war's costs were covered by taxes. The state secretary of the treasury, Karl Helfferich, explained to the Reichstag how the staggering debt was to be met: "Once peace has been concluded, we can present our enemies with the bill for this war which has been forced on us." When victory proved an illusion, German taxpayers after 1918 were presented this bill.

Claims of Teutonic efficiency notwithstanding, Imperial Germany had made absolutely no economic preparations for the war. Despite the fact that the Reich imported all of its manganese, nitrate, and rubber needs; 90 percent of its cotton, wool, and copper requirements; half of its iron ore; and one-third even of its food supplies, nothing had been stockpiled for a national

WAR EXPENDITURES AND MOBILIZATION, 1914–1919

	War Costs and Loans ($ billions)	Forces Mobilized (millions of men)
Austria-Hungary	4.7	9.0
Germany	19.9	13.25
British Empire	23.0	9.5
France	9.3	8.2
Italy	3.2	5.6
Russia	5.4	13.0
United States	17.1	3.8

emergency, nor were there plans to regulate the supply of raw materials and foodstuffs once war broke out.

Two men came to the fore to provide relief. Professor Fritz Haber resolved the lack of imported nitrates for ammunition from Chile by developing (with Robert Bosch) a synthetic method of extracting ammoniac from nitrogen in the air. Walther Rathenau of German General Electric (AEG), shocked in August 1914 to discover that no plans existed to assess the supply and demand of vital war supplies, established within the War Ministry a special War Raw Materials Department to coordinate the procurement of vital war supplies. Both Jews, these men received no thanks from their fatherland: Rathenau was assassinated in 1922 by right-wing extremists; Haber died in enforced exile in 1934.

Imperial Germany slowly moved to what in Britain became known as "war socialism," that is, governmental control of the economy. As early as 1914 Berlin decreed that potato meal should go into a special "K" bread and reduced the fats in diets, because these were badly needed for glycerine for the war effort. Ration cards were printed and eventually issued for meat, bread, and potatoes. A special Exports and Exemptions Office was created to regulate the flow of food. Clemens von Delbrück in October 1915 was placed in charge of an Imperial Potato Office, and Georg Michaelis of the Ministry of the Interior headed a national food supply agency empowered to ration bread and grains.

These amelioratory measures did not, of course, overcome the basic lack of preparedness to fight a protracted war. By 1917 the harvest had fallen to half the level of 1913. The Allied naval blockade (1914–1919), the loss of farmhands to the war effort, and the indiscriminate slaughter of livestock (one-third of cattle and two-thirds of hogs) as a result of soaring prices led to severe shortages. Public protests against the food supply erupted in the spring of 1916. The so-called turnip winter of 1916–1917 reduced daily bread rations to a meager six ounces per person and eggs to one per person every fourteen days. By 1918 available fats were down to 12 percent and meat to 18 percent of peacetime levels. Daily caloric intake had been halved to a thousand calories. Average weight of civilians fell off by 20 percent. The production of cereal crops in Austria-Hungary plunged by half between 1914 and 1915, and early in 1918 industrial workers saw their daily rations of bread reduced first to 7 and finally to 5.8 ounces per day. Many industries managed to retain their labor force only by offering food as part of wage settlements.

The medical consequences of malnutrition were dramatic. Infant mortality in Germany rose 50 percent above the level of 1913. The female mortality rate leaped 51 percent and the overall civilian mortality rate 37 percent. Tubercular-related deaths were up 72 percent. At least 763,000 Germans died as a result of the Allied "hunger blockade."

Soldiers fared no better. In 1917 front-line troops in Austria-Hungary received one ounce of meat per day, those in Germany six ounces. U.S. "doughboys" in France, by contrast, grumbled over their daily allotment of twenty-four ounces of meat. The quartermaster-general of the Austro-Hungarian armed forces advised military personnel that worms in meat, although admittedly not appetizing, nevertheless were not dangerous — and constituted additional protein. The German navy by 1917 served a concoction known as "barbed wire": 75 percent water, 10 percent sausage, 3 percent potatoes, 2 percent peas, 1 percent turnips, and traces of beef, fat, and vinegar.

The war effort demanded ammunition and weapons in hitherto unheard-of quantities. The famous shell shortage of 1915, especially, prompted all governments to expedite the flow of materials to the front. By 1916 the Germans even coined the word *Materialschlachten* (material battles) to denote the new kind of warfare being fought.

After August 1916 the army command of Generals von Hindenburg and Ludendorff sought to mobilize the nation for war. With Colonel Max Bauer acting as liaison to industry and General Wilhelm Groener in charge of a special War Office within the Ministry of War, Hindenburg and Ludendorff set out dramatically to increase armaments production. The so-called Hindenburg Program decreed that the supply of munitions, powder, and steel was to be doubled and that of machine guns and artillery to be tripled. Yet another bureaucratic sinecure, the Weapons and Munitions Procurement Agency, was forged to oversee this mammoth effort. While some historians have argued that an "explosive fusion," a "symbiosis between the military and industry" took place by 1917, much of the available evidence suggests that industry remained the major power in that "fusion." Rupprecht Crown Prince of Bavaria, an army corps commander in France, bluntly stated that "heavy industry set the tone in Germany" and that the military "all danced around the golden calf."

In order to ensure an adequate supply of manpower, Germany adopted draconian measures. Early in the war about 15,000 Belgian skilled workers were conscripted for German industry; 61,500 would follow after 1916. The Reich forced 260,000 Polish workers and an equal number of Allied prisoners of war to labor in German industry and trade. Farm production was augmented by releasing 79,000 German convicts to work the land. Nearly 40 percent of German workers were directed from peacetime industries such as food, printing, and textiles to wartime production in armaments, chemical, and steel plants.

In 1916 Hindenburg and Ludendorff drafted an Auxiliary Service Law designed to mobilize the nation's potential work force. The law expanded military conscription to include all males to the age of fifty, established premilitary training for the nation's youth, closed universities for the duration of the war, shut down factories not directly involved in war production, and instituted national direction of labor. The generals anticipated an immediate surfeit of 200,000 workers as a result.

But this law was not to be. Social Democrats, Progressives, and Centrists in the Reichstag united with trade unionists to revise the original draft. The final act, passed in parliament by a vote of 235 to 19 in December 1916, not only exempted agricultural workers, the medical professions, clerics, and public transport workers but limited compulsory labor service to males between the ages of sixteen and sixty. General Groener estimated that he received only about 60,000 additional workers, mainly women, by April 1917. Deferments from military service for war industries actually rose, from 1.89 million in 1917 to 2.42 million in 1918.

Even so, total manpower mobilization was staggering. Initially about 5 million men (7.5 percent of the population) either volunteered or were drafted for military duty. That figure climbed to 11 million (16.5 percent of the populace) by the end of the war. By 1918 nearly half of all German males between the ages of fifteen and sixty reportedly had been drafted. The reverse side of the coin was that conscription reduced the male industrial work force by 23 percent, from 5.8 million in 1914 to 4.5 million by 1918.

Like German men, German women generally rallied around the war effort in 1914. On July 31 the Federation of German Women's Associations established a National Women's Service (NF) to assist the war effort. The NF encouraged its members to run soup kitchens, establish improvised hospital wards, tend to the rising numbers of orphans, and knit woolen socks for the troops at the fronts. The women offered patriotic lectures on the war and its origins, as well as on the need for a German fleet.

It is not easy to assess the direct contribution that women made to the war effort. Although women were expressly excluded from the Hindenburg Program and the Auxiliary Service Law of 1916, hard reality dictated otherwise. Thousands of women took over jobs in industry vacated by men drafted for the war effort, although not nearly to the same extent as in Britain. A recent estimate claims that 700,000 additional German female workers were employed during the war in the engineering, metallurgical, chemical, mining, and manufacturing industries. By 1918 2.3 million women were at work in industrial enterprises, an increase of 46 percent over 1914. In particular, the female work force — for the most part single women — tripled in such traditionally male industries as iron and steel and doubled in the electrical branch. By 1918 female workers at times outnumbered males in armaments industries. Most women would leave the labor force after the war.

Although the overall percentage of working women remained at peacetime levels, occupational shifts occurred. The number of women employed in peacetime industries such as textiles, for example, fell by half; those working for Alfried Krupp, by contrast, increased tenfold to 28,000 by 1917. The Prussian railroad administration expanded its female work force tenfold to 100,000 by 1918. Nevertheless, nearly half of all employed women remained in the agrarian sector as maids, laborers, and part-time helpers. A great deal of additional research will have to be done before a clearer picture of working women's role during the war emerges.

Over time the war divided the women's movement much as it did overall German society. The small radical group of suffragists around Anita Augspurg — in essence, the core of the Suffrage Union of 1902 — became active in the peace movement and sought an end to the war without annexations or indem-

Welding for Victory: Woman worker at a Berlin munitions plant (1915).

nities. The majority of members of the BDF, however, enthusiastically endorsed the government's various annexationist war aims programs, rejected President Woodrow Wilson's peace note in 1917, condemned the terms of the armistice in 1918, and denounced the Treaty of Versailles in 1919. A right-wing faction led by Martha Zietz and Eleonore Drenkhahn embraced the proto-fascist platform of the German Fatherland party (discussed later in this chapter). Indeed, many of these "conservative" BDF members by 1933 had flocked to the National Socialist movement.

Who "won" and who "lost," overall, as a result of the war effort? Male conscription naturally hit the SPD and its Free Trade Unions hardest: party membership plummeted from just over 1 million in 1914 to 586,000 in 1915 and 243,000 in 1917. Female membership in the SPD declined 60 percent during the war. At Easter 1917 a left-wing splinter faction of the SPD formed the Independent Social Democratic party (USPD), dedicated to ending the war without indemnities and annexations, self-determination for all peoples, universal disarmament, and international arbitration instead of confrontation. The party attracted a politically disparate group ranging from the revisionists Eduard Bernstein and Hugo Haase to the radicals Karl Liebknecht and Rosa Luxemburg. About 100,000 of the SPD rank and file also embraced the new labor party.

The Free Trade Unions had started the war with 2.5 million members, but conscription took a heavy toll; membership fell to 1.2 million in 1915 and only 967,000 in 1916 before rising modestly to 1.1 million in 1917. About 400,000 women were enrolled in the Free Trade Unions by the end of the war. Thousands of former Free Trade Unionists deserted the movement, whose collective bargaining efforts during the war they saw as weak and half-hearted. Many were particularly upset over the Unions' refusal to deploy the general strike as a weapon to force economic and political improvements.

Strikes were infrequent under the "domestic peace" announced in 1914: the police registered only 137 in 1915 and 240 in 1916. But the mobilization of the work force by Hindenburg and Ludendorff, combined with inflation and food shortages, more than doubled the number of strikes to 561 in 1917. Most of the early strikes were occasioned by food shortages and low wages and took the form of hunger riots and looting. After 1916 they concentrated ever more in armaments plants and became increasingly violent.

The truth is that although nominal wages (wages not adjusted to reflect the cost of living) doubled and trebled for most industries over the course of the war — women engaged in the metallurgical sector, for example, enjoyed a 324 percent increase in pay — real wages (which take inflation into account) fell sharply. Workers in peacetime industries fared worst: male wages declined 44 percent, female wages 39 percent. But even in war industries, there was a loss of real income: 23 percent for men and 12 percent for women. This impoverishment radicalized labor. Early in 1917 more than 25,000 workers in Berlin demonstrated for the release of the radical USPD leader Liebknecht, jailed on May 1, 1916, for a "treasonous" speech he had delivered at Potsdam against the war. In April about 200,000 workers in three hundred enterprises in Berlin were joined by half a million workers nationwide to protest the war in general and the declining standard of living in particular. In January 1918 half a million Berlin workers in war industries plants, joined by an equal number throughout Germany, took to the streets to demand better pay, more food, and an end to the war.

Workers were not the only "losers" during the war. Small-scale businesses and consumer-oriented industries suffered declines in output and profits between 1914 and 1916. In the wake of the direction of labor and raw materials after the Hindenburg Program and Auxiliary Service Law of late 1916, they were routinely forced out of the marketplace. The middle class as a whole suffered during the war. The established bourgeoisie of high-ranking civil servants and professionals lost ground in the face of inflation, falling real wages, and declining property values. The new middle class of white-collar employees, perhaps hardest hit by inflation and declining real wages, was "proletarianized." A recent investigation into the domestic impact of the war argues that the German middle and working classes drew closer together in terms of loss of income and standard of living.

War by Numbers: Verdun 1916, U-Boats 1917

At 8:00 A.M. on February 21, 1916, twelve hundred German artillery pieces rained a storm of steel down on French defenders encamped along the east bank of the Meuse River. Eight hours later ten divisions of infantry charged the French positions in waves. Before it was all over the Germans had committed forty-eight divisions to Verdun and had hurled 10 million shells into the Meuse escarpment. German combatants at Verdun included the famous flyer Baron von Richthofen and the novelist Arnold Zweig, future generals Heinz Guderian and Otto von Stülpnagel, and future National Socialists Rudolf Hess and Ernst Röhm. The Germans recorded more than 300,000 casualties.

Verdun, more than any other battle, became synonymous with what the German historian Gerhard Ritter, a junior officer in France during the Great War, termed "idiotic reciprocal mass murder." In fact, Verdun is notorious almost as much for the reasoning that brought it about as it is for the actual carnage. General von Falkenhayn, Moltke's successor as chief of the general staff, on December 21, 1915, had laid out his plan of battle for William II. The general rejected a drive into Russia because it would disperse the German army over the vast expanse of that land. Operations against Italy were ruled out because Falkenhayn viewed the Austro-Hungarian army already as a "cadaver." A drive through the Balkans in the direction of British India he dismissed as peripheral.

That left the Western Front. France, Falkenhayn assured his supreme war lord, was "militarily and economically weakened to the point of exhaustion." The driving force of the enemy coalition was "perfidious Albion." Britain was willing to fight to the last Frenchman and to finance the anti-German coalition until victory had been achieved. Because the relative weakness of the German fleet made a direct strike against the island nation impossible, Falkenhayn opted for an indirect twin strike. At sea German U-boats would launch a major offensive against Britain's vital supply lines; on land the German army would assail "England's tool on the Continent," France. A defeated and demoralized France would sue for peace, as it had in 1870.

Falkenhayn ruled out both Schlieffen's encirclement panacea and current notions of a breakthrough strategy. He settled instead on "an operation limited to a narrow front," that is, a conventional assault against an objective "for the retention of which the French general staff would be compelled to throw in every man they have. If they do so, the French will be bled dry." The medieval fortress salient at Verdun along the Meuse River was selected as the object. It was "immaterial," Falkenhayn lectured William II, "whether we reach our goal." The main objective was to "bleed to death" French forces. The chief of the general staff gave the operation the code name *Gericht* (Court of Justice). Neither the ally at Vienna, nor the German chancellor, nor even corps commanders were apprised of the nature of the undertaking.

Verdun became not only a battle of attrition but also a battle of matériel. More than two hundred trains were required to haul ammunition to the front for the preparatory artillery barrage alone. Thereafter, thirty-four trains stretching fifty kilometers in length would be needed just to resupply the heavy shells for a single division with fifteen batteries of artillery. New tools of war were introduced: steel helmets, flamethrowers, grenade-firing rifles, and a new asphyxiating gas, phosgene. Captain Willy Rohr effectively deployed his new ten-men platoon of storm troopers (*Sturmbattalion*) armed with semiautomatic weapons, hand grenades, and flamethrowers. Ernst Jünger, a veteran of the Great War and one of its most influential subsequent writers, talked about the new "workers of war." Air power was used mainly for reconnaissance. Parachutes were available, but their use frowned upon as "dishonorable" for the new knights of combat, the pilots.

German headquarters was painfully aware that its forces were being destroyed. Routine ten-day casualty reports kept Falkenhayn abreast of events at Verdun: thirty-eight thousand casualties in April, fifty-four thousand in May, another twenty thousand in June at Fort Vaux alone. The Kaiser grew pessimistic as early as mid-March: "This will not end in a great victory." The German army lost its best frontline officers and experienced noncommissioned officers at Verdun. The army was shattered. Desertions increased dramatically. The troops lost faith in their leaders. The "ideas of 1914" were buried in the blood and mud at Verdun. Crown Prince William noted that "the Meuse mill ground up the hearts of the soldiers as much as their bodies." The German official history of the war later spoke of "the catastrophe of the tragedy of Verdun." Few remembered in the fall of 1916 that the first regiments of the Brandenburg III Corps had stormed French positions at Verdun on February 22 to the stirring sounds of patriotic martial music, "Prussia's Glory."

What next? Encirclement had failed at the Marne and in Flanders in 1914. Germany had not made a breakthrough in either the east or the west. Attrition had succeeded all too well, for both the French and the Germans, at Verdun. Was there no way to break the stalemate?

The Imperial German Navy had a plan. At Jutland on the last day of May 1916 it had inflicted great loss on the British Grand Fleet but had not been able to alter the strategic course of the war. In his after-action report of the battle on July 4, Admiral Reinhard Scheer conceded that Britain could not be defeated in this war due to its "great material superiority" in ships and its advantageous "military-geographical position" astride the two exits to the North Sea. Only "the defeat of British economic life — that is, by using the U-boats against British trade" — the commander of the High Sea Fleet informed his Kaiser, could force London to the peace table.

Germany had tried submarine warfare in 1915 and 1916, but repeated incidents involving American lives and ships had led to acrimonious "notes" from Washington. The most famous incident at sea occurred on May 7, 1915, when a German U-boat torpedoed the British liner *Lusitania,* with the loss of 1,200 lives, including 139 Americans.[1] A public outcry in the United States, combined with President Woodrow Wilson's stern warning against any future incidents, prompted Berlin to call off the underwater offensive. But after Verdun, voices mounted in Germany demanding that the new technology be given a chance to prove itself. While Chancellor von Bethmann Hollweg's assistant Kurt Riezler spoke of yet another "leap into the dark," Generals von Hindenburg and Ludendorff, who had replaced the hapless Falkenhayn at the end of August 1916, favored the naval initiative. The head of the Admiralty Staff, Henning von Holtzendorff, accordingly set out to secure expert counsel on the matter.

A modern-day think tank as well as a naval-industrial complex emerged. Academics and civilians joined forces with naval officers to survey the situation. They pored over British import-export statistics, world merchant shipping tonnage reports, insurance risk tables, farmers' almanacs, and even the American *Rye and Seed Quarterly* in order to arrive at the conclusion that wheat imports were the Achilles heel of the British economy. That island kingdom, they argued, would not be able to resist unrestricted submarine warfare for more than six months. Nearly five hundred copies of the "top secret" findings were circulated to men of influence, including Bethmann Hollweg, as well as Hindenburg and Ludendorff.

On December 22, 1916, Admiral von Holtzendorff made these findings his own. Two critical points emerged: the ultimate tonnage of merchant shipping available to Britain and the percentage of the total production of wheat available to it. According to the German experts, world production of wheat was down 9 percent in 1916; wheat rust on the American plains would further reduce that figure in 1917. About 10.65 million of the 20 million tons of Allied and neutral shipping were needed to provision Britain. The German analysts concluded that if 600,000 tons of shipping per month could be destroyed during the first two months of unrestricted submarine warfare and about 500,000 tons per month over the next four months, the British tonnage available for food supplies would decline by 40 percent, "a final and irreplaceable" loss. German victory would be guaranteed by October 1917.

On January 9, 1917, it was decided to launch unrestricted submarine warfare on February 1. William II, Hindenburg, Ludendorff, and Holtzendorff were united in this view. Bethmann Hollweg harbored doubts about the wisdom of the U-boat campaign but endorsed the initiative at Pless that day. Not only was he faced with a solid military-naval front, but as early as October 1916 the pivotal Center party had demanded that he follow the military in this matter.

But what about the United States? Would it not immediately protest any loss of American lives or shipping? The protocol of the meeting on January 9 shows that this issue was fully discussed. Bethmann Hollweg confidently

[1] The *Lusitania* most probably (and illegally) was carrying munitions to Britain.

anticipated "the entry of America into the war." Ludendorff stated that he was prepared "to accept this risk." Admiral Scheer's representative, Captain Magnus von Levetzow, dismissed possible American entry into the war as being "of no importance to the fleet." William II allowed that although he "fully expected America's entry into the war," this was "irrelevant" to the outcome of the struggle. Germany's leaders were convinced that it would take the United States at least a year to gear up for war and to transport an army to Europe. The U-boats would have decided the outcome by then.

Initial successes exceeded expectations. In February 1917 more than 540,000 tons of mainly British shipping were torpedoed; in March the figure reached the target level of 600,000 tons; and April proved to be the best month of the campaign, with 840,000 tons of Allied shipping sent to the bottom. Then disaster struck. On May 10 German submarine commanders for the first time spied convoys: Allied cruisers and destroyers now escorted merchant ships sailing in tight formation across the North Atlantic. German destruction of Allied shipping declined to an average of only 350,000 tons per month. Losses during convoy fell below 1 percent. Worse yet, the hunters became the hunted: depth charges, bomb howitzers and throwers, mine nets, explosive paravanes, flares, and hydrophones doubled the number of U-boats destroyed from twenty during the first half of 1917 to forty-three in the second half of that year.

Reality showed that the German number crunchers had had a narrow focus in their analyses of economic determinants. Apart from overlooking the shipbuilding capacity of the United States and ignoring the amount of neutral and seized tonnage available to Britain, they possessed no clear notion even of how many ships per month Britain required to sustain its industry and feed its citizens. Moreover, because of their preconceived notions of the British national character, they never imagined that rationing would be instituted, that the government would take control of shipping and insurance matters and regulate prices, and that land previously uncultivated could be brought into production. There still persists in Anglo-Saxon historiography the notion that the U-boats almost defeated Britain in the war, but the truth was quite another matter: Britain's daily needs of fifteen thousand tons of cereals could be delivered by a mere four ships. Not even the supply of oats for racehorses was jeopardized by the submarine campaign of 1917.

On April 6, 1917, the United States declared war on Germany as a result of the U-boat campaign. It joined the entente not as an ally but rather as an "associated power" because President Wilson wanted to maintain his diplomatic independence for the future peace settlement. A clumsy attempt by the German Foreign Office of Arthur Zimmermann to entice Mexico (for the recovery of Arizona, New Mexico, and Texas) and Japan (for influence over the western terminus of the Panama Canal) to attack the United States hardly helped matters. At sea not a single loaded eastbound American troop transport was sunk during the entire war. And after some initial interdepartmental wrangling, the

U.S. Navy by 1918 was in position substantially to assist the Allied war at sea both against the U-boats and the German High Sea Fleet.

In fact, just as they had grossly underestimated the British before 1914, German planners in 1917 had dismissed the Americans as negligible. Once more, to use Werner Sombart's words, it was a case of "merchants" against "heroes." Arrogance, hubris, and the supremacy of an engineering mentality had replaced sober analysis in German strategic planning. Stereotyped notions concerning the American love of peace and prosperity as well as abhorrence of war combined to prompt German leaders to dismiss the Republic's soldiers and sailors as untrained and untrainable. American grain reserves, which alone covered the Allied deficit for 1916, were discounted. Nor was the slightest attention paid to the financial power of the Republic. In short, deeply embedded preconceptions from the 1890s of the American "parvenu" precluded sober analysis in 1917.

1918: The Nemesis of Power

The failure of the unrestricted submarine campaign by the fall of 1917 moved German military planners to mount one final, all-out effort to break the military stalemate on the Western Front. The notion was not without merit. In April 1917 the German military had transported V. I. Lenin and his followers from Switzerland to Sweden in a sealed train specifically to foment revolution in Russia. On April 16 the Bolsheviks arrived in Petrograd (St. Petersburg), and after several initial setbacks during the summer carried out a successful revolution on November 7, 1917.[1] Lenin moved quickly (and against his own party) to conclude peace with Imperial Germany in March 1918 at Brest-Litovsk in order to concentrate on spreading his revolution throughout Russia. The end of the war in the east held out the promise of additional troops to Hindenburg and Ludendorff.

But there were danger signs on the horizon. Austria-Hungary was on the point of collapse. In the spring of 1917 Emperor Charles I, who had succeeded Francis Joseph in November 1916, launched secret negotiations with France designed to take Austria-Hungary out of the war. They failed miserably when made public by the French premier, Georges Clemenceau, and strained relations between Berlin and Vienna to the breaking point. Additionally, British forces drove Germany's ally Turkey[2] out of the Middle East while War Minister

[1] By the Gregorian calendar. Under the old Julian calendar then in use, the Bolshevik revolution fell on October 25; hence the term "Great Socialist October Revolution," or simply "Red October."

[2] Turkey had negotiated a defensive alliance with the Central Powers in July 1914 and, after the German cruisers *Goeben* and *Breslau* entered Turkish waters on August 10-11, joined the war against the entente at the end of October 1914.

Enver Paşa pursued illusory campaigns of conquest in the Caucasus. And the United States was beginning to send troops to France at the rate of 200,000 to 300,000 per month. Finally, Hindenburg and Ludendorff had been informed by the Prussian War Ministry that Germany had no reserves. All that remained was the call-up of the 637,000 recruits from the age cohort born in 1899–1900. Could one possibly wait any longer? If so, for what?

Ludendorff code-named his desperate offensive "Michael" in honor of Germany's patron saint. The assault possessed no strategic objective; Ludendorff even forbade his staff to use the word *strategy* in his presence. Despite impressive initial gains in the area around Amiens, Michael ground to a halt for lack of direction and reserves. The army invented the term *abgekämpft* ("fought out") to describe its troops. Many of the latter had stopped to raid bountiful Allied supply depots rather than to press the assault. Nor were the tools of modern industrialized warfare on hand. Germany barely had 30,000 trucks running on wooden or iron tires at a time when the Allies had 100,000 vehicles running on rubber. And while the Reich had but 20 A7V "tanks," the Allies boasted 800 assault vehicles.

The anticipated reinforcements from the east failed to materialize. Ludendorff's megalomania and obsession with empire building as far as the Caspian Sea necessitated the presence of a million German occupation troops in Russia. Among those who did make the trek westward to France, desertions en route in German depots rose from 10 percent in November 1917 to 20 percent in May and 30 percent by August 1918. An estimated 200,000 to 1.5 million deserters roamed Germany. Even the regular army deployed along the Western Front wanted to end the war. On August 8, the "black day of the German army" as Ludendorff put it in the wake of the Allied offensive between Ancre and Avre, seasoned Prussian Guards units met raw recruits with shouts of "strike breakers"! The German army had come to the end of its physical and psychological rope after four years of uninterrupted carnage.

Ludendorff, too, realized that the end was near. His biting rejoinder to a staff colonel who had to inform him that the army had reached the end — "What is the point of all your croaking? What do you want from me? Am I now to conclude peace at any price?" — attests to the intimate connection between war aims and the survival of the Prusso-German state. But the game was up. On August 14 army headquarters agreed that it was senseless to continue the war. On September 29 Ludendorff demanded an immediate armistice. Two days later, just before heading to Sweden in disguise to pen his memoirs, the general informed his officers that he had asked William II to appoint cabinet members from among the ranks of the old *reichsfeindlich* camp of Centrists, Progressives, and Social Democrats — men who in 1917 had already organized themselves into a special parliamentary caucus and who after the war would constitute the backbone of the new republican government. "Let them now conclude the peace that will have to be concluded," Ludendorff crowed. "Let them stew in their own juice." Even in defeat, the German generals showed a remarkably keen sense of self-preservation and a highly developed ability to shift blame for the lost war to those least responsible for either its outbreak or its duration.

In October 1918 Imperial Germany attempted at the eleventh hour to reform its constitutional structure. Admiral Paul von Hintze, state secretary of the Foreign Office, convinced Generals Hindenburg and Ludendorff as well as William II that the war had been lost and that the time had come to initiate a "revolution from above" in order to head off a potential "revolution from below." Only by pursuing such a reformist course, Hintze cogently argued, might the monarchy be saved and the shock and anger caused by the news of Germany's defeat be shifted to building a broadly based parliamentary government. Chancellor Georg Count von Hertling, a seventy-eight-year-old Bavarian conservative, had not been included in these deliberations, and he was now hastily replaced by a more moderate aristocrat, Prince Max, heir presumptive to the throne of Baden.

With the Kaiser's albeit unsteady approval, Max von Baden abolished the hated Prussian three-class voting system, made ministers responsible to the Reichstag, and voided the Kaiser's command authority over the army and navy. With the stroke of a pen, Germany was transformed from its traditional semiauthoritarian to a British-type constitutional monarchy. The Reich's parliamentarians thus were cast in the unenviable role of seeking a new national consensus and guiding the nation toward an uncertain future.

A mirage of hope glimmered for the new government. Throughout October, Chancellor Prince Max appealed to President Wilson for an end to the war on the basis of the Fourteen Points that the U.S. president had enunciated on January 8, 1918, before a joint session of Congress. The Germans put their faith in the first five general points calling for open diplomacy, freedom of the seas, removal of trade barriers, reduction in armaments, and impartial settlement of colonial claims based on the interests of the people involved. Few in Germany understood that the Fourteen Points had been designed in part to serve the needs of psychological warfare. In December 1917 Lenin had called for an end to the war without annexations or indemnities, and Wilson sought to counter the Bolshevik peace drive with one of his own. Even fewer Germans apparently bothered to examine the remaining points, which demanded the restoration of an independent Belgium (Point 7), the return of Alsace-Lorraine to France (Point 8), "autonomous development" for the nationalities of the Austro-Hungarian Empire (Point 10), and recognition of an independent Poland with free access to the sea (Point 13).

At home the year had also brought about a hardening of fronts. Food shortages combined with falling real wages to bring about a wave of strikes. The Independent Social Democrats gained strength in the industrial regions around Cologne and Leipzig, as well as in Silesia. The radicalization of labor as a result of the war boded ill for the future. Fifty strikes per month broke out in 1918. And the story was much the same in Austria-Hungary. In January

1918 industrial strikes prompted by a drastic reduction in bread rations erupted in Wiener-Neustadt and spread to the other industrial areas of Austria, as well as to Hungary. The government was taken completely by surprise. By 1918 the bulk of the army was unreliable, the police powerless. At the last moment Emperor Charles I managed to restore order only by calling in reliable army units to suppress the strikes. It was the beginning of the end of the Austro-Hungarian monarchy.

As a final response to the war, Germany turned to what has been called protofascism. General Ludendorff and Colonel Bauer had come to the conclusion by 1916 that the monarchy was no longer viable. "Total war," they had concluded, could be conducted only with an "absolute military dictatorship." The problem was that Ludendorff could never quite gather up the courage to accept the lead role in such an authoritarian state (*Führerstaat*).

The founding of the Fatherland party by Wolfgang Kapp and Alfred von Tirpitz on September 3, 1917, at Königsberg, the coronation site of the Hohenzollerns since 1701, brought forth the kind of public support that the military could never hope to marshal. The new group represented a distinct departure from existing Wilhelmian political parties. In fact, eschewing the parliamentary system entirely, the Fatherland party sought to become a nationalistic and xenophobic mass movement of the traditional conservative Right and middle classes. Therein it hoped to build on the experiences gained during the *Sammlungspolitik* of the 1870s, 1880s, and 1890s. Specifically, Kapp and Tirpitz sought to revitalize Germany by way of a vast annexationist program. In the west, they sought to bring Holland and Belgium under direct German control. In the east, German domination over Russia and Turkey would extend its influence "as far as the Pacific and the gates of India." By July 1918 the Fatherland party boasted 1.25 million members, far surpassing even the SPD as a mass movement.

The new movement incorporated — in fact, supplanted — the old Wilhelmian pressure groups such as the Pan-German, Colonial, and Navy leagues. It attracted support among peasants' associations, the German Association of the Middle Classes, and the Central Union of German Industrialists. Indeed, heavy industry proved especially supportive in terms of both membership and contributions. A direct link between the Fatherland party and fascism can be established in the person of Anton Drexler. A functionary in one of the 2,536 local branches of the Fatherland party, Drexler went on to become the original founder of the National Socialist party in Munich. Heinrich Class, president of the Pan-German League and an active supporter of the Fatherland party from its inception, added a special flavor to the burgeoning protofascist movement by calling for a "ruthless campaign against Jewry," which he, like Ludendorff and countless others, blamed for having lost the war and ruining "our good but misled people." Class' comments built a bridge from the Second Reich to postwar Germany for the antisemites.

"The General Strike of a Defeated Army"

The final impetus for the collapse of Imperial Germany came from the High Sea Fleet. In late October 1918 Admiral Reinhard Scheer, as well as Admiral Franz von Hipper, the new fleet chief, concocted Operations Plan No. 19, which called for a final desperate naval sortie against the combined Anglo-American surface forces in the North Sea. Scheer decreed that "honor" and the future "existence" of the navy demanded the sacrifice and even considered asking William II to go down with the fleet in mock-heroic style. Instead, on October 29 the stokers in the fleet doused fires in the boilers and raised the red flag of revolt on the heavy units. Hipper, like most other naval officers utterly inexperienced in politics, simply dispersed the rebellious sailors to the various German ports, where they immediately fomented rebellion. By November 5 Lübeck and Travemünde had fallen to rebellious sailors. Hamburg followed the next day. Bremen, Cuxhaven, and Wilhelmshaven surrendered without opposition on November 6. The sailors next headed inland, seizing Cologne on November 7 and then Bielefeld and Hanover.

Thus, the fleet that was supposed to have steered Germany toward glorious times instead launched a revolt. The fleet that the nation had poured its treasure into had remained idle throughout most of the war. The fleet that had poisoned Anglo-German relations now was to be surrendered to the Allies and interned at Scapa Flow in the Orkney Islands, there to await its fate. And the fleet that was to have united the German middle classes in 1848 and again under Tirpitz now spearheaded the nation's dissolution.

On November 8, independent of the sailors' revolt, Kurt Eisner of the USPD established a Constituent Workers', Soldiers', and Peasants' Council at Munich. Eisner hoped eventually to create a democratic and socialist Bavarian republic as a first step toward the founding of a "United States of Germany" including Austria. Eisner dramatically opened the Bavarian archives in order to establish Germany's role in the origins of World War I. Would his example catch on?

The revolt reached Berlin by November 9, but there was to be no "Red October" as in Russia under Lenin. The erstwhile *Reichsfeinde* were now handed power without a shot being fired. Friedrich Ebert from the SPD as chairman of the Council of People's Commissars quietly slipped behind Bismarck's desk at the Chancery. His colleague Philipp Scheidemann on November 9 calmly proclaimed the birth of the German republic from a window in the Reichstag building. Elsewhere throughout the Reich, kings and princes quietly surrendered their authority, which in reality they had exercised in name only since 1871. The king of Saxony, Frederick August III, gladly handed power over to the Socialist Democrats with the immortal line: "Do your filth alone!"

But why a republic in November 1918? Part of the answer lies in the lack of an alternative. On November 9 General Wilhelm Groener, Ludendorff's successor as first quartermaster-general, had informed William II that the army "no longer stands behind Your Majesty!" The Kaiser had boarded his special cream-and-gold imperial train at the Belgian village of Spa the next morning and vanished toward the Dutch frontier — and twenty-two years of rather dignified exile at Doorn. His son, Crown Prince William, was widely regarded as unacceptable. Profligate, politically inept, and morally weak, he appealed at best only to diehard Hohenzollern legitimists. Thus Scheidemann's proclamation of a republic on November 9 met with little resistance, save from Ebert, who was unpleasantly surprised by this unilateral act. And being decent citizens, the Social Democrats helped load fifty wagons of "necessities" to ship to William II at Doorn, along with 60 million marks spending money.

The deed was done. After half a century in opposition to and excluded from all imperial agencies of power, the Social Democrats were asked to pick up the pieces. August 4, 1914, had shown that they had jettisoned Marx for nationalism. Ebert had lost two sons in the war and was not about to preside over the dissolution of the Bismarckian state. Above all, army censors had kept the truth of Germany's defeat from the home front; hence news of the total collapse on the Western Front came as a surprise and shock to nation and government alike. No less an authority than the Conservative leader Ernst von Heydebrand und der Lasa exclaimed: "We have been lied to and deceived." What would the future hold?

Ebert and his colleagues were not in an enviable position in November 1918. At a time when the Allies calculated that a working adult required 2,500 calories per day, German workers were down to less than 1,000 calories, enough to sustain only a two-year-old child. About 250,000 people starved to death in Germany in 1918. Railroad strikes crippled the nation's transport system, and miners' strikes deprived the government of much-needed income from industrial production. Street fighting broke out almost daily in Berlin, Brunswick, Bremen, Eisenach, Erfurth, Gotha, Halle, Hamburg, and Leipzig. In Munich, Kurt Eisner had founded a socialist republic, a strange mixture of French Revolution and Mardi Gras. In the Rhineland Konrad Adenauer, with French support, tried to sustain a movement to separate from Prussia. Active fighting continued with Soviet Russian forces in the Baltic states and East Prussia, as well as with Polish units in Posen (Poznań) and West Prussia. The Bismarckian state seemed on the point of dissolution.

Against this background Ebert concluded the famous pact with General Groener on November 10, 1918: the army promised to bring its forces home in an orderly fashion and to defend the provisional government, while Ebert agreed to recognize the authority of the Prussian officer corps and to suppress the nascent soldiers' councils. In truth, in November 1918 the army found itself in its greatest crisis since the twin disasters of Jena and Auerstädt in 1806. Physical seizure of power was anathema to its tradition of being "apolitical," yet its officers vowed not to suffer the fate of their tsarist brethren in Russia.

Revolution, November 1918: Soldiers on the roof of the Brandenburg Gate.

Groener entered into his pact with Ebert, as he wrote his wife, "so that the cart will not slide further to the Left." The army openly stated its quid pro quo for recognizing the new regime: "The officer corps demands that the government will suppress Bolshevism." Ebert, who on the army question found himself very much in the position of the Liberals in 1848–1849, for the moment gained much-needed support from Groener in restoring law and order and safeguarding the Reich's threatened borders. But in the long run the agreement of November 10 allowed the army to operate virtually as a "state within a state." It was a heavy mortgage.

By December 1918 Germany was in the political position that Russia had been in the previous year. The dual authority that had existed in the Petrograd Soviet and the Provisional Government was mirrored in Berlin by the dual powers of the workers' Executive Council and the government's Council of People's Commissars. The difference was that the German revolution produced no Lenin. Nor did it create armed forces comparable to Leon Trotsky's Red Army or a secret police along the lines of Felix Dzerzhinsky's "Extraordinary Commission to Combat Counterrevolution, Sabotage, and Speculation" (Cheka). Richard Müller, head of the Executive Council, lamented his organization's lack of revolutionary fervor: "Insecure fumbling, fearfully weighing everything without decisively risking anything."

Victims of war and revolution: Children march to demonstrate their plight (November 1920).

The German labor movement assembled in Berlin on December 16, 1918, in order to chart a course for the future. The First German Congress of Workers' and Soldiers' Councils, despite its overtly Bolshevik name, proved extremely moderate. Although it voted almost unanimously to reform the Prussian army and to nationalize heavy industry, it firmly rejected Lenin's form of government by soviets by a vote of 400 to 50 and instead called for elections for a national constituent assembly. Neither Liebknecht nor Luxemburg was elected to the Congress. Only two women were among its 496 delegates.

There was to be no "second" or socialist revolution. The civil service, as in 1806 when Napoleon had occupied Berlin, loyally stayed at its posts. Professor Seeberg, author of the expansive war aims program of 1915 and now rector of the University of Berlin, promised an obedient transition from empire to republic. The theologian Ernst Troeltsch aptly captured the spirit of the German revolution: "Not a person dead in defense of Kaiser and Reich! The bureaucracy has decided to serve the new government! . . . On all faces one could read: Salaries will continue to be paid!" Another keen observer of German events, Walther Rathenau of the electrical giant AEG, spoke of a "revolution by accident." It was all orderly and proper, with an absolute minimum of violence. Nothing more than a political changing of the guard constituted the "revolution" of 1918. "We call the general strike of a defeated army the German revolution," Rathenau presciently noted.

But Ebert and Scheidemann paid a high price for their patriotic service: division of the German labor movement. On December 24, 1918, when the People's Naval Division quartered in the royal stables in Berlin moved to arrest the Council of People's Commissars in retaliation for Ebert's refusal to pay them, Gustav Noske, the SPD's self-appointed bloodhound of the revolution, upon Ebert's orders called in imperial units to crush the revolt. Heavy bloodshed was avoided when Ernst Däumig, leader of the left-wing of the USPD, decreed that one should neither spill blood nor topple a government during the Christmas season.

The repercussions of this Christmas Eve fiasco were severe. On December 27, 1918, the Independent Social Democrats left Ebert's government. Four days later the German Communist party (KPD) was founded, and on January 5 the radical wing of the German workers' movement decided to press for a "second revolution" in Berlin. The so-called Spartacist Uprising[1] of January 6–13, 1919, was marked by incredible incompetence and lack of imagination on the part of the radical workers and their leaders. It was brutally suppressed once more by imperial troops and free-corps units (*Freikorps*) — government-financed volunteer paramilitary units — called in by Noske. Liebknecht and Luxemburg were murdered on January 15 by soldiers from the same units deployed against the People's Naval Division on Christmas Eve 1918; their mutilated bodies were dumped in a Berlin canal. The events of January 1919, in the words of the Austrian Socialist Rudolf Hilferding, constituted the "battle of the Marne" of the German revolution. On the other hand the revolution at last had its martyrs.

Events at Munich also took a turn for the worse. Kurt Eisner was murdered by a right-wing fanatic, Anton Count von Arco-Valley, on February 21, 1919. Early in April a "Soviet Republic" was proclaimed. Its supporters ranged from radical farmers to anarchists and from confidence-men to psychopaths; its program centered around abolishing the civil service and forming a Red Army, to be staffed in large measure by released Russian prisoners of war. The "Soviet Republic" was short-lived. On May 1, 1919, regular army formations augmented by Free Corps units invaded Bavaria. Six hundred people died in the Bavarian civil war.

[1] Liebknecht and Luxemburg from jail after 1916 and 1917, respectively, had secretly smuggled out pamphlets that their followers illegally distributed. The "Spartacus Letters" were named in honor of a Greek slave who had led revolts against Rome from 73 to 71 B.C.

World War I, the "great seminal catastrophe" of the twentieth century, was finally over. It had affected no fewer than thirty-eight states. Twenty-three million men had fought for the Central Powers and 42 million for the Allied and Associated Powers. Austria-Hungary had lost 1.1 million men killed and 3.6 million wounded or taken prisoner, Germany 1.9 million dead and 4.2 million injured or taken captive. The Habsburgs and the Hohenzollerns were in exile. The multinational Austro-Hungarian Empire was disintegrating into individual national states, and the future of the German Empire was in doubt.

Tragically for Germany (and the rest of the world), the transition from war to peace was bridged by a cruel myth. On November 18, 1919, Field Marshal von Hindenburg appeared before a Reichstag Committee of Enquiry to "testify" on the causes of Germany's collapse. It was a triumphant farce. Escorted by an honor guard and formally seated in a chrysanthemum-bedecked witness box, Hindenburg (the "wooden titan") swore before a startled audience that Germany had never been militarily defeated but "stabbed in the back" by certain pacifist and socialist elements — Jews and Marxists. Whereas William II had assured Austria-Hungary of his *Nibelungen* loyalty before 1914, Hindenburg continued the allusion in 1918. "Our exhausted front collapsed just as Siegfried did from the foul spearthrow of the truculent Hagen."[1] Thereafter November 9, 1918, became a synonym for shame and treason. The leaders of the new republic collectively became the "November criminals" in the gutter rhetoric of the Right.

The alleged "November criminals" were confirmed in office by the national elections of January 19, 1919, which brought out a record 83 percent of the voters. The SPD was certain of victory. For the past half-century its leaders had preached the optimistic message that if all citizens were allowed to vote freely and if all restrictions on suffrage were removed, the electorate would deliver a mandate for liberal and social reform.

The returns of January 1919 seemed to bear out that faith. The parties that had coalesced behind the "peace resolution" in July 1917 garnered 76.1 percent of the vote and 329 of 421 seats. The SPD led with 37.9 percent, and the erstwhile Center party, temporarily reconstituted as the Christian People's party, received 19.7 percent. The newly founded German Democratic party, which included Albert Einstein as well as most of the former Progressives, claimed 18.5 percent. The old Conservative party, regrouped as the German National People's party (DNVP), garnered but 10.3 percent of the vote, and while the erstwhile National Liberals, now the German People's party (DVP), were limited to 5.9 percent. It was a clear victory for democratic and republican forces. The only sour note was that among the nearly twenty parties vying

[1] Hindenburg's reference is to Richard Wagner's operatic triumph *Der Ring des Nibelungen*, wherein the mythic Germanic hero Siegfried is struck down by the archvillain Hagen.

for the voters' support, four were regionally based in Bavaria, Brunswick, Hanover, and Schleswig-Holstein, attesting to the fact that the particularism that had plagued the Reich for centuries had not been eradicated.

For the first time in German history, women, who had made up 10 percent of the National Assembly, as well as soldiers voted in a national election. Women voted in record numbers, with nearly 90 percent of eligible females casting ballots in January 1919. And women could now stand for political office. Gertrud Bäumer of the Federation of German Women's Associations took her seat in the National Assembly as a Democratic party deputy.

The National Assembly faced the triple problem of concluding peace, drafting a constitution, and demobilizing the armed forces. It was convened at Weimar in Thuringia, the city of Goethe and Schiller, partly to contrast the Germany of "poets and thinkers" with that of "Prussian militarism" and partly because, while Berlin was being ravaged by ongoing violence, Weimar was under the protection of a "reliable" Free Corps formation. It was also well known to President Ebert and Chancellor Scheidemann that U.S. President Wilson nurtured a strong dislike for Berlin and all that it stood for.

In 1919 the German nation thus embarked on its first experiment with democracy against a backdrop of military defeat, political revolution, and domestic turmoil. Bismarck's Reich of 1871 was on the point of dissolution. William II's erstwhile promise to steer his subjects toward "glorious times" had been shattered by massive loss of life (nearly 2 million men) and a staggering national debt (about 175 billion marks). Prosperity had yielded to unemployment and strikes. And even the brief flirtation with parliamentary monarchy of October 1918 seemed in jeopardy without a monarch in Berlin to anchor the system. The public mood was perhaps best captured by the eminent Berlin historian Friedrich Meinecke: "A fearful and gloomy existence awaits us in the best of circumstances!"

Suggested Readings

There is no single-volume treatment of World War I and Germany in either English or German. On the other hand, the origins of the war have received more than their fair share of debate. An overview can be gleaned from Holger H. Herwig, ed., *The Outbreak of World War I: Causes and Responsibilities*, 5th ed. (Lexington, Mass., and Toronto, 1991). Volker R. Berghahn, *Germany and the Approach of War in 1914* (New York, 1973), details the domestic roots of the war, and Imanuel Geiss, *July 1914: The Outbreak of the First World War. Selected Documents* (New York, 1968), concentrates on the diplomatic record. Fritz Fischer, *War of Illusions: German Policies from 1911 to 1914* (New York, 1975), is a superb treatment of the actual road to war. Samuel R. Williamson, Jr., *Austria-Hungary and the Coming of the First World War* (New York, 1991), is the most recent exploration of Vienna's decision to go to war in 1914.

The issue of German war aims has been exhaustively analyzed. The standard remains Fritz Fischer, *Germany's Aims in the First World War* (New York, 1967). Earlier treatments of the topic include Hans W. Gatzke, *Germany's Drive to the West: A Study of Germany's Western War Aims During the First World War* (Baltimore, 1950); Marvin L. Edwards, *Stresemann and the Greater Germany, 1914–1918* (New York, 1963); and Henry Cord Meyer's classic, *Mitteleuropa in German Thought and Action, 1815–1945* (The Hague, 1964). Those who opposed war have been identified by Francis L. Carsten, *War Against War: British and German Radical Movements in the First World War* (London, 1982).

Military-industrial relations were first studied by Robert B. Armeson, *Total War and Compulsory Labor: A Study of the Military-Industrial Complex in Germany During World War I* (The Hague, 1964), as well as by Gerald F. Feldman, *Army, Industry, and Labor in Germany, 1914–18* (Princeton, 1966). A more recent overview is Gerd Hardach, *The First World War* (Berkeley and Los Angeles, 1977). The greater issue of the war and its impact on German society was first broached by A. Mendelssohn-Bartholdy, *The War and German Society* (New York, 1971). In outline form, Hans-Ulrich Wehler, *The German Empire, 1871–1918* (Leamington Spa, 1985), remains useful. Most stridently, Jürgen Kocka, *Total War: German Society 1914–1918* (Leamington Spa, 1984), offers a Marxist analysis of class warfare during the Great War. The role of women during the war still awaits an English-language treatment. Until one is available, see Richard J. Evans, *The Feminist Movement in Germany, 1894–1933* (London, 1976); and Ute Frevert, *Women in German History: From Bourgeois Emancipation to Sexual Liberation* (New York, 1989).

The career of the wartime imperial chancellor has been defended by Konrad H. Jarausch, *The Enigmatic Chancellor: Bethmann Hollweg and the Hubris of Imperial Germany* (New Haven, 1972). Gerhard Ritter, *The Sword and the Scepter: The Problem of Militarism in Germany* (Coral Gables, 1973), interrupted his grand sweep of the relationship between the German military and "statecraft" in order to dedicate the fourth volume of this set to the defense of Bethmann Hollweg. Martin Kitchen, *The Silent Dictatorship: The Politics of the German High Command Under Hindenburg and Ludendorff, 1916–18* (London, 1976), seeks to establish the link between the military duumvirate and later protofascist developments in Germany.

A brief examination of the German military in the war can be found in Holger H. Herwig, "The Dynamics of Necessity: German Military Policy During the First World War," in Allan R. Millett and Williamson Murray, eds., *Military Effectiveness*, vol. 1, *The First World War* (Boston, 1988). The mythology of Verdun received corrective treatment from two novelists: Arnold Zweig, *Education before Verdun* in 1935, and Edgar Maass, *Verdun*, in 1936. The story of the Habsburg armed forces in the Great War is best told by Gunther E. Rothenberg, *The Army of Francis Joseph* (West Lafayette, Ind., 1976). The war at sea is covered in Holger H. Herwig, *"Luxury" Fleet: The Imperial German Navy, 1888–1918* (London and Atlantic Highlands, N.J., 1987).

The long-term implications of the war as well as the Allied "hunger blockade" are expertly handled by Robert W. Whalen, *Bitter Wounds: German Victims of the Great War, 1914–1939* (Ithaca and London, 1984), and C. Paul Vincent, *The Politics of Hunger: The Allied Blockade of Germany, 1915–1919* (Athens, Ohio, and London, 1985). In a league by itself for erudition is Modris Eksteins, *Rites of Spring: The Great War and the Birth of the Modern Age* (Boston, 1989).

The German "revolution" of 1918 needs an updated examination. Its prehistory has been provided by John W. Mishark, *The Road to Revolution: German Marxism and World War I, 1914–1919* (Detroit, 1967). General treatments of the revolution are by A. J. Ryder, *The German Revolution of 1918: A Study of German Socialism in War and Revolt* (Cambridge, 1967); Ralph H. Lutz, *The German Revolution, 1918–1919* (Stanford, 1922); Charles B. Burdick and Ralph H. Lutz, eds., *Political Institutions of the German Revolution, 1918–1919* (Stanford, 1966); and Francis L. Carsten, *Revolution in Central Europe, 1918–1919* (London, 1972). The German soviet movement has been analyzed by Holger H. Herwig, "The First German Congress of Workers' and Soldiers' Councils and the Problem of Military Reforms," *Central European History* 1 (1968): 150–65. The radical forces and phases are detailed by David W. Morgan, *The Socialist Left and the German Revolution: A History of the German Independent Social Democratic Party, 1917–1922* (Ithaca, 1975); Eric Waldman, *The Spartacist Uprising of 1919 and the Crisis of the German Socialist Movement: A Study of the Relation of Political Theory and Party Practice* (Milwaukee, 1958); and Rudolf Coper, *Failure of a Revolution: Germany, 1918–1919* (Cambridge, Mass., 1955). Events in Munich have been analyzed by Allan Mitchell, *Revolution in Bavaria, 1918–1919: The Eisner Regime and the Soviet Republic* (Princeton, 1965).

C H A P T E R

7

THE UNWANTED REPUBLIC: WEIMAR GERMANY, 1919–1933

400,338,326,350,700,000,000 marks

Cash in circulation, November 1923

The Weimar Republic, Germany's first bid for democracy, failed. To a degree, that failure looms large over the second bid for democracy, the Federal Republic of 1949, and to a lesser degree also over the reunification of East and West Germany in 1990. Why did Germany's first attempt fail? Did special circumstances intervene? Or were there too few people who desired to make democracy work? Weimar faced obvious problems: defeat, revolution, and a dictated peace. President Woodrow Wilson had made it clear to the Germans in October 1918 that he would deal only with new, democratically elected German leaders. Thus the men who had opted for war in July 1914 were relieved of the onerous burden of concluding peace. Moreover, economic disasters — war debts, inflation, and depression — plagued the Weimar state almost from its inception.

The Republic's failure in 1918 to reform the imperial bureaucracy, judiciary, and officer corps hobbled its efforts to democratize these institutions. Although the bureaucracy, as under Napoleon after 1806, loyally conducted the business of those who paid its salaries, neither the legal profession nor the military made any pretense of fondness for the Republic. That numerous organizations, including the armed forces, continued to fly the imperial black-white-red colors alongside (or in place of) the republican black-red-gold standard gave witness to their antirepublican stance. Many Germans mourned the passing of the Hohenzollern monarchy and feared a future under a social-democratic government. The abrupt news of military defeat in October 1918 had come as a shock; the military regime had not prepared the nation. It was perhaps symptomatic of this political ambivalence that Infantry Regiment No. 9 at Potsdam, successor to the prestigious First Guards Regiment on Foot, habitually toasted the Weimar Republic by hailing "His Majesty, the King of Prussia." Indeed, this mixed reaction is corroborated by the realization that the Potsdam regiment lost more men opposing Hitler than any other unit in the army.

To its critics, the Republic began as treason and remained treasonous to all that was "German." To accept Weimar would have meant to exchange elitism for egalitarianism; to admit that sacrifice and war had been for nought; to concede that the Allies had won the Great War not only with bigger battalions and factories but also with ideas. In short, it would have required civil courage. Michael Faulhaber, the cardinal-archbishop of Munich, stated the general rejection of the Republic perhaps most crassly: "The Republic constitutes perjury and high treason."

For its part, the Republic failed to confront the army's stab-in-the-back accusation head-on. It failed to drive home the point to the general public that the real *Dolchstoss* (stab in the back) had been delivered not by the home front, which had bled heavily and sacrificed for four years, but rather by the Kaiser and the imperial government that in 1914 had readily accepted war in the hope of establishing some form of continental hegemony. Additionally, Weimar's supporters failed to stress that the nation had been deceived by the military's refusal in late 1918 to inform either the government or the people about the true state of its predicament. And the first republicans who in 1918–1919 had signed the armistice and then the peace failed to clarify that responsibility for the war rested not with them but with the erstwhile emperor and imperial government. By and large, the academics and professionals who rallied to the Republic after 1918 considered it beneath their dignity to cross swords with the charlatans and mythmakers who confused the public about the true state of affairs. They would pay dearly later for that failure.

The story of the Weimar Republic is one of political selfishness and division. Class interest usually came before the national interest. Factionalism paralyzed the political process in general and parliament in particular. Proportional representation in national elections contributed to the splintering of political groups and increased the distance between electors and deputies. Finally, the split in the German labor movement, the inflation of 1923, and the Great Depression of 1929 demoralized and decimated those who should have been staunch supporters of the Republic: the working and middle classes. In the end, German voters faced a grim choice between conservative authoritarianism and nihilist totalitarianism.

Chaos, 1919–1923

The Republic's first major task was to end the war. On May 7, 1919, the German delegation, which had been kept behind barbed wire at the Hôtel des Réservoirs in Versailles, was handed the eighty-thousand-word draft treaty. It was a sobering document. Instead of the grandiloquent philosophical language of President Wilson's Fourteen Points, the terms were couched in the customary European language used by victors to the vanquished. Alsace-Lorraine was to be given to France, Eupen-et-Malmédy to Belgium, Posen (Poznań) and West Prussia to Poland, Memel (Klaipėda) to Lithuania, and all the German colonies to the Allies. Danzig (Gdańsk) was to become a "free city" under the League of Nations, and a corridor was to cut off East Prussia from the rest of Germany, thereby connecting Poland to the Baltic Sea. France was free to exploit the coal reserves of the Saar for fifteen years, the left bank of the Rhine was to be occupied by the Allies, and plebiscites were to be held in southern East Prussia, northern Schleswig-Holstein, and Upper Silesia to decide the future of those areas of mixed populations. In all, Germany lost one-seventh of its territory and one-tenth of its population. Most serious was the loss of half of its iron ore and a quarter of its coal reserves.

Article 232 of the treaty, which addressed reparations, imposed further economic conditions. Reparations, as yet unspecified as to total amount, were to include 60 percent of Germany's coal production over the next decade; 90 percent of the German merchant fleet; half of all river shipping; all foreign investments and foreign patents; half of all dairy herds; one-quarter of chemical and pharmaceutical output; and almost all modern locomotives and rolling stock. Reparations were designed primarily to rebuild war-torn Belgium and northern France but eventually encompassed the total costs of the war, including future pensions, incurred by the victorious Allies. Germany's major rivers were placed under international control. Some provisions seemed remarkably trivial but ultimately proved lucrative: the French received a monopoly over the terms *champagne* and *cognac*; the Americans gained the rights to Bayer aspirin.[1]

The German fleet was to be surrendered to the Allies and the future navy restricted to fifteen thousand officers and men. Construction of capital ships, naval aircraft, coastal artillery, and U-boats was forbidden. The army was to be limited to 100,000 long-term servicemen and the General Staff disbanded. The treaty prohibited heavy artillery, tanks, gas, and aircraft. An Inter-Allied Military Control Commission was created to ensure that Germany would comply with these conditions.

[1] Bayer, a German corporation, had its U.S. assets seized during the war, and the patent to manufacture aspirin was transferred to various American firms.

THE VERSAILLES SETTLEMENT, 1919

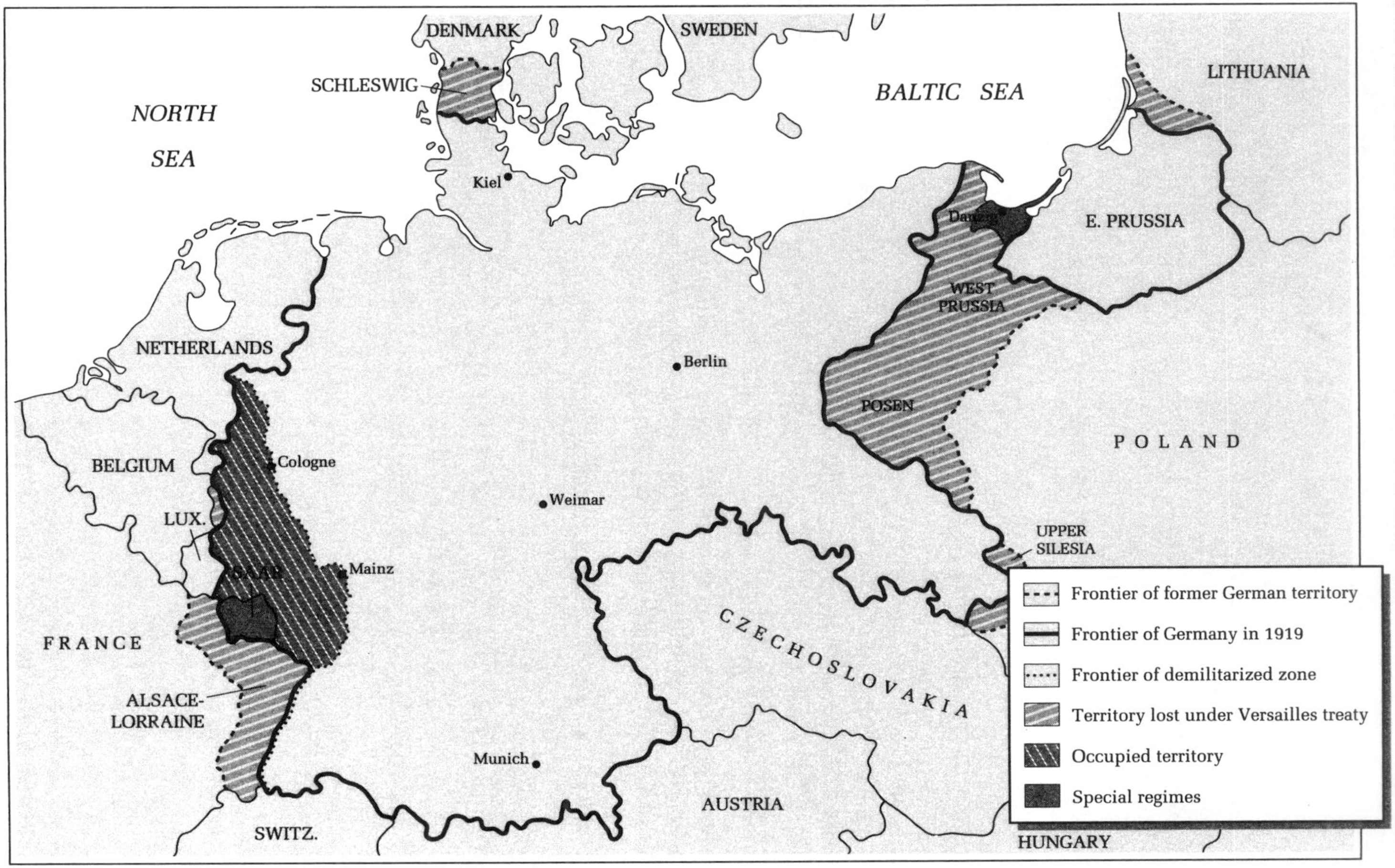

Most galling was Article 231 of the treaty, which forced Germany (and Austria) to assume sole guilt for the war and all its damages. For the first time in history, a nation was saddled with the full onus for starting a war and for paying for all its effects. Not surprisingly, Chancellor Philipp Scheidemann, speaking in the Great Aula of Berlin University, where during the French occupation of Prussia in 1807 Johann Gottlieb Fichte had delivered his famous "Addresses to the German Nation," refused to accept the treaty terms. "What hand will not wither," Scheidemann asked the National Assembly, "that delivers us into such chains?" On June 19, the cabinet split: 7 for, 7 against accepting the treaty.

Was there an alternative, such as a revolt like that of Yorck von Wartenburg (1812)? General Wilhelm Groener, first quartermaster-general of the army, decided the issue by appealing to the nation's future: "Only if we can reasonably maintain the Reich intact is Germany's rebirth possible." Scheidemann resigned, and on June 22 the National Assembly grudgingly bowed to the inevitable and ratified the Treaty of Versailles by a vote of 237 to 138. The document was signed on June 28, 1919, in the Hall of Mirrors at Versailles, on the very table at which Otto von Bismarck in 1871 had created the German Empire. In a grim gesture of defiance, Admiral Ludwig Reuter scuttled the High Sea Fleet interned at Scapa Flow in the Orkney Islands.

Historians basically agree that the Versailles Treaty constituted an unhappy compromise. It was not sufficiently moderate to placate the Germans but not harsh enough to cripple the Reich. French Marshal Ferdinand Foch accurately called it a twenty-years' armistice. Above all, no one in Germany accepted the historical verdict of 1918. From far Left to far Right, Germans were united in their opposition to Versailles. While a special department of the German Foreign Office in the Wilhelmstrasse at Berlin busily sanitized the diplomatic record of 1914 to erase all traces of possible German war guilt, the public clamored for revision of the peace. The popular vocabulary resonated with terms such as the *war-guilt lie*, the *colonial-guilt lie*, *war criminals*, and *the shame and dishonor* of the Versailles *Diktat*.

On a slightly more positive note, on August 11, 1919, the National Assembly ratified a new constitution. Based on the fundamental unitarian principles espoused by German liberals in 1848–1849 in the Paulskirche at Frankfurt, the constitution established the principle of sovereignty of the people in a democracy. A special bill of rights guaranteed freedom, personal liberties, the rights of churches and freedom of religion, and the right of assembly. Additionally, the constitution protected marriage and the family from state interference. To maintain public order and historical continuity, it decreed that judges were irremovable. Supreme authority was vested in the Reichstag, which alone was empowered to pass legislation and to which the chancellor and his ministers were accountable. The chancellor, much like the British prime minister, was responsible for forming a government, proposing legislation, and setting the annual budget. The normal term of parliamentary office was four years.

Looking to the American model, the National Assembly created the popularly elected office of president. Given a term of seven years, the Reichspräsident appointed and dismissed civil servants (including the government) as well as army officers. To safeguard public order, the president received sweeping powers under Article 48 of the constitution to rule without parliament in times of national emergency. The Social Democrat Friedrich Ebert, the Republic's first president from 1919 until his death in 1925, issued no fewer than 134 emergency decrees during his first five years in office. With Paul von Hindenburg's election as president in 1925, the office became much like that of a substitute emperor (*Ersatzkaiser*). Hindenburg clearly expressed his views on the Republic's political structure: "Both hands for the fatherland, but nothing for the parties." In other words, Hindenburg espoused reverence for the nation and disdain for the democratic process.

Given the Republic's system of proportional representation, whereby voters marked their ballots for party lists rather than for individual candidates, parliamentary deputies grew distant from their voters. They failed to develop a special bond of responsibility and care for their constituents, realizing that true political power rested with party chairs and caucuses. Moreover, fragmentation of public opinion encouraged the development of about forty political parties, thereby further splintering an already divided polity.

In fact, the constitution contained several weak spots, apart from the possible misuse of Article 48. Instead of abolishing the old dynastic states and creating several regional states (*Länder)* of equal size, the National Assembly maintained Prussia intact — almost three-fifths of Germany in terms of territory and population. The vast tracts of land owned by the former ruling houses remained untouched. In addition, the special rights of the southern states were abolished, and Berlin assumed greater power over the provinces, including that of levying direct taxes. Centralization, however, proved unworkable, given Weimar's political fragmentation and the resulting inability to forge stable parliamentary majorities. Provisions were made for grass-roots citizens' initiatives through plebiscites and referenda. Commendable though this feature was in theory, in practice it allowed every splinter group and faction to appeal its special interests outside parliament.

In a formula worthy of *Alice in Wonderland*, the first sentence of the constitution stated: "The German Empire is a Republic." Germany's civil servants and officers swore allegiance not to the constitution or the Republic but to the vague notion of the German state, however individually one defined that. Because Hugo Preuss, the main architect of the constitution, was a Jew, the Right denounced Weimar as the "Jewish Republic" (*Judenrepublik*). And even where its heart was in the right place, the Republic left itself open to ridicule. By abolishing all titles and decorations, it forced future leaders to award foreign dignitaries Red Cross medals and retiring officers gold watches. The constitution was never officially abolished by the future National Socialist regime and thus remained on the books until May 8, 1945.

These systemic problems could have been overcome — or ironed out through amendments to the constitution — had the bulk of the populace endorsed the Republic. Instead, the first four years of the Republic, in the words of Foreign Minister Walther Rathenau, were reminiscent of the chaos following the Thirty Years' War, and much like the 1648 postwar scene, Weimar's initial troubles lay in its military system.

The task of demobilizing nearly 10 million soldiers proved difficult and aroused bitterness. Many veterans of the Great War refused to return to civilian life. Instead, they formed numerous volunteer forces, auxiliary volunteer units, and civil guards. Antirepublican and antisocialist, these formations comprised mainly lower-ranking army officers. The best known were the Free Corps (*Freikorps*), active in "defending" Germany's borders against foreign incursion and maintaining domestic order. But dozens of smaller, regional combat leagues also cropped up, with romantic names such as Bayern and Reich, Oberland, Olympia, Viking, Werewolf, Young German Order, and the like. Middle class, conservative, and largely monarchist, these groups took politics to the streets, using assault and even assassination. Numerous anti-Weimar fringe groups, such as the Thule Society and the German Workers' party, had their headquarters in Munich, the mecca of right-wing fanaticism. It was here that Adolf Hitler was to find a political home in the National Socialist German Worker's party (NSDAP).

Early in 1920, Germany still maintained 660,000 soldiers instead of the treaty ceiling of 100,000. Half a million soldiers still needed to be demobilized. Partly to protest this measure, ultraconservatives, embittered officers, and East Elbian agrarians encouraged Wolfgang Kapp, cofounder of the erstwhile Fatherland party, to overthrow the Republic. On March 13 the troops of General Walther von Lüttwitz and the Naval Battalion of Commander Hermann Ehrhardt, forces that had refused demobilization, entered Berlin through the Brandenburg Gate. There to greet them, just by "chance," was the wartime first quartermaster-general of the old imperial army, Erich Ludendorff. The government fled to Stuttgart. Army chief General Hans von Seeckt went on "sick leave." The navy joined Kapp. The trade unions proclaimed a general strike, a call initially followed by only a few because March 13 fell on a weekend.

Kapp foundered on the active resistance of workers as well as on the passive resistance of bureaucrats. Soldiers demand first and foremost to be paid. But employees of the Reichsbank refused to honor Kapp's requests for cash by arguing that no "Chancellor Kapp" existed on their books. When it was suggested to Ehrhardt that he simply seize the requisite funds, the Free Corps leader indignantly replied that he was an officer and not a common bank robber. Additionally, Chancery officials removed the state seal, thereby depriving Kapp of the ability to legitimize orders. Above all, the trade unions' general strike received nationwide support. Soon there was no water or heat in Berlin; food deliveries were suspended; and communications ground to a halt. On March 17 Kapp fled to Sweden; Lüttwitz eventually found refuge in Hungary.

This comic opera would have remained a harmless anecdote in history had it not been for two developments. As Kapp's forces withdrew through the Brandenburg Gate, they commemorated their departure by unleashing a volley of machine-gun fire into the jeering crowd. When the government called for assistance, the Republic's failure to reform the imperial officer corps came home to roost: General von Seeckt bluntly declared that "troops do not fire on troops" for fear of jeopardizing the "comradery of the officer corps." To an exasperated President Ebert, who demanded to know where the army's loyalty lay, Seeckt coldly asserted: "The army stands behind me." Seeckt was thereafter appointed commander-in-chief of the Republic's armed forces (*Reichswehr*).

In the industrial Ruhr region of the Rhineland, the workers not only rose to the challenge of a general strike but even formed a "Red Army" of fifty thousand men. For almost a year, this force remained in the field before finally meeting defeat — at the cost of three thousand dead and 1 billion marks damages — by the same Free Corps forces that had supported Kapp. Social Democratic defense minister Gustav Noske's policy of cooperation with the army thereby was disgraced; the German Democrat Lord Mayor of Nuremberg, Otto Gessler, replaced Noske as defense minister.

The SPD also came to rue its refusal to purge the German judiciary in 1918. Statistical analysis perhaps best reveals the nature of class justice under the Republic. For the period 1918 to 1922, 22 members of the Left were tried for murder: 17 were convicted, and 10 sentenced to die. For the Right, 354 were tried for murder: 1 was convicted, and none was executed. Average incarceration for political crimes by the Left amounted to fifteen years; for the Right, four months.

Indeed, for the first time in history, Germans undertook political murder with reckless abandon. The killings of Rosa Luxemburg, Karl Liebknecht, and Kurt Eisner in 1919 (see Chapter 6) were followed by the murders of the Communist editor Leo Jogiches, the pacifist Hans Paasche, and the Bavarian Independent Socialist deputy Karl Gareis in 1921. An acid attack on Scheidemann barely failed in 1922. In August 1921 Matthias Erzberger was murdered while on vacation in the Black Forest, and in June 1922 Foreign Minister Rathenau was assassinated on his way to work in the Wilhelmstrasse. Children in the streets celebrated in lyrical verse the death of the "goddamned Jewish sow." Most of the killers came from the ranks of Free Corps units such as Oberland and the Brigade Ehrhardt, as well as the latter's successor after the Kapp putsch, "Organisation Consul." Yet when Chancellor Joseph Wirth in the wake of Rathenau's murder asserted in the Reichstag that "the enemy stands on the Right," both the German People's party (DVP) and the German National People's party (DNVP) took offense.

Given the turmoil of the postwar period, the first election of the Republic in June 1920 proved disastrous for its founders. The Social Democratic vote fell by 17 percent, that of the Democratic party by 10 percent. Only the Center party remained constant at around 18 percent. Thus, overall support for the Weimar parties fell from 76 percent in the National Assembly to 47 percent; never again would the three parties enjoy a parliamentary majority. Conversely, the extreme Left (USPD and KPD) tripled its share of the vote to 20 percent, and the Right (DNVP and DVP) managed to double its share to 28 percent — giving the parties opposed to the Republic 48 percent of votes cast. Germany's most famous novelist, Thomas Mann, smugly noted that the June 1920 election constituted a "protest against the present pigsty."

Chaos continued to reign, especially in the financial sphere. Having paid for the war by raising loans, and in the process increasing the money in circulation fivefold, Germany faced a national debt of 154 billion goldmarks (GM) at the end of 1918, not counting pensions, veterans' benefits, war damages, and reparations. In April 1919, Weimar's first budget projected a shortfall of 5 billion GM, an amount equal to the entire federal budget of 1913. Moreover, the Allied occupation of the Rhineland deprived the central government of 30 percent of all taxes and customs revenues.

The Republic saw three possible paths to solvency: raising taxes dramatically to retire the debt, declaring national bankruptcy and thereby reneging on all debts, and borrowing to meet fiscal needs. The first course would cost the ruling parties at the ballot box. The second constituted political suicide, given that the national debt was held mainly by the middle class. This left the third course, which entailed several short-term advantages: it would push responsibility for the economic chaos onto the Allies; mounting debts would "prove" to the Allies that Germany was incapable of paying reparations; and the inflation that was sure to follow would eventually reduce the debt dramatically.

Reparations were of immediate concern to the Republic. The Germans expected to pay 30 billion GM over thirty years, but the French ("The Germans will pay for everything") countered with a figure of 226 billion GM over forty-two years. A compromise was reached at London in May 1921: 132 billion GM, amortized at 6 percent, with annual payments of 2 billion GM in addition to 26 percent of all German exports. The British economist John Maynard Keynes estimated that this amount, constituting 7 percent of German national income, was three times what the Reich could pay. And because the Allies refused to take massive payments in kind (coal, timber, iron, chemicals) for fear of hurting their own domestic industries, the Germans eventually tried to deliver paper notes by the wagon loads. In January 1923 five French divisions, assisted by several Belgian units, invaded the industrial Ruhr to protest lagging cash payments and to ensure future gold deliveries.

The causes for the inflation of 1923 go much deeper than simply reparations. Towering wartime debts, reduced production capacity, and depleted stocks of raw materials and goods combined with the staggering costs of postwar demobilization and unemployment relief to produce steep inflation by 1919. That inflation was intensified when the Reichsbank pursued a policy of freely granting commercial credit and when it accepted at face value the monthly treasury notes that the government issued to plaster over budget deficits. Such free spending fiscal policies bore no relation to the actual value of the mark. Currency in circulation soared. Tax collection lagged behind the depreciation of the currency as a result of the oversupply of paper notes. Soon 1,783 presses churned out paper notes day and night. Inflation gave way to hyperinflation. The dollar rose to 50,000 marks by January 1923; it reached an unfathomable 4 trillion marks by November. A simple one-course meal by mid-October cost 60 million marks; by November, a liter of milk sold for 360 billion marks, bread for 201 billion marks. The entire national debt of 154 billion goldmarks was now reduced to 15.4 pennies in terms of 1914 currency.

Minister of Finance Hans Luther and Reichsbank president Hjalmar Schacht took the drastic step of introducing a new rentenmark, based not on gold but on industrial and agrarian mortgages, at the rate of 1 rentenmark for 1 trillion paper marks, and this solution eventually stabilized the currency. But the cost was great: the impoverishment of a large part of the lower and middle classes, most of whom had put their faith in insurance policies and government war bonds. Because wages and salaries did not keep pace with devaluation, families could not afford food, clothing, and health care. Civil servants, white-collar employees, rentiers — in short, the middle class, all those on fixed income or salary — felt cheated and deceived by the government. In their panic to escape the inevitable slide into the proletariat in the wake of having lost their savings, they turned to political extremes for instant remedy.

There were, nevertheless, winners in 1923. Debtors such as landowners and industrialists gained because inflation destroyed the values of mortgages and bonds. And because the Reichsbank accepted depreciated marks as payment, big business was able not only to shed its debts but also to buy smaller competitors on speculation. Noted industrialists such as Hugo Stinnes in the Ruhr borrowed heavily from the Reichsbank to expand their industrial empires and later repaid the loans at face value with vastly depreciated paper money. The old Wilhelmian policy of industrial concentration and cartelization continued, especially in the chemical and electrical industries.

Diplomatic chaos augmented the economic distress. In March 1921 60 percent of the inhabitants of Upper Silesia voted to stay with the Reich; this notwithstanding, the League of Nations turned much of this area over to Poland in October, greatly weakening Weimar's credibility at home. There was but one way out of isolation for the Republic: resort to the old policy of Frederick William, the Great Elector, of playing East off against West. Ulrich Count von Brockdorff-Rantzau, the Reich's plenipotentiary to the Peace of Paris, had realized this by 1919: "Germany has the choice either to broker between East and West or to provide the battlefield for their struggle."

On April 16, 1922, while in Genoa to discuss reparations problems with British and French leaders — and two months before his assassination — Foreign Minister Walther Rathenau had met with his Soviet counterpart, G. V. Chicherin, at Rapallo and startled the world by signing an accord. By this agreement, Germany and Soviet Russia reestablished diplomatic ties, renounced all past debts and commitments, and granted each other most-favored-nation trade status. This modest accord raised the specter of the old Prussian balancing act between East and West. Additionally, the two "outlaws" of the European state system broke the bonds of isolation imposed on them at Paris in 1919. Brockdorff-Rantzau, newly appointed German ambassador to Soviet Russia, candidly stated that "the calamity of Versailles" could now be "corrected from Moscow." Genoa failed to meet its original goals because French president Raymond Poincaré refused to make the trip from Paris.

The French invasion of the Ruhr to protest the shortfall in German cash reparations payments on January 11, 1923, came at a time of diplomatic and economic turmoil. The Germans resorted to passive resistance, refusing to cooperate with the occupation authorities. Mines and plants shut down, railroads ceased to run. The French countered with mass arrests, jailings, and even summary executions of resistance leaders. They evicted 147,000 German residents, most of them railroad men, from the Ruhr. In six months, production fell by half as 130,000 Ruhr laborers refused to report to work. Iron mills in Lorraine closed when they could not obtain Ruhr coal. Further deportations of German workers to French penal colonies only served to unite the Ruhr populace against the invaders. In March French troops killed thirteen "Marxist" workers at Essen as they protected Krupp automobiles from seizure. German currency became worthless.

Sanity returned on September 26, 1923, when Chancellor Gustav Stresemann announced that he was breaking off the German resistance. Realizing that the German economy had collapsed completely and that potential separation of the Ruhr would jeopardize future recovery, Stresemann worked to stabilize the German currency, to resume reparations payments, and to cooperate with Paris and London because he understood that Germany had no other course available. On November 23, 1923, French president Poincaré accepted a German offer to resume reparations deliveries from Ruhr industrial plants. French and Belgian forces eventually withdrew from German soil.

In the meantime, a number of wildly disparate separatist movements crippled Germany from Upper Silesia to the Palatinate, from Schleswig-Holstein to Bavaria. "Free from Berlin" became the new battle cry. On October 21, 1923, a small, radical group of separatists seized power in a few cities, such as Bonn, Duisburg, Mainz, and Wiesbaden, and with the help of Belgian and French forces proclaimed a "Rhineland Republic." It was widely received with cold contempt, and by January 1924 its leaders had been shot by right-wing civil guards. In Saxony, Minister-President Erich Zeigner appointed Communist ministers to his cabinet "to preclude a military dictatorship by big business"; Thuringia followed suit. Special agents from Soviet Russia arrived to train "proletarian legions" for the coming class struggle. Hamburg experienced an attempted Communist putsch. And in Bavaria, Prime Minister Gustav von

"No, I won't submit to force!" Passive resistance to French / Belgian invaders in the Ruhr (January 1923).

Kahr appointed himself special "state commissar general" in order to lead a conservative national monarchist movement. When the local commander of the army's 7th Division, General Otto von Lossow, refused to obey an order from Defense Minister Gessler to dissolve a radical right-wing newspaper, Kahr instead appointed him "Bavarian territorial commander" and had Lossow's troops swear an oath of loyalty to Bavaria. For the first time since 1871, the German army committed high treason.

How would Berlin react? Chancellor Stresemann was spared having to ask Reichswehr to move against Reichswehr by Zeigner's call for open opposition to the army. On October 30, after asking President Ebert to invoke Article 48, Stresemann sent troops into Saxony and Thuringia to quell Zeigner's bid for a "Red October." When the chancellor declined to move the troops south into Bavaria, the SPD left his cabinet.

Events came to a head on November 8 when Kahr called a meeting at one of the largest beer halls in Munich, the Bürgerbräukeller, to demand the restoration of the Wittelsbach dynasty to the throne. The meeting was interrupted by Adolf Hitler (1889–1945), leader of the two-thousand-member National Socialist German Workers' party (NSDAP), a right-wing splinter faction that sought a romanticized synthesis of the two great waves of the nineteenth century, nationalism and socialism. Aided by about two dozen supporters, Hitler used the occasion of Kahr's monarchist rally to proclaim the start of a "national revolution." Following the example of Kemal Ataturk in Turkey and Benito Mussolini in Italy, Hitler decided to march on the capital with the omnipresent General Ludendorff at his side. The Bavarian monarchist plot ended when Crown Prince Rupprecht refused to be associated with it. Hitler's "beer-hall putsch" failed on the morning of November 9, when police drawn up at the Odeonsplatz in downtown Munich fired on the National Socialists, killing fourteen men.

Stresemann did not survive the national crisis. On November 23 the Reichstag passed a vote of nonconfidence in his government. President Ebert reprimanded his SPD colleagues, "In six weeks you will have forgotten what prompted you to overthrow the chancellor. But you will still feel the consequences of your stupidity after ten years." In fact, in November 1933 SPD leaders had ample time to contemplate their actions behind the barbed wire of Adolf Hitler's concentration camps.

Stabilization, 1924–1929

By contrast to the chaotic early 1920s, the mid–1920s are often referred to as the golden years of the Republic. Industry slowly recovered after the first major loan of $100 million from Wall Street helped to jump-start the sagging German economy. Production rose by 50 percent between 1924 and 1929, and in 1927 the gross national product had regained its prewar level. The Wilhelmian cartelization, which established production quotas, divided up the market, and fixed prices as well as wages, also continued. The United Steel Works controlled 40 percent of all coal, iron, and steel output, while the IG-Farben conglomerate ruled over a similar percentage of German chemical production. A startling example of this concentration is the entrepreneurial empire — fifteen hundred companies and three thousand factories — that the Ruhr industrialist Hugo Stinnes left behind in 1924. Most of the leaders of Germany's major industrial enterprises were authoritarian, anti-Western, and antirepublican. Few favored Stresemann's policy of "fulfilling" Germany's obligations under the Treaty of Versailles.

For Germans, as well as for the rest of the industrialized world, the 1920s were also years of technological wonders. Steam and electricity combined with steel and concrete to produce a technological boom. Automobiles, airplanes, and ocean liners became the most visible symbols of modern technology. The North German Lloyd's passenger liner *Bremen* won the coveted blue ribbon for the fastest North Atlantic crossing to New York on its maiden voyage, only to lose the ribbon to its sister ship, the *Europa*. The super dirigible *Graf Zeppelin* circumnavigated the globe, and the fixed-wing aircraft Junkers G38 and Dornier X inaugurated regular transatlantic passenger service. Europe's first freeway opened between Cologne and Bonn. And the small electric motor revolutionized light industry as well as home and craft work.

Late-nineteenth-century urbanization advanced inexorably as millions of young people continued to flock from countryside to city in search of well-paying jobs in industry and government. Germany was becoming an export-driven manufacturing center. Whereas agrarian production in 1890 had constituted 32 percent of total output, by 1928 it had slipped to just 15 percent. Unfortunately, most German cities were unable to absorb the heavy influx of new workers. More than half the populations of Barmen and Königsberg and roughly 40 percent of families in Berlin and Breslau lived in one-room domiciles.

Real wages lagged behind the cost of living for most of the first half of the Republic and caught up only by 1928. They surpassed the cost of living from 1931 to 1933 because the Great Depression drove prices down considerably.

COST OF LIVING AND WORKERS' WAGES (1928 = 100)

Year	Nominal Wages	Cost of Living	Real Wages
1925	75	93	81
1926	78	93	84
1927	88	97	89
1928	100	100	100
1929	103	101	102
1930	95	97	97
1931	84	89	94
1932	69	80	86
1933	71	78	91

For the first time in German history, women enjoyed legal equality with men. The constitution stipulated that women and men had "basically the same right and duties," that in marriage both sexes enjoyed "equality of rights," and that civil service positions were open for women as well. Women now could vote, join political parties, enter universities and professional schools, and compete in the marketplace. Indeed, women flocked into myriad organizations: 90,000 joined the Union of Rural Housewives and 100,000 the Imperial Union of German Housewives. The Trade Union League of Salaried Employees by 1931 boasted 100,492 female members. Religious organizations especially prospered. The Evangelical Women's Union claimed 1.5 million members, and its political arm, the German Evangelical Women's Federation, with close ties to the German National People's party, was 200,000 strong. The Center party could count on the support of 250,000 volunteers from the Catholic Women's Federation volunteer group, as well as the 1.6 million young women and mothers organized into the church's various lay organizations.

In the marketplace, women, like men, moved off the farms and into the urban industrial, service, and craft sectors. Although the number of women employed stayed steady at around 35 percent, numerically this figure increased by 1.7 million. Under the terms of most wage agreements, however, women continued to earn between 20 and 40 percent less than men, and the wage gap closed only for highly skilled employees. In the field of education, women constituted 16 percent (twenty thousand) of university students by 1931; most found employment as teachers in high schools and in the medical professions.

In the political arena, women were most strongly represented in the Social Democratic party, where usually one Reichstag deputy in ten was female. But the SPD, which since the days of August Bebel had championed the cause of women, failed to attract female workers outside the working classes. In the 1929 Reichstag, for example, the greatest percentages of the women's vote fell to the Center (59 percent), the German National People's party (56 percent), and the German People's party (51 percent). The SPD's female vote stood at 43 percent, that of the Communist party even lower at 37 percent. Female representation in the Reichstag reached a high of 7 percent (forty-one deputies) in 1930. By and large, women voted according to regional traditions: Center party in the Catholic Rhineland and Bavaria, Social Democratic in the traditional strongholds of the labor movement such as Berlin, Leipzig, Magdeburg, and Nuremberg. Female membership in the SPD tripled to 207,000 by 1920 and in trade unions jumped fourfold to 1.7 million. But by 1926 female trade union membership had fallen by more than 60 percent.

Gertrud Bäumer, leader of the Federation of German Women's Associations (BDF), at first rallied to exert a "motherly" influence over German society by seeking membership on film boards, battling what the BDF deemed the moral laxity of Weimar culture. In 1927 the federation worked with the Center party and the SPD to gain passage of the Law for the Combatting of Sexual Diseases designed to inhibit the spread of sexually transmitted diseases by decriminalizing prostitution. Although abortions remained illegal under Article 218 of the Criminal Code, the law nevertheless softened penalties for women who underwent the procedure and stiffened those for the individuals who performed them.

But as time passed, the BDF also moved to the right. By 1932 its 750,000 members embraced Benito Mussolini's corporate state system and sought to organize into female "corporations" of work and occupation. They argued, like Mussolini, that modern legislative bodies should be organized along economic rather than political and regional lines. Such reorganization alone could eliminate the anarchy and class conflict engendered by free capitalism. With ever greater stridency, the BDF advocated the creation of a new national community based on a harmonious underlay of state and social fabric. Not surprisingly, it was among the first volunteer organizations to be taken in by the National Socialist notion of the *Volksgemeinschaft* (national racial community), a concept in vogue among many political parties long before 1933.

The BDF never attracted the Republic's female youth, and its intellectual exclusiveness failed to appeal to the lower middle class. The old Wilhelmian radicals around Anita Augspurg gravitated into the pacifist camp, forming the Women's League for Peace and Freedom and editing journals such as the *Woman in the State*.

Above all, women were caught up in the overall trend toward modernity. Wearing casual clothes, bobbing their hair, and smoking cigarettes, modern women joined the white-collar labor force at levels three times those of the prewar period. Nearly all clerical workers were female; two of three were under twenty-five years of age. Magazines, newspapers, and film celebrated them as young, elegant, and sexy; by 1930 cinemas were selling 6 million tickets per week. As with the Wilhelmian youth movement, health and fitness became important. By 1929 2 million women were enrolled in fitness clubs and an additional 640,000 in gymnastics associations. Youth hostels recorded that females constituted one in every three of their 3.6 million registrants that year.

Critics countered that as a result of this push for modernity, the divorce rate had tripled between 1905 and 1925 to sixty-two per thousand marriages and that abortions, although illegal, numbered around 1 million in 1931. The Right, while appreciating the women's vote, was distressed at the perceived by-products of female emancipation: sexual promiscuity; rising divorce, abortion, and illegitimacy rates; falling birthrate (the two-child nuclear family had become the norm by 1925); greater number of females in the work force; mounting contraceptive use by women; and burgeoning sex literature such as Theodore Van de Veldes' *The Perfect Marriage* (forty-third printing in 1932) and *Eroticism in Marriage* (eleven printings between 1928 and 1931). In short, the chasm between traditional family ties and modern occupational demands deepened under the Republic. It would be cleverly exploited by Hitler.

Two groups in the Weimar Republic — bureaucrats and officers — formed the heart and soul of the German Right. Steeped in Prussian tradition, the civil servants, including the chancellor and his ministers, identified with the state rather than with a particular government. Out of a sense of duty or for financial reasons, most bureaucrats remained at their posts after 1918; only in SPD-controlled Prussia did a few resign rather than serve. Socially and politically homogeneous, the German bureaucracy remained conservative, if not monarchist. In the absence of strong leadership, as existed under Bismarck, officialdom developed its own initiatives, delaying or obstructing unpopular measures through inertia and internal obfuscation. In the end, the civil service did not destroy the Republic; it simply refused to lift a finger to support it.

The officer corps was left leaderless after 1918 when its supreme commander, William II, hastened to the Netherlands. It thus set a new course: to stay above politics and avoid responsibility for the war. General Wilhelm Groener, Ludendorff's successor as first quartermaster-general in 1918, later conceded that "to preserve the instrument clean and the General Staff unencumbered for the future" he had done his level best after the end of the war "to reject all responsibility for the armistice." General Hans von Seeckt bluntly stated, "The army serves the state, only the state; for it is the state." Seeckt's policy was simple: to restore Germany's military power by either abolishing or evading the terms of the Treaty of Versailles. To this end, Seeckt first undertook a careful screening of the four thousand officers allowed under the Treaty of Versailles, weeding out all volunteers, Free Corps, and former front officers in favor of noble and staff officers. Indeed, whereas nobles had constituted but 9 percent of the officer corps during the Great War, by 1925 one in four officers was noble. Concurrently, the percentage of sons of officers in the corps doubled between 1913 and 1925 to 48 percent. Homogeneity and exclusiveness lay at the heart of Seeckt's plan.

From the start, Seeckt viewed the 100,000-man army as temporary, a cadre army wherein lieutenant-colonels led battalions and divisions boasted army corps staffs. In addition, Seeckt augmented the Reichswehr with special "work commandos" as well as with "border and territorial guards" along the Polish border. By 1927 most of these soldiers came from the ranks of the Free Corps, the combat leagues, veterans' organizations such as the Stahlhelm, and paramilitary forces such as the National Socialist Sturmabteilung (SA). They hid their weapons in haystacks and barns. The Inter-Allied Military Control Commission reportedly underestimated the German stock of guns fivefold, of howitzers sevenfold, and of artillery sixfold. On a more grandiose scale, weapons barred by the Treaty of Versailles such as aircraft, artillery, submarines, and tanks were constructed in the Netherlands, Spain, and Sweden by either subsidiaries of German firms or special dummy corporations set up directly with Ministry of Defense funds. Finally, Seeckt secured the training of German officers in forbidden services such as aviation and tank warfare in the Soviet Union.

Difficult relations: General von Seeckt amused by War Minister Gessler (Summer 1928).

Reichswehr leaders spent much of the 1920s planning the wars of the future. They struggled to perfect a strategy that would limit the scale of warfare in order to make it a purposeful instrument of state policy once more. In the end, they concluded that the only alternative was to return to the strategies of the past. Only more arms and more men would ensure victory. Above all, Reichswehr planners sought institutional control of violence. The army was to be the sole bearer of weapons; they would permit no infringement on their monopoly. The roots of the eventual dissonance between Adolf Hitler and the generals thus lay in these planners' designs rather than in the putative clash between conservative Reichswehr and radical National Socialist views.

Above all, bureaucrats and officers loathed the new oligarchy of bigwigs (*Bonzen*) that dominated the Republic's political life. The 1921 edition of *Who's Who* reveals that 61 percent of its entries comprise party politicians and only 23 percent the traditional elites of nobility, officer corps, industrialists, and men of property. Mostly without independent means, the new political elite had entered politics for profit. Its members clung to office for fear of unemployment; hence, participation of one's party in governing coalitions became a matter of personal as well as political survival. Gone were the days when the Prussian novelist Theodor Fontane's rustic squire, Dubslav von Stechlin, could dismiss with good cheer his electoral defeat in Rheinsberg-Wutz at the hands of a Social Democrat with a splendid meal of trout and saddle of venison. "Winning is fine, but sitting down to dinner is much better."

After the turmoil of 1923, a deceptive calm settled over Germany. Although governments changed every eight or nine months on average, a center coalition of democratic, republican support — the erstwhile *Reichsfeinde* under Bismarck — accorded a modicum of continuity. Over time, a routine developed: minority coalition governments existed at the mercy of the Reichstag and with the support of the president. They declined to rule by emergency decree (Article 48) between 1925 and 1930.

The intellectual heart of this Weimar coalition was the Democratic party (DDP) of such men as Albert Einstein, Theodor Heuss, Hugo Preuss, and Alfred Weber, the brother of Max Weber, as well as Gertrud Bäumer of the women's movement. As heirs to the liberal tradition of the 1848 Frankfurt Paulskirche and the Progressives' struggle against Bismarck during the constitutional crisis of 1862–1866, the Democrats stood for pluralism and responsible government. They rejected socialism out of hand and aimed instead at a synthesis of individual freedom and social responsibility. Their greatest success was in drafting the constitution, thus guaranteeing basic civil rights. Their greatest failure was their inability to decentralize the Reich by breaking up historic Prussia. The DDP's political base was the educated middle class (*Bildungsbürgertum*). But the DDP never managed to establish a dynamic program because it attempted to bridge too many competing material interests; in short, it lacked a doctrinaire political program. The Democrats fared poorly at the polls over the course of the Republic; their share of the vote fell from 18 percent in 1918 to 6 percent in 1924, and finally 3 percent in 1930.

THE WEIMAR POLITY

Weimar Coalition	Conservatives	Radical Opposition
DDP	DNVP	KPD
Center Party	DVP	NSDAP
SPD		

Regional splinter parties (Bavarian People's party, Guelphs, Polish party)

The Catholic Center party (*Zentrum*) remained a constant in Weimar politics, taking part in every government until 1932. As under the Empire, it was a diverse social and economic group dedicated to preserving church education as well as lay organizations and the sanctity of the Christian family, while concurrently combating atheism and socialism, state power, and permissive culture. The Center's share of the popular vote stayed level at around 16 percent.

The third leg of this Weimar trinity was the Social Democratic party (SPD). Its attitude and role during the Republic were ambivalent: the SPD took part in half of Weimar's sixteen cabinets yet toppled five of the eight by withdrawing support. As late as 1930, 60 percent of its rank and file consisted of workers, 17 percent of civil servants and white-collar employees. At no time did the SPD gain influence over either Catholic workers or farm laborers. Moreover, the SPD could never decide whether to be a government or an opposition party. Nor did it abandon Marxism to attract more middle-class support. As a result, it seldom passed the 30 percent threshold in national elections.

The SPD's support for the war on August 4, 1914, and its pact with General Groener on November 10, 1918, had alienated its left wing. Until 1922 many of the latter found a new home in the Independent Social Democratic party (USPD), which drew around 6 to 8 percent of the vote. But the radicals on the Left increasingly turned to the Communist party (KPD). After the abortive Spartacist uprising of 1919 and Zeigner's "stillborn revolution" of 1923, KPD membership declined by 1928 from 280,000 to 130,000. Its leader after 1925, Ernst Thälmann, was a willing tool of Moscow, best known for his savage attacks against the "social fascists" of the SPD, whom he would have ample opportunity to meet in Hitler's concentration camps after 1933.

On the moderate Right, Stresemann's German People's party (DVP) was heir to the National Liberals of the Empire. Rebuffed in his bid to join the Democratic party because of his extreme wartime annexationism, Stresemann initially rejected the Republic and the constitution and instead clamored for a plebiscitary monarchy (*Volkskaisertum*). The German People's party's supporters came from the German bourgeoisie — men and women of property and education. It was founded largely with the financial support of powerful industrialists from the Ruhr, and it openly played on middle-class fears of socialism. A popular party slogan went, "From Red chains only the DVP will set us free." The DVP's share of popular votes hovered around 14 percent before dropping off after its founder's death in 1929 to 5 percent in 1930 and 1 percent in 1932.

The major power on the Right was the German National People's party (DNVP), successor to the old German Conservatives, Free Conservatives, and right wing of the National Liberals. Antirepublican and antidemocratic, the German National People's party became a magnet for monarchists, antisemites, and pan-Germans. The DNVP basically longed to restore the lost unity, the "ideas of 1914." *Pluralism* was by definition a divisive term. The DNVP's share of the vote in federal elections was around 18 to 20 percent, until participation

REICHSTAG ELECTIONS, 1920–1933 (IN THOUSANDS)

Party	June 1920		May 1924		Dec. 1924		May 1928		Sept. 1930		July 1932		Nov. 1932		Mar. 1933	
	Votes	Seats	Votes	Seats	Votes	Seats	Votes	Seats	Votes	Seats	Votes	Seats	Votes	Seats	Votes	Seats
KPD	590	4	3,693	62	2,709	45	3,265	54	4,592	77	5,283	89	5,980	100	4,848	81
SPD	6,104	103	6,009	100	7,881	131	9,153	153	8,578	143	7,960	133	7,248	121	7,181	120
Center	3,910	64	3,914	65	4,092	69	3,712	61	4,128	68	4,589	75	4,230	70	4,425	74
DDP[a]	2,334	39	1,655	28	1,920	32	1,479	25	1,322	20	372	4	336	2	334	5
DVP	3,919	65	2,728	45	3,049	51	2,680	45	1,578	30	136	7	661	11	432	2
DNVP	4,249	71	5,697	95	6,206	103	4,382	73	2,458	41	2,177	37	2,959	52	3,137	52
NSDAP	—	—	1,918	32	907	14	810	12	6,383	107	13,769	230	11,737	196	17,277	288

[a] State party after 1930.

WEIMAR CABINETS, 1919–1933

Chancellor	Party	Start	Days	Coalition Partner
P. Scheidemann	SPD	Feb. 13,1919	130	DDP
G. Bauer	SPD	June 21,1919	277	DDP, Center
H. Müller	SPD	Mar. 27,1920	72	DDP, Center
C. Fehrenbach	Center	June 21,1920	317	DDP, Center, DVP
J. Wirth	Center	May 10,1921	165	SPD, DDP
J. Wirth	Center	Oct. 26,1921	384	SPD, DDP
W. Cuno	Indep.	Nov. 22,1922	263	DDP, DVP, Center
G. Stresemann	DVP	Aug. 13,1923	51	SPD, DDP, Center
G. Stresemann	DVP	Nov. 6,1923	48	DDP, Center
W. Marx	Center	Nov. 30,1923	177	DVP, DDP
W. Marx	Center	June 3,1924	195	DVP, DDP
H. Luther	Indep.	Jan. 15,1925	223	DVP, DDP, DNVP, Center
W. Marx	Center	May 16,1926	214	DVP, DDP
W. Marx	Center	Jan. 29,1927	499	DNVP, DVP
H. Müller	SPD	June 28,1928	636	DVP, DDP
H. Brüning	Center	Mar. 30,1930	556	DDP, DVP, DNVP
H. Brüning	Center	Oct. 9,1931	233	DDP, Indep.
F. v. Papen	Center	June 1,1932	170	DNVP, Indep.
K. v. Schleicher	Indep.	Dec. 3,1932	55	DNVP, Indep.
A. Hitler	NSDAP	Jan. 30,1933		DNVP, Indep.

in Chancellor Wilhelm Marx's government in 1927–1928 dropped its popular support to 14 percent. Thereafter, under Alfred Hugenberg, the DNVP moved further to the right on the political spectrum, eventually becoming nothing more than stirrup-holders for Hitler.

The "golden" twenties were strongly shaped by Stresemann, who served as foreign minister from 1923 until 1929, and his policy of "fulfilling" the Versailles terms. Stresemann became the symbol of stabilization and continuity in Weimar. Historians have interpreted him as either the forerunner of today's "good European" or as the reincarnation of Bismarckian duplicity. In truth, he was a bit of both.

Stresemann was both opportunist and tactician, monarchist and expansionist, a statesman desiring the overturn of the verdict of 1918 through détente with France, the establishment of economic stability by way of cooperation with the United States, accommodation with the Soviet Union, and revision of the Reich's eastern borders and a return to Wilhelmian world politics. Stresemann hoped that by fulfilling Versailles terms in the short run he could revise the military and territorial terms of the Versailles settlement in the long run. He sought by a clever (if dangerous) strategy to return Germany to great power status. Specifically, he was prepared to accept the loss of Alsace-Lorraine while concurrently working to regain Eupen-et-Malmédy from Belgium and to coax the coal-rich Saar back to Germany. In the east, he demanded that Danzig, the "corridor," and Upper Silesia revert to Germany. By this policy he hoped to drive a wedge between Poland and France.

Stresemann chafed under the yoke of the Inter-Allied Military Control Commission. He strove to establish "equality in arms" and demanded that the other European powers reduce their armaments to German levels. Unlike most other Germans, Stresemann sought admission into the League of Nations for tactical reasons: Geneva would constitute a splendid forum from which to trumpet Germany's grievances against the 1919 settlement, as well as to focus attention on the complaints of German-speaking residents in Belgium, Czechoslovakia, Denmark, France, and Poland. Above all, Stresemann fervently wished to abolish the Versailles system of international agreements and to replace it with the old European balance of Bismarck, wherein Germany had been the predominant power. In short, he preferred bilateral accords to international consensus: Bismarck reborn.

After 1923 Stresemann set out on his course to restore Germany's sovereignty. In April 1924 the American banker Charles G. Dawes established a regular schedule of German reparations payments, beginning with 1 billion GM and rising to 2.5 billion GM after five years; no total amount was stipulated. Both the national railway system and the Reichsbank were placed under Allied control to ensure payment. In return, Germany received an immediate loan of 800 million GM from the United States, which quickly increased to 3 billion GM by 1925. In fact, throughout the 1920s, American loans each year outstripped German reparations payments. What if the loans were recalled at a time of financial crisis?

The Dawes Plan convinced world leaders that Germany was finally serious about reparations and restored credibility to Weimar politics. In October 1925 Stresemann and French foreign minister Aristide Briand agreed to meet at Locarno, Switzerland, to discuss Franco-German relations. To the pealing of church bells along Lake Maggiore, the two leaders signed a host of accords, the centerpiece of which was the Rhine Pact. Under British and Italian "guarantee," Belgium, France, and Germany agreed to accept their existing borders, to renounce the use of force in revising these borders, and to submit all territorial disputes to international arbitration. In addition, Stresemann accepted freely the permanent demilitarization of the Rhineland. France, in its frenetic search for security, signed alliances with Czechoslovakia and Poland.

Privately, Stresemann emphasized that at Locarno he had managed to maintain a free hand for his eastern policy. In time and with the help of American loans, Germany would recover economic strength and then be free to revise the Versailles dictate, either peacefully or, if need be, by force. The German foreign minister saw Locarno as a "chance to regain German lands in the east," for he had successfully resisted recognizing existing borders with Warsaw and Prague. The following year, Germany was admitted into the League of Nations; Stresemann and Briand shared the Nobel Peace Prize for Locarno; and Stresemann endorsed Briand's pact with his American counterpart, Frank B. Kellogg, to "renounce war as an instrument of national policy."

In April 1926 Stresemann revealed his policy of balancing East off against West by renewing the Rapallo agreement in the Treaty of Berlin. A true "reinsurance treaty," the 1926 accord basically pledged both Germany and the Soviet Union to neutrality in the event that one or the other should be attacked by one or more powers. Additionally, neither party was to join any coalition for the purpose of an economic or financial boycott of the other. As is well known, the eastern tie also served to create the "Black Reichswehr," that is, the testing of forces and weapons barred by the Treaty of Versailles. A German tank school and military pilot-training center in central Russia allowed the Reichswehr to keep abreast of developments in armor and aviation, and eventually Reichswehr units participated in Red Army field maneuvers.

For Stresemann, the combination of Locarno and Berlin, although tying Germany politically to Paris and London, left the question of the Reich's eastern borders open and kept the military free of commitments. Both pacts reflected Stresemann's desire, as he put it in a famous private letter to Crown Prince William of Prussia, "to finesse and to evade the great decisions."

In fact, the euphoric "spirit of Locarno" led Briand and Stresemann in September 1926 to a second meeting at the village of Thoiry along the French-Swiss border, where Briand proposed nothing less than to evacuate the Rhineland and the Saar, as well as to dismantle the Inter-Allied Military Control Commission. Stresemann offered to recompense France for the "loss" of the Saar coal fields and to extend vast loans to cash-poor France. His gesture proved too bold. President Poincaré refused to condone such a drastic revision of Versailles. Thoiry constituted the last major Franco-German diplomatic initiative of the 1920s.

In 1929 reparations were once more reordered, this time by the American banker Owen D. Young. For the first time, both a rate and a total were agreed on: Germany was to pay 2.05 billion GM annually for fifty-nine years, until 1988. In return, the Allies agreed to end their control over the German railway system and Reichsbank. While Stresemann crowed, "We are once again masters in our own house," the Right at home lashed out against what it termed the "enslavement" of two future generations of Germans. In fact, in December 1929, the Right forced a national referendum, the so-called freedom bill, calling for the imprisonment of any government and president to sign the Young Plan. Although the measure failed to attain the required 50 percent of public support, it served its purpose of dividing the nation.

At Geneva in 1929, Briand made a final impassioned plea to Stresemann to put the past behind and to set course for establishing a "United States of Europe." Stresemann countered with a promise to work toward creating a

European postage stamp. He died of a heart attack on October 3, 1929. Three weeks later, Wall Street crashed.

The Republic of Outsiders

It is always risky to seek a direct link between culture and society, for many artists and writers create for the pure aesthetic value of the act. The Weimar Republic not only allowed artists almost complete freedom of expression but also subsidized their labors to an extent previously unknown in German history. Expressionism was too vague and directionless a movement to be related to the socioeconomic conditions of Weimar. Thus, the question of whether the richness of "Weimar culture" was simply an expression of the Republic's liberal policies toward the arts or whether it truly represented that society's deeper concerns and values must remain open.

Ideas do not exist in a vacuum. The shared experiences of total war, defeat, revolution, and civil strife were relived on paper and in film by Weimar's writers and directors. The basic instability of postwar politics similarly resonated in their works. Recurrent themes of alienation, chaos, dissonance, and disease certainly constituted a form of social critique. Writers especially were preoccupied with contemporary social, economic, and political problems. And yet Weimar culture was also elitist. Many of its writers overtly or covertly rejected democracy and longed for a restoration if not of the monarchy then at least of some form of authoritarian government. Nor was Weimar culture targeted to the masses. Bertold Brecht may have hoped that his social satires would inspire the workers, but in reality Brecht's works attracted mainly fellow intellectuals and enlightened bourgeois audiences. High culture and popular culture remained uneasy partners at best in Weimar Germany.

Weimar culture has become synonymous with the search for new values and ideals: its temper was tormented, raffish, and revolutionary. It was the culture of the intellectuals and gained prominence only through the efforts of German émigrés. The general public by and large ignored the avant-garde in favor of the traditional. The top thirty-four best-sellers between 1918 and 1933 included only three writers associated with Weimar culture: Erich Kästner, Thomas Mann, and Erich Maria Remarque. The bulk of the best-sellers consisted of the sea yarns of Felix Count Luckner and Gorch Fock, the national-patriotic ruminations of Hans Grimm and Clara Viebig, and, above all, the adventure stories of Karl May.[1]

German youth, unsettled by a lost war, democratic pluralism, and unemployment in a mass industrial society, continued to be fascinated by Friedrich

[1] Karl May wrote best-sellers about the American Old West without ever leaving his home near Dresden in Saxony. His adventure yarns were immensely popular with young people; Hitler reread the entire May library during the war in the East, 1941–1945.

Nietzsche and with the brief, chiseled poems in which Stefan George transmitted the master to students. George condemned modern industrial society and its egalitarian, democratic trends and demanded instead a new, strictly hierarchical, and aristocratic male order led by artists and writers. In practical terms, youth gravitated to the Free Corps and the various combat leagues; entire companies, even battalions, were filled with the young. At universities, they flocked to the antidemocratic fraternities and by 1929–1930 had captured the student governments of the universities of Erlangen and Greifswald for the NSDAP. Berlin, Breslau, Giessen, Jena, and Rostock would follow the next year. Before 1933 university student unions were the only national organizations completely dominated by the Hitler movement. Such was the state of the academy whence would come the lawyers, judges, and civil servants of the future.

Above all, Weimar culture questioned existing values and traditions. In the sciences, especially, uneasiness percolated as each discovery by men such as Albert Einstein, Max Planck, Werner Heisenberg, Niels Bohr, and Enrico Fermi seemed to undermine comfortable nineteenth-century ideas. The older, Newtonian-Kantian concept of science as a system of knowledge based on a single law of causality increasingly came under fire. It was all confused and confusing to the public at large. Even the new international architectural style developed by Walter Gropius (after the Dutch De Stijl group) at the Bauhaus in Weimar after 1919 employed simplified cubic masses, assembled asymmetrically and utterly unadorned. It rejected the traditional Wilhelmian gilded style and argued that function should drive style. Team design was stressed, and architecture and art were fused in the factory murals of Paul Klee and Wassily Kandinsky. The Right denounced the new style as "cultural bolshevism," and in 1933 Hitler closed the Bauhaus and drove Gropius into exile. Gropius as well as Erich Mendelssohn and Mies van der Rohe would exert great future influence in their new homes in the United States and Brazil, respectively.

The left-wing literati, after years of opposition to William II, became the semiofficial Weimar spokesmen. Hermann Hesse's assaults on middle-class hypocrisy and pleas for an individual standard of values, as expressed in *Demian* (1919) and *Steppenwolf* (1930), stirred Weimar youth, as they would American students during the Vietnam War. Franz Kafka's posthumously published novels, such as *The Trial* (1925) and *The Castle* (1926), unsettled and bewildered readers with their nightmare fantasies of a world of threatening but inexplicable reality. Bertold Brecht's poetic brilliance, especially in his *Three Penny Opera* (1928), provided bright, cynical social satire, and Kurt Tucholsky's bitter attacks on the Republic, which he depicted with penetrating malice as false and lame, were reminiscent of Heinrich Heine nearly a century earlier.

Weimar's brightest stars never embraced the Republic. Tucholsky and his friends at the journal *Weltbühne* were convinced that all that was good and egalitarian resided in Joseph Stalin's Soviet Union. Hesse terminated his membership in the Prussian Academy of Arts due to his "deep distrust of the German Republic," this "rootless and spiritless state created out of the vacuum, the exhaustion after the war." Gerhart Hauptmann, the "poet prince" of the Republic, turned his back on Weimar. Even the self-professed "patron" of the Republic, Harry Count Kessler, was shocked to discover the new Prussian government as little more than "a uniform, shapeless gray mass, like lice." In short, the literati of the Left despised the Republic in large measure because it was boring and dull. Others simply felt isolated in the new democratic societies of the 1920s. When asked, "What should we Austrian writers do now?" the great Austrian poet, playwright, and librettist Hugo von Hofmannsthal replied, "Die."

Ironically, the new republican writers did Weimar a double disservice: they mercilessly revealed the Republic's weaknesses, thereby helping to undermine its authority, and they claimed to embody the essence of republican spirit and offered their opponents ammunition with which to discredit the Republic. Art and literature became political battlefields, polarized into extremes: beauty versus degeneracy, belief versus putrefaction, nature versus asphalt, manliness versus effeminacy, martial music versus "nigger" music (jazz), countryside versus city, discipline versus undiscipline, night versus day. Terms such as *asphalt literature*, *artistic junkyard*, and *corrosive Jewish intelligence* were but a few of the epithets the Right used to deride Weimar culture. Compromise was the first victim of this bitter conflict.

Denunciation of the Republic became the common thread that united intellectuals on both Left and Right. Arthur Moeller van den Bruck in his epic *Third Reich*, which appeared in the year of Adolf Hitler's abortive beer-hall putsch in Munich, denounced the Republic as the triumph of liberalism and capitalism and called for a neoconservative revolution. Oswald Spengler in 1924 described the Republic as "a five-year orgy of incompetence, cowardice and vulgarity." Already in 1918 the first volume of Spengler's classic *The Decline of the West* had predicted the end of European-American "culture" — decay, democracy, plutocracy, and technology — and its replacement with a new "iron age" of brainless but brutal dictators. Blood would battle with gold, Spengler argued, and blood would win. New steel Caesars would rejuvenate the state by sweeping away the debris of the past: capitalism, communism, monarchism, and socialism.

In *Prussian Socialism* (1920), Spengler denounced Karl Marx as the child of liberalism and called for a "third way": a new socialism, reconciled with the Prussian soldierly tradition, wherein everyone would be servant, worker, or soldier and only a few would be both master and servant. Neoconservatives of all shades disliked the Republic, the Reichstag, the League of Nations, and the new European democracy. They enjoyed the support of university students as well as professors, young army officers as well as veterans' organizations — in the end, even of Chancellor Franz von Papen.

A popular literary genre focused on the experience of mass, industrialized warfare in northern France in World War I. It tried to cope with the memories of senseless slaughter by recreating it on paper and in film. Best known is Remarque's *All Quiet on the Western Front*, which sold 640,000 copies in the first three months of 1929. Remarque's message was pacifist: war by definition is evil and meaningless. When *All Quiet on the Western Front* came out in film the following year, the Right viciously attacked its pacifism and eventually forced it to close. More influential in the long run were the novels of Ernst Jünger, especially *Storm of Steel* (1920), in which the former officer of the Great War argued that what counted was "not what we fight for, but that we fight." He called for national resurrection and salvation in the wake of decay and decline. History, Jünger argued, was in a critical phase: the future would bring a new apocalypse.

In 1932, the same year that Aldous Huxley published *Brave New World*, Jünger countered with *The Workers*, a pessimistic tale of the triumph of democracy, as well as a ringing plea for an age of technocracy and its attendant subjugation of the individual to a "pitiless" hierarchy. Jünger's new order would see the dichotomies of private versus public life, of front versus home erased. Material battles would transform the soldier into a "worker of war," and total war would demand total mobilization, total planning, and total obedience.

These writers sowed the seeds from which Hitler's National Socialism would spring. Yet when the promised "Caesar" appeared in 1933, the neoconservatives, including van den Bruck, Jünger, and Spengler, were terribly disappointed in the herdlike mentality and hysterical oratory of his mass movement. These writers had envisaged national salvation through a new intellectual elite and quickly discovered that the Nazi leaders failed to measure up to their high standards. Although antidemocratic and antirepublican, men such as Bruck, Jünger, and Spengler in the end shied away from the total barbarization that National Socialism represented.

Nor was the state of affairs in academia more positive. Philosophers such as Martin Heidegger and Karl Jaspers preached despair and displayed an indifference — if not downright hostility — toward contemporary politics. One of their colleagues, Max Wundt, set the tone for many when he proclaimed, "This state is un-German from root to crown." And what of the historians? With the notable exception of a few young radicals such as Eckart Kehr and Hermann Kantorowicz, Clio's practitioners remained loyal to their roots in the National Liberal, Prussian school as the great applauders of Bismarck and his Reich. They lamented the passing of the Hohenzollern monarchy and yet reveled in the demise of its Habsburg cousin. They toiled long and hard to deny war guilt and to provide the intellectual framework for revisionism.

One of academia's august, if more moderate, members, Friedrich Meinecke, coined the phrase *Vernunfts-Republikaner* (prudent republicans) to denote acceptance of the Republic "out of hard political necessity," but without emotion, conviction, or love. Even the erstwhile critic of the Prussian military system, Hans Delbrück, could not extol the Republic enthusiastically.

Prudent Republican: Thomas Mann ponders a troubled past (1950).

While conceding that he was in a way one of its pioneers, Delbrück nevertheless stated: "One serves the Republic, but one does not love it." The ranks of the *Vernunfts-Republikaner* included the dramatist Gerhart Hauptmann, the religious philosopher Ernst Troeltsch, and the painter Max Liebermann. Like Thomas Mann, they continued to place "General Dr. von Staat" — the Prusso-German veneration of state, military, and formal education — above democracy and Republic.

In fact, Thomas Mann personified the intellectual meanderings of many of the Weimar mandarins. His *Reflections of an Unpolitical Man* (1917) had constituted little more than a polemic upholding German "humanism" against Western "civilization." Mann grew to despise early Weimar. "I hate politics and democracy," he asserted, "which pollute all national existence." Yet by 1922 he realized that German youth yearned for an ideal to serve, and he offered them his own view of a republic, albeit romanticized. Mann lectured the conservative youth at Breslau University that year: "The Republic, democracy, today are such intrinsic realities for us all, each one of us, that to deny them is to deceive."

While Thomas Mann "thought too much" to serve as a rallying point for republicans, his brother Heinrich "played at politics" too much to assume the mantle of Victor Hugo or Emile Zola in his beloved France. Thomas Mann's great Weimar novel, *The Magic Mountain* (1924), depicted disease, death, and ideological debate set in a Swiss Alpine (Davos) tubercular sanitarium. *The Magic Mountain* has been likened to a "delicately carved puppet-theater," a stage on which "everything was discussed and nothing decided." Its list of characters includes the intellectual fanatic who predicts terror and totalitarianism; the psychoanalyst who talks cleverly and lasciviously of the connection between diseases of the body and the mind; the officer who is silent, does his duty, and dies; and the amiable progressive as well as the liberal optimist who remain ineffectual children of the Enlightenment. There, in literary form, was the cast of the Weimar Republic.

Perhaps the true essence of the *Vernunfts-Republikaner* can best be distilled from an anecdote that the journalist-novelist Arthur Koestler recalls making the rounds in 1932 at the Berlin publishing firm of Ullstein. According to the story, there was once an executioner named Wang Lun who lived during the Ming dynasty and whose lifelong goal was to behead a person so quickly that the victim's head remained poised on his neck. After years of practice, Wang Lun in his seventy-sixth year realized his ambition. He dispatched eleven men, with eleven heads rolling in the sand.

> Then came the twelfth man; he began to mount the scaffold, and Wang Lun, with a whisk of his sword, beheaded his victim so quickly that he continued to walk up the steps. When he reached the top, he spoke angrily to the executioner: "Why do you prolong my agony?" he asked. "You were mercifully quick with the others!" It was Wang Lun's great moment; he had crowned his life's work. A serene smile spread over his face; he turned to his victim, and said, "Just kindly nod, please."

In Weimar Germany, the "executioner" came in 1933.

Radicalization and Collapse, 1930–1933

With the accuracy of historical hindsight, one can well say that the Weimar Republic began to disintegrate around 1925. On February 28, President Ebert died of appendicitis after having just defended himself in a particularly vicious libel suit — the last of 173 provoked by charges from the Right that ranged from drunkenness and accepting bribes to pursuing an indecent lifestyle and high treason. Through the clever manipulations of Admiral Alfred von Tirpitz, Field Marshal Paul von Hindenburg agreed to come out of retirement to run for president; in a second runoff election, the seventy-eight-year-old Hindenburg defeated Wilhelm Marx of the Center party, mainly because the Communist leader Thälmann siphoned off 6 percent of the "democratic" vote.

Hindenburg had no love for the Republic, yet as an officer he proved surprisingly loyal to his oath of office. During his first four years as president, he did not once resort to rule by Article 48. But he did gravitate ever more into the circle of his former officers and East Elbian Junkers, who in 1927 managed to help him regain the family estate at Neudeck in East Prussia, which the family had lost shortly after World War I upon the death of Hindenburg's sister-in-law. Above all, three men exercised inordinate influence over him: Otto Meissner, pliant presidential secretary to Ebert, Hindenburg, and Hitler; Colonel Kurt von Schleicher, the coming man of the army who deftly handled politicians and trade unionists alike; and Hindenburg's son, Oskar, a colonel who in the judgment of his military superiors should never have risen above the rank of corporal. Over time, this "camarilla" came to dominate presidential appointments.

In addition, the Republic continued to shoot itself in the foot. In May 1926, in an ill-conceived effort to placate monarchists, Chancellor Hans Luther's government introduced a bill in the Reichstag permitting the flying of a second flag, the black-white-red merchant flag, ostensibly on grounds that the Republic's red-black-gold could not readily be seen at sea. Instead of placating the monarchists, the bill merely served to divide parliament on the flag issue; the Right demanded nothing less than formal abolition of the Republic's colors.

Then there was the matter of the vast territories of the former ruling houses. Whereas Austria had simply confiscated these possessions in the name of the nation, in Germany they had been given to the states in trust. Final disposition was left until later. In January 1926, the SPD and KPD introduced a bill calling for government seizure of such lands without compensation. Income from their resale was to be distributed to veterans, victims of inflation, landless farmers, the unemployed, and the poor. Although a national referendum once more failed to gain 50 percent approval, the issue, like that of the flag, badly divided the nation and fanned the flames of political dissent.

By 1928–1929, leadership in many political parties had shifted to the right. Inflation had soured middle-class voters on the Republic, and proportional representation had alienated voters from their Reichstag deputies. Germans continued to regard reparations payments as unjust, and they widely resented forced semidisarmament. The chaos of pluralism and the splintering of an already divided polity confused and offended bourgeois voters especially. The Center fell under the control of Monsignor Ludwig Kaas, a prelate who targeted the SPD as a primary political enemy; the Center party's parliamentary caucus was led by the conservative Heinrich Brüning. After Stresemann's death the German People's party turned for leadership to Ernst Scholz, who in his first speech in the Reichstag unleashed a verbal attack on the SPD. For its part, the German National People's party in 1928 had turned to former Krupp director and film magnate Alfred Hugenberg, who immediately demanded an end to the "system of caucuses, committees and diffusion of all energies through speeches and counter-speeches" — in short, democracy.

In political terminology, the Führer (leader) cult became trendy. From the Center's Kaas to the Communist's Thälmann, political pundits now spoke of their Führer and his leadership qualities. In the process, the political landscape was neatly divided between good and bad: "good" and "German" were "the ideas of 1914," hierarchy, struggle, war, heroic death, and the notion of a *Volksgemeinschaft*; "bad" and "alien" were "the ideas of 1789," democracy, parliamentarism, pluralism, pacifism, liberalism, and "Europe."

Seen against this background, the Great Depression served as the proverbial last straw. While historians debate its underlying causes — global overproduction, a drop in population growth and a concurrent increase in the work force, the lack of reinvestment in plants, and the failure to adjust to postwar market conditions — the reality for Germans was unemployment and misery. Without the customary influx of American cash loans, the German economy, highly dependent on tumbling exports, collapsed. Industrial production in 1932 was half that of 1928, stocks were off one-third in the same period, and unemployment skyrocketed to 30 percent of the labor force. Unemployment probably touched the lives of nearly one out of every two German people when one considers that women, who were not considered permanent members of the registered labor force, were not included in the official unemployment statistics.

In March 1930 Chancellor Hermann Müller's government attempted to cover the fiscal 1930 deficit of 1.5 billion GM by the twin expedients of reducing unemployment benefits and raising unemployment insurance to 4 percent. Industry refused to pay its share of the proposed new taxes, and labor declined to share the burden alone. Social Democratic opposition to reduced unemployment benefits brought down Müller's coalition government.

UNEMPLOYMENT, 1929–1933

Year	Total	Percentage of Labor Force
1929	1,899,000	8.5
1930	3,076,000	14.0
1931	4,520,000	21.9
1932	5,603,000	29.9
1933	4,804,000	25.9

Unemployment 1930–1933: The deadly curse.

On March 30, 1930, the Center's Heinrich Brüning formed a new government dedicated to a policy of deflation: to cut state expenditures sharply, reduce wages and prices, and raise taxes in the hope of restoring employment and appearing to try to meet reparations payments. Brüning disingenuously left the decision on raising unemployment insurance to 4 percent as well as additional government social grants to the Institute of Labor Exchange and Labor Insurance — in effect, burying it in committee. A balanced budget, Brüning argued, would "prove" both Germany's desire to fulfill the Young Plan and its inability, despite these efforts, to do so.

Brüning revealed in his memoirs that he had even greater domestic aspirations. By shifting his political basis sufficiently to the right to include the German National People's party, the chancellor hoped to gain approval for a return to the Bismarckian constitutional system whereby the Prussian and German executives were fused into one and "*to make possible the peaceful restoration of the monarchy.*" Such romantic notions were complemented in foreign policy by radical revisionism and great power enthusiasm. Brüning sought nothing less than to restore the European pentarchy of pre–1914 (Britain, France, Germany, Russia, and Italy).

Tactically, Brüning packed his cabinet with bureaucratic specialists and resorted to rule by presidential decree, invoking Article 48 five times in 1930, forty-four times the following year, and sixty times in 1932. Brüning's deflationary policies brought about a twenty-point decline in the cost-of-living index between 1930 and 1932, but wages and salaries plummeted precipitously. Civil service salaries in 1931 were reduced three times, with a total monetary decline of 23 percent. Concurrently, existing taxes on income (for bachelors especially), goods and services, sugar, and beer rose, and new ones were levied against mineral water and warehouses.

The chancellor's popularity fell calamitously in the summer of 1931 when, during a state visit to Great Britain, he announced further cuts in state salaries, war pensions, unemployment benefits (which were eliminated for married women), and child support payments, as well as an "emergency" surcharge of 4 to 5 percent on all income. The British were told that this would be "the last sacrifice of the German people for the fulfillment of reparations payments." In short, Brüning tightened the economic screws on the German people in order to promote his basic program to abolish reparations.

In 1931 Austria requested a customs union with Germany in order to escape the ravages of the Great Depression. The French, seeing this (not without cause) as the first step toward eventual German political reunion, reacted angrily by withdrawing their short-term investments from the Creditanstalt in Vienna, one of Europe's largest banks; it collapsed in May 1931. A financial panic ensued in Berlin, highlighted by a run on the banks. On June 13 Brüning was forced to close all financial institutions to halt the run on deposits. As a result, loans to industry and agriculture were blocked, and industrial production slowed to 40 percent of plant capacity.

Brüning's tight-fisted fiscal policy turned a deep recession into depression. Tightening credit instead of loosening it, raising taxes rather than lowering them, cutting public spending rather than priming the pump, and raising tariffs rather than lowering them worsened Germany's economic plight. Similar policies in Britain, France, and the United States brought similar results.

Suddenly, a ray of sunshine appeared on the horizon: on June 30, 1931, President Herbert Hoover announced a moratorium on all reparations payments. This may have been the first "victory" in the chancellor's grand strategy, but mass hunger and mass unemployment at home overshadowed this foreign policy success. By the fall of 1932, one in three Germans (23.3 million) struggled to survive on public welfare. The suicide rate stood at 260 per million people, double that of France and the United States and triple that of Britain. On the streets, Brüning was denounced as the "hunger chancellor." Aloof, cold, and reclusive in the best of times, Brüning ignored the public's distress and confidently claimed to be "one hundred meters from the goal."

Brüning's final act as chancellor was to launch a rearmament program designed to create a Reichswehr of twenty divisions as well as an air force by 1933. At the International Disarmament Conference at Geneva in February 1932, Brüning demanded equal rights for Germany. Failing that, he announced that he was ready to renounce all weapons limitations imposed on Germany in 1919 and to begin training a national militia at the rate of 100,000 men per year.

While negotiations continued at Geneva, domestic affairs ended Brüning's career. In April he managed to oversee President von Hindenburg's reelection against the surprisingly strong candidacy of Adolf Hitler, and even to ban the NSDAP's paramilitary thugs, the brown-shirted storm troopers (SA), from German streets. But a financial scandal — the so-called eastern assistance (*Osthilfe*), which permitted East Elbian squires with government funds to retire short-term, high-interest loans through long-term, low-interest notes — proved too much at a time of mass misery. Abandoned by his own party as well as by Hindenburg and Schleicher, Brüning was forced from office on May 30, 1932.

His successor, fellow Center party deputy Franz von Papen, established a "cabinet of barons" on June 1. In fact, Papen was the creation of army chief General Kurt von Schleicher. Both men sought to tame the burgeoning Nazi movement by bringing all or at least a part of it into their government as a junior partner. Both desired to end parliamentarism and to dismantle Social Democratic and trade union power. Neither enjoyed parliamentary or popular support. Their one political strategy was to end SPD rule in Prussia. On July 20, 1932, Papen, with the open support of the Reichswehr, overthrew the government of Otto Braun, the "red tsar of Prussia," and personally assumed the role of national commissioner for Prussia. Historic Prussia disappeared on a note of supreme irony: its defenders from 1918 to 1932 had been the Social Democrats, the Center, and the Left Liberals, the old Bismarckian enemies of the state; its destroyers in 1932 were the Conservatives, the agrarians, and the army — men such as von Hindenburg, von Papen, and von Schleicher.

That Papen enjoyed no popular support was amply revealed in the elections of July 31, 1932, in which the National Socialists triumphed with 37 percent of the vote and 230 deputies, while the KPD jumped to 14 percent of the vote and 89 deputies. Combined, the two extremist antidemocratic and antirepublican parties polled 51 percent of the vote. Even the Center party turned its back on Papen, who resigned in November 1932. Hitler's man in Berlin, Joseph Goebbels, set the course for the future: "Either vigorous opposition or power. Toleration kills. The SPD serves as a cautionary example."

In fact, German politics no longer were conducted in the Reichstag but rather on the streets. A virtual civil war raged from 1931 to 1933. In 1931 the Prussian police recorded more than 300 political murders. From mid-June to mid-July 1932 alone, it noted 99 dead and 1,125 wounded in 461 political riots. On July 17, 1932, 17 people were killed and more than 100 wounded during a brawl in the Hamburg suburb of Altona. Every weekend, the paramilitary forces of extreme Right (Storm Troopers) and Left (Red Front) terrorized German cities.

Not even parliaments were spared. On May 25, 1932, NSDAP and KPD deputies clashed in the Prussian parliament; on December 7, the same factions in the Reichstag battled each other with ashtrays, spittoons, desktops, and telephones torn from the walls. At the best of times, NSDAP deputies on every

"Where one burns books, one will end by also burning human beings" (Heinrich Heine). Nazi book burning, including Heine's works, Leipzig (May 1933).

possible occasion lustily sang their party anthem, the "Horst Wessel Song," in the Reichstag. The KPD countered equally lustily and frequently with the "Internationale."

Desperate to end the political chaos, President von Hindenburg on December 3 forced General von Schleicher to come out of the shadows and to assume the office of chancellor. The *Tägliche Rundschau*, a Berlin newspaper in the pay of the Reichswehr, summed up the situation as follows: "The best horse has been brought out of the stable, and now the stable is empty."

Like Brüning, Schleicher had a plan. He proposed, much as Frederick the Great had militarily, to conduct a "strategy of the diagonal" politically — that is, to rally army and trade unions to support a "third way" between the diametrically opposed poles of capitalism and communism. Spengler's social-romantic vision of "Prussian Socialism" was to be realized; the old planned union between Bismarck (conservatism) and Ferdinand Lassalle (socialism) revived.

Chancellor von Schleicher's first move was to exploit the split within the National Socialist German Worker's party between Adolf Hitler, who continued to play for all or nothing, and Gregor Strasser, who feared that such a rigid course would destroy the party. Schleicher's clumsy attempt to harness the more moderate elements within the NSDAP failed miserably because Strasser proved too weak to play the role. On December 9, Goebbels called Strasser "a dead man"; on June 30, 1934, Hitler would fulfill that ominous prophecy. Next, Schleicher proposed to broker a "diagonal connection" from SPD to DNVP, including both Free and Catholic trade unions. The Social Democrats, well remembering their persecution between 1878 and 1890, refused to join a coalition government engineered by an army general. Schleicher thus ran out of alternatives.

What next? On October 10, 1931, and again on November 19, 1932, Hindenburg had interviewed Hitler as a possible candidate for chancellor, but each time the president deemed the "Bohemian corporal" fit, at best, to serve as postmaster-general. Moreover, the NSDAP had fared poorly in the national election of November 6, 1932, losing 6 percent, or about 2 million votes, at the polls. Nor had Hitler's party fared better in regional elections, sustaining a stunning loss — for example, of 40 percent of its former support in Thuringia. Although Nazi propaganda made much of the gain of a few percentage points in the elections in the tiny state of Lippe (98,000 voters) on January 15, 1933, in reality the Lippe election had brought about a strengthening of the moderate parties at the expense of the KPD and the DNVP.

Hitler was saved from probable oblivion by the machinations of the "camarilla" that surrounded Hindenburg. Presidential secretary Meissner, former Chancellor von Papen, and son Oskar undermined the president's confidence in Schleicher, on the one hand, and encouraged him, on the other, to turn to Hitler. Crown Prince William of Prussia counseled Hindenburg to take a chance on Hitler. Confused, Hindenburg turned to the Reichswehr: General Werner von Blomberg, military commander in East Prussia, and his staff chief, Colonel Walther von Reichenau, decided the issue in favor of the "Bohemian corporal."

A story perhaps best reflects President von Hindenburg's state of mind at the time. Viewing the NSDAP's torchlight parade through Berlin from the presidential palace on January 30, 1933, Hindenburg reportedly said to Meissner: "I did not know, Ludendorff, that we have so many Russian prisoners of war." A more lucid Joseph Goebbels on January 30 realized the opportunity at hand: "We have arrived at our goal. The German revolution begins!"

Suggested Readings

The standard history remains Erich Eyck, *History of the Weimar Republic*, 2 vols. (London, 1962, 1964). Two older single-volume treatments are William S. Halperin, *Germany Tried Democracy* (New York, 1946), and Arthur Rosenberg, *A History of the Weimar Republic* (London, 1936). Still useful is the third edition of Anthony J. Nicholls, *Weimar and the Rise of Hitler* (New York, 1991). The most recent analyses are Eberhard Kolb, *The Weimar Republic* (Boston, 1988); and Detlev J. K. Peukert, *The Weimar Republic: The Crisis of Classical*

Modernity (New York, 1992). Finally, an anthology has been offered by Ian Kershaw, *Weimar: Why Did German Democracy Fail?* (London, 1990).

Weimar politics has elicited great interest. For the Left, several new treatments have emerged: Richard Breitman, *German Socialism and Weimar Democracy* (Chapel Hill, N.C., 1981); Ben Fowkes, *Communism in Germany Under the Weimar Republic* (New York, 1984); Eve Rosenhaft, *Beating the Fascists? The German Communists and Political Violence, 1929–1933* (Cambridge, 1983); and Richard N. Hunt, *German Social Democracy, 1918–1933* (New Haven, Conn., 1964). The history of the Center was first explored by Klaus Epstein, *Matthias Erzberger and the Dilemma of German Democracy* (Princeton, 1959); a more recent portrait is Bruce B. Frye, *Liberal Democrats in the Weimar Republic* (Carbondale, Ill., 1985). The saga of the Right was first revealed by Lewis J. Hertzman, *DNVP: Right-Wing Opposition to the Weimar Republic, 1918–24* (Lincoln, Neb., 1963); Walter H. Kaufmann, *Monarchism in the Weimar Republic* (New York, 1973); and Klemens von Klemperer, *Germany's New Conservatism: Its History and Dilemma in the Twentieth Century* (Princeton, 1957). See also Andreas Dorpalen, *Hindenburg and the Politics of the Weimar Republic* (Princeton, 1964).

The twin poles of the climactic year 1923 have been expertly treated in political terms by Werner T. Angress, *Stillborn Revolution: The Communist Bid for Power in Germany, 1921–23* (Princeton, 1963), and Harold J. Gordon, Jr., *Hitler and the Beer Hall Putsch* (Princeton, 1972). The German inflation of that year can be studied in two anthologies: Fritz Ringer, ed., *The German Inflation of 1923* (New York, 1969), and Gerald D. Feldman, ed., *The German Inflation Reconsidered* (New York, 1982). Detailed analysis of its impact is provided by Michael L. Hughes, *Paying for the German Inflation* (Chapel Hill, N.C., 1988). A specific treatment of heavy industry and the inflation is Gerald D. Feldman, *Iron and Steel in the German Inflation, 1916–1923* (Princeton, 1977).

The Peace of 1919 has been analyzed from a multinational perspective by Klaus Schwabe, *Woodrow Wilson, Revolutionary Germany, and Peacemaking, 1918–1919: Missionary Diplomacy and the Realities of Power* (Chapel Hill, N.C., 1985). The economic side of the peace has been surveyed by Derek H. Aldcroft, *From Versailles to Wall Street: The International Economy in the 1920s* (Berkeley and Los Angeles, 1977). Two highly revisionistic approaches are provided by Marc Trachtenberg, *Reparations and World Politics* (New York, 1980), and Stephen A. Schuker, *The End of French Predominance in Europe: The Financial Crisis of 1924 and the Adoption of the Dawes Plan* (Chapel Hill, N.C., 1976). The response of German industry in the 1920s to defeat, revolution, and reparations was pioneered by Robert A. Brady, *The Rationalization Movement in German Industry: A Study in the Evolution of Economic Planning* (Berkeley and Los Angeles, 1933); the problem of unemployment can be understood from an anthology by Richard J. Evans and Dick Geary, eds., *The German Unemployed, 1918–1936* (New York, 1987).

The foreign policy of the Weimar Republic, and especially of Gustav Stresemann, attracted numerous scholars after World War II: E. H. Carr, *German-Soviet Relations Between the Two World Wars, 1919–1939* (Baltimore, 1951); Hans Gatzke, *Stresemann and the Rearmament of Germany* (Baltimore, 1954); Henry A. Turner, *Stresemann and the Politics of the Weimar Republic* (Princeton, 1963); and later, Jon Jacobson, *Locarno Diplomacy: Germany and the West, 1925–1929* (Princeton, 1972). Most of the newer reinterpretations have come from German scholars. An exception is Robert G. Grathwol, *Stresemann and the DNVP: Reconciliation or Revenge in German Foreign Policy, 1924–1928* (Lawrence, Kan., 1980). Also worth reading is Fritz Fischer, *From Kaiserreich to Third Reich* (Boston, 1986).

Military history has been relatively neglected. Critical of army-state relations was Francis L. Carsten, *The Reichswehr and Politics, 1918–1933* (Oxford, 1966); much more sympathetic to the generals was Harold J. Gordon, Jr., *The Reichswehr and the German Republic* (Princeton, 1957). A more sophisticated approach was undertaken by Gaines Post, Jr., *The Civil-Military Fabric of Weimar Foreign Policy* (Princeton, 1973). The story of right-wing volunteer forces has been exhaustively detailed by James M. Diehl, *Paramilitary Politics in Weimar Germany* (Bloomington, Ind., 1977), whereas the army's professionalization in the 1920s is expertly dealt with by David N. Spires, *Image and Reality: The Making of the German Officer, 1921–1933* (Westport, Conn., and London, 1984). Two German scholars, Manfred Messerschmidt and Jürgen E. Förster, offer synopses of their larger works in Allan R. Millett and Williamson Murray, eds., *Military Effectiveness*, vols. 2, 3 (Boston, 1988). Students should also consult the provocative essay by Michael Geyer, "German Strategy in the Age of Machine Warfare, 1914–1945," in Peter Paret, ed., *Makers of Modern Strategy from Machiavelli to the Nuclear Age* (Princeton, 1986).

Weimar culture was first examined by Peter Gay, *Weimar Culture: The Outsider as Insider* (New York, 1968), and Walter Laqueur, *Weimar: A Cultural History* (New York, 1974). A more recent interpretation is Ronald Taylor, *Literature and Society in Germany, 1918–1945* (Totowa, N.J., 1980). The history of film has been documented by Thomas G. Plummer et al., eds., *Film and Politics in the Weimar Republic* (New York, 1982), and Siegfried Kracauer, *From Caligari to Hitler: A Psychological Study of the German Film* (Princeton, 1947). Art, literature and theater can be gleaned from Bärbel Schroder and Jürgen Schebera, *The "Golden" Twenties: Art and Literature in the Weimar Republic* (New Haven, Conn., 1988), and John Willett, *Theater of the Weimar Republic* (New York, 1984). A novel interpretation of modernism has been provided by Jeffrey Herf, *Reactionary Modernism: Technology, Culture, and Politics in Weimar and the Third Reich* (New York, 1984).

The last years of the Republic have recently attracted economic interpretations: Harold James, *The German Slump: Politics and Economics, 1924–1936* (Oxford, 1986), and Peter D. Stachura, ed., *Unemployment and the Great Depression in Weimar Germany* (New York, 1986). Neoconservatism and its impact upon the dissolution of democracy was examined by Herman E. Lebovics, *Social Conservatism and the Middle Class in Germany* (Princeton, 1969), and the decline of the liberal center was studied by Larry E. Jones, *German Liberalism and the Dissolution of the Weimar Political System, 1918–1933* (Chapel Hill, N.C., 1988).

The right-wing orientation of German youth has been analyzed by Peter D. Stachura, *Nazi Youth in the Weimar Republic* (Santa Barbara, Calif., 1975), and Michael S. Steinberg, *Sabres and Brown Shirts: The German Students' Path to National Socialism, 1918–1935* (Chicago, 1977). There is no research monograph detailing the role of women in Weimar. Students will have to consult the general overviews by Ute Frevert, *Women in German History: From Bourgeois Emancipation to Sexual Liberation* (New York, 1989), and Richard J. Evans, *The Feminist Movement in Germany, 1894–1933* (London, 1976), as well as the collection of essays edited by Renate Bridenthal et al., *When Biology Became Destiny: Women in Weimar and Nazi Germany* (New York, 1984).

C H A P T E R

8

THE BROWN REVOLUTION: NATIONAL SOCIALISM, 1933–1939

Our Constitution is the will of the Führer.

Hans Frank, May 1936

Adolf Hitler was appointed chancellor of Germany by President Paul von Hindenburg on January 30, 1933. There was no seizure of power (*Machtergreifung*), no bloody revolution. Hitler calmly went from the Hotel Kaiserhof to the Chancery and then to the presidential palace in order to receive the go-ahead to form a cabinet. Joseph Goebbels, who since 1926 had been in charge of conquering "red Berlin" for Hitler, noted in his diary that day: "It is almost as in a dream. The Wilhelmstrasse is ours. The Führer is already working at the Chancery."

Few were alarmed by the appointment. The Social Democrats viewed Hitler as "the pied piper from Braunau," a mere tool of heavy industry and East Elbian landed interests, a prisoner of the German Conservatives. The executive committee of the Communist International at Moscow in December decreed that National Socialism constituted nothing more than "the frank, terroristic dictatorship of the reactionary, chauvinistic, mainly imperialistic elements of finance capital." The army was delighted to have captured the "wonderful human material" of the National Socialist movement. Former defense minister Wilhelm Groener had confidently described Hitler as "a modest, decent human being, who only wishes the best. . . . Our task will be to direct the movement into proper channels." Former chancellor Franz von Papen was even more optimistic: "In two months we will have squeezed Hitler into a corner, and he will squeal." And Papen's successor, Kurt von Schleicher, had already written Hitler and his movement off as "a problem of the past." Only General Erich Ludendorff, Hitler's fellow conspirator in the beer-hall putsch of 1923, expressed alarm. Obviously piqued at having been upstaged by the

"Bohemian corporal," whom he had grown to distrust over the past decade, Ludendorff charged Hindenburg with having delivered Germany into the hands of "the greatest demagogue of all time," who undoubtedly would plunge the Reich "into unfathomable misery."

The French public regarded Hitler's appointment as nothing more than another tedious episode in the turbulent political life of the Weimar Republic. In the United States, the Führer was equated with Benito Mussolini, an ardent anti-Communist. The American public initially viewed Hitler as little more than a joke, but by 1938 he had gained sufficient public stature to be named *Time* magazine's Man of the Year. The British press saw Hitler as just another politician — no better and no worse, yet the *Sunday Times* noted that "no one knows what Hitler stands for."

To be sure, by 1933 Europeans were both curious and wary of the general parameters of fascism: the emphasis on the charismatic leader, the pseudo-religious propaganda, the ardent appeal to youth, the color-shirted paramilitary troops, the constant appeal to a glorious national past, and the deep hatred of all that was foreign and international. All too many accepted at face value the National Socialists' promise to heal internal divisions and to reknit an unravelling society.

Hitler and his brand of National Socialism resulted from and benefited from specific German developments. They were hardly the inevitable by-products of a particular German form of industrial capitalism, plagued by a preindustrial, politically immature German bourgeois elite. Defeat and revolution in 1918, a draconian peace settlement in 1919, inflation in 1923, depression after 1929: these events catalyzed Hitler's eventual rise to power. After 1930 the Führer cleverly exploited the systemic crisis of Weimar's parliamentary democracy. The depression of the early 1930s crystallized the weakness of Weimar's political structure and accelerated the disintegration of its authority. All the while, Hitler and his Nazis offered the nation not only an alternative government but above all an alternative political and social system.

Origins

In a national radio broadcast on April 1, 1933, Goebbels proclaimed the counterrevolutionary[1] nature of the new regime: "We will erase the year 1789 from the pages of history." The National Socialist movement was dedicated to supplanting not only the French Revolution but also liberalism and Marxism — not to mention internationalism, pacifism, and egalitarianism — while con-

1 The Nazis viewed themselves as counterrevolutionary in that their "revolution" was designed to undo the negative effects of both the French Revolution of 1789 and the Bolshevik Revolution of 1917. Much like Marx, Hitler claimed to have perceived the inner workings of history, but instead of class conflict, the motive force, he said, was racial conflict.

currently shunting aside traditional Prusso-German conservatism. It sought to create a new order based on pseudo-racial law, authoritarianism, and expansionism.

National Socialists wanted to create a racially homogeneous Germany by excluding "undesirable" racial groups such as the Jews; to restore Germany's great power status by "revising" the punitive clauses of the Treaty of Versailles; and to overcome the Marxist class struggle by fusing the two great waves of the nineteenth century, nationalism and socialism. That Hitler's adversaries failed to perceive the revolutionary dynamic of National Socialism was to prove a tragedy for both Germany and the rest of Europe. Workers as well as burghers remained in the grip of their ideological conviction that all revolutions were by definition of the Left. Most moderate politicians continued to cling to authoritarianism as a guarantor against the dreaded "revolution from below" — a view expressed in Thomas Mann's notion of General Dr. von Staat.

Few in Germany listened carefully to Hitler's candid statement: "Our party must possess revolutionary character, because the current state of affairs, 'peace and order,' means that we will preserve the present pigsty." It dawned on few that revolution could also come from the Right. Indeed, the emblem of the Hitler movement, the black swastika in a white circle against a blood-red background, constituted a clever homage to the tricolor of Otto von Bismarck's Second Reich of 1871, while concurrently raising to prominence the red of revolution.

The general contours of Hitler's career are well known. Born on April 20, 1889, in Braunau on the river Inn, the son of an Austro-Hungarian customs official, Adolf Hitler was the scion of a family marked by incest and illegitimacy. Variously recorded as "Hiedlers" or "Hüttlers," the Hitlers may well have been of Czech ancestry. The Führer who would later demand genealogical proof of Teutonic ancestry from 60 million Germans did not even know who his grandfather was or whether he had been "tainted" by Jewish blood (probably not). What is known is that after 1933 Hitler did his level best to eradicate all documentary evidence and to murder eyewitnesses from his early days, including Reinhard Hanisch, with whom Hitler sold art works to Jewish art dealers in Vienna, and Father Bernhard Stempfle, who edited parts of *Mein Kampf* in the mid-1920s.

At Linz, the young Hitler saw his first opera by Richard Wagner, *Rienzi*, and was mesmerized by its messianic music. Wagner's Teutonic paganism seemed to Hitler to be the true religion of a heroic Germanic Nordicism. He dreamed of becoming its high priest. "At that hour it began," he later claimed in *Mein Kampf*. Perhaps the most formative years of Hitler's youth were spent in Vienna between 1908 and 1913. There, Hitler lived a twilight existence of make-believe and role playing. Modestly endowed with pensions from his parents' deaths, amounting to 83 crowns per month, the young Hitler sought to pursue a career in art and architecture. He failed, and instead eked out a meager existence at a men's home by selling paintings and postcards.

Soon Hitler slipped into the popular and national (*völkisch*) subculture of Vienna. From the magazine *Ostara* published by the renegade priest Adolf Lanz (alias Jörg Lanz von Liebenfels), Hitler read about blond heroes and "racial hygiene," blue-eyed "Aryans" and swarthy ape-men, and the need to "deport, sterilize, and liquidate" the latter subspecies. From the Pan-German leader Georg von Schönerer, Hitler absorbed the expansionist message, the need to unite Europe's German-speaking peoples, the virtues of Germanic culture and of blood and soil, and the "Heil" greeting. And from the city's popular mayor, Karl Lueger, Hitler took to heart Viennese antisemitism and demagoguery. Never an original thinker, Hitler acted as a sponge, soaking up the hate and anger of fin-de-siècle Vienna: radical, racial, biological antisemitism. He would later synthesize the ideas he absorbed in Vienna into a highly powerful and dynamic set of beliefs.

Above all, Vienna taught Hitler how to hate. Scapegoats abounded: Jews and Marxists, Freemasons and pacifists, and women from all social strata. Life for Hitler became simple. He was always right, others always wrong. When he failed, it was the fault of others. All was black or white, either-or, friend or foe. Later on, part of Hitler's evil genius lay precisely in his ability to turn hate into personified revenge; his own salvation demanded the humiliation and destruction of others. According to psychohistorian Rudolph Binion, the death of Hitler's mother, Klara Poelzl, in 1907, while under the care of a Jewish physician, Dr. Eduard Bloch, and especially the latter's use of gaseous iodoform to treat her cancer, indelibly marked the son.

In May 1913, in order to escape the clutches of the Habsburg military police for his failure to report for military duty, Hitler crossed the border into Bavaria carrying a single suitcase. It is highly interesting to note that the future high priest of social Darwinism and the self-proclaimed "first soldier of the German Reich" entered the Reich clandestinely as a refugee from Austro-Hungarian military authorities. Quickly apprehended by Bavarian authorities and handed over to a Habsburg military court at Salzburg, Hitler in February 1914 was decreed "unfit" and "too weak" for military service in Francis Joseph's army. Hitler returned to Munich where, on August 1, 1914, World War I euphoria swept him along: he volunteered for military service and was posted to the Sixteenth Bavarian Reserve Infantry Regiment.

Military life proved a welcome relief from the drift of Hitler's bohemian existence. He volunteered for hazardous duty, became a message runner at the front, and received the prestigious Iron Cross First Class — on the recommendation of a Jew, regimental adjutant Hugo Gutmann. But Hitler remained a loner, nourished his many hatreds, and was deemed to lack the "leadership qualities" required for promotion to noncommissioned officer rank. He fell victim to a British gas attack south of Ypres during the night of October 13–14, 1918, and heard the news of Germany's surrender at an army hospital at Pasewalk.

Hitler had brooded long and hard about the nature of life and history during the war years, and he emerged from the Great War convinced that "internal internationalism," that is, Marxism and Judaism, had brought about defeat and revolution in 1918. Above all, he put the Jews in a historical context: in order for the "culture producing Germans" to triumph against the "culture destroying Jews," a remorseless struggle for survival needed to be waged and won. Specifically, the Germans needed to develop a race consciousness and a viable national community (*Volksgemeinschaft*) for the inevitable showdown with the "racial enemy" and alleged destroyer of nations, the Jews.

Hitler next accepted a position as instruction officer (*Bildungsoffizier*) in the army, and his new career took him to Munich, the vortex of postwar right-wing fringe groups. There he investigated the miniscule German Workers' party of Anton Drexler for the German army and joined it as party member No. 555.[1] By the summer of 1921 he led it. Two men proved instrumental in furthering Hitler's career. Captain Ernst Röhm, who would eventually head Hitler's paramilitary force, directed demobilized soldiers to the newly renamed National Socialist German Workers' party (NSDAP).[2] Dietrich Eckart, author of *Bolshevism from Moses to Lenin*, introduced Hitler to the cream of Munich society — publishers and art dealers such as Bechstein, Bruckmann, Hanfstaengl, and Lehmann — and helped secure the funds required to purchase a party newspaper, the *Völkischer Beobachter* (People's Observer).

Others were soon attracted to the "king of Munich," who at beer halls and circus tents regaled his audiences with bitter diatribes against Jews and Marxists, the Versailles Treaty, and the "new Babylon" Berlin. General Erich Ludendorff, the first quartermaster-general of the old imperial army listened, as did Gottfried Feder, a populist economist. They were joined by Alfred Rosenberg, author of *The Myth of the Twentieth Century*; Rudolf Hess, deputy leader and fellow frontline soldier; Hermann Göring, last wartime commander of Manfred von Richthofen's famous "Flying Circus"; Heinrich Himmler, unemployed student of poultry farming; and Julius Streicher, teacher and publisher of antisemitic pornography. At best second-raters, these men were given an outlet only by Hitler's movement.

This little band entered German history for one fleeting moment on November 8, 1923, when they subverted a demonstration of monarchical solidarity in the Munich Bürgerbräukeller into a planned "march on Berlin." The next day they staged a parade through Munich that was forcibly halted by police fire. This so-called beer-hall putsch ended in February 1924 in a trial at the Munich Infantry School that afforded Hitler a platform from which to

---

1 The NSDAP started numbering at 501 in order to exaggerate its strength.

2 Hitler added the descriptors "National Socialist" to Drexler's DAP in order to stress the group's goal to incorporate these two great waves of nineteenth-century thought.

broadcast his views. Above all, the events of November 8 and 9 showed Hitler the precarious nature of putsch attempts, and he vowed in the future to pursue a legal strategy, seeking power through the ballot box rather than through the barrel of a gun. His opponents derided his change in tactics by referring to him as "Adolphe Légalité." Nine months' incarceration at Landsberg provided Hitler time to put his thoughts to paper.

Originally entitled "Four and a Half Years of Struggle Against Lies, Stupidity, and Cowardice," *Mein Kampf* (My Struggle) emerged as seven hundred pages of glorified biography, ideological platform, political strategy, and wildly distorted history. Even the most convinced National Socialists found the book practically unreadable. Most foreigners dismissed it as inconsequential. But this "unread best-seller of world literature" — the five hundredth printing appeared in 1939, and 6 million copies were sold by 1945 — laid out the basic program of the Hitler movement.

At the heart of the book lie the concepts of race and *Volk*, both inextricably German in Hitler's mind. Both needed to maintain their purity. Both at all times struggled against evil forces. For Hitler, the social Darwinistic notion of a struggle (*Kampf*) for survival of the fittest was the engine of world history. Peace was an illusion. The "Aryan" constituted the master race; Jews, Slavs, and Negroes (blacks) were subspecies. Eternal combat against the latter was ordained by God: "Insofar as I struggle against the Jews," Hitler wrote, "I fight for the work of the Lord."[1] The Jewish "abscess" particularly needed to be lanced. Because history rewarded those who proved fanatical and destructive — crusaders and witch burners alike — victory eventually would fall to the "Aryan" blonds of Lanz and Schönerer. Democracy was but "the precursor of Marxism," the opium of the weak. In all, the program was a composite of "the ideas of 1914" and an utter distortion of Friedrich Nietzsche's emphasis (see Chapter 4) on the "will to power" on the part of the new *Herrenmensch* (master race). The focus on Nietzsche remained constant: Hitler's last birthday gift to Benito Mussolini in 1943 was *The Collected Works of Nietzsche*.

The methods to power were clear. Propaganda would capture the masses. It needed to be simple and clear, uncompromising and hard-hitting. "The broad masses are not receptive to half-truths and weakness," Hitler claimed. Bright colors, gut words (smash, force, hate, crush, etc.), and stirring music were crucial to success. A coherent ideology (*Weltanschauung*) was essential. "Political parties tend toward compromises; ideologies never. Political parties take into account the action of their opponents; ideologies are infallible." Terror, in the form of paramilitary forces such as the brown-shirted storm section (*Sturmabteilung*, or SA) and the black-shirted protection squad (*Schutzstaffel*, or SS), was necessary to combat international influences.

[1] Hitler was deeply antireligious and used the word *God* as a propaganda ploy so as not to alienate potential supporters. He no doubt meant that the struggle was ordained by history.

Above all, the principle of supreme, unquestioned leadership was central. The *Führerprinzip* removed political and moral responsibility from those who served. Hitler was the embodiment of the will of the German people; thus he expressed their will and was empowered to carry it out. The Führer leads; all others follow. Power flows solely from the Führer. Thus, only he is responsible; he is the ultimate redeemer of the nation. Followers obey and carry out orders. The Nazi jurist Carl Schmitt pathetically noted: "A command is the most beautiful thing in the world!" The *Führerprinzip* integrates all classes and social strata into one harmonious *Volksgemeinschaft*, a national racial community of interests wherein individualism is subsumed into the greater general weal. Those who lie outside the pure *Volksgemeinschaft* must be excised from it.

The symbiotic relationship between the Führer and his people was one of master and followers. While the Göttingen University sociologist Christian von Krockow has depicted this as an erotic power relationship bordering on sadomasochism, it should be remembered that Hitler intended the *Führerprinzip* as a manipulation of the deep-seated German desire to heal a fragmented society that seemed in permanent crisis and to build a better, stable Germany.

Mein Kampf, and especially Hitler's unpublished "Second Book" of 1928, also tackled the issue of foreign policy. As early as 1924, Hitler had developed the notion of the need to conduct a war of conquest against the Soviet Union and to eradicate "Jewish" bolshevism. This concept of requisite expansion (*Lebensraum*) soon hardened into an *idée fixe* buttressed by the geopolitical heartland notions of Professor Karl Haushofer, a former army general whose lectures at the University of Munich Hitler apparently attended. In alliance with Great Britain — another constant in Hitler's foreign policy considerations — Germany would unfold its power as the dominant continental player. Fascist Italy likely would join the crusade against bolshevism. If France opted to stay out, then it too would have to be conquered in order for Germany to avoid a two-front war as in 1914.

Hitler's radical aims in the east, while taking up a theme already aired by Generals Hindenburg and Ludendorff and other rabid annexationists from the Great War, constituted a major point of departure from the moderate revisionists, who sought mainly to overturn the most onerous clauses of the Versailles *Diktat* and to restore the borders of 1914. "The gigantic empire in the east is ready to collapse," Hitler cheerily forecast in *Mein Kampf*. Because he equated Marxism with Judaism, his crusade against the Soviet Union would serve two purposes: the riches of the Ukraine would ensure Germany protection against another naval blockade, and eradication of the "Jewish pest" in the east would remove the "cancer" that was destroying Germanic civilization. In short, a fatal combination of dogma and shrewd calculation permeated Hitler's expansionist program from the start.

As a prerequisite to achieving this megalomaniacal dream, Germany would have to be unified into a true *Volksgemeinschaft* in order to preclude the divisions of 1914–1918. Then, in alliance with Britain and Italy, the hereditary enemy France would have to be crushed. Thereafter, while Britain concentrated on its overseas possessions, Germany would undertake the gigantic war of conquest and racial purification in the east. The spoils of empire — colonies in Africa and the Middle East — would fall into German hands like ripe plums. It is hard to think of another statesman who postulated his basic program so clearly, so early, and in writing.

Reality, however, proved quite another matter. After 1926 the NSDAP, with only 27,117 members throughout the Reich, participated in various regional elections, receiving between 1.5 and 3.7 percent of the vote. In the national elections of 1928, it garnered 800,000 votes (one in eight came from party members), or 2.6 percent of the electorate. But then came the Wall Street crash and the death of Foreign Minister Gustav Stresemann in October 1929. Unemployment soared to 3 million in the winter of 1929–1930, 5 million in the fall of 1930, and 6 million by January 1932. Voters searched for simple solutions to complex questions. The NSDAP vote in Schleswig-Holstein increased sevenfold between 1928 and 1930; a similar pattern arose in Franconia and Oldenburg.

Educated youth turned to Hitler too. At Erlangen and Greifswald universities, the student governments had given NSDAP candidates majorities by 1929; Breslau, Giessen, Jena, Königsberg, Rostock, and the Technical University of Berlin had followed suit in 1930. Overall party membership by that year had doubled to 200,000.

The great breakthrough came in the national elections of September 1930, in which 82 percent of eligible voters participated. Rocked by unemployment and economic misery as a result of the Great Depression, the German electorate turned its back on democracy: the NSDAP vote jumped 800 percent to 6.4 million (18.3 percent) and 107 mandates; that of the Communists (KPD) rose to 4.6 million votes (13.1 percent) and 77 mandates. If one adds to this the votes of the antirepublican German National People's party (2.5 million) and the lesser right-wing splinter parties (2.4 million), it becomes clear that nearly 17 million

NSDAP SHARE OF GERMAN ELECTIONS

Election	Votes (000s)	Percentage	Seats
May 1924	1,918	6.5	32
December 1924	907	3.0	14
May 1928	810	2.6	12
September 1930	6,383	18.3	107
July 1932	13,769	37.3	230
November 1932	11,737	33.1	196
March 1933	17,277	43.9	288

voters, or half of all who turned out for the election, cast ballots for antidemocratic factions. In 1932 Hitler received German citizenship by accepting a senior civil service post from the recently elected NSDAP government in the state of Brunswick.

How does one account for this surprising electoral breakthrough? The years 1930 to 1932 were high drama for many Germans. Politics had shifted from parliament to the streets. Chaos, violence, and even murder became common. Politics polarized into a contest between extreme Left and Right — at the expense of the democratic Center. Most Germans yearned for an end to the crisis management of the Weimar Republic, for an end to the political and social fragmentation of the nation. Many longed for restoration of the national power and prestige stripped from them at Versailles in 1919. All Germans needed jobs and job security. The Nazis cleverly exploited the fear and insecurity harbored by most citizens and concurrently held out the promise of creating a new Germany devoid of political and social divisions — a true national community (*Volksgemeinschaft*).

An analysis of NSDAP members attracted between 1930 and 1933 reveals that workers dominated, with 33.5 percent. Most were employed in handicrafts and small-scale manufacturing and customarily worked in small shops or in government enterprises. Few came from the organized working class. The next largest group of NSDAP members was that of white-collar employees, with 22 percent. Many of these flocked to the NSDAP out of fear of the Marxist Left, frustrated career ambitions, and distress over eroded social prestige and professional security. Agrarian laborers came third, with 14.1 percent, followed by craftsmen, small tradesmen, and self-employed artisans, with 17.3 percent. The typical NSDAP laborer toiled on the land or, especially in Saxony and Thuringia, worked in textile cottage industries. In urban centers, he or she tended to come from the ranks of the unskilled, with high representation from the public services sector (gas, water, electricity, post, railroad).

These Nazi voters typically were people who saw themselves as marginal to a modern industrial society, with no control over their lives. Many cast their ballots for Hitler as a protest against economic distress and as a yearning to return to better times. The NSDAP's newfound support came in part from previous nonvoters but also from young first-time voters and from people who had defected from the traditional conservative parties, such as the DVP and DNVP. Regional analyses have suggested that the Nazis captured the Protestant rural and small-town voters, many of whom were from the lower middle class.

The new National Socialists hailed from east, central, and north Germany, stemming from medium and small towns rather than the industrial metropolises. Thirty-seven percent of party members and 26 percent of party leaders were under age thirty. Hitler at forty-three and Göring at forty were the elders of the movement. Albert Speer and Baldur von Schirach, as well as the SS leader Reinhard Heydrich, were still in their twenties. Heydrich's superior, SS leader Heinrich Himmler, was in his early thirties.

For a brief period in German history, as historian Thomas Childers has argued, the NSDAP became what the traditional parties of the German bourgeois Center and Right, as well as those of the Marxist Left, had failed to provide: the long-sought party of middle-class concentration. The Nazis could well crow that they constituted a true peoples' party (*Volkspartei*). But by 1932 the NSDAP reached the limits of its expansion in terms of class and religion, perhaps the two best predictors of German electoral behavior. The National Socialists failed to make major inroads into the electoral strength of the Catholic Center party; in fact, the latter's vote increased slightly between the elections of September 1930 and July 1932. And although the Nazis did score some gains among industrial workers, electoral sympathies among workers continued to be divided mainly between the SPD and KPD, with the latter (rather than the NSDAP) becoming the principal beneficiary of working-class radicalism.

Hermann Rauschning's claim that "it was the women's vote that brought Hitler to victory" is highly exaggerated. In fact women, who constituted only 5 percent of the NSDAP as late as 1933, tended to vote for the more traditional parties, such as the Center and Conservatives. Only in the March 1933 elections, after Hitler came to power (*Machtergreifung*), did the female vote for Hitler outstrip the male vote. Why did women vote for this predominantly male and antimodern NSDAP, which denounced the feminist movement of the Weimar Republic and yearned for a return to the "children, kitchen, and church" mentality of Wilhelmian Germany? The answer is that they voted not as females but as members of specific social classes, economic strata, and religious groups. Their voting habits, like those of most men, were driven by economic crisis.

As the depression deepened, "Adolphe Légalité" doubled his share of Reichstag mandates to 230 in the national elections of July 1932, garnering no less than 37.3 percent of the vote. He was soon accused of being the front man for big business, an unfounded charge that lingers on in some quarters. Although the NSDAP's financial records were destroyed in the Führer bunker in Munich during the last days of World War II, recent research suggests that although no fewer than 339 captains of industry and banking — including such luminaries as Emil Kirdorf and Fritz Thyssen — gave financial support to the NSDAP, these leaders financed other parties too, including the KPD. In the presidential elections of 1932, for example, 90 percent of political contributions from industry flowed not to Hitler but to Paul von Hindenburg. In short, German business and banking covered all bets. An analysis of one region, the Rhineland, has revealed that 80 percent of all funds raised came from party members. The NSDAP, in fact, was the only political party that charged admission (1 reichsmark) to its meetings.

Despite his tremendous electoral gains of July 1932, Hitler was no closer to victory than he had been in 1930. Although he continued to threaten the government with the street violence of the 2-million-man SA, the national elections of November 1932 brought a net loss of 2 million votes (6.2 percent) for the NSDAP. Goebbels panicked. Early in 1932 he had confided to his diary: "We must attain power in the foreseeable future. Otherwise, we will win ourselves to death in elections." In December 1932 he expressed the same pessimism: "The situation in the Reich is catastrophic."

Hitler was rescued from this conundrum by his appointment as chancellor on January 30, 1933, owing to the intrigues of the "old gang" around Papen and Schleicher, as well as Oskar von Hindenburg, the president's son. The nocturnal torchlight parade on January 30 marked the apparent triumph of the forces of counterrevolution. A fire at the Reichstag on February 27, allegedly set by the Dutch Communist Marinus van der Lubbe, provided Hitler with the necessary pretext to gain emergency powers from Hindenburg to launch his "brown revolution."

Under the auspices of a Presidential Decree for the Protection of *Volk* and State, which remained in effect until 1945, Hitler had KPD functionaries arrested and civil liberties suspended. Remaining on the offensive, Hitler called a national election and used all the powers of incumbency, including terror by the SA and other Nazi irregulars, which civil authorities carefully ignored or condoned, to gain a clear majority in the Reichstag. He was to be bitterly disillusioned: March 1933 brought the NSDAP 17.3 million votes and 288 mandates but not the desired majority.

To offset defeat at the polls, Hitler orchestrated a patriotic passion play designed to demonstrate the close link between National Socialism and Prussian Conservatism. On March 21, the date on which Bismarck had opened the first Reichstag in 1871 — over the graves of Frederick William I and Frederick II at the Potsdam garrison church and with an empty chair reminding all present of the unfortunate absence of William II — Hindenburg and Hitler solemnly shook hands. One side of the church was filled with the admirals and generals of Imperial Germany, including Hindenburg and Crown Prince William; the other was solidly brown and black. Bach chorales were intoned inside the church; artillery rounds split the air outside. The Hindenburg myth thus was wedded to the Hitler myth. That same day, the Nazi's primary newspaper, *Völkischer Beobachter,* proudly announced the creation of the Dachau concentration camp the day before.

Forty-eight hours later, the Reichstag, minus eighty-one KPD deputies, met at the Opera Kroll to take up Hitler's request to pass the Enabling Act, which would grant him emergency powers for four years. The bill required a two-thirds majority for passage. The last chance to salvage the Republic was at hand. Ringed by armed SA and SS units, the deputies cast their ballots. The decisive vote belonged to the Center party. Well remembering the trauma of the *Kulturkampf* under Bismarck, Monsignor Ludwig Kaas instructed Center deputies to vote for the act. Only the SPD went down with honor, refusing to

The Old and the New Germany: Hindenburg and Hitler shake hands over Frederick the Great's tomb.

endorse Hitler. The final vote was 444 to 94. All 288 NSDAP deputies collectively leaped to their feet and sang the party anthem, the "Horst Wessel Song." The road was clear to enact the party's program.

"Seizure of Power"

On April 7, 1933, Joseph Goebbels gloated over the pace of revolution in Germany. "One can say that today history is once more being made in Germany." The history being made was the Nazification of the German state apparatus and society, the so-called *Gleichschaltung*. The latter constituted the true Nazi "seizure of power." Through a series of radical measures, the Nazis banned all political activity save their own, transformed parliamentary democracy into Hitler's personal dictatorship, imposed on the nation a highly centralized system of police rule and state-sponsored terror, and forced traditional elites to embrace the new Nazi ideology.

Under the sweeping powers granted by the Enabling Act and with a shrewd combination of physical terror and public support, the old order was destroyed and replaced by the new. Non-NSDAP governments were forcibly overthrown in Baden, Bavaria, Hesse, Saxony, Württemberg, Bremen, Hamburg, and Lübeck. SA storm troopers assisted in the violent removal of democratically elected officials, and NSDAP supporters stormed city halls. By the end of the year, only one in every seven mayors remained in office. Swastika flags flying over government buildings symbolized the triumph of the revolution. In Prussia alone, about twenty-five thousand people were arrested in March and April as part of a campaign of political terror.

Millions of Germans stampeded to join the NSDAP. As party membership tripled between January and May 1933, the NSDAP became unwieldy, and its composition was radically altered. Civil servants, teachers, and lawyers led the list of newly converted National Socialists. This flood of middle-class recruits led to "embourgeoisement," and their smug satisfaction threatened to weaken the once-radical NSDAP. Fearing for the movement's revolutionary dynamism, Hitler in May closed the NSDAP to further membership, a ban that remained in effect until 1937. Germans quickly discovered that a low party number, signifying early party membership, enhanced one's chances of success in the new state.

Having successfully removed a possible political threat from regional parliaments, the Nazis next tackled labor, another potential center of resistance. On May 1 Hitler invited labor leaders to celebrate the traditional May Day in Berlin and called on workers to join the new classless *Volksgemeinschaft*. The following day the Führer's security forces broke into and looted the offices and presses of the Social Democratic Free Trade Unions. The liberal Hirsch-Duncker unions yielded to Nazi pressure and dissolved themselves that same May; the Christian trade unions followed in June. The German labor movement was reorganized by Robert Ley, head of the NSDAP's Political Office, as the German Labor Front (DAF). Ley at once prohibited strikes and outlawed collective bargaining.

On May 10 Social Democratic party offices were seized, and by June 22 the SPD had been outlawed. Its leaders were forced into exile at Prague; those less fortunate joined KPD functionaries in the concentration camps. Perversely, labor was reunited for the first time since 1919. The non-Socialist parties readily adjusted to the new circumstances. Democrats and Liberals disbanded. The Conservatives proved slow to take the hint, and Hitler had their offices occupied on June 21. The Center party dissolved itself on July 5. Three days later, Hitler, like Napoleon and Mussolini before him, concluded a Concordat with Rome, bringing to fruition long-standing negotiations between the Vatican and the Weimar Republic. Hitler accepted Rome's right to appoint church leaders and the Catholic church's claim to run special schools and other lay institutions. The Vatican recognized the Hitler regime and agreed to the dissolution of the Center party. Partly because of the self-destruction of political parties, the number of newspapers in Germany fell by one-third in 1933. On July 14, the anniversary of the fall of the Bastille in 1789, Hitler declared the NSDAP to be the only legal party in Germany.

Women were not exempt from the *Gleichschaltung* (Nazification of state apparatuses). The Federation of German Women's Associations (BDF) had closed shop by May 1933, its members subsumed into the League of German Girls and the NS-Frauenschaft, headed by Gertrud Scholtz-Klink. Gertrud Bäumer's ideal of 1914, that women owed the nation compulsory labor, was resurrected in the National Socialist Mother's Service. And Bäumer's authoritarian style certainly found emulation in Scholtz-Klink's ruthless energy and unscrupulous subservience to Hitler.

Extraparliamentary pressure groups, many of which had hounded the Weimar Republic into its early grave, were quickly disbanded or absorbed into corresponding NSDAP organizations. Franz Seldte, head of the veterans' movement, joined the NSDAP in April, and two months later the national veterans' organization "Steel Helmet" (*Stahlhelm*) merged with the SA. On April 20 Walter Darré, the NSDAP's agricultural expert, presented his Führer with a special birthday present: forty thousand agrarian cooperatives had joined the NSDAP. And on May 22, German industry, led by Gustav Krupp von Bohlen und Halbach, embraced the *Führerprinzip* and climbed aboard the NSDAP bandwagon by fusing the erstwhile Reich Federation of German Industry with the Association of German Employers to form the Nazi-controlled Reich Estate of German Industry. Jewish businesses faced a nationwide boycott on April 1.

Goebbels, in his new capacity as head of the Reich Chamber of Culture, rigorously enforced the Civil Service Reconstruction Law of April 7, designed to purge government bureaucracies of republicans, Socialists, and Jews. By April 1934, about four thousand Jewish lawyers, three thousand doctors, two thousand civil servants, and hundreds of directors, conductors, musicians, actors, and academics had been removed from government payrolls. More than thirty-seven thousand Jews had left Germany during the first year of Nazi rule. Thomas Mann, himself driven into exile, nevertheless applauded what he called the "desemitization of justice."

Academia also underwent *Gleichschaltung*. Although most German mandarins, including Richard Strauss, Martin Heidegger, and Gerhard Hauptmann, stayed at their posts, others were not as fortunate. Alfred Rosenberg's Militant League for German Culture was instrumental in "cleansing" academia of the likes of Max Horkheimer and Ernst Kantorowicz, Paul Tillich and Karl Mannheim. Other outcasts soon followed: Heinrich and Thomas Mann, Alfred Döblin, Ricarda Huch, and Albert Einstein, to name but a few. Black lists circulated against the writings of Bertolt Brecht, Sigmund Freud, August Bebel, Carl von Ossietzky, and Hugo Preuss, all the way down to Heinrich Heine and Karl Marx. On May 10 German students, accompanied by SA and SS bands, committed to flames the works of Mann and Marx, Freud and Einstein, and Ossietzky and Remarque, among countless others, thereby resurrecting Heine's

Joseph Goebbels explains the New Order in Berlin (August 1934).

century-old prediction: "Where one burns books, there one will end by also burning human beings."

The "brown revolution" set in motion several waves of elitist emigrations. First to go were the Communists, Social Democrats, and trade unionists able to escape the SS dragnet. Next went a flood of political "undesirables" — men such as former chancellors Joseph Wirth and Heinrich Brüning and ministers Gottfried Treviranus and Erich Koch-Weser. A third wave of emigrants consisted of disillusioned former National Socialists, including Otto Strasser and Hermann Rauschning. Finally came the exodus of Jewish refugees. Within a few years, Hitler managed to undo more than a century of assimilation: 330,000 German, 150,000 Austrian, and 25,000 Sudeten Jews would leave their homeland before 1939. Most found shelter in Belgium, Britain, France, Palestine, the Netherlands, and the United States.

One in every four émigrés was an intellectual. No fewer than twenty-four Nobel laureates, including Albert Einstein, Max Born, and Erwin Schrödinger, fled. Prominent social scientists and humanists such as Ernst Bloch, Ernst Cassirer, Herbert Marcuse, and Karl Popper chose exile over persecution. The University of Bonn stripped Thomas Mann of his honorary doctorate; other universities rushed to do the same, now deeming former academic giants "undesirables." Less prominent Austrian and German Jews found refuge from Nazi persecution difficult due to virulent antisemitism abroad, especially in Canada and the United States.

By July 1933 Hitler could well proclaim a successful "end to the revolution." Many of the traditional power elites — nobility, bureaucracy, church, labor — had embraced the new regime, had been "synchronized" or driven underground, or had emigrated. Germany finally achieved centralization. All power emanated from Berlin. The Reich was now divided into ancient Germanic districts (*Gaue*), and regional minister-presidents were replaced by Reich governors (Reichsstatthalter) appointed from Berlin. Regional police forces were subjected to central control. Berliners called the Reichstag — brown-shirted, male dominated, and given to singing Nazi anthems — "the world's largest male glee club."

State and party bureaucracies ballooned as NSDAP members claimed the spoils of victory. At the party level, by 1935 thirty-five *Gau* leaders commanded an army of 827 regional and 21,000 district leaders as well as 260,000 block and cell leaders. In all, 700,000 NSDAP functionaries now lined up at the federal trough. In Munich, capital of the movement, more than 1,600 NSDAP staffers were housed in forty-four buildings. At the state level, Robert Ley's German Labor Front employed 40,000 bureaucrats to manage labor. Ministerial staffs in Berlin grew by 170 percent during the 1930s. No one personified this proliferation of offices and titles more than Hermann Göring: Prussian minister-president, president of the Reichstag, head of civilian aviation, minister of forestry, plenipotentiary for the Four Year Plan (1936, designed to bring rearmament to the point where Germany could conduct a major war in four years), infantry general and later field marshal as well as special Reich field marshal, commander-in-chief of the air force, deputy Führer, and even Reich master of hounds. He was, in short, a man for all seasons.

To the outside world, the Third Reich was a model of Teutonic efficiency and order. Today's historians, however, describe the administrative structure of the National Socialist state as "authoritarian anarchy" or "institutional Darwinism." Indeed, a neofeudal labyrinth of conflicting and redundant state, party, and private bureaucracies vied with each other for power and its rewards. A monocratic *Führerstaat* existed side by side with a polycratic administrative state. Hitler, by way of the ancient tactic of divide and conquer, was able to stand above the fray and to play the role of arbiter down to 1945.

In many ways, Hitler's administrative style was a throwback to his old bohemian days. Concentrated work was replaced by intuition. "Führer directives" took the place of collegial decisions. The cabinet ceased to meet after February 1938, and the luxurious cabinet room in Albert Speer's New Chancery remained unused. Hitler had much in common in terms of work habits, if not of ideas, with another restless ruler, William II. And was *Führer* all that far removed from *Majesty*?

According to the British historian Ian Kershaw, in time Hitler fell victim to his own myth as omnipotent savior of the nation. As early as the 1920s, Hitler had encouraged the development of a Führer cult within the party. After 1933 Hitler transformed this cult into a mass phenomenon designed to accord the Nazi regime legitimation of a beloved leader enjoying the unprecedented adulation and subservience of his people. Hitler's image changed from party leader to that of supreme and infallible national leader. In the public consciousness, the Führer transcended day-to-day politics. He was above party squabbles and misdeeds, an Olympian figure fully preoccupied with rescuing the nation from economic misery and political chaos. But the Führer cult affected Hitler too. By 1936 a quasi-religious, messianic mentality dominated the Führer. Even excesses by the party were excused by the public with the comment: "If only the Führer knew about that . . ." Sycophantic adulations addressed to "Mein Führer" became as much a part of the Hitler cult as the rhythmic "Heil Hitler" chants. And a horde of "little Führers," derisively termed "party bigwigs" (*Bonzen*), radiated in Hitler's glow — and enriched themselves at state expense.

Common folk noted the changes. Regional studies of Bavaria have shown that although most local residents approved of the Nazis' endeavors to overcome the political and social fragmentation of the past and to build a new society, they also noted the "dictatorship of *Bonzen*" and the enrichment of party officials at public expense. The alleged corruption of Nazi labor leaders caught the attention of former trade unionists. What many termed the "pseudo-socialism" of the German Labor Front under Ley drew their ire, and they viewed the idealized *Volksgemeinschaft* as a propagandistic mirage.

In the spring of 1940 Joseph Goebbels baldly summarized the events of the past decade. "Our domestic opponents," he stated, "did not know where we were headed, that our oath of legality was only a ruse. We wanted to come to power legally, but of course we did not want to use [power] legally." He conceded that the existing power elites at any time "could have crushed us"; instead, "they let us pass through the danger zone." It really was that simple.

The Face of Terror

Hans-Ulrich Thamer, a German historian who has written a recent account of the 1930s, *Seduction and Violence*, claims that "30 June 1934 was as important as 30 January 1933 on the road to annihilation and barbarism." During what Hitler later called the Night of the Long Knives, the leadership of his own SA, as well as other diverse opponents of the regime, were butchered at state order throughout the land. On that day, NSDAP, SS, and Reichswehr marched arm in arm down the road to terror. The Night of the Long Knives would constitute a major charge in the Allied case against Nazi war criminals at Nuremberg after World War II.

Ernst Röhm, head of the SA and one of Hitler's very few personal friends from the early Munich days, had called for a "second revolution" — a purge of the Junker-dominated professional officer corps. Röhm sought to transform the SA into a revolutionary army that reflected and promoted the ideas and goals of the revolutionary Nazi movement. He demanded that "the grey rock of the Reichswehr" be "drowned in the brown flood of the SA," and he warned Hitler that the SA would not "tolerate that the German revolution die away" or be "betrayed" by moderates. Revolt simmered within the NSDAP.

Hitler at first attempted to tame his old friend. On December 1, 1933, he invited Röhm to join his government in the hope that ministerial responsibility would moderate Röhm's radical position. But Röhm refused to be silenced. Instead, he used his position within Hitler's cabinet to rail against the "bureaucratization" of the NSDAP and to demand that the SA be reconstituted as a national militia. Privately, Röhm denounced Hitler as an "ignorant corporal" and threatened to mobilize his thirty divisions of brown shirts. Viktor Lutze, one of Röhm's staffers, betrayed the private outburst to Hitler.

The Führer was caught between the hammer of the Reichswehr and the anvil of the SA: the latter was his trusted old guard from the early days of the movement, but the former was indispensable for the technical aspects of planned rearmament and the conduct of future wars of aggression. Hitler resolved this dilemma by forging an unholy alliance between party and army. The Führer's seductive suggestion of a "twin-pillars theory," whereby the party would unify the home front while the soldiers concentrated on military science, rallied Reichswehr to NSDAP.

Indeed, little separated party and army in the early 1930s. Defense Minister General Werner von Blomberg was without scruples, fully devoted to his Führer. In February 1934 he had applied the NSDAP's racial theories to the officer corps and had elevated the party's emblem, the swastika, to be the official symbol also of the army. Chief of the Army General Werner von Fritsch, even after his fall from grace in 1938, admitted that it had been his fervent desire after the Great War "victoriously to wage three battles": against the labor movement, the Catholic church, and the Jews. How could Fritsch have resisted Hitler's temptations? Finally, Colonel Walter von Reichenau expressed the feelings of many army colleagues when he based his support for the NSDAP on cold, rational calculations: "Embrace the new state, only in this way can we preserve the positions befitting us." Official orders to permeate the army with National Socialist doctrine soon emanated from Blomberg.

Hitler's dilemma, then, was to square the circle, how to reconcile Röhm's plans to transform the SA into a revolutionary army with the Reichswehr's demand that it remain the sole bearer of arms in the Nazi state. The Führer quickly discerned in President von Hindenburg's written desire for a Hohenzollern restoration the potential basis for a convenient deal to seal the marriage between party and army. Hitler met with senior army leaders in April aboard the cruiser *Deutschland* and hatched a deal: the Reichswehr would suppress Hindenburg's call for the return of William II from the Netherlands, and Hitler would eliminate the threat from Röhm and the SA.

In June 1934 a series of unforeseen developments forced Hitler to act. On June 17 former Chancellor von Papen at Marburg University warned that Röhm's radical course would end in a Marxist bloodbath and insisted that the transitional stage of Nazi rule permitted by the Enabling Law prepare the way for a future authoritarian state based on Christian principles. Privately, Papen went so far as to ask President von Hindenburg, through his son Oskar, to proclaim a military dictatorship.

Papen's initiative galvanized Hitler into action. Under no circumstances could he allow Papen to create an alliance between Reichswehr officers and Conservatives. Hitler encouraged Röhm to take sick leave at the resort of Bad Wiessee, and with the SA leader safely on leave in Bavaria, the road was clear for the Führer to plot Röhm's demise. SS units were put on alert throughout Germany on the night of June 24–25. Captain Röhm's name was purged from the lists of the Union of German Officers. The Reichswehr lent trucks, guns, and barracks to the SS units under Sepp Dietrich. Himmler and Blomberg circulated black lists of potential candidates for "liquidation." Hitler flew to Essen to disguise his real plans.

On the morning of June 30, 1934, Hitler, whip in hand, led the SS execution squad to Bad Wiessee. Röhm and his staff, many of whom were surprised together in bed, were arrested and transported to Stadelheim prison or to the Dachau concentration camp. Rudolf Hess and Max Amann, Hitler's publisher, vied with each other for the "honor" of killing Röhm. In the end, Hitler gave the order to Theodor Eicke, commandant at Dachau. Eicke also summarily executed another seventeen SA men, as well as Father Stempfle, the editorial assistant for *Mein Kampf*, and Gustav von Kahr, Hitler's fellow traveler in the initial stages of the beer-hall putsch of 1923.

In Berlin, Göring and Himmler directed the terror. Papen was placed under house arrest; two of his senior aides were murdered. Gregor Strasser, a left-wing member of the NSDAP, was executed at SS headquarters in the Prinz-Albrecht-Strasse. Former Chancellor General von Schleicher was shot, along with his wife, at his home. Schleicher's confidant, General Kurt von Bredow, met his death at his residence. In all, accounts were "settled" with nearly a hundred "enemies of the state."

June 30, 1934, proved a milestone as the first state-planned and legalized mass slaughter of the Third Reich. Instead of remonstrances from the army over the death of two of its generals, Blomberg thanked his Führer for this "decisive and brave act"; Hindenburg followed suit. On July 20 Hitler rewarded the SS for its part in the purge by releasing it from SA tutelage, placing it directly under his personal command, and allowing Himmler to raise a division of heavily armed forces. Lutze was repaid for his earlier betrayal of Röhm by being appointed head of the emasculated SA.

Hitler emerged as the real winner of the Night of the Long Knives. With one bloody blow, he had removed the threat from the Left (SA) and the Right (army). On July 13 he brazenly informed the Reichstag that on June 30 he had accepted "responsibility for the fate of the German nation and thereby of the *Volk*" as its "supreme tribune." Corruption, homosexuality, and treason had been exorcised from the Reich. Potential opponents of the regime could now be certain of their fate. At the Nuremberg party rally that fall, a somber Hitler informed the nation: "In the next thousand years, there will be no other revolution in Germany."

Almost as if ordained by the Führer, President von Hindenburg died on August 2, 1934. In a repeat of the "Day of Potsdam" on March 21, 1933, Hitler orchestrated a grand funeral for the "deceased commander" at his "Valhalla," an austere stone temple at Tannenberg in East Prussia, where in 1914 Hindenburg had defeated the tsarist armies. Immediately thereafter, Hitler combined in his person as Führer the offices of president and chancellor. Blomberg and Reichenau at once ordered the armed forces to swear an oath of loyalty to "the Führer of the German Reich and *Volk*"; the civil service quickly followed. A national referendum formally endorsed the events of June–August 1934. "The pied piper from Braunau" now reigned supreme over 60 million Germans.

Pockets of caution, if not of overt resistance, nevertheless remained. One of these was the churches, whose concern over the tactics of the Hitler regime emerged as early as 1934 and would lead to open conflict three years later. Both Catholics and Protestants remonstrated against what they perceived to be the unmasked aggression of the SS against all forms of religion and the atheistic strains of leading National Socialists. Given the Prussian tradition of religious toleration since 1685, which had prompted the most prominent Junker families to protest Bismarck's *Kulturkampf* in the 1870s, a possible alliance of church, nobility, and officer corps loomed by the mid–1930s.

But like other power elites, the churches harbored ambivalent feelings toward National Socialism. Certainly clerics shared the Nazis' nationalism, approved of the NSDAP's opposition to Weimar, respected its emphasis on the family, and endorsed its anticommunism. Haunted by the specter of social revolution by the "godless" Marxists, church leaders looked sympathetically on the regime's law-and-order stance. But the movement's racial doctrines, political practices, and atheistic leanings alarmed many prelates. Nevertheless, they confined their criticism to religious matters, well aware that the public viewed Hitler as a decent man and looked to him for defense against the wild elements in the party. Most Germans at this time regarded Hitler as a God-fearing man.

The Nazis initially were restrained in their dealings with the churches. They recognized the churches' authority over their flock and regarded the organized Protestant and Catholic churches as potential threats to the regime. Thus, they spared churches the violence and persecution directed against the Left and the Jews. Instead, the Nazis adopted a dual strategy: accommodation with high-ranking prelates balanced by beatings and jailing of dissident parish priests.

As with other power elites, the church youth had quickly succumbed to Hitler's magnetism. In 1933 the Protestants sent their 700,000 Youth Group members into the Hitler Youth. Moreover, as early as 1932, Pastor Joachim Hossenfelder had organized a "German Christian" movement, one that soon proclaimed itself to be the "SA of Jesus Christ." Their slogan, "The swastika on our breast, the Cross in our heart," sent a clear message of their intended relations with National Socialism. Theology students and youthful pastors streamed into the NSDAP. On April 23, 1933, Hitler entrusted Ludwig Müller, an army chaplain, with creating a unified "Reich church."

Catholics tended not to be alarmed by Hitler. The Führer had been born a Catholic, paid his obligatory church tax, attended Mass on occasion, and laced his speeches with references to God and Providence. In 1931 the Roman church had lifted its earlier ban on Catholics joining the NSDAP. Two years later, it signed a Concordat with Hitler, guaranteeing the church basic rights of education and investiture while officially recognizing the Hitler state.

This honeymoon between party and churches became strained as the true nature of the new regime emerged. Between 1933 and 1937 the Third Reich relentlessly persecuted the smaller denominations and religious sects: Jehovah's Witnesses in 1933; Anabaptists in 1935; Seventh Day Adventists and Zionist Community in 1936; Free Pentacostalists, Baha'i, Church of the Apostle John, and Bible Faith Fellowship in 1937. Christian Scientists and the Salvation Army would follow in 1941. Pacifist faiths were decimated in 1938 by a federal law making refusal to answer the draft a capital offense. Most Masonic lodges, ranging from the Grand Master Lodge of the Three Globes to the Grand Prussian Lodge of Friendship, were closed between 1933 and 1935. All were accused of having international ties.

Protestant disenchantment with Hitler surfaced as early as September 1933, when Pastor Martin Niemöller, a former U-boat officer and vicar of a prosperous congregation in Berlin-Dahlem, sent his colleagues sixteen theses denouncing the "German Christian" movement. At a national synod at Wittenberg, where Martin Luther in 1517 had nailed his ninety-five theses on the city's church door, Niemöller denounced the regime's racial doctrines and in the name of two thousand fellow pastors appealed for a return to a free, evangelical church.

In November 1933 the "German Christians" replied with a formal call to abolish the Old Testament and the "Jewish" theology of St. Paul while raising Jesus Christ to full "Aryan" status. When half the German pastors (about seven thousand) rallied to Niemöller's side, the Protestant movement began to fragment. On January 4, 1934, Hitler moved to head off religious strife with a gag order on all clerical-political pronouncements.

But Hitler's goal was not to be realized. In May 1934 at Barmen, Niemöller mobilized the newly created "Confessing church" (*Bekennende Kirche*) on the basis of the scriptural foundations contained in the Bible (the so-called Barmen Declaration). Two years later, the Confessing church openly challenged the NSDAP's racial doctrines and accused the party of trying to create a substitute religion built on the glorification of race, a "religion of the blood." Niemöller's epistle was read from the pulpits in Prussia by three out of every four pastors.

Catholic disenchantment with Hitler grew more slowly than that of the Protestants, yet by 1936 it had become abundantly clear to church fathers that Hitler was not holding up his end of the Concordat; the NSDAP and its various organizations were making steady inroads into Catholic lay organizations. In March 1937 Pope Pius XI sent an encyclical written in German, "With Burning Sorrow," to every German parish. The pontiff, like Emile Zola in his famous tract *J'Accuse*[1] of 1898, began every paragraph, "With Burning Sorrow, we see. . .," followed by a litany of National Socialist transgressions against the church. In concluding, Pius XI called on German Catholics to resist the doctrine of race and Hitler idolatry and to uphold Christ, his church, and the primacy of Rome.

Hitler treated Niemöller's and Pius XI's attacks as calls to battle. Noted atheists such as Heinrich Himmler, Wilhelm Frick, and Baldur von Schirach rallied Martin Bormann, section chief in the party chancery, to move against the churches. The resultant measures ran from some 250 public "morality trials" of dissident clerics to beatings and incarceration at Dachau, as well as to the razing of churches as part of "urban renewal." Theologians such as Dietrich Bonhoeffer were forbidden to speak to or write for the public. Niemöller was dispatched to a concentration camp when the German Supreme Court at Leipzig failed to convict him of sedition.

[1] Zola had penned his tract *I Accuse* in defense of Captain Alfred Dreyfus, a Jew wrongly accused of high treason by the French army. It constituted a vitriolic denunciation of high-ranking army officers and government officials who refused to reopen the case in order to view fresh evidence.

It is difficult to discern Hitler's ultimate aims regarding religion. A few clues do emerge, however, from his *Secret Conversations*[1] during the war against the Soviet Union. On one occasion, Hitler promised to "extract retribution to the last farthing" from the churches: "No 'T' will remain uncrossed, no 'I' undotted in the balancing of our accounts." On another occasion, he grimly predicted that he would consider his "life's final task" to be "to solve the religious problem." Bormann in 1941 spoke about an eventual "liquidation of churches." The SS that same year depicted the "politicized church" as successor to the "Marxists of 1918."

Looking back on his turbulent career during the 1930s, Martin Niemöller simply yet powerfully described the invidious manner in which dictatorial regimes prey on disunited populaces:

> When the Nazis came for the Communists, I remained silent, for I was not a Communist. When they incarcerated the Social Democrats, I remained silent, for I was not a Social Democrat. When they came for the Catholics, I did not protest, for I was not a Catholic. When they came for me, there was no one left to protest.

The Idealized *Volksgemeinschaft*

Aside from occasional objections, most Germans favored the new regime. The Nazis had restored stability and provided jobs. They fostered a new classless atmosphere and promised to restore Germany's international power and respect. A public opinion poll in the Federal Republic of Germany in the 1970s still ranked the Third Reich second in popularity to the Wilhelmian Empire among historic regimes. The truth is that Hitler was able to proceed because of overwhelming public support. Plebiscites registering approval ratings of more than 99 percent may have been inflated, but they nevertheless reflected a tidal wave of public approval.

For the average German citizen, the period after 1933 brought law and order, peace and prosperity. By 1938 unemployment had fallen to 1.9 percent — compared with 26.4 percent in the United States and 12.9 percent in Britain — in large part due to Hitler's pump-priming public works projects and rearmament (discussed later in this section). More than 1.3 million women had joined the labor force since 1933. Trains ran on time, streets were safe and clean, stores overflowed with food and dry goods, and "asocials" were safely tucked away for "reeducation" in concentration camps. The few public excesses of the NSDAP were blamed on overly zealous party *Bonzen*. The

[1] This book, published posthumously, records Hitler's discussions with his elite circle at the Russian front, 1941–1944.

Führer was seen to stand above it all. In short, the NSDAP's slogan, "Germany Awake," was being realized.

The Olympic Games in the summer and winter of 1936 showed the world a nation on the march, a dynamic and united national community that had put defeat, revolution, inflation, and unemployment behind it. Conspicuous consumption became the order of the day for party leaders. Goebbels treated a thousand guests to a special "night of lights" on the Pfaueninsel in Berlin. Joachim von Ribbentrop hosted seven hundred guests under a tent at his villa at Berlin-Dahlem, where "Pommery champagne of the best quality flowed in rivers." Göring, not to be outdone, had a miniature eighteenth-century village reconstructed in the garden of his ministry. Amid the euphoria of the Olympics, Hitler issued a tart directive: "The German Army must be able to deploy in four years; German industry must be on a war footing in four years."

National Socialist views on domestic affairs had been shaped by two vividly contrasting historical experiences: the national solidarity of August 1914 and the collapse of the home front in November 1918. Hitler vowed to recreate the former and to preclude the latter. To this end, the new regime struggled after 1933 to forge a coherent, authoritarian national base. It tried to guarantee a basic minimum of food and consumer production in order to avoid domestic hunger and political unrest. But the armaments plants' rising demand for raw materials and the hard currency to acquire them sharply curtailed consumer production as early as the mid–1930s. War in 1939 would bring price controls to prevent rapid inflation and rationing to avoid the excesses of black marketeering as during World War I. Nazi propaganda made much of the fact that Hitler had replaced the class-driven, democratic, pluralistic Weimar system by a genuine *Volksgemeinschaft*.

Labor, which was crucial for future armaments production, had been reshaped into the German Labor Front on May 10, 1933. To the delight of all National Socialists who took the second word in the party's title to heart, labor was elevated and celebrated in the Law to Order National Work. The *Führerprinzip* was thereby applied to the workplace: in place of the "Marxist" system of confrontation between labor and capital, there now existed in theory a harmonious system in which "plant leaders" headed the "plant community," to which the "followers" owed obedience and loyalty. Special "shop councils" and "social courts of honor" were established to uphold the honesty of designated "trustees of work." Although the system appears cumbersome, it served the interests of the state by furthering the integration of labor into the nation.

To make the new social order more palatable, the Strength Through Joy (KdF) program, based on Mussolini's vast national recreation agency *Opera Nazionale Dopolavoro*, was institutionalized nationwide. Under its auspices, the state undertook to direct the leisure activities of the masses. It organized concerts, films, theaters, games, and exhibitions and offered them at greatly reduced prices to the public. By 1939 nearly one German in two had participated in Strength Through Joy. A special fleet of cruise ships, whose flagship was named after the Swiss National Socialist leader Wilhelm Gustloff, offered week-long cruises to Madeira. For those of lesser means (and perhaps greater party devotion) there were pilgrimages to Berchtesgaden, site of Hitler's mountaintop retreat. In raw numbers, KdF participation rose from 2.3 million people in 1934 to 10.3 million by 1938. At 60 reichsmarks for a seven-day cruise to Norway, its programs were within the reach of most laborers, who averaged 180 reichsmarks per month. SS reports claimed that nearly one in five KdF travelers was a worker. Regional studies suggest that the public by and large viewed KdF as the "great achievement of the Third Reich."

The program also sought to exert pressure on employers to improve the work environment. Building inspections, better ventilation, additional washing facilities, and clean cafeterias highlighted the Beauty of Labor program directed by Albert Speer within the KdF. By 1940 Beauty of Labor had redecorated twenty-six thousand workshops, provided eighteen thousand canteens and restrooms, and built three thousand factory sports facilities. Additionally, Nazi labor policies emphasized equal educational opportunities, job competitions, social mobility, and promotion based on merit. Strength Through Joy was designed to stabilize Germany's chronically precarious socioeconomic balance by eliminating social fragmentation and the class system. It also accorded the state a splendid chance to extend surveillance of its subjects to the workplace. It remains an open question how many workers were positively affected by KdF and thus reconciled to the regime.

Some prominent government figures, especially Goebbels, scoffed at this catering to mass tastes, and many cafés proudly displayed signs stating that they did not serve KdF groups, yet Strength Through Joy was probably the most successful social program devised by the Third Reich. By paying heed to the demands of modern industrial society for greater mobility, KdF became the precursor to the present-day German tourism boom.

The impact of National Socialist labor policies on German workers is difficult to gauge because of the regime's unique combination of subsidies and controls. Standard indicators such as the wage scale mean little in a closed system of wages and prices, where rabid fear of inflation led to massive government support for basic goods and services. Overall, wages and salaries in 1937 claimed a smaller share of the national product than they had in 1928, while profits in trade and industry claimed a larger share. Gross income per taxpayer declined 3 percent between 1933 and 1940. Piecework was favored over flat wages by the state; the job rather than the worker was paid. Highest wages were in the metal trades, machinery, and electrical goods, with the lowest in brewing, papermaking, and woodworking. Chemicals, hard-coal mining, and rubber assumed the middle positions. Finally, it is estimated that the cost of food absorbed up to 50 percent of the average worker's income.

Hitler's first economic priority after 1933 was to reduce and eventually to abolish unemployment. He used a two-pronged strategy: government-sponsored public works programs and an unprecedented rearmament program.

Hitler cared little about economic theories and simply demanded that the Reichsbank make available the requisite funds for reconstruction and rearmament. Hjalmar Schacht complied and pumped 12 billion reichsmarks into the German economy between 1933 and 1938. Defense expenditures rose from 4 percent of public outlays in 1933 to 50 percent by 1938; highway appropriations skyrocketed from 3 million reichsmarks in 1933 to 916 million in 1938. Unemployment fell by 2 million in 1933, and full employment was attained by 1935.

The idealized *Volksgemeinschaft* was most consistently touted by Nazi pundits in the agrarian sector. The farmer became the darling of Nazi ideology, with its emphasis on blood and soil (*Blut und Boden*) and the superior virtue of rural life. Radical agrarian reformers demanded nothing less than the creation of a new "peerage of blood and soil." The NSDAP's agrarian ideology was antimoney, antiartistocratic, antibourgeois, and anticity. Its antiurban animus was transformed by the Nazi state after 1933 into firm promises of total control of markets and prices, creation of new homesteads, and enhancement of farm security through generous credit provisions and population redistribution to the land.

In practice, the Third Reich produced fixed prices and guaranteed domestic markets but did little else for German farmers. The law on the New Formation of German Peasantry in June 1933 left the big estates untouched. The price of agricultural land doubled between 1932 and 1938. The number of new homesteads created, which had increased annually during the Weimar Republic, fell steadily throughout the Third Reich. Farm income lagged behind nonfarm income by at least 10 percent, and farm wages amounted to half those paid in industry and trade. The number of farm laborers fell by about 300,000 (3 percent) in the 1930s. Farm debt rose for small and middle-sized farms.

Contemporary observers described farmers as poor, coarse, dirty, and overworked. Their farms lacked sanitation, efficient use of fertilizer, good bookkeeping, and mechanization. More than half the farms in Germany had no running water. Agricultural education was eschewed by the youth: the number of university students of agriculture and veterinary science fell by 20 percent between 1932 and 1939.

German farmers needed mechanization, rationalization of ownership, and subsidized cooperatives. They received flattering rhetoric, thundering denunciations of mechanization, and stirring pleas to work harder and longer for increasingly little reward. In 1940 Max Rumpf, a German expert on agrarian conditions, concluded that farmers were overworked, technically inefficient, and ignorant. National Socialism had done little to improve their lot.

Aside from farmers and workers, women were perhaps most directly affected by the social policies of the Third Reich. National Socialist policy regarding women was highly ambivalent, a synthesis of reactionary and progressive policies. Hitler hailed mothers as the "most important citizens" of his state, provided they were "Aryan," healthy, and loyal. In 1933 Goebbels stated unequivocally that "a woman's first and most fitting place" was the family and that her "most glorious duty" was to "present her people and her country with a child." Thereby, both Hitler and Goebbels harked back to the "three Ks" of William II: *Kinder, Küche, Kirche* (children and kitchen, but not necessarily church).

The Hitler movement resurrected the old Weimar notion of community as well and even deployed the language of the Federation of German Women's Associations when it equated childbirth with military service. At the grassroots level, women by the millions joined new National Socialist mass organizations such as the German Women's Organization (*Deutsche Frauenschaft*), the German Women's Welfare Organization (*Deutsches Frauenwerk*), the League of German Girls (*Bund Deutscher Mädchen*, or BDM), the German Labor Front, and the People's Welfare (*Volkswohlfahrt*). More than two-thirds of all married working men and more than one-third of all female employees labored, generally without pay, on farms and in family businesses. Yet women also entered the registered labor force after unemployment had virtually been eliminated by 1937. The percentage of women in the overall work force climbed slowly from 34 percent in 1933 to 37 percent by 1939. Wages for women, however, remained 30 to 35 percent below those of males.

A quick glance at the German women's movement reveals the pyramidal structure of NSDAP organizations. Of the movement's 3.3 million members, one-third held an official position or title. There were 223,024 unit leaders, 59,802 cell leaders, 22,593 local leaders, 725 district leaders, and 32 *Gau* (regional) leaders. A similar structure organized the 600,000 girls of the BDM in 1933. Ten girls constituted a team, four teams a company, four companies a group, three to five groups a ring, four to six rings an *Untergau*, and twenty of the latter an *Obergau*. Thirty-five *Obergaue* answered directly to the Leader of Reich Youth, Baldur von Schirach. Berlin underground wit interpreted the initials BDM to stand for "union of German mattresses" or "soon to be German mother" in obvious and off-color allusion to the alleged sexual promiscuity of the Nazi girls' movement.

The East German novelist Christa Wolf's autobiographical *A Model Childhood* offers excellent insights into the life of a thirteen-year-old in the Young Girls (*Jungmädel*) branch of the BDM. Wolf, whose parents ran a grocery store during the Nazi period, describes how ten-year-old "Nelly" reacted to her first evening with the *Jungmädel* and what fun it was

> to become so familiar with the new word by repeating it to herself: "comradeship" meant the promise of a loftier kind of life . . . far removed also from the white figure in the store smock who was standing outside waiting for Nelly. . . . Where Mickey [the team leader] sang and played and marched with them and taught them games, there was something her mother couldn't give her, something she didn't want to miss.

Despite their participation in the NSDAP's mass organizations, women were excluded from membership in the party executive, the army, and the higher rungs of the civil service. By the mid–1930s, they no longer served

The idealized Brown *Volksgemeinschaft*: Nazi poster invites women to join the movement.

as judges, prosecutors, and lawyers. Around 1935 women constituted only 9 percent of the civil service, not surprising given that the Republic's 1932 Law on the Legal Position of Female Public Servants had effectively forced them out of the civil service. Women were denied high political office, and their access to professions was limited by a 1933 quota that permitted but 10 percent female students at universities. Schools concentrated studies for women on home economics and crafts, giving rise to the notion of a "pudding degree" (*Puddingabitur*) in place of Humboldt's august university-entrance degree. The reintroduction of official brothels was a further insult to the women's movement.

Because the Hitler state, like that of Frederick II, needed future soldiers, in 1938 a new law, much like the Prussian Civil Code of 1794, granted divorce without cause after three years' separation. Penalties for abortions were stiffened, and contraceptives became hard to find. On the other hand, 25,000 sex education centers were established by 1938 for those who required educational and psychological counselling. These measures notwithstanding, the average number of children per marriage did not rise during the Third Reich, and the average household size of 3.6 people in 1933 actually declined to 3.27 by 1939. The fertility rate between 1934 and 1939 was 20.4 births per thousand people, the same as in 1924. In fact, the two-child nuclear family remained the norm in the 1930s.[1]

Like Mussolini, Hitler rewarded motherhood. As early as 1933, interest-free loans of 1,000 reichsmarks were designed to get women out of the workplace and back into the home to bear children, and in 1936 a heavy tax was levied on childless couples. Conversely, by 1938 more than 2.5 million fathers and mothers enjoyed governmental child-support payments. A Reich Mothers' Service by 1936 provided not only training for mothers-to-be but also trips and vacations for mothers and their children. And on Mothers' Day 1939, 3 million women received the Cross of Honor of the German Mother: bronze for four to five children, silver for six to seven, and gold for eight or more.

On the less savory side, the eugenic theories of the League for the Protection of Motherhood from the first decade of the twentieth century were resurrected. The July 1933 Law on the Prevention of Hereditary Diseases in Children — which established compulsory sterilization of men and women with mental deficiencies, epilepsy, schizophrenia, deafness, blindness, and hereditary physical disabilities — was soon expanded to include alcoholism, prostitution, drug abuse, criminality, and long-term welfare dependence. By 1939 about 320,000 citizens had been sterilized. Abortion for "eugenic reasons" was introduced in 1935, and three years later abortion on demand was extended to all Jewish women. During World War II, the SS confidently reported that the general public supported "racial hygiene" practices and even "mercy killings," as long as doctors and patients alike agreed to the measures.

In 1935 SS leader Heinrich Himmler established fourteen homes for "racially acceptable women bearing illegitimate children." The stigma of the unwed mother was erased, at least in theory and within the SS. Under the Spring of Life (*Lebensborn*) program, young girls were exhorted to "donate a child to the Führer"; pre- and postnatal care were available to all. When the need to correct infertility arose, women could use the services of a *Zeugungshelfer* (literally, "procreation helper") provided by the SS. Hitler endorsed the program and during the war took delight in commenting on the "enhanced

[1] The increase in the number of German children born in the 1930s was due to a 20 percent increase in the number of marriages above the mean for the 1920s.

racial levels" in formerly "degenerate" regions such as Berchtesgaden, the Bohemian Forest, and the Masurian Lakes.

In a famous decree of October 1939, Himmler deemed it the "sublime task of German women of good blood" to "become mothers to children of soldiers setting off to battle," even if this lay beyond the bounds of law and outside the sphere of marriage. Conversely, SS men were admonished not to forget their duty to the fatherland: "Only he who leaves a child behind can die with equanimity." Over the ten years of its existence, *Lebensborn* registered about twelve hundred births, half of them illegitimate.

The ultimate effect of the *Lebensborn* program remains unclear. The SS as a whole failed to rise to the challenge: 61 percent of the SS were bachelors in 1939, while the married cohort (ninety-three thousand men) produced an average of only 1.1 children per family. Part of the answer to this low reproduction rate lies in the ages of the SS: two-thirds of its officers were bachelors under forty. The remaining one-third senior officers apparently fell victim to the middle-class materialistic malaise of having fewer children as prosperity increased. Given Himmler's great emphasis on utter secrecy with regard to the Spring of Life program, it is not surprising that few reactions from female participants in the program were documented.

Overall, then, the NSDAP's women's policy constituted a highly ambivalent confluence of policies that were modernist — a youth program, divorce laws, welfare measures, and state-sponsored volunteer organizations — and traditionalist — education, employment, and labor practices.

Hitler's controls extended to areas beyond labor, women, and the family. Every German was to be brought within earshot of the Führer's voice by mass production of a one-station radio, the People's Receiver (*Volksempfänger*). In addition, Hitler, who greatly admired Henry Ford, wished to initiate serial production of low-cost (1,000 reichsmarks) "KdF automobiles" that could cruise at 100 kilometers (about 65 miles) an hour on the new freeways (*Autobahnen*); in short, a car was to be put within the reach of every German family. When established automakers protested that they could not meet these specifications, Hitler ordered Ley's German Labor Front to build a new automobile plant at Wolfsburg. Although only a few prototypes of Ferdinand Porsche's "Volkswagen" were produced for the military under the Third Reich, the beloved "beetle" would become a major component of the West German "economic miracle" after the war.

Hitler's attitude toward popular culture was highly ambivalent. To be sure, there were the obligatory party and youth films, including perhaps the best known, *Hitler Youth Quex*,[1] but they did not fare well at the box office. Viewers instead flocked to theaters mainly to see historical re-creations, the so-

[1] This screen apotheosis of the Hitler Youth martyr Heinz Norkus told the story of a frail proletarian youngster who yearned to become a member of the Hitler Youth. "Quex" realized his dream, only to perish at the hands of Communist thugs while distributing NSDAP pamphlets.

called Frederick the Great and Bismarck films. In sharp contrast to the Soviet Union, where films about Lenin and Stalin became a cottage industry, not a single picture with Hitler as its central character was ever shot. The closest was Leni Riefenstahl's *Triumph of the Will*, a classic cinematographic record of the 1934 party rally at Nuremberg. Traditional operas and plays, albeit by Germanic composers and authors, remained as popular as ever.

Contemporary novels also maintained their appeal. While the regime railed against "Americanism" in general and "nigger culture" (or jazz) in particular, German readers by the thousands bought translations of the works of Virginia Wolfe, William Faulkner, and Ernest Hemingway. Margaret Mitchell's *Gone with the Wind* was a best-seller in the Third Reich. John Steinbeck's *Grapes of Wrath* likewise delighted German readers; its filmed version became a favorite of Hitler, who saw it as "evidence" of the decline of the American "blood and soil" community. Apparently, what mattered most to the regime was not so much what the public read, saw, and heard but rather the regime's power to dictate the nation's leisure activities. Robert Ley, head of the German Labor Movement, smugly proclaimed in 1938 that only sleep remained a purely private matter in the Third Reich.

Architecture, too, revealed the National Socialist ideal of popular culture. In an attempt to outdo the pyramids along the Nile and the victory arches along the Tiber, Hitler ordered Albert Speer, his favorite architect, whom he eventually entrusted to carry out his massive rebuilding schemes, to draw up great granite and marble monuments designed to reflect the grandeur of National Socialism "for millennia." Nuremberg was to receive a Congress Hall seating 60,000 for party rallies for the next eight hundred years, as well as a stadium for 405,000 people. Berlin was budgeted to get 60 million reichsmarks per annum for twenty years in order to reconstruct the city as a fitting "world capital." A Congress Hall for 250,000 people would serve as the Führer's temple. It has been calculated that Hitler's architectural gigantism for Berlin and Nuremberg alone would have exhausted every marble pit from Finland to Italy and from Spain to the Urals. In 1942 the giant construction cranes in Nuremberg were sent to Auschwitz to build IG-Farben's chemical plants designed to exploit slave labor (Jews and Soviet prisoners of war).

Indeed, the annual September party rallies at Nuremberg became the greatest spectacles of popular political culture. Hitler would deliver up to twenty speeches and review fifty thousand workers (spades at arms) as well as attend army maneuvers. The "blood flag" that the Führer had carried on November 9, 1923, would be unfurled for the ceremonious swearing in of new SA and SS units. Parade after parade followed band after band. An entire nation seemed on the march. French journalists were convinced that the new man, the *homme hitlerien*, had been forged in the crucible of the new *Volksgemeinschaft*.

Hitler took special delight in addressing the thousands of youths gathered at the Nuremberg Stadium each year. Indeed, the new regime paid its greatest attention to youth and their education. While young people in Britain, France,

Triumph of Terror: The SS on parade at Nuremberg (1936).

and the United States suffered hopelessly in the grip of the Great Depression, the Hitler state gave youth a sense of mission and an assurance of inheritance. Regional and national festivals, athletic competitions, and pastoral hikes effectively integrated youth into the state. Youth's anthem proclaimed that it was on the march, that its flag was more precious even than life. Hitler constantly assured the young that everything he did was for their benefit; in time, the torch would be passed to them. Much of this rhetoric and activity harked back to the youth movement of the Wilhelmian era.

But there were dark undertones to the regime's slavish veneration of youth. Gregor Strasser had given youth its slogan long before the *Machtergreifung* in 1933: "Stand aside, old ones!" Thereafter, the party indoctrinated the young with its concepts of race, blood, soil, honor, mission — and hatred of all that was alien and "undesirable." Hitler envisaged nothing less than a new youth, made of steel. He vowed to "eradicate millennia of domestication" and to forge an "athletic youth." Above all, the Führer wished once again to see "the free, glorious beast of prey sparkle in their eyes."

In order to mobilize German youth, Hitler had appointed Baldur von Schirach "Youth Leader of the German Reich" on June 17, 1933. Within months, Schirach concentrated the diverse youth groups, ranging from the 70,000 Boy Scouts to the 700,000 Protestant Youths, into four party organizations commanded by 400,000 male and female youth leaders. For those between the ages of ten and fourteen, there was the German People's Youth

(*Deutsche Jungvolk*) for boys and the Federation of German Young Girls (*Bund Deutscher Jungmädel*) for girls; for those between the ages of fourteen and eighteen, the Hitler Youth for boys and the League of German Girls for girls. In 1934 Saturdays were officially proclaimed "youth days," and in December 1936 the party's youth movement, which encompassed 60 percent of all young Germans, was transformed into an official state agency. By 1938 nearly 9 million boys and girls were officially enrolled in the Hitler Youth.

Education remained highly traditional in the Third Reich. Most teachers and professors remained at their posts and joined the NSDAP. Students continued to move from the elementary schools (*Volksschule*) to the two-tiered high school system of *Gymnasium* and *Realgymnasium*. The *Abitur* (diploma) continued as the university entrance certificate. And university students came from the same social strata as before 1933: children of upper- and middle-class civil servants constituted half the university student population between 1933 and 1939. Although the Nazis in 1938 made available select university admissions for non-*Abiturienten* with good records in the Hitler Youth or Labor Service, the results were barely visible: these students made up only 1 percent of all university enrollments by 1939.

Outside the normal school system, a host of competing special schools had been established as early as 1933–1934 by Hitler, Himmler, Hess, Röhm, and Ley to educate youth along National Socialist lines. The SS set up the so-called National-Political Training Institutions (*Nationalpolitische Erziehungsanstalt*, or "Napola") for boys between the ages of ten and eighteen. Resurrecting the ideals of the old Prussian Cadet Schools, these institutions were designed to educate the future administrative and military elites of Germany. Most students came from civil service (26 percent) and salaried employee (22 percent) backgrounds. For boys aged twelve or over who had distinguished themselves in the *Jungvolk*, the junior branch of the Hitler Youth, Schirach established special "Adolf Hitler Schools." Although social standing played no part in the selection of students, 80 percent of all pupils stemmed from the solid middle class; one-third came from families engaged in commerce and trade. Instruction centered on "racial hygiene," biology, leadership qualities, administration, and geography.

The top graduates of the Napolas and the Adolf Hitler Schools could enroll in special indoctrination courses, each lasting a year, at three so-called *Ordensburgen* (castles of a knightly order). Only married party members between the ages of twenty-three and thirty qualified. As educators of the new "nobility of the nation," these pseudo-Germanic, castlelike academies stood directly under NSDAP control. To give the *Ordensburgen* historical continuity and direct the attention of their pupils to the future "Greater German Empire" in the east, the final year of course work was held at the Marienburg, the ancient headquarters of the Teutonic Knights, who in the thirteenth century had been sent by the papacy to colonize Slavic lands. Alfred Rosenberg, the self-styled ideologue of National Socialism, even planned to establish a special

NSDAP University, but this project never materialized. Indeed, the entire party school system defies evaluation due to its brief existence.

The broad scope of National Socialist designs on the nation's human material was perhaps best expressed by Hitler in a speech at Reichenberg in December 1938:

> This youth learns nothing else but to think German, to act German; and when these boys and girls at age ten come into our organizations in order for the first time to experience fresh air, then four years later they will graduate from the Jungvolk into the Hitler Youth, and there we will again have them for four years. Especially then, we will not surrender them into the hands of our old class begetters, but instead will take them at once into the party, the Labor Front, the SA or the SS. . . . And when they have been there for eighteen months or two years, and still have not become totally committed National Socialists, we will send them into the Labor Service. . . . And whatever then still remains of class consciousness or social snobbery after six or seven months will be dealt with by the army for two years — and when they return from there after two, three or four years, to make sure that they will not backslide, we will again take them into the SA, SS, and so on; and they will never again be free for the rest of their lives.

It would be difficult to imagine the Free German Youth of the German Democratic Republic without this precursor.

Into the Darkness: The SS State

A black shadow quite literally hung over Germany: Heinrich Himmler's SS. From modest beginnings in the 1920s, the *Schutzstaffel* emerged full-blown in 1934 after its role in the Night of the Long Knives. By 1937 Himmler commanded a five-headed hydra. The General SS consisted of civilian security forces with rudimentary military training. The Reserve SS assisted the regular police and prepared for future front-line duty. The Death's Head Units, originating from concentration camp guards, persecuted "asocial" elements and upheld racial standards. The Security Service (SD) under former naval officer Reinhard Heydrich was entrusted with "ideological intelligence" for both party and state. And the Race and Settlement Main Office supervised the maintenance of racial purity and devised policies for the colonization of future conquered territory in the east. A consummate empire builder, Himmler later would expand his domain to include the formidable Armed SS (*Waffen-SS*), heavily armed forces that, after the abortive attempt on Hitler's life in the summer of 1944, would rise to equal status with army, navy, and air force. The motto of the SS, "Loyalty Is My Honor," revealed its simplistic mentality.

The SS represented a perfect fusion between party and state. An ideological combat unit with direct ties to the Führer, it was the purest manifestation

"Loyalty Is My Honor": Heinrich Himmler of the SS (1938).

of National Socialist thought and power. Systematized terror became the SS's primary accomplishment. In the person of Himmler, the organization's corporate outlook represented a strange composite of antique and modern thought, romantic and rational practices. In the catacombs of Himmler's head-quarter castle, the Wewelsburg near Paderborn, the SS juxtaposed the most sophisticated electronic surveillance equipment available with pseudo-runic rituals dating back to the ancient Germanic tribes. Relentless waves of mass executions stood in stark contrast to Himmler's adamant opposition to hunting (as a dedicated environmentalist wishing to preserve the purity of the forest). Idolization of modern technology and communications was balanced against fears of destroying the traditions of a highly romanticized German medieval past, much like the youth movement before 1914.

Himmler's ideal SS recruit was racially healthy, physically alert, and tall. Somehow, he said, recruits "had to possess the desired blood." In order to maintain a homogeneous and exclusive SS "family," Himmler as early as 1931 had stipulated that those in the SS intending to marry seek his approval. In addition to examining the "racial hygiene" of the prospective bride, Himmler also demanded that she submit a picture of herself in a bathing suit. By 1935 all SS upper-echelon leaders (and soon every recruit) had to offer proof of racial purity (non-Jewish ancestry). The following year, Himmler decreed marriage between the ages of twenty-five and thirty to be ideal. Berlin underground humor was quick to react: the "ideal Aryan"[1] was described as being as blond as Hitler, as thin as Göring, and as athletic as Goebbels. It might also have included as handsome as Himmler.

Although most SS volunteers were men who spied their chance for rapid promotion in a new ideological force — and hence did not hail from the traditional elites of property, education, and birth — a surprising number of nobles nevertheless enlisted. By 1938 the German nobility, including the hereditary princes of Mecklenburg, Waldeck-Pyrmont, and Hesse, provided almost one-fifth of the members of the SS elite. With the annexation of Austria in 1938, composition of the SS took on a decidedly south German flavor.

On Hitler's birthday in 1934, Himmler was entrusted with command of the Prussian Secret State Police (*Gestapo*). On June 17, 1936, Hitler appointed him head of all German police forces. As Reichsführer-SS and Chief of the German Police, Himmler was subject only to the commands of his Führer. The *Gestapo*, especially, was placed beyond the reach of all legal authorities. Under Adolf Eichmann, a special subsection (IV B4)[2] of the division within Reinhard Heydrich's SD dealing with Catholicism, Protestantism, and Freemasonry would later gain special notoriety as executors of the "Jewish question."

The SS set out on the road to terror with the arrest of more than twenty-five thousand people in Prussia alone in the aftermath of the Reichstag fire on February 28, 1933. In order to handle the flood of internees, on March 20 Himmler ordered construction of a concentration camp, or *Konzentrationslager* (KZ), at

---

1 The word *Aryan* is a linguistic term referring to the Indo-European group of languages. Its root comes from Sanskrit and means "noble." In the nineteenth century it was given racial connotations by writers such as Houston Stewart Chamberlain. Hitler equated the word *Aryan* with "pure" and *Jew* with "impure."

2 In September 1939 the *Gestapo* became Section IV within the newly created Reich Main Security Office (RSHA) of the SS; B4 became the subsection of the *Gestapo* dealing with Jews, Catholics, Protestants, and non-German ethnic groups.

The Aryan Ideal: Hermann Göring.

the former munitions factory at Dachau. Others, all with the motto *Arbeit Macht Frei* (Work Liberates) emblazoned above their entrance gates, followed at Oranienburg, Esterwegen, Sachsenhausen, Buchenwald, and Papenburg, to name but several. A special female KZ eventually was established at Ravensbrück, north of Berlin. By the end of July 1933, nearly thirty thousand political prisoners were housed in these rudimentary concentration camps. Hitler personally warded off all legal inquiries into the nature of the camps.

"Work Liberates": Dachau, 1933.

In July 1934 Theodor Eicke, Dachau's first commandant, was promoted to "Inspector of Concentration Camps and SS Guard Units." His pupils at Dachau had included Rudolf Höss, future commandant of Auschwitz. Under Eicke's supervision, each camp was regulated by about 120 SS Death's Head volunteers; another one thousand to twelve hundred guards were stationed nearby in barracks. Inmates were identified by colored triangular patches on their uniforms: red for political offenders, black for "asocials," purple for Christian fundamentalists, green for common criminals, blue for would-be emigrants, and pink for homosexuals. Jewish prisoners in addition received a yellow patch, thus according them a six-sided Star of David. The KZ system faced its most severe test in November 1938, when about thirty-five thousand Jews arrived in the wake of a national pogrom.

National Socialism did not possess a coherent "Jewish policy" before 1938, apart from a general desire to make Germany *judenrein* (free of Jews). The entire Jewish policy remained erratic, selective, and arbitrary. Each government office employed its own "specialist" on the "Jewish question," and each proceeded at its own pace. This confusion was due partly to rivalry that existed throughout the 1930s between party and state and partly because Hitler did not want to jeopardize economic development and foreign trade by excluding Jews from the nation's business sector too rapidly. It also resulted from the inability of party and state leaders to define a clear, unified concept regarding how to "solve the Jewish question."

Generally, the NSDAP was sharply divided into "radicals" (hardliners) and "rationalists" (or gradualists). The former included men such as Goebbels, Ley, and Streicher; the latter, Himmler and Heydrich. Hitler, while ranting about the need to make Germany *judenrein*, cleverly remained above the fray and refused to become embroiled in these bureaucratic turf squabbles, retaining the final decision for himself. In the meantime he encouraged his minions to curtail the civil rights of Jewish citizens, restrict their occupational spheres, and trigger sporadic anti-Jewish demonstrations. The regime's policy regarding Germany's 530,000 Jews has been depicted as one of "creeping persecution." Tragically, many Jews misread this lack of a coherent national "Jewish policy" as lack of intent and clung, however hopelessly, to the illusion that they might escape persecution and eventually endure in Germany.

Under the "Aryan Paragraphs" of the Civil Service Reconstruction Law of April 1933, Jews were expelled from all government and public institutions; the conscription law of March 1935 expressly barred their service with the armed forces. The Nuremberg racial laws of September 1935 deprived "non-Aryans" of full citizenship, forbade marriage between Jews and "Aryans," prohibited service by "Aryan" women in Jewish homes, and even outlawed "heavy petting" in public among diverse racial groups. These edicts seem to have been received by the general public with benevolent indifference. In 1938 Germany's annexation of Austria (*Anschluss*) exacerbated the "Jewish question" by adding 200,000 Austrian Jews to the Greater German Reich.

Who was a Jew? The Nuremberg "racial laws" offered no clear answer. On November 14, 1935, a First Decree to the Reich Citizenship Law clarified matters somewhat: a "Jew is someone who is descended from three full-blooded Jewish grandparents." But what was the basis for being classified a full-blooded Jew? The First Decree offered this interpretation: "belonging to the Jewish religion." Was this a *racial* policy? As villages vied with one another to rid themselves of Jews, the party received countless inquiries concerning specific measures to be taken against Jewry. The Second Decree, on December 21, 1937, simply suggested that Jews be formally barred from all occupations and socially isolated.

And what about Hitler? In April 1937, during a speech to regional NSDAP leaders, Hitler slyly hinted at his own "Jewish policy":

> The final goal of our overall policy is naturally clear to all. Whenever I act, I am concerned not to undertake a step that will hurt us. You know, I always venture right to the edge of what is permissible, but never over it.

Using an analogy from boxing, Hitler assured his listeners that he did not immediately threaten an opponent with force simply for the sake of fighting. Growing more animated, he accorded a look into the future of the German Jews: "I want to annihilate you." Finally, Hitler averred that he would back the Jews into a corner, from which they could not retaliate: "I will thrust my dagger into your heart."

Matters came to a head early in November 1938. On November 7 Herschel Grynszpan, fearing for the safety of his parents who, as Polish Jews, had been expelled from Germany by Hitler on October 27, shot Ernst vom Rath, an official at the German embassy in Paris. Rath died of his wounds two days later. The NSDAP elite was gathered in Munich to celebrate the abortive beer-hall putsch of 1923. News of the assassination fell like a bomb. Goebbels, in trouble with his Führer over the elitist nature of his propaganda as well as his many extramarital affairs, seized the initiative, and the SA spied its chance to regain the status it had lost during the Night of the Long Knives on June 30, 1934. With Hitler's verbal approval, Goebbels launched a nationwide pogrom. Its cause and intent were clear: a secret report of the Supreme Party Court in February 1939 held Goebbels to be the instigator of the pogrom and acknowledged that while "the party was not to appear to outsiders as originator of the demonstration, in reality it had organized them and carried them out."

On the night of November 9, 1938, the SA, armed with hammers, axes, and crowbars, went about its grisly work. They destroyed 267 synagogues, 844 stores, and 171 private dwellings; ransacked countless apartments, unceremoniously dumping their contents on the streets below; and murdered at least ninety-one Jews. Michael Lucas, a butcher, recorded the night's activity at the small village of Hoengen near Aachen:

> After a while, the Stormtroops were joined by people who were not in uniform; and suddenly, with one loud cry of, "Down with the Jews," the gathering outside produced axes and heavy sledgehammers. They advanced towards the little synagogue . . . burst the door open, and the whole crowd, by now shouting and laughing, stormed into the little House of God. . . . When the first rays of a cold and pale November sun penetrated the heavy dark clouds, the little synagogue was but a heap of stone, broken glass and smashed-up woodwork.

The SS arrested about thirty-five thousand Jews the next day and dispatched them to Dachau, Sachsenhausen, and Buchenwald. The almost uninterrupted sound of breaking glass that night gave rise to the term *Kristallnacht* (Crystal Night) for the pogrom.

Not all Germans remained unmoved by these events. South German Catholics, especially, regarded the display of violence as an affront to German "culture and decency." Many regretted the wanton destruction of property. In Württemberg Pastor Julius von Jan sermonized about the "nation's infamy" as a result of Crystal Night, and in Berlin Father Bernhard Lichtenberg of St. Hedwig's Cathedral spoke out from the pulpit against the atrocities. Jan was brutally beaten by an angry Nazi mob and imprisoned; Lichtenberg died in Nazi captivity in 1943.

On November 12 in Berlin, Göring, in his capacity as head of the Four Year Plan, castigated the orgy of destruction in the presence of Goebbels. Spontaneous violence was anathema to the regime, he said. Instead, Göring moved "blow-by-blow" to destroy German Jewry. He imposed a collective fine of 1 billion reichsmarks on the "Israelite community" for the damages of *Kristallnacht*; appropriated all Jewish insurance money to the state; forbade Jews to

"Crystal Night": Ravaged Jewish-owned stores in Berlin (November 1938).

possess stocks, bonds, jewelry, and paintings; and severely curtailed their use of public facilities and transportation. Finally, Göring, acting on Hitler's orders, decreed that in the future the "Jewish question" would be transferred to the SS. Thus, while Goebbels crowed that "the radical position has carried the day," in reality the "rationalists" — that is, the practitioners of "cold terror" — had triumphed. Authorities in Swabia, Franconia, Lower Bavaria, and the Upper Palatinate reported that most citizens expressed "fullest understanding" for this "legal punishment" of the Jews.

A Central Agency for Jewish Emigration was established by the SS early in 1939, but the problem was that most other countries maintained stiff immigration restrictions and quotas. Attempts to send Jews to Argentina, Canada, Chile, Colombia, Cuba, Paraguay, and the United States largely proved fruitless. Although Britain accepted more than 10,000 German Jewish children, it concurrently exerted diplomatic pressure on Greece, Rumania, Turkey, and Yugoslavia not to allow ships with Jewish immigrants to depart for Palestine. Roughly 170,000 Jews left the Reich before emigration was banned on October 23, 1941. Most went to Belgium, Czechoslovakia, Denmark, France, and the Netherlands, where the German assault of 1939–1940 would again subject them to German control.

Biological, racial antisemitism, as outlined by Hitler in *Mein Kampf*, was gaining momentum. At the meeting on November 12, 1938, Göring had warned that in case of "external conflict, a great reckoning with the Jews would result." On the sixth anniversary of the *Machtergreifung*, Hitler informed the Reichstag as well as foreign diplomats in Berlin that any future war would result in the destruction of German, indeed European, Jewry. The road to Auschwitz was open.

Suggested Readings

The vast literature on National Socialism and Adolf Hitler almost defies description. Two splendid introductions are Allan Mitchell, *The Nazi Revolution: Hitler's Dictatorship and the German Nation* (Lexington, Mass., 1990), and Jeremy Noakes and Geoffrey Pridham, eds., *Nazism: A History in Documents and Eyewitness Accounts*, 2 vols. (New York, 1990). The early history of the Führer is provided by Bradley F. Smith, *Adolf Hitler: His Family, Childhood, and Youth* (Stanford, 1967); of his movement, by Dietrich Orlow, *The History of the Nazi Party, 1919–1933*, 2 vols. (Pittsburgh, 1969–1973). By far the best overview of the Hitler regime is Karl Dietrich Bracher, *The German Dictatorship: The Origins, Structure, and Effects of National Socialism* (New York, 1970); but Martin Broszat, *The Hitler State: The Foundation and Development of the Internal Structure of the Third Reich* (London, 1981), is valuable as well.

The best-known biography of Hitler remains Alan Bullock, *Hitler: A Study in Tyranny* (New York, 1964), which offers much of the same as an earlier treatment by Konrad Heiden, *Der Fuehrer: Hitler's Rise to Power* (Boston, 1944). A more recent comprehensive biography is Joachim Fest, *Hitler* (New York, 1974). William Carr, *Hitler: A Study in Personality and Politics* (New York, 1979), provides some interesting insights, as do Ian Kershaw, *The "Hitler Myth": Image and Reality in the Third Reich* (Oxford, 1987), and Sebastian Haffner, *The Meaning of Hitler* (Cambridge, Mass., 1983). Psychohistory rests with Rudolph Binion, *Hitler Among the Germans* (New York, 1976); Robert G. L. Waite, *The Psychopathic God: Adolf Hitler* (New York, 1977); and Walter C. Langer, *The Mind of Adolf Hitler: The Secret Wartime Report* (New York, 1972).

The question of the NSDAP's electoral base has been addressed by Richard F. Hamilton, *Who Voted for Hitler?* (Princeton, 1982), and Thomas Childers, *The Nazi Voter: The Social Foundations of Fascism in Germany, 1919–1933* (Chapel Hill, N.C., 1984). Michael Kater, *The Nazi Party: A Social Profile of Members and Leaders, 1919–1945* (Cambridge, Mass., 1983), has examined the composition of the party's leadership. Everyday life in Nazi Germany has been explored by Richard Bessel, ed., *Life in the Third Reich* (New York, 1987); Ian Kershaw, *Popular Opinion and Political Dissent in the Third Reich* (Oxford, 1983); Detlev Peukert, *Inside Nazi Germany: Conformity, Opposition and Racism in Everyday Life* (New Haven, Conn., 1989); and Benjamin C. Sax and

Dieter Kuntz, eds., *Inside Hitler's Germany: A Documentary History of Life in the Third Reich* (Lexington, Mass., and Toronto, 1992).

Regional studies abound. The classic for decades has been William Sheridan Allen, *The Nazi Seizure of Power: The Experience of a Single German Town, 1922–1945* (Chicago, 1965). New investigations have emerged since: Geoffrey Pridham, *Hitler's Rise to Power: The Nazi Movement in Bavaria, 1923–1933* (New York, 1973); Jeremy Noakes, *The Nazi Party in Lower Saxony, 1921–1933* (London, 1971); and Johnpeter Horst Grill, *The Nazi Movement in Baden, 1920–1945* (Chapel Hill, N.C., 1983).

The "brown revolution" history was pioneered by David Schoenbaum, *Hitler's Social Revolution: Class and Status in Nazi Germany, 1933–1939* (New York, 1966), and Ralf Dahrendorf, *Society and Democracy in Germany* (New York, 1967). More recent interpretations are Richard Grunberger, *The 12-Year Reich: A Social History of Nazi Germany, 1933–1945* (New York, 1971), and Tim Mason, *Social Policy in the Third Reich* (New York, 1990). The role of youth in Hitler Germany rests with Walter Z. Laqueur, *Young Germany: A History of the German Youth Movement* (New York, 1962), and Peter D. Stachura, *Nazi Youth in the Weimar Republic* (Santa Barbara, Calif., 1975). The labor movement remains a stepchild of historical investigation; students must still rely on Max H. Kele, *Nazis and Workers: National Socialist Appeals to German Labor, 1919–1933* (Chapel Hill, N.C., 1972), and on the more recent biographical treatment by Ronald Smelser, *Robert Ley, Hitler's Labor Front Leader* (Oxford, 1988). By contrast, women's history has been blessed by Jill Stephenson, *Women in Nazi Society* (London, 1975), and *The Nazi Organization of Women* (London, 1981), as well as Claudia Koonz, *Mothers in the Fatherland: Women, the Family, and Nazi Politics* (New York, 1987). See also the survey by Ute Frevert, *Women in German History: From Bourgeois Emancipation to Sexual Liberation* (New York, 1990).

National Socialism's appeal to the agrarian sector can be studied in Timothy Tilton, *Nazism, Neo-Nazism, and the Peasantry* (Bloomington, Ind., 1975), and John Farquharson, *The Plough and the Swastika: N.S.D.A.P. and Agriculture in Germany, 1928–1945* (London, 1976). The symbiotic relationship between industry and Nazism has benefited greatly from the recent investigations by Henry A. Turner, Jr., *German Big Business and the Rise of Hitler* (New York, 1985); Avraham Barkai, *Nazi Economics: Ideology, Theory and Policy* (New Haven, Conn., 1990); John Gillingham, *Industry and Politics in Nazi Germany* (New York, 1985); and, more narrowly and apologetically, Peter Hayes, *Industry and Ideology: IG Farben in the Nazi Era* (Cambridge, 1987). Also of interest is Richard J. Overy, *The Nazi Economic Recovery, 1932–1938* (London, 1982).

The history of the connection between religion and National Socialism began with studies of Catholicism: Gordon C. Zahn, *German Catholics and Hitler's Wars* (New York, 1962), and Guenter Lewy, *The Catholic Church and Nazi Germany* (New York, 1964). The overall Christian reaction to Hitler was pioneered by John S. Conway, *The Nazi Persecution of the Churches, 1933-45* (New York, 1968). See also the more recent treatment by Ernst Christian Helmreich, *The German Churches Under Hitler: Background, Struggle, and Epilogue* (Detroit, 1979).

The world of academia and art has not been neglected. Geoffrey J. Giles, *Students and National Socialism in Germany* (Princeton, 1985); Gilmer W. Blackburn, *Education in the Third Reich: A Study of Race and History in Nazi Textbooks* (Albany, N.Y., 1985); and Jacques R. Pauwels, *Women, Nazis and Universities: Female University Students in the Third Reich, 1933–1945* (Westport, Conn., and London, 1984), have offered the first English-language treatments of schools, students, and curricula. The scientific community has been studied by Alan D. Beyerchen, *Scientists Under Hitler: Politics and the Physics Community in the Third Reich* (New Haven, Conn., 1985); and architecture by Barbara Miller Lane, *Architecture and Politics in Germany, 1918–1945* (Cambridge, Mass., 1985). Henry Grosshans, *Hitler and the Artists* (New York, 1983), has tackled the thorny issue of the Führer's views on art, and David Welch, *Propaganda and the German Cinema* (New York, 1985), has examined National Socialism's clever exploitation of film.

The role of antisemitism in the Third Reich has been outlined by Sarah Gordon, *Hitler, Germans and the "Jewish Question"* (Princeton, 1984). Still useful is Karl A. Schleunes, *The Twisted Road to Auschwitz: Nazi Policy Toward German Jews, 1933–1939* (Urbana, Ill., 1970). The road from persecution to annihilation has most recently been surveyed by Avraham Barkai, *From Boycott to Annihilation: The Economic Struggle of German Jews, 1933–1943* (Hanover, N.H., 1989), and François Furet, ed., *Unanswered Questions: Nazi Germany and the Genocide of the Jews* (New York, 1989). Of particular interest to students is Werner T. Angress, *Between Fear and Hope: Jewish Youth in the Third Reich* (New York, 1988).

CHAPTER

9

"WORLD POWER OR DEMISE": HITLER'S FOREIGN POLICY, 1933–1945

For the good of the German people, we must wish for war every fifteen or twenty years.

Adolf Hitler, August 1941

The alpha and the omega of National Socialism was war. All that Hitler and his paladins did was designed toward this end. The seizure of power, the "brown revolution," the creation of a *Volksgemeinschaft*, the attack on internationalism in the form of churches, Jews, and Marxism, the institutionalization of terror under the SS: all were but steps to create a united domestic base from which Hitler could conduct his expansionistic foreign policy.

Rivers of ink have been spilled over Hitler's foreign policy. Was he a madman pursuing messianic visions? Or was he merely a traditional German statesman in the mold of Bismarck or Stresemann? Did Hitler have a clear timetable of aggression, or was he the consummate opportunist, taking only what others offered? This chapter will argue that Hitler possessed a general strategy to revise the Versailles *Diktat*, as well as a bold design to seize territories in order to build a Greater German Empire from the Pyrenees to the Urals but that he acted flexibly and opportunistically in implementing these plans.

Perhaps no other major statesman in history has ever revealed his program, in both writing and speeches, as clearly and as often as Hitler. One can almost sympathize with the Führer's outburst in August 1939 — "Idiots, have I ever told a lie in my life?" — when he was informed by Birger Dahlerus, a Swedish middleman during the Polish crisis, that London did not trust Hitler's words. Once more, Joseph Goebbels hit the mark in the spring of 1940, when he reviewed the events of the 1930s:

> In 1933, a French minister should have said (and had I been French minister-president, I would have said): the man who wrote the book *Mein Kampf*, in

> which this and that is written, has become chancellor. We cannot tolerate that man in our neighborhood. Either he goes, or we march. That would have been totally logical.

Of course, the French declined to act accordingly and instead permitted Germany "to pass unimpeded through the risk zone" of revising Versailles. Europe paid the price.

Hitler possessed definite, fixed views on foreign policy even before he came to power in 1933. These centered on two related systems of ideas: the doctrines of race and space. Hitler nurtured a virulent, vulgarized version of social Darwinism. The rise and fall of civilizations, he believed, was directly related to their success or failure in maintaining racial purity. Human beings, like plants and insects, either survived or perished. This was a simple law of nature, one that had nothing to do with morality and everything to do with the will to fight, with struggle (*Kampf*). To Hitler, space translated into agriculturally usable land. In the eternal struggle for space, the stronger won, seized the space, proliferated in that space, and then extended that space yet again. Thus, by definition expansion was limitless: in the end, there could only be total victory or utter defeat, *Weltmacht* or *Niedergang*.

The key to Hitler's foreign policy was European Russia. There was the requisite living space (*Lebensraum*), and there resided the major negative force in the struggle for survival, European Jewry. Bolshevism was merely the latest configuration of the timeless "Jewish conspiracy" to dominate the world. Hence, only a war of racial-biological extermination against the "Jewish-Bolshevik conspiracy" could secure the future for Germany. Hitler had no love for those revisionists who desired restoration of "the borders of 1914"; his radical revisionism aimed to extend the Reich's borders at least as far east as the Ural Mountains.

Hitler offered no specific timetable of aggression. There was no clock that he wound up in 1933 and then stood back and allowed to unwind. In his foreign policy means, Hitler was an opportunist, a manipulator of events. He cleverly exploited the favorable international situation facing Germany in the 1930s. Britain and France were determined to avoid a repetition of the slaughter of 1914–1918 by any and all means; the former was concerned primarily about maintaining its far-flung empire, and the latter sought safety behind the massive fortifications of its Maginot Line. After 1919 the United States had withdrawn into isolation. The Soviet Union was beset by internal upheaval. Thus Hitler's strategy was clear: to stress Germany's peaceful intentions while covering its true goals, to avoid creating a unified opposition while gaining Britain and Italy as allies — and all the while preparing Germany for a war of conquest. The critical issue was whether Hitler would be able to impress his ideas on events, or whether events and realities would reshape his ideas.

Revising Versailles

Three days after being appointed chancellor, Adolf Hitler convened a meeting of high-level military planners at the office of General Kurt von Hammerstein-Equord, chief of the army. In surprisingly candid terms, the Führer stated that his overall program centered on "conquest of *Lebensraum* in the east" and its "ruthless Germanization." Step by step, he laid out the general contours of his program: reordering of the German state by "extirpating Marxism" and reestablishing the nation's "will to arms," reclaiming political power under the slogan "build up of the armed forces," and finally deploying that armed might to acquire *Lebensraum*.

There were no objections. In fact, Hitler's general policy was in line with the "revisionist" policies of his listeners: restoration of the borders of 1914, if need be by a new partition of Poland; return of Imperial Germany's colonies that were taken at Versailles; and establishment of a German-dominated *Mitteleuropa*, as envisaged by Friedrich List in the 1840s and enunciated by Chancellor Theobald von Bethmann Hollweg in September 1914. Hitler's reference to "Germanization" of eastern territories harked back to the eastern colonization schemes put forth by Generals Paul von Hindenburg and Erich Ludendorff, among others, in 1917–1918.

Hitler's foreign policy strategy was to destroy the multinational Versailles system and to force each of its members to conclude bilateral agreements with Berlin. To achieve this end, he sought to isolate France by way of agreements with Britain and Italy and to push ahead with German rearmament at utmost speed. Once the latter goal had been achieved, Hitler devised the twin tactics of public rhetoric and naked force. The Führer would conduct a policy of driving his adversaries to the brink of war in crisis after crisis that he manufactured without ever giving them a hint whether he was prepared, as he undoubtedly was, to resort to armed force to press his case.

Hitler made his first major move on the European chessboard on October 14, 1933, when he withdrew Germany from the League of Nations. By following the Japanese precedent of May 1933, Hitler stressed that the League constituted nothing more than a screen for Anglo-French enforcement of the Versailles *Diktat*. A national referendum brought 95 percent approval for this measure. Next, Hitler dumbfounded the West on January 26, 1934, by signing a ten-year Non-Aggression Pact with Poland, wherein both states renounced the use of force to settle potential differences.[1]

That Hitler was still a novice at international relations became evident in the summer of 1934 and involved the "birthplace of National Socialism,"

---

[1] Marshal Józef Piłsudski apparently took *Mein Kampf* seriously and in 1933 had proposed a preemptive strike against Hitler's Germany. His French ally rejected the idea out of hand. Thus Piłsudski decided to come to terms with Hitler.

Austria. It was only natural that Hitler would look to his homeland, which he referred to by the supposedly Carolingian name *Ostmark* (Eastern March), for expansion. Almost every visitor to his retreat at Berchtesgaden at some point was led to the large picture window and shown the magnificent view toward Salzburg, "the home of the Führer."

After a lengthy Austro-German war over visa fees, Britain, France, and Italy had united on February 17, 1934, to guarantee Austria's territorial integrity. The Austrian chancellor, Engelbert Dollfuss, used this blank check to launch a massive attack against the Social Democrats, which culminated in the destruction of the Social Democratic stronghold in Vienna. In the process, Dollfuss created an authoritarian, semifascist regime, establishing close ties with Benito Mussolini's Italy and banning the Nazi party in Austria in the summer of 1934.

Frustrated, Austrian National Socialists on July 25 murdered Dollfuss in a particularly brutal fashion. Although Hitler took delicious delight in this removal of a troublesome opponent, he apparently did not direct the actions of the Austrian Nazis that day. And when an angry Mussolini mobilized Italian forces on the Brenner pass, Hitler backed down and denied involvement in the assassination. Lacking armed might, Hitler was forced to acknowledge the limits of his power.

January 1935 proved more auspicious for the Führer. The coal-rich Saar region, which under the Treaty of Versailles had been given to France in 1919 to exploit for fifteen years, held a referendum to decide its future: 91 percent of the vote fell to Hitler's Germany. It was a smashing victory. For the first time, an area beyond the control of the German police voted freely to join the Hitler state.

Undoubtedly emboldened by the Saar vote, Hitler went on the offensive in his assault on the Versailles *Diktat*. On March 16, 1935, he informed the rest of the world that Germany would introduce male conscription and raise an army of thirty-six divisions (550,000 men). Concurrently, Hitler announced that Hermann Göring would now build an air force (*Luftwaffe*). In reality, this merely gave public notice of the air force's acquisition program of July 1, 1934, which had called for the construction of 17,015 aircraft at a cost of 10.5 billion reichsmarks (RM). On March 17 Hitler orchestrated a mammoth memorial day for Germany's fallen warriors from the past, designed much like the Day of Potsdam in March 1933 to express the fusion of the new Third Reich with historic Prussia.

The West reacted by meeting at Stresa in Piedmont, Italy, on April 14 and forging a common front. Britain, France, and Italy denounced the German unilateral decision on conscription and expressed joint interest in maintaining Austria's independence. Hitler hardly noticed. It is interesting that his March 16 announcement fell on a Friday, when Hitler knew that the cabinet in London was off for the weekend and thus unable to react immediately to his bold offensive. He would repeat that stratagem in the future.

But before Hitler could resume the offensive, the British decided to negotiate a further break in Versailles. On June 18, 1935, London agreed that Berlin could build a surface fleet 35 percent the size of the Royal Navy, as well as a U-boat force equal to that of Britain, should Hitler see this as necessary. The Führer later declared that June 18 had been the "happiest day of his life" and hailed his special envoy, Joachim von Ribbentrop, as "greater than Bismarck." The Anglo-German naval agreement outraged the French, who accused the British of having abandoned Versailles and destroyed the Stresa front. At best, it can be argued that the British foreign secretaries, John A. Simon (to June 1935) and Sir Samuel Hoare, negotiated the agreement in an attempt to test whether Hitler was, in fact, willing to enter into collective agreements designed to preserve peace. Perhaps British leaders also acted in response to domestic political pressures for disarmament and in the hope of heading off a future German claim for parity by putting a limit on German rearmament in this most vital field. Hitler, for his part, viewed the accord as but the first step on the road toward an eventual Anglo-German alliance. In October 1936, he appointed Ribbentrop ambassador to the Court of St. James's and sent him off with the admonition: "Ribbentrop, bring me the English alliance."

In reality, Hitler and Ribbentrop steered divergent courses. Frequent contact with British leaders had convinced Ribbentrop that an alliance with "perfidious Albion" lay beyond the possible — or desirable. Instead, Ribbentrop developed the alternate notion of a Berlin-Rome-Tokyo accord and on November 25, 1936, moved in that direction by signing an alliance with Japan; Italy joined the so-called Anti-Comintern Pact on November 6, 1937. The German Foreign Office, which had not been consulted, denounced Ribbentrop's initiative as the "private adventure of a dilettante."

Hitler, on the other hand, chased the elusive dream of a British alliance throughout his career; Albert Speer termed it the "red thread" that ran through all of the Führer's calculations. Hitler dispatched no fewer than six special envoys to Britain during the 1930s. In 1936 he offered to meet Prime Minister Stanley Baldwin on a ship in the middle of the North Sea and even "to fly to Chequers to meet the English prime minister." Despite temporary setbacks, such as the abdication of the "English National Socialist," Edward VIII, due to machinations of the "reactionary, Jewish, anti-German clique" in London, Hitler stayed the course.[1] The "deal" that he proposed was simple: Britain would concentrate on its overseas empire while Germany received a free hand on the Continent. To this end, Hitler even offered the British use of a squadron of German battleships against the United States, Britain's most dangerous

[1] Although Edward VIII undoubtedly viewed Nazi Germany positively and maintained contacts with Hitler both before and after his abdication, his alleged sympathy toward fascism was greatly exaggerated by Hitler, who erroneously believed that the king personally directed British foreign policy.

global rival. That it had been Britain's national policy for three centuries to preserve the balance of power in Europe by preventing continental hegemony by any single nation was blithely ignored by Hitler.

The British were convinced that the Soviet Union posed the greatest long-term threat to Europe, so they were willing to meet Hitler more than halfway. On November 19, 1937, Lord Halifax, the future foreign secretary, offered to reintegrate Germany, the outcast of Versailles, into the European concert and sweetened the offer with a willingness to negotiate critical issues such as Danzig, Austria, Czechoslovakia, and the former German colonies. While most German "revisionists" in the army and the foreign service would have jumped at the offer, Hitler turned it down. The Führer wanted a formal alliance with England to pursue a policy of grandiose conquest in the East; amelioratory revisions of Versailles were not ends in themselves. The British, however, refused to offer Hitler such an alliance, and slowly the German leader came around to the realization that he would have to proceed without — but, he hoped, not against — Great Britain.

German-Italian relations improved, and conversely the Stresa front collapsed, after October 1935, when Mussolini invaded Ethiopia. In this first "fascist war," which featured concentration camps, mass executions, use of gas, and aerial strafing of women and children, Italy could well have been defeated had Britain closed the Suez Canal to Italian ships and had other nations — the United States, especially — cut off Italy's vital foreign oil supplies. Hitler, in fact, originally had supported the Ethiopians with supplies valued at over 4 million RM, perhaps in retribution for Mussolini's anti-German stance during the Austrian crisis of 1934, but eventually spied his chance to lure the Italian dictator into the German orbit by supporting Italy's war effort. In the process, Hitler, recognizing the ineffectiveness of the League of Nations and collective security, was able late in 1935 to escape from his self-imposed isolation.

Perhaps the last chance to stop Hitler came in the spring of 1936. On March 7, in another weekend surprise, three lightly armed German infantry battalions moved into the demilitarized Rhineland. How would the French react? Once more, Hitler was playing brinksmanship. His diplomats urged caution. His generals were apprehensive lest the French retaliate. General Alfred Jodl at Nuremberg recalled that as a colonel in March 1936 he had felt "like a gambler who has placed his entire fortune at roulette on red or black." We know today that the German units had orders to stage a fighting withdrawal in the case of serious opposition.[1] And although Hitler was willing to let it come to war with France, which possessed the strongest army in Europe, the presence along the Rhine of a single German division supported by a mere two squadrons of the newly founded air force hardly offered victory.

[1] The persistent story that German troops had orders to withdraw in case of French opposition is only partially correct and utterly misleading: the withdrawal was to be a tactical defensive move, not a return to an earlier position. Thus Hitler fully accepted the possibility of war.

The French backed off, delivering the final blow to Versailles and Locarno. Complacent behind their Maginot Line and overestimating Hitler's forces, they missed a splendid chance to rebuff German aggression. For Hitler, March 7 was "the most exciting day of his life." The nation agreed, according the NSDAP slate 98.8 percent of the vote during the national elections of March 29, 1936. The British scholar Ian Kershaw claims that the Rhineland coup laid the basis for the Hitler myth. While diplomats and generals feared setbacks or defeat, Hitler alone promised victory. On March 14, 1936, the Führer noted: "With phantasmagoric certainty I proceeded along the road dictated to me by Providence." Once more, his cautious diplomats and soldiers had been proved wrong. Once again, Hitler had shown them that an aggressive foreign policy was vital to national integration.

The summer of 1936 brought Hitler an unexpected chance to test the resolve of Britain and France. On July 25, while attending a performance of Richard Wagner's *Siegfried* at Bayreuth, two plenipotentiaries sent by General Francisco Franco-Bahamonde of Spain asked Hitler for aid in the unfolding Spanish Civil War.[1] Without consulting the Wilhelmstrasse, Hitler agreed at once to dispatch twenty transport planes, six fighters, and twenty antiaircraft guns to Spain. The German effort eventually would grow to six thousand men in the form of a special expeditionary corps, the Condor Legion. Although Göring and Ribbentrop feared "complications" from Britain, Hitler had once again taken advantage of a crisis to advance his case.

But why Spain? First and foremost, the Spanish Civil War diverted attention from Central Europe to the periphery of the Continent. In addition, Hitler could well use the mineral riches of Spain and its African possessions, to which he laid claim in return for further aid to General Franco. But above all, the chance to test the mettle of the West proved decisive: if London and Paris would not fight to preserve democracy in Spain, how could they be expected to take a stand over Poland or the Soviet Union?

Events in Spain further cemented the emerging German-Italian cooperation. On November 1, 1936, Mussolini officially proclaimed a Berlin-Rome axis; on September 28, 1937, he received a triumphant reception in Berlin. In what turned out to be the last grand orchestration of public spectacle, the two dictators approached Berlin by train on separate tracks to show the parallelism of their movements. The capital's main streets were lined with four rows of white pillars mounted with eagles, swastikas, busts of Caesar, and fasces[2] and sixty

[1] On July 18, 1936, Spanish military officers rebelled against the Left Republican government of Manuel Azaña. The war ended in March 1939 with the surrender of Madrid and Valencia to General Franco. About seven hundred thousand people died during the war in battle; a further thirty thousand were executed or assassinated; and fifteen thousand died in air raids. Germany and Italy supported Franco; the Soviet Union backed the Republicans; Britain and France opted for nonintervention.

[2] A bundle of rods surrounding an axe with protruding blade, the fasces was a badge of authority for Roman magistrates. It has long appeared on the U.S. dime, and Mussolini revived it as a symbol for his movement in the 1920s.

thousand SS men. More than fifty-five thousand square yards of bunting had been woven into intertwining German and Italian flags, each the height of a building. One million people turned out for the occasion. Mussolini, overcome by the pomp, at once ordered the "goose-step" adopted by the Italian army. Hitler proclaimed "Germany is once again a world power."

In many ways, 1937 proved critical for Hitler. At home, he faced opposition from both Protestants (Martin Niemöller) and Catholics (Pius XI) over his attacks on Christianity (see Chapter 8). As a sign of quiet army protest against the regime's attacks on religion and its racial idolatry, church parades and Sunday services became obligatory in the army. Furthermore, many commanders, especially General Ludwig Beck, chief of the General Staff, feared that rearmament was proceeding much too quickly and might lead to war prematurely. And at the Wilhelmstrasse, diplomats expressed their growing concern that they were being bypassed in serious negotiations by party officials such as Göring, Hess, and Ribbentrop.

Ernst von Weizsäcker, head of the Foreign Office's political division, realized that a "new era" was at hand: after four years of domestic reform, Hitler was turning his attention beyond the Reich's borders. To be sure, Weizsäcker was concerned mainly with the pace, rather than the content, of Hitler's "revisionism." Although Weizsäcker shared his Führer's basic program — creation of a "Greater Germany" including the Polish corridor, Upper Silesia, the Sudetenland, and Austria — he nevertheless was concerned whether Hitler would remain on an "evolutionary course" or would resort to "revolutionary" means. In other words, was Hitler leading Germany to precipitous calamity?

The answers to these questions came on November 5, 1937. At a secret conference in the Chancery, Foreign Minister Konstantin von Neurath, Defense Minister Werner von Blomberg, army chief General Werner von Fritsch, air force head Hermann Göring, and naval commander Admiral Erich Raeder were subjected to a four-hour monologue by Hitler. It was pure *Mein Kampf.* After ruling out self-sufficiency (*Autarkie*), overseas colonies, and expanded foreign trade as solutions to Germany's need for *Lebensraum*, Hitler announced that expansion of the Germanic "racial core" could come only in Europe, specifically, in the western parts of the Soviet Union. The question was when and how. The answer: Germany's "space question" needed to be solved "at latest by 1943–45," and "only by use of force." The path led through Czechoslovakia and Austria; the West would not intervene.

Hitler had convened the meeting, as he put it, to "open the throttle" with regard to foreign policy. Dissatisfied over the slow pace of rearmament, he had designed the November 5 session to test his top diplomatic and military leaders' resolve to step up the pace of "revisionism."

The meeting served its purpose. Beck was "decimated." Neurath allegedly fainted. Raeder left the session "white as a sheet." When the admiral asked his fleet chief to work out the practical implications of Hitler's statements, Admiral Rolf Carls replied: war with Britain, France, the Soviet Union and probably "one-half to two-thirds of the world." Although Blomberg remained enchanted with his Führer and continued to press for war readiness, Fritsch was livid over the pace and the tone of Hitler's instructions. Göring engaged Colonel Friedrich Hossbach, who had taken minutes of the meeting, in a lengthy discussion over its intent.

Hitler, who departed immediately for Berchtesgaden after the meeting, had got precisely the information he wanted. He denounced Neurath's Foreign Office as "a hodgepodge of hirelings" and deemed the generals to be "supine yard dogs" rather than "ice-cold, unpleasant men such as I have in the party." They were not the stuff with which to conduct wars.

Hitler got his chance to purge the diplomatic and officer corps early in 1938. Blomberg's marriage on January 12 to Erna Gruhn, a women with a "certain past," as well as falsified charges of "homosexuality" levied against Fritsch, gave Hitler the necessary pretext. Blomberg, whom Hitler strangely viewed as too soft on planned expansionism, was forced to resign. Fritsch was suspended from active duty. The top echelons of the military declined to revolt, partly because German generals shared the basic contours of Hitler's expansionist program and partly because political revolt was anathema to them.

Looking for possible successors, Hitler ruled out Göring as "totally unsuitable" to head the armed forces. Before leaving office, Blomberg rendered his Führer a last service by suggesting that Hitler personally assume command of the armed forces. For good measure he not only gave his Führer a list of sixteen generals lacking sufficient National-Socialist "vigor" but even suggested that his "office boy," General Wilhelm Keitel, head a new Supreme Command of the Armed Forces (OKW). General Walther von Brauchitsch, who assured Hitler that he was "ready to do anything," replaced Fritsch as army chief. The Defense Ministry was abolished.

At the Wilhelmstrasse, the ubiquitous Ribbentrop replaced Neurath, and more fervent Hitler supporters received the ambassadorial posts of Rome, Tokyo, and Vienna. Walter Funk, another NSDAP cipher, succeeded Hjalmar Schacht at the Ministry of Economics. Thus, the *Gleichschaltung* (Nazification of the state apparatus) was complete. The last possible centers of opposition to the Nazis had been destroyed. The Führer was now surrounded by pliant yes men. The last cabinet meeting of the Third Reich on February 5, 1938, approved these changes.

This bloodless coup at home permitted Hitler in the spring of 1938 to step up his attacks on Austria. Nineteenth-century Pan-German longings for a "greater German" (*grossdeutsch*) unification combined with Göring's desire to lay his hands on vital Austrian industries to speed up the process. On February 12, the Führer summoned Austrian chancellor Kurt von Schuschnigg to Berchtesgaden and subjected him to a classic Hitlerian diatribe, ending with the charge that the entire history of Austria had been but one "uninterrupted betrayal" of the German *Volk*. The meeting ended with Schuschnigg's

Home again: Adolf Hitler returns to Vienna (March 1938).

agreement to let Austrian National Socialists into his government — specifically, their leader, Arthur Seyss-Inquart, as special "security minister" — and to coordinate the Austrian economic and military systems with Germany. On returning to Vienna, however, Schuschnigg had second thoughts. On March 9, he decided to hold a national referendum on March 13 over the future of Austria as a last desperate measure to preserve its independence.

Hitler was furious about Schuschnigg's use of his own tactic of plebiscites and on March 10 signed Directive No. 1, the invasion of Austria code-named Operation Otto. Schuschnigg resigned the next day, and Seyss-Inquart seized all government ministries in Vienna. Mussolini declared his disinterest in the fate of Austria, and Hitler gratefully assured the "Duce": "I will never forget this . . . never, never, never, come what may."

March 12, 1938, must have been high drama for Hitler. In his open-air Mercedes, he crossed the border into Braunau, his birthplace. From there, he toured through flower-bedecked villages to Linz, where he signed the document formalizing the annexation of Austria (*Anschluss*). The next day, millions cheered his triumphant entry into Vienna, the scene of his most bitter disappointments as a youth. From the balcony of the Hofburg Palace, Hitler informed a delirious crowd of 200,000 people that he had brought the 6.5 million residents of his homeland "home to the Reich." Cardinal Theodor Innitzer, the Catholic primate of Austria, welcomed Hitler to Austria.

Austria paid a heavy price for the *Anschluss*. An initial wave of arrests by the Germans netted 76,000 suspected opponents of annexation — not only known leaders of the labor movement but also the heads of Austrian patriotic groups. The Austrian bureaucracy was purged of at least 6,000 civil servants in the ministries of education and police. That night, SS units, with the help of

Austrian antisemites, rounded up 1,500 of Austria's 183,000 Jews and deported them to concentration camps in Germany; countless others, including Sigmund Freud, went into exile.

Bismarck's work was undone; the *grossdeutsch* solution finally had the upper hand. The Habsburg's crown and other insignia were removed to Nuremberg. A national referendum in the newly proclaimed "Greater German Empire" in April 1938 brought a vote of 99 percent in favor of the *Anschluss*. In addition to Austria's iron pits, Germany gained much-needed gold and foreign currency reserves of 1.4 billion RM from the Treasury in Vienna. More important to Hitler, Czechoslovakia now faced Germany on three sides.

In all his mental perambulations of the "Czech question," Hitler consistently placed emphasis on the eventual destruction of Czechoslovakia as a sovereign state, and not on the plight of the Sudeten Germans in the northwest corner of the state and their fate. In fact, Hitler cared little for the 3.5 million Sudeten Germans. In 1919 they had voted for inclusion in the new Austrian Republic, but the statesmen at Paris had instead insisted they be given to the Czechoslovak state as a security buffer. Here was another chance to undermine the Versailles *Diktat*.

Fourteen days after the annexation of Austria, Hitler met with the Sudeten-German leader, Konrad Henlein, to discuss the "Sudeten question." Four weeks later, General Keitel was instructed to prepare Case Green, a potential invasion of Czechoslovakia.

Czechoslovakia was in an unenviable position. Although its major ally, France, was obliged by treaty to defend Czech independence, political and military leaders in Paris agreed that France could not "give military assistance to Czechoslovakia" owing to the strength of the German fortifications along the Rhine. In London, the Foreign Office firmly believed that some conciliatory steps needed to be taken to assuage the Sudeten-German minority in Czechoslovakia. Above all, Britain possessed no continental army with which to resist Hitler's advances. Paris and London thus restricted themselves to offering Prague repeated expressions of loyalty.

On May 20, 1938, Czechoslovak president Edvard Beneš precipitated a crisis when he mobilized his country's army in the wake of a statement by Prime Minister Neville Chamberlain of Britain hinting at possible "border revisions" at Czechoslovakia's expense. Was Chamberlain's comment a bluff? Hitler became indignant when on May 22 news reached him of Britain's and France's reiteration of their obligations to maintain Czechoslovak neutrality. On May 30 he announced his "irreversible decision" to crush Czechoslovakia "by military action"; execution of Case Green was set for anytime after October 1. For the first time, Hitler officially informed his military planners that war with Britain might be a possibility. The Führer cleverly intensified the crisis throughout the summer of 1938 through escalating rhetoric and threats against Prague.

Chamberlain twice flew to Germany in September 1938 to discuss the "Sudeten question" with Hitler. Britain mobilized its reserves as well as its fleet, mounted antiaircraft guns on major government buildings, and dispatched schoolchildren from urban centers to the countryside. In France, one in three Parisians fled the capital in a fear-crazed exodus. Surely European cities would be leveled at the first sign of war. Chamberlain expressed the views of many when he proclaimed: "How horrible, fantastic, incredible it is that we should be digging trenches and trying on gas-masks here because of a quarrel in a far-away country between people of whom we know nothing."

On September 29, at a conference in Munich hastily arranged by Benito Mussolini, Chamberlain agreed to the transfer of 3.5 million Sudeten-Germans and their lands to the Third Reich. With the loss of strategic border areas and their fortifications, Czechoslovakia now lay open to invasion. Hitler, instead of being delighted at this surrender, felt cheated of the spoils of victory. "That fellow," Chamberlain, he informed Schacht on his return to Berlin, "has spoiled my entry into Prague." In fact, Hitler had wanted to force war on Czechoslovakia in the firm belief that Britain and France would stand idle. Thus humbled by their abandonment of an ally, they would hardly be positioned to oppose the Führer's further plans in eastern Europe.

The Munich conference has become synonymous with appeasement of Hitler. On the surface, the Führer had won all down the line: Czechoslovakia, the only viable democracy to emerge from the Paris settlements of 1919, had been sacrificed by Britain and France, two of its sponsors; the French system of alliances in eastern Europe had been undermined; the Soviet Union had been kept out of the European concert; and the basis had been laid for the total destruction of the remainder of Czechoslovakia. But a rational strategy lay behind Chamberlain's policy. At home, spending on public housing was pulling Britain out of the depression; would he jeopardize this progress by shifting outlays to armaments production? Overseas, the Admiralty desperately needed funds to upgrade the critical base at Singapore and saw little need to sacrifice the Far East in order to resist Hitler. And finally, he thought, the greatest danger to Europe lay not in Germany but rather in the Soviet Union. It made sense to Chamberlain to "appease" Hitler in what was, after all, his backyard to invite him into a European coalition against Bolshevism. Perhaps the British prime minister remembered July 1914, when a local crisis in eastern Europe had escalated into a European war. The tragedy of Chamberlain's and his advisers' plan was that they failed to realize that Hitler could not be appeased, no amount of revision of Versailles would deter him from his grand schemes of conquest in the east.

The British cabinet quickly learned how seriously Hitler took the Munich accord. On March 14, 1939, the Führer summoned to Berlin the new Czech president, Emil Hácha (whose main accomplishment was having translated Rudyard Kipling's *Jungle Book)*, to discuss the "Czech question." After a night of verbal abuse, Hácha signed an agreement "placing the destiny of the Czech people and nation confidently in the hands of the Führer of the German Reich." On March 15, a triumphant Hitler rushed to Prague to survey his new acquisition. From the Hradčany Castle, the palace of the kings of Bohemia, the

THE DESTRUCTION OF CZECHOSLOVAKIA, 1938–1939

erstwhile Habsburg subject pronounced with egotistical relish: "Czecho-Slovakia has ceased to exist." Neurath was rescued from oblivion and appointed "Reich protector" of Bohemia and Moravia. Eight days later, Hitler seized Memel (Klaipeda) on the eastern shores of the Baltic Sea from Lithuania, for good measure, and assumed responsibility for "the protection of the political independence of Slovakia."

From a military-industrial perspective, Hitler had greatly expanded his capacity to undertake war. While Chamberlain fumed that as "a joint signatory of the Munich Agreement" he should have been entitled to "consultation," Germany took over 1,465 Czech airplanes, 710 tanks, and 1,649 artillery pieces. The Bank of England handed Prague's gold reserves of £6 million to Berlin. Now possessing 15 percent of the world's industrial production, Germany ranked second only to the United States. The "Greater German Empire" outflanked Poland on three sides.

Hitler was almost embarrassed by the choices open to him early in 1939. Should he turn first against France and Britain in order to clear his western front before tackling the Soviet Union? Or should he turn east now? If he set the latter course, would Poland assist him?

As early as October 1938, Ribbentrop had approached Polish ambassador Józef Lipski with an offer: if Poland ceded to Germany the free city of Danzig and a German corridor across the Polish corridor, and joined the anti-Communist camp, Hitler was willing to cement German-Polish relations by extending the 1934 Non-Aggression Pact for twenty-five years. The Poles were unreceptive. Foreign Minister Józef Beck's official stance was "not one millimeter nearer to Berlin than to Moscow." In fact, the Poles dreamed of leading a "third Europe," an eastern bloc stretching from the Baltic Sea to the Dardanelles.

Matters took on urgency on March 21, 1939, when Ribbentrop pressed Lipski to discuss Danzig and the corridor. The Poles again refused to enter into any accord with the Germans. Then Chamberlain seized the initiative on March 31, 1939, by announcing that Britain would "guarantee" Polish sovereignty. Hitler was dumbfounded at first ("what now?") but recovered quickly. Case White, the planned "final reckoning with Poland" for "centuries to come," was set for September 1. On April 28 Hitler abrogated the Non-Aggression Pact with Poland of 1934, as well as the Anglo-German Naval Agreement of 1935. He had decided on war and feared only that at the last moment, some "swine" would once again suggest negotiation.

All eyes turned to Moscow. How would Joseph Stalin react to these latest threats? Despite having been rebuffed by London and Paris in his support of Republican Spain and even though he had not been invited to Munich, Stalin nevertheless was willing to talk with western leaders — but on his own terms. Stalin had informed Chamberlain that he made Polish participation a prerequisite in a multilateral antiaggression front against Hitler, and hence the prime minister could well conceive of his "guarantee" of Polish independence as the necessary step toward this end. But the minute that the British gave their "guarantee," Stalin saw no need to enter into an anti-Hitler coalition: Chamberlain's unilateral action on March 31 ensured that any German attack on Poland would embroil Britain and France in a war with Germany. The Soviet Union could stand by and "mediate" at some appropriate point of its own choosing.

Moreover, the British did not press high-level talks with Stalin. Neither Foreign Secretary Lord Halifax nor any other cabinet minister went to Moscow. Instead, two minor Whitehall officials took a slow boat (three weeks) to Leningrad and then on to Moscow by slow train. An exasperated Stalin replaced M. M. Litvinov, the architect of collective security, with V. M. Molotov, "old iron pants," thereby signaling a change in course. Moreover, he informed the Eighteenth Congress of the All-Union Bolshevik Party, "Britain and France have repudiated the policy of collective security."

Hitler read the signal.[1] On August 14 Ribbentrop cabled Moscow that he was ready to come for talks. Three days later, Stalin adjourned his negotiations with the British and French. Ribbentrop arrived in Moscow on August 23. In three hours, he and Stalin agreed to a ten-year Non-Aggression Pact, as well as

[1] Repeated Soviet attempts to enter into discussions with Nazi Germany — the latest as late as February 1937 — had failed due to Hitler's disinterest.

a secret codicil amounting to a fourth partition of Poland along the rivers Narew, Vistula, and San. In the Baltic region, Ribbentrop agreed to Stalin's demands for Finland, Latvia, and Estonia, while Ribbentrop coveted Lithuania. Finally, Germany recognized Soviet claims to Bessarabia in the Balkans. Ribbentrop saw the pact as the capstone of his anti-British diplomacy.

For Hitler, this "pact with Satan" averted the possibility of a two-front war as in 1914 and guaranteed him uninterrupted supplies of vital Soviet raw materials. Stalin gained breathing space and was given access to German industrial and chemical patents.

Still, Hitler had not given up hope for an alliance with Britain. On August 25 he once again extended his offer: in return for a free hand on the Continent, he would "guarantee" the British Empire. No reply. Four days later, a nervous Hermann Göring cautioned his Führer against playing *vabanque*, that is, for all the chips on the table. Hitler coldly cut Göring off: "I have always played *vabanque* throughout my life." In fact, Hitler had now decided to have what he called his "little war." General Franz Halder, Beck's successor as chief of the General Staff, laconically noted in his diary: "30.8. — Poles in Berlin. 31.8. — blowup. 1.9. — use of force."[1]

Hitler's "Little War"

At 4:45 A.M. on the morning of September 1, 1939, the German armored cruiser *Schleswig-Holstein* opened fire on Polish fortifications near Danzig as German troops crossed the border into Poland. In Berlin, Adolf Hitler began the war with a lie, informing the Reichstag that regular units of the Polish army had fired on German territory. "Since 5:45 we are returning the fire!" Having donned his "sacred and most dear" uniform from the Great War, Hitler vowed not to take it off until he met with either victory or death. Paraphrasing Frederick the Great's "first servant of the state" concept, Hitler declared: "I now wish to be nothing other than the first soldier of the German Reich." Forty-eight hours later, Britain and France declared war on Germany.

September 1939 was not August 1914. There was no euphoria, no bands, no flower-bedecked rifles, no women passing out sandwiches or shaming young men to volunteer for service. Instead, Hitler was met with silence and sullen resignation by Berliners he met on his way to the Reichstag. In fact, the invasion of Poland stood in opposition to Hitler's overall "program," for he had sought to "revise" Versailles by way of lightning wars against isolated opponents on the Continent under the umbrella of British neutrality. September 1939 was not the war he wanted in terms of either timing or the lineup of powers.

---

[1] These German dates refer to August 30 and 31 as well as to September 1.

Again, unlike 1914, there was to be no "war guilt" controversy concerning the origins of World War II. Hitler had wanted what he called his "little war" ever since Munich 1938. He, rather than big business or the military, had pushed for it. On November 23, 1939, he laid out for his service chiefs the meaning of the war. After once again reminding them that "struggle is the destiny of all being," Hitler equated the conflict to "the final act of the Great War." After a twenty-year hiatus, "today we will write the second act of that drama." In short, Hitler stressed the continuity in German foreign policy aims from William II to himself. Moreover, he announced his "irreversible" decision after Poland to attack Britain and France in order to clear his western flank before tackling the Soviet Union. At stake was nothing less than "the destiny of the nation." Once more, the either-or mind-set from the Vienna days prevailed. The renowned Prussian historian, Otto Hintze, detected something "alien" and "totally amoral" in Hitler: "This man really does not even belong to our race. There is something reminiscent of an extinct primate about him."

How well was Germany prepared for war in 1939? In contrast to its lack of readiness in 1914, when it had made absolutely no economic preparations for war, the Third Reich had made great strides toward putting the economy on a war footing between 1935 and 1939. Nevertheless, nagging supply problems remained: critical war materials such as nickel, tungsten, molybdenum, and manganese as well as rubber and oil had to be imported; only in coal was Germany self-sufficient.

The military, especially, was keenly aware of the severe burden that motorization placed on the economy. The demand for petroleum products, for example, rose from 527,000 tons in 1933 to 1,312,000 tons in 1937. By the summer of 1938, Germany had on hand but 25 percent of the fuel that it required, enough to sustain war for four months. That same year, 70 percent of high-grade iron had to be imported. Supplies of rubber were down to one-sixteenth of requirements. Neither the new synthetic fuel (Leuna) nor synthetic rubber (Buna) plants ever reached demand levels, although Buna did meet German needs from 1940 on.

The year 1937 had proved critical. The Reich had reached the limits of its financial and material resources, its factories were running at full capacity, and the pool of available labor had been exhausted. Hitler had recognized its plight: "Germany is living in a time of bitter struggle over foodstuffs and raw materials." In 1936 Hermann Göring had launched the Four Year Plan to enable the Reich to conduct a major European war in four years, partially by developing alternatives to vital raw materials in short supply in Germany. Well aware that full concentration on armaments production would seriously deplete the nation's reserves of hard currency and raw materials, Göring had counseled that national bankruptcy by 1940 could be avoided only by war. In other words, a victorious war ending with monstrous reparations to be paid by and vital raw materials to be taken from its losers was the only solution to overcoming chronic raw materials shortages, as well as alleviating the "social tensions" occasioned by shortfalls on the domestic market. The *Blitzkrieg* (lightning warfare) was devised not so much as military doctrine but as a response to "the mounting dichotomy between military aspirations/economic possibilities and increasing social pressures." Germany was not driven to war as a result of economic necessity; rather, the political decision to conduct a war for continental hegemony produced the overheated war economy that reached bankruptcy by 1937.

The heart of the problem was that Germany lacked the requisite foreign currency and gold to import war materials. The changeover from an export to a war economy deprived the nation of its main source of hard currency: exports fell from 12 billion RM in 1930 to 4.5 RM billion in 1937. Consequently, cash reserves dipped from 2.8 billion RM in 1930 to 70 million RM in 1936–1937. The Supreme Command of the Armed Forces in 1938 estimated that Germany held but 1 percent of the world's gold and financial reserves, compared to 54 percent for the United States and 11 percent each for Britain and France. Between 1937 and 1939, industry completed only three of every five orders due to lack of raw materials. By January 1939 all service branches had to absorb a 30 percent cut in raw material allocations. Nor did the diffusion of industrial control among the War Ministry's economic staff, the Plenipotentiary for the War Economy (1935), and Göring's office for the Four Year Plan (1936), not to mention local *Gau* leaders and the SS, expedite production.

The occupation of Prague in the spring of 1939 had shown that the solution to the Reich's supply problems was conquest. Germany was able to lay its hands on 500 million RM in gold reserves as well as 2.9 billion RM in raw materials. The Balkans were rich in copper, lead, zinc, and bauxite, and Rumania could supply wheat and oil. Seizing the western regions of the Soviet Union would remove all economic shackles forever.

The European phase of the war in 1939–1940 unfolded virtually as Hitler expected. The German assault on Poland featured the *Blitzkrieg*: while the air force destroyed much of its Polish counterpart on the ground in the first two or three days of the war, Stuka dive bombers attacked major concentrations of Polish forces and civilian centers, spreading terror and disorder. Thereafter, German armored and motorized spearheads rapidly broke through Polish army lines and destroyed communications and supplies in the rear. Finally, through the gaping holes created by the tank (*Panzer*) units streamed columns of motorized and nonmotorized infantry. General Erwin Rommel described the new doctrine as "the art of concentrating strength at one point, forcing a breakthrough, rolling up and securing the flanks on either side, and then penetrating like lightning, before the enemy has time to retreat, deep into his rear."

On September 17 Stalin, fearing that Hitler would occupy Poland entirely and thus deprive the Soviet Union of the spoils agreed on in the Ribbentrop-Molotov pact the preceding month, invaded Poland from the east. Ironically, German and Soviet forces met at Brest-Litovsk, where in March 1918 Imperial

Germany had dictated a draconian peace to the Soviets. A triumphant Hitler entered Danzig on September 19 and announced, "Poland will never rise again." The fourth partition of Poland took place on September 28: Stalin took what Poland had seized from the Soviet Union in 1921, and Hitler acquired western and central Poland. In a secret codicil to the Nazi-Soviet compact, Stalin also received Estonia, Latvia, and Lithuania (incorporated as Soviet republics in August 1940). Both conquerors took vengeance on the Poles. Soviet secret police units (NKVD) set about eradicating the Polish intelligentsia and officer corps. In 1943, German units in the Katyn forest near Smolensk uncovered the remains of four thousand Polish officers murdered by the Soviets in the spring of 1940.

The Germans were barbaric and systematic. Covered by a special amnesty issued by Hitler and General von Brauchitsch, five special SS execution units (*Einsatzgruppen*) roamed the Polish countryside and murdered preselected doctors, priests, civil servants, country squires, and merchants. Reinhard Heydrich of the Security Forces (SD) crowed as early as September 27 that only 3 percent of the Polish intelligentsia survived. His superior, Heinrich Himmler, somewhat prematurely proclaimed: "The East belongs to the SS." The western regions of Poland were reconstituted as the "Warthegau," and 1.4 million Germans eventually were "resettled" there. Concurrently, more than 1 million Poles were forcibly removed to the "General Government" under Hans Frank, the later staging area for the Holocaust. Hitler was well satisfied: "There shall be only one master for the Poles: the Germans. . . . Hence, all representatives of the Polish intelligentsia are to be murdered. That sounds harsh, but it simply is a law of life."

As a harbinger, on September 21 Heydrich developed his initial blueprint for the Polish (and later European) Jews. The Jews were to be herded into special "reservations" through the auspices of Councils of Jewish Elders (*Judenrat*) for eventual concentration in five ghettos at Warsaw, Cracow, Lublin, Radom, and (after June 1941) Lwów. While not yet using the term *final solution*, the head of the SD spoke menacingly of "subsequent measures" and alluded to the "final aim" of German policy with regard to European Jewry.

Hitler's partners Italy and Japan had remained on the sidelines in September 1939; hence Germany's dependence on Soviet raw material deliveries increased dramatically to offset the effects of the naval blockade that Britain (as in 1914) had instituted against Germany. On October 9, 1939, Hitler, in a rare memorandum to Göring, Raeder, Brauchitsch, Keitel, and Halder, announced his decision to turn west, preferably that same fall. Resorting to reasoning reminiscent of General Erich von Falkenhayn's at Christmas 1915 to justify the Verdun offensive, Hitler stated that the defeat of France would force Britain to conclude peace and to leave the Continent to Germany. Looking beyond the clash with Paris and London, the Führer declared that the greatest obstacle to his goal "to create a European continental imperium under German leadership" from the Pyrenees to the Urals was posed by the two flanking powers, the United States and the Soviet Union. "No treaty and no accord," he informed his military paladins, could secure lasting Soviet neutrality. Hence, he decided to defeat the western democracies before turning against the Soviet Union. "The main thing is the will to crush the enemy." The operation was set for November 12.

The German generals, well remembering the stalemate and trauma of 1914–1918, objected and demanded time to study the Polish campaign and to refit their combat units. Hitler grew furious and announced his intention to root out the defeatist spirit that reigned at General Staff headquarters at Zossen. He demanded "fanatical decisiveness" from his military leaders. "I will not be frightened away by anything, and will destroy anyone who is against me."

Bad weather caused no fewer than twenty-nine postponements of the attack in the West (code-named Case Yellow). To create a diversion, on April 9, 1940, German air, land, and sea units stormed Denmark and Norway in Operation Weserübung. All the while, planning for the war against France continued unabated. Although most generals favored some revised form of the old Schlieffen plan of 1914 — a giant sweep through Belgium and northern France and an attack on Paris from the west — General Erich von Manstein offered Hitler an alternative scheme: a crescent-like sweep through the densely forested (and hence lightly defended) Ardennes forest up to the English Channel. Eschewing Schlieffen's obsession with concentration on the right wing, Manstein counseled a surprise attack against the enemy center and disruption of its dispositions. Hitler proved receptive and instructed the army to reformulate its plans for Case Yellow in line with Manstein's bold concept.

On the morning of May 10, 1940, as Winston S. Churchill was driving to Buckingham Palace to be sworn in as Britain's new prime minister, the Germans struck in the west. Eighty-nine divisions, including 3,000 armored vehicles, invaded Belgium and the Netherlands, taking both in five days. Farther south, an additional forty-four divisions, including three tank corps, in two days crashed through the Ardennes forest. On May 14 the *Luftwaffe* leveled Rotterdam; 30,000 civilians died during an action designed simply to create civilian panic and terror. The Germans reached the Meuse River on May 13, the Oise River four days later. General Halder noted: "Führer is terribly nervous. Frightened by his own success." By May 20 the Germans were at the Somme River, site of the slaughter of 1916 in which the Germans had lost 650,000, the British 420,000, and the French 195,000 men. Four days later, however, Hitler committed his first major mistake: by halting General Heinz Guderian's tank units at the Le Bassée Canal, he allowed the British to evacuate 340,000 troops from the beaches at Dunkirk. This tactical blunder notwithstanding, German troops entered Paris on June 14. Forty-eight hours later, General Henri Pétain, hero of the French defense of Verdun in 1916, formed a

GERMANY'S WESTERN CAMPAIGN, 1940

collaborationist government, eventually sited at Vichy. Benito Mussolini had joined the war on June 10: "I need a few thousand dead so that I can attend the peace conference as a belligerent."

On June 22, 1940, Corporal Adolf Hitler of the erstwhile Sixteenth Bavarian Reserve Infantry Regiment sat in the same chair in the same railroad car at the forest of Compiègne, where twenty-two years earlier Marshal Ferdinand Foch had dictated the armistice conditions to the representatives of Imperial Germany. Hitler's terms by contrast were surprisingly moderate: Alsace-Lorraine and Eupen-et-Malmédy were returned to the Reich; Luxembourg was annexed outright; Belgium came under a German military commander; and the Netherlands received a Reich commissioner. Two-thirds of France remained unoccupied. Twelve German generals were promoted to the grade of field marshal; Göring to the special rank of Reichsmarschall. General Keitel, head of the OKW, celebrated his Führer as "the greatest military commander of all time," thereby adding the cult of military genius to the Hitler myth. And while Göring "liberated" the champagne cellars of Reims, Hitler toured Paris in the company of artists and architects. He was not impressed.

Hitler had attained all that Wilhelmian planners had ever dreamed of: a German-dominated Europe of 200 million people and a colonial empire in Central Africa a possibility. Eastern Europe and the Balkans lay open to German dominance. Surely Britain would now accept the "deal" that Hitler had repeatedly offered: to concentrate on the Empire and to leave Europe to Germany. If it did not, Admiral Raeder was ready with an alternative: the German Navy would strike at "perfidious Albion" indirectly by way of a strategic diversion in the Mediterranean, perhaps thereby creating a German land bridge to India.

Hitler was not interested in such a traditional European program. He had spoken and written for the last two decades about *Lebensraum* and "resettlement" in the east, using terms such as *extirpation* and *liquidation* to define the parameters of his racial-biological wars of extermination. He was not to be derailed. Already in June 1940, flushed with victory over France, he informed Keitel that conquest of Soviet Russia, by comparison, would constitute "child's play." Early in July, Hitler toyed with the idea of invading the Soviet Union in the fall, while the United States was still unprepared for war and tied down by Japanese expansion in the Pacific.

But what about Britain? Historians have failed to reach consensus on whether Hitler ever intended to invade the island nation (Operation Sea Lion). Probably not. Although German landing craft were assembled throughout the summer of 1940 on the southern shores of the English Channel and although the *Luftwaffe* in August and September conducted an aerial assault on first military and later civilian targets, Hitler never personally participated in the operation. Instead, and uncharacteristically, he left all planning to his admirals and generals, who could not even agree on a potential landing site. In the end, Hitler probably hoped once again to bluff Britain into a deal.

July 1940 became the turning point in Hitler's planning. On July 31, he confided his decision to the generals:

> England's hope is Russia and America. If the hope for Russia disappears, America also disappears [as a factor] because Japan will be revalorized tremendously. . . . But if Russia is destroyed, then England's last hope will have been erased. Germany will then be the master of Europe and the Balkans. Conclusion: Russia must be finished off. Spring 1941. The sooner we destroy Russia, the better.

Therewith, the European war assumed global dimensions. The invasion of the Soviet Union would deny Britain its last possible continental ally, and it would free Japan to expand in the Pacific, thereby depriving the United States of the ability to meddle in Europe in behalf of Britain. On September 27, 1940, Hitler signed the Tripartite Pact with Japan and Italy to prepare for the future.

Germany, Italy, and Japan considered themselves to be "have-not" countries. All three coveted true great power status by way of territorial expansion. Italy by force of arms sought Mediterranean hegemony (*spazio vitale*) and mastery over the Middle East. Mussolini, arguing that Italy was "a prisoner of the Mediterranean," demanded that it acquire free connections with the oceans. The "bars" of the prison were Corsica, Tunis, Malta, and Cyprus; the "sentinels" were Gibraltar and Suez. Only by breaking these Anglo-French "bars" could Italy march to the Indian Ocean, "joining Libya with Ethiopia through the Sudan." Above all, Mussolini was anxious to recreate the grandeur of Rome and to remake the Italian people into a cruel and domineering master race.

Japan harbored similar expansionist ambitions. It coveted the vast resources of Southeast Asia (oil, rubber, bauxite, tin) and hoped to establish an autarkic empire under the guise of a Greater East Asian Co-Prosperity Sphere. In July 1937 the Japanese military unleashed a fateful war for the greatest prize of all, China. Victory in China would accord Japan raw materials as well as a market for its ailing economy; resettlement areas for a population that was increasing at the rate of more than 1 million people per year; security against armed Soviet incursions into China; and an opportunity to export "superior" Japanese culture and values. Thus expansionism, if little else, was the cement that held the so-called Rome-Berlin-Tokyo Axis together.

If Hitler needed any further impetus to buttress his decision to invade the Soviet Union, he received it on November 12–13 from an unlikely source, Soviet Foreign Commissar V. M. Molotov. During secret discussions in Berlin, Molotov, in Hitler's words, "let the cat out of the bag" by demanding immediate Soviet dominance over Finland, Rumania, and Bulgaria, as well as the Turkish straits. Later he would request control over Hungary, Yugoslavia, German-occupied western Poland, and the strategic waterways separating Denmark from Sweden. Obviously, such Soviet war aims were incompatible with Hitler's own plans. On December 17, the Führer instructed General Alfred Jodl, army chief of staff: "We must solve all European continental problems in 1941, since the USA by 1942 will be positioned to intervene." The next day, Hitler signed Directive No. 21, Operation Barbarossa, the invasion of the Soviet Union — his "real war" at last. The German nation was to be prepared to conduct a total war against its primary ideological and racial foe.

The Home Front

Adolf Hitler's wartime domestic policies were driven by the desire to avoid the catastrophes of the Great War: unrest, rebellion, revolution, and the alleged "stab in the back" by Jews and Marxists. To prevent this last threat, Hitler in the 1930s had driven "undesirables" into either emigration or concentration camps. In order to head off industrial unrest, the Führer insisted that consumer production not suffer drastically on account of the changeover to a wartime economy, even after the tide had turned against him in 1941–1942.

By and large, Hitler's domestic economic plan succeeded. Not only were there no widespread strikes, rebellions, and revolutions as in 1917–1918, but the consumer index as late as 1943 remained at the last peacetime level; only in 1944 did it begin to drop.

In fact, officials of the Third Reich had gradually prepared the nation for wartime conditions before 1939. Lofts were ordered cleared of all combustible materials, gas masks made mandatory in homes, and sandboxes as well as fire stations established in most neighborhoods to control damage from incendiary bomb attacks. Moreover, a point system designed to regulate the distribution of foodstuffs as well as restaurant, travel, and holiday usage was implemented before 1939. This strategy was extended after the start of the war into a formal system of rationing fats, meats, butter, cheese, milk, marmalade, and sugar. Items such as dog food and Christmas decorations eventually were added to the rationing cards.

Because Denmark, France, and the Netherlands were forced to triple their export of agricultural products to Germany, weekly allocations of vital foodstuffs remained at tolerable levels. Bread rations fell only from 2,400 grams in September 1939 to 2,225 grams by October 1944; fats from 270 to 218 grams; and meat most dramatically from 500 to 250 grams. Potato and vegetable consumption increased in the absence of dairy products, fish, and meat from daily diets.

The costs of the war were financed in large measure by ruthless exploitation of occupied territories. In addition to plunder and tribute carried off at regular intervals, German-occupied lands had to pay for their occupation costs and provide lines of credit to Berlin. The reichsmark was pegged artificially high against foreign currencies to enable Germany to purchase more foreign-produced goods. Unlike the Great War, World War II was not financed by vast domestic loans, nor did taxes rise precipitously. Apart from a tax on beer,

INDUSTRIAL OUTPUT, 1939–1944 (1939 = 100)

Year	Total	Armaments and Supplies	Consumer Goods	Housing
1939	100	100	100	100
1940	97	176	95	53
1941	99	176	96	36
1942	100	254	86	23
1943	112	400	91	—
1944	110	500	86	14

tobacco, brandy, and champagne, the government levied a 50 percent surcharge on income tax only for those whose revenues exceeded the 234 RM floor. In November 1939 official holidays, overtime pay, and night pay were restored to workers.

As the male labor pool declined because ever greater numbers of young men were drafted for military service, so-called foreign workers (*Fremdarbeiter*) and prisoners of war increasingly replenished the supply. Over the course of the war, 7 million laborers (including 1.5 million women) were forcibly recruited: 4 million from the Soviet Union, 1 million from Poland, the rest from Belgium, France, Italy, and the Netherlands. The workers from the eastern regions, especially, were denied legal rights and detained in concentration camps if they complained. Their existence has been compared to that of slave peasants (helots) in ancient Greece. The immense scope of the German slave labor program is strikingly borne out by Himmler's plans to use at least 12 million such "helots" in the postwar era, which according to Albert Speer's calculations would have required the construction of 12,061 permanent barracks for just one-third of this cohort.

By 1944 one in every five workers in Germany reportedly was either a prisoner of war or a *Fremdarbeiter*. They were detailed to the agrarian sector (44 percent), chemical industries (28 percent), and machine plants (26 percent) of the "Greater German Empire." Their labors accounted for one in every four tanks, trucks, and howitzers produced.

Women became increasingly important to the German war effort. Hermann Göring, as head of the Four Year Plan, yearned to tap into the available pool of 6.4 million German women not in the work force. In 1938 he had created a special Reich Labor Service, whereby young men and women between the ages of eighteen and twenty-five were called on to render six months service before seeking gainful employment. For women, this service was to occur either on

CIVILIAN LABOR MOBILIZATION (millions)

Year	German Men	German Women	Foreigners, Prisoners of War
1939	24.5	14.6	0.3
1940	20.4	14.4	1.2
1941	19.0	14.1	3.0
1942	16.9	14.4	4.2
1943	15.5	14.8	6.3
1944			
Spring	14.2	14.8	7.1
Fall	13.5	14.9	7.5

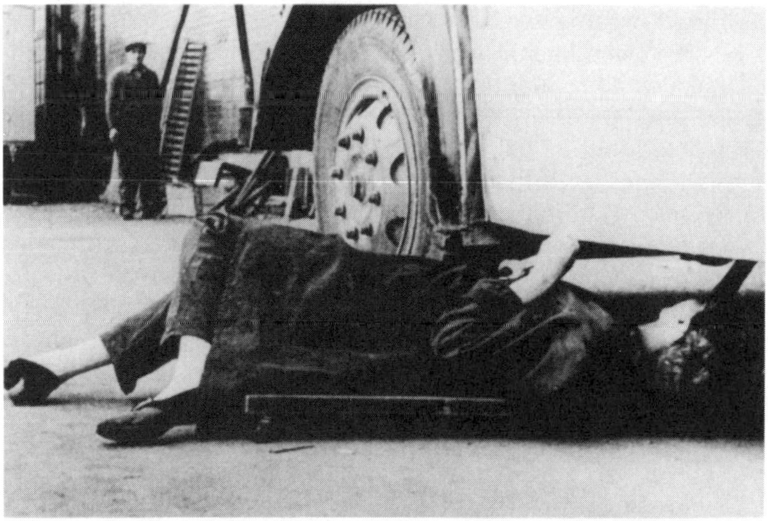

Women at War: Auto mechanic in Vienna (May 1944).

farms or in domestic homes. A year later, Göring established guidelines to call up women between the ages of fourteen and sixty for service in war-related industries. But Göring's efforts, as well as similar ones later in the war by Albert Speer, ran up against Hitler's refusal to sacrifice the National Socialist ideal of women to hard reality. Additionally, Hitler was constrained by the realization that drafting women for national labor would have adverse effects on the morale of both the home and fighting fronts.

The exigencies of total war eventually forced the Third Reich to compromise on the women's issue. The number of women in the work force slowly rose from 37.4 percent in 1939 to 48.8 percent by 1943. On average, there were 2.6 million women in the German labor pool between 1939 and 1944, and of these, just over 1 million worked the land.

Perhaps the most dramatic effect of the war on women's work was the shift from domestic to war-related industries. Between 1939 and 1943 the number of women employed in consumer industries fell by 300,000 to 1.3 million; those in war-related industries doubled to 1.5 million during that same period. By 1943 all women between the ages of seventeen and forty-five had to register for national service, but exemptions remained high: it is estimated that only 500,000 women were freshly mobilized for war production by 1945. Industry provided them with day care centers, nurseries, social services, and six-week maternity leaves. Females also returned to universities in large numbers and by 1943–1944 comprised 61 percent of all students. About 3,500 women volunteered for and were trained by the SS as concentration camp guards; their behavior differed little from that of their male colleagues.

The brunt of organizing the industrial war effort fell to two men: Fritz Todt and Albert Speer. As minister of armaments and munitions, Todt in 1941 had subdivided war production into five committees: munitions, tanks, machines, guns, and general military supplies. Yet whereas Todt's authority had been restricted to the final stages of production, Speer after February 1942, with Hitler's backing, established a system of production rings to supervise all stages of production. Both Todt and Speer were driven by two general goals: concentration as well as rationalization of production, and restoration of the independence of private industry under a program of decentralization. The latter aim gradually watered down the forced integration of the private and governmental sectors under Göring's highly centralized Four Year Plan.

Resorting to the improvisations of Walther Rathenau in 1914–1915, Speer established special "rationalization committees" to streamline production from labor and raw materials allocations to the energy supply. Speer tried to bring about uniformity in the production of airplanes, guns, and tanks. Overall, production rose fully 300 percent between 1942 and 1944 and reached its zenith in the fall of 1944, at the very height of the Anglo-American aerial assault on Germany. In 1943 Hitler promoted Speer at the age of thirty-eight to the post of minister of armaments and war production. With the special support of the Führer, Speer struggled — not always successfully — to gain control over air force and navy production as well as the OKW's economic division under General Georg Thomas. Furthermore, Speer managed to rid his staff of the NSDAP and bureaucratic old guard and to replace them with his own "apolitical specialists." Half in irony, Speer later likened this move toward reliance on young technocrats to "parliamentarization."

But the economic picture was not all that rosy. The National Socialist chaos of competing neofeudal rivalries could not be swept away overnight. Speer remained nominally subservient to Göring as head of the Four Year Plan and hence could do little when Göring, in his capacity as chief of the air force, ordered reallocations in production to favor his service branch. In addition, General Thomas at the OKW managed to retain a good deal of independence from Speer, and Fritz Sauckel, plenipotentiary for labor allocation after March 1942, with the aid of Martin Bormann jealously guarded the labor supply against Speer's demands. Finally, party *Bonzen* throughout Germany proved reluctant to surrender their personal control over men and materials in their *Gaue.*

Both Todt and Speer realized early in 1942 that the war had been lost in economic terms. Joseph Goebbels' call in February 1943 for total war was more intention than reality. Nor did the Third Reich find much-needed succor in 1945 from the suggestions of Reichsführer-SS Heinrich Himmler that armaments plants be relocated on the floors of German lakes and that synthetic fuels be produced from the roots of pine trees. And even with the resources of most of continental Europe at its disposal, German industry lacked the base to compete with the grand coalition arrayed against it.

ARMAMENTS PRODUCTION, 1943

State	Outlays ($ billions)	Aircraft	Tanks	Artillery
Germany	13.8	25,220	10,700	109,300
England	11.1	26,300	7,500	132,100
United States	37.5	30,912	16,508	38,386
Soviet Union	13.9	34,900	24,100	178,700

The war had a great social and cultural leveling effect on Germany. Rationing reduced most strata of society to similar levels of caloric intake and consumer consumption, and the Allied Bomber Command did not discriminate on the basis of birth, income, or education. Goebbels cleverly expounded that general equality and national solidarity as a result of the war effort served to strengthen the concept of the *Volksgemeinschaft*. Although 13 million men had been mobilized by late 1944, the war, oddly enough, solidified home life. Secret SS reports on the home front revealed that most Germans had retreated into private life in response to the war, had closed ranks against outside forces and influences, and had settled into a desperate struggle to survive the carnage as a family unit. By a shrewd combination of seduction (sustained levels of consumer production) and force (police terror and intimidation), Hitler, incredibly, kept the nation at war until the bitter end. His campaign against the Soviet Union, however, stretched Germany's workforce and material resources to their utmost limits.

The World War: 1941

Hitler took great pains to explain the precise nature of Operation Barbarossa to his top planners. On January 9, 1941, he informed them that only with the "immeasurable treasures" of the "gigantic Russian area" could Germany become secure from blockade and "in position to sustain the struggle against continents." After the defeat of Soviet Russia, Hitler argued, Japan would expand in the Pacific, forcing the United States to concentrate on the Americas. Britain would finally join Germany as a "junior partner." The Führer envisaged nothing less than a final *Weltblitzkrieg*: a triple pincer movement via North Africa, the Middle East, and the Caucasus into Afghanistan and India.

Lest there be any doubt about the nature of the war in the east, Hitler bluntly informed two hundred army officers that in this "struggle between two ideologies," there could be no talk of "the old tradition of soldierly comradery. We are dealing with a war of annihilation." On May 13, 1941, Hitler released his soldiers from all legal responsibilities for their actions in the upcoming war. On June 6 he ordered that Soviet commissars were "in all cases to be dispatched at once by arms." Army and SS leaders agreed on the need for special SS commandos (*Einsatzgruppen*) to liquidate the Russian Jews, as they constituted the "biological root" of Bolshevism. Even a "moderate" such as General Erich Hoepner, who later would join the German resistance movement, accepted this line of reasoning: "It is the old struggle of Germans against Slavs, the defense of European culture against Muscovy-Asiatic inundation, the warding off of Jewish Bolshevism." Hitler confided to Mussolini that he had always loathed the Nazi-Soviet Treaty of August 1939 but that he was now "once again intrinsically free" as a result of this decision.

Operation Barbarossa was temporarily delayed by two Italian initiatives. In April 1941 a German army made a detour to Yugoslavia and Greece to rescue Italian forces from impending annihilation. Concurrently, General Rommel was dispatched to North Africa on a similar mission. The delay did not threaten pending German operations in the Soviet Union. After all, General Erich Marcks' plan predicted victory in the east at best in seven, at worst in nine, weeks. Marcks' optimistic prognosis, with which Hitler fully concurred, was almost borne out by events.

On June 22, 1941, one year to the day after the French armistice at Compiègne, 150 German divisions dealt the Soviet Union a staggering blow. Within two months, Field Marshal Wilhelm von Leeb's Army Group North pinned Soviet forces against the Baltic Sea and besieged Leningrad. Army Group Center, commanded by Field Marshal Fedor von Bock, moved from Warsaw and advanced spectacularly: Minsk fell by July 10 with the loss of 290,000 prisoners and Smolensk nine days later with an additional 100,000 prisoners. Army Group South, headed by Field Marshal Gerd von Rundstedt, drove into the Ukraine in textbook operations: more than 665,000 Soviet troops surrendered at Kiev on September 19; an equal number capitulated at Vyazma on October 7. During November General von Manstein invaded the Crimea, while General Wilhelm von Kleist seized Rostov.

Euphoria combined with megalomania reigned at Hitler's headquarters near Rastenburg in East Prussia. Even the usually cautious General Halder expressed confidence on July 3 that "the campaign against Russia will be won within fourteen days." On July 14 Hitler assured the Japanese ambassador, General Hiroshi Oshima, that the war would be over in six weeks and that Berlin and Tokyo ought to formulate plans "jointly to annihilate" the United States. The Führer spoke of the Urals as the future border of the "Greater Germanic Empire of the German Nation" — an obvious throwback to the Holy Roman Empire — and resurrected plans from the Great War to annex the Crimea, which was to be renamed "Gothenland." Further, he expressed his "total determination" to raze Leningrad and Moscow as Rome had once done with Carthage. Two days later, he informed army and party leaders of his plans to subdivide the Soviet Union into four "commissariats": Eastland, Muscovy, the Caucasus, and the Ukraine, "firstly to rule, secondly to administer, and

OPERATION BARBAROSSA

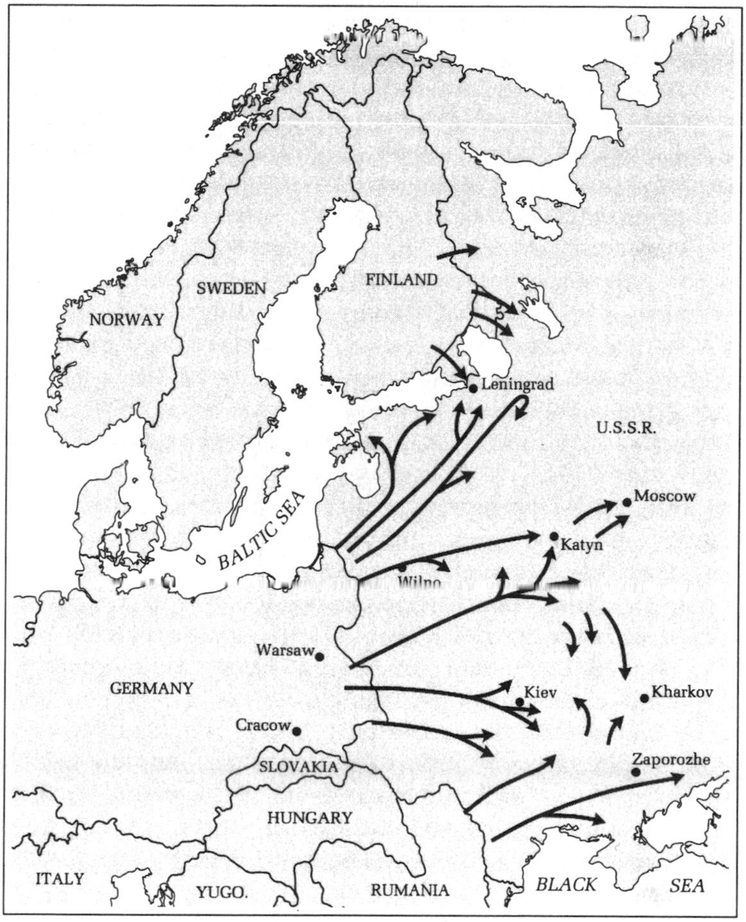

thirdly to exploit." Never again, he assured his listeners, would a military power be allowed to rise west of the Urals. "Iron rule must be and must remain: Never may others than Germans be permitted to bear arms." By July 14 Hitler was so confident of victory that he ordered priorities in armaments production to be shifted to the air force and the navy.

Albert Speer was given orders to translate the impending triumph into architectural wonders. Berlin would become nothing short of the "capital of the world" where, in a monstrous assembly hall, topped by a dome 250 meters in diameter, Hitler would hold his world court. Initially, the dome was to be crowned with an eagle clutching a swastika in its claws 290 meters above ground; Hitler now changed the swastika to a globe, which, in Speer's words, "Hitler did not wish to possess merely as a symbol." A central train station would dwarf Grand Central Terminal in New York; a North-South Axis would be twice as broad as the Champs Elysées in Paris; and an Arch of Triumph, at 117 meters high and 170 meters wide, would double the dimensions of its counterpart in the French capital.

Hitler also harbored more sinister plans. During the night of July 11–12, 1941, harking back to Dietrich Eckart's work *Bolshevism from Moses to Lenin*, the Führer informed his innermost circle that Bolshevism was but the "illegitimate son of Christianity; both are the offspring of Judaism." Religion and National Socialism, he told his listeners, were incompatible. As for "the ridiculous hundred million Slavs," Hitler proposed to turn them into carriers of water and hewers of wood; they would not be inoculated against diseases or taught how to read or write, and the males would be sterilized. The brutal nature of the war in the east, for which Hitler suspended the Geneva Convention, can be strikingly demonstrated by a single episode: the 707th Infantry Division, operating in White Russia, in its monthly report for October–November 1941 stated that it had shot 10,431 out of a total of 10,940 "captives," while suffering but 7 casualties.

If Hitler ever had a chance to win the war in the east, it would have been with the support of the indigenous populations, many of whom were receptive to ending Stalinist rule. Instead, he announced that he had come not as liberator but as conqueror and refused, as he put it, to wage war by "Salvation Army methods." Instead, thousands of Russians were summarily executed by army and SS firing squads. More than 3 million Russian prisoners of war died in German detention camps from starvation, illness, and exhaustion by May 1944. The SS *Einsatzgruppen* repeatedly noted the staunch support they received from senior military commanders such as Generals Erich Hoepner, Walther von Reichenau, Gerd von Rundstedt, and Karl-Heinrich von Stülpnagel, among others. Russians and Ukrainians countered this barbarization with partisan warfare, which proved especially effective against the German rear echelon supply system.

On July 15 Himmler shaped prevailing German views on the future order in the Soviet Union into "General Plan East": in thirty years, more than 30 million Russians would be "relocated" behind the Urals and their lands "resettled" by Germans. The rest of the Slavs would be "racially leached" and "scrapped" over time. Sixteen days later, Göring, probably acting on verbal orders from Hitler, instructed Heydrich to commence preparations "for a total solution of the Jewish question in the German sphere of influence in Europe." Heydrich was instructed to submit "an overall plan" analyzing all aspects "of the intended final solution of the Jewish question." For the first time the phrase *final solution* appeared in official use. Internally, the SS referred to the July 31 missive as Führer Order No. 1 on the Jewish Question. In July Himmler increased the numbers of troops engaged in executions on the eastern front sixfold, to nineteen thousand.

The face of defeat: A German soldier in straw boots leaves Stalingrad for an uncertain fate.

But the Soviet Union had first to be defeated, and conquest was not proving easy. Desperate Soviet counterattacks forced Rundstedt out of Rostov in November. Central Russian forces, now commanded by Marshal Georgi K. Zhukov, halted the German advance in the suburbs of Moscow. As temperatures plunged to forty degrees below zero Fahrenheit, German armor was immobilized, and men froze. Nevertheless, German generals, undoubtedly remembering the halt at the Marne in September 1914, opted to push the last reserves into the assault on Moscow. When the capital refused to fall, Hitler ordered that the line fifty miles west of Moscow be held at all cost. The price proved terribly high to Germany: 831,000 casualties by December 31. Hitler once more held to his old social Darwinistic all-or-nothing mind-set. On November 27, 1941, he informed the Danish foreign minister, Erik Scavenius, that "if the German people are no longer sufficiently strong and prepared to sacrifice their own blood for their survival, then they shall perish and be annihilated by another, stronger power."

Having already discovered such lack of "strength" and willingness to "sacrifice" among his generals, Hitler in December 1941 personally assumed command of the German army. Over time, he would fire half his generals for similar lack of conviction, in the process reducing the General Staff, in the words of General Halder, to nothing more than "letter carriers." Comparing his own position in the winter of 1941 to that in which Generals Paul von Hindenburg and Erich Ludendorff had found themselves in 1917, Hitler decided on a bold offensive similar to Operation Michael in the spring of 1918. The summer of 1942 would bring a final, desperate German drive into the oil and grain reserves of southern Russia. Hitler termed the offensive his "last chance to alter destiny."

Before Hitler could launch his operation, he received word over the BBC Radio in London that his ally, Japan, on December 7, 1941, had attacked the U.S. naval base at Pearl Harbor. While his military planners scrambled to find Pearl Harbor in an atlas, Hitler rushed to Berlin and in a "heroic gesture" on December 11 declared war against the United States.

What prompted this act? Germany was required under the auspices of the Tripartite Pact of September 1940 to declare war only if Japan were attacked by a third party. Foreign Minister von Ribbentrop opted for the declaration of war on grounds of prestige: "A great power . . . declares war itself." Admiral Raeder counseled war for practical reasons: "The situation in the Atlantic will be eased due to the successful intervention of Japan."

Hitler himself was driven by a combination of factors. He had long resented U.S. interference in European affairs and had developed a visceral dislike of President Franklin D. Roosevelt, whom he denounced as a "lout" and a syphilitic aristocrat and whom he compared to the equally "mentally insane" Woodrow Wilson. Additionally, a declaration of war now would demonstrate Germany's solidarity with the Japanese and perhaps keep them from making a separate peace with the United States later. By declaring war on the United States, Hitler, who undoubtedly desired to finish the eastern campaign the following year, hoped to force it to divide its resources equally into Atlantic and Pacific components and thereby prevent it from decisively intervening in Europe in 1942. In other words, if the campaign in 1942 in the east succeeded, Hitler would control a blockade-safe "Fortress Europe" against which the Americans would be powerless. Again, it was all or nothing.

Götterdämmerung

The German campaign in the east in 1941 had exacted a terrible toll in men and matériel. The semiofficial German history of the war concludes that 3,254 armored vehicles, 121,529 trucks, and 14,648 pieces of artillery were lost between June and December 1941. The invading army of June 22 boasted about 3 million men: by the end of the year, 831,000 German soldiers were listed as killed, missing, or wounded. Numerous divisions reported that they were down to 50 percent of strength. Reserves were exhausted. The death toll would rise dramatically as the harsh winter of 1941–1942 set in.

The National Socialists harbored a morbid fascination with heroic death. In all likelihood, Richard Wagner's apocalyptic vision of a "Twilight of the Gods" greatly appealed to Hitler, who instructed Wilhelm Kreis to design monstrous *Totenburgen* (castles of the dead) from the Vistula to the Dnieper rivers. Kreis was ordered to draw up plans for a gigantic Berlin Hall of Soldiers, where the great captains of Germany, both past and present, were to be interred; for his part, Hitler desired to be laid to rest in a tower in Linz. Somber ceremonies were highlighted by torchlight and mystical rituals.

The darkest side of National Socialism came to the fore after events shifted in the war late in 1942. A German advance into the Caucasus along a 500-mile front, personally commanded by Hitler, ground to a halt before Stalingrad on the Volga River. On November 9, 1942, Hitler, in Munich to celebrate the abortive beer-hall putsch of 1923, confidently boasted: "We already have Stalingrad." On November 19–20, two Soviet army groups crept to the north of the city; five days later, they had encircled it. A prestigious objective, Stalingrad became the Verdun of World War II. By February 2, 1943, General Friedrich Paulus and the Sixth Army surrendered, having been denied by Hitler repeated requests to retreat: 165,000 prisoners and more than 1,000 tanks were taken by Marshal Zhukov's forces. Hitler compared Stalingrad to the Greeks at Thermopylae;[1] Goebbels to Frederick the Great's desperate defense of his crown during the latter stages of the Seven Years' War. The SS noted "deep depression" among the general populace and a feeling that Stalingrad was the "beginning of the end." Indeed, this defeat destroyed the Hitler myth.

Almost concurrently, early in November 1942 British General Bernard L. Montgomery's 8th Army drove Rommel's Afrika Korps back from El Alamein in Egypt, costing the Reich 60,000 men and 500 tanks. At the same moment, Anglo-American armies landed in Morocco and Algeria. Hitler knew that the game was up. Late in 1942, he confided to General Jodl that "victory could no longer be attained." Yet the Führer, ever the social Darwinist, was firmly resolved to carry the war to its final, devastating conclusion.

The summer of 1943 brought little cheer to Hitler. On July 5 he launched a desperate attack against six Soviet armies around Kursk, hoping to preclude a general Soviet advance that summer. The action quickly degenerated into a great battle of attrition. The Soviets counterattacked on July 12 and by early August switched to a general offensive around Kursk that destroyed the German Army Group Center (70,000 men and 3,000 tanks lost).

Finally, during the summer of 1943, Admiral Karl Dönitz, Raeder's successor as head of the navy, lost the Battle of the Atlantic. The U-boats had inflicted

[1] To halt the Persian advance into Greece in the spring of 480 B.C., King Leonidas of Sparta with about seven thousand hoplites and archers defended the pass at Thermopylae to the last man. The heoric action allowed time for the Peloponnesian states to augment and organize their forces.

staggering losses on Allied shipping on the vital North Atlantic run — 500,000 tons per month between June and November 1942 — but they were unable to gain the desired advantage in the battle of logistics. By 1943 Dönitz's vaunted submarine force was no longer able to ravage Allied supply routes because of stronger air-sea protection: 3,546 merchantmen in sixty-two convoys crossed the North Atlantic without a single loss. Allied countermeasures to the U-boat threat, such as convoy, radar, aerial patrols, depth charges, electronic intercepts, and special naval "killer groups" — combined with Dönitz's insane insistence on maintaining constant contact by radio with his submarines — took a devastating toll on the U-boats: 784 vessels were destroyed at sea, and of the 40,900 men recruited for the submarine branch, 28,000 were killed and 5,000 taken prisoner.

Hitler's reaction to these reversals was a fanatical determination to fight to the end. On November 9, 1942, he informed the "old guard" gathered at Munich that "only one thing remains, and that is *Kampf*," to "fight and fight again." The word *capitulation*, Hitler averred, did not exist in his vocabulary. And whereas the army of Imperial Germany had "laid down its arms at fifteen minutes to twelve, as a matter of principle, I always stop only at five minutes past twelve." On another occasion, Hitler let it be known that he would not "shed any tears for the German people": life was simple, the strong won, the weak deserved to perish. "I am also as cold as ice in this: if the German people are not willing to take an active part in their self-preservation, good: then they shall cease to exist."

In 1943 Joseph Goebbels acknowledged that the Third Reich was on a course of total destruction: "We have burned our bridges." Again, it was all or nothing. "We will go into history books either as the greatest statesmen or as the greatest criminals."

The final *Götterdämmerung* took many forms. Arrests at home soared: fifteen thousand in October 1941 alone, ten times the rate in 1935–1936. Military courts meted out barbaric justice in order to keep the war going: whereas the U.S. Army in war handed down 763 death sentences overall and executed a single soldier for desertion, the *Wehrmacht* meted out fifty thousand death sentences and executed nearly six thousand soldiers for desertion. Under the provisions of the infamous "night and fog" decree[1] adopted by SS and army in September 1941, about seven thousand people, mainly French, were deported to Germany as potential enemies in occupied territories. Soviet prisoners of war starved or froze to death on a massive scale or were consigned to special

[1] On December 7, 1941, Hitler and General Wilhelm Keitel issued a secret order designed to suppress resistance movements in Belgium, France, Denmark, the Netherlands, and Norway. Suspected resisters were to be arrested quietly and to disappear in the "fog of the night." In all, 6,639 people were arrested and 1,793 sentenced to death.

sections in concentration camps. And nearly 5 million men and women recruited from German-occupied Europe labored under inhumane conditions in industrial plants supervised by Franz Sauckel's labor allocation enterprise.

In fact, the nature of the camps was changing rapidly. In February 1940 work was begun on the former barracks of the Austro-Hungarian army at Auschwitz to transform them from a camp for political prisoners and prisoners of war to a possible industrial hub, and finally to a complex of thirty-nine camps housing more than 100,000 inmates — in short, a center for annihilating Jews. A satellite camp at Birkenau consisted of 250 wood and stone barracks. German industries such as IG-Farben and Siemens Schuckert relocated plants to take advantage of this free labor supply. In the fall of 1941 additional camps sprang up in eastern Poland at Bełżec, Majdanek, Sobibór, and Treblinka, among others. At the height of the Holocaust in 1943, Auschwitz and Birkenau averaged about 120,000 prisoners. Thus, the Holocaust became a major phase of the war.

On January 30, 1939, Adolf Hitler had informed Reichstag deputies that, were "international Jewish financiers" to force war on Germany, it would end with "the annihilation of the Jewish race in Europe." He kept his word. Yet Hitler's only order for mass killings came on September 1, 1939, when he decreed the "mercy killing" of the physically and mentally disadvantaged. Under the "euthanasia" program (code-named T4), about eighty thousand people were killed in six centers. Chemists from the Reich Criminal Investigation Office experimented with carbon monoxide to poison those slated for death. When church opposition in August 1941 forced the SS to cancel the program in Germany, it was merely shifted to the eastern camps (code-named 14f13). For the rest of the killing, Hitler preferred to issue verbal commands couched in euphemisms such as *final solution* and *actions*. Those who know the nature of the regime and Hitler's relationship with his underlings unanimously agree that the Holocaust could not have been carried out without the Führer's knowledge and consent.

Hitler probably gave the order to carry out the "final solution of the Jewish question" (*Endlösung*) at the height of his victory euphoria in the summer of 1941. Plans for the "physical final solution" of Soviet Jews had circulated in military planning as early as March 1941. In mid-June Reinhard Heydrich instructed his SS *Einsatzgruppen* of their duty to murder "all Jews employed in the [Soviet] state or party apparatus." During the first five months of the campaign in the east, Heydrich's forces reported the "liquidation" of 380,000 Jews by mobile execution squads. The death camps in Poland were established in the fall of 1941, and in October former "T4" personnel arrived to direct killing operations using gas. The first gassing of Jews took place at the Chełmno concentration camp in western Poland in December 1941.

On January 20, 1942, Heydrich chaired a meeting at Wannsee, a Berlin suburb, to coordinate the "final solution." Acting on Göring's directives of July 31,

"Final solution": Hungarian Jews being selected for death or slave labor at the railroad siding at Auschwitz-Birkenau (1943).

1941, which Heydrich announced were the direct result of "instructions from the Führer," the head of the SD targeted Europe's 11 million Jews[1] (1.4 million had already been murdered) for "liquidation." Adolf Eichmann, head of Department IV B4 in the *Gestapo* within the SD, was empowered to begin the mass roundup and transportation of European Jews to the east. At his trial in Jerusalem in 1961 Eichmann spoke of his "uncommon joy" in "solving" a world-historical "problem" by killing 6 million European Jews.

At Wannsee, the main governmental bureaucracy (Interior, Foreign Office, Chancery, Four Year Plan, East Ministry, Justice, and the General Government in Poland) became accessories to the "final solution." This seduction and corruption of the Reich bureaucracy at Wannsee was later acknowledged by the

[1] Experts on the Holocaust agree that Heydrich's figure was probably too high and that there were about 9 million Jews in Europe at the time.

Prussian conservative, Ewald von Kleist-Schmenzin, when he coined the phrase: "Unprincipled as a German civil servant, godless as a Protestant cleric, and dishonorable as a Prussian officer." Above all, at Wannsee Heydrich served notice that he was to be regarded as the principal architect of the "final solution."

Did the Führer know about the slaughter? As early as August 1941 Gestapo chief Heinrich Müller ordered all SS execution squads to send Hitler "constant reports" about their "work in the east." In 1942 Hitler alluded to the destruction of European Jewry in no fewer than four public speeches. In December 1942 Himmler sent Hitler a detailed report of the work of the special *Einsatzgruppen* and claimed 336,211 Jews as victims to date. In addition, Himmler and Heydrich of the SD, as well as commandant Höss at Auschwitz, routinely commented on Hitler's direct involvement in the Holocaust. Goebbels was equally blunt: "The Führer has ordered the final solution of the Jewish question." When senior camp commanders, wary that no paperwork existed on the Holocaust, demanded written instructions, Martin Bormann, head of Hitler's chancery, in July 1943 curtly informed them that all matters pertaining to the *Endlösung* were to be verbal.

Hitler remained absolutely consistent to the end. The "Political Testament" that he dictated on April 29, 1945, not only admonished Germans "punctiliously to observe the racial laws" and to fight on against "the poisoner of all the nations of the world, international Jewry" but blamed the entire course of the lost war on "international Jewry and its helpers." Future generations, however, would in time be grateful "that I extirpated the Jews from Germany and Central Europe." Little wonder that Elie Wiesel, a Nobel Prize-winning author and survivor of the Holocaust, in his book *Night* has one of the camp inmates sardonically state: "I've got more faith in Hitler than in anyone else. He's the only one who's kept his promises, all his promises, to the Jewish people."

Most victims of the Holocaust went to their deaths too stunned and terrorized to resist. Yet some were defiant, cursing their German tormentors. Others plotted escape. Some resisted actively.

The behavior of the perpetrators of the Holocaust defies rational explanation. It is too simplistic to dismiss them as psychopaths or sadists. Many readily accepted the ideological foundations of the regime's obsession with racial purity. Some acted out of a distorted sense of executing a higher good. Others, placed outside their peacetime social environment, took at face value Himmler's repeated assurances that they were not engaged in criminal activity. Still others rationalized that the barbarization of warfare in the east had already removed all normal conventions and constraints. And some acted out of self-serving careerism.

Reichsführer-SS Heinrich Himmler addressed the question of how one could undertake such a monstrous policy at Posen (Poznań) in October 1943. He informed senior SS officers that he had come to them to speak "quite frankly" on a "very grave matter," one that "we will never speak of publicly": the "extermination of the Jewish race." Having noted some demoralization among them, Himmler assured SS leaders that he recognized their service to Germany: "To have stuck it out and at the same time, apart from exceptions caused by human weakness, to have remained decent, that is what has made us hard. This is a page of glory in our history which has never to be written and which never will be written." He lauded his listeners for having "cauterized" the Jewish "sepsis" and for a task well done. "We had the moral right, the duty to our *Volk*, to destroy this people which wanted to destroy us." One wonders whether the irony of this attempt at racial "purity" ever dawned on SS leaders with such "German" names as Globocnik, Skorzeny, Wisliceny, and Zelewsky.

Ordinary Germans were not totally ignorant of the "final solution." Deportations were conducted in broad daylight, and local police were involved. Transports were seen and heard. Jews next door disappeared overnight. Hundreds of thousands of German soldiers on leave from the Russian front told of mass executions in the east. German soldiers from the west reported the large-scale roundups and deportations of Belgian, Dutch, and French Jews. And the SS reported that Hitler's dark references to the "final solution" were picked up by the general populace.

Perhaps the final comment on the Holocaust should be left to one of its intended victims. Dr. Zalman Grinberg, survivor of the Kovno ghetto and the death marches, told Dachau survivors in May 1945, nearly a month after their liberation by American forces: "Hitler has lost every battle on every front except the battle against defenceless and unarmed men, women, and children. He won the war against the Jews of Europe. He carried out this war with the help of the German nation."

In the last year of the war, the Third Reich decided not to spare even its own people. With Goebbels' creation of a last manpower reserve — the *Volkssturm* consisting of all males between the ages of fifteen and sixty, roughly analogous to the *Landsturm* established during the War of Liberation after 1806 — more and more German men were sucked into destruction. At another level, the Allied bombing offensive against German cities claimed 500,000 civilians. "Fortress Europe," in the words of President Roosevelt, possessed no "roof." Only Goebbels could see profit in the "bombing terror," informing his listeners that thereby "the last remaining class barriers" were being torn down and that bourgeois Europe had, in fact, been destroyed by Allied Bomber Command!

The bombing campaign over Germany reached its deadly climax between January 1944 and January 1945. U.S. Army Air Forces alone flew 755,000 sorties in which they dropped 1.4 million tons of bombs. Given the highly inaccurate nature of aerial bombing even in daylight attacks, Allied pilots often dropped their loads indiscriminately in and around major German cities. The results were mixed. Petroleum and chemical industries were hit hardest: the supply of aviation fuel plunged to 10 percent of need by September 1944, and the flow of ammunition to the fronts virtually ceased early in 1945. The U.S. Strategic Bombing Survey conducted after the war concluded that the attack on Germany's transport system, which started late in the war, was also a success: the critical resupply of the fronts had stopped almost completely by September 1944. Coal stocks were reduced to eighteen days by October 1944. The aerial assault on other vital industries was less effective. German electric power systems were given too low a priority in strategic bombing and hence managed to maintain power production almost to the end of the war. Less than 17 percent of all capital stocks and only 6.5 percent of machines were destroyed, according to the Strategic Bombing Survey. In addition, 14 percent of Allied bombs dropped on Germany failed to explode. Thus, it is safe to conclude that strategic bombing was a major factor in defeating Germany but not decisive alone.

The effect of bombing upon civilian morale is almost impossible to gauge. Public opinion surveys conducted by the SS secret service revealed that Allied destruction of German cities strengthened the populace's resolve to fight on to the bitter end. But what German would report another sentiment to the SS in 1944? It would not be far off the mark to suggest that the ready surrender to the Allies of industrial areas in western Germany during the last months of the war in part resulted from the devastating effect of Allied bombing on German morale and production.

In many ways June 1944 proved to be the darkest month of the war for German armed forces. On June 6 the greatest amphibious assault known to history (Operation Overlord) began along the Normandy coast in France. More than 4,000 Allied ships landed 176,000 troops and their gear after nearly 10,000 aircraft had dropped 10,000 tons of explosives on the German defenders. And on June 22, 1944, the third anniversary of Operation Barbarossa, the Soviets launched a massive offensive against Army Group Center, in which they mauled twenty-eight German divisions (381,000 men) and destroyed 2,000 tanks.

It was only a matter of time before Hitler's "little war" ended. By the end of July, Allied forces broke out of their beachheads and in August liberated Paris. That same month, the U.S. 7th Army (nearly 100,000 soldiers) landed on the Côte d'Azur in southern France and drove up the Rhône Valley in order to protect the Allies' southern flank in France. By September 1944 Allied forces under the command of General Dwight D. Eisenhower closed on the German border.

Operation Overlord finally galvanized the German resistance. A loose collection of disparate workers, civil servants, and officers without a solid base, the resistance had spent most of its time debating the nature of a future German state. Its members could never quite come to grips with the need to murder the head of state. One such resistance group was the Wednesday Society in Berlin consisting of renowned academics such as the historians Hermann Oncken and Friedrich Meinecke, the noted surgeon Ernst Friedrich Sauerbruch, and former minister Wilhelm Groener. Another resistance center was

Finis Germaniae? The Reichstag Building (1944–1945).

organized by Helmuth James von Moltke at his estate Kreisau in Silesia and consisted of civil servants, clergy, and workers — men who were morally and politically outraged by the Nazi's reign of terror and who feared for Germany's future.

Several German Communists, such as Anton Saefkow in Berlin, Franz Jacob in Hamburg, and Theodor Neubauer and Magnus Poser in Thuringia, organized regional workers' resistance movements. They were joined by the so-called red orchestra of Harro Schulze-Boysen and Arvid Harnback that sought to establish contacts with the Soviet Union. And finally there was the "white rose" student group, led by Hans and Sophie Scholl, that distributed anti-Nazi leaflets at Munich University and established contact with other university students opposed to the regime. The SS managed to destroy most of these resistance groups between 1942 and 1944.

More promising was the resistance movement within the army, mainly because its members had occasional contact with Hitler and finally resolved that the Führer's death was necessary to Germany's salvation.[1] Its most active members included Henning von Tresckow, Claus Schenck von Stauffenberg, Friedrich Olbricht, and former chief of staff Ludwig Beck. In a note to Stauffenberg, Tresckow attested to the officers' motivations:

> The assassination must be attempted, regardless of cost. Even if it should fail, something must be done in Berlin. For it no longer is solely a question of our immediate goals but of showing the world that the German resistance movement dared to take the decisive step. Compared with this, nothing else matters.

On July 20, 1944, Colonel von Stauffenberg detonated a bomb at Hitler's headquarters, but it failed to kill the Führer. The planned seizure of power throughout German-controlled Europe (Operation Valkyrie) similarly failed.

Hitler decided to unleash the last revolutionary energy of his movement against the resistance: "This time we will deal with them in the manner to which National Socialists are accustomed." A special People's Court under Roland Freisler dispatched instant justice in accordance with Hitler's instructions: "I want to see them hanged, hanged like cattle." On August 8, 1944, the first eight officers from the resistance condemned to death were hanged by piano wire in the meat locker of the Plötzensee Prison in Berlin. The officers' wives and children were also condemned to death. Hitler railed against "the 'vons' who call themselves aristocrats"; in the end, he turned against the Junker elite that had constituted the backbone of Prussia since the time of the Great Elector. The "twin-pillar theory" of army and party was a dead letter. The great tragedy, according to Hans-Ulrich Thamer, a recent German historian of the Nazi regime, is that more people died during the bombings, deportations, forced marches, and collapse of the military fronts in the last few months of the war than had died during the previous four years of the war.

But nothing could deter the bitter end for Germany. The promised "wonder weapons" such as the V1 and V2 rockets, while deadly to those targeted, were no match for Allied and Soviet artillery and tanks. The death of President Roosevelt on April 12, 1945, had no impact on the Allies' demand for Germany's "unconditional surrender."[2] Nor did Hitler's "Nero Order"[3] of March 19, 1945, ordering the total destruction of Germany, slow the Allied offensive.

---

1 Army officers had made about half a dozen abortive attempts on Hitler's life between 1938 and 1943.

2 Goebbels, reading to his Führer from Thomas Carlyle's *History of Frederick II of Prussia*, likened Roosevelt's death to that of the Tsarina Elizabeth in 1762, the so-called Miracle of the House of Hohenzollern.

3 Hitler's "Nero" order of March 19, 1945, demanded the total destruction of German communications and transport systems, shipping, bridges, industrial plants, postal service, and the like, through dynamiting or burning.

On April 25, 1945, U.S. and Soviet forces met at Torgau on the Elbe River. Although the German Navy rescued 2 million residents of East Prussia, nearly 3 million died fleeing from the advancing Red Army.

On April 30, the "first soldier of the German Reich" deserted, along with his wife of one day, Eva Braun, by committing suicide in his bunker in Berlin. World War II ended as it had started, with a lie: Admiral Dönitz reported by radio to the nation that its Führer had sustained "heroic death in battle."

The nightmare was finally over. The "Thousand-Year Reich" had lasted just twelve years. The European civil war of 1914 had exhausted itself. Hitler's megalomania had brought the Red Army to the Elbe River. Central Europe was divided between the two flanking powers, the United States and the Soviet Union. Both the European order and the German nation-state lay in ruins. Perhaps as a final, perverse irony, the man who had wanted to extirpate European Jewry actually helped create the state of Israel.

The human cost of the war was staggering. Globally, 55 million people died. Germany sustained 3.76 million military dead, 4 million wounded, and 500,000 missing in action. The Soviet Union claimed 7.5 million in military losses, as well as 12.5 million in civilian dead. Of its 5.7 million prisoners of war, 3.3 million died during internment. Most of Europe from Paris to Moscow lay in ashes; more than a hundred major German cities had been leveled. Adolf Hitler's prophesy at the start of the war, that in ten year's time one would not recognize Germany again, had found terrible fulfillment. Few expected the "German question" ever to resurface.

Suggested Readings

The expansionistic impulses of National Socialist ideology have been examined by Eberhard Jäckel, *Hitler's World View: A Blueprint for Power* (Middletown, Conn., 1972). In more traditional terms, the war aims program of the Third Reich is traced by Norman Rich, *Hitler's War Aims*, vol. 1, *Ideology, the Nazi State, and the Course of Expansion*, and vol. 2, *The Establishment of the New Order* (New York, 1973). The most detailed analysis of Hitler's foreign policy has been offered by Gerhard L. Weinberg, *The Foreign Policy of Hitler's Germany*, vol. 1, *Diplomatic Revolution in Europe, 1933–36*, and vol. 2, *Starting World War II, 1937–1939* (Chicago, 1970, 1980). A forceful assault upon appeasement has been launched by Williamson Murray, *The Change in the European Balance of Power, 1938–1939* (Princeton, 1984). The best guide to that policy is Wolfgang J. Mommsen and Lothar Kettenacker, eds., *The Fascist Challenge and the Policy of Appeasement* (London, 1983).

Two senior German scholars provide abridged versions of their major findings: Andreas Hillgruber, *Germany and the Two World Wars* (Cambridge, Mass., 1981), and Klaus Hildebrand, *The Foreign Policy of the Third Reich* (Berkeley and Los Angeles, 1973). The classic account of Austro-German relations in 1938 is by Gordon Brook-Shepherd, *The Anschluss: The Rape of*

Austria (London, 1963). Hitler's views with regard to America have been analyzed by Holger H. Herwig, *Politics of Frustration: The United States in German Naval Planning, 1889–1941* (Boston and Toronto, 1976).

Economic preparations for war can be studied in Berenice Carroll, *Design for Total War: Arms and Economics in the Third Reich* (The Hague, 1968); for the early period of rearmament, see R. J. Overy, *The Nazi Economic Recovery, 1932–1938* (London, 1982). Less satisfactory are Burton H. Klein, *Germany's Economic Preparations for War* (Cambridge, Mass., 1959), and Alan Milward, *The German Economy at War* (London, 1965). The German buildup has been expertly detailed by Wilhelm Deist, *The Wehrmacht and German Rearmament* (London, 1981).

The relationship between Hitler and the generals has received a great deal of attention. Students will still do well to consult the older works by Gordon A. Craig, *The Politics of the Prussian Army, 1649–1945* (New York, 1956), and John W. Wheeler-Bennett, *The Nemesis of Power: The German Army in Politics, 1918–1945* (London, 1953). More recent treatments are by Esmonde M. Robertson, *Hitler's Pre-War Policy and Military Plans, 1933–1939* (New York, 1967); Robert J. O'Neill, *The German Army and the Nazi Party, 1933–1939* (London, 1966); and, especially, Omer Bartov, *Hitler's Army: Soldiers, Nazis and War in the Third Reich* (New York, 1991). Three brilliant essays are provided by Klaus-Jürgen Müller, *The Army, Politics and Society in Germany, 1933–45: Studies in the Army's Relation to Nazism* (New York, 1987). Charles S. Thomas, *The German Navy in the Nazi Era* (London, 1990), has offered the first English-language account of party and navy, and Williamson Murray, *Luftwaffe* (Baltimore, 1985), reveals the shortcomings of the German air force.

Students of the German military in the Third Reich need to be cautioned about the extensive memoir literature, much of which was penned by the generals, along with such sympathetic historians as Basil Liddell-Hart, *The Other Side of the Hill: Germany's Generals, Their Rise and Fall, with Their Own Account of Military Events, 1939–1945* (London, 1948), and Harold Deutsch, *Hitler and His Generals: The Hidden Crisis, January–June 1938* (Minneapolis, 1974), to serve as apologia. The theme of almost all is that if the generals had had their way, Germany would have won the war. Two examples why care should be taken must suffice. The head of military intelligence in the east, Reinhard Gehlen, actually penned his "memoirs," *The Service: The Memoirs of General Reinhard Gehlen* (New York, 1972), in 1944 in an effort to obscure the fact that his office repeatedly and grossly underestimated Soviet capabilities. Germany's two leading admirals — Erich Raeder, *My Life* (Annapolis, 1960), and Karl Dönitz, *Memoirs: Ten Years and Twenty Days* (London, 1959) — had Admiral Erich Förste ghostwrite their memoirs so that no conflict in their interpretations of the war at sea should emerge. Thus, readers will look in vain for the bitter conflict that raged between the two concerning the deployment of "big ships" or U-boats.

The story of the German military is currently being written by a team of scholars at the Military History Research Office at Freiburg; six volumes in

German are out, and the first two have appeared in English with Oxford University Press: *Germany and the Second World War* (London, 1990, 1991). A sample of their work can be gleaned from Wilhelm Deist, ed., *The German Military in the Age of Total War* (Leamington Spa, 1985), as well as from two articles by Manfred Messerschmidt, "German Military Effectiveness between 1919 and 1939," and Jürgen E. Förster, "The Dynamics of the *Volksgemeinschaft*: The Effectiveness of the German Military Establishment in the Second World War," in Allan R. Millett and Williamson Murray, eds., *Military Effectiveness* (Boston, 1988), vols. 2, 3.

German exploitation of European labor has been chronicled by Edward L. Homze, *Foreign Labor in Nazi Germany* (Princeton, 1967), and the effects of the war — and specifically the Allied bombing campaign — are examined in Earl R. Beck, *Under the Bombs: The German Home Front, 1942–1945* (Lexington, Ky., 1986). Theo Schulte, *The German Army and Nazi Policies in the Soviet Union* (New York, 1988), and Omer Bartov, *The Eastern Front 1941–45: German Troops and the Barbarisation of Warfare* (New York, 1986), have exploded the myth of the "decent" German military as opposed to the "evil" National Socialist occupation policies in the east. Readers should also consult Albert Speer, *Inside the Third Reich* (New York, 1970), as an insider's account by one of the few thinking members of the NSDAP elite.

The notoriety of the SS drew the attention of scholars early on: Gerald Reitlinger, *The S.S.: Alibi of a Nation, 1922–1945* (London, 1956); George H. Stein, *The Waffen SS: Hitler's Elite Guard at War, 1939–1945* (Ithaca, NY, 1966); Heinz Höhne, *The Order of the Death's Head: The Story of Hitler's SS* (New York, 1970); and Charles Sydnor, Jr., *Soldiers of Destruction: The SS Death's Head Division, 1933–1945* (Princeton, 1977). The most recent scholarly interpretation is Bernd Wegner, *The Waffen-SS: Organization, Ideology and Function* (Oxford, 1990). A superb general overview of Himmler's empire remains Helmut Krausnick and Hans Buchheim, eds., *Anatomy of the SS-State* (New York, 1968).

The men and women who paid the ultimate price for resisting Hitler have been examined by Peter Hoffmann, *The History of the German Resistance, 1933–1945* (Cambridge, Mass., 1979). The carnage to Germany in terms of human lives has been revealed sympathetically by Martin K. Sorge, *The Other Price of Hitler's War: German Military and Civilian Losses Resulting from World War II* (Westport, Conn., 1986). The Holocaust was first chronicled by Raul Hilberg, *The Destruction of European Jews* (New York, 1961). Students should also consult Martin Gilbert's exhaustive *The Holocaust: A History of the Jews of Europe during the Second World War* (New York, 1985), and Leni Yahil, *The Holocaust: The Fate of European Jewry* (Oxford, 1990). Hitler's role in the "final solution" has been established by Gerald Fleming, *Hitler and the Final Solution* (Berkeley and Los Angeles, 1984). The most recent examination is by François Furet, ed., *Unanswered Questions: Nazi Germany and the Genocide of the Jews* (New York, 1989).

C H A P T E R

10

A HOUSE DIVIDED: GERMANY, 1945–1960

Article I. The dignity of people is inviolable. It is the duty of all state power to respect and to defend it.

Basic Law, 1949

The shadow of the failure of the Weimar Republic hung over German politicians after 1945. Would a second attempt at democracy be possible? Would it succeed? Or would traditional elites combine once more with radical popular movements to bring about another authoritarian and antidemocratic government? And what policy toward Germany's future would the two major Allies, the Soviet Union and the United States, adopt? Would the former seek to impose a Soviet-style system in its zone of occupation? And would the latter duplicate its free-market capitalist economy in its sector?

In fact, history now favored the democratic cause. The center of economic and political power in Germany shifted to the Rhine as a result of the nation's division in 1949 — into the Federal Republic of Germany (FRG) at Bonn and the German Democratic Republic (GDR) at East Berlin — and the loss of many of its eastern lands (East Prussia, West Prussia, Pomerania, and Silesia). The nation's religious center of gravity had also moved, from the Protestant east to the Catholic west. The military had been broken and discredited; there could be no "state within a state," as had existed under General Hans von Seeckt in the 1920s. And the traditional Prussian conservative power elites had lost their economic basis and political power. By Order No. 46 of the Allied Control Commission of February 23, 1947, the historic state of Prussia was dissolved because "since time immemorial [it] has been the pillar of militarism and reaction in Germany."

Nor would there be a "stab-in-the-back" debate as had occurred after 1918 — that is, the charge that the civilians had sold out the military by forcing a surrender. The German military surrendered unconditionally to the Western Allies at Reims on May 7, 1945, and two days later to the Soviets at Berlin-Karlshorst. Most Germans hastily turned their backs on the recent past and looked inward instead. Few mourned the lost regime. Visitors to Germany in 1945 noted sardonically that Adolf Hitler must have been the only National Socialist! There was no resistance to Allied occupation, no partisan warfare, no Nazi combat leagues ("Werewolves") or guerrillas to harass the occupiers. Silence and submission on the part of a physically and morally decimated nation met the Allies as they entered Germany.

During the first four years of the postwar period, policymakers in London, Moscow, Paris, and Washington largely determined German affairs. Yet step by step, politicians in Berlin and Bonn began to establish two sovereign German states: one within the framework of West European and North Atlantic economic and defense systems and the other in alliance with the Soviet Union and the Warsaw Pact. Intra-German relations suffered accordingly.

Most important, the two German states developed distinct socioeconomic and political systems. East Germany abolished private property and industry in favor of a centrally directed and planned socialist system. West Germany, in contrast, turned to a social-market economy that featured private initiatives and encouraged free-market competition yet offered generous social programs. Eventually two quite different and separate states came to represent the one common German nation.

"Hour Zero"

German historians use the term *hour zero* to refer to both the near total desolation of their land and the start of its rebuilding in 1945. The term is not without merit. In the last four months of the war alone, the Western Allies flew 404 bombing raids, dropping 500,000 tons of bombs. These attacks severely damaged each of Germany's sixty-one major cities and rendered 14 million families homeless. Eighty percent of Cologne and 50 percent of Hamburg, for example, were laid waste. The German communications system was crippled, and 90 percent of the railroad network destroyed (10,000 locomotives and 112,000 freight cars bombed). German experts calculated that their nation lay under 523 million cubic yards of rubble.

Hunger and disease as had not been seen since the seventeenth century followed the destruction. Nine out of ten children in Cologne were underweight in 1945. Daily adult rations in Essen consisted of two pieces of bread, two potatoes, and one spoon of milk soup. Whereas the United Nations estimated that 2,500 calories per day were required to sustain a working adult, the norm in the American zone during the winter of 1946–1947 was 1,330, in the British zone 1,146, and in the French zone, only 900. Typhoid, diphtheria, whooping cough, tuberculosis, and sexually transmitted diseases ravaged the population. And while the territories of the future Federal Republic of Germany had lost one-quarter of their former food supplying areas, their population in 1945 was 20 percent larger than it had been in 1938.

One of the major reasons for this burgeoning population was the human tragedy of forced removals and resettlements. Germany in 1945 resembled an anthill. More than 7 million people recruited for slave labor under the Third Reich had to be repatriated, as did the 700,000 survivors of the concentration and extermination camps. Two million war widows sought work and shelter, and 2 million wounded men crowded often bombed-out hospitals and barracks. Nearly 12 million German prisoners of war needed to be demobilized and returned to normal life. And almost 7 million Germans were evicted from former German areas and marched into the new American and British zones of occupation. The refugees included 3.5 million Germans from Poland, 2.5 million from Czechoslovakia, 500,000 from Hungary, and 150,000 from Austria. All required food, clothing, and housing at Allied expense. Britain estimated that it spent £200 million for foodstuffs and raw materials between 1945 and 1948 in its zone alone.

What was to become of Germany? In the fall of 1944, U.S. Secretary of the Treasury Henry Morgenthau, Jr., had put forth a "Program to Prevent Germany from Starting a World War III." This plan basically aimed to reduce Germany to an eighteenth-century pastoral state through territorial dismemberment and economic destruction. President Franklin D. Roosevelt and Prime Minister Winston S. Churchill feared that the Morgenthau Plan would allow Soviet hegemony in Europe. U.S. Secretary of War Henry Stimson also opposed it and believed that an economically strong Germany, whatever its future territorial shape, was vital to European recovery. Thus in 1945 the Western Allies possessed no firm plans for Germany, beyond the decision reached at Yalta in

POPULATION SHIFTS TO WEST GERMANY, 1946–1949 (in thousands)

State	Refugees	Displaced	Evacuees
Bavaria	1,914	390	624
Baden and Württemberg	698	101	193
Hesse	656	83	369
North-Rhine, Westphalia	1,095	56	580
Lower Saxony	1,812	165	657
Schleswig-Holstein	956	49	465

THE DIVISION OF GERMANY AT POTSDAM, 1945

February 1945 to divide the country as well as its capital into four zones of occupation, to dismantle German heavy industry, and to demand reparations for war damages.

In April 1945 the U.S. Joint Chiefs of Staff agreed that Germany had to be so weakened that it could never again pose a threat to world peace. Their decree, JCS–1067, proposed demilitarization, de-Nazification, decentralization, and democracy. Execution of this Morgenthau Plan fell to the Allied Control Council, established at Berlin in June 1945, a labyrinth organization of 12 directorates and 170 subsections. In July 1945 the Allied leaders, meeting at Potsdam, agreed to split East Prussia between the Soviet Union and Poland

and to place other former German lands east of the Oder and Neisse rivers under Polish administration. What remained of Germany was divided among the victorious Allies: one-third was put under Soviet rule and the remaining two-thirds under American, British, and French control.[1]

The Soviets, commanded by Marshal Georgi K. Zhukov, set out to destroy in their sector what they termed the "monopoly capitalism" that had nurtured National Socialism. Specifically, the Soviet Military Administration for Germany, known by its German acronym SMAD, took over all banks in its new occupation zone, confiscated accounts with more than 3,000 reichsmarks, invalidated private as well as public debts, and socialized control of the major industries and transport and banking systems. SMAD dismantled about 1,400 industrial plants by the end of 1946 and demanded reparations in the amount of $10 billion. It seized available livestock and expropriated 7,000 large estates (of more than 300 acres each) as well as 243,000 acres of fertile land belonging to prominent officials from the erstwhile Third Reich. A monstrous bureaucracy embracing 50,000 employees, SMAD ran the Soviet sector by issuing more than 1,000 decrees in less than a decade, a performance that rivaled that of Joseph II in Austria in the 1780s.

The Soviets established cabinet-level ministries recruited from four major political factions: the Communists (KPD), Liberals (LDPD), Social Democrats (SPD), and Christian Democrats (CDU). The Red Army also returned to Germany former KPD activists such as Walter Ulbricht (Berlin), Gustav Sobottka (Schwerin), and Anton Ackermann (Dresden). These men installed politically reliable German prisoners of war from the Soviet Union as local and regional mayors and governors. The old KPD had been reconstituted on June 11, 1945, with the blessings of SMAD, but on April 21–22, 1946, to create a one-party system, Marshal Zhukov merged the KPD and SPD into the new Socialist Unity party (SED). It would rule until 1989.

As 1945 gave way to 1946, SMAD undertook an economic and social revolution from above. It nationalized private companies under the aegis of Soviet joint stock companies (SAG), transforming firms such as IG-Farben, Mannesmann, Siemens, and AEG, as well as large banks, into state enterprises. After 1945 SMAD also seized properties belonging to so-called Nazi activists and war criminals. In the agrarian sector, Soviet authorities parceled out, without compensation to their former owners, large estates of more than 100 hectares (247 acres), which encompassed 35 percent of all arable land, in lots of between 1 and 25 acres to about 550,000 poor farmers. By 1947 more than half of all former private enterprises had passed into state control. SMAD sold the SAGs to the German Democratic Republic in 1953.

---

[1] Joseph Stalin refused to recognize France as a victorious power, but the United States gave France a portion of its zone of occupation both in Germany and in Berlin.

Nor did the bureaucracy escape the purges. About 520,000 former National Socialists reportedly were weeded out between 1945 and 1948. Half of the 40,000 teachers in the Soviet zone were deemed politically unreliable. And 85 percent of all lawyers and judges had lost their jobs in the fall of 1945. The Soviets accused about 45,000 Germans of Nazi activities and sentenced one-third to labor camps. But the state needed experienced administrators, and hence de-Nazification quickly ground to a halt; SMAD ended it in February 1948. Western observers caustically noted that the SED thereby became the "big friend of little Nazis."

In the West, French occupation under the umbrella of a *délégation supérieure* encompassed the Saar, Palatinate, and parts of the Rhineland, Baden, and Württemberg and controlled about 12 percent of the German population. The French military commander, General Pierre Koenig, a veteran of the desert war in North Africa, demanded that Germany be decentralized and that the Saar, which France had occupied in February 1946, as well as the left bank of the Rhine, be "administered" by France. Koenig hence resuscitated the 1920s plans of President Raymond Poincaré. French policy generally sought to turn the western German lands from Constance to Cologne into a buffer zone, to weaken German industrial capacity permanently, and to force the surrender of the coal-rich Ruhr to France. General Koenig refused to cooperate not only with local German authorities but also with his American and British allies. The French-occupied territories were ruthlessly used: more than 80 percent of all their exports went to France. Historians later referred to these lands as "exploitation colonies."

The British occupation sector, commanded by Field Marshal Bernard L. Montgomery, victor of the Battle of El Alamein (1942), encompassed Prussia's former western possessions as well as the northern lands of the former Third Germany — that is, the non-Austrian and non-Prussian lands of the Holy Roman Empire. It was the most populous zone and the most heavily industrialized and destroyed. The British military administration proceeded to rule through the twin policies of centralization and democracy from below. By the summer of 1946 it had already established the three future states (*Länder*) of Schleswig-Holstein, North Rhine–Westphalia, and Hanover. Hanover would soon include Brunswick, Oldenburg, and Schaumburg-Lippe and be reconstituted as Lower Saxony. In August 1945 the British encouraged the creation of trade unions and allowed non-Nazi German officials to run cities and villages. In January 1947 the British established a common economic administrative unit (Bizone) with the Americans. British authorities permitted the first state elections in their occupation zone in April 1947.

The American zone consisted mainly of Bavaria, Hesse, and the northern parts of Baden and Württemberg and was administered by the Office of Military Government for the U.S. Zone (OMGUS), effectively run by General Lucius D. Clay. Without clear direction from Washington, OMGUS rigorously proceeded with democratization, decentralization, de-Nazification, and demilitarization. It emplaced American mandate governments in its occupation zone in May 1945 and allowed political parties by September. OMGUS permitted communal elections in January 1946 in an attempt to win Germans for democracy.

De-Nazification proved the most controversial aspect of American postwar administration. By the end of 1945, more than 100,000 suspected Nazis were interned in American camps in Bavaria and 90,000 in the British zone. In January 1946 the Allies decreed removal from office of all former NSDAP members and Germans openly hostile to Allied occupation. Discovery of the NSDAP's membership catalogue in a Munich paper factory greatly facilitated these efforts. Furthermore, the Americans stipulated that all Germans over the age of eighteen complete a questionnaire about their past before receiving a ration card and work permit. Respondents fell into five categories: major offender, offender, lesser offender, fellow-traveler, and untainted. By the summer of 1946, more than 1.6 million Germans had filled out questionnaires, and nearly 400,000 lost their jobs as a result of the information they provided. The total number of questionnaires diligently researched by the 545 American "courts" and 22,000 staffers reached 3.7 million by 1949, when jurisdiction over de-Nazification was transferred to the new Federal Republic at Bonn. Another 3 million questionnaires were processed in the British and French zones of occupation. The effort ultimately foundered on the inaccurate and even misleading information submitted on the forms.

Recent scholarship has revealed that the German churches played a prominent role in supplying former Nazis with documents exonerating them of crimes committed under the Hitler regime. Germans derisively termed these papers *Persilscheine*, named after the leading brand of laundry detergent. It has also come to the light that the Western Allies all too willingly used former SS officials to hunt for communists in territories formerly under German occupation. Thus "ratlines" were established through which men such as Adolf Eichmann, the architect of the "final solution," and Klaus Barbie, the "butcher of Lyon," escaped prosecution and went into exile.

The activities of the International Military Tribunal, conducted at Nuremberg between November 1945 and October 1946, turned out to be more promising. The Allies charged twenty-four major NSDAP organizations and members — with the exception of Adolf Hitler, Joseph Goebbels, and Heinrich Himmler, who had committed suicide at the end of the war — with crimes against peace and humanity, as well as with planning aggressive wars. Twelve received death sentences. Although some legal experts have decried the Nuremberg trials for handing down ex post facto judgments, there is general consensus that the heinous nature of the crimes committed by the Third Reich demanded legal action. Between 1945 and 1949, American authorities alone conducted twelve major follow-up trials of National Socialist lawyers, industrialists, doctors, and diplomats, resulting in more than 5,000 convictions and 486 executions. Finally, about 50,000 German nationals faced trial in the non-German lands where they stood accused of war crimes. In 1955 the Federal Republic of Germany received jurisdiction over Nazi war criminals.

In contrast, the process of de-Nazification in Austria, which the victorious Allies also occupied, was slow and incomplete. Above all, Austrian scholars quickly propagated the half-truth that their state had been the first victim of Nazi aggression in 1938. They also mounted a highly successful campaign to sanitize public discourse about the years 1938 through 1945, to disassociate Austria from German national and even cultural traditions, and to popularize clichés about Austrian distinctiveness in the form of largely Disneyesque images of their nation as one of Lipizzaner stallions, Vienna choir boys, Salzburg Mozart festivals, and *The Sound of Music.* These Austrian apologists depicted National Socialism as a German import and tried to bury its Austrian roots. Austrians thus chose not to confront the recent past but to ignore it.

Part of the reason for this self-exculpation lay in politics. In 1945 the 600,000 Austrian members of the Nazi party, SS, and SA outnumbered the membership of any other political party and with their immediate families constituted one-quarter of the population. No government could afford to offend their potential political clout, especially when a general amnesty in April 1948 returned the vote to 360,000 of these former Nazis. Four decades would elapse before Austrians had to face their Nazi past.

Political life in Germany returned to the American, British, and French zones by 1945–1946. In April 1945 Kurt Schumacher refounded the old Social Democratic party at Hanover on the twin principles of democratic socialism and parliamentary democracy. At its first party convention the following month, the SPD demanded the creation of "a planned, socialist economy" in any future German state. Not surprisingly, the western occupation authorities frowned on this development and in the summer of 1948 blocked a Social Democratic attempt to socialize the coal industry in North Rhine–Westphalia.

In December 1945 Konrad Adenauer and Jakob Kaiser created the Christian Democratic Union (CDU) at Bad Godesberg from the ranks of the old Catholic Center party, as well as a residue of anti-Nazi liberals and conservatives. The CDU thus constituted a Catholic-Protestant alliance made up mainly of middle-class elements. Attempts to revive the Bavarian People's party of the Weimar Republic proved unsuccessful. At Würzburg in October 1945, Joseph Müller, a former member of the German resistance and concentration camp inmate, formed a new political party, the Christian Social Union (CSU). The CSU's supporters were mainly prosperous farmers, merchants, tradesmen, and small industrialists. By agreement with the CDU, the organization restricted its political activities to Bavaria.

In December 1948 at Heppenheim the old German middle class of education and the professions, former stalwarts of the National Liberals with a sprinkling of Democrats and Progressives, founded the Free Democratic party (FDP).

The party championed individual initiative and private property. Theodor Heuss, a South German liberal and former Reichstag deputy under the Weimar Republic who had voted for the Enabling Law in 1933, became its first chairman.

Political Division, 1945–1961

Two men symbolized the two German states — the FRG and the GDR — that emerged by 1949: Konrad Adenauer and Walter Ulbricht, respectively. One could hardly have found more antipodal persons. Ulbricht was born the son of a tailor in Leipzig in 1893 and raised a "red" and an atheist. Adenauer was born in 1867 into a family of well-to-do judicial civil servants in Cologne and cemented his future career by marrying into the Cologne patriciate. Ulbricht learned the carpenter's trade, joined the SPD in 1912, was drafted into the German army, and in 1917 was jailed for being absent without leave. Adenauer spent the war in Cologne and in 1917 succeeded his uncle as lord mayor, the youngest man to hold such an august office in Imperial Germany. A party hack during the Weimar Republic, Ulbricht joined the Communist party in 1919, became district leader in Thuringia in 1921, and entered the KPD's Central Committee two years later. Adenauer continued as lord mayor of Cologne until 1933, in 1923 playing a suspect role during the French occupation of the Rhineland (he apparently sought to separate his Catholic homeland from Protestant Prussia). Both men found themselves on the outside in 1933. Ulbricht went into exile in Paris in 1933 and Moscow in 1938, the year that Adolf Hitler stripped him of German citizenship. Adenauer was removed from public office in 1933 and spent much of the Nazi years in self-imposed exile at his Rhöndorf residence in the Rhineland.

Both men enjoyed meteoric careers after World War II. When the German Democratic Republic was founded in 1949, Ulbricht was appointed one of three deputies to Minister-President Otto Grotewohl. But Ulbricht's real power lay with the Socialist Unity party. Already in January 1949 he had headed the five-member "little secretariat" of the party's Politburo, an elite within an elite. Administrative reform of the party in 1950 brought Ulbricht the office of secretary-general of the SED, and six years later he assumed leadership of the GDR's Defense Council. Upon the death of President Wilhelm Pieck in 1960, Ulbricht abolished that office and appointed himself head of a twenty-eight-member State Council, thereby combining in his person the three most important posts in the GDR: the Defense Council, State Council, and SED. Adenauer served as chancellor of the Federal Republic of Germany from 1949 to 1963, as its foreign minister from 1951 until 1955, and as the Christian Democratic Union's leader from 1950 until 1966. Adenauer died in 1967, Ulbricht in 1973.

In some ways, Ulbricht's path to power was smoother than that of Adenauer's. At the international level, the growing estrangement between the

United States and the Soviet Union during the period of the cold war provided Ulbricht the stage on which to show his devotion to the Soviet Union, and the presence of more than 300,000 soldiers of the Red Army supplied the backing that he failed to receive from the populace. Above all, Ulbricht knew what he wanted: to "create socialism on German soil." He understood that this goal could best be accomplished through a powerful Communist party ruling with an iron fist ("democratic centralism") while concurrently maintaining the fiction of democracy. "Everything has to look democratic," he decreed, "but everything has to be controlled by us."

Ulbricht quickly discovered that he lacked popular support. Regional elections, relatively free of coercion, in the five *Länder* under Soviet occupation in October 1946 brought only 47.5 percent of the popular vote for the SED. In addition, returns in "red" East Berlin revealed a disastrously low showing of 29.8 percent, compared with 43.6 percent for the traditional party of labor, the SPD. Moscow took alarm at these numbers and encouraged Ulbricht to press for "democratic centralism" in the form of one-party rule. The economic and political recovery in the western zones of occupation further fueled the Soviet Union's worry that a West German state might emerge. Stalin's attempt in 1948 to blockade Berlin (see pages 369–370) in part reflected a reaction to the Soviets' belief that German developments were slipping out of their control.

The Socialist Unity party took these fears to heart. In the fall of 1949, with the assistance of the Communist Party of the Soviet Union, the SED drafted a constitution for the Soviet zone that called for the creation of a "united, peace-loving, antifascist, democratic German republic." On October 7, 1949, the SED presented its constitution to the Third People's Congress for Unity and a Just Peace, which immediately ratified it. The document forged the German Democratic Republic out of the old states of Brandenburg, Mecklenburg, Saxony, Saxony-Anhalt, and Thuringia and adopted the basic constitution of the Weimar Republic. There would be no fewer than four redrafts of the constitution after 1949. In 1952 Ulbricht recast the GDR into fourteen districts. He used a combination of threats and physical force to reform the CDU and LDP parties along accepted (and subservient) lines and added the German Democratic Peasant's party (DBP) and German National Democratic party (NDPD) to the list of "block" parties under the umbrella of the National Front of Democratic Germany. Even mass organizations such as the Federation of Free German Unions (FDGD) and the Free German Youth (FDJ) were allowed to elect representatives to the People's Chamber (*Volkskammer*).

But what counted most in the GDR was control of the administrative process by the Socialist Unity party. Ulbricht had hit upon a widely used communist ploy immediately after the elections of October 1946: unitary lists. Electors could either approve or disapprove a list of candidates prepared by the SED. Free elections were anathema to the party. Although a "mere" 66.1 percent of East Germans endorsed the SED's first slate of candidates in 1949, no fewer than 99.7 percent of the voters supported Ulbricht's "German Democratic National Front" slate in the GDR's first national elections. Negative votes were equated with asocial behavior. On the surface, at least, the presence of half a dozen "parties" on the unitary lists gave a semblance of pluralism.

Real power remained with the SED. In a pyramidal scheme highly reminiscent of the Nazi's political machine, the Socialist Unity party organized its roughly 2 million members into 75,000 cells, which answered to more than 250 city and county organizations. The SED supervised these county organizations by fifteen district directorates. Holding party congresses every three or four years, the SED elected 150 to 200 members of its Central Committee, which, in turn, filled the fifteen to twenty-five seats on the Politburo, responsible for ideological and political policy. Thus the GDR slavishly followed the Communist Party of the Soviet Union in both ideology and structure.

The SED's most urgent task was to bring about socialism in Germany. Ulbricht argued that only the Soviet Union had already established true socialism on its soil and that the GDR remained one step behind. Because elements of the old bourgeois-capitalist society still lingered in the East German "people's democracy," Ulbricht argued that he had no choice but to rule in the name of the workers until the SED established true socialism between the Elbe and Oder-Neisse rivers. Yet by 1968 Ulbricht felt sufficiently confident of the GDR's progress toward socialism that he redrew the constitution. Article 1 boldly proclaimed the German Democratic Republic "a socialist state which under the leadership of . . . its Marxist-Leninist party is building socialism."

For the first ten years of the GDR, Ulbricht insisted that there was a common German history and should be a single (albeit socialist) German nation. In 1959, however, he added a hammer and protractor as a symbol of demarcation to the black-red-gold German flag shared by both German states. Many West Germans refused to accept that after 1949 the GDR was a sovereign state, preferring instead to call it the "east zone" or simply the "zone." Bonn politicians as late as the 1960s still talked of the "Soviet zone," and the powerful national press of Hamburg publisher Axel Springer placed quotation marks around the German initials for the "zone" (DDR) until 1989.

Whatever West Germans may have wished to believe, the GDR was a sovereign state and moved quickly to assert its right to undertake diplomatic initiatives. In June 1950 Ulbricht traveled to Prague and signed agreements stating that no border disputes existed between the GDR and the Czechoslovak People's Democracy and formalizing the expulsion of Germans from Czech border areas. One month later, Ulbricht recognized the Oder-Neisse line as the border between the GDR and Poland. Relations with the Soviet Union were normalized. A host of agreements on trade and the exchange of scientific information in 1950 and 1951, to be capped in 1955 by a cooperative agreement on the peaceful use of atomic energy, prepared the way for diplomatic relations between East Berlin and Moscow. On January 25, 1955, the Soviet Union unilaterally declared that it ceased to be at war with Germany. In May it invited the GDR to become one of the founding members of the Soviet-backed eastern defense system, the Warsaw Pact. And on September 20, 1955, Moscow formally recognized the sovereign status of the GDR. The division of Germany into two nations was complete.

Ulbricht had little difficulty in creating an army for the Warsaw Pact. Already in 1948 he had established a clandestine "army" under the guise of the People's Barracked Police (KVP) and in 1955 quickly recruited from its ranks 100,000 men for the new National People's Army (NVA). The latter increased by 40,000 men after the construction of the Berlin Wall in 1961 (see pages 396–397), and the following year universal male conscription was introduced in the GDR. Although the German Democratic Republic, like its western rival, initially had to resort to "Hitler generals" to staff the highest command positions, by 1956 four of five officers were loyal SED party members.

Over the last fifteen years of his reign, Ulbricht faced four major crises. Rapid economic and political recovery in West Germany constantly brought unfavorable comparisons, both within and without the GDR, between the two German socioeconomic systems. Reconstruction and reparations forced the East German leader to demand ever greater production from his work force and to maintain artificially low wages. Contacts between the two German states were tenuous at best as they groped toward normalization of both intra-German and intra-Allied relations. And prospects of better wages and living conditions in the west prompted many East German laborers to abandon the GDR. In fact, Ulbricht's first crisis was domestic. In June 1953 thousands of East Berlin construction workers demonstrated and went on strike to object to higher work norms (see pages 381–382). Hundreds of thousands of fellow workers throughout the GDR quickly joined them, and only Soviet military might restored order.

Ulbricht's second crisis originated with Moscow. At the Twentieth Party Congress of the Soviet Communist Party in 1956, Secretary-General Nikita S. Khrushchev began his assault on the barbaric legacy of Joseph Stalin. Ulbricht, caught completely off-guard, at once penned a lead editorial in the state's official newspaper, *Neues Deutschland*, that Stalin had never been a "classic Marxist." He also announced a new five-year plan of "modernization, mechanization, and automation" and promised a 30 percent rise in real wages as well as a forty-hour workweek. Many East Germans interpreted Ulbricht's statement as a signal for change. The philosopher Ernst Bloch, the economist Fritz Behrens, and the nuclear physicist Robert Havemann called for a "third way" between East German authoritarianism and West German capitalism, one they dubbed "socialism with a human face." But the bloody suppression of the Hungarian revolt of 1956 by Soviet tanks quickly ended all reform aspirations in the Soviet-controlled states of Eastern Europe. A wave of suicides and forced expulsions from the SED signaled the return to hard-line "normalcy."

The third crisis was international. In the 1960s Ulbricht secured recognition for the GDR by a host of African and Asian states and formulated the so-called Ulbricht Doctrine. East Berlin demanded that friendly nations refuse to recognize the Federal Republic at Bonn as long as the latter declined to treat the GDR as a sovereign equal. In 1968 Alexander Dubček, the chairman of the Slovak Communist party who replaced Klement Gottwald as leader of the Czechoslovak Socialist Republic (ČSSR), sought to introduce "socialism with a human face" during the so-called Prague Spring, a period of hope for reform of the old Stalinist Communist system in Czechoslovakia. Ulbricht was not amused. On August 21 units of the National People's Army joined other Warsaw Pact forces and invaded the ČSSR in order to restore socialism under the umbrella of the Brezhnev Doctrine. Named for the new Soviet leader, Leonid Brezhnev, the doctrine stated that it was the duty of all socialist nations to come to the aid of any country where socialism was threatened. But the sight of German units invading Czechoslovakia — in the footsteps of Hitler's legions of 1939 — did little to enhance the global image of the German Democratic Republic.

The fourth crisis centered on intra-German relations. By 1960 more than 2 million GDR residents (in a country of 17 million people) had fled to the Federal Republic in search of freedom, jobs, and prosperity. The steady exodus grew to twenty-five hundred people per day in late 1960, and the loss of this largely highly skilled labor pool threatened the GDR with technological and economic chaos, if not collapse. The mass emigration resulted in the construction of the Berlin Wall[1] in 1961 and evoked several notable exchanges of caustic accusations and bitter acrimony in the intra-German debate. Ulbricht denounced the Federal Republic as a "neofascist" and "imperialist" tool of the United States and vilified the Social Democratic party as a class traitor and a "social-fascist" organization.

Yet Ulbricht was too shrewd a politician not to realize that the GDR lay far behind the Federal Republic in production and standard of living. In June 1963, with the help of Erich Apel, chairman of the State Planning Commission, he introduced the New Economic System, designed to restore some initiative to decision making and to reduce the multiple layers of the economic apparatus. But a downturn in the Soviet economy prompted the Kremlin to turn to its East European satellites for help. In December 1965 the GDR was forced to sign a new trade agreement with the Soviet Union, whereby Moscow delivered raw materials at near world prices and procured finished products from East Germany at bargain levels. Observers both at home and abroad widely attributed Apel's suicide that month to this exploitation of East German productivity.

Nor did intra-German relations improve. In May 1970 a meeting at Kassel between East German president Willi Stoph and West German chancellor

[1] Shortly after midnight on August 13, 1961, East Germany began to erect a concrete and barbed wire barrier along the 100-mile border between East and West Berlin. The Wall eventually was extended along the entire boundary between the GDR and FRG and enhanced with electronic detection devices, armed guards, guard towers, mines, automatic firing devices, and patrol dogs.

Willy Brandt proved a disaster. Stoph bluntly demanded an immediate payment of 100 billion deutsche marks as "compensation" for Bonn's "luring away" the people of the GDR between 1949 and 1961. Tensions reached an all-time high in 1971 when Ulbricht was forced out of office by a new generation of GDR leaders eager for modernization and economic streamlining.

In the West, Konrad Adenauer after 1949 also had to rely on elderly politicians from the Weimar years. Many were in their late sixties — Adenauer was in his early eighties — and during the first two years of the Federal Republic's existence, twenty-three deputies died of heart attacks and circulatory ailments. Adenauer's most bitter rival, Kurt Schumacher, led the Social Democratic party. A survivor of eight years at the Dachau concentration camp under Hitler, Schumacher was a mixture of German patriot and socialist pundit. He demanded not only that western Germany join other socialist European states in a defense league against Soviet expansion but also that Germany be restored to the borders of 1937. His supporters ranged from former communist Herbert Wehner to labor leader Fritz Erler and political activist Willy Brandt, as well as to middle-class intellectuals such as Karl Schiller and Carlo Schmid.

Like Ulbricht, Adenauer had a firm vision of the future. A Catholic patriarch with strong opinions augmented by cynicism and sarcasm, Adenauer cared about neither Nazi skeletons in his government's closet nor unscrupulously mobilizing fears of Soviet Russia to attain his goals. He nurtured a strong distrust of the political savvy of most of his countrymen and demanded little more than that they regularly go to the polls and vote CDU/CSU.

Above all, Adenauer accepted the political reality of both U.S. superpower status and French fears of a German revival. He was encouraged in October 1946 by Secretary of State James F. Byrnes' famous speech at Stuttgart assuring Germans that the United States would remain in Europe as well as help western Germany get back on its feet. "Germany is part of Europe," Byrnes stated, "and recovery in Europe will be slow indeed if Germany and her great resources of iron and coal is turned into a poorhouse." Here was a clear renunciation of the Morgenthau Plan. Yet Adenauer understood fully that any future German state could operate only within the parameters of Allied policy. Those limits were clearly defined during the Berlin crisis of 1948.

The former German capital had been partitioned in 1945. Eight of its twenty districts, or about 40 percent of the city, formed the Soviet zone; the rest was parceled out among Britain, France, and the United States. On June 23, 1948, the Soviets registered their objection to West German currency reform (see pages 384–385) by cutting the 2.5 million West Berliners off from the western powers under the pretext of road, rail, and canal "repairs." Additionally, the Soviets curtailed all supplies of food and electricity to West Berlin.

Western military action was out of the question. The 6,500 Allied troops in West Berlin were no match for the 17,000 Soviet soldiers in East Berlin, augmented by 300,000 Red Army units in the Soviet zone, that surrounded Berlin.

Berlin Air Bridge: American planes unload at Tempelhof (1948–1949).

But General Clay, determined not to let Stalin get his way, warned, "If Berlin falls, Western Germany will be next." On July 26, 1948, the Western Allies began an air bridge to West Berlin via the three air corridors allowed them by international agreement. Over the next eleven months, 212,621 flights brought 1.7 million tons of supplies to keep the 920,000 West Berlin families alive. West Berlin's mayor, Ernst Reuter, and General Clay became symbols of the will of Berliners to survive and of the Allies' refusal to be intimidated by Soviet measures. In May 1949 Stalin announced that all necessary "repairs" had ended. In a face-saving measure, the Soviet dictator agreed that West Berlin could remain under Anglo-French-American rule but that the Soviet Union would have no formal relations with any future West German state.

The Berlin crisis provided Adenauer his first opportunity to move toward restoring German sovereignty. In June at Koblenz German political leaders opted to form a "parliamentary council" to draft what was to become the Basic Law (*Grundgesetz*) of the Federal Republic of Germany. But there were initial pitfalls. On July 1, 1948, the three military governors of the Western Allies at Frankfurt proposed that the eleven German state premiers convene in September to frame a constitution. This plan (the "Frankfurt Documents") alarmed the German state leaders; any formal constitution would recognize permanent division of the country. Like their colleagues in the east, the West German premiers turned to the Weimar Republic for a model in drafting the actual constitution. But unlike leaders east of the Elbe River, they favored a pluralistic, democratic state.

From September 1948 to May 1949 the Parliamentary Council convened at the Museum Koenig in Bonn amid stuffed bears, gorillas, and chimpanzees to hammer out the Basic Law for the future state. The council's sixty-five members included four women. Most delegates, like those who had met a century earlier at the Paulskirche in Frankfurt, were civil servants, lawyers, judges, and professors. The final draft of the Basic Law was accepted on May 8, 1949, by a vote of fifty-three for and twelve against and was ratified by the various West German states on May 23.[1]

The Parliamentary Council established a bicameral system. The federal parliament (*Bundestag*) is elected every four years by universal, equal, and direct suffrage accorded all Germans eighteen years and older (Articles 38–39). Deputies are selected equally by proportional representation from party lists and single-member districts. The *Bundestag* drafts and passes legislation and selects the chancellor. The latter decides national policy, nominates the cabinet, and implements laws passed by the *Bundestag*, to which he is directly responsible. To avoid the political splintering of Weimar, it was decreed (before the elections of 1953) that parties had to receive 5 percent of the national vote or win at least three single-member districts in order to be seated in the *Bundestag*. And to head off the negative votes of no confidence that had marked the political disarray of the final three years of the Weimar Republic, West German constitutionalists drafted a "constructive vote of no-confidence" (Article 67) whereby the opposition has to demonstrate its agreement on a new cabinet before it can topple an existing government. The federal council (*Bundesrat*) is elected by the legislatures of the various *Länder* according to their total population. Its major function is to approve or reject laws passed by the federal parliament, although it can also initiate legislation (Articles 50–51).

Well remembering the misuse of presidential powers (Article 48) during the Weimar Republic, the Parliamentary Council redefined the office of the *Bundespräsident*: the federal president wields no emergency powers and is not elected directly. Rather, the president is elected by the Federal Convention, which comprises *Bundestag* deputies plus an equal number of representatives elected from state parliaments. The *Bundespräsident* represents the Federal Republic internationally, concludes foreign treaties, countersigns federal laws, and appoints cabinet members, federal judges, military officers, and senior civil servants. He or she serves for five years (Article 54). The Federal Constitutional Court at Karlsruhe, modeled on the U.S. Supreme Court, was created to ensure the constitutionality of all federal, state, and local legislation (Articles

[1] The Bavarian state legislature voted 101 to 63 against ratification but quickly passed a bill stating that Bavaria would recognize the Basic Law once two-thirds of the other federal states had ratified it.

93–94). Article 88 grants the *Bundesbank* the right to issue and manage the currency. The national flag is black-red-gold, the colors of nineteenth-century liberalism and nationalism.

Recalling Germany's role in starting World War II, the Bonn legislators decreed that future German military forces could be deployed only in defensive wars (Articles 87a, 115a–115f), and that these forces could not prepare for or conduct offensive operations (Article 26). And remembering the now 18 million Germans living in the GDR, the West German constitutionalists in Article 23 stipulated that the Basic Law would apply automatically to new states added to the Federal Republic.

The Basic Law reversed the traditional preeminence in Germany of state over local and individual rights. Freedom, equality, and responsibility of the individual citizen were recognized as sacrosanct. Article 20 of the Basic Law stipulates that the Federal Republic is "a democratic and social federal state." Control over public education rests with the states. Freedom of religion is guaranteed (Article 4), as are the rights of the family (Article 6). Men and women are legally recognized as equals (Article 3).

The Western Allies accepted the Basic Law, with the caveat that it not include "Greater Berlin," and transformed their military governors into high commissioners (1949–1954). In September 1949 they drafted the Occupation Statute, which gave them the right to replace the West German government if it transgressed against the newly established democratic order. The Parliamentary Council narrowly chose Bonn (33 to 29 votes) over Frankfurt as the temporary capital of the new state, pending reunification and restoration of Berlin as the German political center. Adenauer was elected chancellor by a plurality of one vote, and the FDP leader Heuss was chosen federal president.

The first elections in the Federal Republic were held in August 1949. On July 21 Adenauer had launched his campaign at Heidelberg Castle by posing a simple choice: "Will Germany become Christian or socialist?" The voters responded positively to him. The anticipated SPD landslide turned instead into a narrow victory for Adenauer's CDU/CSU coalition with 31 percent of the vote. The SPD came in second with 29.2 percent. And the FDP, which opted to join Adenauer in a coalition government, held the balance with 11.9 percent.

Adenauer's penchant for autocratic decision making became evident at once. Instead of entrusting administration of the new state to young, democratic civil servants, Adenauer turned to experienced veterans of the Third Reich. Most visibly, he chose Hans Globke, an ex-NSDAP party member and councillor in the Ministry of the Interior from 1932 to 1945, to run his chancery. By selecting one of the architects of the infamous Nuremberg racial laws of 1935 as his closest adviser, the chancellor tainted the Federal Republic with charges of pro-Nazi sympathies from the start. Furthermore, 60 percent of all governmental section chiefs appointed by the Adenauer government between 1950 and 1953 were former NSDAP members. Most opted to serve the new state in order to preserve their social status and careers, thereby continuing the

ELECTIONS IN THE FEDERAL REPUBLIC OF GERMANY

Year	CDU/CSU	SPD	FDP	KPD
August 1949				
% of vote	31	29.2	11.9	5.7
Seats	139	131	52	15
March 1953				
% of vote	45.2	28.8	9.5	2.2
Seats	243	151	48	0
September 1957				
% of vote	50.2	31.8	7.7	—
Seats	270	169	41	—
September 1961				
% of vote	45.3	36.2	12.8	—
Seats	242	190	67	—

Prusso-German tradition of 1806, 1919, and 1933 of bureaucratic obedience to authority. De-Nazification became the first victim of West German sovereignty.

To rationalize this reliance on former servants of the Hitler regime, West German pundits created the *Betriebsunfall* (industrial accident) concept. They argued, rather ingenuously, that Hitler had been brought to power not by specific socioeconomic forces but by pure accident. After a twelve-year reign of terror, the Nazis had disappeared from the scene quite as suddenly. In this manner, Bonn politicians depicted National Socialism as an "errant" or "deviant" system that lay outside the mainstream of German history. The British high commissioner, Sir Ivone Kirkpatrick, was not duped: "Whenever I travelled, I ran into ghosts of Hitler's Reich, men who had occupied positions in the administration, in industry, or the society of the day."

The German Protestant church was particularly sensitive to concerns over Germany's unsavory past. At Stuttgart on October 19, 1945, it expressed "deep anguish" over the "untold suffering" that had been "visited on peoples and countries." In promising a new beginning, church leaders such as Martin Niemöller, survivor of nearly a decade's incarceration in Hitler's concentration camps, acknowledged the sins of the past: "We accuse ourselves of not having professed our faith more courageously, prayed more truly, believed more joyously, and loved more urgently." Neither Jews nor the Holocaust received specific mention in the document. The Catholics proved less repentant and during the debates over the Basic Law insisted on the validity of Hitler's Concordat with Rome in 1933.

Adenauer's first government was also keenly aware of the potential political clout of the Union of Expellees and Dispossessed (BHE), organized in 1950 to lobby for Germans who had lost their homes in the east. In June 1950 the Union won 23.4 percent of the vote in regional elections in Schleswig-Holstein and three years later sent twenty-seven deputies to the *Bundestag* at Bonn. But by 1957 it was unable to clear the 5 percent hurdle, and its former voters moved on to the CDU and Adenauer.

From the start, the Federal Republic avoided the political polarization of the late Weimar years. The KPD won 5.7 percent of the national vote in 1949 but in the next election fell well below the minimum level, with 2.2 percent. In 1956 the Federal Constitutional Court at Karlsruhe ordered the Communist party dissolved as an antidemocratic organization. Nor did the extreme Right fare better. The German Reich party (DRP) in 1949 garnered only 1.8 percent of the vote, and the Socialist Reich party, a neo-Nazi splinter faction, was banned by the Karlsruhe court as antidemocratic before the 1953 elections.

Adenauer's greatest success came in the area of foreign policy — that is, in restoring German sovereignty and embedding the Federal Republic within the European community. The chancellor made it clear that he viewed the eastern "zone" as an artificial creation propped up by Soviet armed might and declared that Bonn alone was responsible "for the fate of the 18 million Germans who live in the Soviet zone." Bonn, Adenauer argued, represented the "only legitimate state organization of the German people." Accordingly, intra-German relations were handled not by the Foreign Office but by a special Ministry for All-German Affairs. The Basic Law granted automatic citizenship to all ethnic Germans and included provisions for eventual reunification, an option that few Germans in 1949 considered realistic.

Adenauer beleived that the road to eventual sovereignty lay in his ability to integrate the Federal Republic into the West European state system. But because the Federal Republic was not a sovereign state in 1949, the chancellor had to resort to interviews with journalists as his main avenue of diplomatic communication. The initiative for "German policy" thus rested not in Bonn but in Washington, Paris, and London. Adenauer was wily enough to exploit this political subservience to tame his parliamentary opposition. During critical debates he would suddenly hold up an American diplomatic cable demanding German compliance on a particular issue; the "cable" often turned out to be the menu from the Hotel Königshof in Bonn.

In November 1949 Adenauer set out to restore German sovereignty by concluding the "Petersberg Agreement" with Britain, France, and the United States. Therein, Bonn promised to cooperate with the West in economic and political matters and to forgo weapons of any kind. In return, the Allies agreed to halt plant demolitions in mid–1951. Kurt Schumacher of the SPD denounced the agreement and accused Adenauer of being "the chancellor of the Allies."

Undeterred, Adenauer in May 1950 signed a compact with French foreign minister Robert Schuman[1] "to place all Franco-German coal and steel production under a common authority." The real force behind the European Coal and Steel Community was the French politician Jean Monnet, who argued that it was best for France to "bind Germany economically and politically in the structure of Western Europe" before the Germans were strong enough to dictate terms. The Schuman Plan effectively launched the integration of the Federal Republic into Western Europe.

The next opening for Adenauer came on June 25, 1950, when seven North Korean infantry divisions invaded South Korea. The Korean War (1950–1953) turned the cold war hot. The United States was now committed in the Far East and anxious to ease its military burden in Europe. As early as December 3, 1949, Adenauer, fearing the expansion of the East German "police" to seventy thousand men, had published an article in the *Cleveland Plain Dealer* holding out the prospect that Germany might provide a contingent for a future European army. The United States quickly approved the suggestion, and Prime Minister Churchill endorsed it in August 1950. Armed with Anglo-American approval, Adenauer created a special office within his chancery under Herbert Blankenhorn to plan German rearmament. Like Ulbricht in the east, he felt that he had no choice but to turn for expertise to former Hitler generals such as Hans Speidel, Adolf Heusinger, and Gerhard von Schwerin.

On August 30, 1950, Blankenhorn's office drafted one of the key documents of German sovereignty. The paper called for the creation of a West German border patrol force (*Bundesgrenzschutz*) and a West German military contingent as part of an all-European army. Adenauer's shrewd linking of rearmament with political independence quickly paid off. In September 1950 the Allied High Commissioners agreed that Bonn could now conduct its own foreign policy and establish a Foreign Office. Additionally, the various German states no longer had to submit their legislation to the commissioners for approval.

In the meantime, Blankenhorn, after adding former Generals Wolf von Baudissin and Johann A. von Kielmannsegg to his office, convened a strategic retreat at the Benedictine monastery Himmerod in the Eiffel. The resulting Himmerod Memorandum in October 1950 became the founding charter of the future *Bundeswehr*. Welcomed by West German veterans' associations especially, it called for the complete "rehabilitation" of the reputation of the German soldier and for the military equality of the Federal Republic within a future European army. Baudissin was largely responsible for including in the document a statement that the new German force was to be "integrated" into the democratic state.

Opposition to German rearmament came on two fronts. France's minister-president, René Pleven, demanded the total amalgamation of all contingent

[1] As an Alsatian, Schuman had fought in the German army in World War I and with the Free French during World War II.

forces into a European Defense Community, in effect denying Adenauer sovereignty for his own forces. At home, veteran, youth, and church groups protested rearmament. On October 10, 1950, Minister of the Interior Gustav Heinemann, who also served as head of the Protestant Synod of Germany, resigned from the cabinet in protest. Pastor Niemöller, now church president of Hesse-Nassau, led public protests. Young people repeated the slogan "without me" to let their feelings be known.

But Adenauer ultimately had both the political will and the necessary parliamentary clout to push rearmament through the *Bundestag.* The anticipated rewards came to him in short order. On July 9, 1951, Britain, France, and the United States declared the state of war with Germany ended. In April 1952 the Federal Republic was allowed to adopt as its national anthem the third stanza of the "Deutschlandlied," which spoke only of pious concepts such as unity and freedom and avoided the references to broad German borders in the first stanza. And on May 26, 1952, the Western Allies concluded the General Treaty with Bonn, recognizing German rearmament. The 1949 Occupation Statute was formally abrogated, and the Allies promised Bonn joint defense of the Federal Republic and West Berlin in case of attack. Schumacher denounced the General Treaty as an Allied "victory" over the German people, arguing that sovereignty had been surrendered to London, Paris, and Washington.

Stalin reacted between March and May 1952 with three notes offering a peace treaty, reunification for Germany as an "independent, democratic, peace-loving state," and restoration of the civil rights of former Nazi officers not accused of war crimes, provided that the future German state undertake no military alliances and accept the Oder-Neisse line as its eastern border. Stalin's initiative came as a complete surprise and proved highly seductive to Germans. Although Schumacher and the SPD jumped at the bait, Adenauer remained skeptical. As in the past, he demanded that the German borders of 1937 be restored and that the nation be integrated into the western alliance system. Above all, he argued prophetically that the time to negotiate with the Soviets was not yet at hand:

> When a new order comes in Europe — and it will come — then we must also insist on a new order in East Europe, including the [Soviet] satellite states. We must enter into discussions with the Soviets only . . . when the West is strong, so that the Soviets will listen to us and to the West.

Adenauer, realizing that Stalin's offer was a last-minute ploy to block formation of a West European joint army, rejected it. The German Democratic Republic reacted by sealing its borders with the Federal Republic and blaming Adenauer for the division of Germany.

The electorate shared Adenauer's position and in September 1953 rewarded the CDU/CSU coalition with 45.2 percent of the vote. The SPD received 28.8 percent. The road to integration into West Europe seemed clear. At the last moment, however, the French National Assembly refused to endorse the formation of an all-European defense force on August 30. Adenauer termed it a "black day for Europe." But Washington and London had worked out a fallback position: German inclusion in the North Atlantic Treaty Organization (NATO). In the so-called Germany Treaty of October 1954, Bonn agreed not to develop nuclear or biological weapons; Britain, for the first time in its history, decided to station forces permanently in Europe; and Britain as well as the United States recognized full sovereignty for the Federal Republic.

On October 23, the Paris Accords formally recognized the Anglo-American initiative. The Federal Republic was admitted into NATO and agreed to contribute a military contingent (*Bundeswehr*) of 500,000 troops. The British first secretary-general of NATO, Lord L. H. "Pug" Ismay, perhaps put it best when he stated that NATO was designed to keep the Americans in, the Russians out, and the Germans down. Once again, the SPD objected to Adenauer's bold initiative. Once again, its efforts came to naught. Conscription as well as American-controlled nuclear weapons came to the Federal Republic in 1957. Noted Nobel laureates in physics such as Max Born, Otto Hahn, Werner Heisenberg, and Max von Laue protested in vain against the introduction of atomic weapons on German soil.

Adenauer now marched from one triumph to the next. The Soviet Union agreed to end its occupation of Austria in 1955, signaling a thaw in its relations with the West. On October 23, 1955, two-thirds of the residents of the French-occupied Saar voted to reject continued association with France; the Saar became a federal German state on January 1, 1957. Secretary of State Walter Hallstein in the Foreign Office revealed Bonn's new-found independence by decreeing that the Federal Republic would break diplomatic relations with any state, except the Soviet Union, that recognized both German states. Bonn implemented the so-called Hallstein Doctrine for the first time in October 1957 by breaking relations with Yugoslavia.

In the fall of 1955 Adenauer visited the Soviet Union in a bold attempt to normalize relations between the two nations and to seek the release of 98,229 suspected German prisoners of war still in the Soviet Union. The Soviets countered that there were only 9,626 Nazi "war criminals" left in Soviet camps. Adenauer had no choice but to accept this figure and successfully negotiated their return to Germany. More than 1.2 million German soldiers were listed as missing in the Soviet Union. They have never been accounted for, their fate subsumed into the improvement of German-Soviet relations. At the height of the negotiations, Adenauer attended the ballet *Romeo and Juliet*. In a highly symbolic gesture, as the heads of the feuding Capulet and Montague families embraced on stage, Adenauer softly placed his hands in those of the Soviet leader N. A. Bulganin. Formal diplomatic relations were established between Bonn and Moscow.

In March 1957 West Germany joined France and Italy as well as the Benelux states[1] in the Treaties of Rome to found the European Economic Com-

[1] The economic union since 1947 of Belgium, the Netherlands, and Luxembourg.

munity. Under the dynamic leadership of the Belgian foreign minister, Paul-Henri Spaak, a European commission headquartered at Brussels began to hammer out joint economic policies, and the Common Agricultural Policy was established to extend massive subsidies to impoverished European farmers. German voters endorsed these European initiatives in 1957 by returning Adenauer's government as the only one in German history ever to score more than 50 percent of the popular vote. The SPD continued to hover at the 30 percent barrier. The various splinter parties, which had garnered 28 percent of the vote in the Federal Republic's first election in 1949, ceased to be a political force. By 1965 their share of the vote had fallen to 3.6 percent.

Perhaps because of its inability to break the 30 percent electoral barrier, in 1958 the SPD at Bad Godesberg decided to undertake the first major revision of its policy since it had met at Erfurt in 1891. Indeed, the venerable workers' party had fallen on hard times. Membership had declined from 875,000 in 1947 to 585,000 in 1954. Its Marxist slogans, red flag, and "comrade" form of address seemed out of place in the Germany of the 1950s. Led by younger men such as Ernst Reuter and Willy Brandt, the SPD cast aside its Marxist cloak and vowed to become the party of reform rather than revolution. In order to appeal beyond its traditional labor vote, the SPD decided to become a pragmatic, issues-oriented mass party. Its platform statement, "as much economic freedom as possible, as much economic planning as necessary," was a clear departure from Schumacher's socialist policies since 1945. In June 1960 the SPD's ideologue Herbert Wehner publicly proclaimed that the SPD recognized all existing diplomatic accords and that it supported the principle of self-defense. The party's electoral success would come in due time.

The Road to Recovery: The GDR, 1945–1961

Although the German Democratic Republic and the Federal Republic of Germany both started from the depths of destruction and despair, two distinct socioeconomic systems emerged. British authorities estimated in November 1945 that Germany had been returned to its preindustrial status as a result of day and night bombing raids. The balance between the highly industrialized Rhineland, Berlin, and Silesia, on the one hand, and the traditional bread basket of central and east Germany, on the other, had been destroyed by occupation and partition. Twenty million people were on the road, seeking work or shelter or loved ones. Black market barter replaced currency dealings. And Allied postwar demolition of factories further impoverished an already ravaged people.

Nowhere were reparations demands more systematically enforced than in the Soviet zone. Half of all exports from eastern Germany in 1946 supposedly took the form of reparations to the Soviet Union. East German scholars claim that total reparations paid to the Soviet Union until 1953 amounted to $4 billion; western estimates range as high as $14 billion. Worse, the lands of the

Soviet zone possessed few natural resources apart from some soft coal and potash deposits. Yet 18 million people had to find work, food, and shelter.

Relief came in January 1954 when the Soviet Union canceled all remaining reparations payments and limited military occupation costs to no more than 5 percent of the East German budget. Moreover, the more than 200 SAGs — with the exception of uranium producers — were turned over to the Ulbricht regime. Most became "people-owned enterprises" (VEB), with the result that less than 4 percent of industry remained in private hands by 1960. A symbiotic economic relationship developed between the Soviet Union and the German Democratic Republic after 1950 with the creation of the East European Council for Mutual Economic Aid (Comecon). Soviet-style five-year plans became the norm. The Soviet Union supplied the requisite raw materials and fuels at world prices, while East Germany returned manufactured goods (mainly heavy machinery) below market value, thereby significantly underwriting Soviet economic development. The GDR's first Five Year Plan, launched in 1950, emphasized heavy industrial production. Central economic direction from East Berlin ensured that uneconomical and highly polluting coal and steel plants remained in operation and that labor, skilled and unskilled, was directed to them. East Germany collectivized agriculture in 1959–1960; consequently, 90 percent of all rural work was done by "agricultural production cooperatives" (LPG) within three years.

To create the desired "socialist mentality," the Ulbricht regime established mass organizations such as the FDGD labor movement, the Free German Youth, and the Democratic Women's League (DFB). The Free German Youth embraced people between the ages of fourteen and twenty-five, and membership soared from under 20 percent in 1955 to nearly 90 percent in 1960 and 98 percent by 1983. Above all, a cult of personality surrounded Ulbricht just as it enveloped Joseph Stalin in the Soviet Union. And the SED ruled supreme. "The party is always right," proclaimed a 1949 East German hymn.

Churches remained outside the mainstream of GDR life. About two-thirds of East Germans who maintained church affiliation were Protestants (mostly Lutherans), and church membership sufficed to exclude young people from

COLLECTIVIZATION IN THE GDR, 1952–1967

Year	Number of Collectives	Percentage of GDR's Area
1952	1,906	3.3
1954	5,120	14.3
1956	6,281	23.2
1958	9,637	37.0
1960	19,261	84.2

The idealized Red *Volksgemeinschaft*: Workers of the transformer factory "Karl Liebknecht" help bring in the harvest of the collective farm "Thomas Müntzer" near Morin (August 1952).

higher education and party membership. In fact, the state systematically attacked churches, often shutting up their buildings or turning them over to the Free German Youth. The state introduced special "youth consecration" to replace Christian confirmation. Clergymen throughout the land were instructed to sever all contacts with their West German counterparts. Church property remained in a state of disrepair, awaiting decay. Eventually the church would become a refuge for dissenters, a haven for both the peace and environmental movements.

Absolute obedience to the state was enhanced in 1950 with the creation of the Ministry for State Security (Stasi), usually headed by a member of the Politburo.[1] The Stasi's internal security arm alone employed about 30,000

[1] General Erich Mielke commanded the Stasi from 1958 until 1989.

persons. Section VI monitored tourists and special visitors, Section VII spied on the regular police, and Section VIII conducted illegal house searches. Still other sections kept tabs on the youth movement, the army, church groups, and athletes. The Stasi's most glamorous unit was Section XV, the foreign intelligence arm. For nearly three decades, it was run by Marcus Wolf, allegedly the master spy Karla in John Le Carré's spy novels. At its height in 1988 Stasi ranks had swelled to 160,000 members.

The Socialist Unity party was a massive bureaucratic apparatus whose membership increased from 680,000 in 1945 to roughly 2 million by 1980. A professional political oligarchy controlled the important positions in party, state, industry, science, culture, and the military. Whereas the state espoused the principle of equality, the party claimed a monopoly on power and truth. Apart from its overt Communist philosophy, the Ulbricht state possessed many of the authoritarian forms of the old Prussian *Obrigkeitsstaat*.

Conformity of view was ensured by 185 district party schools, 15 regional party schools, and the national Karl Marx party university. Special privileges ranging from villas in the Berlin suburb Wandlitz to automobiles and consumer shops closed to workers and farmers made party careers highly attractive. Purges ensured that only the most loyal or pliant remained party members. In 1950, for example, Ulbricht evicted about 150,000 members of a suspect "Tito clique"[1] from the SED. In 1952 the German Democratic Republic created the special State Commission for Cultural Affairs to direct the state's cultural and literary life. Hitlerian terms such as *degenerate* and *decadent* were reintroduced to describe Western art, in particular. "Socialist realism" in the form of factory murals and pastoral landscapes became the desired art form.

Ulbricht surpassed the efforts of the Federal Republic in the areas of higher education and women's work in the 1950s. The East German leader added twenty-five new institutions of higher learning to the existing fifteen polytechnical and six humanistic universities. The number of university students doubled to 57,500 between 1951 and 1954 alone; more than half came from farmer and worker families. Ulbricht's regime also tailored education to the needs of working mothers, eventually providing day care for more than half of all children up to the age of three and kindergarten for nearly 90 percent of those aged three to six. Additionally, the state introduced six months' maternity leave and, after 1972, one year of unpaid "baby leave" along with job guarantees and insurance benefits. By the end of the 1970s, 87 percent of all women in the GDR were gainfully employed, compared to 52 percent in the FRG.

In the area of sports, the Ulbricht state used women athletes to showcase the "workers' and peasants' state" at the Olympic Games. It is not far off the

[1] The Yugoslav communist leader Josip Broz Tito had broken with Moscow in 1948, and thereafter the term *Titoism* was used to denounce all "anti-Soviet deviationism."

mark to suggest that the Olympic world power GDR was mainly a female power. Ulbricht had cynically reasoned that a world-class athlete could do more for the GDR than an industrial worker. East Germany had inherited this pronounced emphasis on sport as a symbol of national prominence from the Third Reich. In short, each German state had its outward symbol of world status: Olympic gold in the GDR, deutsche marks in the FRG.

Yet to many of its residents, the GDR remained an artificial and unloved creation. Ulbricht tolerated no freedom of speech, association, or movement and outlawed collective bargaining for workers. A deep gulf divided workers from managers: whereas a metal worker in 1951 earned less than 300 marks per month, managers on average received 4,000 marks. Between 1950 and 1961 nearly 3 million East Germans voted with their feet by resettling in the West. Most of those who left were highly trained and under twenty-five years of age. Those who stayed retreated into private life and turned their television aerials toward the West. The GDR's ringing appeals to traditional Prussian values of sacrifice, work, and authority were all too familiar from the recent past. The old bureaucracy seemed merely to have changed clothes: communist red had replaced Nazi brown. Insecurity, lack of identity, and a sense of inferiority to the West marked the public attitude in the GDR. It became fashionable for East Germans to espouse Immanuel Kant's Prussian motto: "Argue as much as you like, and about what you like; just obey!" "Socialism with a human face" remained at best a distant mirage.

The year 1953 was a watershed for the German Democratic Republic. Joseph Stalin died in March, leaving East German leaders without direction. Sensing a thawing of domestic rule by Stalin's successors, a reform faction within the Socialist Unity party headed by Rudolf Herrnstadt and Wilhelm Zaisser demanded a "new course" of emancipation from the Soviet Union. Ulbricht briefly toyed with the notion of reform. Nationalization of industry was temporarily halted, and economic output shifted to a 30 percent increase in consumer production. Incentives to return were offered to the 182,000 workers who had crossed into the West in 1952 alone. But a concomitant 10 percent increase in work quotas demanded of all GDR workers immediately erased the positive impact of these concessions.

On June 16–17, 1953, East German workers took to the streets to demand reforms. Mythology enshrouds the revolt. For the Federal Republic, June 17 clearly showed that the Ulbricht state was but an artificial Soviet creation devoid of popular support; the date became a national holiday. For the German Democratic Republic the uprising was but "fascist provocation against the GDR"; it used the event to conduct yet another purge of party and state. In truth the revolt was marked not by centralized direction but by spontaneity. Recently opened SED and police archives reveal that on June 17 about 140 government buildings (city halls, SED, and police headquarters) were stormed and 593 industrial plants struck by 496,765 workers. The largest protests occurred in East Berlin, Halle, and Leipzig. At the height of the uprising,

Red Terror: Soviet tanks suppress the Berlin workers' revolt (June 17, 1953).

industrial workers led strikes in 270 cities and communities from Berlin to Karl-Marx-Stadt and Magdeburg to Görlitz. Steel and construction workers marched in solidarity with railroad and chemical workers. Their demands ranged from reduction of work quotas to lower food prices, from free elections to resignation of the Ulbricht government.

Ulbricht was afraid to face the proletariat. Instead, Soviet tanks restored order in Berlin by June 18. More than 200 civilians and 100 police were killed. Soviet authorities arrested 6,000 people, including 3,500 workers; the total included 238 West Berliners and 42 West Germans. Ulbricht's eventual response was twofold: concessions to the workers and repression of suspected leaders. On June 21 the Central Committee of the SED reverted to the previous work quotas, lowered public transportation fees, and increased pensions as well as health coverage. In October the SED reduced food prices 20 to 25 percent and introduced state-financed credit to enable young couples, in particular, to purchase furniture, cars, and appliances.

The other side of the coin was yet another massive purge of the party. In July the Central Committee of the SED ousted Herrnstadt and Zaisser from its ranks and later that year their supporters at the grass-roots level. Between one-half and two-thirds of all district and county party leaders reportedly lost SED membership; twenty were executed. At the same time, Ulbricht stripped his National Front partners of all independence. Show trials of leading members of the CDU and LDPD drove home the message of repression to East Germans. Ideological indoctrination within the party and state apparatus was stepped up. So-called flight from the republic became a criminal offense in 1957. Reaction had its reward: when the Ulbricht regime finished counting the ballots in the October 1954 election, 98.4 percent of East Germans had approved the SED unitary list.

In July 1958 Ulbricht launched a final economic offensive. He assured the delegates to the SED's party congress that the German Democratic Republic would surpass the Federal Republic's standard of living in three years. The State Planning Commission within the Ministerial Council was ordered to meet Ulbricht's demand for economic parity with West Germany. That goal proved unreachable. Labor productivity in the GDR remained at least 30 percent — and perhaps as much as 50 percent — lower than in the FRG, and the east's standard of living lagged fully 40 percent behind that in the west. The commission succeeded only in nationalization and collectivization; 90 percent of all industrial and food production now came from "people-owned enterprises" and "agricultural production cooperatives," respectively.

"Economic Miracle": The FRG, 1945–1961

The western occupation zone, like its eastern counterpart, emerged from the ravages of war only slowly. In 1946 industrial production stood at one-third of its 1936 level. Ration cards dictated consumer production. Curfews proscribed nightlife. Allied regulations required formal permits for travel from state to state or zone to zone, but urban dwellers organized so-called hamster tours whereby they went from farmhouse to farmhouse begging food in exchange for personal valuables. Black marketeering flourished: Chesterfield and Lucky Strike cigarettes were common currency, and everything from shoes to hats, fruit to meat, and jewelry to bathtub gin was offered for sale. In Stuttgart in 1947, black market prices ranged from 85 reichsmarks for a pack of cigarettes to 150 RM for a pound of butter, to 250 RM for a pound of meat. A common slogan summed up the prevailing spirit: "Each for himself, God for all." Prostitution and rape were widespread, especially in the French and Soviet zones. Reportedly, 300,000 births resulted from this violence perpetrated against women.

Foreign aid fueled the western zones' economic recovery. On June 5, 1947, U.S. Secretary of State George C. Marshall at Harvard University announced the massive European Recovery Program, which allocated $1.5 billion to the western sectors. These funds were intended to stimulate German economic recovery, which, in turn, would ease the heavy costs of military occupation and civilian housing and food. At the same time, France received $2.7 billion and Britain $3.1 billion in American aid. Although the money provided under the Marshall Plan constituted only 7 percent of Germany's overall capital and material needs, it nevertheless served as a psychological boost and a catalyst to economic recovery. Rationing and other economic controls were lifted in June 1948.

Full recovery took decades and is usually attributed to Professor Ludwig Erhard, a disciple of the so-called Freiburg school of economics. In 1942 surviving members of Pastor Martin Niemöller's Confessing church had approached several economists at the Freiburg University, including Walter Eucken and Wilhelm Röpke, to devise a blueprint for German economic restructuring in a post-Hitlerian world. Erhard, through Professor Alfred Müller-Armack at Freiburg, became the beneficiary of these wartime deliberations. Often depicted as a dogmatic academic and "an American invention," Erhard in fact was neither. Rather, he was a pragmatic politician who realized the need to build up consumer industries in the new Germany, to foster economic competition, and to encourage industrial growth as long as it did not lead to the cartels and monopolies of the past.

Erhard appreciated the need to operate between the U.S. government's call for a tough line on economic decentralization and General Clay's wish to stimulate German recovery to allay the costs of occupation. He also understood that Germany's two major parties clamored for state control of the economy. The SPD demanded a centrally planned economy with public ownership of most resources and basic industries. Surprisingly, the CDU also endorsed state economic control. In February 1947 at Ahlen, the party executive demanded that large cartels be broken up, iron and coal syndicates nationalized, and industrial workers granted the right to codetermine wages and conditions of work as well as social benefits.

But Erhard stayed the course. Bit by bit he convinced Adenauer of the need to create a free market economy with generous social programs. Erhard counseled elimination of all rationing, an end to price controls, liberalization of the market, and "competition among producers in favor of consumers." Perhaps Adenauer overcame his initial opposition to Erhard's liberal economic views when he realized that the United States would never support a socialist Germany. Whatever the case, in April 1949 at Düsseldorf Adenauer adopted Erhard's concept of a "social market economy," a term coined by Müller-Armack of the Freiburg school.

Erhard shrewdly understood that although aerial bombing had demolished much of Germany's housing and transportation network, it had destroyed only 19 percent of its capital stock and 6.5 percent of its machinery. He also valued the Marshall Plan funds' power to jump-start the German economy. Finally, Erhard acknowledged the abundant skilled labor pouring into the western zones in the form of refugees from either former German lands in the east or from the Soviet zone.

Fiscal order was restored on June 18, 1948. U.S. military occupation authorities, working closely with Erhard, gave every west German in their zone sixty newly printed deutsche marks (DM) and declared the old reichsmark null and void, though Germans could exchange small amounts of the old reichsmarks for new deutsche marks at a ten-to-one ratio. The next day, Erhard, acting without any formal authority, announced over German radio that most consumer goods would be removed from government pricing controls and allowed to seek their free market value. He informed a startled nation that all outstanding debts could be written off up to 90 percent of face value and that anyone with savings of more than 5,000 RM would be investigated by the Treasury. Finally, he announced that German authorities would create a new *Bank Deutscher Länder*, soon renamed the *Deutsche Bundesbank*, as a federal bank to issue and manage the new currency. Allied leaders at Frankfurt endorsed this bold initiative, but only after formally chastising Erhard for having failed to seek their permission before making his historic broadcast.

This radical restructuring, much like Hjalmar Schacht's equally drastic currency reform in 1924, primarily hurt those who had managed to save a little — small and middle-class investors. But the gains were dramatic. The black market disappeared overnight as stores, stocked with goods, anxiously awaited a clientele armed with real money. Over 90 percent of the old reichsmarks were withdrawn from circulation. By June 20 both the British and French zones had joined this American initiative. Only the Soviets refused to honor the new marks. Currency reform in effect brought about an economic trizone as the French joined the Anglo-American bizone of 1947. It also paved the way for the creation of the Federal Republic one year later. When political union of the three western occupation zones came about in September 1949, the regions were already united fiscally and economically.

For women, there was no "hour zero" in 1945. In Berlin alone, nearly fifty thousand "rubble women" began the dreary task of cleaning up the debris of years of bombing. More than 4 million German men had died in the war, and another 12 million were prisoners of war. The upshot was that there were 7.3 million more women — most between the ages of twenty and forty — than men in Germany in 1945. Five years later there still remained 3.3 million war widows. Many of the latter concluded what were called "uncle marriages," cohabitating with a man rather than marrying in order to keep war pensions. More than 6 million women worked in the American and British zones alone in 1947. The divorce rate jumped from 11 percent in 1946 to 19 percent in 1948 as families cracked under the physical and psychological strain of the lost war.

The year 1950 revealed how long the road to recovery would be. Two million Germans were unemployed and 17 million on some form of welfare. Six million German families still lacked permanent housing. The national debt stood at 13.5 billion DM, of which 7 million DM constituted postwar loans. Nearly 2 billion DM remained on the books as payments from the Dawes and Young plans of the 1920s. And although the United States eventually agreed to reduce the German debt to 7.5 billion DM, Bonn still faced annual payments of between 567 million and 765 million DM.

COST OF LIVING AND WAGES IN THE FRG, 1950–1970 (1962 = 100)

Year	Money Wages[a]	Cost of Living	Real Wages
1950	41.9	78.7	53.2
1954	56.1	85.2	65.8
1958	71.6	92.6	77.3
1962	100	100	100
1966	134.0	112.8	118.8
1970	179.9	123.7	145.5

[a] Money wages reflect the face value of wages paid to employees. Real wages are money wages adjusted for inflation and thus indicate actual purchasing power.

Erhard's "social market economy" in time produced the West German "economic miracle." Seven million new workers found jobs, and unemployment fell to 1.2 percent by 1960. In the 1950s the West German growth rate stood at 8.6 percent per year, an incredibly high rate of sustained growth when measured against current "successful" rates of around 2 percent per year. Over the long period of recovery from 1950 to 1985, the gross national product increased a hundredfold to 1,845 billion DM, exports soared from 8.4 billion to 537 billion DM, and the balance of trade went from a deficit of 3 billion DM in 1950 to a surplus of 112.6 billion DM in 1985. Disposable family income grew by 400 percent between 1950 and 1970.

Two major pieces of legislation sought to distribute wealth equitably: the Law for the Equalization of Burdens (LAG) in May 1952 compensated war-related losses, and the February 1953 Refugee Law created federal housing and job-training projects. Under the terms of the LAG, those with property valued above 5,000 DM were assessed a "contribution" amounting to half the estimated assets value, to be paid over thirty years. By 1986 more than 3 million prosperous West Germans had paid 139 billion DM to roughly 10 million less affluent countrymen (those bombed out or refugees from eastern lands). About 67 percent of relief funds went to the homeless and 23 percent as compensation for war damages or losses.

Housing shortages nevertheless continued to plague the Federal Republic. As early as August 1945, German authorities had established an emergency fund to help defray the cost of housing millions of refugees in Bavaria, Lower Saxony, and Schleswig-Holstein. But five years later, there were only 10.1 million residences for 16.4 million families. West German Housing Construction Acts in 1950 and 1956 resulted in the building of 4.5 million new dwellings. Critics uniformly condemn Germany's "wretched postwar architecture," with its monotonous rows of multiple-occupancy housing spaced to suit the range of gantry cranes and its relentless patterns of joints and stereotypical windows set into the center of each wall panel. The new "urbanity" favored

The new "urbanity": The Hansa Quarter in West Berlin (1957).

concentration over dispersal, density over looseness, and metropolitan flair over hygienic greenery. The endless sprawling suburbs of low- and high-rise structures became a testimonial to neglected architectural opportunities.

This banal development in part stemmed from the town planning boards' lack of power. Landowners formed private lobbies and dominated the planning process, demanding indemnification payments for land in redevelopment areas not at current but rather at potential market value. Consequently, builders had to render this expensive land financially profitable by constructing as many housing units as possible on every plot. Public antipathy toward town planning only encouraged the tyranny of private property owners. And Bonn made little money available for architectural innovation. Scientific building research in the Federal Republic was a paltry 0.002 percent of total

"Made in Germany": The VW beetle becomes the symbol of the "economic miracle."

building volume, at a time when industry invested two thousandfold this amount in research. Succor came only in the 1960s with the rise of so-called citizens' initiatives in the areas of town planning and the environment.

The newfound prosperity of the "economic miracle" manifested itself in a mad rush of consumer spending. The number of cars in West Germany rose from 12 per 1,000 citizens in 1950 to 412 per 1,000 in 1984. Highway volume ballooned thirtyfold. The Volkswagen "beetle" became the symbol of "made in Germany" exports. Half a million tractors appeared in the countryside, along with an equally dramatic increase in mechanical threshers and harvesters. Television sets in West German homes between 1955 and 1958 alone multiplied eightfold to 2 million. By 1962, one-half of all German homes had refrigerators, two out of three had vacuum cleaners, and every third home had a washing machine. In addition, the tourism craze of the Nazi's Strength Through Joy program was not only renewed but increased: in 1987 German tourists spent 42 billion DM seeing the world.

Prosperity also brought stability and an end to class struggle. The Confederation of German Trade Unions (DGB), founded at Bielefeld in March 1947, managed to gain for German workers one-third of all seats in the boardrooms of major companies in 1952. Under the terms of this Works Constitution Act, employees gained the right to codetermination in social welfare issues, work and vacation time, and collective bargaining. Strikes became rare; real wages doubled. The workweek steadily shrank to below forty hours, the state provided social services, and housing and transportation became readily available. In 1957 so-called dynamic rents were introduced. That year, by tying rents to wage and price indexes, Bonn boosted average rents 65 percent.

The sociologist Helmut Schelsky claims that the Adenauer years created a "leveled-off, middle-class society." Other sociologists coined the term *deproletarianization* to describe the West German labor movement. The Federal Republic, with few exceptions, ceased to have traditional upper and lower classes. Many noble families quietly dropped the *von* from their names. Social discrepancies leveled off, and one could speak of a country with a single middle class consisting of skilled blue-collar and white-collar workers. And although the Federal Republic never used sports to try to legitimize its existence, in 1954 its world championship in soccer at Bern, Switzerland, symbolized the nation's return to grace and prestige.

The Federal Republic's newfound wealth could not erase all the sins of the recent past. In September 1952 Adenauer concluded an agreement with the state of Israel whereby West Germany agreed to distribute 3.5 billion DM to the Jewish state as "compensation" for the Holocaust. Only 11 percent of Germans agreed with the measure, and almost forty members of Adenauer's own party abstained in the *Bundestag* when the bill came up for approval. Nevertheless, Adenauer realized that much of the world demanded that Bonn atone for the barbarism perpetrated by the Third Reich, and he extended "compensation" to individual families as well. By 1980 the Federal Republic had awarded 80 billion DM to Jewish victims of the Third Reich; the figure is expected to pass 100 billion DM by the year 2000. The establishment of the Institute for Contemporary History at Munich in 1953 to assist Germans in "conquering the past" advanced German-Israeli relations another step in the right direction by confronting the Nazi past through books and films (rather than by hiding it).

After two decades of war and black-market conditions, many German women in the late 1950s opted for a return to a more traditional role as housewife and mother. Sociological surveys suggest that most Germans were turning inward, seeing the family and home as a castle, a retreat from the outside world. These surveys also reveal the emergence of a new concept of marriage as a partnership in which both spouses are fundamentally equal.

Young women finally managed to storm the bastions of education. Whereas in 1960 only one of four girls completed secondary school, that figure had doubled to one of two, where it remains today. In 1979 numerical gender equality was attained for the prestigious *Gymnasium* that led to university admission. In 1960 a mere 4.4 percent of eligible women between the ages of nineteen and twenty-one became university students; twenty years later that figure had quadrupled to 16 percent, and in 1991–1992 stands at 33 percent. Overall, the percentage of women at German universities rose from 24 percent in 1960 to 37 percent in 1980. Women pursued careers in education and the humanities, generally eschewing the applied sciences and engineering (4 percent) as well as physics, chemistry, and computer sciences (20 percent).

The legal position of German women had also improved dramatically. Article 3 of the 1949 Basic Law guaranteed equal rights for men and women. Six years later, the West German Federal Labor Court decreed equal pay for equal work. And in July 1958, the same court under the Equal Rights Law struck from the Civil Code all sections granting males special roles in the upbringing of children, administration of joint property, and disposal of wealth. By 1976 women could choose their original surname as the family name. One year later they gained the right to "no-fault" divorce, which had existed since 1938 in the Third Reich.

The pace of reconstruction in both German states in the period 1945 to 1960 was astounding. Seldom has a nation risen so quickly from the ashes of defeat and destruction. The Bonn regime systematically repaired transportation and communications systems, underwrote housing construction, promulgated a new constitution, and achieved near-full employment. Whereas Adenauer firmly embedded the Federal Republic in the West European and North Atlantic economic and defense systems, Ulbricht's German Democratic Republic developed into the Soviet Union's most reliable and productive trade and defense partner in Eastern Europe.

But the nation remained divided and intra-German relations fragile at best, in truth reaching their nadir by the end of the 1950s. As the decade closed, bitter acrimony set in. Whereas Adenauer conducted a policy of "maintained tensions" by limiting all contacts with East Germany, which he continued to refer to as the "zone," Ulbricht deliberately closed his border with West Germany, which he called the "revanchist puppet state" of the United States and NATO. The two German leaders joined the cold war with egotistical relish and developed policies ("Ulbricht Doctrine" and "Hallstein Doctrine") declaring any recognition of the "other" German state by a third power an unfriendly act. By 1960 few Germans took public rhetoric in Berlin and Bonn concerning future reunification seriously.

Ulbricht's charge to the SED's Fifth Party Congress in July 1958 to catch and then surpass West German industrial output within five years remained a distant mirage. Embittered by failed government promises of better wages and housing, about 3 million East Germans had left the GDR by 1960 to seek prosperity (and freedom) in the land of Ludwig Erhard's "economic miracle." Most of the refugees were professional people and skilled workers under twenty-five years old. Consequently, the GDR's population declined from 19 million in 1945 to 17.8 million by 1960; conversely, that of the FRG rose from 40 million in 1948 to 55 million by 1960.

The flight of skilled citizens to the West threatened the very existence of the German Democratic Republic. Production norms set at the 1958 party congress could not be met, and the GDR fell ever further behind the FRG in industrial output. The loss of 3 million young people shifted the age balance in East Germany toward the elderly, thereby putting greater strains on the nation's social security system. And the SED's attempt to consolidate the distinct (and, it claimed, superior) socioeconomic system of the "first German workers' and farmers' state on German soil" — the party's very legitimacy — was seriously jeopardized. Indeed, Ulbricht and his minions writhed at the specter of thousands of their citizens turning their backs on the GDR every month by 1961. Clearly, drastic measures would be necessary to stem the flood of what Ulbricht denounced as "flight from the Republic."

Suggested Readings

The general contours of the Allied occupation have been sketched in by Michael Balfour, *Four-Power Control in Germany and Austria* (London, 1956); Nicholas Balabkins, *Germany Under Direct Controls: Economic Aspects of Industrial Disarmament, 1945–1948* (New Brunswick, N.J., 1964); and John E. Farquharson, *The Western Allies and the Politics of Food: Agrarian Management in Postwar Germany* (Leamington Spa, 1985).

The Soviet administration of East Germany has been analyzed by Henry Krisch, *German Politics Under Soviet Occupation* (New York, 1974); Carl J. Friedrich, *The Soviet Zone of Germany* (New Haven, Conn., 1956); John G. Nettl, *The Eastern Zone and Soviet Policy in Germany, 1945–1950* (Oxford, 1951); and Gregory W. Sanford, *From Hitler to Ulbricht: The Communist Reconstruction of East Germany, 1945–1946* (Princeton, 1983). More detailed studies include Robert Slusser, ed., *Soviet Economic Policy in Post-War Germany: A Collection of Papers by Former Soviet Officials* (New York, 1953); Wolfgang F. Stolper and Karl W. Roskamp, *The Structure of the East German Economy* (Cambridge, Mass., 1960); and Frieda Wunderlich, *Farmer and Farm Labor in the Soviet Zone of Germany* (New York, 1958).

Understanding the U.S. occupation of Germany begins with Lucius D. Clay, *Decision in Germany* (Garden City, N.Y., 1950); a critical survey is provided by Edward N. Peterson, *The American Occupation of Germany: Retreat to Victory* (Detroit, 1978). The Marshall Plan has been detailed by John Gimbel, *The Origins of the Marshall Plan* (Stanford, 1976); Michael J. Hogan, *The Marshall Plan: America, Britain, and the Reconstruction of Western Europe 1947–1952* (Cambridge, 1987); and Charles S. Maier, *The Marshall Plan and Germany: West German Development Within the Framework of the European Recovery Program* (New York, 1991). American attempts to "reeducate" Germans are handled by Nicholas Pronay and Keith Wilson, eds., *The Political Reeducation of Germany and Her Allies After World War II* (London, 1985).

De-Nazification was satirized by the novelist Ernst von Salomon, *Fragebogen (The Questionnaire)* (New York, 1954). The Nuremberg trials have been placed in perspective by Bradley F. Smith, *Reaching Judgement at Nuremberg: The Untold Story of How the Nazi War Criminals Were Judged* (London, 1977). The Berlin crisis of 1948 has been examined by Avi Shlaim, *The United States and the Berlin Blockade 1948 to 1949: A Study in Crisis Decision-Making* (Berkeley, 1983).

Allied foreign policy with regard to Germany starts with John H. Backer, *The Decision to Divide Germany: American Foreign Policy in Transition* (Durham, N.C., 1978). The cold war perspective can be gleaned from Charles S. Maier, ed., *The Origins of the Cold War and Contemporary Europe* (New York and London, 1978), and, especially, John L. Gaddis, *Strategies of Containment: A Critical Appraisal of Postwar American National Security Policy* (New York, 1982). The British position has been worked out by Donald C. Watt, *Britain Looks to Germany: British Opinion and Policy Towards Germany Since 1945* (London, 1965), and Alec Cairncross, *The Price of War: British Policy on German Reparations, 1941–1949* (Oxford, 1986). A recent reappraisal is Josef Becker and Franz Kipping, eds., *Power in Europe? Great Britain, France, Italy and Germany in a Postwar World, 1945–1950* (New York, 1986). French occupation policies were first elucidated by F. Roy Willis, *The French in Germany, 1945–1949* (Stanford, 1962).

The early history of the German Democratic Republic was undertaken by Jean Edward Smith, *Germany Beyond the Wall: People, Politics . . . and Prosperity* (Boston and Toronto, 1967), and David Childs, *East Germany: Politics and Government* (London, 1969). The Berlin revolt of 1953 has been examined by Arnulf Baring, *Uprising in East Germany* (Ithaca, N.Y., 1972). See also Wolfgang Leonhard, *Child of the Revolution* (London, 1956). Carola Stern, *Ulbricht: A Political Biography* (London, 1965), looks at the GDR's founder. The Socialist Unity party has been studied by Jonathan Steele, *Socialism with a German Face: The State That Came in from the Cold* (London, 1977); Peter C. Ludz, *The Changing Party Elite in East Germany* (Cambridge, Mass., 1973); and Martin McCauley, *Marxism-Leninism in the German Democratic Republic: The Socialist Unity Party (SED)* (London, 1979).

Study of the Adenauer era begins with Konrad Adenauer, *Memoirs, 1945–1953* (London, 1966). A general introduction is provided by Michael Balfour, *West Germany* (London, 1968); Edgar Alexander, *Adenauer and the New Germany: The Chancellor of the Vanquished* (New York, 1957); Arnold J. Heidenheimer, *Adenauer and the CDU: The Rise of the Leader and the Integration of the Party* (The Hague, 1960); and Ralf Dahrendorf, *Society and Democracy in Germany* (New York, 1967). Adenauer's major political rival has been examined by Lewis J. Edinger, *Kurt Schumacher: A Study in Personality and Political Behavior* (Stanford, 1965).

The West German "economic miracle" has been analyzed by Volker R. Berghahn, *The Americanisation of West German Industry, 1945–1973* (Leamington Spa, 1986), and Eric O. Smith, *The West German Economy* (New York, 1983). The West German political system is detailed by Herbert Doring and Gordon R. Smith, eds., *Party Government and Political Culture in Western Germany* (London, 1982); Kenneth H. F. Dyson, *Party, State and Bureaucracy in Western Germany* (Beverly Hills, Calif., 1977); and Eva Kolinsky, *Parties, Opposition and Society in West Germany* (New York, 1984). For the SPD, see Douglas A. Chalmers, *The Social Democratic Party of Germany: From Working-Class Movement to Modern Political Party* (New Haven, Conn., 1964); and for the CDU, Geoffrey Pridham, *Christian Democracy in Western Germany: The CDU/CSU in Government and Opposition, 1945–1976* (London, 1977).

Ekkehart Krippendorff and Volker Rittberger, *The Foreign Policy of West Germany: Formation and Contents* (Beverly Hills, Calif., 1980), is a useful primer for West German foreign policy since 1945. The early years of Bonn's foreign affairs are discussed in Wolfram F. Hanrieder, *West German Foreign Policy, 1949–1963* (Boulder, Colo., 1980). German-American relations can be gleaned from Roger Morgan, *The United States and West Germany, 1945–1973: A Study in Alliance Politics* (London, 1974).

German rearmament has been researched primarily by West German scholars. For the English reader, Donald Abenheim, *Reforging the Iron Cross: The Search for Tradition in the Armed Forces* (Princeton, 1989), offers a good introduction to the problem of "militarism" in postwar Germany. Architecture and reconstruction are discussed and depicted in Wolfgang Pehnt, *German Architecture, 1960–1970* (London, 1970).

CHAPTER

11

TWO STATES, ONE NATION, 1961–1989

In the ten years that have elapsed since the end of the Second World War, two sovereign states have been created on German territory — the German Democratic Republic and the Federal Republic of Germany. Each of them has its own economic and social order. The sovereignty rights of each of them have been recognized by other states.

N. A. Bulganin, July 1955

By 1960, the two German states were well on the road to economic recovery and political stability. Konrad Adenauer had firmly emplaced the Federal Republic (FRG) in the Western camp through membership in the North Atlantic Treaty Organization (NATO) and the European Common Market, and Walter Ulbricht had implanted the German Democratic Republic (GDR) as a Soviet satellite in the Warsaw Pact and the Council for Mutual Economic Aid (Comecon). Both founding fathers still ruled their respective states: Adenauer at Bonn and Ulbricht at East Berlin. But both men were nearing the ends of their careers, and a younger generation, represented by men such as Ludwig Erhard and Erich Honecker, waited in the wings to assume the reins of power.

The division of Germany seemed virtually unresolvable. In July 1955 the victorious Allies had met at Geneva to discuss the "German question," and the Four Powers concluded that no solution existed. Soviet leaders N. A. Bulganin and Nikita S. Khrushchev paid a visit to East Berlin on their way back to Moscow and assured Ulbricht that reunification was not simply a German matter but one that could be achieved only through collective security in Europe. Specifically, both Kremlin leaders asserted that there now existed two sovereign, separate German states with quite distinct socioeconomic systems. This so-called two-states theory dominated German affairs for the next three decades. And the construction of the Wall dividing first West from East Berlin and then West from East Germany in August 1961 offered physical evidence of the seemingly permanent division of Germany.

As the world's attention shifted from Berlin and Germany to Vietnam and Cuba, Angola and Namibia, torn by national and socialist liberation movements, German leaders were forced to redefine their states' places in the international system. Even Berlin ceased to be the focal point of cold war tensions in a bipolar Soviet-U.S. world. Slowly but steadily, Bonn and East Berlin groped toward normalization of relations. The FRG's *Ostpolitik* (eastern policy), most closely associated with the SPD leader Willy Brandt, brought cultural, trade, and transit agreements with the GDR. Both German states were admitted to the United Nations and the Olympic movement. Intra-German trade flourished as the Federal Republic offered generous financial support to the GDR in return for measures easing intercourse between the two German states' residents.

Nevertheless, the Wall remained, with its concrete barrier, barbed wire, electronic sensors, mines, guard dogs, and armed guard towers. Few Germans expected reunification within their lifetime, and most accepted the hard reality that Moscow and Washington, rather than Bonn and East Berlin, held the keys to Germany's future. In short, only policies enunciated in the two world capitals could overcome the national division.

"A Socialist State of Workers and Farmers": The GDR, 1961–1989

The real founding date for both German states was August 13, 1961. On that day many hopes for possible reunification were shattered as twenty thousand East German army and police units began constructing a concrete wall between East and West Berlin. In time, the barrier would extend along the entire border between East and West Germany as well. Barbed wire, mines, electronic detection devices, guard dogs, motorcycle patrols, machine guns, and even helicopters would eventually end all physical intercourse between the two German states.

For thirty years the Wall symbolized the postwar division of Germany. Before its construction, nearly half a million people in Berlin crossed relatively freely from one occupation zone into another every day. More than fifty thousand East Berliners had worked or studied in West Berlin. But at least 2 million East Germans had also taken advantage of the open border to seek a better life in the West, and their exodus undermined the German Democratic Republic's economy. Repeated Soviet threats to limit Western access to Berlin only served as a catalyst for many of the refugees. In the first three months of 1961, thirty thousand GDR residents fled their state. In early August another twenty-five hundred deserted the "first socialist state on German soil." Despite

"No one has any intention of building a wall": Walter Ulbricht (June 1961).

publicly declaring in June 1961 that "no one has any intention of building a wall," in August 1961 Ulbricht obtained permission from the Warsaw Pact states to construct the "antifascist protective wall." Supervision fell to Erich Honecker.

Honecker, who would succeed Ulbricht in 1971, was born in 1912 at Neunkirchen in the Saar to a family of coal miners. He had joined the KPD during the Weimar Republic and risen through the ranks in the Communist youth movement. Arrested by the Nazis in Berlin in 1935, Honecker spent the next decade incarcerated at the Brandenburg-Görden prison. From 1946 to 1955 he headed the Free German Youth, spent 1956–1957 in the Soviet Union, and in 1958 was elevated to the Politburo and entrusted with supervising the GDR's defense and security systems. Upon replacing Ulbricht in 1971, Honecker appointed his second wife, Margot, minister of education and the sole female member of the Politburo. By 1976 Erich Honecker was secretary-general of the SED and chairman of both the Defense Council and State Council. Honecker, in good proletarian tradition, listed his occupation as "roofer" and that of his wife as "telephonist."

The East German leader saw himself as representing a new, highly educated elite that was replacing the *apparatchiks*, or party hacks, of Ulbricht's time. Increasingly technical experts and plant managers rather than party functionaries were determining economic policies, and professional competence rather than political reliability was determining the individual's place in society. On the other hand, the SED remained above the law and aloof from society regarding its citizens as units of production in a revolution conducted from above. In Honecker's "highly developed socialist society," the SED leadership still controlled the forces of production, organized the economy, defined professional opportunities, set standards of living and social services, established wages and prices, and developed culture, education, recreation, and sports.

Honecker had a keen, if slanted, sense of German history. In 1974 he rewrote the East German constitution, jettisoning the notion of a single German nation and replacing it with the concept that Germany had always consisted of two nations, one bourgeois and the other proletarian, with no common ground between them. The following year Honecker renegotiated the 1955 and 1964 friendship agreements with the Soviet Union and for the first time dropped any reference to eventual German reunification. In 1981 the East German leader refined his theory of the "two Germanies." As he put it, although two German states coexisted, there was but one German nationality. The dichotomy would end once the proletariat in the Federal Republic embraced "socialist reconstruction" along East German lines. Only when West German workers "take in hand the socialist transformation of the Federal Republic," Honecker assured his party elite, could the "question of unification" be "asked completely anew!"

Erich Honecker has also been described as a "Red Prussian." He restored, both physically and intellectually, many of Prussia's historical traditions and heroes. With the exception of the Soviet helmet, East German forces wore traditional *Wehrmacht* uniforms, ceremonial daggers, boots, and badges, and paraded down Unter den Linden in East Berlin with the Prussian "goose step," led by a traditional Prussian martial band. The military reformers of the post–1806 period were honored as precursors of socialist reforms; one of them, Gerhard von Scharnhorst, even had a medal cast in his honor. The Russo-Prussian solidarity of 1812 against Napoleon was resuscitated through the highly visible and prestigious Association for German-Soviet Friendship.

In 1983 the celebrations that marked the five hundredth anniversary of the birth of Martin Luther, chaired by Erich Honecker, denoted that the sixteenth-century enemy of the peasants' rebellions had a place in the pantheon of East German heroes. Recalling "Frederick the Great," Honecker restored Schadow's equestrian statue of Frederick II to its place of honor on Unter den Linden. Even the nationalist gymnast Friedrich Jahn was included in East German history. Given time, Otto von Bismarck, too, may well have been rehabilitated.

When Honecker replaced Ulbricht in May 1971, he viewed the economy as his main challenge. Having come to power largely because Ulbricht had lost favor with Kremlin leaders over his refusal to accept a slight thaw in East-West relations, Honecker understandably championed Marxist-Leninist orthodoxy. He immediately denounced East German writers who "doubt everything, doubt all authority." Concurrently, he nationalized all remaining private and semiprivate enterprises, primarily in the food and textile sectors, which employed 2 million people and accounted for 14 percent of national income.

Honecker quickly accomplished his stated goal of state socialism. In 1972 the SED announced that 99.4 percent of all East German workers toiled in state-run *Volkseigene Betriebe*, or VEB plants. Eight years later Honecker unified groups of these "people-owned enterprises" into horizontal or vertical cartels called *Kombinate*, each employing between twenty thousand and forty thousand workers. Having fully nationalized all East German industries, Honecker felt sufficiently confident to renew the provisions of the New Economic System of Planning and Management of the Economy that Ulbricht had introduced in 1963, to allow his technological elite greater flexibility in determining production, prices, and wages.

Honecker entrusted the education of the GDR's technological elite to his wife, Margot. As head of the Ministry of People's Education, she centralized admissions, courses, textbooks, and examinations. After 1964, all children attended elementary school (*Grundschule*) and then secondary school for four years. The following year Margot Honecker established special ten-year Comprehensive Polytechnical Secondary Schools to create "conscious, socialist citizens." Only after a solid grounding in the three "R's," as well as Russian, history, and Communist civics, did students specialize in "polytechnical instruction." The latter included practical work in factories and on farms for four hours per week so that students balanced theoretical school instruction with contacts with agrarian and industrial producers.

The traditional German universities that the GDR inherited — Berlin (1809), Leipzig (1409), Halle (1694), Jena (1558), Rostock (1410), Greifswald (1456), and Dresden Technological University (1890) — were radically restructured. Admission depended as much on family origin, with preference given to the offspring of workers and farmers, as on intellectual ability. Traditional faculties were abolished and replaced by sections on Marxism/Leninism, history, chemistry, science, engineering, and mathematics. Councils of representatives from the Socialist Unity party, the Free German Youth, and, where appropriate, industrial or agrarian combines ran the sections. Although traditional rectors still headed the universities, real power rested with the Ministry for Universities and Vocational Colleges — that is, with the SED. Under Ulbricht, the GDR's seven universities had been supplemented by forty-seven university-level special institutions, such as the Medical Academy at Dresden, the Music College at Berlin, and the Sports University at Leipzig.

The Sports University quickly gained world fame — and notoriety. It identified prospective athletes at age five or six, devised special medical programs for their development, and augmented their physical performance with drugs banned by the International Olympic Committee and other international sporting associations. Successful athletes were showered with rewards ranging from cars to apartments. Most belonged to military, police, or industrial "clubs" in order to maintain the fiction that they were amateurs. And most worked for the State Security Service (Stasi). Those who failed to achieve world standards of competition were thrown back into the normal system.

The Olympic Games revealed the success of the GDR's sports system and provided Honecker an opportunity to trumpet the superiority of socialism. After competing at Melbourne (1956), Rome (1960), and Tokyo (1964) as part of an all-German team, the GDR became a member of the Olympic Committee in 1965 and was allowed to appear at Mexico (1968) as a separate squad. The GDR's sports elite, trained primarily at Leipzig, in 1980 dominated both the Summer Games at Moscow (second in medals only to the Soviet Union) and the Winter Games at Lake Placid (first in total medals).

Power under Honecker remained with the SED. In 1981 the party encompassed 2.17 million members, of whom almost one in four was listed as a member of the labor force. Among workers in the SED, 34 percent were women. The real brokers of power, however, remained in the Politburo, whose members became ever more elderly: the average age in 1971, fifty-nine, rose to sixty-four by 1986. The faithful were rewarded with special villas in Wandlitz near Berlin, Volvo state limousines, and access to special shops stocked with Western goods. SED coffers bulged with foreign currency through the proliferation of special Intershops and hotels that accepted only hard currency, charged exorbitant transit and visitors' fees, and maintained an official (and highly artificial) exchange rate of parity between East and West German marks. The West German magazine *Der Spiegel* claimed that at the 1981 party conference, all delegates received a pocket calculator, leather writing case, digital watch, flower vase, and cognac dispenser.

In return for their status, SED party hacks eulogized Honecker on every occasion, according their leader standing ovations and prolonged, tumultuous applause as well as thirty or more official accolades whenever he addressed them. Nevertheless, this never-ending self-adulation could not conceal the fact that the SED had changed from a revolutionary party of struggle and change to a hide-bound administrative party of bureaucrats and *Bonzen*. The SED machinery's very size and complexity militated against reform.

In foreign policy Honecker desperately sought to gain international recognition for the GDR, and he succeeded. In 1971 only twenty-six states recognized the East Berlin regime; that number had risen to 121 by 1976. Moreover, in 1973 both German states gained admittance into the United Nations. Two years later, the GDR became a signatory to the Helsinki Conference on European Security and Cooperation (CSCE), by which the heads of thirty-three European states recognized the status quo (and hence the permanent division) in Europe.

Honecker's most visible foreign policy activity took place in the so-called Third World. Following the Soviet example, East Germany supported nationalist and socialist liberation movements throughout the world. Ulbricht had recognized Fidel Castro's revolution in Cuba in 1963, and in the 1970s Honecker offered generous credits to Havana and agreed to purchase Cuban products (mainly sugar) in order to help its dictator withstand the U.S. blockade of the island. The GDR's first military "advisers" in black Africa were dispatched to the Congo (Brazzaville) in 1973; others soon followed to Nigeria, Namibia, Ethiopia, Angola, Zimbabwe, and Mozambique. Members of the East German People's Army also traveled to Syria, Algeria, Iraq, and Libya; Western observers monitored GDR ammunition shipments to Ethiopia, Tanzania, and Mozambique. In 1973 the GDR, which refused to recognize the state of Israel, permitted Yassar Arafat's Palestine Liberation Organization (PLO) to establish an office on its territory. And by 1978 more than two thousand East German specialists had taken over the security of the People's Republic of South Yemen. In return, the Honecker state gained not only the appreciation of Moscow but also access to much-needed oil, coal, and other raw materials.

Intra-German relations, however, caused Honecker the most concern. The "eastern policy" of FRG foreign minister Willy Brandt (SPD), launched in the mid–1960s (see pages 415-419), threatened to isolate Honecker as West German ministers were welcomed not only in London, Paris, and Washington but also in Budapest, Prague, Warsaw — and Moscow. Nor could Honecker halt news from West Germany. Apart from the fact that most East German television aerials continued to face west, more than 1 million West Germans visited the GDR each year and another 1 million West Berliners undertook day trips to East Berlin each year. Conversely, by 1975 more than 1.3 million East German pensioners and another 40,000 below pensionable age but on "urgent family business" were permitted to travel to the Federal Republic. Intra-German telephone calls rose from 700,000 in 1970 to 16.7 million by 1978 as a result of transit agreements reached between Bonn and East Berlin in the wake of Brandt's *Ostpolitik*.

Honecker, alarmed by this near-free exchange of information, responded with a policy of delimitation (*Abgrenzung*). The Stasi impaired the work of foreign journalists in the GDR and deported many for unfavorable reporting. Honecker doubled fees for intra-German travel in 1980. As early as September 1970 the East German leader had launched a vigorous program of indoctrination in the press and schools and on radio and TV in order to stress the rudimentary differences between the GDR and the FRG. His specific aim was to disabuse East Germans of the pervading notion that a common German nation and culture existed. Because of the persistence of capitalism in West Germany and the development of socialism in East Germany, Honecker averred, the two German states had grown apart, developing different consciousness and undergoing different experiences. He personally exorcised the word German from the East German vocabulary and replaced it with the German acronym DDR ("German Democratic Republic"); East Berlin now became the *Hauptstadt der DDR* (capital of the GDR). In 1978 GDR leaders made military training in schools mandatory, presumably to guard against West German "revanchism" and "imperialism," and ordered schools and the media to stress GDR patriotism and love of the Soviet Union. At the same time, Honecker truncated the East German Protestant church from the all-German Evangelical church, based in the Federal Republic, and reorganized it into the League of Evangelical Churches in the GDR at East Berlin.

Abgrenzung failed to produce the desired result. Although many East Germans took pride in their economic achievements — the second leading industrial power in the Comecon block — and their Olympic triumphs, they remained bitter, sullen, alienated, and angry over the SED's continued monopoly of power. Many rejected both the GDR and the FRG and viewed themselves primarily as Germans belonging to a theoretical "Germany." They recognized unitary-slate elections as a mockery of democracy — in June 1986, for example, the SED-approved single slate won 99.94 percent of the national vote — and decried the emphasis on military training in schools. They began to question why their standard of living and level of production lagged about 30 percent behind that of West Germany, despite the fact that they labored almost three hundred hours per year more than their West German counterparts. Many continued to maintain a fictional relationship with their state: "You act as though you are paying us, and we act as though we are working for you." And many were shocked by the public suicide by immolation of Pastor Oskar Brüsewitz in August 1976, an obvious sign that pressures were building up within Honecker's own League of Evangelical Churches.

Above all, East Germans looked longingly at the gradual softening of communism in Hungary under János Kádár ("goulash communism") and the development after August 1980 of the Solidarity movement of Lech Wałęsa in Poland. Even the model Soviet Union was undergoing reform. Leonid Brezhnev died in November 1982 and was followed by the brief reigns of Yuri Andropov (to February 1984) and Konstantine Chernenko (to March 1985), and finally by the reform dynamism of Mikhail Gorbachev.

Honecker, at age seventy-three, remained stiff, conservative, and unimaginative. The new Soviet leader, at age fifty-four, possessed great energy, a forceful personality, and a flexible mind, and he was a master of maneuver. Above all, he possessed a vision of the future radically different from that of his Kremlin predecessors (and Honecker). The Soviet leader apparently had concluded that the Soviet Union's East European satellites had reached the end of their economic and military abilities and that the GDR in particular was in economic decline. Gorbachev accepted that the Federal Republic was solidly tied to the West and that the Wall was a hindrance to improved German-Soviet relations, a barrier against future sources of credit and high technology. Additionally, Gorbachev realized that the European Community, led by the Federal Republic and France, was rapidly emerging as a new continental and global power. Whereas he earlier had reminded Europeans that the Soviet Union was part of the "European house" in an attempt to lure them away from U.S. influence, Gorbachev now desperately sought to gain admittance for his crumbling state to that very "house," newly centered not at Moscow but at Brussels.

Under a policy of "restructuring" (*perestroika*), Gorbachev aimed to revamp the Soviet state so that it could compete economically with the West. Specifically, he tried to loosen the Soviet Union's highly centralized system of economic planning and management by scaling back the power of Moscow's top-heavy state corporations and ministries. With the help of foreign investment, joint ventures, and Western consumer goods, Gorbachev moved to institute "socialist-market" cooperatives as well as private family businesses and farms. And his parallel program of "openness" (*glasnost*) promised liberalization of expression and the political process. To be sure, Gorbachev did not demand full democratization of Soviet society and firmly endorsed the Communist party's monopoly of power, but he suggested that the Soviet people be permitted to "make public what everyone knows but no one dares say out loud." He suggested that the founder of the Soviet Union had demanded nothing less. "We want more openness about public affairs in every sphere of life," Gorbachev announced, "Truth is the main thing. Lenin had said: More light! Let the party know everything. As never before, we need no dark corners where mold can reappear."

On several occasions, Honecker sought to encourage the Soviet leader to disband his revisionist development. When he failed, Honecker reverted to hard-line rule in the GDR. In Bismarckian fashion he denounced members of the East German peace movement, named Swords into Plowshares, as "enemies of the state." In 1986 he depicted environmentalists who protested the dumping of West German refuse in the GDR against cash payments as "enemies of the state." Two years later, Honecker ordered the Stasi to step up its surveillance of all churchgoers and to arrest those who used God's houses for "political purposes." The Stasi even managed to penetrate the West German postal system and to monitor its long-distance telephone network.

In 1986 Honecker launched a new Five-Year Plan in a bold attempt to modernize East German key technologies such as computers, robotics, nuclear energy, laser application, and biotechnology. But decades of neglect of the nation's infrastructure obstructed the attempted modernization. The rail network lagged woefully behind that of West Germany. Trucks and cars remained of poor quality and insufficient quantity. Spare parts proved hard to come by and gasoline expensive and inferior. Consumer goods such as cars, washing machines, and colored televisions were in short supply, and when available after several years' wait, exorbitantly priced. The sewage system failed to meet the needs of a modern industrial society, and environmental protection had long been ignored in favor of higher productivity. Housing had suffered, and the functional new urban centers featured uniform concrete-slab construction with monotonous regularity of styles.

East German industry quickly discovered that its plants were too obsolete and inefficient to compete head-on with Western technology. Vast state subsidies alone permitted the GDR to participate in global markets. And East Germany was becoming ever more dependent on West German lines of credits. In 1984, as a result of a state visit the previous year by Bavarian Minister-President Franz Josef Strauss, who wished to play an international role independent of Bonn, Honecker had received bank credits of 2 billion deutsche marks to prop up his failing industries.[1] But borrowing led to further borrowing, and by 1989 the East German national debt, most of it owed to the Federal Republic, stood at a staggering 300 billion DM. The GDR, in the eyes of many European leaders, was economically propped up and politically stabilized only by West German support. Many West German scholars today believe that the GDR managed to survive as long as it did mainly as a result of this massive infusion of West German cash.

In perhaps one of the least savory intra-German developments, Honecker initiated a program of releasing political prisoners for cash. In 1983, for example, the GDR set free 20,000 East German political prisoners in return for nearly 2 billion marks; the average price per prisoner in the 1980s amounted to about 50,000 marks. As late as 1988 Bonn purchased freedom for 1,094 persons in exchange for 320 million marks. A popular joke about the special intra-German relationship made the rounds in East Berlin in the late 1980s: How have the two German states divided Karl Marx's legacy? *Answer*: The West has the Capital and the East has the Manifesto.

To the end, Honecker refused to condone criticism. A case in point is that of Rudolf Bahro, an SED party member since 1954, who in 1977 had dared to criticize existing practices in the GDR and to suggest alternatives. In a book entitled *The Alternative in Eastern Europe*, published by a company owned by West German trade unions, Bahro had accused the ruling elite in the Politburo of having disrupted traditional horizontal lines of communication and having reduced the GDR to a "subaltern" status with regard to both the Soviet Union and West Europe. Society, Bahro warned, was about to crack under the SED's policy of domination and submission. Individual initiative had been subsumed into collective monotony. Bahro demanded the creation of a new "League of Communists" to make planning accountable to the people, to humanize education and work, and to unleash the energetic mental capacity ("surplus consciousness") of East German citizens. Change, in the GDR as well

[1] In return, the East German leaders dismantled automatic-firing weapons and mines along the Wall separating the two German states.

as in Eastern Europe, Bahro argued, was inevitable. The Honecker regime responded by arresting Bahro and sentencing him to eight years' incarceration for betraying party and state. The GDR clearly had no place for those who "doubt everything, doubt all authority."

Cultural Challenge and Revival

When eminent non-Nazis such as the dramatist Bertold Brecht, the novelist Arnold Zweig, the poet Johannes R. Becher, the historian Ricarda Huch, and the philosopher Ernst Bloch returned to East Germany after World War II, continuity in literature and the arts seemed ensured. But their individualistic writings, denounced as "formalism," and their failure to put the working class at the center of their labors quickly ran afoul of the Ulbricht regime's demand for "socialist realism" along Soviet lines. Control over culture was thus turned over to the new State Commission for Affairs of Art.

In April 1959, in the wake of the "liberal" Hungarian revolution three years earlier, the East German denizens of culture called a meeting at Bitterfeld, near Halle, to establish new guidelines that would bind artists and intellectuals to the state. Industrial workers, untainted by the "bourgeois" writings of James Joyce or Franz Kafka, were encouraged to take up the pen and to lay the foundation of a socialist culture in the German Democratic Republic. Concurrently, established writers were sent into factories to discover the reality of work and to gain artistic impulses for "socialist realism." Although many writers privately deplored this approach, in April 1964 Ulbricht convened a second conference at Bitterfeld and personally demanded the creation of socialist and popular culture.

East German writers responded by turning to examinations of Germany's past and the role of the individual under totalitarianism. The regime initially tolerated their efforts. In 1958 Bruno Apitz in *Naked Among Wolves* recounted his experiences at Buchenwald concentration camp, and Christa Wolf in *Divided Heaven* that same year explored the attitudes, pro and con, of a young woman (Rita) toward life in the former German capital before the Wall. Torn between joining her fiancé in West Berlin and life in East Berlin, Rita returns to the GDR — only to attempt suicide in a railway yard. In a hospital, she recalls her reasons for returning. GDR censors viewed the novel favorably, and Wolf was considered briefly for a position on the SED's Central Committee.

In 1968, however, Wolf's autobiographical *Thoughts About Christa T.* aroused the regime's ire because it championed the rights and privileges of the individual in a lifeless society directed by party *Bonzen.* Erich Honecker, then the Politburo member entrusted with overseeing the armed forces and the security service, denounced the novel as too pessimistic. Stefan Heym's *Day X*, a work about the June 1953 workers' revolts, had to be published in West

Germany because of its "obvious errors." The most popular novel of the 1960s was Erwin Strittmatter's *Old Beehead*, the story of a wily peasant who founds his own tiny agricultural cooperative, only to see it demolished by party bureaucrats who demand that it merge with a larger agricultural commune.

Regime and writers collided head-on in November 1976 when Honecker, now head of both party and state, forced Wolf Biermann, whose critical songs and satirical verses had infuriated him, to emigrate to West Germany. The regime could not tolerate the iconoclastic Biermann. Vital and irreverent, disrespectful and impatient with elders still caught up in the ideology of the 1930s, Biermann alienated what he called the "office elephants" of the SED with his antiestablishment ballads (paralleling those of Joan Baez in the United States). Biermann's expulsion was protested by a hundred prominent East German artists, thirty of whom were immediately excluded from the country's writer's union as "asocials." Christa Wolf and Stefan Heym were blacklisted for their critical verses. In 1979 Honecker restricted the ability of East German writers to publish in the West by laying claim to their royalty payments and threatening them with incarceration if they ignored his injunction.

East German bureaucrats faced an unusual situation: they were constantly confronted with their larger, more prosperous, and more democratic neighbor. Honecker and his minions interpreted every challenge to official SED ideology as a threat to their state's stability. Conversely, East German writers fully appreciated the yearning of the general public for their writings. The poet Günter Kunert, who followed Biermann to West Germany in 1979, perhaps put it most succinctly when he noted that the East German reader "seeks for something in literature that he cannot find elsewhere . . . for reference to what has imprecisely been called the sense of existence."

In the Western Allied occupation zones, writers had lamented this lack of a "sense of existence" as early as 1945. They referred to the end of World War II as "point zero" (*Nullpunkt*), or total cultural emptiness.[1] They deplored the seemingly insatiable cravings of German youth for American jeans and hamburgers, the rock 'n' roll of Elvis Presley, and the movies of James Dean. Material prosperity became the cherished goal for the young. "Don't Fence Me In" was the ballad of a generation seeking space. The "American dream" lay just over the horizon. Many German writers feared the development of a "skeptical generation," one that saw little utility in and felt little enthusiasm for the literary and political process.

Such pessimism was hardly warranted. West German youth revealed its political acumen in the late 1960s, and German writers in September 1947 established the vibrant Group 47, named after its founding year, that burst on the literary scene in grand fashion in the 1950s. Their avowed goal was indi-

[1] The writers' notion of a cultural "point zero" was adapted by later historians who spoke of 1945 as constituting "hour zero."

vidual reckoning with the recent tormented past, and their efforts climaxed with the publication of three important novels in 1959.

Heinrich Böll, a liberal Catholic on the political Left, led the assault on what he termed the corrupting influences of church, state, power, the modern media, and society in general. *Billiards at Half Past Nine* launched Böll on a career that would be capped by the Nobel Prize in literature in 1972. The novel's plot line, paralleling that of Thomas Mann's 1901 classic *Buddenbrooks*, for which Mann had received the Nobel Prize, traces the family history of the Fähmels, noted Cologne architects, through the course of a single day (September 6, 1958). Robert Fähmel plays billiards with the bellboy Hugo at the Hotel Prinz Heinrich and ruminates about his past. Through Robert, Böll, who served six years with German forces in France and the Soviet Union, assaults the false heroics of German life and rediscovers a world of the wounded, poor, and suffering. The "lambs" in Robert's past have either been killed by those in power or died in the bombed city. Those who have "partaken of the hosts of the beasts," including the monks of St. Anthony who endorsed the Nazis, continue to thrive and wield power without remorse or contrition. Many are high officials in the Bonn government. Through the Fähmels, Böll managed to link the tragedy of German history from William II through Weimar to Hitler and finally to Adenauer. Böll did not want his countrymen, in the early throes of the "economic miracle," to forgot their past.

Günter Grass' *The Tin Drum* was the second blockbuster novel of 1959. The Danzig-born sculptor, painter, poet, and playwright, whose expertise stretched from jazz to fish cookery, had grown up a member of the Hitler Youth, had been wounded in action during the war, and later became a personal friend of the SPD leader Willy Brandt.

The central character in Grass' novel is the hunchback Oskar. Haunted by memories and anxieties from the past, Oskar, with the aid of a child's drum, recounts his political past in a West German mental institution. While searching for his lost drums, Oskar witnesses the destruction of the Danzig synagogue during Crystal Night on November 9, 1938, and finds his Jewish friend Markus, who had provided drums to Oskar at reduced prices, murdered in his shop by SA storm troopers. After defending the Polish post office at Danzig on September 1, 1939, Oskar joins a troupe of acrobats entertaining German forces in Normandy, only to be disturbed by the sudden arrival of Canadian troops on D-Day, June 6, 1944. Thus, Grass comes to grips with Nazism and the lost war. Oskar's lament about the "mere economic miracle" of Ludwig Erhard in the 1950s stands in stark contrast to his positive evaluation of Hitler's Reich. Oskar's refusal to grow symbolizes what Grass saw as the stunted development of Germany. In the end, Grass' work reflected the uneasy feeling of a generation unwilling to face the failed and inhuman ideology of the recent past.

Uwe Johnson's *Speculations About Jacob*, the third major work of 1959, tackled the issue of postwar division, the cold war, and the individual under totalitarian rule. Educated in Nazi-occupied Poland and later at Leipzig and

"Point Zero" surpassed: Günter Grass of the "Group 47" in 1961.

Rostock universities, Johnson was deeply troubled by the East Berlin revolt in 1953 and the Hungarian uprising of 1956; he had emigrated to West Germany before the Wall was built in 1961 in order to publish his works. Jacob Abs, a railroad dispatcher, is the central character in *Speculations*. East German state security (Stasi) wants to recruit Jacob's girlfriend Gesine, who works in the West for NATO. Jacob's loyalties are torn. Out of a sense of duty and joy in his technical expertise, Jacob helps dispatch Soviet troops to Hungary to crush the 1956 uprising. Revolted by his own actions, Jacob flees to West Berlin, only to be alienated by its crass materialism and unrepentant Nazis. He returns to East Berlin and is run over by a locomotive. Was it suicide? The reader is left to ponder the question. Johnson's message, especially for West Germans, was that underneath the iron-fisted rule of the SED, perhaps a more compassionate, humane way of life was possible.

Postwar German literature sought to depict the historical, national, and social experience of the past, as well as to explore the conflict between individual freedoms and totalitarian suppression. It mirrored the uneasiness of the 1950s — a time of economic experimentation, national transition, and political uncertainty.

German theater, especially operatic theater, also underwent a period of introspection and change. The Wagner festivals at Bayreuth under the Third Reich had been heavily infected with Nazi ideology. Adolf Hitler had extended his special patronage to the Wagner family and the Bayreuth pageants, with the result that Richard Wagner's Nordic theosophies deteriorated into *völkisch* rituals celebrating Germanic blood and soil. In the early 1950s the Wagner clan at Bayreuth experimented with abstract forms of theater: the *Nibelungen* characters appeared on stage in business suits or plastic jump suits as often as they did in traditional armor and breastplates. Symbolically, this change helped integrate cultural and political history: the smart business suit represented pluralistic and affluent West German society every bit as much as *Nibelungen* armor plates under Hitler had depicted an ancient and heroic *völkisch* past.

German film in the 1970s and 1980s further tackled the problems of Germany's Nazi past and reconstruction. Rainer Werner Fassbinder's 1979 premier of *The Marriage of Maria Braun* appealed to a young generation that had been taught about the deeds of their parents, the "Auschwitz generation," who had bequeathed them the Third Reich as an unwanted legacy. The parents' collective denial of the past and satisfaction with the economic miracle of Adenauer and Erhard exploded on the screen.

Fassbinder's main character, Maria, married a soldier, Hermann Braun, at the end of World War II. Presumed missing in action, Hermann returns from the war and surprises Maria, who is in bed with a black American occupation soldier. In the ensuing fight, Maria kills her lover, but Hermann takes the blame for the murder. Maria promises her husband a "real life" when he is released from prison. In the meantime, she pursues economic success single-mindedly through the textile factory owner Oswald. Her dream of the great eternal love ends when she discovers that Hermann had "sold" her to Oswald. The film ends with Maria and Hermann blown up in their villa through a gas explosion.

Fassbinder suggests that Maria's fate mirrored that of the nation. Both were conquered and reconstructed. Both were materially well off but in the process had lost their souls. Practical survival through accommodation takes precedence over human traits such as memory and mourning. Just as Maria looks for her missing husband by listening to a monotonous voice over the radio calling out the names and identification numbers of missing soldiers, the nation looks for its scattered subjects. The theme of nationalism is chillingly addressed when the camera surveys a landscape of destroyed houses: the strains of the German national anthem can be heard; they stop, then start again, and finally break off, suggesting the half-devastated, crippled German nation.

The film's treatment of German rearmament is devastating. As Chancellor Adenauer assures a nation over the radio, "I do not want an army, we've had enough deaths," Maria's family eats, comments on the quality of the potato salad, and exchanges recipes. Food is more important than politics; the nation under reconstruction shows a deficient political awareness. But near the end of the film, Adenauer proudly trumpets: "We have the right to rearm — as much as we can, as much as we want." At a restaurant, Maria lurches to her feet, stumbles, and vomits.

The year 1979 brought to German viewers the American television docudrama "Holocaust." Almost 20 million Germans saw at least one episode, and the series evoked a strong reaction. Most Germans, and especially the younger ones, were shocked by the explicit footage of Germans under the Third Reich indiscriminately murdering Jews. Was the Holocaust their national inheritance?

In 1984 Edgar Reitz captivated the nation with a sixteen-hour reply, "Heimat"; at least 25 million Germans saw at least one episode, and 9 million viewed the entire saga. The German term *Heimat* (homeland) denotes the site of one's lost childhood, family, and identity, all that is not distant and foreign, an ideal that evokes romantic harmony between the rural dweller and nature. Reitz offered his fellow countrymen a nostalgic image of radical regionalism replete with peasant characters and dialect, "everyday history" (*Alltagsgeschichte*) centered on everyday functions such as eating and drinking, working and worrying, celebrating and crying, falling in love and marrying, raising children and dying. The film thus conjured up past associations of the Nazi's vision of "blood and soil" and offered future nightmares of European integration and cultural homogenization.

"Heimat" is set in the mythical southern Rhineland village of Schabbach (in reality, Hunsrück) and revolves around the figure of Maria (born in 1900), who marries Paul Simon when she is nineteen, spends her entire life in the village, and dies there at age eighty-two, lonely and worn out. Reitz offered Germans images of the hominess of a secure childhood in the country; the power of village life to establish deep bonds; the appeal of strenuous but unalienated manual labor; the charm of local eccentrics; but also the smug narrow-mindedness of simple provincials and their hostility to all that is not "local" (*heimisch*). In the end, Reitz reveals the destruction of *Heimat* as the result of the gnawing tension between staying and leaving, the longing for distant places and homesickness, and the search for material wealth and the simple richness of home. The values of *Heimat*, according to Reitz, have been destroyed and turned into memories by World War II and reconstruction. The film had a profound impact on the German populace of the 1970s, which had turned its energies away from Vietnam, Cuba, and China and toward new dangers at home: pollution of the land, water, and air, nuclear power plants, and NATO missiles.

The Search for Stability: The FRG, 1961–1989

Like Ulbricht in East Berlin, Konrad Adenauer at Bonn also faced discontent in the early 1960s. *Der Alte* ("the ancient one") was in his mid-eighties, and many Germans felt that the time had come for him to step down in favor of a younger, more dynamic leader. In October 1962 a scandal involving freedom of the press rocked Adenauer's government. The Hamburg journal *Der Spiegel* published leaked government documents showing that some units of the *Bundeswehr* were not combat ready. Defense Minister Franz Josef Strauss, with Adenauer's approval, arrested several editors of *Der Spiegel* and ordered police searches of the magazine's Bonn and Hamburg offices. Strauss was forced to resign as a result of a nationwide outcry against such heavy-handed measures. Adenauer retired as chancellor on October 15, 1963.

For fourteen years West Germany had known only one chancellor. With iron will and single-minded determination, Adenauer had forged the Federal Republic literally out of the smoldering ashes of war. His greatest and boldest political accomplishment was accepting German partition as the price for integrating the Federal Republic into the Atlantic and West European communities. *Der Alte* broke with the traditional East-West seesaw politics of the German Foreign Office and argued that reunification could come about only over time and as a result of Western strength. History proved him right.

Ludwig Erhard, Adenauer's successor, sought to base his government on harmony of interests and integrity. Unlike the authoritarian Adenauer, Erhard hoped to establish direct contact with the West German people and to become a "people's chancellor" (*Volkskanzler*). In international relations, he gave his foreign minister, Gerhard Schröder, freedom to begin exploring an opening with the East. Through a policy of small steps, the Erhard government in 1963–1964 concluded trade agreements with Poland, Rumania, Hungary, and Bulgaria.

Erhard, however, had succeeded Adenauer in troubled times. In 1966 the extreme right-wing National Democratic party (NDP) of Adolf von Thadden gained 8 percent of the vote in Hesse and Bavaria. Two years later it scored another triumph, with 10 percent of the ballots cast in Baden-Württemberg. The NDP would slide into political oblivion by 1983 with only 0.2 percent of the national vote, but its gains in the 1960s nevertheless concerned and embarrassed Erhard. Additionally, the German economy slipped into recession in 1966: unemployment rose, productivity declined, and high expectations of continued material prosperity could not be met.

In fact, the German economy was making a transition from production to services industries. Coal yielded to oil. Steel declined. Ruhr and Saar became examples of "rust belt" decay. Electronics and high technology dominated the market. For most Germans, these changes brought uncertainty and fear. Many believed that the nation was descending into another crisis like the depression of 1929. Erhard could not allay these fears, and on December 1, 1966, the

The "people's chancellor": Ludwig Erhard in retirement (1973).

father of the West German "economic miracle" yielded to the "Great Coalition" of CDU/CSU and SPD headed by Chancellor Kurt-Georg Kiesinger (CDU) and Vice-Chancellor Willy Brandt (SPD). It was a watershed in German politics as the two major parties after years of bitter debate joined forces to guide the Federal Republic toward better times.

Led by Karl Schiller, the new minister of economics, the Great Coalition introduced sweeping economic reforms. The *Bundesbank* conducted a rigorous inflation-fighting strategy and encouraged labor and management to adopt a more cooperative approach in wage and price negotiations. The Great Coalition rebuilt the national railroad system to accommodate high-speed electric trains and to stimulate domestic industry. As a result of these measures, Schiller first stabilized and then strengthened the mark, increased exports sharply, and brought inflation under control. New job training programs gradu-

COMPOSITION OF THE WEST GERMAN LABOR FORCE
(percentage)

Sector	1950	1960	1970	1980	1985
Farming, forestry and fishing	24.7	13.6	8.5	5.5	5.4
Manufacturing	42.6	47.7	48.8	44.1	41.0
Services	18.4	21.2	25.2	31.9	35.3
Trade, transport	14.3	17.5	17.5	18.5	18.3

ated highly productive workers. Economic recovery was so swift that the Federal Republic by the end of the 1960s experienced a severe shortage of labor, which it resolved by recruiting 3.4 million "guest workers" from Spain, Portugal, Italy, Yugoslavia, and Greece.[1] Kiesinger and Brandt augmented these domestic measures by further opening up relations with East Europe: in 1967 the Federal Republic established formal diplomatic relations with Rumania and Yugoslavia.

Unfortunately for the Great Coalition, the 1960s saw international turmoil. U.S. involvement in the Vietnam War evoked massive student protests, in both the United States and Europe. French students demonstrated against government cuts in education, and a new German generation, just reaching political maturity, showed its displeasure with the existing political process by forming an "extraparliamentary opposition" (APO) outside the customary political system. The APO's energies were focused in the summer of 1967 by the state visit of the shah of Iran, widely seen as an oppressive monarch who relied on the secret police to prop up his peacock throne. To protect Shah Reza Pahlavi against expected demonstrations by thousands of Iranian students living in the Federal Republic, Bonn instituted tight security measures.

The shah's visit sparked a series of students revolts, culminating on June 2, 1967, in the police slaying of Benno Ohnesorg of the Free University of Berlin. Taking the anti–Vietnam War protest movement at Berkeley as their model, students across West Germany rose to denounce "police brutality" in Germany and "American imperialism" in Vietnam. They founded the Socialist German Student Union (SDS), as well as the Socialist University Union, to protest materialism and consumerism and what they considered an impersonal technological society. Additionally, they denounced the alleged exploitation of workers, who took little note of them, and called for permanent revolution.

Largely children of affluent, professional families, the student leaders saw themselves as heirs to the *Burschenschaften* of the post-1815 period, as well as

[1] Schiller was also concerned about the declining German birthrate: the number of children born per year dropped from 1.04 million in 1965 to 811,000 in 1970, and to 601,000 by 1975.

the youth protest (*Wandervögel*) under William II. They took their theoretical framework ("the cult of violence") from the Marxist Frankfurt school of Herbert Marcuse and Wilhelm Reich. Their slogan was "Be realistic, demand the impossible!" Supported by East German funds, the APOs organized student riots. When one of their leaders, Rudi Dutschke, was shot at in April 1968, his followers burned the offices and plants of Axel Springer's conservative newspaper empire, as well as a department store in Frankfurt.

Official reaction was swift. In May 1968 the *Bundestag* passed a series of emergency laws that beefed up police powers and accelerated the system of justice under which the protest leaders could be tried. Armed with these new powers, the police forcibly cleared houses occupied by the radical students. Because institutions of higher learning were considered ungovernable, power over universities shifted from politicians to the professional bureaucracy. Above all, law-and-order-minded German citizens were shocked by these displays of student radicalism.

The protest movement had an impact on Germany. Demonstrations and citizens' initiatives thereafter became accepted political practice. Above all, the movement forced the West German establishment to reexamine inherited traditions and practices, to confront the possibility of change, and to come to terms with the demands of a younger generation for greater freedom within the Federal Republic's polity. Educational reforms totally altered the traditional university system. The *Ordinarienuniversität*, where all power had rested with tenured professors (*Ordinarien*), was transformed into the *Gruppenuniversität*, where decisions were made by a "tri-parity" system encompassing tenured professors, the junior faculty (*Assistenten*) and staff, and students. The number of universities grew, and the student body dramatically increased.

A new feminism also emerged in West Germany at the time of the student revolts. In 1968 the Berlin Action Council for the Liberation of Women was formed. Its members vowed to end the "exploitation" of women in society and the family, to demand "wages for housework," to end all gender-determined division of labor, and to take the Marxist class struggle "into marriage." Specifically, the women demanded that one-half of all skilled and professional jobs be reserved for them and that Article 218 of the legal code prohibiting abortions be repealed ("My belly belongs to me"). The Berlin Council declared its intention to form an extraparliamentary action group to pursue its program. In the meantime, women adopted the idea of consciousness-raising groups from the United States as a vehicle for changing attitudes.

The movement scored some major gains. Shelters for battered women arose in Berlin, and today there are more than a hundred in West Germany alone. Feminist magazines such as *Courage* and *Emma* did a brisk business, with circulations in 1981 of 60,000 and 100,000, respectively. The total number of German university students increased from 291,000 in 1960 to 1.3 million by 1984, with women making up nearly 40 percent of the student population (but less than 10 percent of the faculty). And in 1976 public protests by women resulted in a new law granting abortions up to the twelfth week of pregnancy.

The radicalism of the 1960s, however, quickly gave way on German front pages to a bold new diplomatic initiative. In the wake of the September 1969 elections, which had given the CDU/CSU 46.1 percent of the vote, the SPD 42.7 percent, and the FDP 5.8 percent, the SPD abandoned the Great Coalition and formed a "social-liberal" alliance with the FDP. Brandt became the first Social Democratic chancellor since 1930 and Helmut Schmidt the first SPD defense minister since 1920; Walter Scheel of the FDP took the posts of vice-chancellor and foreign minister. For the first time in German history, eighteen-year-olds voted in November 1972, and 80 percent of new voters between eighteen and twenty cast their ballots for the SPD/FDP coalition.

Brandt's appointment was a milestone in history: he saw his chancellorship as the final end of World War II. Brandt's supporters referred to his victory as a second "zero hour," a chance for true democratic reconstruction after twenty years of uninterrupted CDU/CSU rule. They pointed with pride to Brandt's credentials as an anti-Communist, citing his at-times heroic defense of democracy and freedom while mayor of West Berlin in the 1960s. The novelist Heinrich Böll depicted Brandt as the first chancellor to lead the German people "out of the master race tradition." Yet Brandt's detractors drew attention to his illegitimate birth as Herbert Frahm in Lübeck in 1913 — he had changed his name to Willy Brandt in 1933 in order to escape detection and arrest by the Gestapo — and to his "unpatriotic" wartime activity as a Norwegian partisan. Above all, the SPD's elevation to governing party confirmed its abandonment of revolutionary rhetoric at Bad Godesberg in 1958.

In October 1969 the new SPD-FDP coalition government of Brandt and Scheel launched its program of eastern policy (*Ostpolitik*). There had long been debate in leading circles at Bonn concerning the ultimate direction of West German foreign policy. The Atlanticists, CDU men such as Ludwig Erhard and Gerhard Schröder, had argued that German-U.S. relations were crucial to German prosperity and security. The Gaullists, centered on the CSU leader Franz Josef Strauss and the CDU politician Josef-Hermann Dufheus, had countered that Europe's interests were not necessarily always those of the United States. Strauss and Dufheus were attracted by Charles de Gaulle's vision of a new "Europe of fatherlands" and saw the French president as a useful counterforce to the established Soviet-U.S. bipolar world.

Adenauer had initially been willing to court de Gaulle and in January 1963 signed a highly symbolic Franco-German friendship treaty designed to bury centuries of mutual hostility. Furthermore, Adenauer, although thoroughly in favor of European integration, saw profit in de Gaulle's 1963 veto of Britain's application for membership in the Common Market, as this move dynamited what Adenauer called the "Potsdam" constellation of 1945. With France safely detached from the Anglo-U.S.-Soviet camp, there could be no fear of renewed Allied incursions on West German sovereignty. But in the end, the German chancellor accepted that only the United States could guarantee West German interests. De Gaulle's allusion during a state visit to Moscow in the summer of 1966 to a possible Franco-Soviet "condominium" over Europe greatly alarmed Adenauer, who quickly issued renewed pledges of German-U.S. solidarity. There would be no Franco-German "special path" (*Sonderweg*). Even de Gaulle admitted that the United States was preferable to the Soviet Union: "Whiskey is stronger than vodka."

In 1969 Brandt and Scheel offered a third way, that of the "new realists." The security of the NATO alliance, they argued, permitted a policy of détente with the Soviet government of Leonid Brezhnev. Brandt and Scheel called for relaxation of the Hallstein doctrine (see page 376), political and economic stability for West Berlin, access to the former German capital, and more "humane" contacts with the German Democratic Republic. But they also appreciated the existence of widespread opposition among the West German populace to formal recognition of both the GDR and the Oder-Neisse border with Poland. Most important, the Brandt-Scheel government recognized that the road to *Ostpolitik* ran through Moscow.

The first thaw in Soviet-German relations came in the sphere of international trade. In February 1970 the Soviet Union agreed to supply the Federal Republic over a period of twenty years with 52 billion cubic meters of natural gas from Siberia. The West German Mannesmann group contracted to provide the Soviets 1.2 million tons of large-diameter steel pipes, and a consortium of seventeen German banks offered Moscow 1.2 billion marks in credits. The terms of the arrangement were doubled in July 1972.

In July 1970 Scheel and Egon Bahr, the state secretary in Brandt's chancery who since 1963 had quietly advocated a policy of "change through rapprochement," traveled to Moscow and in August reached an agreement whereby West Germany and the Soviet Union renounced the use of force in settling outstanding differences, recognized the Oder-Neisse border between Poland and Germany, and accepted in principle the establishment of formal relations between the two German states. In December Chancellor Brandt signed a treaty with Poland recognizing the Oder-Neisse demarcation line as final. While he was in the Polish capital, Brandt symbolically kneeled at the memorial to the savage German suppression of the Warsaw ghetto uprising in 1943. The writer Günter Grass, a native of Danzig, accepted the permanent loss of his birthplace and lauded Brandt's "courageous" political act. *Time* magazine voted Brandt its Man of the Year for 1970.

Not all West Germans shared this veneration of Brandt. Many feared that he was moving too fast and giving up too much in return for little. The German-Polish pact contained no provisions for financial restitution or even a formal apology for the Polish expulsion of millions of Germans from their ancestral homelands after 1945. And although Warsaw agreed to permit the remaining 300,000 Germans in Poland to be repatriated to West Germany, this process quickly deteriorated into bitter wrangling as the Polish Communist

Mastering the Past: Chancellor Brandt kneels at the memorial to the Warsaw ghetto uprising (December 1970).

leader Edward Gierek extorted cash payments of 2.3 billion marks from Bonn for the relocation of 125,000 Germans. The Vatican continued to insist on the validity of its Concordat with Adolf Hitler in 1933 and did not appoint Polish bishops to the former German dioceses in East Prussia, Silesia, and Pomerania until June 1972. Brandt countered by arguing that because Hitler's Germany had caused Europe's destruction between 1939 and 1945, the onus for restoring Europe rested with the Federal Republic.

The third leg of Brandt's *Ostpolitik* concerned Berlin. Since the construction of the Wall in 1961, East German police had routinely harassed West Germans traveling between the Federal Republic and West Berlin. Visa fees, obligatory daily monetary conversions at par, car searches, and long delays were standard practice at the three border crossings allowed the West. In September 1971 Brandt succeeded in getting Britain, France, the Soviet Union, and the United States to initial a Quadripartite Agreement regulating communications and traffic between the Federal Republic and West Berlin. Intra-German discussions on the status of Berlin concluded that same month with extensive agreements in September and December concerning postal and telephone communications as well as "unimpeded" traffic between the FRG and West Berlin. Throughout the negotiations, Brandt steadfastly refused to recognize the GDR's claim to determine Berlin's status.

The *Bundestag* began debates on the eastern treaties, with Moscow and Warsaw, in February 1972. Opposition came from Franz Josef Strauss, leader of the Bavarian CSU, and Helmut Kohl, deputy chairman of the CDU, in particular. The right wing of the FDP, headed by Erich Mende, who liked to remind fellow deputies that he had been awarded the German army's highest decoration during World War II, threatened to rebel against Scheel and join the CDU/CSU in voting against the treaties. The treaties were headed for an apparent impasse: whereas 82 percent of West Germans polled in 1972 favored *Ostpolitik*, the CDU/CSU opposition had won regional elections in Bavaria, Rhineland-Palatinate, Schleswig-Holstein, and Baden-Württemberg and thus was positioned to block ratification of the treaties in the Federal Chamber (*Bundesrat*).

At this critical juncture, Soviet leader Leonid Brezhnev and his foreign minister, Andrei Gromyko, let it be known that the Soviet Union would refuse to ratify the recent transit agreement ensuring West German access to Berlin unless the two eastern pacts were ratified. This threat notwithstanding, the CDU/CSU on April 27 launched a final assault against *Ostpolitik* by introducing a "constructive vote of no-confidence" against Brandt. The party's candidate, Rainer Barzel, fell two votes short of the required 249 (out of 496) votes needed to pass.[1] The Moscow, Warsaw, and Berlin agreements were ratified by the *Bundestag* on May 17, 1972. CDU and CSU abstained from the final vote. Mende deserted the FDP and joined the CDU.

In the fall of 1972 Brandt moved to consolidate his political position at home and to complete his "eastern policy" in Europe. In September he took the constitutionally spurious step of moving a vote of confidence in the *Bundestag*, with the stated goal of calling an election should it fail. Brandt guaranteed failure of the motion (248 to 233) by having cabinet members absent themselves from the vote; elections were called for November 19.

While the election campaign raged in the Federal Republic over *Ostpolitik*, Brandt negotiated a treaty with the East German leader Erich Honecker. Brandt had met twice with GDR Minister-President Willi Stoph in 1970 but had accomplished little. The meeting at Erfurt (home of the Lutheran Reformation of the sixteenth century and birthplace of the SPD in 1891) was sidetracked by thousands of East Germans chanting Brandt's name; that at the Schlosshotel in Kassel (where Napoleon III had been held captive in 1870–1871 and Adolf Hitler had stayed in the 1930s) had been disrupted by demonstrations against Stoph and the GDR. In 1972 there were no symbolic public meetings between the two German leaders, and they initialed the Basic Treaty eleven days before the West German elections. Honecker guaranteed West Germans unfettered access to West Berlin and conceded that administrative and economic bonds tied the former capital to the Federal Republic. He refused, however, to recognize West Berlin as part of the FRG. Brandt, in turn, agreed that two sovereign German states now existed and that East Berlin was the capital of the GDR.

---

[1] Herbert Wehner, the SPD party chief, later admitted that "people were paid" to preserve the Brandt government.

The elections of November 19, 1972, confirmed the "social-liberal" coalition in office. The SPD gained six seats and the FDP eleven; the CDU/CSU lost seventeen seats. On December 21 Brandt signed the Basic Treaty. A last-ditch attempt by Bavaria in May 1973 to have the treaty declared unconstitutional by the Federal Constitutional Court at Karlsruhe failed, and the Basic Treaty became law that month. In June 1973 both German states were admitted into the United Nations.

Brandt's "eastern policy," in the chancellor's own words, was a "synthesis of practical thoughts and idealistic aspirations." It eased tensions in Central Europe and made West Germany an active partner in global détente. Above all, *Ostpolitik* greatly expanded Bonn's options in the East, without, however, endangering the Federal Republic's Western orientation. In 1971 Brandt received the Nobel Peace Prize for his bold initiative, the first German so honored since the writer Carl von Ossietzky in 1936.[1]

But at home, Brandt ran afoul of economic issues. Although the German growth rate stood at a healthy 7.5 percent in 1969, massive government spending drove inflation up to 5.3 percent by 1972. Alarmed, Economics Minister Schiller demanded budget cuts of 2.5 billion marks in 1972 but encountered severe opposition from his colleague Helmut Schmidt, whose defense budget stood to lose 800 million marks. Moreover, Brandt was reluctant to cut domestic programs for fear of alienating the left wing of his own party. Per capita spending on education skyrocketed between 1965 and 1970 from 264 to 453 marks; social spending, in terms of the gross national product, rose 21 percent in the 1970s.

Unexpected foreign developments also affected the German economy. On October 6, 1973, Egypt and Syria attacked Israel. The Yom Kippur War resulted in the complete defeat of both Arab states, and on October 16, Middle East oil producers reacted with sharp reductions in oil exports to the West. The Federal Republic's key industries, largely fueled by imported Mideast oil, slumped. German oil imports tripled in cost to 32.8 billion marks by 1974 — and doubled again by 1980. The chancellor's popularity at home rapidly deteriorated as Germans were asked to conserve fuel by reducing speed on the national highways and as Bonn doubled the price of gasoline at the pump.

Additionally, international terrorism first reared its ugly head during Brandt's term in office. In September 1972 eight heavily armed Arab terrorists broke into the Israeli athletes' village during the Olympic Games at Munich and demanded the release of two hundred Arab prisoners from Israeli jails. A rescue attempt resulted in a dozen deaths, including those of nine Israeli

[1] Ossietzky could not personally receive the Nobel Peace Prize for 1935 in 1936 because he was incarcerated (since February 1933) in the Papenburg concentration camp by Hitler. Ossietzky died on May 4, 1948, in custody in a public hospital of the tuberculosis he had contracted at Papenburg.

athletes when their rescue helicopter blew up. The incident proved a great embarrassment to Germans and Jews alike.

The final blow to Brandt's prestige was mainly of his own making. As early as May 1973 West German internal security forces had warned the chancellor that his personal adviser, Günter Guillaume, was an East German "mole." Brandt refused to heed the warning and was publicly embarrassed in April 1974 when the arrested Guillaume confessed to being an officer of the East German National People's Army. A humiliated Brandt resigned on May 6, 1974. Scheel was elected to the office of federal president; his post as foreign minister went to Hans-Dietrich Genscher of the FDP.

Helmut Schmidt succeeded Brandt as chancellor. Known as a tough negotiator and a "doer" (*Macher*), Schmidt was a practitioner of the art of the possible. The new chancellor in short order reaped the remaining benefits of Brandt's *Ostpolitik*. On July 10, 1974, after four years of difficult negotiations, Czechoslovakia and the Federal Republic established formal diplomatic relations by jointly declaring the Munich Agreement of 1938 null and void. And in the summer of 1975 Schmidt joined the Conference on European Security and Cooperation at Helsinki and, along with Honecker, signed an agreement safeguarding human rights and furthering European economic cooperation.

Yet, like Brandt, Schmidt faced troubled times domestically. The mid–1970s witnessed the development of urban terrorist bands. From 1974 until 1977 the Red Army Faction (RAF) conducted acts of individual terror designed to destabilize the Federal Republic. Its leaders advocated terrorism as a "necessary" antidote to what they denounced as the "consumer terror" allegedly embedded in West Germany's prosperous society. They also wished to abolish the institution of marriage and to replace the nuclear family with large-scale communes. Robbery, arson, and murder became the main weapons of the RAF, which was headed by a troika of students. Ulrike Meinhof, born in 1934, one year after Adolf Hitler's rise to power, was the daughter of academics at Jena University in East Germany; she studied literature and philosophy at Marburg and Münster and became editor of a radical student newspaper, *konkret*. Andreas Baader, son of a historian killed on the Russian front in World War II, was a high school dropout who went to West Berlin to escape military service. There he met and married Gudrun Ensslin, who introduced him to the SDS movement. Ensslin, daughter of a Lutheran pastor, became the actual leader of the RAF. The murder of Benno Ohnesorg in 1967 launched her terrorist career. "You know what kind of pigs we are up against," she proclaimed to friends, "that is the generation of Auschwitz. . . . They have weapons and we don't. We must arm ourselves."

During its reign of terror, the Red Army Faction murdered thirty people, kidnapped numerous others, and bombed U.S. and German government installations. In January 1972, as a result of the RAF's reign of terror, the Bonn government instituted loyalty oaths for all civil servants as a condition of employment. Baader, Meinhof, and Ensslin were arrested in 1972 for crimes ranging from robbery to murder. Meinhof hanged herself in prison in 1976. An

"Cult of Violence": Wanted poster for leaders of the Red Army Faction.

attempt by some Middle East associates to rescue Baader and Ensslin in October 1977 by hijacking a Lufthansa passenger plane failed when special West German antiterrorist forces rescued both passengers and plane at Mogadishu in Somalia. The wave of terrorism that gripped the nation quickly subsided: Baader shot himself and Ensslin hanged herself while both were in jail. The recent opening of East German Stasi documents will undoubtedly reveal the degree to which the Red Army Faction was subsidized by the Honecker regime.

The Schmidt administration also faced the ire of a growing environmentalist movement. Acid rain, pollution of rivers and lakes, the threat of nuclear accident and waste storage, and the desire of the United States to station nuclear weapons and intermediate-range missiles on German soil resulted in the formation of the Green party in 1978. An amalgam of ecology-minded young people, pacifists, opponents of the arms race, and macrobiotic food devotees, the environmentalist Greens became the collective home of Germans' discontent with the three major parties. Most of its members were young (under thirty-five) and held university degrees; they were doctors, administrators, and social workers. In 1983 the Green party entered the *Bundestag* with 5.6 percent of the national vote; four years later they had increased their vote to 8.3 percent.

The social-liberal coalition unraveled in the early 1980s. The Schmidt-Genscher partnership failed to function smoothly because of personal differences between the two dominant leaders of the SPD and FDP. Schmidt's own party was badly divided over the issue of stationing U.S. missiles on German soil to counter the threat of Soviet intermediate-range SS-20 missiles in East Europe and by the chancellor's promise to increase real defense spending by 3 percent per year. Major economic policy differences developed between the Social Democrats and the Free Democrats, who demanded that rising inflation be brought under control by massive spending cuts. Schmidt, fearing that cuts in social programs would cause a rebellion of the left wing of his own party, demanded on September 17, 1982, that the four FDP ministers in his cabinet resign; otherwise, they would be dismissed. All four promptly complied. On October 1 a "constructive vote of no-confidence" (256 to 235 votes) brought Helmut Kohl, the avuncular former CDU minister-president of the Rhineland-Palatinate, to the chancery. Genscher, whose FDP had deserted its coalition partner and voted with the CDU/CSU, remained in the new "christian-liberal" government as foreign minister.

The Fourth Reich?

The political about-face (*Wende*) of 1982 was confirmed by the elections of 1983, when the CDU/CSU increased its share of the vote to 48.8 percent, although the FDP fell to 7.0 percent, partly because voters disapproved of its facile switch of political partners.[1] The SPD's share of the popular vote plummeted to 38.2 percent as many of its younger voters turned instead to the Green party. Additionally, Helmut Schmidt's caustic treatment of the party's left wing (confirming his nickname "Schmidt the Lip") over their opposition to

[1] Kohl, like Brandt in 1972, used the questionable tactic of calling a motion of confidence and defeating his own government in order to force an election.

the stationing of U.S. nuclear-tipped missiles on German soil had reduced the SPD to bitter internecine squabbles. It has yet to recover its erstwhile poise and voter appeal of the Brandt years.

Helmuth Kohl remained firmly committed to two ideals. As head of the CDU government in the Rhineland-Palatinate, he had championed states' rights in the face of Brandt's centnalization of power at Bonn. Second, he fully shared Adenauer's policy of tying West Germany to the Common Market and NATO. In his inaugural address on June 23, 1983, Kohl announced that relations with the East would be tougher, more realistic, and less charitable. He refused to "accept the division of our Fatherland" and demanded relations with the GDR on the basis of "self-determination." Despite the two German states, the new chancellor proclaimed, "there is only one German nation." Finally, Kohl suggested that a unified Germany join an integrated Europe. "We need European unification, just as the peoples of Europe need the elimination of the division of Germany."

But foreign policy had long been Kohl's weak suit. Although he had been an early critic of Brandt's *Ostpolitik*, his foreign minister, Genscher, a refugee from Halle in East Germany and a survivor from the Brandt-Scheel coalition, pursued *Ostpolitik* vigorously after 1982. And whereas Kohl initially distrusted the reform zeal of Mikhail Gorbachev in the Soviet Union, comparing the Soviet leader to Nazi propaganda chief Joseph Goebbels, Genscher eventually asked his partners in London, Paris, and Washington to take Gorbachev and his reforms seriously.

Kohl's first leadership challenge came in 1983 during the so-called great missile debate. The United States sought to counter the Soviet SS-20 danger to Europe by asking the Federal Republic to permit Washington to station Pershing II and cruise missiles on German soil. Kohl agreed and in the fall of that year asked parliament to grant him the necessary authority. This measure evoked a storm of protest, and in October nearly 400,000 people, most of them young, demonstrated against the missiles at Bonn for nearly a week. Noted writers such as Günter Grass and Heinrich Böll joined the crowds — and the SPD — to denounce the American move. But Kohl had the necessary votes in the *Bundestag*, and the missile bill passed in November 1983. The Federal Constitutional Court upheld the vote in December 1984.

A second crisis centered on the Kohl government's attempt to forge a new national identity. Throughout the 1970s, the teaching of history in German schools had been relegated to the periphery of curricula. The historian Hellmut Diwald, echoing the earlier lament of Johann Wolfgang von Goethe in the 1790s, asked: "Germany — what is it?" Michael Stürmer, professor of history at Erlangen University and occasional speech writer for Chancellor Kohl, demanded nothing less than an official history that stressed the positive aspects of Germany's past. Lavish historical exhibitions detailing the medieval Hohenstaufen empire (1150–1250) at Stuttgart in 1977 and the Prussian legacy at Berlin in 1981 reinforced this search for historical identity. But the popular showing of the American television series "Holocaust" in 1979 identified a darker national past.

The 1980s brought a wave of Nazi revivalism. In 1983 the tabloid *Der Stern* caused a national sensation by publishing the (albeit forged) "diaries" of Adolf Hitler. The death of Dr. Josef Mengele, who had brutally determined the fate of hundreds of thousands of Jews at Auschwitz, evoked a flood of apologias by Germans who denied Nazi crimes and who sought to depict the German people as "victims" of Nazism. And the death at Spandau of the last Nazi war criminal, Hitler's deputy "Führer" Rudolf Hess, even prompted accusations from West German right wing circles that Hess had been the victim of Allied political murder.

A series of highly symbolic acts catapulted West German anguish over its Nazi legacy onto the international stage. In January 1984 Chancellor Kohl visited Israel and observed that as the first chancellor of the postwar generation, he enjoyed "the grace of late birth" (1930) and thus had been too young for involvement in any of the crimes committed by Germans under the Third Reich. The speech was almost universally interpreted as an attempt by Kohl to escape responsibility for German actions between 1933 and 1945.

No sooner had the brouhaha over the Israel visit died down than Kohl sought to repeat his symbolic act of shaking hands with French president François Mitterand at the 1916 battlefield of Verdun. That same year, the chancellor decided to mark the fortieth anniversary of the end of World War II in 1985 by shaking hands with the American president Ronald Reagan at the military cemetery in Bitburg, site of nearly fifty graves of *Waffen-SS* soldiers. Kohl had been deeply offended by his exclusion from Allied celebrations in Normandy commemorating the fortieth anniversary of the D-Day landings of June 6, 1984, and he determined in 1985 to cement German-U.S. friendship with a public display of postwar reconciliation. Instead, the Bitburg visit produced another round of charges that Kohl remained insensitive to Germany's Nazi past.

President Richard von Weizsäcker undertook damage control. The German federal president, elected in 1984, had served with the illustrious Potsdam Ninth Infantry Regiment, which had lost a high number of officers opposing Hitler, during the war. He had been forced to come to grips with Germany's dark past while defending his father, Ernst von Weizsäcker, state secretary in the German Foreign Office from 1938 to 1943, before the International Military Tribunal at Nuremberg in 1945–1946. On May 8, 1985, the fortieth anniversary of the German surrender in Europe, Weizsäcker used the power of his office to remind his countrymen of "the inhumanity and tyranny of the National Socialist regime." That road to terror, the president tartly stated, had started on January 30, 1933. Weizsäcker spoke openly of the Holocaust and pointedly noted that "too many of us claimed that they had not known anything about it." Finally, Weizsäcker asserted that "there is no such thing as the guilt or innocence of an entire nation"; "guilt, like innocence, is not collective but personal." The president's office was flooded with 1.5 million requests for the speech.

But a new storm was just over the horizon. That same month, the noted Cologne historian Andreas Hillgruber published a slender volume entitled *Two Kinds of Demise*, in which he equated the Holocaust with the defeat of the German *Wehrmacht* by the Red Army in 1944–1945. The disappearance of Germany from the East and the Holocaust, Hillgruber suggested, had weakened Western civilization by destroying its vital Central European component—both German and Jewish. On June 6, 1986, the forty-second anniversary of D-Day, Ernst Nolte published a sensational article in the *Frankfurter Allgemeine Zeitung* entitled "A Past That Will Not Go Away," in which the Berlin political theorist argued that the Holocaust was neither unique nor a German national crime. Instead, Nolte suggested, the Holocaust was comparable to other national atrocities, most notably the Turks' massacre of Armenians in 1915 and Joseph Stalin's massacre of independent landowners (*kulaks*) and Ukrainians between 1929 and 1933. The twisted road to Auschwitz, Nolte mused, ran through Stalin's "Gulag Archipelago."

This academic initiative erupted with dramatic effect into the so-called historians' quarrel (*Historikerstreit*) of 1985–1988. A number of historians such as Klaus Hildebrand, Hagen Schulze, and Michael Stürmer joined Hillgruber and Nolte in questioning whether all Germans could be held responsible for Nazi crimes, whether Nazi atrocities were unique, and whether these lamentable excesses were but part of a greater "banality of evil." On the other side of the debate, the philosopher Jürgen Habermas, ably assisted by historians such as Hans and Wolfgang Mommsen and Hans-Ulrich Wehler, charged that Hillgruber and Nolte, in particular, sought to "trivialize" the "final solution" as part of a broader new German nationalism. Habermas argued that these conservative scholars were conducting a "strategy of moral relativization" designed not only to deny guilt for the Holocaust but eventually to deny the Holocaust itself. Habermas queried whether Hillgruber, Nolte, and Stürmer were engaged in inventing a usable past for what they deemed to be the "ahistorical" German generation of the 1980s. Rudolf Augstein, editor of *Der Spiegel*, maliciously charged that the revisionist historians were "constitutional Nazis."

As the *Historikerstreit* raged, Philipp Jenninger, the CDU president of the *Bundestag*, marked the fiftieth anniversary of the Crystal Night of November 1938 with a formal speech that seemed to many to promote understanding of and justification for this act of savage repression of Jews. Jenninger was forced to resign as yet another storm of international and domestic protest rocked the Kohl government.

President von Weizsäcker once more sought to calm troubled waters. In October 1988 he addressed the annual meeting of German historians and unequivocably reminded the nation's scholars: "Auschwitz remains unique. It was perpetrated by Germans in the name of Germany. This truth is immutable and will not be forgotten." Few newspapers failed to note that the Holocaust and the German division were intimately related because the nation's division (and hence the legitimacy of the GDR) was the direct consequence of the war started by Nazi Germany in 1939.

As President von Weizsäcker struggled valiantly to remind his countrymen of their historical burden, the Nazi past finally entered public debate in Austria. In 1985 the prominent Kiel historian Karl Dietrich Erdmann stimulated Austro-German debate on the "German question" by calling for a new concept of German comparative history embracing three states (Austria, the Federal Republic, and the German Democratic Republic), two nations (Austria and the German states), and one *Volk* (German). Erdmann's Austrian colleagues, who in the mid–1980s tried to revive Habsburg nostalgia in order to conceptualize it as essentially non-German, countered by denouncing the Kiel historian's initiative as an attempted "historiographical *Anschluss*." They redoubled their efforts to create a distinct non-German Austrian history.

But the debate could not be restricted to academic circles. In June 1985 the right-wing Austrian Progressive party (FPÖ) of Jörg Haider at Salzburg under the slogan "Rejuvenate Austria Politically" propagated the notion of a common cultural Germany encompassing Austria, the FRG, the GDR, and Switzerland. The FPÖ's 414-point program was liberally laced with references to "*Volk* and family," "*Volkstum* and *Heimat*," and "German *Volks- und Kulturraum*" (national and cultural sphere), all reminiscent of Nazi verbiage. Haider demanded that the German language be placed on a par with English and French in European councils and denounced Austrian nationhood as an "ideological monstrosity." While supporting such general concepts as the family, clean air, pure water, less urban noise, and more law and order, Haider also demanded an end to further immigration into Austria and expulsion of the suspected 100,000 illegal foreign workers in Vienna alone. FPÖ supporters are mainly in their twenties, with skilled workers and young academics constituting a majority of members.

In the November 1986 national elections, the FPÖ gained nearly 10 percent of the vote and helped elect Kurt Waldheim, a former officer in the German *Wehrmacht* during World War II, as federal president. Waldheim's election sparked international protest and boycott of the Austrian president largely because Waldheim, the former United Nations secretary general, had lied (and continued to lie) about his Nazi past. In March 1989 the FPÖ scored major gains in regional elections in Tyrol, Salzburg, and Carinthia, where Haider formed a coalition government.

Apart from the international reaction to the search for a new historical identity, the Kohl administration suffered from the same malaise that gripped Republican administrations in the United States in the 1980s: political corruption and scandals. In Bonn these problems centered on the Ministry of Defense. In 1988 the Ministry of Defense was caught permitting a Kiel shipyard to deliver building plans for U-boats to South Africa, despite legal injunctions against the sale at home and a United Nations embargo against Pretoria. During investigation of this case, it was discovered that the ministry had actually sold submarines to Argentina and India under Chancellor Schmidt. At the end of 1989 news broke that West German chemical concerns had sold plants to Libya that could easily be converted to produce military gas.

Late in 1990 and early in 1991 Kohl received evidence that the Federal Republic had sold weapons and munitions to Iraq and that private German firms had constructed Saddam Hussein's personal bunkers. Additional news that parts of Hussein's poison gas arsenal stemmed from Germany proved extremely embarrassing to Bonn, as the Iraqi dictator had targeted these weapons primarily against Israel. Further investigation revealed that some of the material was delivered by firms that still refused to pay compensation to the millions of slave laborers they had deported to eastern plants during the Third Reich. Finally, in March 1992 Defense Minister Gerhard Stoltenberg resigned when news broke that he had dispatched nineteen Leopard I tanks to Turkey, despite a specific *Bundestag* prohibition of November 1991 against the delivery.

The scandals were not restricted to the defense establishment. In 1984 President Rainer Barzel of the FRG had resigned in the wake of revelations that he had accepted generous sums of money from the Flick industrial group of companies, which had financed the Nazis at the end of the Weimar Republic, for personal services. One year later German courts found Otto Count Lambsdorff of the coalition partner FDP guilty of having wrongfully diverted Flick money to FDP party funds.[1] And in 1987 CDU Minister-President Uwe Barschel of Schleswig-Holstein laid down his office when evidence surfaced that he had spied on and tried to slander his SPD opponent, Björn Engholm. Barschel later committed suicide in Geneva. Young voters in particular decried the wave of political scandals.

Kohl paid the price for these scandals in the federal elections of January 1987. In the worst electoral defeat for the CDU/CSU since 1949, Kohl's party lost 2 million votes, mainly to the FDP (800,000) and the SPD (400,000); 800,000 voters opted not to vote at all. Yet for some West Germans the CDU had strayed from its conservative roots. In 1988 Franz Schönhuber, a Bavarian television personality, founded the Republicans as a new right-wing political party. The following year Schönhuber's party surprised many analysts by winning 7.5 percent of the vote in West Berlin communal elections, largely on the platform of opposition to the numerous Turks and other foreign laborers living in the city. Even more alarming, Schönhuber won just over 10 percent of the

[1] The SPD also had used illegal transfers from its Friedrich-Ebert-Foundation to fund political tricks. Even Werner Nachmann of the Central Council of Jews in Germany had embezzled 33 million marks of West German "restitution" money during the 1980s.

vote in West Germany's most prosperous state, Baden Württemberg. Was the Republicans' victory a harbinger?

In truth, the Germany of the late 1980s had changed radically from that of the Adenauer years. Nearly two of every three Germans were born after 1945. Germans had become world travelers. Men's hair was short or long, bleached or colored. Gays and lesbians paraded openly and organized politically. Cohabitation was accepted. About 3 million foreign workers, mainly from Spain, Italy, Yugoslavia, and Turkey, still resided in Germany, despite attempts to repatriate them to their homelands by way of cash payments. Above all, the German economy continued its success story. In 1988 exports amounted to 323 billion DM, compared to U.S. exports of 322 billion DM and Japanese exports of 265 billion DM. This fact is especially astounding given that the U.S. population was four times and the Japanese twice that of the Federal Republic. In fact, in the late 1980s, the Federal Republic and the German Democratic Republic combined boasted Europe's highest exports ($353 million) and the world's fourth highest gross domestic product ($1 billion).

The brightest spot in the Kohl administration remained Hans-Dietrich Genscher, Bonn's foreign minister who emerged from the elections of 1987 convinced that historic changes in Germany's relations with the Soviet Union were achievable. In February 1987 Genscher bluntly admonished Kohl: "Help Gorbachev!" In a major policy announcement on February 6, Genscher spoke of the possibility of a major turning point in East-West relations and argued that it would be "a mistake of historic dimensions for the West to let this chance slip just because it cannot escape from a way of thinking which invariably expects the worst from the Soviet Union." The only question was whether Helmut Kohl would be able to master a major international crisis.

INCOME DISTRIBUTION IN THE FEDERAL REPUBLIC

Year	National Income (billion DM)	National Income per Capita (DM)
1950	76.9	1,640
1955	141.0	2,865
1960	222.3	4,259
1965	358.5	6,115
1970	530.4	8,745
1975	803.6	12,997
1980	1,148.6	18,656
1985	1,420.0	23,270

Suggested Readings

Comparative histories of East and West Germany are few and far between given the fact that Western scholars were never allowed to use SED archives. There are, however, two general surveys: Lawrence L. Whetten, *Germany East and West* (New York, 1980), and Henry A. Turner, Jr., *The Two Germanies Since 1945* (New Haven, Conn., 1987).

The most recent reexaminations of the GDR are by David Childs, *The GDR: Moscow's German Ally* (London, 1983); Martin McCauley, *The German Democratic Republic Since 1945* (London, 1983); and A. James McAdams, *East Germany and Détente: Building Authority After the Wall* (Cambridge, 1985). Erich Honecker, *From My Life* (Oxford and Toronto, 1981), tells the "success story" of the GDR from the perspective of its top leader. More general and balanced is David Childs, ed., *Honecker's Germany* (London, 1985). The Socialist Unity party has been studied by Jonathan Steele, *Socialism with a German Face: The State That Came in from the Cold* (London, 1977); Peter C. Ludz, *The Changing Party Elite in East Germany* (Cambridge, Mass., 1973); and Martin McCauley, *Marxism-Leninism in the German Democratic Republic: The Socialist Unity Party (SED)* (London, 1979). Historical writing in the GDR has found a student in Georg G. Iggers, ed., *Social History of the GDR: New Orientations in Recent East European Historiography* (New York, 1989).

An exhaustive treatment of West Germany since 1945 has been provided by Dennis L. Bark and David R. Gress, *A History of West Germany*, 2 vols. (Oxford, 1989). A recent single-volume examination is Michael Balfour, *West Germany* (London, 1982). The West German political system has been studied by Kendall Baker, Russell J. Dalton, and Kai Hildebrandt, *Germany Transformed: Political Culture and the New Politics* (Cambridge, Mass., 1981); Klaus von Beyme, *The Political System of the Federal Republic of Germany* (New York, 1982); Klaus von Beyme and Manfred G. Schmidt, eds., *Policy and Politics in the Federal Republic of Germany* (Aldershot, 1985); David Childs and Jeffrey Johnson, *West Germany: Politics and Society* (New York, 1981); Russell J. Dalton, *Politics in West Germany* (Boston, 1989); Peter J. Katzenstein, *Policy and Politics in West Germany* (Philadelphia, 1987); and H. G. Peter Wallach and George K. Romoser, eds., *West German Politics in the Mid-Eighties: Crisis and Continuity* (New York, 1985). Developments in Austria after 1945 have been analyzed by William T. Bluhm, *Building an Austrian Nation: The Political Integration of a Western State* (New Haven, Conn., 1973).

Two interpretations of Willy Brandt's *Ostpolitik* are by William E. Griffth, *The Ostpolitik of the Federal Republic of Germany* (Cambridge, Mass., 1978), and David M. Keithly, *Breakthrough in the Ostpolitik: The 1971 Quadripartite Agreement* (Godstone, 1986). See also Willy Brandt, *People and Politics: The Years, 1960–1975* (Boston, 1978). For Brandt's successor, see Jonathan Carr, *Helmut Schmidt: Helmsman of Germany* (London, 1985), and Wolfram F. Hanrieder, ed., *Helmut Schmidt: Perspectives in Politics* (Boulder, Colo.,

1982). Specialized studies of West Germany's role within the Western alliance include David Gress, *Peace and Survival: West Germany, the Peace Movement, and European Security* (Stanford, 1985), and Wolfram F. Hanrieder, *Germany, America, Europe: Forty Years of German Foreign Policy* (New Haven, Conn., 1989).

The West German "economic miracle" in the post-Erhard era has been analyzed by Edwin Hartrich, *The Fourth and Richest Reich* (London, 1980), and Frank Vogl, *German Business After the Economic Miracle* (London, 1973). Popular opinion has been studied by Elisabeth Noelle-Neumann, ed., *The Germans: Public Opinion Polls, 1967–1980* (Westport, Conn., 1981). For the emergence of the environmentalist Green party, see Werner Hulsberg, *The German Greens: A Social and Political Profile* (London, 1988), and Gerd Langguth, *The Green Factor in German Politics: From Protest Movement to Political Party* (Boulder, Colo., 1986). Terrorism in the Federal Republic has been detailed by Jillian Becker, *Hitler's Children: The Story of the Baader-Meinhof Terrorist Gang* (Philadelphia, 1977).

Broad swemps of German culture and society have been undertaken by Charles B. Burdick, Hans-Adolf Jacobsen, and Winfried Kudszus, eds., *Contemporary Germany: Politics and Culture* (Boulder, Colo., 1984), and John Ardagh, *Germany and the Germans: An Anatomy of Society Today* (New York, 1987). More detailed studies include Keith Bullivant, *Realism Today: Aspects of the Contemporary West German Novel* (Leamington Spa, 1987); Peter Demetz, *Postwar German Literature: A Critical Introduction* (New York, 1970); and K. Stuart Parkes, *Writers and Politics in West Germany* (London, 1986). The German cinema has been superbly analyzed by Anton Kaes, *From Hitler to Heimat: The Return of History as Film* (Cambridge, Mass., 1989); see also the older work by John Sanford, *The New German Cinema* (London, 1980).

The thorny issues of German rearmament and military strategy have been dealt with by Montecue J. Lowry, *The Forge of West German Rearmament: Theodor Blank and the Amt Blank* (New York, 1990); Stephen F. Szabo, ed., *The Bundeswehr and Western Security* (New York, 1990); and Julian Lider, *Origins and Development of West German Military Thought*, 2 vols. (Brookfield, Vt., 1986–1988). The role of the military in civilian society is discussed by Donald Abenheim, *Reforging the Iron Cross: The Search for Tradition in the Armed Forces* (Princeton, 1989).

CHAPTER 12

"THE GREAT SOCIALIST OCTOBER REVOLUTION,"[1] 1989

Skepticism is the first duty of the citizen.

Proletarians of the World: Please Forgive Me. Karl Marx.

GDR banners, 1989

The year 1989 started out routinely for Erich Honecker and the German Democratic Republic (GDR). On February 6 a young locksmith was gunned down at the Berlin Wall trying to escape. A month later another proletarian fatally crashed his home-made balloon while trying to cross into West Germany. On June 12 the Chinese Foreign Ministry warmly thanked the GDR for its solid support during the massacre of students in the Square of Heavenly Peace in Beijing. August would witness the celebration of the twenty-eighth anniversary of the construction of the Berlin Wall. A confident Honecker still expected the imminent rise of the West German workers against their capitalist overlords. Above all, the GDR planned large-scale rallies for October 7 to commemorate the fortieth anniversary of its founding in 1949. Arm in arm with Soviet leader Mikhail Gorbachev, Honecker planned to use this august occasion to reaffirm socialist solidarity and brotherhood before assembled Socialist Unity party (SED) dignitaries at the Palace of the Republic in East Berlin.

But storm clouds were gathering on the horizon. In Poland the Solidarity labor movement of Lech Wałęsa, which since June 1989 was in a coalition government with the Communist party of General Wojciech Jaruzelski, openly challenged the Communists' right and ability to rule. A strong reform element in Hungary, led by Károly Grósz and Imre Poszgay, had ended János Kádár's

[1] The Bolshevik revolution in 1917 fell on October 25 under the old Julian Calendar then in use in Russia, and hence the term "Great Socialist October Revolution."

nearly thirty-two-year rule as Hungarian Communist leader in May 1989. With liberal reformer Poszgay in the lead, Hungary, which for years had practiced a "softer" East bloc variant of "goulash communism" and strongly sought economic ties to the West, announced on May 2 that it would dismantle parts of the fortifications along its 221-mile border with Austria.

Most threatening, Soviet leader Gorbachev not only continued to push his twin policies of economic restructuring (*perestroika*) and openness (*glasnost*) but in June 1989 paid a highly successful state visit to Bonn. The "Gorbomania" that swept the Federal Republic could hardly have been comforting to Honecker. And in July 1989, speaking before the Council of Europe at Strasbourg, Gorbachev revoked the Brezhnev Doctrine, whereby the Soviet Union since 1968 had reserved the right to "protect" socialism in any of its satellite countries that strayed from the prescribed course. Moreover, the Soviet president prophesied a time of "change in the future as well" for East European lands other than Poland and Hungary. It was "inadmissible," Gorbachev lectured European leaders, for any state to "limit the sovereignty" of any other.

Hungary's dismantling of the iron curtain, which had divided Europe for forty years, caught the attention of thousands of East Germans vacationing in Hungary, a legal privilege that they enjoyed as fellow members of the Warsaw Pact. By July 16 about thirty enterprising GDR citizens had taken refuge in the West German embassy in Budapest in hopes of making their way to the Federal Republic (FRG) via Hungary. Within a month their number increased sixfold; another thirty thousand East Germans flocked to Hungary ostensibly on vacation but also in the hope of reaching the Federal Republic from there. On August 14 the East German writer Monika Maron warned of a malaise in the land. Why were these people fleeing the "first workers' and peasants' state" on German soil? "They have more to eat than the Poles, more money than the Hungarians; they live incomparably better than the Russians, Ukrainians, and the Uzbeks." Her warning fell on deaf ears in East Berlin.

The exodus out of the GDR continued unabated and extended to Czechoslovakia. By August 18 the West German embassy compound at Prague was fully occupied by refugees from the GDR, and more than eight hundred less fortunate souls crowded the area just outside its gates. On August 24 several hundred GDR citizens took advantage of a brief opening in the Austro-Hungarian border as a result of a "Europe Day" celebration to charge across the frontier into Austria; concurrently, about three thousand East German citizens undertook the illegal, and still dangerous, crossing.

Swamped by thousands of refugees from the GDR and pressured by both German states to solve this mounting problem, Budapest on September 11 rescinded its transit agreement with the GDR, under which Hungary would have been obliged to return all East Germans to Honecker. Károly Grósz and Imre Poszgay thereby effectively legitimized the exodus. In the ensuing weeks more than fifty-seven thousand East Germans, legally as vacationers or illegally as refugees, passed through Hungary en route to Austria, where special trains whisked them on to West Germany. Hungary, the first East European

A tear in the Iron Curtain: East German refugees bolt from Hungary to Austria near Sopron (August 1989).

state to tear down the iron curtain, became the main conduit for this intra-German traffic.

The story was much the same, although somewhat less dramatic, in Czechoslovakia. The initial group of fifty GDR refugees on August 18 at the West German embassy in Prague quickly swelled to twenty-five hundred within a month. Caught between East German demands to return the refugees and West German pressure to permit them to depart for the Federal Republic, Czechoslovak officials weighed their options. On October 1 the West German foreign minister, Hans-Dietrich Genscher, announced from the balcony of his embassy in Prague that the now six thousand refugees of the GDR were free to go to West Germany, albeit only via the GDR.

Erich Honecker had insisted on this condition to maintain the fiction that the refugees were leaving the GDR directly and with his official sanction. The refugees had their GDR passports revoked and were officially escorted out of East Germany as "undesirables." But even this face-saving ploy backfired. Nearly five thousand people gathered at the Dresden station to meet the transit trains, and many attempted to jump onto the moving cars. Within forty-eight hours, about ten thousand East Germans arrived in the Federal Republic via Prague through their former homeland. Emergency shelters sprang up throughout the Federal Republic to house the tens of thousands of new "citizens." East Germans who had stormed the West German embassy in Warsaw were flown to the Federal Republic in Polish airplanes.

At home, Honecker maintained a firm stance. On September 5 he informed his people that he would tolerate no reforms along existing East European and

Soviet lines. The Wall, Honecker averred, would stand for another hundred years. Nor should East Germans forget the lesson of Tiananmen Square in Beijing. Honecker reminded his subjects of an old socialist saying: "Neither ox nor ass can retard the course of socialism." And when the grass-roots democratic movement *Neues Forum*, founded on September 5, appealed to Honecker for official recognition, General Erich Mielke, head of State Security Service (Stasi), brusquely rejected its request.

Mikhail Gorbachev arrived in East Berlin on October 6. As at Bonn in June, he was met by passionate cries of "Gorby! Gorby!" The next day, at the Palace of the Republic to celebrate the fortieth anniversary of the founding of the German Democratic Republic, Gorbachev warned of the vulnerability of the hard-line East German regime. "Attempts to unify and to standardize social developments," the Soviet president informed Honecker's assembled SED elite, "belong to the past." Every people had the "sovereign" right to select its own "developmental modes." Alluding to recent events in Poland and Hungary, Gorbachev cautioned Honecker that "life punishes those who delay."

On October 8 Gorbachev waded into massed East German crowds and assured them that time was on their side. "We know our German friends well. We know their ability to think creatively, to learn from life, and to make changes when necessary." His words were quickly taken up by the populace, which read them as a mandate for reform. As the massive flight of East Germans to West Germany continued unabated, tens of thousands of GDR citizens took to the streets to vent their anger at and frustration with the regime, shouting "*Glasnost*" and "Democracy, Now or Never." Police and Stasi weighed in with rubber truncheons and water cannons; hundreds were injured in what became the largest uprising since June 1953.

Nor was East Berlin isolated in its popular protests. Throughout September and October thousands of residents of Leipzig had mounted Monday evening prayer meetings at historic St. Nicholas Church, where Johann Sebastian Bach had once played the organ and directed the choir. On October 9 about 70,000 citizens of Leipzig took to the streets to demand reform. Within a week the number of protesters at Leipzig swelled to 200,000. Other young people gathered at the Church of the Redeemer at East Berlin to vent, with the help of rock music, their unhappiness with the regime.

Honecker, in ill health due to a kidney ailment, initially sought to use force against the demonstrators. He was dissuaded from doing so by members of his own Politburo, who, perhaps remembering the uprisings of June 1953, doubted their ability to suppress popular revolts without Soviet military might. Eventually Honecker capitulated to popular pressure. On October 18, after eighteen years of supreme power, he laid down his offices as head of both state and party. Egon Krenz, Honecker's "crown prince," picked up the uneasy coronet. Still the "quiet revolution" continued in the streets of Dresden and Leipzig, where crowds, now in the hundreds of thousands, demanded change. For the first time ever, East Berliners held vigils to honor those killed at the Wall.

On October 29 prominent artists and writers such as Christa Wolf, Stephan Heym, Stephan Hermlin, Volker Braun, and Daniela Dahn, to mention but a few, gathered at the Church of the Redeemer to demand fundamental reform of both the German Democratic Republic and the Socialist Unity party. They sought free elections, freedom of assembly and the press, the separation of party and state, the abolition of the power monopoly of the SED, demolition of the Wall, an end to all special privileges for the party elite, and adherence to minimum environmental standards. Education Minister Margot Honecker resigned on November 2 due to "personal reasons."

The "great socialist October revolution" of 1989 now entered its final, critical phase. On November 4 one million people jammed the streets of East Berlin to denounce what they termed Honecker's "errors, omissions, and crimes." The novelist Christa Wolf summed up their mood by citing two of the most prominent popular slogans: "Democracy, Now or Never" and "We Are the People." The reformers were highly alarmed by the continuing exodus and feared that the moment might already have passed to reform the GDR from within. They had every reason to be fearful. After November 5 fifteen thousand East German refugees arrived within forty-eight hours in Bavaria alone. By November 6 about two hundred former GDR residents crossed the border from Czechoslovakia to Bavaria every hour. The exodus included fifteen hundred doctors and more than four thousand medical personnel. Hospitals threatened to close in East Germany. Public services such as garbage collection, sanitation, telephone, transportation, and communications collapsed for lack of workers.

The pace of demands for change escalated. Minister-President Willi Stoph resigned on November 7. The twenty-one-member Politburo followed the next day. By November 8 more than ten thousand people per day were arriving in Czechoslovakia from the German Democratic Republic, on their way to the Federal Republic. Makeshift tents and "floating hotels" (ships) in West Germany could barely provide shelter for the ever-growing flood of refugees.

On November 9 the dam burst: new Politburo member Günter Schabowski announced late that evening that the borders to West Berlin and West Germany would be opened. A true *Volksfest* (people's festival) ensued. People met, embraced, and danced on and at the Wall. The next day East Germany announced that it would begin to dismantle the Wall, that international symbol of oppression and internment. Bonn immediately proclaimed that it was making available to individual GDR citizens crossing the intra-German border not 300 million marks "welcome money" (*Begrüssungsgeld*), as previously promised, but 800 million marks.

There was no turning back. On November 12, the first weekend after the fall of the Wall, 1 million GDR residents flooded into West Germany; that number would soar to 8.6 million in four days. Although most went as tourists, a growing number decided to stay in the Federal Republic. "Welcome money" for 1990 was immediately raised to 1.3 billion marks, shortly to be increased yet again to 3 billion marks. Conversely, the East German mark,

Volksfest on the Wall (November 10, 1989).

formerly officially pegged by the GDR at par with its West German counterpart, fell to a ratio of twenty-to-one. The Bonn government asked all West German stores to remain open during nights and weekends to accommodate the shoppers. The first incidents of disgruntlement appeared as a result of this mass influx of East Germans (dubbed *Ossis*) into West Germany. In several West German cities *Wessis* burned East German Trabant cars to protest this wave of "foreign" shoppers.

Where had the Stasi been all this time? We may never know the answer. Perhaps Mielke and his top lieutenants were too old to meet the challenge. Perhaps they realized that it would be suicidal to move against hundreds of thousands of demonstrators. Perhaps they were prisoners of their lifelong

Marxist obsession with the deterministic, unalterable course of history. All we know is that Mielke's headquarters were flooded with accurate reports about the extent and danger of the street demonstrations. Perhaps, like the U.S. intelligence apparatus in recent years, Stasi was unable to digest this wealth of information and was immobilized by the sheer weight of evidence arriving and awaiting analysis. Mielke paid the price.

On December 7 Mielke's once-dreaded organization was formally disbanded by the so-called Round Table, a loose political confederation consisting of former East German unitary bloc parties such as the Liberals (LDPD), Christian Democrats (CDU), German National Democrats (NDPD), and German Democratic Peasants (DBD), as well as of new citizens' movements such as New Forum, Democracy Now, Democratic Awakening, Alliance 90, and the Green party. Remnants of the former Socialist Unity party, soon to be renamed Party of Democratic Socialism (PDS), also joined the Round Table under its new leader, Gregor Gysi. All agreed to hold elections in the GDR in March 1990.

The one man who did not panic was Helmut Kohl. On November 28 the West German chancellor, until then widely derided for his jovial incompetence, seized the moment by announcing new "confederative structures" between the two German states in a ten-point plan. Kohl called for an end to the division of Germany, with the reunified state to be firmly imbedded within the framework of the European Community. For internal political reasons (the potential vote of erstwhile "dispossessed" Germans from the east) Kohl declined to recognize the Oder-Neisse line as the Federal Republic's border with Poland. However, President Richard von Weizsäcker, in order to defuse international concerns over renewed German expansionism, demanded that the chancellor immediately recognize the Oder-Neisse border between Poland and Germany. Kohl's bold initiative found resonance among the East German population. On December 11 tens of thousands took to the streets in Leipzig, chanting "We Are One People" and "Germany, United Fatherland." Overnight the terms of the national debate were changing.

Two salient observations emerge. President Gorbachev's decision not to intervene in East German affairs, a total renunciation of the Brezhnev Doctrine, made reunification possible. The physical dynamism of the East German majority made it necessary. The chants of "Germany, United Fatherland" and "We Are One People" appeared only after the fall of the SED old guard.

Many East German reformers were shocked by this dramatic change in the streets, the sudden transformation of chants from being *the* people to those of being *one* people. On December 18, 150,000 people used the occasion of a silent march not only to commemorate the victims of Stalinism but also to step up their demands for reunification. Revelations concerning the ostentatious life-style of SED *Bonzen* behind the secure walls of their villas at Wandlitz, combined with news that State Secretary Alexander Schalck-Golodkowski reportedly had absconded with as much as 100 million marks earned in secret weapons deals with countries such as Iran, swept away the last remnants of SED legitimacy.

On December 18 Stoph's successor, Minister-President Hans Modrow, met with Kohl in Dresden to chart the future. Modrow at first tried to save the GDR as a sovereign state, arguing that its existence was vital to the balance and security of Europe, and requested a new line of 15 billion marks credit from Kohl to permit the GDR to ride out the crisis. The East German leader's bold offensive fizzled: Soviet leaders in Bonn concurrently inquired how the Federal Republic could help Moscow survive the winter of 1989.

Thus disarmed, Modrow agreed to release all political prisoners by Christmas, to open the Brandenburg Gate, symbol of twenty-eight years of German division, to establish a three-to-one exchange rate between the two German currencies, to embark on economic cooperation, and to formalize cultural exchanges. That same day, Gustav Husak's hard-line Communist regime at Prague was toppled by the moral power of Václav Havel and the public demonstrations of Civic Forum (the so-called velvet revolution). Chancellor Kohl celebrated his complete political triumph on December 22 at the reopened Brandenburg Gate before 300,000 wildly cheering Germans.

Thereafter the story of the German revolution is almost anticlimactic. World leaders scrambled frantically to catch up with German events. While British and French statesmen urged a cautious, slow approach to the "German question," U.S. president George Bush assured London, Paris, and Moscow that German reunification posed no security problems to Europe — after Kohl agreed late in November to sign a treaty with Warsaw recognizing the Oder and Neisse rivers as the border between Germany and Poland.

Throughout the winter of 1989, Chancellor Kohl, dubbed "Adenauer's grandson" in CDU quarters for his adherence to *der Alte's* foreign policy concept, fought off all attempts to convene a four-power conference to deal with German affairs. He feared that such a step would reconvene the 1945 Potsdam coalition of Britain, France, the Soviet Union, and the United States and in the process diminish Bonn's hard-won sovereignty rights. "We do not need four midwives." Kohl dealt from a position of strength because he knew that neither Moscow nor Washington was interested in a divided Germany anymore. Quite the opposite: the continued division of Germany was now regarded as an obstacle to European stability. The GDR had become the object rather than the subject of global politics.

By January 1990 Gorbachev in principle accepted German unification, with the caveat that this be accomplished outside the framework of the NATO defense system. Newly elected Czechoslovak president Václav Havel gave his blessings to German reunification that same month — at Munich, no less, scene of his country's shameful dismemberment in 1938. In February 1990 the World War II Allies (Britain, France, the United States, and the Soviet Union) began discussions with the two German states at Ottawa ("Two-Plus-Four Talks") to end the division of Germany.

A final remaining hurdle were the elections scheduled for the German Democratic Republic. On March 18, 1990, to the surprise of many, East Germans turned their back not only on the old SED, now reconstituted as the Party of Democratic Socialism, but also on the venerable SPD as well as on the more moderate parties loosely organized within the Round Table. They returned instead a solid endorsement (48.1 percent) of the Alliance for Germany headed by the CDU, which garnered 40.6 percent of the vote. In May the two CDU leaders, Kohl at Bonn and Lothar de Maizière at East Berlin, signed an agreement, effective July 1, 1990, acknowledging the social and economic union between the two German states. Once again it remained for the rest of the world to catch up with German events and formally to end the division of Germany — and thereby, World War II in Europe.

In June Kohl smoothed the path of reunification by extending an immediate line of credit of 5 billion marks to the Soviet Union. The following month he visited Gorbachev and calmed lingering Soviet fears of Germany's future military role by promising to reduce overall (East and West) German forces to 370,000 men. Undoubtedly realizing that a united Germany within a supranational defense alliance was preferable to a sovereign German army, Gorbachev reconsidered and permitted Germany to remain in NATO. Quite possibly he had recognized that the Soviet Union no longer had the power to resist German developments. Perhaps he realized that German unification was the price to pay for lasting cooperation with the West. Money once more greased the wheels of change. Kohl agreed not only to finance the stationing of Soviet troops in East Germany to the tune of $8 billion but also the costs of their withdrawal by 1994. Kohl was now conducting what amounted to a bilateral summit conference with the Soviet leader; the spirit of Potsdam 1945 was dead.

With Gorbachev's agreement to grant Germany full sovereignty in hand, Kohl had won his case. On September 12, 1990, Britain, France, the United States, and the Soviet Union and the two German states concluded a treaty at Moscow granting unified Germany full sovereignty. Unification (formally termed "accession") under Article 23 of the West German Basic Law of 1949 became official on October 3, 1990, the new German national holiday. Brandenburg, Mecklenburg-West Pomerania, Saxony, Saxony-Anhalt, and Thuringia became the newest German *Länder*. In late November thirty-two European states plus Canada and the United States, formally recognized German reunification and the termination of the division of Europe at the Conference on Security and Cooperation in Europe (CSCE) at Paris.

Mild opposition to German reunification came mainly from Israel and Poland. The latter had joined the Two-Plus-Four Talks for matters pertaining to future German-Polish relations. World War II and the cold war were finally over. On October 2 the old Allied military *Kommandatura* in Berlin was dissolved.

GERMANY, 1993

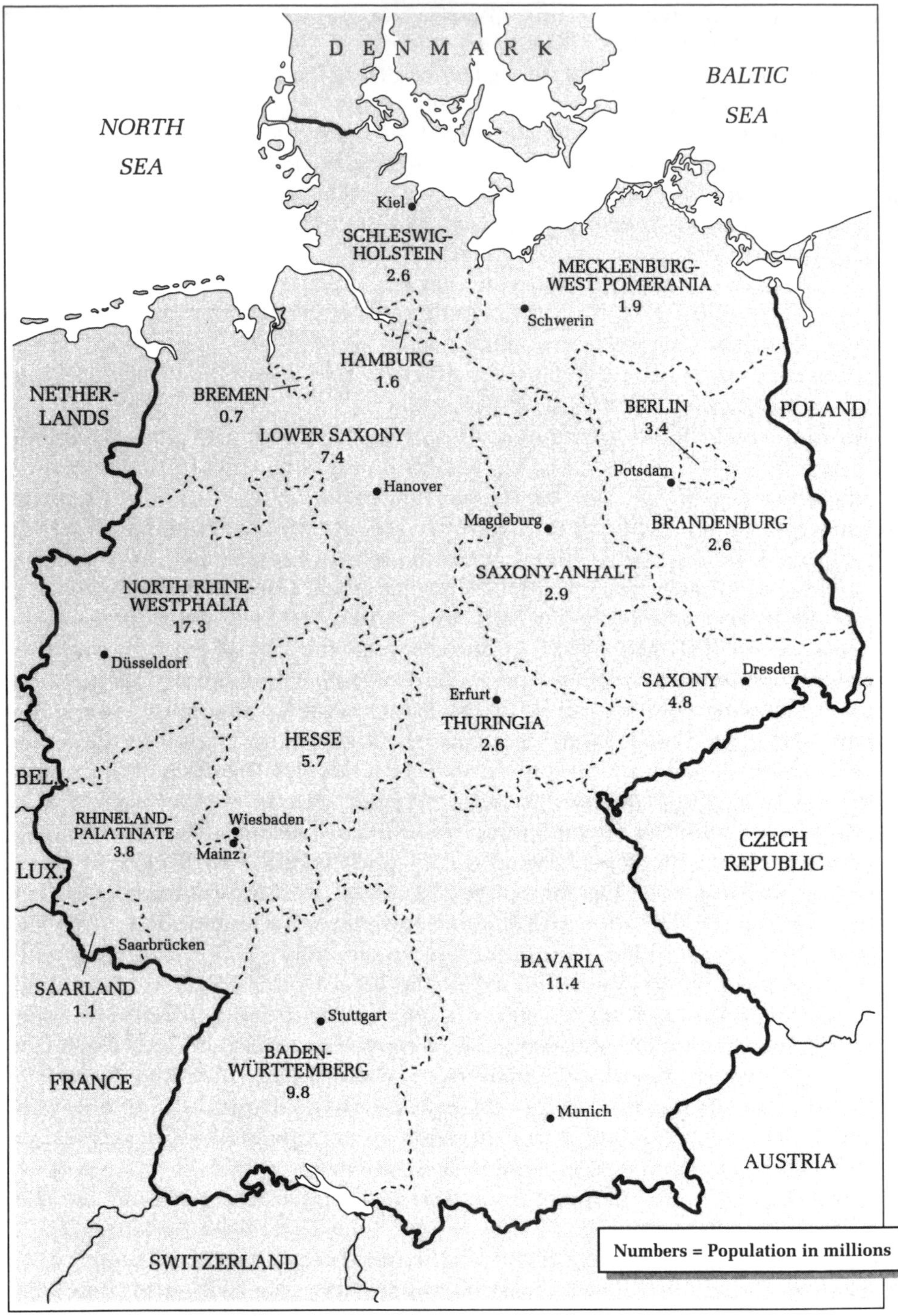

German unification, at best only a distant mirage before 1989, had come about in less than a year.

All-German elections on December 2, 1990, gave the reigning coalition government of Christian Democratic Union, Christian Social Union, and Free Democratic party an overwhelming victory: 54.8 percent of the vote and 392 seats in the new 662-member *Bundestag.* Both Kohl's CDU and Genscher's FDP received a greater percentage of the vote in East than in West Germany. Oskar Lafontaine's SPD, with 33.5 percent of the vote, its lowest since 1957, remained in its customary role of loyal opposition. Once again the SPD had missed the historical moment. While vociferously criticizing Kohl's reunification plans, Lafontaine had failed to put forth a constructive alternative. The greatest loser, however, was the Green party of West Germany, whose 3.9 percent of the vote disqualified it from sitting in parliament. The radical Right (NPD) polled only 0.3 percent of all ballots. The Party of Democratic Socialism (formerly SED) received a disappointing 2.4 percent of the vote. But a last-minute decision by the Federal Constitutional Court at Karlsruhe to waive the 5 percent minimum vote for parties surpassing that level alone in the former GDR lands allowed the old SED to take its seventeen seats in the *Bundestag.* Chancellor Kohl could well speak of a "day of joy." After extensive debate, the *Bundestag* agreed to relocate the nation's capital in Berlin in the coming decade.

Chancellor Kohl's understandable euphoria was forced off front pages by events in the Middle East. In February 1991 a U.S.-dominated United Nations coalition attacked Iraq as punishment for Saddam Hussein's invasion of oil-rich Kuwait on August 2, 1990. What would West Germany, a staunch NATO supporter, do in response to pleas for help from Washington? Kohl weighed his options carefully and ultimately promised financial but not military support. While cries of ingratitude and disloyalty arose in some Western quarters, most notably in Washington, the sight of iron-crossed German armored units charging across the Middle East desert near the borders of Israel would hardly have enhanced Bonn's image.

The hangover from unification followed immediately. More than forty years of industrial mismanagement, pollution, and other environmental disasters in the former German Democratic Republic came to light for the first time. Transportation and communications networks dating from the 1920s were unable to service the high-speed and high-technology demands of German business and government establishments. Banks and credit unions could not cope with the instant changeover to deutsche marks. Hotels and restaurants in the former GDR lands were utterly unprepared to handle the immediate rush of visitors.

Above all, the heavily polluting industrial plants, most dating from the time of the Weimar Republic, had to be closed down at once because none met West German or European Community environmental standards. Additionally,

East German industry was denied guaranteed markets in East Europe and the Soviet Union in the wake of the collapse of Comecon. As a result, unemployment immediately soared to almost one industrial worker in three. Accustomed for forty years to having the state regulate their lives, many East Germans felt helpless to cope with the vicissitudes of a free market economy.

For West Germans, many of whom had been wary of the costs of reunification from the start, the staggering price of reunification (139 billion marks to June 1992) threatened higher taxes and a reduction in their standard of living. Many West Germans were especially bitter because Kohl, parroting U.S. president George Bush's November 1988 campaign promise ("Read my lips, no new taxes!"), had assured his countrymen that reunification would not translate into additional taxes. But in December 1990, Kohl realized his poor judgment in promising no new taxes and reversed his policy, imposing a "temporary" 7.5 percent surcharge on income tax; it remains in place.

By reneging on his promise of no additional taxes, Kohl alienated many West German voters. A rare but massive strike of communications, public, and transport workers in May 1992 was mainly a protest against the escalating cost of reunification. The chancellor's biting comment that Germany had become the land of "vacation workers" did little to restore labor calm.[1]

But as bewildering and as unsettling as reunification might have been to many old German Democratic Republic stalwarts, for East Europeans it offered a new economic haven. Whereas 388,000 East Germans had headed westward in 1989, the next year about 400,000 ethnic Germans arrived in the united Germany from Poland, Rumania, and the Soviet Union. It is estimated that due to their ethnic origins, 3 million more are legally eligible to claim German citizenship under the 1949 Basic Law. Moreover — and quite apart from the 360,000 Soviet forces and their 200,000 dependents stationed on German soil — a steady illegal invasion of Poles, Rumanians, Bulgarians, Yugoslavs, Iranians, Gypsies, Turks, Iraqis, and even Afghans continues unabated. Germany, with the most liberal refugee laws in Europe (Article 16 of the Basic Law), has become a magnet for all shades of asylum seekers: 193,000 in 1990, more than 225,000 in 1991, and nearly 500,000 in 1992. The German-Polish border along the Oder and Neisse rivers has become the European equivalent of the "cactus curtain" between Mexico and the United States along the Rio Grande. And although the federal border police (*Bundesgrenzschutz*) during the summer of 1991 alone prevented 9,000 Poles from crossing into Germany, the Interior Ministry at Bonn believes that 42,000 others successfully entered the country. Political unrest and economic chaos in East Europe and the former Soviet Union threaten to put an even greater strain in the future on the German border police.

[1] German workers are the highest paid in the world and enjoy an average workweek of twenty-nine hours, six weeks of annual vacation, and an extra month's salary at Christmas.

A potentially still more menacing time bomb looms in the archival records of the extensive personal surveillance system conducted by Stasi. At the height of General Mielke's reign, the SED's "sword and shield" employed 86,000 full-time and 110,000 part-time officers, troops, and informants. In fiscal 1988 Mielke's budget of $2.25 billion constituted 16 percent of state expenditures. Between 1950 and 1989, the Stasi spied on 6 million Germans, two-thirds of whom resided within its own borders.

Although the Stasi managed during its last days in power to shred no fewer than 936 sacks of sensitive documents at its Central Archive on the Normannenstrasse, the remaining files are so extensive that their curator, Joachim Gauck, estimates that it would take one archivist 128 years to catalog them. In raw terms, if one accepts the benchmark figure that one yard of documents contains 10,000 sheets of paper, remaining Stasi files would stretch about 120 miles.

The Stasi files were made available to the public on January 1, 1992, and 300,000 *Ossis* and *Wessis* immediately applied for permission to examine them. First indications suggest that international terrorist organizations such as the Palestine Liberation Organization and the Red Army Faction had been generously financed by Mielke and that they were accorded a safe haven in the former GDR. In June 1992 it was discovered that the Stasi had paid professional killers six-figure sums to assassinate political opponents in the Federal Republic. These recent revelations also document the pervasive nature of Stasi activity. Perhaps most tragically, thousands of East German families face painful disclosures of their unsavory past. Star athletes routinely spied on fellow teammates and coaches. Teachers regularly reported on "conspicuous" children to Section VIII of the Stasi, detailed to monitor "dangerous persons" in schools. Corrupted priests reported confessionals to Mielke. Brothers reported on sisters, spouses on each other. University deans and department heads informed on their faculty. West German churches bribed Mielke's minions in order to maintain contacts with their GDR brethren.

And there remains the fate of former Stasi officers and informants, especially in the light of the fact that, late in 1991, a first group of former GDR border guards was convicted for shooting would-be escapees. West German authorities have now doubled their erstwhile estimate that the Stasi shot about two hundred East Germans trying to escape the GDR. Larger political questions also remain. In August 1992 Russia and Chile returned Erich Honecker from his retreat in the Chilean embassy in Moscow to German authorities to account for his infamous "shoot-to-kill" order to East German border guards. Honecker, along with General Mielke and former Minister-President Willi Stoph, went to trial on charges of manslaughter in November. In January 1993 Honecker's trial was dismissed because of his ill health, and it is unclear whether Mielke and Stoph can be convicted of acts that were not considered crimes under the laws of the former GDR. Moreover, both Mielke and Stoph are taking full advantage of the lenient German legal system to obtain frequent trial interruptions by claiming ill health.

The careers of numerous East German politicians, including its first democratically elected prime minister, Lothar de Maizière, have been ruined by allegations of former Stasi activity. Rumors of erstwhile Stasi contacts threaten to topple Manfred Stolpe, the premier of Brandenburg, and Gregor Gysi, the head of the Party of Democratic Socialism. West German security forces alone know to what degree former Stasi agents were behind the 1992 race riots in the former GDR. Are such uprisings intended to destabilize the united Germany? One may well wonder whether de-Stasification will be as painful as de-Nazification was after 1945. At the very least, the State Security Service personified Franz Kafka's nightmare vision of anonymous and omnipresent forces threatening humanity by inexplicable and inhuman powers.

Above all, the question remains of what the future will hold for the new Germany. Which aspects of its past will it shed, and which will it seek to maintain? Will Germany become a European partner, or Europe a German partner? Will the new Germany remain content to be a full member of NATO, the European Community, and the Conference on Security and Cooperation in Europe — that is, firmly embedded in the European security and economic system — or will it seek to resurrect the old seesaw policy of playing East off against West? And will NATO and the CSCE survive the Gorbachev revolution in their present forms? Such questions defy resolution. They do, however, demand a framework of reference.

Several factors suggest that present-day Germany is not a repeat of the constellation of 1815 and its resultant convolutions, as some scholars and pundits have suggested. Nor is it 1871 yet again. In fact, the German revolution of 1989–1990 was not a masterstroke of superior statecraft as conducted by Otto von Bismarck in 1870–1871 but rather a gift of history, one — albeit vital — part of the great process of disintegration of the Soviet Union initiated by Gorbachev. Kohl's studied "Europeanization of the German question," as revealed through the Two-Plus-Four Talks, alone distinguishes this unification from its forerunner.

For the first time in its history, Germany has been unified with rather than against the approval of its neighbors. The former Soviet Union, Poland, Czechoslovakia, and Hungary today accept Germany as both a vital cog in the European state system and a great economic power. For the first time ever, Germans have both freedom and unity. Ludwig Bamberger's rhetorical query in 1866 of his Rheinhesse voters, "But is unity not in and of itself a piece of freedom?" need haunt Europeans no longer. Nor do Germans have to ponder whether they are defined by national tradition or by the constitutional form of their government. They are citizens of the longest democratic experiment on German soil.

The German state today, in the words of Bismarck, is "saturated." Few Germans dream of a "fourth" Reich. Few wish to restore the Franconian, Hohenstaufen, Hohenzollern, or Hitlerian empires. With the exception of several dwindling Sudeten and Silesian groups, there is no public call for a return of "lost territories" as under the Weimar Republic. Konrad Adenauer's policy of Western integration destroyed the foundations of the old *Mitteleuropa* policy. Most Germans have little time for annexationism. If there is a debate, it is not between *Kleindeutsch* or *Grossdeutsch* but rather between *Kleineuropa* and *Grosseuropa* supporters — that is, between those who wish either to exclude or to include East Europe in the European Community. Conversely, and unlike 1871, there are no Danish, French, or Polish minorities in Germany.

In a nutshell, as of October 3, 1990, the Federal Republic with its current borders, including the Oder-Neisse line, is the only real alternative. Few Germans see their unified country as a stepping-stone to greater dreams. Youth in particular regard it primarily as a transitory stop on the road to a United States of Europe. Past references to the existence of three German states — East and West Germany as well as Austria — have all but abated, for most Germans have accepted the fact that Austria is not a German state simply because it does not want to become one. The Federal Republic has ceased to be a revisionist power situated at the crossroads of Europe.

Finally, Germany today is irrevocably tied to the West. Gone is the diplomatic, economic, geographical, military, and political ambivalence of the past. The sudden collapse of the Soviet Union, combined with European integration, has, in effect, denied any future Machiavellian dealers in the German Foreign Office the diplomatic leeway to maneuver between the super powers. This is all the more remarkable in the light of Chancellor Helmut Schmidt's state-of-the-nation address in 1979, in which he reminded his countrymen of their peculiar predicament:

> The idea that one day a state of 75 million Germans could arise in the middle of Europe arouses concern in many of our neighbors and partners in Europe. . . . We ought not overlook the fact that, in the eyes of others, the German division is today part of the European balance of power that secures peace in Europe. . . . In our geopolitical position and with our recent history, we Germans cannot allow ourselves a political schizophrenia. . . . Readiness for reality is needed if our will to peace is to prevail.

Calls throughout 1989 for a neutral Germany were quite rightly warded off by Chancellor Kohl. All of Europe can sleep much better with Germany firmly embedded in NATO, the European Community, the Conference on Security and Cooperation in Europe — and without nuclear, biological, or chemical weapons.

If the fear of German expansionism has been put to rest, so too has the concept of the German special path, or *Sonderweg*. In 1933 Germany was the only Western industrial state to abandon democracy during the height of the Great Depression. A plebiscitary, pseudo-legitimate *Führerstaat* was all too easily built upon the solid foundations of the old Prusso-German authoritarianism

(*Obrigkeitsstaat*). But the end of World War II also saw the end of any chance for *Sonderweg*. Prussia disappeared from the map, and its Junker class was largely destroyed or disempowered. Nationalism was disgraced, militarism soundly defeated. The late-nineteenth-century tradition of illiberalism in time yielded to the acceptance, even by the established elites, of a functional, democratic state. The old bureaucratic edifice of 1807, 1918, and 1933 survived, but so did the federalism of 1871. After nearly half a century of Western parliamentarism, one can only hope that democracy, pluralistic toleration, and a sense of legality and legitimacy abound in Bonn and that they will continue to do so after the capital has been relocated to Berlin by the end of the century.

The flag of the new Germany is black-red-gold: the tricolors of Jena University and the Wars of Liberation 1813–1815, of the Wartburg 1817, of Hambach 1832, of the Revolutions of 1848–1849, and of Weimar 1919–1933. Moreover, it is historical irony that the Federal Republic's three major political parties — Christian Democrats, Social Democrats, and Free Democrats — are successors of the erstwhile Bismarckian *Reichsfeinde* of Center, SPD, and Progressives, respectively.

Daunting challenges remain for Germany. Because the German Democratic Republic was incorporated into the Federal Republic — and the reunited nation is thus the "Federal Republic of Germany" — there was no "middle ground" or "third way," for which many East German reformers had hoped. The choices consisted of continued state socialism or the West German social market economy. West Germans today refer to reunification in terms of a new *Anschluss* (as had been the case with Austria in 1938). Although a feeling of triumph persists in many West German quarters, East Germans often see themselves as the victims of colonization.

Former GDR citizens will stimulate the development of social equality and programs and bring a sense of both patience and modesty to the unified Germany, but they will also carry with them the impedimenta of their past: lack of compromise, lack of tolerance, illiberalism, economic chaos, and environmental destruction. Long-pent-up emotions are already surfacing as 16 million Germans for the first time try to come to grips with the entire "Auschwitz" syndrome. No longer can the Holocaust be justified by East Germans as the logical outcome of (West) German capitalism and militarism.

The 16 million citizens of the erstwhile German Democratic Republic went straight from twelve years of National Socialist totalitarianism to forty-five years of Communist totalitarianism — in all, fifty-seven years of dictatorial rule. They can hardly be expected to embrace the give-and-take of parliamentary government overnight. Additionally, the effects of nearly five decades of Communist propaganda will take years to erase.

The shadow of terrorism lurks over Germany. Are there still Stasi operatives at work? If so, do they continue to support the Red Army Faction? Obviously, the latter has been hard at work capitalizing on East German discontent aroused by the problems of economic, political, and social integration. The

Red Army Faction's brutal slaying in 1991 of the Federal Trustee for East German properties, Detlev Rohwedder, does not augur well for the future. The mistrust and terror created by General Mielke and his minions will take decades to overcome.

Unification will demand social and economic sacrifices. Over the next decade West Germans will have to carry the brunt of the financial burden, perhaps as high as 30 billion marks per quarter in fiscal 1992, but they will also have to learn to develop patience toward and understanding for their new brethren, two qualities that are rare commodities in today's fast-moving world. In June 1992 President Richard von Weizsäcker called for a new "equalization of burdens" as had occurred in May 1952, requesting that West Germans mobilize their private reserves of 3 trillion marks to pay for East German reconstruction. The response to his plea has been ice cold. Chancellor Kohl has declared that spending one-quarter of German tax revenues for reconstruction is a sufficient burden for the state. West German companies are disinclined to invest heavily in the new federal states, and much of the money channeled into reconstruction ends up in the coffers of West German firms rebuilding the former GDR's long-neglected infrastructure. And the almost insurmountable problem remains of property ownership rights in the lands of the erstwhile GDR.

East Germans, long used to a centrally directed economy within the sheltered Comecon system, will have to accept the pains of global competition. East German heavy industry, with its outdated equipment, overmanned work staff, poor-quality production, and inefficient marketing system, is in no position to compete in world markets. Unemployment in 1991–1992 ran at around 30 percent. Yet it should be remembered that the current economic crisis is due not so much to reunification as to decades of SED mismanagement and neglect. All too many East Germans in 1989 had demanded reunification for economic reasons: adoption of the powerful mark, equalization of the standard of living between the two German states, and gainful employment at West German wage levels. Reality has rudely dashed these excessive expectations.

In the short run, East Germans will have to accept that their wages and standard of living will be lower than those of the old Federal Republic but modestly higher than they were under Honecker. They will have to struggle to bring about economic growth, a rise in their standard of living, an equitable distribution of wealth, and effective political power. They will have to accept the often irritatingly slow pace of democracy and the opaque vicissitudes of pluralism. If two German states still exist, they do so only in the sense of Benjamin Disraeli's classic analogy from nineteenth-century England, *Sybil, or the Two Nations*: one rich, one poor. Marxism may well be dead, but the material dialectic is alive and well.

The issue of political integration remains. Most West Germans see themselves as *Bundesdeutsche* (Germans of the Federal Republic) rather than simply as "Germans." Most East Germans see themselves primarily as "Germans"

The cost of communism: Polluting power plants near Cottbus (1990).

rather than as *Bundesbürger* (citizens of the Federal Republic). West Germans have accepted pan-Europeanism, travel extensively throughout the Continent, and have learned its major languages. East Germans, to whom the Honecker regime had bequeathed a strong sense of German heritage, will have difficulty adjusting to pan-Europeanism. They cannot be expected to make the quantum leap to thinking and being "Europeans" overnight. For the citizens of both German states, will the sense of belonging to a European community over time supersede the identity of country and nation? West German publicists such as Hans Magnus Enzensberger (*Europe, Europe*) openly warn that European Community bureaucrats at Brussels threaten to erase regional traditions and distinctiveness.

And then there is the fact that both East and West Germans grew up on a political fiction: the state-sponsored notion that each had traversed a *Sonderweg* since 1945. For East Germans this revolved around the conviction that the GDR constituted the first "workers' and peasants' state" on German soil. For West Germans it centered on Bonn's claim that the Federal Republic had overcome the nationalism and militarism of the past. Now that both German states are one nation again, it will be interesting to see what sort of national mythologies will evolve to serve as a bond between them.

Few politicians on either side of the Elbe River have addressed the critical question of the future image and character of their state. Most have taken refuge behind the comfortable thought that their state will continue as the Federal Republic of Germany. That is a myth. In 1990 the *Bundesrepublik Deutschland* of Adenauer and Erhard, Brandt and Kohl came to a dramatic, sudden, and unexpected end. Over time the comfortable, conservative, and mainly Catholic CDU/CSU bloc will have to devise a platform that will attract former East German voters permanently. The party's coalition partner, the Free Democrats, will have to find bourgeois voters in a long-standing "workers' and peasants' state." The political center of gravity will shift. The new Germany will be more northern, more eastern, more German, more Protestant, and more social.

It will also move its political center of gravity to the right. The Republican party of Franz Schönhuber in May 1992 gained nearly 10 percent of the vote in communal elections in West Berlin (just over 8 percent in Greater Berlin), thereby maintaining its earlier gains in the capital.[1] Schönhuber, who idealizes Benito Mussolini's Italy of the 1920s, has attracted twenty thousand members to his party. Most are in their early twenties and despise what they call the "postmodern world"; Schönhuber proudly sees his movement as the revolt of grandparents (Third Reich) and grandsons (present day) against the fathers (the Germans of the "economic miracle"). The Republicans want a "Germany for Germans" only and equate a multicultural society with a multicriminal society. In Austria the Progressive party (FPÖ) of Jörg Haider, which in October 1990 gained 16.5 percent of the national vote and claims popular support by one in every five Austrians, shares many of the Republicans' views.

Antiforeign sentiment raged throughout Germany during 1992, especially in the former GDR, where it was launched by the vulgar radicalism of Austrian-born Gerd Honsik. Honsik's "stop-foreigners" movement appeals not only because it argues that jobs should be reserved for unemployed East Germans but also because the GDR had nurtured an authoritarian, nationalistic, and xenophobic society. The "stop-foreigners" movement seeks the expulsion of the 2 million Turkish foreign laborers (*Gastarbeiter*) from German soil. It insists that Germany has never been a land of immigrants but rather a distinct (and superior) nation in cultural terms.

The antiforeigners' phenomenon finds support also among the nearly 2 million ethnic Germans who have returned to the country from their former homes in Eastern Europe since reunification. Like many other immigrants, these new arrivals tend to defend and uphold the traditional religious beliefs, social habits, language, and social morals of the Germany they left two or three centuries ago. A final target of resentment are the 1 million refugees (about 500,000 in 1992 alone) who have flocked to Germany from other countries under the protection of its liberal asylum laws. Most are forbidden to work and live in makeshift camps awaiting a final court ruling on their status. This group, more than any other, is the target of popular resentment against all aliens. In fact, a spiral of hatred has developed: the *Wessis* look down on their narrow-minded, pandering *Ossi* cousins; the East Germans denounce the ethnic

[1] Voter protest against the established parties also brought the Democratic Socialists (formerly SED) 11 percent of the (mainly East) Berlin vote.

The Unmasterable Past? A neo-Nazi in Cottbus on guard (1991).

Germans from the East as "Polacks"; both eastern and ethnic Germans seek to deny foreign laborers a fair share in society; and the foreign laborers fear that the refugees will threaten their hopes for social and economic integration.

Large-scale unemployment in the former GDR and antiforeign sentiment throughout the nation have provided grist to the racist mills of the disparate neo-Nazi (and skinhead) movements. Almost daily television coverage accords the roughly forty thousand hard-core German rightists publicity and importance far beyond their influence and power. But Bonn is not Weimar, as evidenced by the marches of hundreds of thousands of democratic supporters and police in Berlin, Düsseldorf, Frankfurt, and Hamburg in December 1992. Unlike Weimar, Bonn is not immobilized by rightist violence: in November 1992, the Social Democratic party under its new leader, Björn Engholm, endorsed Chancellor Kohl's call for a tightening of Germany's liberal asylum laws, which in 1949 were intended to provide a future haven for Germans living in the Soviet zone and the lands annexed by Poland and the Soviet Union. The new laws, passed in December, will permit asylum only to those who can prove that they were the victims of political persecution in their native lands.

The united Germany is smaller than the state of Montana but contains 78 million rather than 800,000 inhabitants. Put differently, Germany cannot continue to absorb half a million asylum seekers per year. Its taxpayers cannot be expected to continue to house, feed, and support this army of economic refugees at an average cost of $10,000 per person. Once the domestic discontent aroused by the flood of asylum seekers is removed, the neo-Nazis and their fellow travelers on the Right will have less fertile ground to sow their seeds of hatred. Nor should it be overlooked that, per capita, there are more right-wing extremists in Belgium, France, Italy, Spain, and the United States than in Germany.

For the rest of Europe there is no escaping the reality that the new Germany will be poised to assume a greater role in the Continent's affairs by the year 2000 at the latest. Straddling Central Europe, Germany is the bridge between East and West; many of Europe's commercial lifelines pass through its territory. Economically, Germany ranks third in the world, with no foreseeable relative decline. It currently provides more than half of all economic aid ($70 billion) to the Commonwealth of Independent States (the former Soviet Union) and is the largest single investor (one-third) in Czechoslovak privatization of industry. With a population of 78 million, Germany surpasses Britain, France, and Italy each by at least 20 million. Few have forgotten French premier Georges Clemenceau's tart remark that the major problem with Germans was that there are 20 million too many of them.

A new national feeling is afoot in Germany and a need for a new national identity. Chancellor Kohl's unguarded verbal slip — "We *are* somebody once again" — has set off fears of revitalized German power throughout Europe. Kohl's plan to revise the 1949 constitution in order to permit German forces to deploy beyond the nation's borders, albeit under United Nations supervision, has alarmed not only Poles but many Germans as well. Bonn's hasty and unilateral recognition of Croatia and Slovenia during the disintegration of Yugoslavia, not to mention its call for military means to end the Balkan crisis, reflects a desire by Germany to conduct an independent foreign policy. U.S. political leaders are greatly concerned about the future of NATO by the May 1992 announcement that Bonn and Paris will create a joint Franco-German army corps.

With the collapse of the German Democratic Republic, Bonn inherited a massive stockpile of weapons: twenty-four hundred tanks, fifty-four hundred airplanes, seventy ships, and fifty-one thousand army vehicles. Given the past scandals in the Federal Republic's Ministry of Defense concerning armaments sales overseas, this matériel represents a tempting source of quick revenue. Bonn will have to develop considerable maturity in judgment concerning its disposal of these arms; above all, the federal government will have to understand that arms sales require *Bundestag* approval.

The challenges facing Germany are not insurmountable, and their solutions are readily discernible: as much domestic federalism and as little centralization as possible; a shift in economic power from the Federal German Bank (*Bundesbank*) to a future European Central Bank with a common European currency (ECU); and as much political power and sovereignty as possible to Europe and its multinational organizations. Chancellor Kohl understands all this. At the medieval Dutch city of Maastricht in December 1991, he led the charge by eleven nations (except Britain) to create a single European currency by 1999, a social charter covering workers' rights, a common European defense policy, more joint action in foreign affairs, a common immigration and asylum policy, and a European police intelligence agency (Europol) to combat drug trafficking and organized crime. This landmark agreement, which is intended to amend the 1957 Treaties of Rome, hopes to establish a European Union of 340 million people by the end of the decade. Not even the program's narrow defeat in a Danish national referendum in June 1992, followed by victories in Ireland and France, has deterred Kohl from pursuing Konrad Adenauer's policy of European integration. In fact, the *Bundestag* approved the Maastricht Treaty by a landslide vote (543–17) in December 1992.

The critical question is whether the European Community will be able (and willing) to integrate the lands of the former Warsaw Pact and the Soviet Union into its network ("management of Soviet decline"). Put differently, how will the EC react to the economic, political, and financial independence (and poverty as well as debt) of the Baltic states, Russia, and Ukraine? Without stability in the East, there can be no stability in the center of Europe. Without rejuvenated economies in the East, the flood of guest workers to the West will continue unabated. Associated agreements reached at Prague in December 1991 between the EC on the one hand and Czechoslovakia,[1] Hungary, and Poland on the other to forge a tariff-free European trading bloc within a decade are at least promising. But without nuclear disarmament in the former states of the Soviet Union, the threat of nuclear war will forever hang over Europe.

France may hold part of the solution to Europe's development. To be sure, Paris has lost its role as diplomatic bridge between Moscow and Washington, and its once-vaunted nuclear deterrent (*force de frappe*) has been rendered superfluous by German reunification and the demise of the Soviet state. France will have to reassess its future diplomatic role and seek new allies. Perhaps President François Mitterrand's staunch support of European integration at Maastricht in 1991 and in the national referendum in 1992, his willingness to forge a joint army corps with Bonn, and his dramatic trip to Bosnia-Herzegovina in June 1992 are signs of this reorientation of French policy.

Above all, there is no sense of the "end of history"[2] at Bonn. There remain countless tasks for German policymakers: rebuilding East Germany, reconstructing the former states of the Soviet Union, disposing nuclear arsenals, cleaning up the environmental catastrophe of the GDR, controlling East-West

[1] The division of Czechoslovakia into independent Czech and Slovak republics on December 31, 1992, poses new problems for the European Community.

[2] In 1989 former U.S. State Department policy planning staff deputy director Francis Fukuyama suggested in a provocative essay, "The End of History?," in *The National Interest*, Nr. 16 (Summer 1989), pp. 3–18, that the near-global triumph of liberal democracy had ushered in a "posthistorical" age.

migration, and integrating the European economic and political systems. Much of the future is unclear. While a good portion of the world struggles to deal with ethnic, religious, and national movements of disintegration, the recently reunified nation between Rhine and Oder seeks to discover its identity, equilibrium, and foreign policy role. In Bonn, there is a growing concern that the 1990s may be much like the years preceding 1914: pregnant with choice and dangers alike.

German leaders have to be acutely aware that all their actions will be judged in the light of the recent past. Chancellor Kohl's ability to convince the *Bundestag* to relocate the capital in Berlin, for example, evoked negative memories not only of William II's Second Reich but also of Adolf Hitler's Third Reich. Kohl's active role in August 1991 in removing Frederick the Great's remains to Potsdam divided the nation and revived remembrances abroad of German militarism. The current veneration in certain sectors of the Federal Republic of all things Prussian will hardly allay European fears of the revitalization of an authoritarian Germany. And Kohl's slowness in confronting the neo-Nazi street violence in 1992, despite calls for swift government action by President von Weizsäcker and millions of German citizens, prompted numerous charges that Bonn was going the way of Weimar. Fair or not, every German action will be viewed in Warsaw and Prague, London and Paris, Moscow and Minsk, in terms of the signals that it sends forth.

The Federal Republic remains the inheritor of what the American historian Charles Maier has termed its "unmasterable past." Although Maier restricted the concept to the 6 million victims of the Holocaust, this dreadful phase of German history was vastly overshadowed by the equally "unmasterable" World War II. No one wishes to pass the iniquities of the fathers on to the children and down to the third or fourth generations, but German actions between 1939 and 1945 resulted not only in the deaths of 5 million of their own but also in those of 20 million Soviets. Monuments from the Pyrenees to the Urals attest to this slaughter. The state of Israel in particular will keep the legacy of the Holocaust alive.

Finally, it is perhaps fitting to return to the epigraph of the first chapter of this book. Therein the young writers Johann Wolfgang von Goethe and Friedrich Schiller in 1795–1796 had expressed their concerns about the new spirit of nationalism aroused by the French Revolution:

> You Germans hope in vain to develop yourselves into a nation; instead — and you can do it — develop yourselves more freely into human beings.

With time and skillful management, the two former German states should be able to accomplish both.[1]

[1] Given the recent nature of the events discussed in this chapter, there does not yet exist a body of English-language literature for reference. Most of the material was gleaned from the German press, particularly from six articles entitled, "Germany's Past; Germany's Future," in the newspaper *Die Zeit* between September and December 1990.

APPENDIX

GLOSSARY

Abgrenzung	delimitation of East from West Germany in the 1970s.
Abitur	high school graduation certificate with university entrance.
ancien régime	Europe before the French Revolution in 1789.
Anschluss	union; annexation of Austria, 1938.
Apparatchik	East German party hack.
Aufklärung	German enlightenment.
Autarkie	self-sufficiency.
Bauernschutz	"peasants' protection" under Frederick II.
Bekennende Kirche	Confessing church (post-1934).
Besitzbürgertum	propertied middle class.
Betriebsunfall	industrial accident; used after 1949 to explain Hitler's rise to power.
Biedermeier	modest bourgeois lifestyle before 1848.
Bildunsgbürgertum	educated middle class.
Blitzkrieg	lightning warfare (1939–1945).
Bonze	party boss; bigwig.
Bundesbürger; Bundesdeutsche	citizens of the Federal Republic of Germany.
Bundespräsident	federal president (1949–).
Bundesrepublik	Federal Republic (1949–).
Bürgertum	middle class; bourgeoisie.
Burschenschaft	fraternity; corps (post-1806).
"Deutschlandlied"	German national anthem.
Diktat	dictate; German term to denounce the Versailles Treaty, 1919.
Dolchstoss	stab in the back; right-wing term to explain loss in World War I.
Einheitsstaat	unitary state.
Einsatzgruppen	SS execution squads (1939–1945).
Endlösung	final solution; German euphemism for the Holocaust (1941–1945).
Fremdarbeiter	foreign worker (during World War II).
Führer	leader (specifically, Adolf Hitler).
Führerprinzip	principle of authoritarian rule (by Adolf Hitler).
Führerstaat	authoritarian state.
Führertum	cult of (charismatic) leadership.

Gau	district, province (ancient Germanic; National Socialist).
Gestapo	secret state police (Prussian after 1933).
Gleichschaltung	coordination; synchronization; Nazification of German state apparatus after 1933.
Götterdämmerung	Twilight of the Gods; Wagnerian opera; term for end of the Nazi regime, 1945.
Grossdeutsch	greater Germany; unification including Austria.
Grundgesetz	Basic Law; West German constitution 1949, amended 1990 for East Germany.
Grundherrschaft	manorial system.
Gutsherrschaft	self-managed Junker estate in Prussia.
Gymnasium	classical high school leading to university.
Herrenmensch	master race.
Historikerstreit	historians' quarrel (West Germany, 1985–1988).
"Horst Wessel Song"	Nazi party anthem.
Judenrat	Jewish Council of Elders.
judenrein	free of Jews; Nazi policy after 1933.
Kampf	struggle; fight (as in Hitler's book, *Mein Kampf*, or "My Struggle").
Kinder, Küche, Kirche	children, kitchen, church (used by William II and Hitler to define role of women).
Kleinbürger	lower middle class.
Kleindeutsch	lesser Germany; unification without Austria.
Kleinstaaterei	particularism of German states after 1648.
Kombinate	East German cartels.
Kristallnacht	Crystal Night; November 1938 pogrom.
Kulturkampf	cultural struggle between Bismarck and the Roman Catholic church, 1870s.
Land (Länder)	German province(s) after 1949; states or countries after 1648.
Landsturm	elderly home defense force.
Landwehr	citizen army or reserve.
Lebensborn	Spring of Life (SS breeding program).
Lebensraum	living space; German eastern expansion.
Leibeigenschaft	serfdom.
Machtergreifung	seizure of power; alleged of Hitler in January 1933.
Mitteleuropa	central Europe; concept of German domination after 1840s.
Nullpunkt	point zero; term used by German writers to denote 1945.
Obrigkeit	executive authority.
Obrigkeitsstaat	authoritarian state.
Ordensburg	castle of a knightly order; highest Nazi party school.

Ostpolitik	eastern policy; associated with West German chancellor Willy Brandt.
Realgymnasium	nonclassical high school.
Realschule	scientific high school (modern period).
Rechtsstaat	state based on the rule of law.
Reichsfeinde	Bismarckian term for enemies of the state.
Robot	feudal service (Bohemia, Czechoslovakia).
Sammlungspolitik	politics of concentration (of agrarians and industrialists).
Schutzstaffel	protection squad (SS); Nazi black-shirted paramilitary force.
Sonderweg	special path; denotes German historical development deviant from Anglo-Saxon "norm".
Staatssicherheitsdienst	East German state security service (Stasi).
Stände	estates of the realm.
Sturmabteilung	storm section (SA); Nazi brown-shirted paramilitary force.
Totenburgen	castles of the dead; Nazi burial crypts.
Vernunfts-Republikaner	prudent republicans; Weimar term for republicans of reason rather than of conviction.
Volk (völkisch)	tribe, race, nation (ancient Germanic term used especially by the Nazis).
Völkischer Beobachter	*People's Observer*, Nazi party newspaper.
Volksgeist	ancient Germanic folk spirit.
Volksgemeinschaft	national racial community; Nazi ideal.
Volkskirche	"people's church," or responsive popular church.
Volksschule	elementary (or primary) school.
Volkssturm	people's storm; last Nazi military reserve.
Waffen-SS	armed SS.
Wandervögel	birds of passage; denotes German youth movement under William II.
Wehrmacht	German army under Adolf Hitler.
Weltanschauung	philosophy of life.
Weltblitzkrieg	global lightning warfare (Hitler's concept).
Zersplitterung	splintering; term for German disunity after 1648.
Zollverein	customs union.

CHRONOLOGY

962–1806	**Holy Roman Empire (HRE)**

SEVENTEENTH CENTURY

1618–1648	**Thirty Years' War**
1648	Peace of Westphalia (October 24)
1661–1715	Reign of Louis XIV in France
1640–1688	Frederick William, Great Elector of Brandenburg
1685	Revocation of the Edict of Nantes (October 18)
	Potsdam Edict of Toleration (November 8)
1689–1697	**War of the League of Augsburg**

EIGHTEENTH CENTURY

1697–1718	Charles XII of Sweden
1697–1733	Augustus II of Saxony, king of Poland
1701–1714	**War of Spanish Succession**
1701	Frederick William I, crowned king of Prussia at Königsberg (to 1713) (January 18)
1713	Pragmatic Sanction of Charles VI, Austria (April 19)
1713–1740	Frederick William I of Prussia
	Pietism in Prussia
1723	Prussian General Directory (January 1)
1733	Prussian canton system (September 15)
1737–1794	Legal reforms of Samuel von Cocceji
1740–1780	Maria Theresa of Austria
1740–1786	Frederick the Great of Prussia
	Height of the Enlightenment
	Baroque and rococo age
1740–1742	First Silesian War
1742–1745	Emperor Charles VII of Bavaria (HRE)
1744–1745	Second Silesian War
1746	First Directory (of Commerce) created by Maria Theresa
1749	General Directory founded at Vienna (May 2)
	Bauernschutz in Prussia (August 12)
1756	Convention of Westminster (January 6)
	Austro-French Diplomatic Revolution (May 1)
1756–1763	**Seven Years' War (Third Silesian War)**

1763	Peace of Hubertusburg (February 15)
	Prussian General School Regulation (August)
1763–1786	*Rétablissement* of Frederick the Great
1765	Royal Transfer and Loan Bank, Berlin (June 17)
1766–1768	Legal reforms of Maria Theresa
1772	First Polish partition (August 5–16)
	Prussian *Seehandlung* (bank) founded in Berlin (October)
1774	Johann Wolfgang von Goethe's *Sorrows of Young Werther*
1775–1783	29,000 Germans sent to fight in America
1776	Adam Smith's *Wealth of Nations*
	Friedrich Maximilian Klinger's *Sturm und Drang*
1778	War of Bavarian Succession (Potato War)
1770s, 1780s	Freemasons, Illuminati, Rosicrucians
1780–1790	Joseph II of Austria
1781	Austrian Edict of Toleration (October 13)
	Austrian serfdom patent; transfer of peasants to crown's jurisdiction (November 1)
1785	Immanuel Kant's *Critique of Reason*
	German Princes' League (July 23)
1786–1797	Frederick William II
1788	Joseph II joins Russo-Turkish War (February)
1789	**French Revolution begins (June)**
1790	Edmund Burke's *Reflections on the French Revolution*
1792	Austro-Prussian alliance against France (February 7)
	Battle of Valmy (September 20)
1793–1794	The Terror (France)
1793	Lazare Carnot's *levée en masse* (August)
	Second Polish partition (September 23)
1794	Prussian Civil Code (to go into effect June 1) completed (February 5)
1795	Treaty of Basel between Prussia and France (April 15)
	Third Polish partition (October)
1797–1840	Frederick William III
1799	Napoleon Bonaparte's coup (November 9)

NINETEENTH CENTURY

1803	Secularization and mediatization of German church lands
1804–1814	**Emperor Napoleon I**
1806	Confederation of the Rhine (July 12)
	Holy Roman Empire dissolved (August 6)
	Battles of Jena and Auerstädt (October 14)

1807	Franco-Prussian Peace of Tilsit (July 7)
	Kingdom of Westphalia created (August 18)
	Prussian Reform Edict (October 9)
1807–1808	Johann Gottlieb Fichte's *Addresses to the German Nation*
1808	Bavarian Constitution (May)
	Prussian Municipal Ordnance (November 19)
1810	Freedom of Trade and Occupation acts (October)
	University of Berlin opened (October)
	War Academy opened in Berlin (October 15)
1812	Emancipation of Prussian Jews (March 11)
	Napoleon invades Russia (June 24)
	Russo-Prussian Convention of Tauroggen (December 30)
1813	Battle of Nations at Leipzig (October 16–19)
1814	Universal male conscription in Prussia (September 3)
1814–1815	**Congress of Vienna**
1815	Battle of Waterloo (June 18)
	Holy Alliance (September 26)
1815–1866	**German Confederation**
1817	Student demonstrations at the Wartburg (October 18)
1819	Prussian customs law (*Zollgesetz*) (January 1)
	Karlsbad Decrees (September 20)
1820	Vienna Final Act (May 15)
1830	Carl von Clausewitz's *On War*
	Revolution in France and Belgium (July 27–29)
1831	Start of the Polish uprising (January)
1832	Hambach festival (May 27)
	Six Articles repressing freedoms (June 28)
1833	Heidelberg students storm Frankfurt (April 3)
1834	**German *Zollverein* (customs union) (January 1)**
1835	First German railroad (Nürnberg to Fürth) (December)
1837	Göttingen Seven constitutional crisis (November 1)
1840–1861	Frederick William IV
1841	August Heinrich Hoffmann von Fallersleben's "Deutschlandlied"
1844	German Catholic reform movement
	Silesian weavers' revolts (June)
1847	Ludwig Jahn's *Turnerbund*
	Prussian United Diet convened (February 3)
1848	**Karl Marx and Friedrich Engels publish *The Communist Manifesto* (February)**

	Paris revolution against Louis Philippe (February 24)
	Revolution in Vienna (March 13)
	Revolution in Berlin (March 18)
	Louise Otto's *Frauen-Zeitung* (April)
	National Assembly at Frankfurt (May 18)
	Vienna retaken by royal forces (October 26)
	Berlin retaken by royal forces (November 10)
1848–1916	Francis Joseph I of Austria
1849	Frederick William I of Prussia declines the German crown (March 27)
1850	Prussian Constitution (January 31)
	Austrian Olmütz Punctation to Prussia (November 29)
1850s, 1860s	Modern German banks founded
1853–1856	**Crimean War**
1859	**Austro-Italian War (April)**
	Charles Darwin's *Origin of Species*
	National Union of liberals founded (September 16)
1861–1888	William I of Prussia
1862	Otto von Bismarck appointed Prussian premier (September 22)
1862–1867	Prussian constitutional crisis
1863	German General Workers' Association founded at Leipzig (May 23)
1864	**Austro-Prussian War with Denmark (February–October)**
1865	Bad Gastein Convention (Austro-Prussian) (August 14)
	German General Women's Association (October)
1866	**Start of the Austro-Prussian War (June 14)**
	Battle of Königgrätz (July 3)
	Peace of Nikolsburg (July 26)
	Indemnity Bill (September 3)
1867	Austro-Hungarian Compromise (March 1)
1867–1871	**North German Confederation**
1869	Social Democratic Workers' party founded at Eisenach (August 7–9)
1870–1871	**Franco-Prussian War**
1870	Bad Ems dispatch (July 13)
	France declares war on Prussia (July 19)
	Battle of Sedan (September 2)
1871	**German Empire proclaimed at Versailles (to 1918) (January 18)**
	Constitution of the German Empire (April 16)
1871–1888	Emperor William I
1873–1887	*Kulturkampf* (with the Catholic church)
1873–1896	German "Great Depression"

1873	Falk's Laws against the Catholic church (May)
	Uniform German civil and criminal code drafted (finalized and ratified December 21, 1876)
1875	German railroad nationalization begins
	Reichsbank (federal bank) established (March)
	"War-in-sight" crisis (April)
	German Social Democratic party's reform program at Gotha (May 22)
1877	Bad Kissingen Dictate (June 15)
1878–1879	"Refounding" of the Reich
1878	Congress of Berlin (June–July)
	Anti-Socialist Laws (to 1890) (October 21)
1879	Agrarian and industrial tariffs introduced (July 12)
	German High Court of Appeals opened at Leipzig (October 1)
	Dual Alliance (Germany and Austria-Hungary) (October 7)
1882	Italy joins the Dual Alliance (May 20)
1883	Rumanian alliance with Austria-Hungary and Germany (October 30)
1883–1889	Otto von Bismarck's social legislation (health and accident insurance, old age pensions)
1884	German protectorates in the Cameroons, Togo, and German South-West Africa (April)
1885	German protectorates in German East Africa and New Guinea (February)
1887	Reinsurance Treaty with Russia (June 18)
	Colonial League founded (December 19)
1888	Three Emperors' Year:
	Death of William I (March 9)
	Frederick III (1888) (March–June)
	William II (to 1918) (June 15)
1890	Otto von Bismarck dismissed by William II (March 18)
	Anti-Socialist Laws end (October 1)
	Liberal reform era of Chancellor Leo von Caprivi
	Sammlungspolitik (Johannes von Miquel)
1891	Pan-German League founded (April 9)
1893	Franco-Russian alliance (January 17)
	Agrarian League (BdL) created (February 18)
1894	Federation of German Women's Associations (BDF)
	Blue Rider art movement in Munich
1898	Eduard Bernstein's "revision" of Marx
	Sezession art movement in Berlin
	"New course" of Bernhard von Bülow and Alfred von Tirpitz
	Kiaochow in China leased as colony (March)

	First Navy Law passed (April 10)
	German Navy League founded (April 30)
1899	*Kyffhäuser* veterans' movement founded (September)
1899–1902	**Boer War in South Africa**

TWENTIETH CENTURY

1900	Prussian Civil Code enacted (January 1)
	Second Navy Law passed (June 14)
	German expedition to suppress the Boxer Rebellion in China (August)
1901	*Wandervögel* youth movement created (November 4)
1904	Anglo-French *entente cordiale* (April 8)
1904–1905	**Russo-Japanese War**
1905	Björkö meeting (William II, Nicholas II) (July 23)
1905–1906	First Moroccan Crisis
	Schlieffen plan drafted
1906	Universal male suffrage in Austria (December 1)
1907	Eulenburg scandal
	Anglo-Russian entente (August 31)
1908	*Daily Telegraph* affair (October)
	Bosnia-Herzegovina annexed by Vienna (October 7)
1911	Second Moroccan crisis initiated (July)
1912	Lord Haldane mission to Berlin (February)
1912–1913	Army Bill debate
	Balkan Wars
1913	Zabern (Saverne) crisis (October–November)
1914–1918	**World War I**
1914	Archduke Francis Ferdinand assassinated (June 28)
	German "blank check" to Vienna (July 5)
	Austro-Hungarian ultimatum to Serbia (July 23)
	Vienna declares war on Serbia (July 28)
	Russia mobilizes (July 30)
	Germany declares war on Russia (August 1)
	Germany declares war on France (August 3)
	Britain declares war on Germany (August 4)
	Battle of Tannenberg (August 26–31)
	First Battle of the Marne starts (September 5)
	Theobald von Bethmann Hollweg's war aims program (September 9)
	Battle of the Masurian Lakes (September 9–10)
	Battle of Lemberg (September 12)
	Turkey joins the Central Powers (October)

1915	Treaty of London (Italy enters the war) (April 26)
	Lusitania torpedoed (May 7)
	Bulgaria joins the Central Powers (September 6)
	Germany defeats Serbia (November)
1916	Germany attacks Verdun (to November) (February 21)
	Start of Battle of Jutland (May 31)
	Rumania joins the Entente (August 27)
	Paul von Hindenburg and Erich Ludendorff command the army (August 29)
	Hindenburg armaments program
	Death of Francis Joseph (succeeded by Emperor Charles I to 1918) (November 21)
	Auxiliary Service Law (December)
1916–1917	"Turnip winter" in Germany
1917	"Unrestricted submarine warfare" starts (February 1)
	Revolution in Russia (March)
	V. I. Lenin goes to Russia via the German "sealed train" (April)
	United States declares war on Germany (April 6)
	German Independent Social Democratic party (USPD) formed (April 11)
	German fleet rebellion (June)
	Reichstag peace resolution (July 19)
	Theobald von Bethmann Hollweg dismissed (July)
	Fatherland party founded (September 3)
	Bolshevik revolution in Petrograd (November 7)
1918	Berlin labor strikes (January)
	President Woodrow Wilson's Fourteen Points (January 8)
	Peace of Brest-Litovsk (March 3)
	Operation Michael in France (March 21)
	Peace of Bucharest (May 7)
	Allied counteroffensive (July 18)
	Erich Ludendorff demands an armistice (September 29)
	Constitutional reform in Germany (October 28)
	Fleet revolt in Wilhelmshaven (October 29)
	Kurt Eisner's council government in Munich (November 8)
	Philipp Scheidemann proclaims a republic (November 9)
	Ebert-Groener pact (November 10)
	William II goes into exile in the Netherlands (November 10)
	Armistice at Compiègne (November 11)
	Council of People's Commissars in Berlin (November 12)
	William II abdicates (November 28)

	First German Congress of Workers' and Soldiers' Councils at Berlin (December 16)
	People's Naval Division rebels in Berlin (December 24)
	Independent Socialists leave the government of Friedrich Ebert (SPD) (December 27)
	Communist party (KPD) founded (December 31)
1919	Spartacist uprising in Berlin (January 6–13)
	National Assembly elected (January 19)
	Soviet Republic in Bavaria (April)
	Treaty of Versailles signed (June 28) (ratified August 11)
	Weimar Constitution adopted (July 31)
1919–1933	**Weimar Republic**
	Bauhaus architecture at Weimar
1920	Wolfgang Kapp's putsch in Berlin (March 13)
1922	Rapallo Treaty (Germany, Soviet Union) (April 16)
	Walther Rathenau murdered (June 24)
1923	Franco-Belgian invasion of the Ruhr (January 11)
	Hyperinflation to November
	Separatist revolts in Rhineland (October)
	Communist revolt in Saxony, Thuringia (October)
	Adolf Hitler's beer-hall putsch in Munich (November 8–9)
1924	Germany accepts Dawes Plan (August 29)
1925	Death of President Friedrich Ebert (February 28)
	Paul von Hindenburg elected president (April 25)
	Locarno pact (Stresemann-Briand) (December 1)
1926	Treaty of Berlin (renews Rapallo) (April 24)
	Germany joins the League of Nations (September 8)
1929	Germany accepts Young Plan (August 6)
	Death of Gustav Stresemann (October 3)
	Wall Street crash (October 23)
1930	Heinrich Brüning becomes chancellor (March 30)
	NSDAP gains ninety-five seats in parliament (September 14)
1931	Austro-German customs union proposed (March)
	Herbert Hoover moratorium on reparations (July 1)
1932	Paul von Hindenburg reelected president (April 10)
	Franz von Papen becomes chancellor (June 1)
	Papen seizes Prussian government (July 20)
	NSDAP doubles seats to 230 in elections (July 31)
	NSDAP loses 6 percent in elections (November 6)
	Kurt von Schleicher succeeds Papen as chancellor (December 3)
1933	**Adolf Hitler appointed chancellor (January 30)**

	Reichstag fire (February 27)
	NSDAP gets 288 seats but no majority (March 5)
	Dachau becomes first concentration camp (March 20)
	Day of Potsdam (March 21)
	Enabling Act ratified; *Gleichschaltung*, or Nazification, begins (March 23)
	Civil Service Reconstruction Law (April 7)
	Trade unions abolished (May 1–2)
	Concordat with Rome (July 8)
	NSDAP declared only legal party (July 14)
	Germany leaves the League of Nations (October 14)
1934	German-Polish Non-Aggression Pact (January 26)
	Barmen Declaration (Confessing church) (May)
	SA purge (Night of the Long Knives) (June 30)
	Austrian Nazis kill Chancellor Engelbert Dollfuss (July 25)
	Death of President Paul von Hindenburg (August 2)
	Adolf Hitler becomes Führer and chancellor (August 19)
	German Labor Front founded (October 24)
1935	Saar votes to join Third Reich (January 13)
	Universal male conscription announced (March 16)
	Creation of air force announced
	Anglo-French-Italian Stresa front (April 14)
	Anglo-German naval agreement (June 18)
	Nuremberg "racial laws" proclaimed (September 15)
	Italy invades Ethiopia (October)
1936	Summer and winter Olympics
	Remilitarization of the Rhineland (March 7)
	Heinrich Himmler becomes chief of all police (June 17)
	Start of Spanish Civil War (to 1939) (July)
	Four Year Plan announced (October 19)
	Berlin-Rome "axis" (November 1)
1937	Pope Pius XI encyclical "With Burning Sorrow" (March)
	Adolf Hitler outlines foreign policy views at Hossbach conference (November 5)
	Anti-Comintern Pact formed (November 6)
1938	Start of purge of army and Foreign Office (January)
	Anschluss (March 11–12)
	Munich conference (appeasement) (September 29)
	Germany occupies Sudetenland (Case Green) (October 1)
	Crystal Night (*Kristallnacht*) (November 9)
1939	Germany occupies Czechoslovakia (March 15)

	Germany occupies Memel (March 23)
	Nazi-Soviet Non-Aggression Pact signed (August 23–24)
	Germany invades Poland (Case White) (September 1)
	Adolf Hitler issues "euthanasia" order (September 1)
	Britain and France declare war (September 3)
1939–1945	**World War II**
1940	Germany invades Denmark and Norway (Operation Weserübung) (April 9)
	Germany invades Belgium, Holland, Luxembourg, and France (Case Yellow) (May 10)
	French armistice at Compiègne (June 22)
	Battle of Britain (August)
	Tripartite Pact (Germany, Italy, Japan) (September 27)
1941	General Erwin Rommel lands in Africa (February 9)
	Germany invades Yugoslavia and Greece (April)
	Hitler issues "commissar" order (June 6)
	Germany invades the Soviet Union (Operation *Barbarossa*) (June 22)
	"Final solution" enacted (summer)
	Atlantic Charter signed (August 11)
	Japan attacks Pearl Harbor (December 7)
	Hitler declares war on the United States (December 11)
	Hitler takes command of the *Wehrmacht* (December)
1942	Wannsee conference on "final solution" (January 20)
	Albert Speer becomes armaments chief (February 13)
	Battle of El Alamein (November 5)
	Battle of Stalingrad begins (December)
1943	Sixth Army surrenders at Stalingrad (January)
	Joseph Goebbels calls for "total" war (February)
	Afrika Korps (Erwin Rommel) surrenders (May)
	Battle of Kursk begins (July 5)
	Benito Mussolini falls from power (July 26)
1942–1943	Germany loses Battle of the Atlantic
1944–1945	Height of Allied bombing offensive
1944	Operation Overlord: Allied landings in Normandy (D-Day) (June 6)
	Soviets destroy Army Group Center (June 22)
	U.S. landings in southern France (July)
	Attempted plot on Hitler's life (July 20)
1945	**Yalta Conference (February)**
	Hitler issues "Nero" order (March 19)
	U.S. issues JCS–1067 on German occupation after the war (April)
	German SPD refounded

	U.S. and Soviet forces meet at the Elbe River at Torgau (April 25)
	Adolf Hitler commits suicide in Berlin (April 30)
	Germany surrenders to Allies (May 7–9)
	Allied Control Council in Berlin (June 5)
	Potsdam Conference (July 17)
	West German CSU founded (October)
	Protestant "Stuttgart" guilt declaration (October 19)
	International Military Tribunal at Nuremberg begins (November)
	West German CDU founded (December)
1945–1949	Soviet Military Administration for Germany (SMAD)
	Office of Military Government for the U.S. Zone (OMGUS)
	De-Nazification; Allied questionnaires on German Nazi activities
1946	East German SPD and KPD merged into Socialist Unity party (SED) (April 21–22)
1947	U.S. and Britain form Bizone (January 1)
	West German trade unions (DGB) reestablished (March)
	Elections in British Zone (April)
	Marshall Plan announced (June 5)
	Group 47 (novelists) formed in West Germany (September)
1948	Currency reform in American zone (June 18)
	Berlin blockade by Soviets (to May 1949) (June 23)
	Allied air bridge to West Berlin begins (July 26)
	Parliamentary Council meets at Bonn (to May 1949) (September)
	West German FDP founded (December)
1949	Basic Law ratified at Bonn (May 23)
	Federal Republic of Germany (FRG) with temporary capital at Bonn created
	Konrad Adenauer elected chancellor of FRG (September 15)
	German Democratic Republic (GDR) created at East Berlin under Walter Ulbricht (to 1990) (October 7)
1950	Schuman Plan (Franco-German coal and steel community) (May)
	Start of Korean War (to 1953) (June)
	East Germany–Czechoslovakia pact (June)
	East Germany–Poland pact (July)
1952	Joseph Stalin notes on Germany (March–May)
	West German Law for the Equalization of Burdens passed (May)
	German General Treaty signed; German rearmament agreed to by Western Allies (May 26)
	Konrad Adenauer signs agreement with Israel on restitution payments (September)
1953	West German Refugee Law passed (February)

	Workers' uprising in East Berlin (June 16–18)
1954	Soviet Union ends GDR reparations (January)
	Soviet Union recognizes GDR sovereignty (March 25)
	Germany Treaty: West ends occupation (October 23)
	Paris Accords: West Germany joins North Atlantic Treaty Organization (October 23)
1955	Warsaw Pact established with GDR (May 11–14)
	N. A. Bulganin-Nikita S. Khrushchev "two states, one nation" speeches (July)
	FRG establishes relations with Soviet Union (September 23)
1956	National People's Army created in GDR (January 18)
	Nikita S. Khrushchev's speech on "crimes of the Stalin era" (February)
	Hungarian uprising (October)
1957	Saar returned to Germany (January 1)
	Hallstein Doctrine announced at Bonn
	Treaties of Rome (forerunner of European Economic Community) (March 25)
1958	SPD reform program at Bad Godesberg (November)
1959	Novels by Heinrich Böll, Günter Grass, and Uwe Johnson
1961	**Berlin Wall constructed (August 13)**
1963	Franco-German Friendship Treaty (January)
	Konrad Adenauer leaves office; Ludwig Erhard succeeds as chancellor (October 15)
1966	Ludwig Erhard resigns as chancellor (November 30)
	"Great Coalition" of Kurt-Georg Kiesinger and Willy Brandt (December 1)
1967	Extraparliamentary opposition (APO) (June)
1968	Prague Spring (January–August)
	Warsaw Pact forces invade Czechoslovak territory (August 21)
1969	SPD/FDP coalition government formed (September 28)
	Chancellor Willy Brandt begins *Ostpolitik* (October)
1970	Moscow Treaty renouncing force (August 12)
	West German–Polish Treaty signed (December 7)
1970s	**East German policy of delimitation (*Abgrenzung*)**
1971	Erich Honecker succeeds Walter Ulbricht as East German Communist leader (May 3)
	Quadripartite Agreement on Berlin (September)
1972	*Bundestag* ratifies eastern treaties (May 17)
	Munich Olympics terror (September)
	Basic Treaty between East and West Germany signed (December 21) (ratified May 1973)

1973	Both German states enter United Nations (June)
	Yom Kippur War; Arab oil embargo (October 6)
1974	Willy Brandt resigns; replaced by Helmut Schmidt as chancellor (May 6)
	German-Czechoslovakia treaty voiding the Munich Agreement of 1938 (July 10)
1974–1977	Red Army Faction terror in FRG
1975	West Germany ratifies Helsinki Conference on European Security and Cooperation agreements (July)
1976	Erich Honecker expels Wolf Biermann (November)
1978	Green party established (July)
1980	Solidarity movement in Poland (August)
1982	Helmut Schmidt replaced by CDU / CSU-FDP coalition of Helmut Kohl and Hans-Dietrich Genscher (October 1)
1983	Missile debate in West Germany
1984	Chancellor Helmut Kohl in Israel ("grace of late birth" speech) (January)
1985	Mikhail Gorbachev becomes Soviet Communist party head; begins *perestroika* and *glasnost* (March)
	Kohl-Reagan visit to Bitburg cemetery (May)
1985–1988	"Historians' quarrel" over German identity rages
1986	Kurt Waldheim elected Austrian president; rise of Jörg Haider (FPÖ) (November)
1989	Hungary begins to dismantle the Iron Curtain (May 2)
	East Germans flood to Budapest, Prague (summer)
	New Forum founded in GDR (September 5)
	Fortieth anniversary of East Germany (October 7)
	Demonstrations in East Berlin, Leipzig
	Erich Honecker resigns (October 18)
	Willi Stoph and Politburo resign (November 7–8)
	Berlin Wall falls; Brandenburg Gate opened (November 9)
	Helmut Kohl puts forth ten-point unity plan (November 28)
1990	Alliance for Germany wins GDR national elections (March 18)
	Two-Plus-Four Talks concluded in Moscow treaty (September 12)
	Reunification ("Accession" of the GDR to the Federal Republic of Germany); new national holiday (October 3)
	Kohl-Genscher coalition wins all-German elections with 54.8 percent of the vote (December 2)
1991	Maastricht agreements on European unity (December)
1992	Opening of the former East German State Security (Stasi) files (January 1)

	Nationwide strike of German communications, public service, and transport workers (May)
	Denmark rejects the Maastricht (European union) Treaty (June)
	Former East German leader Erich Honecker returns to Berlin from Moscow to stand trial for his "shoot-to-kill" order at the Wall (August)
	German parliament ratifies the Maastricht Treaty (December)
	Neo-Nazi violence; anti-Nazi demonstrations
1993	Erich Honecker goes into exile in Chile (January)

INDEX

*Note: A repeated page number followed by *n* indicates that a separate reference appears in a footnote as well.